GUINNESS WORLD RECORDS 2020

Mononofu is equipped with an air gun on its right arm that shoots sponge balls at c. 140 km/h (87 mph).

▶ LARGEST HUMANOID VEHICLE

Inspired by the giant robots of the classic anime series *Mobile Suit Gundam*, engineer Masaaki Nagumo (left, with assistant Go Sakakibara above) and agricultural equipment manufacturer Sakakibara-kikai (all JPN) created the towering *Mononofu*. It measures 8.46 m (27 ft 9 in) tall and 4.27 m (14 ft) from shoulder to shoulder, as verified on 7 Dec 2018 in Kitagunma, Gunma Prefecture, Japan. Turn to p.173 for more – and don't miss our special *GWR 2020* gallery of ground-breaking robots on pp.146–67.

CONTENTS

Welcome to the 2020 edition of the world's best-selling annual book, fully updated for a new decade with thousands of the latest records. In 11 superlative-packed chapters, we celebrate the most astonishing, mind-blowing and inspiring achievements... and give you the chance to take on some record challenges of your own.

The colour-coded chapters organize records into 11 key categories.

The book is crammed with eye-popping imagery from all around the world, as well as some exclusive, never-before-seen photos.

How big? Discover the true scale of some of our biggest and smallest record holders wherever you see the 100% icon.

100%

GWR is supported by a panel of international experts with a wide range of specialist subjects, from archaeology to zoology. Meet some of our consultants on pp.250–51.

In the SNAPSHOT features, we gave our digital artists a unique challenge: London has always been the home of GWR, so what would it look like if a few iconic records – such as the **tallest statue**, the **largest space station** and the wealth of the **richest person** – were placed next to some of the city's most famous landmarks? The results are in, and they're quite astounding…

In 2016, Gabriel Medina (BRA) lands the **first successful backflip at a Surfing World Championships event**. He is awarded a perfect score of 10) at the 0i Rio Pro in Rio de Janeiro, Brazil.

Whichever day you were born, you'll find a record that was achieved on that date in our birthday calendar.

DO TRY THIS AT HOME!

If bagging a GWR title is on your wish list, then head to our new VIRAL SPORTS chapter. From yo-yoing and speed-cubing to juggling and bottle-flipping, you'll find a selection of try-at-home records. Plus, go online to meet the current record holders – such as blindfolded bottle-flipping champion Josh Horton (above) – who share their expertise on how to get your name in the world's most famous record book.

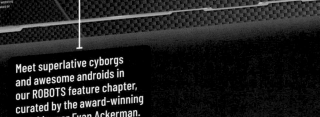

BIONICOPTER

CONTINUE THE STORY ONLINE @ GUINNESSWORLDRECORDS.COM

Whenever you see this symbol, visit our website at **guinnessworldrecords.com/2020** for bonus video content. Our video team has curated a selection of clips from the world's most awe-inspiring and jaw-dropping record holders, so don't miss the chance to see the records come to life.

Meet superlative cyborgs and awesome androids in our ROBOTS feature chapter, curated by the award-winning tech blogger Evan Ackerman.

EDITOR'S LETTER

Welcome to *Guinness World Records 2020* – fully revised and updated for the new decade…

This year has seen our Records Management Team process more than 100 applications each day, covering every conceivable subject matter. As always, the rigorous review process means that only between 5% and 15% of applications make it through each year. So while it's a regrettable "no" for **"most emails unread"** and

"longest time in the shower", I'm pleased to give a thumbs-up to 5,103 successful claims for the past 12 months.

In addition to the thousands of applications we receive annually, we also solicit superlative facts and figures from a wide pool of consultants and advisors. This year, our Senior Editor Adam Millward has doubled our efforts in widening our team of experts, and I'm pleased to welcome on board the likes of the School of Ants, the Berkeley

BLUE PETER

CBBC flagship series *Blue Peter* staged a special show to mark the launch of *Guinness World Records 2019*. DJ Greg James (far left) and presenter Radzi Chinyanganya (left) joined in the fun with the **most toots of a party blower in one minute (team of two)** – 78 – while Ruairidh Forbes (all UK) achieved the **fastest time to prepare three envelopes** – 36.14 sec.

A LEAGUE OF THEIR OWN

On 30 Jun 2018, Jamie Redknapp (UK) achieved the **highest-altitude football dropped and controlled** – 38.92 m (127 ft 8 in) – in Borehamwood, Hertfordshire. He had broken his wrist during an earlier attempt after it was hit by a football dropped by comedian Romesh Ranganathan, but soldiered on to claim the record on Sky One's *A League of Their Own* panel show.

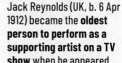

ANT & DEC

Anthony McPartlin (above left) and Declan Donnelly (right, both UK) – better known as Ant & Dec – are the proud owners of the **most consecutive National Television Awards for Best Presenter** – a staggering 18, as of 22 Jan 2019. The Geordie duo have hosted smash hits for ITV such as *SMTV Live*, *Pop Idol*, *Ant & Dec's Saturday Night Takeaway* and *Britain's Got Talent*.

MINI MARK

In celebration of World Book Day on 7 Mar 2019, GWR superfan Alasdair Samson dressed up as adjudicator Mark McKinley (see below) – complete with blazer, stopwatch, clipboard and beard! "Mini Mark" was so convincing that he received an invite to GWR HQ to meet the man himself.

JACK REYNOLDS

Jack Reynolds (UK, b. 6 Apr 1912) became the **oldest person to perform as a supporting artist on a TV show** when he appeared on Channel 4's *Hollyoaks* aged 107 years 2 days. He was presented with his certificate by GWR's Mark McKinley (below). The intrepid great-grandfather is also the **oldest person to ride a zip wire**, aged exactly 106 years, on 6 Apr 2018.

CESC FÀBREGAS

GWR caught up with Spanish midfield maestro Cesc Fàbregas to present him with his certificates for the **fastest time to achieve 100 assists in the English Premier League** – 293 matches, playing for Arsenal and Chelsea – and **most football volley passes in 30 seconds by a pair** – 15, achieved with Jamie Redknapp.

JAN 1 US President Theodore Roosevelt celebrates the first day of 1907 with the **most handshakes by a head of state (single event)**. He greets 8,513 people at an official White House function.

JAN 2 At Twickenham, UK, in 1932, Gerhard Hamilton "Gerry" Brand kicks the **longest rugby union drop goal** – 77.7 m (255 ft) – for South Africa against England.

WIZARDING WORLD

On 28 Feb 2019, Victoria Maclean (UK) had her **largest collection of *Wizarding World* memorabilia** verified at 3,686 items in Neath, West Glamorgan, UK. Maclean (above left), who has been collecting items relating to the *Harry Potter* and *Fantastic Beasts* franchises for 18 years, was presented with her certificate by GWR's Sofia Greenacre.

SURESH JOACHIM

In 2018, GWR HQ opened its doors to record holders to honour their achievements and hear their amazing stories. Among them was Suresh Joachim (CAN, b. LKA, centre), holder of GWR endurance titles including the **longest duration balancing on one foot** – 76 hr 40 min – and the **greatest distance dribbling a basketball in 24 hours** – 177.5 km (110.2 mi).

SCRAMBLED!

During filming for a Valentine's Day special on CITV's *Scrambled!*, presenter Kerry Boyne (UK, far left, with GWR's Anna Orford) achieved the **fastest time to sort 30 coloured flowers into vases** – 44.92 sec – on 23 Jan 2019. The flowers and vases came in five colours: green, orange, pink, blue and yellow.

hope to inspire millions of people to strive towards their own personal goals. It doesn't matter what you want to achieve in life – whether it's climbing Mount Everest, rowing the Atlantic or sorting jellybeans using chopsticks – if it fulfils our criteria, we're committed to recording it.

So, if you want to be a record-breaker and get your name in the world's most popular annual book, you can start by getting in touch via the website at **guinnessworldrecords.com**. Just be sure to give us plenty of notice, as we'll have at least another 99 applications to consider that day…

6 NATIONS SIN BIN

On 21 Jan 2019, Welsh fly-half James Hook (UK) caught a rugby ball after it had been fired from a machine at 100.58 km/h (62.49 mph) on BBC Cymru Wales's *6 Nations Sin Bin* in Cardiff, UK. Hook saw off the challenge from Welsh international rugby stars including Shane Williams, Rachel Taylor, Andy Powell and former record holder Gareth Thomas.

Our video team has been busier than ever, recording hundreds of hours of material for the GWR YouTube channel. Look out for the ▶ icon throughout the book – where you see this button, it means there's accompanying footage, which you'll also find listed on the website.

Another new section in *GWR 2020* is "Snapshot". You can find these poster-like features at the beginning of each chapter. Our editors have worked closely with 55Design – and GWR's 3D artist Joseph O'Neil – to put record-breakers such as the **tallest statue** and the **largest space station** into visual context by measuring them against famous London landmarks. Why London? The UK capital has been the home of the *Guinness World Records* book for 65 years.

By celebrating the best in human achievements, we

Seismology Lab and the Royal Botanic Gardens, Kew, to name just three.

Also new to Guinness World Records this year is robotics consultant Evan Ackerman. Part of the team at the Institute of Electrical and Electronics Engineers, Evan has curated our special feature chapter on robots, which starts on p.146.

As always, our talent scouts have been out and about, visiting car shows, dog festivals, videogame conventions and marathons. Look out for features on bubbles (pp.90–91) and fire (pp.92–93). At our visit to SkillCon 2018 in Las Vegas, Nevada, USA, we were wowed by combat jugglers, footbaggers and speed-cubers – turn to our "Viral Sports" section from p.98 to see the spectacular results. You can also watch our exclusive SkillCon videos at **guinnessworldrecords.com/2020**.

STRICTLY COME DANCING

As part of *Strictly Come Dancing's* (BBC) Annual Strictly Pro Challenge, Oti Mabuse (ZAF) achieved the **most jive toe-heel swivel steps in 30 seconds** – 48 – on *Strictly: It Takes Two* on 19 Oct 2018. Oti saw off competition from fellow dancers Luba Mushtuk and Amy Dowden to claim the title. She is pictured below with host Zoe Ball (right) and GWR's Sofia Greenacre.

Craig Glenday
Editor-in-Chief

HUGH JACKMAN

In 2018, GWR Editor-in-Chief Craig Glenday presented megastar Hugh Jackman (AUS) with his certificate for **longest career as a live-action Marvel superhero** – 16 years 232 days as of 3 Mar 2017, playing Wolverine. Hugh shares the record with his *X-Men* co-star Patrick Stewart (UK, aka Professor Xavier).

JAN 3 In 1996, aviation photographer Ryuji Furusho (JPN) begins his quest to achieve the **most airlines flown on**. By 13 Jan 2014, he has increased his tally to 156.

JAN 4 Lakshan Wanniarachchi (LKA) takes on the **most simultaneous Scrabble opponents** – 40 – in Colombo, Sri Lanka, in 2015. He beats 31 players to qualify for the record.

5

POWER YOUR CURIOSITY

Guinness World Records is on a mission... to inspire people to be more adventurous by exercising their innate sense of curiosity!

"Curiosity is the essence of human existence," said NASA astronaut Eugene Cernan, the **last human to walk on the Moon**. "I don't know what's over there around the corner. But I want to find out!" It's this drive – to learn more about the universe, the world around us, and even ourselves – that inspires everyone at GWR.

Here, we share some of the projects that we've been involved in over the past year. Our hope is that you'll be inspired to unleash your own record-breaking power. What motivates you? What are **you** curious about? Whatever it is, it can probably be channelled into a GWR title...

In Oct 2018, we teamed up with KidZania – the indoor city run by kids – to give visitors the chance to attempt official GWR titles. We set record challenges as part of their STEAM Week (promoting science, technology, engineering, and mathematics), all of which were broken multiple times throughout our time there. As STEAM Week came to an end, our on-site adjudicator Sofia Greenacre crowned several new record holders, including those listed below. A huge thank-you to everyone who took part!

- Ilia Ahmadi-Shooli (IRN, below):
  Fastest time to complete a buzz-wire course – 14.60 sec

- Ektoras Crisp (UK):
  Fastest time to stack a 10-large-brick right-angle LEGO® tower – 17.93 sec

Guinness World Records' Editor-in-Chief Craig Glenday and *Gamer's Edition* Editor Mike Plant paid a visit to MCM Comic Con in London in Oct 2018. There, they hosted an inspiring Q&A with special-effects guru Julian Checkley, whose Batman outfit has the **most functional gadgets on a cosplay suit** (23), and robot engineer James Bruton, who created the **tallest 3D-printed sculpture of a human** (3.62 m; 11 ft 10 in).

We also had the chance to stage some record attempts and prize giveaways. Congratulations to *Fun Kids Breakfast Show* host Sean Thorne (below left) on setting two records playing *WWE 2K19* (2K Games): the **fastest time to win a custom eight-man battle-royale match** (1 min 46 sec) and **fastest time to win a fatal four-way ladder match** (2 min 23 sec).

Julian's Batman outfit has functioning smoke bombs, batarangs, a grapnel gun, UV lamp and tracking device.

YouTube

Providing 24/7 access to record-breaking is our YouTube channel, which this year passed the milestone of 1 billion views! There are more than 2,000 videos for you to enjoy, and we're uploading new content all the time. Subscribe now and get access to our monthly "Best of..." videos, "Meet the Record Breakers" profiles and a ton of user-generated content sent in directly from our record holders as evidence. If you're inspired to break a record of your own, you might even find yourself profiled one day! Find us at **youtube.com/guinnessworldrecords**.

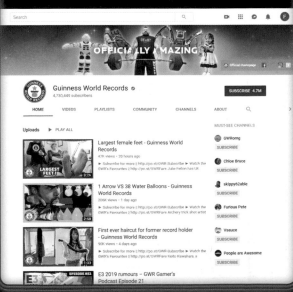

JAN 5 At a dance studio in Vienna, Austria, Elena Sofie Sterlini (AUT) achieves the **longest duration twerking** in 2018. She dances for a marathon 2 hr 1 min.

JAN 6 In 2017, Jon Lovitch (USA) constructs the **largest gingerbread village** – consisting of 1,251 buildings – as displayed at the New York Hall of Science in Corona, New York City, USA.

national schools partnership

In conjunction with the National Schools Partnership, GWR launched the "Read Big, Dream Big" campaign in 2018. The aim of this literacy project was to help young readers to set ambitious goals while developing their reading, writing and speaking skills. Pupils learnt about record-breakers through reading *GWR 2019* and taking part in curriculum-linked classroom activities.

A competition also challenged the pupils to create a poster and write about how the record-breakers in *GWR 2019* had inspired them to "Read Big, Dream Big". In first place was Lily from Saxlingham Primary School in Norwich, Norfolk, who won a tablet and GWR goodie-bag. Lily's poster celebrated her favourite record holder: Betty Goedhart, who – at 84 years 249 days– is the **oldest performing flying-trapeze artist**!

Cath Kidston OFFICIAL ATTEMPT

GUINNESS WORLD RECORDS® TITLE

LARGEST CREAM TEA PARTY

HOSTED BY MARY BERRY

Every year, schools, charities, companies and even entire towns get together to break records. This year was no exception, and we were proud to help a number of record-breaking organizations with their charitable efforts.

On 1 Jul 2018, home furnishers Cath Kidston (UK) celebrated their 25th anniversary by throwing the **largest cream tea party** for 978 people at Alexandra Palace in London, UK. Culinary icon Mary Berry (right, centre) joined in the fun, which raised money for Friends of the Elderly.

On 23 Nov 2018, GWR teamed up with Heathrow Airport, British Airways and Aerobility (all UK) to stage the **heaviest aircraft pulled 100 m by wheelchair (team)**. In all, 98 wheelchair users hauled a Dreamliner 787-9 weighing some 127.6 tonnes (281,309 lb)!

This year, we relaunched our Kids website with the help of our Startopian friend Ally Zing. He's a "fizzing ball of energy" who's come to Earth in search of the Officially Amazing!

GWR Kids has been fully re-designed and updated, and is packed with exclusive photo features, videos, activities and more, all carefully curated by our Editorial team. So pop by **kids.guinnessworldrecords.com** and have a go at some record-breaking science experiments, create your own animal hybrids (pandolphin, anyone?) and download free superlative posters.

If you prefer your record-breaking on the move, you can also find us on PopJam, Instagram, Twitter, Facebook and Snapchat. Whatever platform you choose, there are more than enough records to satisfy even the most curious among you.

JAN 7 — In 1972, the Los Angeles Lakers win their 33rd game in a row - the **most consecutive NBA wins**. The streak, which began on 5 Nov 1971, is ended by the Milwaukee Bucks two days later.

JAN 8 — Ashrita Furman (USA) adds the **fastest mile on can-and-string stilts** to his epic list of GWR titles in 2011. He completes the course in 11 min 55 sec in Ottawa, Ontario, Canada.

7

GWR DAY

MOST MAMBA TRICKS PERFORMED WHILE SKIPPING FORWARDS IN 30 SECONDS

Hijiki Ikuyama (JPN) performed 24 mamba tricks in half a minute as he skipped in Tachikawa, Tokyo, Japan. A mamba trick involves a brief release of one handle of the rope, which is thrown aside while the other end continues in motion. The released handle completes a 360° revolution on its own beside the jumper and is then caught again by the same hand, readying the rope to be skipped over once more.

Trick-shot specialists the Harlem Globetrotters (USA) regularly rack up new world records on GWR Day. Below, Julian "Zeus" McClurkin scores the **most blindfolded basketball slamdunks in one minute** (5). See below for more of their GWR Day feats!

Each year, thousands of people around the world attempt a mind-boggling variety of challenges as part of Guinness World Records Day. This annual day of record-breaking was inaugurated in 2005 to mark the anniversary of GWR becoming the **best-selling annual book**. It's your chance to have a go at an official GWR title while highlighting a good cause, raising money for charity, bringing together friends or colleagues, or just for fun. Here are some of 2018's successful attempts...

For all the action, check out the GWR Day videos on our website at guinnessworldrecords.com/2020

LARGEST COLLECTION OF STAMPS FEATURING AUTOMOBILES

Nabil Karam (LBN) has accumulated 3,333 different stamps bearing images of cars, as verified in Zouk Mosbeh, Lebanon. He's shown above with GWR's Editor-in-Chief Craig Glenday (left) and adjudicator Talal Omar (right).

This isn't the first mega-collection that Karam has put together. He's also the current owner of the **largest collection of model cars** (37,777) and **dioramas** (577).

Most people sport-stacking (multiple venues)

For its 13th annual "STACK UP!" event – held on 8 Nov 2018, the same as GWR Day – the World Sport Stacking Association (WSSA) rose to the challenge once again by getting more people stacking and de-stacking plastic cups (pictured right) than ever before. In total, 624,390 stackers gathered at 2,833 schools and organizations located across 25 different countries, with the majority (569,928) based in the USA.

The WSSA first achieved this record 12 years previously with a total of 81,252 participants, in celebration of GWR Day 2006 – meaning a seven-fold increase in attendance for the 2018 event!

LARGEST ULTRAVIOLET (UV) BLACKLIGHT PAINTING

Guinness World Records was proud to use GWR Day to support the inspiring work carried out by the UK charity YoungMinds – and literally shine a light on the challenges faced by youngsters with mental-health issues. With the help of artist Livi Gosling (UK), a team of volunteers from YoungMinds created a 453.22-m² (4,878-sq-ft) ultraviolet painting in Milton Keynes, Buckinghamshire, UK. UV paintings appear white under natural light; their design only emerges under blacklight. And why the image of a tree within a head? Because "just like a tree, mental health is something that needs to be nourished so that it can be healthy and blossom," Livi explained.

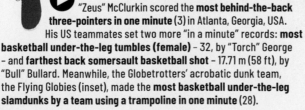

HARLEM GLOBETROTTERS AND FLYING GLOBIES

"Zeus" McClurkin scored the **most behind-the-back three-pointers in one minute** (3) in Atlanta, Georgia, USA. His US teammates set two more "in a minute" records: **most basketball under-the-leg tumbles (female)** – 32, by "Torch" George – and **farthest back somersault basketball shot** – 17.71 m (58 ft), by "Bull" Bullard. Meanwhile, the Globetrotters' acrobatic dunk team, the Flying Globies (inset), made the **most basketball under-the-leg slamdunks by a team using a trampoline in one minute** (28).

JAN 9 The **first underground railway system** opens in London, UK, in 1863. The initial stretch of the Metropolitan line runs 6 km (3.73 mi) between Paddington and Farringdon Street.

JAN 10 In 2013, Quvenzhané Wallis (b. 28 Aug 2003) becomes the **youngest Oscar nominee for Best Actress**, aged 9 years 135 days. She was just six when she appeared in *Beasts of the Southern Wild* (USA, 2012).

▶ MOST FRONT-SPLIT SPINS IN A WIND TUNNEL IN ONE MINUTE

Indoor skydiving instructor Danielle "Doni" Gales (AUS) performed 55 spins while maintaining a front split at iFLY Downunder in Penrith, New South Wales, Australia. It's a tough physical challenge, but the 23-year-old feels that her other main passion had prepared her for it. "I've danced my whole life, I was born and raised into it," she told GWR. "That definitely helped my progression with flying."

Fastest time to assemble five PLAYMOBIL figures

Hu Yufei (CHN) put together a quintet of PLAYMOBIL figures in just 59.88 sec at the Shanghai Kids Fun Expo held in Shanghai, China.

Other Chinese visitors to the event also set a string of Guinness World Records titles, including: **fastest time to make 21 Play-Doh noodles** (39.32 sec, by Jin Zuan); **fastest time to sort 30 toy vehicles** (20.92 sec, by Xu Qin); and **fastest time to change the covers on a child safety seat** (1 min 58.44 sec, by Qi Haifeng).

Most bounce juggles in one minute (three basketballs)

Luis Diego Soto Villa (MEX) made 213 bounce juggles in 60 sec with a trio of balls in Mexico City, Mexico.

▶ FASTEST TIME TO SOLVE THREE RUBIK'S CUBES SIMULTANEOUSLY USING THE HANDS AND FEET

Que Jianyu (CHN) unscrambled a trio of Rubik's Cubes at once with his hands and feet in just 1 min 36.39 sec in Xiamen, Fujian Province, China.

On the same day, he hung from a pole to record the **fastest time to solve a Rubik's Cube upside down** (15.84 sec).

▶ LARGEST LEGO®-BRICK RING SUNDIAL (SUPPORTED)

Playable Design (CHN) unveiled a fully functioning sundial measuring 2.91 m (9 ft 6 in) in diameter and 0.8 m (2 ft 7 in) in thickness. It was built from 45,000 pieces of LEGO DUPLO®. Sundials are one of the oldest timekeeping devices, dating back to at least *c.* 1500 BCE.

Most times to bounce a ping-pong ball against a wall with the mouth in 30 seconds

Ray Reynolds (UK) launched a table-tennis ball against a wall and caught it again on the rebound, using only his mouth, a total of 34 times in half a minute in London, UK.

▶ Longest duration skipping while hula hooping

Zhang Jiqing (CHN) jumped a skipping rope for 1 min 32.653 sec – while hula hooping – at the Beijing Chaoyang Normal School in Beijing, China. Zhang attempted this record aged 63 years to prove his strength and fitness as part of GWR Day. He skipped 142 times during the challenge.

Most doughnuts stacked in one minute (blindfolded)

Katie Nolan (USA) stacked seven doughnuts while unsighted on ESPN's *Always Late with Katie Nolan* in New York City, USA, on 7 Nov 2018.

▶ Fastest time to wrap a person in cling film

YouTuber "Dekakin" (JPN) took just 1 min 59.71 sec to cling-wrap Ichiho Shirahata – a member of idol group "Gekijo-ban" Gokigen Teikoku – in Minato, Tokyo, Japan.

▶ Most lights used in a permanent light and sound show

The Wenzhou Mountain Light Show in Zhejiang, China, is a tourist attraction that uses 707,667 lights to illuminate the mountainside, buildings, bridges and other features on both sides of the River Ou. It was installed by Beijing Landsky Environmental Technology Co., Ltd (CHN) and confirmed as an official world record on GWR Day 2018.

▶ LONGEST DISTANCE TO STRETCH HOME-MADE SLIME IN 30 SECONDS

Japanese vlogger "Yocchi" (above centre) from "BomBom TV" extended a piece of slime to 3.87 m (12 ft 8 in) in Tokyo, Japan.

On the same day, a group from "BomBom TV" achieved the **longest distance to stretch home-made slime in 30 seconds (team of eight)** – 13.78 m (45 ft 2.5 in).

> More than three months of work, involving input from astronomers and engineers, went into making this giant timepiece!

▶ FARTHEST WHEELCHAIR RAMP JUMP

Aaron "Wheelz" Fotheringham (USA) pulled off a 21.35-m (70-ft) wheelchair ramp jump at Woodward West in Tehachapi, California, USA. During the day, he also made the **tallest quarter-pipe drop-in on a wheelchair** and **highest wheelchair hand plant**, both at 8.4 m (27 ft 6 in).

JAN 11 In 2016, Li Xingnan (CHN) executes the **highest wall-assisted backflip** – 3.70 m (12 ft 1 in) – on the set of *CCTV – Guinness World Records Special* in Beijing, China.

JAN 12 A harlequin macaw named Zac achieves the **most canned drinks opened by a parrot in one minute** in 2012, prising open 35 sodas in 60 sec using only his beak in San Jose, California, USA.

MOST-WATCHED GWR VIDEOS

Adorable animals, death-defying stunts, unbelievable humans and crazy talents... whatever you love to watch, nobody brings you closer to the action than GWR. Find us on social media, wherever you are in the world. Here, we've compiled lists of our most popular videos on YouTube – which one is *your* favourite?

In recent years, the explosion of social media has enabled GWR to reach out and connect with audiences around the world. Whether you look for us on YouTube, Facebook, Instagram or PopJam, you're guaranteed to find eye-popping footage of all things Officially Amazing. And we love to hear from our community of viewers, posters and sharers, who always have an opinion on record-breaking!

In Nov 2018, we celebrated the total viewing time for GWR videos on YouTube passing the 1-billion-hour landmark. Our most popular video – in which managers from appliance and electronics company Aaron's (USA) toppled the then-record for **largest human mattress dominoes** – has been viewed more than 46 million times alone (see far right). We're always on the lookout for the next must-watch video, and every month our digital team compiles a round-up showcasing the freshest and best footage.

We're especially proud of our "Meet the Record Breakers" series, which offers an exclusive insight into the stars behind the feats. Being given access to these record holders allows us to learn about their incredible stories first-hand. Check out the most popular videos on YouTube below.

GWR GOES GLOBAL

Since they first began in 1998, official GWR television shows have been seen in more than 190 territories around the globe – from North America to the Middle East, Asia and Australia. Here, Sultan Kösen (TUR), the **tallest man** (see pp.58–59), appears on China's *CCTV - Guinness World Records Special* alongside fellow record-breakers.

MOST-WATCHED "MEET THE RECORD BREAKERS" VIDEOS ON YOUTUBE

	VIDEO	POSTED	VIEWS
1.	**Longest fingernails on a single hand (ever)**	29 Sep 2015	15,317,359
2.	**Woman with the longest legs**	9 Sep 2017	9,256,334
3.	**World's Tallest Dog**	12 Sep 2012	7,163,951
4.	**Batman Cosplay Breaks World Record**	24 Aug 2016	6,910,558
5.	**Martial arts master attempts katana world record – Japan Tour**	2 Mar 2017	5,981,577
6.	**Can Head's skin sucks... literally**	31 Mar 2016	4,468,971
7.	**Tallest high top fade**	14 Sep 2017	4,331,221
8.	**World's Tallest Horse**	12 Sep 2012	3,872,814
9.	**Britney Gallivan: How many times can YOU fold a piece of paper?**	26 Nov 2018	3,720,518
10.	**The Pull Up Guy**	5 May 2016	3,439,371

All figures correct as of 18 Feb 2019

The *Guinness World Records* book – the **best-selling annual** of all time – isn't the only place to discover incredible feats. We also capture or collect records on video to share with our millions of online fans. Look out for this "play" symbol as you read *GWR 2020* – any record it appears beside has a tie-in video not to be missed. Watch them all at:

www.guinnessworldrecords.com/2020

JAN 13 In 1981, schoolgirl Donna Griffiths (UK) starts sneezing and will not stop until 16 Sep 1983, a total of 976 days later – the **longest sneezing fit**. She sneezes 1 million times in the first year alone.

JAN 14 Competitive eater Patrick "Deep Dish" Bertoletti (USA) achieves the **most cloves of garlic eaten in one minute** - 36 - in 2012 at Sierra Studio in East Dundee, Illinois, USA.

TOP 25 MOST-WATCHED GWR VIDEOS ON YOUTUBE

VIDEO	POSTED	VIEWS
1. **Largest human mattress dominoes**	7 Apr 2016	51,446,906
2. **Stretchiest skin in the world!**	12 Jan 2009	37,396,345
3. **Longest bicycle**	10 Nov 2015	19,648,054
4. **Most wet T-shirts put on in one minute**	8 Jun 2015	16,606,141
5. **Parkour – Highest wall-assisted backflip**	11 Nov 2016	15,851,965
6. **Longest Female Legs**	11 Mar 2009	15,345,386
7. **Longest fingernails on a single hand (ever)**	29 Sep 2015	15,317,359
8. **The highest cricket ball catch of all time**	5 Jul 2016	14,783,638
9. **Most mini dominoes toppled**	29 Jul 2014	14,222,140
10. **Tallest Man In The World: Xi Shun**	14 Apr 2008	12,675,322
11. **Most layered bed of nails sandwich**	5 Feb 2016	12,287,653
12. **Most Spiders On A Body For 30 Seconds**	27 Jul 2007	11,882,364
13. **The world's longest tongue**	9 Sep 2014	10,990,528
14. **Book Dominoes**	16 Oct 2015	9,473,611
15. **Woman with the longest legs**	9 Sep 2017	9,256,334
16. **Tightest parallel parking record beaten at new Mini launch**	31 May 2012	8,766,424
17. **Farthest flight by hoverboard**	22 May 2015	8,694,963
18. **Farthest distance wall running (parkour)**	30 Nov 2012	8,581,682
19. **USA Olympians attempt the Largest bubblegum bubble world record**	31 Jul 2016	8,025,513
20. **World's Tallest Dog**	12 Sep 2012	7,163,951
21. **Batman Cosplay Breaks World Record**	24 Aug 2016	6,910,558
22. **Loudest Purring Cat**	21 May 2015	6,751,925
23. **Fastest time to pierce 4 coconuts with 1 FINGER!**	11 Apr 2013	6,682,935
24. **Ultimate Guinness World Records Show – Episode 2: Beer Steins, Bananas and Human Cube**	5 Apr 2012	6,660,398
25. **Most costume change illusions in one minute**	30 Sep 2016	6,640,954

All figures correct as of 18 Feb 2019

The record for **largest human mattress dominoes** has since been raised to 2,016 people, by Stylution Int'l and Ayd Group (both CHN) on 23 Jul 2016.

The total time viewers have spent watching GWR videos on YouTube amounts to approximately 2,500 years.

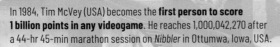

JAN 15 In 1984, Tim McVey (USA) becomes the **first person to score 1 billion points in any videogame**. He reaches 1,000,042,270 after a 44-hr 45-min marathon session on *Nibbler* in Ottumwa, Iowa, USA.

JAN 16 A team of 10 surgeons carries out the **first jawbone transplant** in 2003 at the Istituto Regina Elena in Rome, Italy. The operation, on an 80-year-old patient, takes 11 hours.

PLANET EARTH

MOST SALT-TOLERANT PLANT

The green algae *Dunaliella salina* can survive at salinity levels ranging from 0.2% to 35%, making it the **most salt-tolerant eukaryote** (any organism with cells that contain a nucleus). The algae is also remarkably heat-tolerant, able to endure temperatures from 0°C to 40°C (32–104°F). It is found worldwide, usually in habitats such as oceans, brine lakes and salt marshes.

In hostile conditions – such as increased saltiness, extreme temperatures or reduced nutrient content – *D. salina* produces increased amounts of the natural red-orange pigment beta-carotene, which helps to protect it. This aerial view shows *D. salina* after such a transformation at Yuncheng Salt Lake (aka "China's Dead Sea") in Shanxi Province.

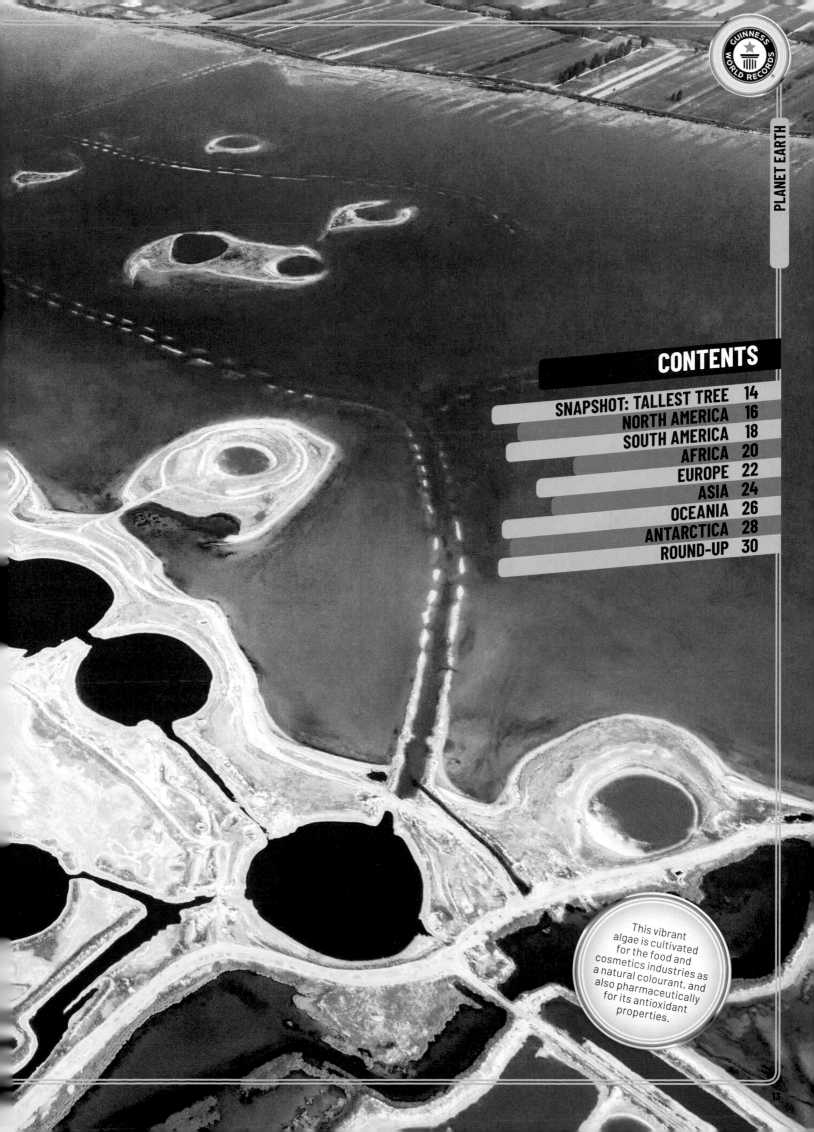

CONTENTS

This vibrant algae is cultivated for the food and cosmetics industries as a natural colourant, and also pharmaceutically for its antioxidant properties.

SNAPSHOT

TALLEST TREE

The western USA is home to the skyscraping redwoods, statuesque trees that outgrow almost all others and can live for more than 2,000 years. Let's imagine one standing alongside London's Palace of Westminster – home to the Houses of Parliament. How would it measure up against the world's most famous clock tower?

Redwoods grow straight and very tall. They require humid conditions to flourish and are found only in a 720-km-long (450-mi) band running along the fog-prone Pacific coast of the USA, from southern Oregon to northern California.

The distinction of being the world's **tallest tree species** is shared between redwoods, eucalypts (aka gum trees) and Douglas firs – all of which can exceed 113 m (370 ft). The **tallest tree** today is a coast redwood (*Sequoia sempervirens*) named Hyperion, it measured 115.85 m (380 ft 1 in) as of 2017. It was first discovered by Chris Atkins and Michael Taylor (both USA) in Redwood National Park, California, USA, in 2006.

Why do redwoods grow so tall? A mild climate, heavy rainfall, summer fogs (which help to reduce evaporation from the leaves), fertile soils and protection from the wind by nearby redwoods all play their part.

Climb into the uppermost branches of a coast redwood and you'll find a host of other plants within the complex canopy. Known as "epiphytes", they include moss, lichen, huckleberry bushes and even other trees such as pines. The lack of soil way up there doesn't hold them back: redwoods produce an abundance of leaves, which eventually fall and settle on their branches, where they rot. The resulting compost provides a fertile base for plant growth. This high-rise ecosystem is home to many animals too, including insects, salamanders and even small mammals such as voles.

Hyperion is nearly 20 m (65 ft) taller than the Elizabeth Tower – better known as "Big Ben", the famous tower that stands at the northern end of Westminster Palace. Strictly speaking, Big Ben isn't the name of the tower, but of the 13.7-tonne (30,200-lb) bell that hangs within it, which first rang out in 1859. Placing Hyperion next to this iconic edifice gives you a sense of just how high majestic redwoods can grow – though admittedly it would make it trickier for Londoners to tell the time...

GREAT REDWOODS FROM TINY CONES GROW...

They're only around 2.5 cm (1 in) long, but these diminutive objects can give rise to majestic trees hundreds of feet tall. The cones have a spiral pattern of plates (or "scales"), within which are 50–60 seeds, each a mere 3–4 mm (0.11–0.15 in) long. These remain inside for eight to nine months, until mature. At this point, the cone turns from green to brown and the scales open to release the seeds.

100%

The roots of a coast redwood aren't that deep, but can easily spread for around 30 m (100 ft). That's just under one-third the height of the Elizabeth Tower (left).

A LONDON EYE VIEW OF GIANT TREES

Hyperion (illustrated on the left) may be the tallest tree now, but the tallest tree ever (right) would have overshadowed it. The all-time record for a standing tree is widely debated, but a prime contender is the 146.3-m (480-ft) eucalypt surveyed by a Mr G Klein in Black Spur near Healesville in Victoria, Australia. It was noted by the then-government botanist of Victoria, Baron Ferdinand von Mueller, in 1867. Both trees are shown here alongside the 135-m-tall (443-ft) London Eye ferris wheel, which sits beside the River Thames; see also pp.190–91.

NORTH AMERICA

Tallest mountain

From sea level, Mauna Kea on the island of Hawaii, USA, reaches 4,205 m (13,796 ft) – almost 2 km (1.2 mi) short of North America's *highest* peak (see below left). But what sits above the surface is only the tip of the "iceberg", as Mauna Kea continues several kilometres underwater. In fact, measured from the lowest point of the local seafloor, the mountain's total height is *c.* 10,205 m (33,480 ft), which is taller than Everest by a full 1.3 km (0.8 mi).

The waters around Hawaii also boast the **largest marine protected area**, based on IUCN criteria. The Papahānaumokuākea Marine National Monument was expanded in 2016 by the then-US President Barack Obama to 1,508,870 km² (582,578 sq mi).

Legally protected from commercial fishing and mining, the reserve is a haven for marine life – not least the world's **largest sponge**. Discovered by two remotely operated vehicles in 2015, the minivan-sized glass sponge is 3.5 m long, 2 m high and 1.5 m wide (11 ft 5 in x 6 ft 6 in x 4 ft 11 in).

Largest grasslands

The Great Plains form a 3-million-km² (1.15-million-sq-mi) north-to-south belt through the heart of the USA. Spanning from the Rocky Mountains to the Missouri River, the vast prairie land is bigger than Argentina – the eighth-largest country. Some of its most famous residents are the herds of roaming buffalo (see p.39).

Deepest plant

In Oct 1984, while exploring an uncharted seamount off San Salvador Island in The Bahamas by submersible, retired Smithsonian botanists Mark and Diane Littler (both USA) collected a type of coralline red algae growing at 269 m (882 ft) below the surface. The maroon-coloured plants were capable of photosynthesis, despite 99.9995% of sunlight being filtered out at that depth.

Largest measured tornado

The USA is infamous for its storm season (Jun–Nov), particularly in the strip of states that lie between Texas and South Dakota known as "Tornado Alley". On 31 May 2013, a twister with a span of 4.18 km (2.59 mi) – an area big enough to fit more than 1,900 soccer pitches – struck El Reno in Oklahoma. The superstorm was measured by the US National Weather Service.

During a four-day storm outbreak over southern USA, the World Meteorological Organization logged 207 distinct twisters on 27–28 Apr 2011, the **most tornadoes in 24 hours**.

Highest tides

Separating the provinces of Nova Scotia and New Brunswick on Canada's Atlantic coast, the Bay of Fundy experiences the highest tides in the world on average. During the spring equinox, the mean tidal range can be as extreme as 14.5 m (47 ft 6 in).

POPULATION
579 million

TOTAL AREA
24.71 million km²

COUNTRIES
23

HIGHEST MOUNTAIN
Denali: 6,190 m

LARGEST LAKE
Superior: 82,414 km²

LONGEST RIVER
Missouri: 4,087 km

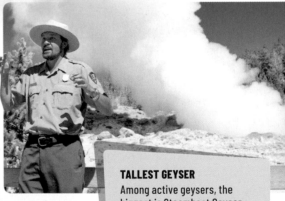

HIGHEST CONCENTRATION OF SLOT CANYONS

Slot canyons are chasms in sedimentary rock created by sandstorms and flash floods, distinguished by very narrow openings. The Colorado Plateau in south-west USA has more slots than anywhere else on Earth – possibly as many as 10,000. Shown above is the Upper Antelope Canyon in Arizona, one of the most photographed slot canyons in the world.

Most northerly volcano

The 2,276-m (7,467-ft) Mount Beerenberg sits on the island of Jan Mayen in the Greenland Sea at 71°N. It most recently erupted in 1985.

Heading north, the barren Devon Island in Canada's Baffin Bay lies at a latitude of 75.1°N. With much of its 55,247-km² (21,331-sq-mi) surface covered in ice and glacial gullies, it's the **largest uninhabited island**.

Farther north still is Oodaaq, a tiny islet off northern Greenland that was first spotted in 1978. Located at 83.67°N, it has been described as the **most northerly land**, though some geologists argue that it's a transitory gravel bank rather than true "land".

LARGEST FRESHWATER LAKE BY SURFACE AREA

The biggest of North America's five Great Lakes, Lake Superior (above) covers 82,414 km² (31,820 sq mi) on the US-Canada border. It is 406 m (1,332 ft) at its deepest.

The **largest lake in a single country**, meanwhile, is Superior's neighbour Lake Michigan, with an area of 57,800 km² (22,300 sq mi) entirely within the USA.

WETTEST DESERT

Although it can reach 40°C (104°F) in the summer, the Sonoran Desert receives between 76 mm (2.9 in) and 500 mm (19.6 in) of rainfall annually, with certain regions prone to higher precipitation levels. Spread across southern Arizona and California, USA, and parts of the Mexican states of Sonora and Baja California, this desert is unusual in that it experiences two wet seasons: one in Dec–Mar and another in Jul–Sep.

TALLEST GEYSER

Among active geysers, the biggest is Steamboat Geyser in Yellowstone National Park, Wyoming, USA. Its jets can reach in excess of 91.4 m (300 ft) tall.

It's not the **tallest geyser ever**, though: that accolade goes to New Zealand's Waimangu Geyser, which in 1903 shot to heights of around 460 m (1,500 ft) every 30–36 hr. However, it has been dormant since 1904.

JAN 17 In 1989, Shirley Metz and Victoria "Tori" Murden (both USA) become the **first women to reach the South Pole by land**, as part of the 11-person South Pole International Overland Expedition.

JAN 18 The **first game of college basketball** is played between the University of Iowa and University of Chicago (both USA), at Iowa City Armory, USA, in 1896.

LARGEST LAND GORGE

The 446-km-long (277-mi) Grand Canyon in Arizona, USA, is one of North America's most iconic geographical features. It was carved out over millions of years by the Colorado River, which still flows through its base. The chasm plunges to depths of 1.6 km (1 mi), and the north and south rims span between 0.5 and 29 km (0.3–18 mi) apart.

It would take more than 1 quadrillion US gal (3.7 quadrillion litres) of water to fill up the Grand Canyon. If you poured all the water from every river on Earth into this gigantic gorge, it would only reach around half full!

GREATEST TREE GIRTH

A 2,000-year-old Montezuma cypress (*Taxodium mucronatum*, inset and below) in Santa María del Tule, Oaxaca, Mexico, had a circumference of approximately 36.2 m (118 ft) when measured in 2005. Local legend has it that the "Árbol del Tule" was planted by an Aztec storm god.

The **greatest tree girth ever** was 57.9 m (190 ft) for a European chestnut (*Castanea sativa*) on Mount Etna, Sicily, Italy, as recorded in 1780. The trunk still exists, but is now in several parts.

LARGEST GYPSUM CRYSTALS

The "Cave of the Crystals" – only discovered in 2000 – sits beneath Mexico's Chihuahuan Desert. A combination of mineral-saturated water and intense heat radiated from magma under the cavern has provided the perfect climate for gypsum to flourish over 500,000 years. The largest crystals measure 11 m (36 ft) long – about the same as a school bus.

JAN 19 In 2010, the People's Government of Yichun City in China create the **tallest ice sculpture**. The dinosaur sculpture measures 16.22 m (53 ft 2 in), nearly three times the height of an adult giraffe.

JAN 20 Democrat John F Kennedy (b. 29 May 1917) is inaugurated President of the United States in 1961 aged 43 years 236 days – the **youngest elected president**.

SOUTH AMERICA

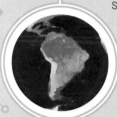

POPULATION
422.5 million

TOTAL AREA
17.84 million km²

COUNTRIES
12

HIGHEST MOUNTAIN
Aconcagua: 6,962 m

LARGEST LAKE
Titicaca: 8,372 km²

LONGEST RIVER
Amazon: 6,400 km

Longest continental mountain range

Stretching 7,600 km (4,700 mi) along the western coast of the continent, the Andes mountain range is often called the "spine of South America". It lays claim to around 100 peaks that exceed 6,000 m (20,000 ft).

The Andes is also a hotspot for nature. A global study into bird diversity across the major mountain ranges, published in the journal *Nature* in Jan 2018, revealed that the Andean Cordillera is home to no fewer than 2,422 species of bird, making it the **most biodiverse mountain range for avifauna**.

Highest commercially navigable lake

Lake Titicaca lies 3,810 m (12,500 ft) above sea level, straddling the Bolivia-Peru border. It's located on the Altiplano – the world's second-largest plateau after the Tibetan Plateau in Asia. With a maximum depth of 180 m (590 ft), it's more than deep enough for even large cargo ships to cross it.

Longest sustained dry period

As well as being the location of the **driest place** (see below right), Chile – the **narrowest country** – has also endured the longest duration without receiving a single drop of rain. According to the World Meteorological Organization, no precipitation fell in the city of Arica between Oct 1903 and Jan 1918 – a total of 172 months, or more than 14 years!

Highest active geyser field

At 4,300 m (14,107 ft) above sea level, El Tatio in northern Chile comprises more than 80 active geysers, as well as mud pools and hot springs. Spread across some 30 km² (11.5 sq mi), it's the largest geyser field in the southern hemisphere. Owing to the high elevation, water boils here at 86.6°C (187.8°F) – in contrast to 100°C (212°F) at sea level.

El Tatio is also home to the **most regular geyser**. Over six days in 2012, "El Jefe" ("The Boss"), as it's known, was recorded erupting 3,531 times; between eruptions, there was a mean interval of just 132.2 sec.

Largest lagoon

Lagoa dos Patos ("Duck Lake") sits on the coast of Rio Grande do Sul in southern Brazil. At 280 km (174 mi) long and 9,850 km² (3,803 sq mi) in area, it's separated from the Atlantic Ocean by a thin strip of sand. Its name comes from the many waterfowl that flock here, including ducks, herons, grebes and flamingos.

Newest impact crater on Earth

On 15 Sep 2007, a chondrite (stony meteorite) struck a dry riverbed near the town of Carancas, south of Lake Titicaca in Peru, leaving a depression 14.2 m (46 ft 7 in) across and at least 3.5 m (11 ft 5 in) deep. It's one of very few impact events to have been witnessed first-hand by humans.

FARTHEST MOUNTAIN PEAK FROM EARTH'S CENTRE

Everest (see p.25) is the **highest mountain** in terms of metres above sea level, while Hawaii's Mauna Kea (see p.16) is the **tallest mountain** from its submarine base, but Mount Chimborazo in Ecuador exceeds both, if measuring from Earth's core. A slight bulge around the Equator means that the summit of this Andean peak is 6,384.4 km (3,967.1 mi) from the centre of our planet – beating Everest by just over 2 km (1.2 mi).

Highest concentration of lightning

Based on observations between 1998 and 2013, storms occur 297 nights of the year at Lake Maracaibo in Venezuela, resulting in 233 lightning strikes per sq km annually. This is caused by hot, humid air interacting with the surrounding mountains.

Smallest desert

With a total area of 105,200 km² (40,600 sq mi) – a similar size to the US state of Kentucky – Chile's Atacama Desert is the smallest on Earth.

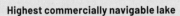

LARGEST BROMELIAD

From the same family as the pineapple, Queen of the Andes (*Puya raimondii*) is an alpine plant native to high altitudes in Bolivia and Peru. The yucca-like leaves can grow 4 m (13 ft) off the ground, but its towering flower spike reaches 12-15 m (39 ft 4 in-49 ft 2 in). It's also the **slowest-flowering plant**, taking as long as 80-150 years to produce its first and only bloom, after which it dies.

DRIEST PLACE

Between 1964 and 2001, the average annual rainfall for the meteorological station near the Chilean town of Quillagua in the Atacama Desert was only 0.5 mm (0.01 in). By comparison, on the same continent, the Amazon Basin (see opposite) receives around 4,260 times more precipitation per year on average.

LARGEST SALT FLAT

At around 10,000 km² (3,860 sq mi), Salar de Uyuni in south-west Bolivia is roughly 100 times the size of the Bonneville Salt Flats in Utah, USA. Once part of a giant prehistoric lake bed, the hypersaline water evaporated over many millennia. Today, it contains an estimated 10 billion tonnes (11 billion US tons) of salt.

JAN 21 At the 2012 Northern Ireland Scrabble Championship in Belfast, UK, Singapore's Toh Weibin amasses the **highest score recorded in a Scrabble tournament** – 850.

 JAN 22 Bipin Larkin – the thrower – and Ashrita Furman – the catcher (both USA) – achieve the **most knives caught in one minute** (56) in New York City, USA, in 2015.

If only the upper drop of Kerepakupai Merú (Angel Falls) is counted – as some hydrologists would have it – then the 948-m (3,110-ft) Tugela Falls in South Africa would take the overall title. Tugela is currently the **tallest multi-tiered waterfall**.

TALLEST WATERFALL

Venezuela's Kerepakupai Merú – aka Salto Ángel, or Angel Falls – has been measured at 979 m (3,212 ft). Bursting out of the sheer cliff face of the Auyán Tepui (a tabletop mountain), the water plunges 807 m (2,648 ft) into the canyon below – the **longest single waterfall drop**. The plummet is so extreme that by the time the water reaches the canyon floor, most of it has vaporized into mist. This seeps through the ground before emerging downstream in a series of smaller cascades, which make up the total height, though this is debated (see fact above left).

LARGEST TROPICAL RAINFOREST

Spanning nine South American nations, and with an expanse of at least 6.24 million km² (2.4 million sq mi), the Amazon rainforest hosts more than 10% of the total global species of flora and fauna.

Winding 6,400 km (3,976 mi) through the forest, the Amazon River pumps out 200,000 m³ (7.1 million cu ft) – or 80 Olympic swimming pools – into the Atlantic every second, making it the **largest river (by flow)**.

LARGEST WETLAND

The Pantanal occupies some 160,000 km² (61,776 sq mi) – almost four times the size of Switzerland – spread over Brazil, Paraguay and Bolivia. The region is celebrated for its biodiversity, playing host to green anacondas (the **heaviest snakes**) and capybaras (the **largest rodents**) – see p.49 – as well as exotic plants such as *Victoria amazonica*, the **largest water lily** (pictured above).

JAN 23 Pakistan's Hanif Mohammad bats for 16 hr 10 min for his score of 337 against the West Indies at Bridgetown, Barbados, in 1958 – the **longest individual Test cricket innings**.

JAN 24 In 1986, *Voyager 2* completes the **first flyby of Uranus**. The probe comes within 81,500 km (50,640 mi) of the cloud tops of the planet and calculates that one Uranian day lasts for around 17 hr.

AFRICA

POPULATION
1.256 billion

TOTAL AREA
30.37 million km²

COUNTRIES
54

HIGHEST MOUNTAIN
Kilimanjaro: 5,895 m

LARGEST LAKE
Victoria: 59,947 km²

LONGEST RIVER
Nile: 6,695 km

Longest-inhabited continent

Known as the "cradle of humanity", Africa is the site on which human ancestors, as well as the great apes, first evolved millions of years ago. In 2017, remains of skulls and jawbones of at least five modern humans (*Homo sapiens*) dating back some 315,000 years were found in a desolate region of Morocco at Jebel Irhoud – a former mine 100 km (62 mi) west of Marrakesh. Until this find, scientists believed that *H. sapiens* first appeared in East Africa more than 100,000 years later.

Today, Africa is also recognized as the **continent with the most countries**: 54.

Oldest mountain range

The Barberton Greenstone Belt in South Africa, aka the Makhonjwa Mountains, is formed of rocks dating back 3.6 billion years. The mountains reach an altitude of 1,800 m (5,905 ft) above sea level. Mount Kilimanjaro – Africa's tallest peak – is estimated to be "only" 2.5 million years old.

Oldest island

Located off the south-east coast of Africa, Madagascar became an island approximately 80–100 million years ago, when it split off from the Indian subcontinent. With an area of 587,041 km² (226,657 sq mi), it is the world's fourth-largest island.

Longest rift system

The East African Rift System is around 4,400 km (2,730 mi) in length, with an average width of 50–65 km (31–40 mi). The escarpments around the edge of the valley have an average height of 600–900 m (1,970–2,950 ft). This extensive feature is thought to begin in the Gulf of Aden and extends to Mozambique in south-east Africa. It has been forming for around 30 million years, as the Arabian Plate pulls away from the African Plate.

Longest lake

Lake Tanganyika is 673 km (418 mi) long and Earth's second-deepest lake after Lake Baikal (see p.24). Straddling the borders of Zambia, Tanzania, the Democratic Republic of the Congo and Burundi, the width of this narrow body of water ranges from 16 to 72 km (10–45 mi).

The **deadliest lake** (i.e., the one responsible for most deaths without drowning) is Lake Nyos in Cameroon. On the night of 21 Aug 1986, between 1,600 and 1,800 people and many animals died after a large release of carbon-dioxide gas there.

Deepest river

In Jul 2008, scientists from the US Geological Survey and the American Museum of Natural History discovered that the Congo River, flowing through central Africa, has a maximum depth

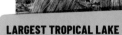

LARGEST TROPICAL LAKE

With a surface area of approximately 59,947 km² (23,146 sq mi) based on 2016 data, Lake Victoria (aka Nam Lolwe, Nyanza, Nalubaale or Ukerewe) is the biggest lake located in the tropics. Containing around 2,424 km³ (581.5 cu mi) of water – around 327 times the volume of Loch Ness in Scotland, UK – it is the main source of the Nile, the world's **longest river**.

of at least 220 m (721 ft). The deepest point in the River Thames in London, UK, is about 20 m (65 ft).

Largest diamond mine

At 1.18 km² (0.45 sq mi), Botswana's open-pit Orapa mine is the size of 165 soccer pitches. In 2017 alone, Orapa produced approximately 9.8 million carats (1,960 kg; 4,320 lb) of the gem, according to Paul Zimnisky Diamond Analytics.

In 2014, the Okavango Delta became the 1,000th site to be named on UNESCO's World Heritage List.

LARGEST "STONE FOREST"

The Grand Tsingy in western Madagascar is a 600-km² (231-sq-mi) forest consisting of sharp limestone pinnacles from the Jurassic period. Over time, this limestone has been eroded by rain to form a dramatic landscape comprising jagged peaks that reach up to 90 m (295 ft) tall.

LARGEST INLAND RIVER DELTA

The 40,000-km² (15,444-sq-mi) Okavango Delta in Botswana is a vast wetland fed by river floodwaters from the Angolan highlands. An area exceeding 14,000 km² (3,860 sq mi) is flooded at least once a decade. The region is home to lions, elephants, 400-plus species of bird and some 70 fish species. The *mokoro*, a type of dug-out canoe, is the traditional means of transport in the delta.

JAN 25 In Owensboro, Kentucky, USA, a hair growing from the belly of Elaine Martin (USA) is measured at 16.77 cm (6.6 in) in 2013 – the **longest abdomen hair**. She calls it "a sight to see!"

JAN 26 In 1972, Yugoslavian airhostess Vesna Vulović miraculously survives after the DC-9 plane she is working on explodes in mid-air – at 10,160 m (33,333 ft), the **highest fall survived without a parachute**.

The Sahara is larger than the USA and occupies approximately twice the area of the Amazon rainforest.

LARGEST HOT DESERT

Nearly an eighth of the world's land surface is arid, experiencing rainfall of less than 25 cm (10 in) per annum. No hot desert is bigger than the Sahara (see p.28 for the **largest desert** overall). At its longest, it is 5,150 km (3,200 mi) from east to west, while north to south it is between 1,280 km and 2,250 km (800–1,400 mi). It covers 9.1 million km² (3.5 million sq mi).

Two-thirds of Africa has been reduced to desert or dry land, making it the **continent most affected by desertification**; around one-third of Africa has undergone moderate to severe desertification. There are a number of natural causes, including climate variation and soil erosion. But human activities such as over-intensive farming, deforestation and even the migration of refugees have exacerbated the process. In the inset above, desert sands are reclaiming the interior of a house in Kolmanskop, an abandoned former diamond-mining town in southern Namibia.

OLDEST DESERT

The Namib is a 2,000-km-long (1,242-mi) coastal desert spanning Angola, Namibia and South Africa, and receives less than 10 mm (0.39 in) of rain per year. It has been arid or semi-arid for at least 80 million years, a condition caused by descending dry air cooled by the Benguela ocean current.

FASTEST LAVA FLOW

Mount Nyiragongo is a shield volcano in the Democratic Republic of the Congo. When it erupted on 10 Jan 1977, the lava – which is very fluid here owing to low silica content – burst through fissures on its flank and travelled at speeds of up to 60–100 km/h (37–62 mph).

Within Nyiragongo's crater (above) is the **largest lava lake**; it is approximately 250 m (820 ft) across and 600 m (1,970 ft) deep.

JAN 27 In 2018, the Kaligi Ranganathan Montford Group of Schools (IND) brings together the **most people solving Rubik's Cubes** - 3,997 - at Jawaharlal Nehru Stadium in Chennai, India.

JAN 28 The **largest ice-cream-scoop pyramid** is built by Diplom-Is (NOR) in Strömstad, Sweden, in 2017. The finished structure measures 1.1 m (3 ft 7 in) tall and contains 5,435 scoops of ice-cream.

EUROPE

POPULATION
727.7 million*

TOTAL AREA
9.89 million km²*

COUNTRIES
51*

HIGHEST MOUNTAIN
Elbrus: 5,642 m

LARGEST LAKE
Ladoga: 17,700 km²

LONGEST RIVER
Volga: 3,530 km

*Only includes European portions of transcontinental countries

Smallest country

The State of the Vatican City (Stato della Città del Vaticano) – an enclave within Italy's capital, Rome – occupies a mere 0.44 km² (0.17 sq mi). That means it could fit almost eight times into Central Park in New York City, USA. Its sovereignty was recognized by the Italian government under the terms of the Lateran Treaty on 11 Feb 1929. Vatican City also has the **shortest land boundary**; its total frontier with Italy amounts to 3.2 km (1.9 mi).

Longest continuously erupting volcano

Mount Stromboli, which sits on an eponymous island in the Tyrrhenian Sea off western Italy, has come to be called the "Lighthouse of the Mediterranean" owing to the unparalleled regularity of its eruptions. It has been known for uninterrupted volcanic activity since at least the 7th century BCE, as first documented by early Greek settlers. Around 170 km (105 mi) south of Stromboli lies fellow record-breaking volcano Mount Etna (see opposite).

Deepest subterranean body of water

In 2015, Polish cave diver Krzysztof Starnawski plunged to 265 m (869 ft) in the flooded Hranice Abyss in the Czech Republic – but he didn't reach the bottom. A year later, he piloted an ROV (remotely operated vehicle) into the cave system, which revealed the depth to be at least 404 m (1,325 ft).

Longest-lasting lightning flash

On 30 Aug 2012, a cloud-to-cloud lightning bolt travelled c. 200 km (124 mi) over south-east France, lasting for 7.74 sec. For context, the average lightning bolt lasts 0.2 sec. This record was verified by the World Meteorological Organization in 2016.

Longest chalk reef

Diver Rob Spray and a team of conservationists discovered a c. 300-million-year-old reef in 2010. Containing tide-carved arches and gullies, the natural feature stretches for more than 32 km (20 mi) off the coast of Norfolk, UK.

Strongest natural whirlpools

In the narrow Saltstraumen strait that connects Skjerstadfjorden and Saltfjorden in northern Norway, tidal waters can reach 40 km/h (25 mph). At peak flow, the tidal race produces powerful maelstroms that can reach around 10 m (32 ft) wide and 5 m (16 ft) deep. The currents are at their strongest during a full moon.

Largest reed bed

The Danube River Delta, stretching across the Black Sea coast of Romania and Ukraine, is a UNESCO Biosphere Reserve and Europe's largest wetland. It's also the location of a 1,563-km² (603-sq-mi) reed marsh – the equivalent area of 3,552 Vatican Cities (see above left). As well as hosting many animal species, especially birds, the reeds serve as a vital natural filtration system before river water flows into the sea.

Largest brackish sea

Covering 377,000 km² (145,560 sq mi), the Baltic Sea in northern Europe is the world's largest body of brackish water (i.e., a blend of fresh and salt water). Its mean salinity ranges from 0.23 to 3.27% – also making it the **least salty sea**. For comparison, seawater on average contains around 3.5% salt. The reduced salinity is the result of a high quantity of freshwater run-off entering the Baltic Sea from surrounding countries.

LARGEST STEAM RINGS

Lava and ash aren't the only things produced by Europe's largest active volcano (see right). Occasionally, Mount Etna also emits massive vortex rings of steam that can span 200 m (650 ft) across and float up around 1 km (0.6 mi). The rare phenomenon is thought to be caused by "rapid pulses of gas" being expelled out of small circular vents at high pressure.

MOST BLUE FLAG BEACHES

Forget the Caribbean or Australia... the country with the most Blue Flag beaches is Spain, with 590 as of 30 Jul 2018. Managed by the Foundation for Environmental Education (FEE), the international voluntary programme assesses beaches on strict criteria such as water quality, visitor education and environmental management.

LARGEST CLONAL COLONY OF MARINE PLANT

In 2006, a vast meadow of Neptune grass (*Posidonia oceanica*) – aka Mediterranean tapeweed – was discovered just south of Ibiza, in Spain's Balearic Island group. This species of seagrass forms large fields on the ocean floor; the record colony was around 8 km (5 mi) across. The self-replicating plant is estimated to be at least 100,000 years old.

LARGEST CORK TREE

Planted in 1783 in Águas de Moura, Portugal, the Whistler Tree yielded 825 kg (1,818 lb) of raw cork in 2009 – enough for 100,000 wine bottles! The material forms part of the bark of cork oaks (*Quercus suber*) and is harvested every nine years or so. In 2018, this superlative specimen, which gets its name from the calls of the many birds that reside in its branches, was declared the European Tree of the Year.

JAN 29 Jim Bolin (USA) unveils the **largest golf tee** in 2013. It stands 9.37 m (30 ft 9 in) tall and has a head diameter of 1.91 m (6 ft 3 in) when it is measured in Casey, Illinois, USA.

JAN 30 In 2018, a total of 17,303 participants learn how to adopt a zero-waste lifestyle at the **largest recycling lesson**. The event is staged by Virudhunagar Toastmasters Club (IND) in Tamil Nadu, India.

LONGEST RECORD OF VOLCANIC ERUPTION

Although Europe is far from the volatile "Ring of Fire" – the **largest volcanic zone** on Earth that abuts countries bordering the Pacific Ocean – it's not devoid of volcanic activity.

The first record of an eruption at Mount Etna, on the Italian island of Sicily, dates back some 3,500 years to 1500 BCE. The continent's largest volcano, standing 3,329 m (10,921 ft) tall, has since erupted more than 200 times.

Most recently, the stratovolcano flared up in Sep 2013 and it has been erupting to some degree ever since. On 24 Dec 2018, ash began to spew from the side of Etna – the first "lateral eruption" the volcano had seen in more than a decade. It went on to trigger a 4.8-magnitude earthquake, as well as many smaller tremors.

LARGEST DEEP-WATER CORAL REEF

Røst Reef, off Norway's Lofoten islands (pictured), lies across an area of seabed equating in size to 14 soccer pitches. At 300–400 m (984–1,312 ft) below the surface, it comprises mainly *Lophelia* stony coral, which attracts an array of marine life quite different to that found in tropical-reef habitats.

MOST TORNADOES BY AREA (COUNTRY)

Between 1980 and 2012, England logged 2.2 tornadoes per 10,000 km² (3,861 sq mi) annually – compared with 1.3 twisters per year in the entire USA. Around 95% of England's tornadoes fell in the EF0–EF1 range (105–175 km/h; 65–109 mph). Pictured is the aftermath of an EF2 twister (up to 220 km/h; 137 mph) that struck Birmingham, UK, in Jul 2005.

ASIA

Largest lake
Situated on the border of south-eastern Europe and Asia, the Caspian Sea has a total coastline of 7,000 km (4,350 mi) and covers 371,000 km² (143,244 sq mi) – about the same area as Japan. The Caspian Sea is an endorheic or "terminal" lake, meaning its water does not discharge into the sea.

Deepest lake
Lake Baikal is a 636-km-long (395-mi) freshwater lake in a rift valley in Siberia. In 1999, an international team of hydrographers and limnologists reassessed previous data to create a more accurate, digitized bathymetric map of the lake. It was found to reach depths of at least 1,642 m (5,387 ft).

Baikal contains some 23,615 km³ (5,665 cu mi) of water – almost double that of Lake Superior in North America – making it also the world's **largest freshwater lake by volume**.

Tallest sand dunes (free-standing)
Megadunes in the Badain Jaran Desert of Inner Mongolia, northern China, have an average height of 330 m (1,082 ft), but have measured as much as 460–480 m (1,509–1,574 ft) – taller than the Empire State Building. Geologists have found a high water content within the sand there, which aids structural integrity – partly explaining their great height.

Largest continuous sand desert
The Rub' al Khali ("Empty Quarter") sand sea – or "erg" – covers an approximate area of 560,000 km² (216,200 sq mi) within the Arabian Desert. Rub' al Khali is predominantly located in Saudi Arabia but also spills over into adjacent areas of Oman, Yemen and the United Arab Emirates.

Also found in Saudi Arabia is the Al-Ahsa Oasis, which occupies some 85.4 km² (32.9 sq mi) and is irrigated by the flow of more than 280 artesian springs. The **largest oasis**, it boasts 2.5 million date palms.

Longest natural arch
A subclass of arch known as a natural bridge, Xian Ren Qiao ("Fairy Bridge") was formed by the Buliu River carving through limestone karst terrain in Guangxi Province, China. An expedition by The Natural Arch and Bridge Society in Oct 2010 measured its span at around 120 m (400 ft).

Largest single flower
Native to south-east Asia, *Rafflesia arnoldii* measures up to 91 cm (3 ft) across and weighs up to 11 kg (24 lb), while its petals are 1.9 cm (0.75 in) thick. *Rafflesia* has no leaves, stem or roots. It grows instead as a parasite on jungle vines. It's sometimes known as the "corpse flower" owing to the rancid stench it emits to attract flies – a feature it shares with the **tallest flower** (see pp.30–31).

Fastest-rising mountain
Located in northern Pakistan in the western Himalayas, Nanga Parbat is growing upwards by 7 mm (0.27 in) per year. The 8,125-m (26,656-ft) peak is the world's ninth-tallest mountain.

SMALLEST SEA
Found on the fringes of oceans, a sea is typically a body of salt water that is partially enclosed by land. Located in Turkey, the Sea of Marmara (above) is 280 km (174 mi) long and around 80 km (50 mi) across at its widest point. Its total surface area is 11,350 km² (4,382 sq mi), with an average depth of 494 m (1,620 ft).

The **largest sea** is also located in Asia: the South China Sea, which measures around 3.5 million km² (1.35 million sq mi).

POPULATION
4.463 billion

TOTAL AREA
44.58 million km²

COUNTRIES
49*

HIGHEST MOUNTAIN
Everest: 8,848 m

LARGEST LAKE
Caspian Sea: 371,000 km²

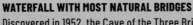

LONGEST RIVER
Yangtze: 6,300 km

*Excludes Pacific island states of Oceania (pp.26–27)

WATERFALL WITH MOST NATURAL BRIDGES
Discovered in 1952, the Cave of the Three Bridges in Tannourine, Lebanon, contains a waterfall that plunges 255 m (836 ft) past three natural stone bridges. It can only be seen during March and April, when the snows are melting. The waterfall cuts through limestone formed in the Jurassic period, around 160 million years ago.

GREATEST RAINFALL IN 48 HOURS
On 15–16 Jun 1995, the town of Cherrapunji in India received 2.493 m (8 ft 2 in) of rain in two days, as verified by the World Meteorological Organization. A high-altitude town in the Indian state of Meghalaya, Cherrapunji's elevation of 1,313 m (4,308 ft) contributes to its high level of annual precipitation.

LARGEST TREE-BORNE FRUIT
Native to the Indo-Malayan region, the jackfruit tree (*Artocarpus heterophyllus*) bears fruit that is typically 0.9 m (2 ft 11 in) long and weighs around 34 kg (74 lb 15 oz) – about 250 times heavier than an orange. The **heaviest jackfruit** on record tipped the scales at 42.72 kg (94 lb 2.9 oz) on 23 Jun 2016.

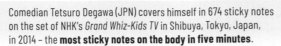 **FEB 2** Comedian Tetsuro Degawa (JPN) covers himself in 674 sticky notes on the set of NHK's *Grand Whiz-Kids TV* in Shibuya, Tokyo, Japan, in 2014 – the **most sticky notes on the body in five minutes**.

 FEB 3 Elisabeth Windisch (DEU) presents the **largest jelly candy** for measurement at Schmitt Waagenbau GmbH in Düsseldorf, Germany, in 2014. It weighs a colossal 512 kg (1,128 lb 12 oz).

At its highest point, Hang Son Đoòng is more than twice the height of the Statue of Liberty!

LARGEST CAVE

Based on overall dimensions, Hang Son Đoòng ("Mountain River Cave") is the largest single cave passage. It measures around 200 m (656 ft) high, 150 m (492 ft) wide and at least 6.5 km (4 mi) long. It is located in Phong Nha-Ke Bàng National Park, Quang Bình Province, Vietnam.

The cave, whose entrance can only be reached via a descent (inset), was discovered in 1991 by local farmer Ho Khanh. However, it took him another 18 years before he was able to retrace his steps and find it again. In Apr 2009, he led a team of British cavers on a six-hour journey through the jungle to Hang Son Đoòng, allowing them to make a partial survey of the cave.

HIGHEST MOUNTAIN

Everest (aka Sagarmatha or Chomolungma) in the Himalayas, on the Tibet–Nepal border, rises 8,848 m (29,029 ft) above sea level. However, Everest is not the **tallest mountain** (see p.16).

As a continent, Asia has the **greatest vertical extent**: 9,278 m (30,439 ft) from Everest's tip to the Dead Sea at the foot of the Jordan Valley, which lies 430 m (1,410 ft) below sea level.

LONGEST-BURNING METHANE CRATER

Nicknamed "The Door to Hell", the 30-m-deep (98-ft) Darvaza Crater has been ablaze since 1971. It is situated in a natural gas field in Turkmenistan's Karakum Desert – some 250 km (155 mi) north of Ashgabat. It is thought that the ground caved in during drilling, and that the crater was intentionally set alight to burn off leaking methane gas.

The **first person to explore the Darvaza Crater** was adventurer George Kourounis (CAN), who descended to the base in Nov 2013 in an insulated aluminium suit (pictured).

FEB 4 In 1994, multiple world record holder Paddy Doyle (UK) achieves the **most burpees in one hour** – a punishing 1,840 – at the Bull's Head pub in Polesworth, Birmingham, UK.

FEB 5 In 2016, Didga and owner Robert Dollwet (USA/AUS) complete the **most tricks performed by a cat in one minute** – 24. Didga's routine includes high-fiving, spinning and riding a skateboard.

OCEANIA

Oceania is a geographic region in the south Pacific Ocean that contains numerous island nations including New Zealand and New Guinea. By far the largest territory in Oceania is the island continent of Australia. The figures in the panel (below left) relate to Oceania as a whole.

POPULATION
38.3 million

TOTAL AREA
8.5 million km²

COUNTRIES
14

HIGHEST MOUNTAIN
Puncak Jaya:
4,884 m

LARGEST LAKE
Lake Corangamite:
234 km²

LONGEST RIVER
Murray: 2,508 km

Smallest continent
For most sources, including GWR, the record holder is mainland Australia, with a west-to-east width of some 4,042 km (2,511 mi) and an area of 7,617,930 km² (2,941,299 sq mi).

With a mean elevation of just over 330 m (1,082 ft) above sea level, Australia is also the **flattest continent**. Its highest point is Mount Kosciuszko, measuring 2,228 m (7,310 ft). This is around half the height of Puncak Jaya, aka Carstensz Pyramid, on New Guinea, which is the tallest peak in Oceania.

Largest ephemeral lake
Unlike the permanent Lake Corangamite (see info bar, left), Kati Thanda-Lake Eyre in South Australia usually contains little or no water, but occasionally floods owing to heavy monsoon rains. At its fullest, this salt-flat basin can turn into a temporary inland sea with an area of around 9,690 km² (3,740 sq mi).

Largest atoll
The Kwajalein Atoll, one of the Marshall Islands in the central Pacific, is a slender ring-shaped reef 283 km

LARGEST SOLITON CLOUD
Soliton clouds are rare formations that maintain their shape while moving at a constant velocity. The longest regular occurrence of this are the backward-rolling "Morning Glory" clouds, which form in the Gulf of Carpentaria, Australia. They can reach 1,000 km (620 mi) long and 1 km (0.6 mi) high, and travel at up to 60 km/h (37 mph).

(176 mi) in length. It encloses a lagoon measuring 2,850 km² (1,100 sq mi) – an area larger than Luxembourg.

Longest sea cave
Surveys of Matainaka Cave – on New Zealand's South Island – conducted in Oct 2012 established its total length as 1.54 km (0.95 mi). The cave, formed by the wave action of the ocean, is still growing gradually longer.

Tallest sea stack
Sea stacks are coastal rock columns formed by wave erosion. Ball's Pyramid, near Lord Howe Island in the Pacific Ocean, rises 561 m (1,840 ft) – taller than the CN Tower in Canada. In 2001, scientists climbing the remote outcrop discovered a small colony of Lord Howe

Island stick insects (*Dryococelus australis*) – the **rarest insect**. Previously thought to be extinct, the species is now listed as Critically Endangered, with an estimated population of 9–35 left in the wild.

Tallest coastal sand dune
Mount Tempest on Moreton Island, off south-east Queensland, stands 280 m (918 ft) tall – three times the height of the Statue of Liberty.

Largest hot spring (surface area)
Frying Pan Lake – aka Waimangu Cauldron – in New Zealand spans up to 200 m (656 ft) and covers around 38,000 m² (409,000 sq ft). Its acidic water averages 50–60°C (122–140°F).

Fastest surface wind gust
The strongest surface wind measured by an anemometer is 408 km/h (253 mph). The gust was logged at an automatic weather station on Barrow Island, Western Australia, on 10 Apr 1996, during Tropical Cyclone Olivia. The speed was ratified by the World Meteorological Organization in 2010.

TALLEST ORCHID
Pseudovanilla foliata, an orchid that grows in the decaying trees of Australian rainforests, has been recorded at 15 m (49 ft) off the ground. The climbing plant is a saprophyte, i.e., it feeds on dead and rotting organic matter.

Uluru was originally part of an ancient mountain range. The surrounding peaks have been gradually eroded away.

LARGEST SANDSTONE MONOLITH
Uluru, also known as Ayers Rock, rises 348 m (1,141 ft) above the desert plain in Northern Territory, Australia. The famous landmark is estimated to be 600 million years old and measures 2.5 km (1.5 mi) long and 1.6 km (1 mi) wide. Uluru's red hue is caused by the rusting of the iron content in the rock at its surface.

LARGEST PRODUCER OF NATURAL DIAMONDS BY VOLUME (SINGLE MINE)
According to figures provided by Paul Zimnisky Diamond Analytics, the Argyle Diamond Mine in Western Australia produced 17.1 million carats of natural diamonds in 2017. It is also the only known source of pink diamonds. However, dwindling reserves mean the mine is set to close in 2020.

FEB 6
In 1952, Queen Elizabeth II succeeds to the throne upon the death of her father, King George VI. As of 21 Apr 2019, she has reigned uninterrupted for 67 years 74 days – the **longest-reigning queen**.

FEB 7
At Super Bowl XLIV in 2010, placekicker Matt Stover (USA) appears for the Indianapolis Colts aged 42 years 11 days – the **oldest Super Bowl player**. He scores five points, but the Colts lose.

LONGEST REEF

The Great Barrier Reef (GBR), off north-eastern Australia, is 2,027 km (1,260 mi) in length, roughly the distance between the UK and Malta. The GBR is, in fact, a "reef system" comprising some 2,900 separate colonies that cover 207,200 km² (80,000 sq mi). Living coral grows on dead polyps that can date back as much as 20 million years.

The reef is a diverse but fragile ecosystem that faces numerous threats – not least "bleaching", where warming ocean waters cause symbiotic algae to be expelled, leaving the coral white. A 2018 study revealed that the GBR suffered an unprecedented nine-month marine heatwave in 2016, during which almost 30% of coral in the reef died off.

OLDEST TROPICAL RAINFOREST

The Daintree Rainforest in Queensland, Australia, covers around 1,200 km² (463 sq mi) and is part of the Wet Tropics of Queensland. It represents the largest single contiguous block of rainforest in Australia and is estimated to be 180 million years old, dating it to the Jurassic period.

LARGEST FLARED SLOPE

Found on the north face of Hyden Rock in Western Australia, Wave Rock is roughly 110 m (360 ft) long and up to 12 m (39 ft) high, giving it an approximate exposed area of 1,320 m² (14,200 sq ft). It is composed of 2.7-billion-year-old granite, which has been eroded by acidic conditions in the soil that used to cover it.

FEB 8

The world's **largest wedding cake** is made by chefs at the Mohegan Sun Hotel and Casino in Uncasville, Connecticut, USA, in 2004. It weighs 6.818 tonnes (15,032 lb).

FEB 9

The Gevora Hotel is inaugurated in Dubai, UAE, in 2018. The gold-coated building has 528 rooms over 75 floors and measures 356.33 m (1,169 ft) in height, making it the **tallest hotel**.

ANTARCTICA

Fewest countries in a continent

Antarctica has no native population, and no countries are recognized below the latitude of 60°S.

Although various countries have claimed parts of Antarctic territory, a 1959 treaty now signed by 53 nations pledges to keep the continent open for peaceful scientific investigation and precludes military activity.

According to the British Antarctic Survey, if omitting its ice shelves, Antarctica has an average elevation of 2,194 m (7,198 ft) above the OSU91A Geoid (a means of measuring sea level that takes into account Earth's irregular shape). This makes it the **highest continent**.

Largest desert

A "desert" is simply an area that has no or very little rainfall. By this definition, the largest desert is the Antarctic Ice Sheet, which covers more than 99% of the 14-million-km² (5.4-million-sq-mi) continent of Antarctica.

Each year, the region receives an average of just 50 mm (2 in) of "water equivalent" precipitation (e.g., rain, snow and hail) – decreasing farther inland; this means that Antarctica is the **driest continent**.

Not surprisingly, the Antarctic Ice Sheet is the **coldest desert**. The British Antarctic Survey states that winter temperatures on the coast average -20°C (-4°F), while in the interior it can sink to -60°C (-76°F) and beyond. Antarctica has also experienced the **lowest temperature on Earth** of all time (see right).

Ironically, however, despite its desert status, the Antarctic Ice Sheet is also the **largest single body of fresh water**: *c.* 30 million km³ (7.2 million cu mi), or around 70% of the world's total – albeit frozen. That's almost 400 times the volume of the Caspian Sea, the **largest lake** (p.24).

Most southerly sand dunes

Sand dunes are not exclusive to hot deserts. Reaching heights of 70 m (230 ft), the dunes of Victoria Valley in Antarctica lie at roughly 77.3°S.

Thickest floating ice

Rutford Ice Stream lies on the eastern flank of the Ellsworth Mountains in West Antarctica. Radio-echo-sounding data obtained in Jan 1975 by Dr Charles Swithinbank and members of the British Antarctic Survey showed that the stream is 1,860 m (6,102 ft) thick at the grounding line – the point at which it starts to float. This is at roughly 77.6°S, 84.2°W, where the stream flows into the Ronne Ice Shelf.

PROFILE

POPULATION
0

TOTAL AREA
14 million km²

COUNTRIES
0

HIGHEST MOUNTAIN
Mount Vinson: 4,892 m

LARGEST LAKE
Subglacial Lake Vostok: 15,000 km²

LONGEST RIVER
Onyx: 32 km

FASTEST KATABATIC WIND

These winds are caused by cold, dense air from high altitude flowing downhill under the force of gravity. The fastest examples are found around the coastal escarpment of Antarctica. Writing in 1915, geologist and explorer Douglas Mawson – who led the 1911–14 Australasian Antarctic Expedition – described witnessing estimated instantaneous wind speeds in excess of 270 km/h (168 mph) at Cape Denison in Commonwealth Bay, Antarctica.

LOWEST TEMPERATURE ON EARTH

On 21 Jul 1983, temperatures at Russia's Vostok research station in Antarctica plunged to -89.2°C (-128.6°F), which is 54°C (93.6°F) colder than the winter average there. In 2018, satellites recorded even colder temperatures of -98°C (-144°F) in the East Antarctic Plateau. However, the World Meteorological Organization maintains that all such measurements should be taken at a standard height in a sheltered weather station. GWR is therefore awaiting confirmation from ground tests before ratifying these reports.

Least sunshine

The South Pole sees no sunlight for 182 days of the year. For six months, the Sun never even rises above the horizon. The North Pole, meanwhile, receives no sunlight for 176 days.

Largest glacier

The Lambert-Fisher Glacier is around 96.5 km (60 mi) wide and 402 km (250 mi) long – making it also the **longest glacier**. It was discovered in 1956 by an Australian aircraft crew during a photo-survey mission.

Remotest tree

There is a Sitka spruce (*Picea sitchensis*) on the subantarctic Campbell Island whose nearest companion is more than 222 km (138 mi; 119.8 nautical mi) away on the Auckland Islands. It is known locally as the Ranfurly tree, after the Governor of New Zealand who supposedly planted it in 1901. However, a 2017 study suggests it was planted later.

HIGHEST OCCURRENCE OF DIAMOND DUST

"Diamond dust" is a ground-level cloud composed of ice crystals that form in the presence of a temperature inversion – i.e., when warm air above the ground combines with colder air lower down. Plateau Station, a now-disused US research base on the central Antarctic Plateau, can experience an average of 316 days each year during which diamond dust clouds are produced.

FEB 10
In 2013, the Skydive Dubai club (UAE) achieves the **most skydivers to parachute from a balloon simultaneously** when 25 of its members take to the air above Dubai.

FEB 11
Mujtaba Hassan Mughal (PAK) reclaims his record for the **most walnuts smashed with nunchuks in one minute** in 2018, crushing a total of 118 in Karachi, Pakistan.

HIGHEST ANTARCTIC MOUNTAIN

The peak of Mount Vinson reaches 4,892 m (16,050 ft) above sea level. Part of the Sentinel Range of the Ellsworth Mountains, around 1,200 km (745 mi) from the South Pole, Vinson was first ascended by a combined team from the American Alpine Club and the National Science Foundation in 1966. Today, it is part of the Seven Summits climbing challenge; of all the peaks on the list, it is the most remote and was the last to be conquered.

Mount Vinson is the least-climbed of the Seven Summits, partly because of the –30°C (–22°F) average temperature and high winds that scour the landscape.

CLEAREST SEA

On 13 Oct 1986, scientists from the Alfred Wegener Institute in Bremerhaven, Germany, measured the clarity of the Weddell Sea off Antarctica. They lowered a Secchi disc – a 30-cm-wide (1-ft) marker designed to help gauge the transparency of water – into the sea until it could no longer be seen. The disc remained visible until it reached a depth of 80 m (262 ft) – about 1.5 times taller than Nelson's Column in London.

LARGEST ICE SHELF

The Ross Ice Shelf was discovered by Captain James Clark Ross (UK) in 1841. Covering an area of around 472,000 km² (182,240 sq mi) of the Ross Sea – a large bay in the Pacific section of Antarctica – it is the largest piece of floating ice in the world. The edge of the shelf is more than 600 km (372 mi) long and 10–15 m (32–49 ft) tall, and presents a near-vertical face to the Southern Ocean.

FEB 12 In 2002, a team of palaeontologists led by Professor Peter Doyle (UK) announce the discovery of the **oldest vomit** – a 160-million-year-old meal regurgitated by an ichthyosaur, a giant marine reptile.

FEB 13 At the 2011 Grammy Awards in Los Angeles, California, USA, E! Entertainment (USA) organizes the **largest gathering of Lady Gaga impersonators**: 121 lookalikes pose for the "Paparazzi".

Deepest documented underwater volcanic eruption
In Dec 2015, an autonomous underwater vehicle was searching for hydrothermal vents west of the Mariana Trench – the **deepest point in the ocean** – in the Pacific. At around 4,450 m (14,600 ft) below sea level, it discovered a 7.3-km-long (4.5-mi) stretch of dark, glassy lava – the result of a recent deep-sea eruption. This was further explored by remotely operated vehicle dives in 2016, and the findings were published in *Frontiers in Earth Science* on 23 Oct 2018.

Longest underwater cave system explored
In Jan 2018, divers confirmed that the 264-km (164-mi) Sistema Sac Actun and the 84-km (52-mi) Dos Ojos system, both in Mexico's Yucatán Peninsula, are connected by a previously unexplored channel. As of Jul 2018, the combined length of this submarine cave system had been measured at 353 km (219.3 mi), as confirmed by the local Quintana Roo Speleological Survey. In common with current cave-naming protocol, once it is proved that two or more systems join up, the resulting cave adopts the name of whichever of them is the largest.

HOTTEST MONTH (SINGLE LOCATION)
The year 2018 saw record-breaking high temperatures across the world. From 1 Jul to 31 Jul, the average daily temperature in Death Valley, California, USA, was 42.3°C (108.1°F), based on readings at a weather station near the Furnace Creek Visitor Center. On four consecutive days (24–27 Jul), it exceeded 52.7°C (127°F).
During a 24-hr period on 26 Jun in the coastal city of Quriyat (inset) in Oman, the air temperature did not drop below 42.6°C (108.7°F) – the **highest low temperature**. The hottest point within the same day was 49.8°C (121.6°F).

OLDEST LIVING INDIVIDUAL TREE
The most ancient trees are the bristlecone pines (*Pinus longaeva*) of the White Mountains in California, USA. Over time, wind, rain and frost deform these trees into twisted shapes (example below). The oldest specimen – named "Methuselah" – was found by Dr Edmund Schulman (USA) and, in 1957, was dated at more than 4,800 years old.

Largest single cave chamber (volume)
The Miao Room is part of the Gebihe cave system, located in Ziyun Getu He National Park, Guizhou Province, China. In 2013, a British-led geology team funded by *National Geographic* mapped the cave with 3D laser scanners and calculated its volume to be 10.78 million m³ (380.7 million cu ft) – large enough to accommodate Egypt's Great Pyramid of Giza four times over.

Longest rainbow observation
On 30 Nov 2017, members of the Atmospheric Sciences department at Chinese Culture University (TPE) studied at least one rainbow (and at one point, four) for an unbroken 8 hr 58 min. The sightings took place from multiple observation decks at the university, on a mountainside in Yangmingshan, Chinese Taipei. The elevated setting, atmospheric conditions and daytime angle of the sun created ideal conditions for the display.

Highest nature reserve
Founded in 1988, Mount Qomolangma National Nature Preserve extends to the summit of Everest (8,848 m; 29,029 ft), the **highest mountain**. Located within China's borders, it covers around 33,810 km² (13,054 sq mi) of the central Himalayan range in the Tibet Autonomous Region.

This is just an example of a bristlecone pine. The precise location of "Methuselah" is kept secret in order to protect it from vandals.

LARGEST MACROALGAL BLOOM
Seaweed is a form of large marine algae, sometimes termed "macroalgae". In Jun 2018, levels of *Sargassum* brown seaweed reached an all-time-high monthly mean coverage of 6,317 km² (2,439 sq mi) – an estimated wet biomass of at least 8.9 million tonnes (9.8 million US tons). The bloom stretched some 8,300 km (5,157 mi), from the Gulf of Mexico to the west coast of Africa. Shown above, workers remove *Sargassum* at Soliman Bay Beach in Tulum, on Mexico's Yucatán Peninsula.

FEB 14 In 2014, a group of 651 singles looking for love take part in the **largest speed-dating event**, held at the TELUS Spark science centre in Calgary, Alberta, Canada.

FEB 15 Driving a vehicle named *Oxygen*, "Slammin'" Sammy Miller (USA) clocks 399 km/h (247.93 mph) on the frozen Lake George in New York, USA, in 1981. It's the **fastest speed in a rocket-powered ice sled**.

At around 400 m (1,310 ft) below sea level, the **lowest nature reserve** is Enot Tsukim Nature Reserve (aka Ein Feshkha), alongside the Dead Sea. Although this body of water is too salty for plants to survive, the 5.8-km-long (3.6-mi) swampy region on its shore – the **lowest wetlands** – is considered an oasis and has lower salinity because of fresh groundwater flowing in from the Judaean Mountains. However, the wetlands are threatened by a continuing drop in the level of the Dead Sea.

Also located in Israel, south-west of the Dead Sea below Mount Sodom, is Malham Cave. On 28 Mar 2019, it was declared the **longest salt cave**, at an estimated 10 km (6.2 mi). The announcement was made by The Hebrew University of Jerusalem

LARGEST TROPICAL PEATLANDS

The Cuvette Centrale peatlands – located in the Congo Basin – cover some 145,500 km^2 (56,180 sq mi), which is more than double the size of Ireland. These swamps contain an estimated 30 billion tonnes (33 billion US tons) of CO_2 – or 20 years' worth of current fossil-fuel emissions in the USA. Cuvette Centrale is one of the planet's most important "carbon sinks" – any area that absorbs more carbon than it releases.

(ISR), following a two-year survey. Salt caves are rare and typically measure no more than around 0.8 km (0.5 mi) in length.

Greatest rainfall in one minute

According to the World Meteorological Organization, on 4 Jul 1956 a downpour of 31.2 mm (1.23 in) fell in 60 sec in Unionville, Maryland, USA.

Oldest biological pigments

At an estimated 1.1 billion years old, the most ancient natural biological colours are pink, red and purple, according to a study published in *Proceedings of the National Academy of Sciences* on 9 Jul 2018. The pigments were extracted from shale rock beneath the Sahara desert in the Taoudeni Basin, Mauritania, and predate other known natural pigments by more than 0.5 billion years.

DEEPEST CAVE

In Mar 2018, a group of Russian speleologists led by Pavel Demidov and Ilya Turbanov descended to the bottom of the Veryovkina Cave in the South Caucasus region of north-west Georgia, recording its depth as 2.21 km (1.37 mi). The team collected samples of a number of rare – and some never-before-seen – troglophilic (cave-dwelling) species during the 12-day expedition.

TALLEST FLOWER

The titan arum (*Amorphophallus titanum*) grows taller than any other bloom. In Oct 2018, GWR's Adam Millward (inset, far right) visited Kew Gardens in London, UK, to present a certificate marking the species' superlative height. At around 3 m (9 ft 10 in) tall, the Kew specimen fell just short of the all-time record: Louis Ricciardiello (USA, above) grew a 3.1-m-tall (10-ft 2-in) *A. titanum*, as confirmed on 18 Jun 2010 in Gilford, New Hampshire, USA.

Titan arums are also called "corpse flowers" because of their foul odour, comparable to that of rotten flesh. The stench can be detected as far as 0.8 km (0.5 mi) away. For this reason, it's regarded as the **smelliest plant** too.

NEWEST OCEAN ZONE

A study of coral-reef ecosystems published in *Nature* on 20 Mar 2018 described a distinct marine faunal biome – the "rariphotic zone" – lying 130–309 m (426–1,014 ft) below the ocean surface. Defined by its scarcity of light, it was previously referred to informally only as a "coral reef twilight zone". Pictured below is *Stichopathes*, a hitherto unknown species of coral discovered here.

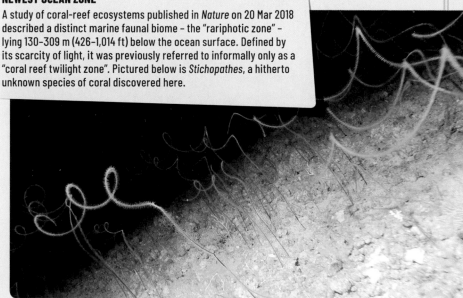

MOST BIODIVERSE TROPICAL GRASSLAND (FLORA)

The Cerrado – a wooded savannah that covers some 20% of Brazil – contains a wider array of flora than any other grassland habitat, with at least 6,500 species of vascular plant. The comparative study was published in *Philosophical Transactions of the Royal Society B* on 8 Aug 2016. The biome also hosts a wealth of fauna, including the maned wolf (*Chrysocyon brachyurus*) – South America's largest canid.

FEB 16 Saeed Abdul Ghaffar Khouri (UAE) pays 52.2 million dirhams ($14.2 m; £7.2 m) for the **most expensive car licence plate** - made up of the single digit '1' - at an auction in Abu Dhabi, UAE, in 2008.

FEB 17 In 1989, chess Masters Ivan Nikolić and Goran Arsović (both SRB) face off in Belgrade, now the capital of Serbia, for a 20-hr 15-min epic that features the **most moves in a chess game**: 269.

31

ANIMALS

SHORTEST HORSE (MALE)

Bombel measures 56.7 cm (1 ft 10 in) to the withers (i.e., the ridge beneath the shoulder blades), as measured on 24 Apr 2018 at Kaskada Stable in Łódź, Poland. This is shorter than a greyhound! Bombel is a miniature Appaloosa owned by Katarzyna Zielińska (POL). Although his parents were average-sized, it was clear after just a couple of months that Katarzyna's pint-sized pony was something special. But in order to qualify for a GWR title, she had to find a horse-measuring device small enough for him!

Sadly, 2018 saw the death of Thumbelina, the **shortest horse (female).** The miniature sorrel brown mare, owned by Kay and Paul Goessling (both USA), measured 44.5 cm (1 ft 5.5 in) to the withers. Thumbelina famously became big news around the world when she met the then-**tallest horse**, Radar – who stood 7.5 times taller than her – in 2006 (below).

Once a month, Bombel travels to a children's hospital to visit the patients. "The kids can brush his tail, brush his mane – they just love playing around with him!" explained owner Katarzyna.

CONTENTS

Track down our wildlife videos at
guinnessworldrecords.com/2020

LARGEST CROCODYLIFORM EVER

By weight, crocodiles are the largest reptiles on Earth today. However, they're not a patch on their giant prehistoric cousins. These "super-crocs", which lived around 112 million years ago in the Mid-Cretaceous, would make a *big* impression today if brought back from extinction, *Jurassic Park*-style. Here, we imagine what it might look like if the mighty *Sarcosuchus imperator* – the biggest of them all – escaped from ZSL London Zoo...

Crocodiles and alligators are often called "living fossils" – creatures that have changed very little over millions of years.

But while today's crocodilians share the traits of *some* of the beasts in their ancestral family tree, in other ways they're quite different. The distinction between past and present crocs is

perhaps most starkly illustrated by *Sarcosuchus*. At up to 12.2 m (40 ft) long, it was the **largest crocodyliform ever** – the all-time giant of the extended crocodile family.

Today's **largest crocodilian** – and the **heaviest reptile** – is the saltwater crocodile (*Crocodylus porosus*). Adult males average 4.9 m (16 ft) in length, though can grow to 7 m (22 ft 11 in) and weigh up to 1,200 kg (2,645 lb).

Size isn't the only thing that differentiated past and present crocs,

though. For instance, some early species were the size of a pet cat and never stepped in water, while others had finned tails and lived in the sea.

Collectively, crocodilians have varied greatly over time, but a few key characteristics have endured across the millennia. Given their evolutionary success, that's hardly a surprise. We can't forget that they were some of the few reptiles to survive the extinction event that wiped out around 80% of life on Earth.

A RIVAL FOR THE TITLE?

Sarcosuchus wasn't the only colossal croc found lurking in ancient swamps... In fact, *Purussaurus brasiliensis*, which lived in South America some 8 million years ago, may have been even larger. This relative of modern caimans measured 10–13 m (32–42 ft) according to some estimates, though scant fossil evidence means the upper limit is contested. See how today's average "saltie" and human would have sized up to *Purussaurus* below.

Sarcosuchus' teeth were as long as 15 cm (6 in)!

Putting aside the size of *Sarcosuchus* – visualized here by a scaled-up saltwater croc – the prehistoric predator was morphologically similar to modern crocodiles. One feature that distinguished it, though, was a bulbous end to its snout, possibly used for smell and vocalizations.

LARGEST CROCODILE IN CAPTIVITY

At 5.48 m (17 ft 11 in) from nose to tail tip, saltwater crocodile Cassius would only be about half the length of *Sarcosuchus*, but he is nevertheless the biggest accurately measured croc alive today. Despite reports of larger specimens in the wild, these are typically "guestimates" based on brief sightings and impossible to verify. Believed to be around 100 years old, Cassius was caught in Australia's Northern Territory in 1987 and moved to Marineland Melanesia on Green Island, where he has resided ever since.

THE BONES OF THE MATTER

We long knew that *Sarcosuchus* was big, but it was only in 2000 that US palaeontologist Paul Sereno established *how* big. On a dig in Niger, he unearthed a 1.8-m-long (6-ft) skull, along with most of its spine, indicating a body length of at least 11–12 m and a mass of 8 tonnes (17,600 lb). Above is a *Sarcosuchus* skeleton on display at the National Museum of Natural History in Paris, France.

DESERT

100%

Most heat-tolerant land animal
In the wild, *Cataglyphis* desert ants from the Sahara in North Africa can survive critical body temperatures of 53°C (127°F), while during lab tests, Australia's red honey ant (*Melophorus bagoti*) briefly reached 56.7°C (134°F). The peak internal body temperature that humans can tolerate before suffering heatstroke is 40°C (104°F).

Desert ants have evolved several ways to keep cool, including long legs to lift their bodies away from the super-hot sand and high speed to minimize exposure to the sun.

In fact, the Saharan silver ant (*C. bombycina*) is the **fastest-running ant**. It can reach bursts of 1.8 km/h (1.1 mph) – or 100 times its body length per second. That's akin to a man of average height sprinting at around 650 km/h (400 mph)!

Smallest fox
Another Saharan resident is the fennec fox (*Vulpes zerda*) – mostly found in Algeria and Tunisia. With a maximum body length of 40 cm (1 ft 3 in), it's the size of a small domestic cat and less than half as long as the more widespread red fox (*Vulpes vulpes*), the **largest fox**. Fennecs' pale fur helps to reflect sunlight, while their huge ears radiate body heat.

Longest-lived rodent
One way to escape the relentless heat is to go underground. That's what East Africa's naked mole rats (*Heterocephalus glaber*) do, living in sprawling subterranean networks that can comprise several kilometres of tunnels. With immunity to many diseases, including cancer, and the ability to survive with very limited oxygen, these extraordinary animals can live for at least 28 years (a good age for a hamster is three).

Mole rat society is as peculiar as their anatomy. Their co-operative ("eusocial") colonies, like those of bees, have a single breeding queen, and individuals perform duties that benefit the collective. This also makes them the **most eusocial mammals**.

Driest habitat for a crustacean
While many of the better-known crustaceans – such as crabs and lobsters – live in or near water, not all of these hard-shelled invertebrates conform to that lifestyle. The desert woodlouse (*Hemilepistus reaumuri*) inhabits dry terrain in the Middle East and North Africa. It can forage at temperatures up to 37°C (98°F). A vital part of the desert food chain, there can be as many as 480,000 woodlice per hectare in some areas.

SMALLEST OWL
Native to dry regions of Mexico and south-west USA, elf owls (*Micrathene whitneyi*) average 12–14 cm (4.7–5.5 in) long and weigh less than a tennis ball. Once thought to dwell exclusively in holes burrowed out of saguaro cacti (inset), we now know they also live in trees and occasionally even fence posts.

Most venomous lizard
Gila monsters (*Heloderma suspectum*) of Mexico and the USA have an LD_{50} value of 0.4 mg/kg. LD_{50} (lethal dose, 50%) scores are a measure of venom potency, based on the amount of toxin required for a fatal dose in half of test subjects. It would take 0.4–0.6 ml – less than one-tenth of a teaspoon – of their venom to kill a human. Luckily, these shy lizards are unlikely to ever expend that much in a natural bite. Their range is shared with the Maricopa harvester ant (*Pogonomyrmex maricopa*). With an LD_{50} of 0.12 mg/kg, it has the **most toxic insect venom** – some 20 times stronger than honeybee venom.

Fastest spider
The Moroccan flic-flac spider (*Cebrennus rechenbergi*) has an ingenious way of evading predators on the sand dunes where it lives. Using a series of forward and backward flips – or "flic-flac" as the trick is called by circus acrobats – this arachnid can clock 6.12 km/h (3.8 mph).

> Red kangaroos are the **largest marsupial newborns**. That said, the jelly-bean-sized joey is a mere 0.75 g (0.02 oz) when born!

MOST VENOMOUS SNAKE
Australia's small-scaled snake (*Oxyuranus microlepidotus*) – aka inland taipan – has an LD_{50} (see above) of just 0.01–03 mg/kg. It typically has 60 mg (0.002 oz) of venom stored in its glands, though one male yielded 110 mg (0.003 oz) – enough to kill 125 people! Despite its deadliness, no human fatalities have been attributed to this species to date, probably owing to its remote habitat.

LARGEST MARSUPIAL
Emblematic of Australia's outback, red kangaroos (*Macropus rufus*) are 2.5 m (8 ft 2 in) long from head to tail. An adult male weighs 22–85 kg (48-187 lb), while females are slightly smaller. Kangaroos are perhaps best known for their hopping skills, a super-efficient means of covering vast distances that requires very little exertion. The **longest kangaroo jump**, observed in 1951, was 12.8 m (42 ft) – about the length of three VW Beetle cars.

FEB 18 In Kerala, India, Abheesh P Dominic (IND) achieves the **most coconuts smashed with one hand in one minute** – 122 – in 2017. He breaks a record that had stood for five years.

FEB 19 In 1994, Mark Kenny (USA) fulfils a lifetime ambition by securing a GWR title, achieving the **fastest 50 m walking on hands**: 16.93 sec. Mark has been performing inverted perambulism since the age of 11.

LARGEST HORNED TOAD

Horned toads – or more accurately horned lizards – are found in deserts, dunes and prairies across the USA and Mexico. Growing to lengths of 20 cm (7.8 in), the long-spined horned lizard (*Phrynosoma asio*) from Mexico's Pacific coast is the largest member of the genus. A flat face and rounded body – a trait which is emphasized by their habit of self-inflating when scared – are two features that led to these reptiles' amphibian association.

Horned lizards have a rather gruesome defence tactic to deter predators... They can pump blood into sinuses below their eyes until they rupture, causing blood to squirt out as far as 1.5 m (5 ft)!

LARGEST JERBOA

Jerboas are desert rodents that use their long back legs to hop – much like kangaroos (see opposite). Their getaway technique often involves jumping in various directions – up to 3 m (9 ft 10 in) at a time – in a bid to throw off their pursuer. Mainly found in the arid steppe of central Asia, the great jerboa (*Allactaga major*) has a body length of 18 cm (7 in), with a 26-cm-long (10.2-in) tail that acts as a balancing aid during leaps.

FASTEST INVERTEBRATES

Despite being referred to as sun spiders, solifugids are not true spiders, though they are arachnids. In short bursts, these desert-dwellers from North Africa and the Middle East can reach 16 km/h (10 mph). That's faster than most of us can sprint – excluding professional athletes such as the **fastest man**, Usain Bolt.

LARGEST CAMEL

With huge padded feet, long eyelashes and built-in food tanks (their humps are stores of fat), camels are well adapted to desert life. At up to 3.5 m (11 ft 5 in) long and 2.4 m (7 ft 10 in) tall at the shoulder, dromedaries (one-humped camels) slightly outsize their Bactrian (two-humped) kin. Only feral groups exist in the wild today, the **largest population** of which is in Australia, numbering 300,000 camels.

FEB 20 Catherine (1952), Carol (1953), Charles (1956), Claudia (1961) and Cecilia (1966) are all born to Carolyn and Ralph Cummins (USA) on this date, the **most siblings born on the same day**.

FEB 21 Steve Fossett (USA) completes the **first solo Pacific crossing by balloon** in 1995. He sets out from Seoul, South Korea, on 17 Feb and lands at Mendham in Saskatchewan, Canada, four days later.

GRASSLAND

TALLEST ANIMAL

Found in dry savannah and open woodland areas of sub-Saharan Africa, fully grown male giraffes (*Giraffa camelopardalis*) reach heady heights of 4.6–5.5 m (15–18 ft). A third of this great stature is typically attained by the 1.5–1.8-m (5–6-ft) neck – the **longest neck on an animal**. The feature is used for courtship, battling rivals and – in tandem with a huge tongue that extends some 45 cm (1 ft 5 in) – to reach juicy foliage in the treetops.

Largest land animal

Adult male African bush elephants (*Loxodonta africana*) weigh around 5.5 tonnes (12,125 lb) – about the same as five dairy cows – and can measure 3.7 m (12 ft 1 in) tall at the shoulder.

These heavyweight herbivores claim several size-based records. They boast the **heaviest brain for a land mammal** – 5.4 kg (11 lb 14.4 oz), nearly four times weightier than a human brain – as well as the **heaviest noses**. The multipurpose trunk, used for everything from slurping water to communicating with other elephants and manipulating objects, weighs up to 200 kg (440 lb).

Fastest primate

Patas monkeys (*Erythrocebus patas*) spend most of their time foraging on the ground in semi-arid areas of Africa. Their skeletons and muscles have evolved so they can make a quick getaway, enabling them to run at speeds up to 55 km/h (34 mph).

Longest terrestrial animal migration

For species whose primary food is grass, moving around to find fresh pasture is a way of life. The Grant's caribou (*Rangifer tarandus granti*) – which can amass in their hundreds of thousands – has been known to cover 4,800 km (2,982 mi) over the barren tundra and plains of Canada and Alaska, USA. As massive as caribou herds get, theirs is not the **greatest land migration** by numbers. That title goes to blue wildebeest (*Connochaetes taurinus*). Each year, some 1–2 million of these grazers embark on an annual circuit between Tanzania and Kenya, which requires them to traverse the crocodile-infested Mara River.

Largest venomous land animal

With adult males averaging 2.59 m (8 ft 6 in) long and weighing 79–91 kg (174–200 lb), the Komodo dragon (*Varanus komodoensis*) of Indonesia is also the **largest lizard**. Although it was long known that its saliva contains pathogenic bacteria, it was only in 2009 that venom-secreting glands were found in its lower jaw.

Longest tongue for a land mammal

The giant anteater (*Myrmecophaga tridactyla*) inhabits various terrains in Central and South America, but to the south of its range (e.g., Uruguay, Brazil and Argentina) it favours temperate pampas grasslands. One of its defining features is a worm-like tongue covered with tiny barbs and sticky saliva that extends up to 61 cm (2 ft) beyond its mouth – six times the **longest human tongue**. It's perfect for winkling out ants and termites from their nests.

With a total body length of 1.2–2 m (3 ft 11 in–6 ft 6 in), inclusive of its big bushy tail, the giant anteater is also today's **largest pilosan** – a group of New World mammals that includes anteaters, tamanduas and sloths.

Heaviest flying bird

Sharing African plains with the **largest bird** of them all (see opposite) is the kori bustard (*Ardeotis kori*). Despite weighing up to 18.1 kg (40 lb), kori bustards are still capable of flight – unlike ostriches – though they will only do so as a last resort. They prefer to stalk bugs and reptiles in tall grass.

Smallest butterfly (wingspan)

Found in grassveld areas of South Africa, the dwarf blue (*Oraidium barberae*) weighs less than 10 mg and its wings measure 1.4 cm (0.55 in) across.

MOST ABUNDANT WILD BIRD

Native to Africa, the red-billed quelea (*Quelea quelea*) has an estimated adult population of 1.5 billion; by comparison, there are thought to be "only" 400 million pigeons globally. These birds are known as "feathered locusts", owing to their ability to decimate vast swathes of farmland. A 1-million-strong flock can ruin 10 tonnes (22,000 lb) of crop in a day.

MOST SUCCESSFUL PREDATOR

African painted dogs (*Lycaon pictus*) live in 10–30-strong packs on sub-Saharan savannah. A combination of adaptability, teamwork and opportunism means that 50–85% of hunting forays result in a kill. Their odds far exceed those of other group hunters, such as lions and hyenas, each with a hit rate of around 30%.

LARGEST WILD EQUID

The Grévy's zebra (*Equus grevyi*) is the biggest species of the horse family, ignoring domestic breeds. It weighs up to 450 kg (992 lb) and stands 140–160 cm (4 ft 7 in–5 ft 2 in) at the withers.

With only some 2,680 Grévy's zebra left on the plains of Kenya and Ethiopia, it's also the **rarest zebra species**. There are fewer Cape mountain zebra (*E. zebra zebra*), but this is currently considered a subspecies.

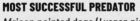

FEB 22 In 2002, Jan Hempel (DEU) performs the **longest backwards jump from a standing position** – 2.01 m (6 ft 7 in) – in Munich, Germany, for *Guinness World Records – Die Show der Rekorde*.

FEB 23 Russia's *Mir* experiences the **first fire on a space station** in 1997, caused by lithium perchlorate "candles" that supply it with oxgyen. The crew come close to escaping *Mir* in their Soyuz "lifeboat".

FASTEST ANIMAL ON LAND (LONG DISTANCE)

Although a cheetah could beat any terrestrial animal in a sprint, its rapid pace can't be maintained for more than about 30 sec. The antelope-like pronghorn (*Antilocapra americana*), on the other hand, is in it for the long haul. The North American ungulate has been recorded cruising at 56 km/h (35 mph) for 6.6 km (4.1 mi).

A cheetah's entire body is built for speed. Long legs and a flexible spine allow for a massive stride, while non-retracting claws provide traction. The large tail also acts as a counterbalance during sudden turns.

FASTEST ANIMAL ON LAND (SHORT DISTANCE)

Adapted to exploit large, open spaces in Africa and Central Asia, the cheetah (*Acinonyx jubatus*) can exceed 100 km/h (62 mph) in pursuit of prey such as antelope. On 20 Jun 2012, a female named Sarah ran the **fastest 100 m by a land mammal**. From a standing start, she completed the course, set up by Cincinnati Zoo at Mast Farm in Clermont County, Ohio, USA, in 5.95 sec – outpacing Usain Bolt's record-setting sprint by 3.63 sec.

100%

FASTEST BIRD ON LAND

While cheetahs use speed to catch their dinner, the ostrich (*Struthio camelus*) uses its sprinting ability to avoid *becoming* dinner. At full pelt, the world's **largest bird** (see the **largest bird ever** on pp.54–55) is able to clock 72 km/h (45 mph).

Speed isn't much use if you don't see danger coming... Fortunately, the ostrich has the **largest eyes for a land animal**. A diameter of 5 cm (2 in) from cornea to retina means that its eyeballs are bigger than its brain!

LARGEST TERRESTRIAL MIGRANT

Symbolically tied to the USA's Great Plains – the **largest grasslands** (see p.16) – tank-like American bison (*Bison bison*) are North America's biggest land animals, weighing around 1 tonne (2,200 lb). Commonly called buffalo, they move with the seasons, heading to higher elevations in spring. These giant grazers came close to being hunted to extinction in the 1800s, but their population has recovered to around 500,000 today.

FEB 24 In 1988, Luciano Pavarotti (ITA) sings the part of Nemorino in Donizetti's opera *L'elisir d'amore* at Berlin's Deutsche Oper in Germany. He is applauded for 1 hr 7 min and takes the **most curtain calls** (165).

FEB 25 In 1956, a white leghorn in Vineland, New Jersey, USA, lays the **heaviest chicken egg**. It weighs 454 g (16 oz) – nine times greater than the average – and incorporates a double yolk and double shell.

Largest species of non-big cat

The puma (*Puma concolor*) is the fourth-biggest feline – only the tiger (see p.44), lion and jaguar are larger – although it is not generally classed as a "big cat". It grows up to 2.75 m (9 ft) long and an adult male can weigh as much as 100 kg (220 lb).

It's also the **mammal with the most names** – more than 40 in the English language alone. These include cougar, panther and mountain lion, while the terms painter and catamount are used east of the Mississippi River, USA.

Most herbivorous monkey

Despite its formidable canine teeth, the gelada (*Theropithecus gelada*) from Ethiopia's Highlands is a grazer, with grass constituting up to 90% of its diet. This Old World monkey is one of the most terrestrial primates.

It's not the **highest-living primate**, though. The coniferous forests of the Yun Ling Mountains in Tibet and Yunnan Province, China, are home to the black snub-nosed monkey (*Rhinopithecus bieti*), which is known to venture to elevations of 4,700 m (15,419 ft).

Smallest placental mammal baby relative to adult body size

A newborn giant panda (*Ailuropoda melanoleuca*) is pink and hairless. It weighs 60–200 g (2–7 oz), making it around 1/900th its mother's size; by contrast, a human baby is nearer 1/20th the weight of an adult female.

Most southerly ungulate

No other ungulate (hoofed mammal) is found farther south than the guanaco (*Lama guanicoe*). Their range extends to Isla Navarino (latitude 55°S) off Tierra del Fuego in Argentina – the southernmost point of South America. Like the vicuña (see right), these grazers are smaller relatives of llamas, at up to 1.1 m (3 ft 7 in) tall. See the **most northerly ungulate** on p.51.

MOST VARIED DIET FOR A BEAR

The spectacled, or Andean, bear (*Tremarctos ornatus*) of South America eats at least 305 plant species – mostly bromeliads and fruit, but also cacti, mosses, ferns, orchids, bamboo and 17 crop plants. Moreover, it eats at least 34 types of animal: 22 mammals, nine insect species, one bird, one annelid (ringed worm) and one mollusc. Documented at a latitude of 23°S in northern Argentina, it is also the **most southerly bear species**.

Most northerly primate

Japanese macaques (*Macaca fuscata*) inhabit the mountainous Jigokudani area of Honshu, Japan, near the city of Nagano (36.6°N). Excluding humans, no primates live farther north. Also called snow monkeys, they survive the -15°C (5°F) winters by bathing in volcanic hot springs.

Smallest deer

Native to the Andes of Colombia, Peru and Ecuador, the northern pudu (*Pudu mephistophiles*) is the smallest member of the Cervidae family. It reaches 35 cm (1 ft 1 in) at the shoulder and weighs less than 6 kg (13 lb 3 oz). The Malay mouse-deer (see p.45) is smaller but isn't a true deer.

Shortest camelid

Vicuñas (*Vicugna vicugna*) are closely related to the llama. On average, adults of the species stand 90 cm (2 ft 11 in) tall at the shoulder.

Found at altitudes of up to 4,800 m (15,750 ft) in the high Andes of South America, the vicuña is also the **highest-living wild camelid**.

LARGEST BIRD OF PREY

Male Andean condors (*Vultur gryphus*) have a maximum wingspan of 3.2 m (10 ft 6 in) and weigh 7.7–15 kg (17–33 lb) – as heavy as a four-year-old child. These vultures inhabit the Andean Cordillera from Venezuela south to Tierra del Fuego in Argentina. Being so hefty, they prefer to live in high, windy areas where they can glide on air currents.

FINEST ANIMAL FIBRE

Endemic to the Tibetan Plateau, the chiru (*Pantholops hodgsonii*) has silky undercoat hairs that are as narrow as 7–10 micrometres in diameter – one-tenth the width of an average human hair. The fine fur provides much-needed insulation in the exposed steppe, which can drop to -40°C (-40°F) in winter. The trade in the chiru's sought-after wool (known locally as *shahtoosh*) has led to dramatic declines in its numbers. With a population estimated at less than 150,000, the species is currently listed as Near Threatened by the IUCN.

FEB 26 In 2014, *In the Name of the King 3: The Last Mission* is released. It is German director Uwe Boll's 10th movie based on a videogame – the **most prolific videogame-licence franchise director**.

FEB 27 TangoTab and Friends (USA) achieve the **most people making sandwiches simultaneously** – 2,586 – at the Kay Bailey Hutchison Convention Center in Dallas, Texas, USA, in 2016.

HIGHEST-LIVING PREDATORS ON LAND

The rarely seen snow leopard (*Uncia uncia*, below), whose range extends across 12 countries in mountainous regions of central and southern Asia, has been photographed at an altitude of 5,800 m (19,000 ft). In the 1990s, a puma was observed at around the same elevation in the South American Andes.

The snow leopard is also the **least dangerous big cat to humans**, with only two confirmed attacks.

The snow leopard has the **longest tail on a big cat relative to body size**. At up to 1 m (3 ft 3 in), the tail is about half its overall length.

HIGHEST-LIVING LIZARD

The Theobald's toad-headed agama (*Phrynocephalus theobaldi*) – aka snow lizard – has been recorded as high as 5,200 m (17,060 ft) on the Tibetan side of Mount Everest and up to 5,400 m (17,716 ft) in western Tibet. Females give birth to live young – a trait that is more common among reptiles native to extreme habitats.

HIGHEST-LIVING SPIDER

In 1924, a species of jumping spider belonging to the family Salticidae was found at a height of 6,700 m (21,981 ft) on Everest in Nepal. It proved to be an unknown species, which in 1975 was finally described and named the Himalayan jumping spider (*Euophrys omnisuperstes*). Its Latin name aptly translates as "highest of all".

HIGHEST-LIVING UNGULATE

The Siberian ibex (*Capra sibirica*, below) lives at greater altitudes than any other ungulate – at elevations up to 6,700 m (21,981 ft) above sea level on the steep slopes and alpine meadows of the Himalayas. Nearby, on the Tibetan Plateau, wild yaks (*Bos mutus*) are found at similarly lofty elevations of 6,100 m (20,013 ft), which makes them the world's **highest-living bovines**.

FEB 28 At the 2016 Mediterranean Dive Show, freediver Aleix Segura Vendrell (ESP) achieves the **longest time to hold the breath voluntarily (male)** – 24 min 3.45 sec – in Barcelona, Spain.

FEB 29 In 2004, Dale Webster (USA) catches a wave for the 10,407th day in a row, claiming the record for the **most consecutive days surfing**. His streak continues until 2015 – a total of 14,641 days.

OPEN OCEAN

Largest fish

Measurements of the elusive whale shark (*Rhincodon typus*) vary wildly from study to study, as well as between regions. Those examined to date have measured 4–12 m (13–39 ft) long, although one exceptional female specimen found off India in 2001 was 18.8 m (61 ft 8 in) long. These plankton-feeding gentle giants dwell in the warmer areas of the Atlantic, Pacific and Indian oceans.

Largest predatory fish

Fully grown great white sharks (*Carcharodon carcharias*) average 4.45 m (14 ft 7 in) in length and generally weigh 520–770 kg (1,150–1,700 lb). There are also unauthenticated claims of specimens up to 10 m (33 ft) long.

The **largest shark ever** was the 16-m-long (52-ft) *Carcharodon megalodon* ("big tooth"), which died out some 2.6 million years ago. It's so-named for good reason: its teeth could be double the size of the great white's!

Newest shark

As documented in the journal *Marine Biodiversity* in Aug 2018, the newest species of shark described is the eastern pygmy false catshark (*Planonasus indicus*). Found at depths of 200–1,000 m (656–3,280 ft), the shark is native to the waters off south-western India and Sri Lanka.

Heaviest jellyfish

Jellyfish are composed almost entirely of water and soft parts, making it hard to obtain accurate weights. But based upon its body size, volume and combined tentacle mass, the lion's mane jellyfish (*Cyanea capillata*) has an estimated maximum weight exceeding 1,000 kg (2,200 lb).

Deepest-living fish

A cusk eel (*Abyssobrotula galatheae*) has been collected from the Puerto Rico Trench, on the boundary of the Caribbean Sea and the Atlantic Ocean, at a depth of 8,370 m (27,460 ft). This is only around 500 m (1,640 ft) less than the height of Mount Everest.

The **deepest dive by a mammal**, on the other hand, is 2,992 m (9,816 ft) for a tagged Cuvier's beaked whale (*Ziphius cavirostris*) near the coast of southern California, USA, in 2013.

Rarest cetacean

The total wild population of vaquita (*Phocoena sinus*) was around 30 individuals in Nov 2016. Numbers are thought to be falling annually by as much as half owing to inbreeding and accidental trapping in fish nets. The vaquita – a species of porpoise – is confined entirely to the northern portion of the Gulf of California, off north-west Mexico.

Longest-lived mammal

The bowhead whale (*Balaena mysticetus*) is a baleen (toothless) species native to Arctic and subarctic waters. A 1999 study carried out by the Scripps Institution of Oceanography and the North Slope Borough Department of Wildlife Management (both USA) estimated an age of 211 for one specimen. They calculated this with a process known as aspartic acid racemization (AAR), which analyses amino acids in eye lenses. Given the accuracy range of this technique, they suggest the 211-year-old could have been anywhere from 177 to 245. Discover an even longer-lived fish on p.55.

Most aerial spins by a dolphin

Dolphins are famous for playfully leaping out of the water, but certain species are more acrobatic than others. The aptly named spinner dolphin (*Stenella longirostris*) can rotate seven times in a single leap.

Largest eye

The Atlantic giant squid (*Architeuthis dux*) has the largest eye of any animal – living or extinct. It has been estimated that a specimen from Thimble Tickle Bay, Newfoundland, Canada, in 1878 had eyes measuring 40 cm (15.75 in) – almost double a volleyball's diameter.

LONGEST FISH MIGRATION

Many fish species undertake marathon annual journeys between their feeding grounds. The longest straight-line distance known to have been covered by a fish is 9,335 km (5,800 mi), by a bluefin tuna (*Thunnus thynnus*). It was dart-tagged off Baja California, Mexico, in 1958 and caught 483 km (300 mi) south of Tokyo, Japan, in Apr 1963.

HEAVIEST BONY FISH

Adult sunfish of the genus *Mola* ("millstone" in Latin) weigh around 1,000 kg (2,200 lb) and span an average 1.8 m (6 ft) between fin tips. The largest specimen on record is a bump-head sunfish (*Mola alexandrini*; example pictured) caught off Kamogawa, Chiba, Japan, in 1996. It was 2.72 m (8 ft 11 in) long and weighed 2,300 kg (5,070 lb) – heavier than an adult black rhino!

For many years, this supersized individual was generally thought to be an ocean sunfish (*Mola mola*), but a study led by Etsuro Sawai of Hiroshima University, Japan, identified it as a bump-head in the journal *Ichthyological Research* on 5 Dec 2017.

BLUE WHALE (*BALAENOPTERA MUSCULUS*)	
RECORD	MEASUREMENT
Largest animal	160 tonnes (352,740 lb); 24 m (78 ft)
Heaviest tongue	4 tonnes (8,818 lb)
Largest lungs	5,000 litres (1,320 US gal) capacity
Largest heart	199.5 kg (440 lb); 1.5 m (5 ft)
Longest animal penis	2.4 m (8 ft)
Slowest mammalian heart rate	4–8 beats per min

FASTEST SHARK

The shortfin mako (*Isurus oxyrinchus*) has recorded swimming speeds exceeding 56 km/h (34.8 mph). Mako sharks hunt by swimming below their prey to avoid detection, before lunging vertically upwards to attack.

The shortfin mako is also the **highest-leaping shark**, capable of propelling itself at least 6 m (20 ft) out of the water, though even higher jumps have been reported.

MAR 1 In Chennai, India, Bhargav Narasimhan (IND) achieves the **fastest time to solve five Rubik's Cubes (one hand)** in 2015 – a blistering 1 min 23.93 sec.

MAR 2 In 2017, Lyudmila Darina (RUS) squeezes the **most people inside a soap bubble** - 374 - in Omsk, Russia. The 2.5-m-tall (8-ft 2-in) bubble is made from water, soap, glycerin and thickening agents.

DEEPEST DIVE BY A CHELONIAN

Chelonians or Testudines are an order of reptiles comprising turtles, terrapins and tortoises. In May 1987, a leatherback turtle (*Dermochelys coriacea*) was recorded at a depth of 1,200 m (3,937 ft) off the US Virgin Islands.

In 2006-08, satellites tracked a tagged leatherback on a 20,558-km (12,774-mi) journey from its nesting site on West Papua, Indonesian New Guinea, to feeding grounds off the coast of Oregon, USA. This is the **longest reptile migration**.

Grimpoteuthis are unique among octopuses in their ability to swallow prey such as worms and small crustaceans whole, rather than tearing and grinding them.

DEEPEST OCTOPUS

Dumbo octopuses (*Grimpoteuthis*) live as far down as 4,865 m (16,000 ft), close to the ocean floor. Their 20-cm-long (7.8-in) bodies are soft, semi-gelatinous and capable of resisting the great pressure found at such depths. The dumbo owes its name to the fins extruding from its mantle, reminiscent of the big-eared Disney character. It swims by moving its fins, pulsing its webbed arms or expelling water from a funnel for jet propulsion.

LARGEST RAY

The Atlantic manta ray (*Mobula birostris*) has an average wingspan of 6 m (19 ft 8 in). The largest individual wingspan recorded is 9.1 m (29 ft 10 in) – wider than a tennis court! Atlantic manta rays are also called "devil rays", owing to the hornlike cephalic fins on their heads. They are solitary swimmers, usually found near the ocean surface.

LOUDEST ANIMAL SOUND

The unidirectional clicks produced by sperm whales (*Physeter macrocephalus*) underwater can be as powerful as 236 decibels – about 44 times the loudness of a thunderclap. Sperm whales use these clicks for echolocation while hunting prey in the low-light depths. They can detect each other's vocalizations tens of kilometres away.

RAINFOREST & WOODLAND

Smallest reptile

Three species of Madagascan pygmy chameleon share this record: the Nosy Bé pygmy chameleon (*Brookesia minima*, above), the Nosy Hara pygmy chameleon (*B. micra*) and the Mount d'Ambre pygmy chameleon (*B. tuberculata*). Adult males of all three species can measure as little as 14 mm (0.5 in) from snout to vent (cloaca); females are slightly larger.

Heaviest parrot

The flightless kākāpō (*Strigops habroptilus*) is confined to three forested islets off New Zealand. Males are bigger than females and weigh up to 4 kg (8 lb 13 oz) at maturity. Such a weight is partly caused by its ability to build up body fat for energy stores.

At 1 m (3 ft 3 in), the **longest parrot** is South America's hyacinth macaw (*Anodorhynchus hyacinthinus*).

Heaviest insect

Four species of goliath beetle (family Scarabaeidae) – *Goliathus regius*, *G. meleagris*, *G. goliatus* (=*G. giganteus*) and *G. druryi* – outweigh all other insects. In one series of males, the lengths from the tips of the small frontal horns to the end of the abdomen reached 11 cm (4.3 in), with weights of 70–100 g (2.5–3.5 oz). All are endemic to equatorial Africa.

Largest deer

In Sep 1897, a male Alaskan moose (*Alces alces gigas*) standing 2.34 m (7 ft 8 in) tall at the shoulders and weighing an estimated 816 kg (1,800 lb) was shot in Canada's Yukon Territory. Females average 1.8 m (5 ft 10 in) tall.

The **largest antler spread**, or "rack", on record is 204.8 cm (6 ft 8.6 in) for a moose that was hunted near Redoubt Bay in Alaska, USA, in Dec 1958.

▶ LARGEST WILD CAT

Male Siberian or Amur tigers (*Panthera tigris altaica*) typically measure 2.7–3.3 m (8 ft 10 in–10 ft 9 in) from nose to tail tip and weigh 180–306 kg (397–674 lb). The heaviest-known wild specimen was 384 kg (846 lb) when measured in 1950.

By contrast, the **smallest wild cat** is the rusty-spotted cat (*Prionailurus rubiginosus*) from India and Sri Lanka. It has a head-and-body length of 35–48 cm (1 ft 1 in–1 ft 6 in) and weighs around 1.5 kg (3 lb) – less than half the weight of a domestic cat.

GREATEST EYE SPAN (RELATIVE TO BODY SIZE)

Stalk-eyed flies (family Diopsidae) have longer eyestalks and spans between their eyes than any other animals. In some species, this distance can actually exceed the body length. A large male specimen of Malayan stalk-eyed fly (*Cyrtodiopsis whitei*, example above), native to the Indian subcontinent and south-east Asia, had a body length of 7.5 mm (0.29 in) and an inter-eye span of 10.5 mm (0.41 in).

Smallest bear

The Malayan sun bear (*Helarctos malayanus*) lives in subtropical India and south-east Asia. Adults grow up to 1.5 m (4 ft 11 in) long, stand 70 cm (2 ft 3 in) at the shoulder and weigh 30–65 kg (66–143 lb) – less than a fifth of the weight of a mature male grizzly.

Despite its size, this species has the **longest tongue for a bear**: 25 cm (9.8 in). It's used to extract honey and bugs from tree trunks and nests.

The **longest mammalian tongue (relative to body size)**, meanwhile, is that of the tube-lipped nectar bat (*Anoura fistulata*) from high-altitude cloud forests in Ecuador. Its tongue can grow to 8.49 cm (3.3 in), which is 1.5 times the total length of its body. Read about the **longest tongue for a mammal** overall on p.38.

Longest weaning period for a mammal

No other mammal weans its offspring for longer than the orangutans (genus *Pongo*) of Borneo and Sumatra. A 2017 study suggests that these apes can nurse young to at least 8.8 years old.

Most amphibians by country

Of the 7,965 or so known species of amphibians in the world, Brazil is home to at least 1,154 (as of Feb 2019), meaning that it harbours around 14.5% of all amphibians within its borders.

Among them are the **most transparent amphibians** – the so-called glass frogs (family Centrolenidae) of Central and South America. Their partly clear abdominal skin resembles frosted glass, allowing for their internal organs and green bones to be seen from below.

LARGEST LEMUR

The indri (*Indri indri*) can grow to 72 cm (2 ft 4 in) long. Its head and body account for some 90% of this, as it is almost tailless. Weighing as much as 7.5 kg (16 lb 8 oz), it is tree-dwelling and inhabits the eastern rainforests of Madagascar. All 100-plus lemur species are endemic to this African island, including the extinct, gorilla-sized *Archaeoindris fontoynontii* – the **largest lemur ever** at up to 200 kg (440 lb)!

 MAR 5 Cámara de Comercio Santa Rosa de Cabal (COL) presents the **longest chorizo** – measuring 1,917.8 m (6,291 ft 11 in) – at Parque Bolívar in Santa Rosa de Cabal, Colombia, in 2011.

LARGEST PRIMATE

The male eastern lowland gorilla (*Gorilla beringei graueri*) of the eastern Congo has a standing height of around 1.75 m (5 ft 9 in) and can weigh 163 kg (360 lb). It lives in tropical forests, in both low-lying and mountainous terrain. Since the 1990s – when there were around 17,000 individuals – poaching, mining and logging, along with civil unrest in the Democratic Republic of the Congo, have depleted the species' population. There may be fewer than 4,000 left, according to the Wildlife Conservation Society and Fauna & Flora International.

Gorillas construct the **largest mammalian nests**. Every day, these great apes build a new ground-based sleeping area from branches and leaves. The temporary beds are circular and span some 1.5 m (4 ft 11 in).

Eastern lowland gorillas are one of four subspecies of these great apes. Their cousins, the western gorillas (*G. gorilla*), numbered around 316,000 as of 2018, but are still classed as Critically Endangered.

LONGEST FEATHERS ON A WILD BIRD

The Reeves's pheasant (*Syrmaticus reevesii*), from the mountain forests of China, has central tail feathers that can exceed 2.4 m (8 ft), which is larger than the wingspan of a golden eagle! If the pheasant throws these feathers up in flight, they act as a brake, enabling the bird to swiftly alter its trajectory to evade an attacker.

MOST COMPLEX COLOUR VISION IN AN INSECT

According to research published in 2016, the common bluebottle butterfly (*Graphium sarpedon*) has 15 types of colour receptor in its eyes, sensitive to ultraviolet and human-visible light. This is compared with only two photoreceptors in the eyes of cats, dogs and horses, three in humans, and four in most birds. Native to southern Asia and Australia, this butterfly is often found flying in the rainforest canopy.

SMALLEST UNGULATE

The smallest hoofed mammal is the lesser Malay mouse-deer, or chevrotain (*Tragulus kanchil*), growing up to 55 cm (1 ft 10 in) long, with a shoulder height under 25 cm (10 in) and a maximum weight of 2.5 kg (5 lb 8 oz). Primarily nocturnal and inhabiting dense tropical forests in south-east Asia, it is rarely encountered. Mature males are identified by their fang-like upper canines, which protrude from the jaw.

MAR 6 Driving a 9,072-kg (20,000-lb) monster truck in Dubai, UAE, Ian Batey (UK) flattens 61,106 soda cans to earn the title for **most cans crushed with a vehicle in three minutes** in 2010.

MAR 7 At the 2010 Academy Awards ceremony, Kathryn Bigelow (USA) becomes the **first female to win an Oscar for Best Director**. She is honoured for her film *The Hurt Locker* (USA, 2008).

FASTEST-MOVING CRUSTACEAN ON LAND

The tropical ghost crabs of the genus *Ocypode* (*O. quadrata* shown above) inhabit burrows above the high-tide mark on sandy beaches, mostly bordering the western Pacific and Indian oceans. Despite running sideways rather than forwards, they have been timed at 4 m/s (13 ft/s).

Densest fur

The coat of the sea otter (*Enhydra lutris*) has 100,000–400,000 hairs per cm² (650,000– 2,600,000 hairs per sq in). The thickness varies across the animal's body – the fur on its paws, for example, being less dense. Sea otters live in the north-east Pacific, off the coasts of Canada, the USA and Russia.

Fastest-eating fish

The bay pipefish (*Syngnathus leptorhynchus*), blue-striped pipefish (*Doryrhamphus excisus*) and longspine snipefish (*Macroramphosus scolopax*) can each detect and gulp down prey in just 2 milliseconds. These fish are able to achieve such speedy strikes owing to elastic recoil-powered tendons, allowing for rapid head and snout movements, before engulfing their food (typically small crustaceans) via suction.

Largest cuttlefish

The giant cuttlefish (*Sepia apama*) grows up to 1 m (3 ft 3 in), including extended tentacles. The animal lives at depths of 100 m (328 ft) and occurs along south-east Australia, on reefs, seagrass fields and the sandy sea floor. Like other cephalopods, it changes the colour of its skin as a form of communication.

Oldest breeding sea bird (specimen)

Aged at least 68 years old, a female Laysan albatross (*Phoebastria immutabilis*) named Wisdom laid an egg at the Midway Atoll National Wildlife Refuge in the Pacific Ocean in Dec 2018. She has been monitored by conservationists for decades and, if all goes well, this could be her 37th chick. These birds generally only live to around 40 years of age.

Most venomous fish

Stonefish (family Synanceiidae) are native to shallow coastal waters of the Indo-Pacific. One species, *Synanceia horrida*, has the largest venom glands of any known fish. Neurotoxin injected from just three to six of its 13 dorsal spines can be a fatal dose for humans.

Venom is injected via a bite or sting, whereas poison is ingested. The **⊙ most poisonous fish** are the pufferfish (family Tetraodontidae), which live in the Red Sea and Indo-Pacific waters. Their bodies contain tetrodotoxin, just 16 mg (0.0005 oz) of which could kill a 70-kg (154-lb) human. Despite this, some consider this fish – known as *fugu* in Japan – a delicacy, when prepared correctly!

Strongest-known biological material

Limpets "excavate" rock for food using tiny teeth with a tensile strength of 4.9 gigapascals (GPa) – stronger than any other natural substance and most man-made materials too. The teeth are comprised of nanofibres formed from the iron-based mineral goethite. This discovery, published in the Royal Society journal *Interface* in 2015, displaced spider silk as the strongest biomaterial, with its upper limit of 4.5 GPa. For context, Kevlar has a tensile strength of 3–3.5 GPa.

Rarest species of penguin

Listed as Endangered by the IUCN since 2000, the Galápagos penguin (*Spheniscus mendiculus*) has an estimated population of just 1,800– 4,700, as per the last census in 2009.

Living on the Galápagos Islands, which straddle the Equator, this is also the **most northerly penguin**.

SMALLEST SEA HORSE

On average, adult Satomi's pygmy sea horses (*Hippocampus satomiae*) are only 13.8 mm (0.5 in) long, making them smaller than a human fingernail. Formally described as a new species in 2008, these diminutive marine fish inhabit the seas around Indonesia's Derawan Island, which lies off Borneo.

100%

LARGEST GREEN TURTLE ROOKERY

During the breeding season, up to 60,000 female green turtles (*Chelonia mydas*) migrate thousands of kilometres to lay their eggs on Raine Island, north of Queensland, Australia. More than 15,000 individuals can nest at any one time on the 1.8-km-long (1.1-mi) beach of this small island on the Great Barrier Reef, the world's **longest reef** (see p.27).

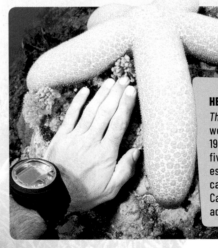

HEAVIEST STARFISH

Thromidia catalai is native to the western Pacific Ocean. On 14 Sep 1969, a specimen of this hefty five-armed species weighing an estimated 6 kg (13 lb 3 oz) was caught off Ilot Amédée in New Caledonia. It was later given to an aquarium in the capital, Nouméa.

SHORTEST LIFESPAN FOR A FISH

The seven-figure pygmy goby (*Eviota sigillata*), also known as the adorned dwarf goby, has a maximum recorded longevity of just 59 days. It is native to tropical coral reefs in the Indian and Pacific oceans. Its exceptionally fleeting lifespan also makes this goby the **shortest-lived vertebrate** overall.

MAR 8 In 2004, Manuel Pérez Pérez (ESP) presents the **heaviest sweet potato** in Güime, Lanzarote, Spain. The supersized spud tips the scales at 37 kg (81 lb 9 oz).

MAR 9 In Los Angeles, California, USA, in 2017, Ali Spagnola (USA) bounces into the record books with the **fastest 100 m on a space hopper (female)** – 38.22 sec.

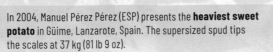

LARGEST PELICAN

The Dalmatian pelican (*Pelecanus crispus*) can grow to 1.8 m (5 ft 10 in) long, weigh 12 kg (26 lb 7 oz) and have a wingspan of 3.2 m (10 ft 5 in). Its wide distribution ranges from southern Europe to China.

It doesn't boast the **longest bill**, however. That title goes to the Australian pelican (*P. conspicillatus*) – its beak can measure up to 47 cm (1 ft 6 in) long, about the same as a newborn baby!

Dalmatian pelicans live in river deltas, estuaries and lakes. The biggest colony, with c. 1,400 breeding pairs, is at Lesser Prespa Lake on the border of Greece and Albania.

HEAVIEST MORAY EEL

In terms of mass, the giant moray eel (*Gymnothorax javanicus*) is the largest of the morays, weighing up to 30 kg (66 lb) – akin to a nine-year-old child! This species grows up to 3 m (9 ft 10 in) long. Giant morays reside in lagoons and on the fringes of coral reefs in the Indo-Pacific region, and have been known to occasionally attack divers.

LONGEST DIVE FOR A SEA COW

Also known as sirenians, sea cows are an order of aquatic ungulates consisting of the manatees and dugong. The longest confirmed dive by a sirenian is 24 min, for a West Indian manatee (*Trichechus manatus*, right) in Florida, USA.

The **largest sirenian ever** was the Steller's sea cow (*Hydrodamalis gigas*). Adults were 8–9 m (26 ft 2 in–29 ft 6 in) long and weighed up to 10 tonnes (22,046 lb) – far larger than any modern-day sirenian. Hunted by sailors for its meat, fat and hide, this slow-moving marine mammal had been driven to extinction by 1768, just 27 years after its discovery.

MAR 10 At the 2009 Attukal Pongala festival in Kerala, India, the **largest annual gathering of women** draws 2.5 million participants. The event is organized by Attukal Bhagavathy Temple Trust (IND).

MAR 11 In 2001, Catherine Hartley and Fiona Thornewill (both UK) set out from Ward Hunt Island in Canada on the **fastest ski journey to the North Pole (female)**. They arrive just 55 days later.

47

RIVERS, LAKES & WETLANDS

Smallest freshwater fish
In 2006, scientists announced the discovery of a transparent relative of the carp, since named *Paedocypris progenetica*. It was found living in highly acid peat swamps in Sumatra and Sarawak in Malaysian Borneo. The smallest adult specimen so far recorded was a 7.9-mm-long (0.31-in) female; the smallest mature male was 8.2 mm (0.32 in).

Longest journey for a freshwater fish
The European eel (*Anguilla anguilla*) undertakes a marathon journey of between 4,800 km and 6,400 km (3,000 and 4,000 mi) to spawn. It spends 7 to 15 years in European rivers and lakes, then rapidly changes into breeding condition, becoming silver and growing a longer snout and larger eyes. The much-altered animal then commences a voyage to the western Atlantic and its spawning grounds in the Sargasso Sea. The entire journey takes approximately six months.

Anadromous fish are those that are born in fresh water, migrate to the sea as juveniles and then return to fresh water to breed. The **largest anadromous fish** is the beluga sturgeon (*Huso huso*), which

fully grown is 2.3 m (7 ft 6 in) long on average and weighs as much as 130 kg (286 lb). It's found in the Black Sea (spawning in the Danube River), the Caspian Sea (Ural River) and the Sea of Azov (Don River).

Fastest flying insect
In short bursts, the Australian dragonfly (*Austrophlebia costalis*) can reach a top speed of 58 km/h (36 mph), which is faster than a galloping horse.

The giant helicopter damselfly (*Megaloprepus caerulatus*) of Central and South America is the **largest dragonfly**. It can reach 12 cm (4.7 in) long, with a 19.1-cm (7.5-in) wingspan.

Longest beaver dam
Located in Wood Buffalo National Park in Alberta, Canada, is an 850-m-long (2,788-ft) beaver dam. This massive structure is more than twice the length of the Hoover Dam on the Colorado River. It was first spotted in 2007 by environmental researcher Jean Thie (CAN) while he was studying satellite photographs of the region. After reviewing old images, Thie concluded that the dam must have been constructed by several generations of beavers, who had probably been working at the site since the mid-1970s.

FASTEST WATERFOWL
Among ducks, geese and swans, Africa's spur-winged goose (*Plectropterus gambensis*) is the fastest in flight, clocked at 142 km/h (88 mph). They get their name from bony "spurs" on their wing joints, used to fight rival birds. This species is also the **most toxic waterfowl**. It sequesters a poison called cantharidin in its body from the blister beetles that it sometimes eats. As little as 10 mg of this toxin can be fatal to humans.

Most cold-tolerant amphibian
The Siberian salamander, aka Siberian newt (*Salamandrella keyserlingii*) and Schrenck newt (*S. schrenckii*) can both endure lows of -35°C (-31°F) in the permafrost of Siberia. These cold-blooded animals are able to cope with these extreme conditions thanks to natural "anti-freeze" chemicals that replace the water in their blood, allowing them to become frozen solid during the winter but then thaw out in the spring. The Schrenck newt

lives primarily in Russia's Sikhote Alin region, while the range of the Siberian salamander extends much farther.

The **most heat-tolerant amphibian** is the Japanese stream treefrog (*Buergeria japonica*). Its tadpoles have been found in hot springs (*onsen*) at temperatures as high as 46.1°C (114.9°F) on Kuchinoshima Island, a volcanic islet in Kagoshima Prefecture, Japan. Living in such hot water may help to expedite their growth and also improve immunity.

▶ LARGEST AMPHIBIAN GENOME
A genome contains all of a species' genetic material. The axolotl (*Ambystoma mexicanum*), aka the Mexican salamander, has a genome containing 32 billion base pairs (basic units of DNA) – at least 10 times more than are present in the human genome. This Critically Endangered amphibian retains juvenile traits for life and is notable for being able to regenerate body parts.

LARGEST RIVER DOLPHIN
The boto (*Inia geoffrensis*), from the Amazon and Orinoco rivers of South America, grows to 2.6 m (9 ft) long. It owes its rosy hue to blood vessels under the skin that regulate body temperature. River dolphins are more flexible than their ocean cousins, helping them to navigate around trees when rivers flood.

LARGEST FLAMINGO COLONY
The soda lakes of East Africa host a permanent population of 1.5–2.5 million lesser flamingos (*Phoeniconaias minor*), mostly in northern Tanzania. Their distinct colouring comes from the algae that they eat, which thrive in the **most alkaline lakes**, in the Rift Valley of Kenya and Tanzania. The water has a pH level of 10–12, which is enough to blister human skin.

MAR 12 Kazuyoshi Miura (JPN, b. 26 Feb 1967) becomes the **oldest professional soccer player to score a competitive league goal** when he nets for Yokohama FC aged 50 years 14 days in 2017.

MAR 13 David Smith Jr (USA) – aka "The Bullet" – achieves the **farthest distance by a human cannonball** when he's shot 59.43 m (195 ft) at Raymond James Stadium in Tampa, Florida, USA, in 2018.

The 6-m (19-ft 8-in) anaconda seen above was photographed in Venezuela in 2012. This species spends much of its life in the water (see inset right, taken in Rio Formoso, Brazil).

HEAVIEST SNAKE

The green anaconda (*Eunectes murinus*) inhabits swamps, rivers and floodplains in South America and Trinidad. A female shot in Brazil in *c.* 1960 was estimated to weigh 227 kg (500 lb) – about the same as an upright piano – and was 8.45 m (27 ft 8 in) long. Most herpetologists today are more conservative when discussing this species' size, putting the upper length limit at around 7.5 m (24 ft 7 in). Anacondas' varied diet includes fish, birds, reptiles and mammals, such as capybaras (below).

LARGEST SNAPPING TURTLE

Native to the Americas, these reptiles are so-named for their propensity to snap their beak-like jaws if threatened. The largest of their kind is the USA's alligator snapping turtle (*Macrochelys temminckii*), which can exceed 100 kg (220 lb) and measure 60-80 cm (1 ft 11 in-2 ft 7 in) long. To hunt, they wiggle a worm-like appendage on their tongues to lure fish.

LARGEST RODENT

The capybara or carpincho (*Hydrochoerus hydrochaeris*) has a head-and-body length of 1-1.3 m (3 ft 3 in-4 ft 3 in), about the same as a border collie, and can weigh 79 kg (174 lb). This giant rodent is found in the basin of the Paraná and Uruguay rivers and in the wetlands of Argentina and Brazil. A social creature, it lives in families of 10–20 individuals.

MAR 14 In 2015, illusionist Rick Smith Jr (USA) wows crowds at the Great Lakes Science Center in Cleveland, Ohio, USA, with the **highest throw of a playing card** – 21.41 m (70 ft 3 in) into the air.

MAR 15 On Fuji TV's *Bikkuri Chojin 100 Special #2* in 2009, competitive eater Takeru Kobayashi (JPN) achieves the **most hot dogs eaten in three minutes** – six – in Kashiwa, Japan.

TUNDRA & ICE

MOST NORTHERLY OWL

Native to the Arctic regions of Eurasia and North America, the snowy owl (*Bubo scandiacus*) ventures farther north in search of prey - mainly small or medium-sized birds and mammals - than any other bird. One of very few birds to spend much of the year in the high Arctic zone, the snowy owl has been recorded at a latitude of 82°N on Canada's Ellesmere Island during the bitter-cold darkness of mid-winter.

Largest bear ever

The tyrant polar bear (*Ursus maritimus tyrannus*) stood 1.83 m (6 ft) at the shoulder, with a body length of 3.7 m (12 ft 2 in) and an average weight of 1 tonne (2,200 lb) – making it nearly three times heavier than an adult male grizzly bear (*U. arctos* spp.). Evolving from an isolated population of Arctic brown bears in the late Pleistocene epoch (250,000–100,000 years ago), this fossil subspecies was the **largest terrestrial mammalian carnivore ever**. Find out about its modern-day record-breaking descendant below.

Longest whale tooth

In the past, the single (very rarely paired) spiralled ivory tusk of the male narwhal (*Monodon monoceros*) was thought to be the horn of the fabled unicorn. Narwhal tusks attain an average length of roughly 2 m (6 ft 6 in), but can exceed 3 m (9 ft 10 in) and weigh up to 10 kg (22 lb). Narwhals live exclusively in cold Arctic waters.

Longest walrus tusks

The tusks of a walrus (*Odobenus rosmarus*) are greatly enlarged upper canine teeth and typically measure around 50 cm (1 ft 7 in) long. In 1997, two superlative tusks were discovered at Bristol Bay in Alaska, USA. The right-hand tooth measured 96.2 cm (3 ft 1.8 in) in length, while its partner was shorter by 2.5 cm (1 in).

Fewest eggs per year for a penguin

Both the emperor penguin (see opposite) of Antarctica and the king penguin (*Aptenodytes patagonicus*) of southern South America produce only a single egg per annum. All other penguin species lay two.

New Zealand's erect-crested penguin (*Eudyptes sclateri*) has the **greatest egg dimorphism for a bird (same clutch)**. Its second egg (the "B egg") can be as much as 80–85% heavier than its first (the "A egg").

Commonest penguin

The macaroni penguin (*Eudyptes chrysolophus*) is a crested bird found on subantarctic islands and the Antarctic Peninsula. There are some 6.3 million breeding pairs, but owing to a steep drop in population since the 1970s it is listed by the IUCN as Vulnerable.

Longest migration by a bird

The Arctic tern (*Sterna paradisaea*) breeds north of the Arctic Circle, flying south to the Antarctic for the northern winter and back again. This trip covers *c.* 80,400 km (50,000 mi), or nearly twice Earth's circumference.

Smallest reindeer subspecies

Adult Svalbard reindeer (*Rangifer tarandus platyrhynchus*) are as short as 0.8 m (2 ft 7 in) at the shoulder and weigh 80 kg (176 lb) – about half the weight of other reindeer subspecies. They are native to Norway's Svalbard islands in the Arctic Circle.

Coldest body temperature for a mammal

In 1987, Brian Barnes at the University of Alaska Fairbanks (both USA) recorded a body temperature of -2.9°C (26.7°F) in hibernating Arctic ground squirrels (*Urocitellus parryii*). The North American rodents can survive sub-zero by somehow "supercooling" their body fluids prior to hibernation, filtering out water molecules that would otherwise turn to ice.

The **richest bear milk** is that of the polar bear. It contains up to 48.4% fat – vital to help cubs endure their bitterly cold environment.

MOST DANGEROUS PINNIPED

The suborder Pinnipedia comprises walruses, sea lions and seals. The carnivorous leopard seal (*Hydrurga leptonyx*) is the only species with a reputation for unprovoked attacks on humans. There is evidence of these seals lunging through cracks in the ice to snap at people's feet, and at least one reported attack on divers. Below, a leopard seal captures an unfortunate Adélie penguin.

LARGEST BEAR

Adult male polar bears (*U. maritimus*) typically weigh 400–600 kg (880–1,320 lb), with a nose-to-tail length of up to 2.6 m (8 ft 6 in).

The species is found at latitudes of 65–85°N, making it the **most northerly bear**. It also has the **largest home range for a land mammal**: adult females in Hudson Bay, Canada, have vast territories that can cover some 350,000 km² (135,135 sq mi) – about the size of Germany.

MAR 16 The **greatest rainfall in 24 hours** is recorded in Cilaos, on the Indian Ocean island of Réunion, in 1952. A total of 1,870 mm (73.6 in) of rain falls in a single day-long period.

MAR 17 In 2011, Reza Pakravan (IRN) completes the **fastest crossing of the Sahara by bicycle** - 13 days 5 hr 50 min 14 sec. Having set out in Algeria on 4 Mar, he finishes his epic journey in Sudan.

Research published in 2018 revealed a trial involving the tagging of 20 emperor penguins with satellite transmitters in the Ross Sea in 2013. One individual remained submerged for 32 min 12 sec – the **longest underwater dive by a bird**.

LARGEST PENGUIN

The emperor penguin (*Aptenodytes forsteri*) inhabits the frozen continent of Antarctica. Males tend to be slightly larger than females, standing up to 1.3 m (4 ft 3 in) tall and weighing as much as 45 kg (99 lb).

The species incubates its single egg for a period of 62–67 days – the **longest incubation for a penguin**. Unusually, this is carried out by the male alone.

LARGEST PINNIPED

Even bigger than polar bears are the bulls of the southern elephant seal (*Mirounga leonina*), native to subantarctic islands. They average 5 m (16 ft 4 in) long from the inflated trunk-like snout (which inspired their common name) to the tips of the tail flippers. They can weigh a staggering 3,500 kg (7,716 lb) – more than seven grand pianos!

MOST NORTHERLY UNGULATE

The musk ox (*Ovibos moschatus*) lives in the tundra of mainland Canada, islands of the Canadian Arctic, and up to the northern tip of Greenland – as far as 83°N. It has evolved several features to survive on the harsh landscape, such as snowshoe-like spreading hooves and an annual layer of thick underwool (*qiviut*), which is eight times warmer than sheep wool.

MAR 18 The **longest underwater kiss in apnoea** (i.e., while holding the breath) is shared by Michele Fucarino and Elisa Lazzarini (both ITA) and lasts 3 min 24 sec in Rome, Italy, in 2010.

MAR 19 In 1877, the **first Test cricket match** comes to an end at the Melbourne Cricket Ground in Victoria, Australia. A Grand Combined Melbourne and Sydney XI beat an English touring side by 45 runs.

DOMESTIC ANIMALS

Most paws offered alternately by a dog in one minute
Jack Russell terrier Jacob "shook hands" with his owner, Rachael Grylls (UK), a total of 80 times in Exeter, Devon, UK, on 17 Feb 2018.

Most dogs walked simultaneously by an individual
On 17 Jun 2018, professional dog trainer Maria Harman (AUS) took 36 hounds on leashes for "walkies" around Wolston Creek Bushland Reserve in Queensland, Australia.

Most consecutive items caught by a dog
Hagrid, a Leonberger, snapped up nine sausages in a row, thrown by owner David Woodthorpe-Evans (UK), in Salford, UK, on 6 Sep 2018.

Longest tongue on a dog
Mochi, a St Bernard owned by Carla and Craig Rickert (both USA), has an 18.58-cm-long (7.3-in) tongue, as measured in Sioux Falls, South Dakota, USA, on 25 Aug 2016.
Incredibly, that's around the same length as the **smallest cat ever**! A male blue-point Himalayan-Persian named Tinker Toy – owned by Katrina

MOST TRICKS PERFORMED BY A PIG IN ONE MINUTE
A miniature pig named Joy and her owner, Dawn Bleeker (USA), completed 13 tricks in 60 sec in Newton, Iowa, USA, on 16 Jan 2018. Joy's feats included picking a ring off its stand (above), unrolling a rug and even playing a toy piano with her nose.

and Scott Forbes of Taylorville, Illinois, USA – was 19 cm (7.5 in) long and 7 cm (2.7 in) tall when fully grown.

Longest jump by a cat
Surpassing the previous mark by some 30 cm (1 ft), Waffle the Warrior Cat (USA) leapt 2.13 m (7 ft) in Big Sur, California, USA, on 30 Jan 2018.
The **longest jump by a rabbit**, meanwhile, measured 3 m (9 ft 10 in) and was achieved by Yabo, handled by Maria B Jensen (DNK), on 12 Jun 1999 in Horsens, Denmark.

Oldest rabbit
Born on 9 Feb 2003, Mick the agouti rabbit was aged 16 years 7 days as verified on 16 Feb 2019. Rescued from an animal shelter in 2004, he now lives with Liz Rench (USA), her dog Sheri and two other pet rabbits in Berwyn, Illinois, USA.

Fastest tortoise
A leopard tortoise named Bertie reached 0.28 m/s (0.92 ft/s) at Adventure Valley in Brasside, County Durham, UK, on 9 Jul 2014. He "ran" the 5.48-m (17-ft 11-in) course in 19.59 sec.

Highest jump by a miniature horse
Castrawes Paleface Orion, owned by Robert Barnes (AUS), cleared a 108-cm (3-ft 6-in) jump in Tamworth, New South Wales, Australia, on 15 Mar 2015. That's quite a feat when you're only 93 cm (3 ft 1 in) to the withers!

Longest horns on a yak
On 23 Dec 2018, the horns of a yak named Jericho measured 3.46 m (11 ft 4 in) from the tip of one across his head to the tip of the other. He lives on a farm in Welch, Minnesota, USA, with Hugh and Melodee Smith (both USA).

Fastest time to jump 10 hurdles by a llama
Caspa, owned by Sue Williams (UK) cleared 10 hurdles in 13.96 sec at Arley Hall in Cheshire, UK, on 6 Sep 2017.

MOST TRICKS PERFORMED BY A RABBIT IN ONE MINUTE
A four-year-old mixed-breed rabbit named Taawi completed 20 tricks with his owner, Aino Kivikallio (FIN), in Turku, Finland, on 15 Dec 2018. Shown below are two of them: "roll the ball" and "jump over an obstacle". Aino has trained Taawi using positive reinforcement, rewarding him with treats for learning activities.

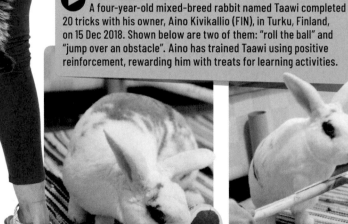

LONGEST DOMESTIC CAT
On 22 May 2018, Barivel measured 120 cm (3 ft 11 in) long in Vigevano, Pavia, Italy. The Maine Coon is shown above with his owner, Cinzia Tinnirello (ITA).
The **longest domestic cat ever** was Mymains Stewart Gilligan (aka "Stewie"), at 123 cm (4 ft). He lived with Robin Hendrickson and Erik Brandsness (both USA).

SHORTEST BULL
Humphrey (right), a male miniature zebu, measured 67.6 cm (2 ft 2 in) tall on 27 Apr 2018, as confirmed at Kalona Veterinary Clinic in Iowa, USA. His devoted owners are Joe and Michelle Gardner (both USA).
The **shortest cow** is a female Vechur named Manikyam, who stood 61.1 cm (2 ft) from the hoof to the withers on 21 Jun 2014 in Kerala, India. She is owned by Akshay N V (IND).

MAR 20 In 2010, doctors confirm that Akshat Saxena (IND) has 14 fingers (seven on each hand) and 20 toes (10 on each foot) – the **most fingers and toes (polydactylism) at birth**.

MAR 21 Dr Mark Temperato (USA) has the **largest drum set** verified at 813 pieces in 2013 in Lakeville, New York, USA. His kit took 20 years to acquire and includes multiple snares, cowbells and cymbals.

MOST TRICKS PERFORMED BY A DOG IN ONE MINUTE

Hero the Super Collie and Sara Carson (CAN) completed 49 tricks in 60 sec in Palmdale, California, USA, on 18 Feb 2018. The gifted canine can perform a wide range of stunts, including catching a frisbee in mid-air, skateboarding and balancing on Sara's feet. The duo appeared on *America's Got Talent* in 2017, coming fifth.

MOST HORNS ON AN ANIMAL

The Jacob sheep is a domestic breed in the UK and North America, though it's thought to have originated in the Middle East. Ewes and rams commonly have four horns, but some have as many as six. Among those with four horns, one pair usually grows vertically – often exceeding 60 cm (2 ft).

On the same show as Simba, Lenny "The Batdog" recorded the **fastest time to jump five hurdles while skateboarding by a dog** - 2.46 sec.

MOST INSTAGRAM FOLLOWERS FOR A CAT

Nala Cat is still Instagram's favourite feline, with 4.03 million followers as of 29 Apr 2019. Adopted by her owner Varisiri Methachittiphan (USA) from a shelter, the Siamese/tabby mix has captivated the web with her wide blue eyes, cute headgear and a penchant for curling up in boxes.

MOST RIBBON BOWS UNDONE BY A DOG IN ONE MINUTE

On 20 Nov 2018, Jack Russell Simba loosened eight bows tied around presents on the set of *La Notte dei Record* in Rome, Italy. Simba was trained by her owner, Valeria Caniglia (ITA).

 MAR 22 At the 1997 World Figure Skating Championships, Tara Lipinski (USA, b. 10 Jun 1982) wins the ladies' individual title aged 14 years 285 days, becoming the **youngest figure skating world champion**.

 MAR 23 In 2012, Morecambe Community High School (UK) stages the **largest egg-and-spoon race** in Lancashire, UK. Cameron Ball leads home the 1,445-strong field in a time of 28.59 sec.

Smallest dinosaur footprints
On 15 Nov 2018, *Scientific Reports* announced the discovery of didactyl (two-digit) tracks an average of 10.33 mm long and 4.15 mm wide (0.4 in x 0.16 in) – see left. The petite prints, made by a dinosaur about the size of a sparrow, were found near Jinju City in South Korea. The tracks, which could have been made by an adult or a juvenile, have been assigned to a new genus and species known only from trace fossils that has been named *Dromaeosauriformipes rarus*. The dromaeosaurs lived in the Cretaceous period (145 to 66 million years ago).

100%

Largest bird ever
The elephant birds of Madagascar became extinct around 1,000 years ago. The largest of these was *Vorombe titan* ("big bird"), which grew to a height of 3 m (9 ft 10 in). It is estimated to have weighed as much as 860 kg (1,895 lb) – with an average weight of 642.9 kg (1,417 lb) – as described in a paper in *Royal Society Open Science* on 26 Sep 2018. For the current **largest bird**, see p.39.

Newest ape
As documented in the journal *Science* in Jun 2018, the now-extinct gibbon *Junzi imperialis* is not only the latest ape species to come to light, but also the **newest genus of ape**. The gibbon's remains were part of an animal menagerie excavated in 2004 from a tomb some 2,200–2,300 years old, located near the former royal capital of Xi'an in Shaanxi Province, China.
During the 18th century, the species underwent the **first known ape extinction caused by humans**, brought about by deforestation, hunting and the pet trade.

Newest crocodile
In Oct 2018, a study in the journal *Zootaxa* revealed the Central African slender-snouted crocodile (*Mecistops leptorhynchus*) to be the latest species of crocodile, distinct from its West African counterpart (*M. cataphractus*). The reptile favours freshwater rivers and is found from Cameroon and Gabon in the west to Tanzania in the east.

First known "exploding" ants
The *Colobopsis cylindrica* group are tree-dwelling carpenter ants from south-east Asia, commonly referred to as "exploding ants". They exhibit a self-sacrificing defensive act that involves rupturing their own bodies to cover rival insects with a sticky, irritating fluid that prevents them from attacking the ants' colony.

First beluga whale sanctuary
Marine wildlife charities Whale and Dolphin Conservation and the SEA LIFE Trust (both UK) have collaborated to turn Klettsvik Bay at Heimaey Island, off south-west Iceland, into the first open-water reserve for the beluga whale (*Delphinapterus leucas*). The natural inlet in which the SEA LIFE Trust Beluga Whale Sanctuary is based covers an area of 32,000 m² (344,445 sq ft) – about the same as 25 Olympic-sized swimming pools – and is 9.1 m (30 ft) at its deepest.

Oldest spider ever
The longest-lived spider for which there is evidence was "Number 16", a female *Gaius villosus* trapdoor spider endemic to Australia. As noted in the journal *Pacific Conservation Biology* dated 19 Apr 2018, she was first recorded in Mar 1974 by Australian arachnologist Barbara York Main and last seen alive c. Apr 2016, making her at least 43 years old. The ancient arachnid resided in North Bungulla Nature Reserve near Tammin, Western Australia.

Oldest animal megafossils
"Megafossils" are ancient organic remains large enough to be seen by the naked eye. The earliest known example of an animal megafossil is *Dickinsonia*, a genus of soft-bodied, oval organisms that lived c. 558 million years ago and grew up to 1.4 m (4 ft 7 in) long. For decades, scientists were unsure whether such life forms were animals, giant single-celled organisms or something else

FASTEST MAMMAL IN FLIGHT
Native to southern USA, Mexico, Central America and South America, the Brazilian free-tailed bat (*Tadarida brasiliensis*) can reach ground speeds of 44.5 m/s (160.2 km/h; 99.5 mph) when flying. An aerodynamic body shape and narrow wings are believed to contribute to its aerial prowess. These measurements were taken from an aeroplane in Jul 2009 near the Frio Bat Cave, close to the town of Concan in Texas, USA.

OLDEST CHIMPANZEE TWINS
Pictured below as juveniles are twin sisters Golden and Glitter with their mother, Gremlin. Born on 13–14 Jul 1998, they were aged at least 20 years 117 days as of 8 Nov 2018.
The siblings live in Tanzania's Gombe Stream Chimpanzee Reserve, the location of the ◎**longest-running wild primate study**. It was initiated in 1960 by primatologist Dr Jane Goodall (UK, below right) in what is now Gombe National Park, and continues today, 59 years later, under the Jane Goodall Institute. In excess of 165,000 hours of data has been collected during observations of more than 320 chimps.

100%

▶ LARGEST BEE
Wallace's giant bee (*Megachile pluto*) can reach 4.5 cm (1.7 in) long, including the mandibles. Entomologists feared that this species had become extinct in the wild, but in Jan 2019 the above female was spotted by a US-Australian team on Indonesia's North Moluccas islands. It's the first live example to be filmed. At a quarter its size, a honey bee is also shown above to provide context.

MAR 24 The **longest goldfish** measures 47.4 cm (1 ft 6.6 in) from snout to tail-fin end – longer than a bowling pin – in Hapert, Netherlands, in 2003. It is owned by Joris Gijsbers (NLD).

MAR 25 In 2012, movie-maker James Cameron (CAN) makes the **deepest crewed descent (solo)** – 10,898 m (35,755 ft) – on board a "vertical torpedo" submersible in the Pacific Ocean's Mariana Trench.

OLDEST LAND ANIMAL

Jonathan, a Seychelles giant tortoise (*Aldabrachelys gigantea*), lives on the remote South Atlantic island of St Helena. He is believed to have been born in around 1832, making him *c.* 187 years old in 2019. Jonathan's age has been reliably estimated from the fact that he was said to be "fully mature" (and thus at least 50 years old) when he first arrived from the Seychelles in 1882.

Longest animal cryobiosis
"Cryobiosis" describes the dormant state that some organisms enter when their environment becomes unfavourable. In May 2018, the journal *Doklady Biological Sciences* revealed that two species of nematode (roundworm) found frozen in Arctic permafrost soil 41,000–42,400 years old were reanimated after being cultivated in a lab. The worms – *Panagrolaimus* aff. *detritophagus* and *Plectus* aff. *parvus* – were collected in 2015 near the Alazeya River in north-eastern Russia.

LARGEST HORN SPREAD FOR A STEER EVER
Sato, a nine-year-old longhorn steer, had a horn spread (the distance between his horn tips) of 3.2 m (10 ft 6 in) on 30 Sep 2018, as confirmed in Bay City, Texas, USA. This is roughly the same distance as three baseball bats laid end to end. His owners are Scott and Pam Evans (both USA).

entirely. In 2018, however, a biochemical study led by the Australian National University detected fossilized cholesterol within organically preserved *Dickinsonia* fossils, confirming that they were animal in nature.

Shortest time for a vertebrate to reach sexual maturity
The turquoise killifish (*Nothobranchius furzeri*) is native to seasonal pools in Mozambique and Zimbabwe. Owing to the short-lived nature of its habitat, it has evolved to be capable of reproducing in 14–15 days, as reported on 6 Aug 2018 in *Current Biology*.

MOST SUCCESSFUL FELINE PREDATOR
Observations of the black-footed cat (*Felis nigripes*) reveal that up to 60% of its hunts result in a kill – even though it's one of the world's smallest wild cats (see also p.44). Endemic to South Africa, Namibia and Botswana, the feline's diverse diet includes small mammals, invertebrates, reptiles, birds and their eggs. On an average night, an adult *F. nigripes* kills 10–14 rodents or small birds.

There are (scientifically unconfirmed) reports from local hunters that this fluffy squirrel preys on chickens and even deer!

LONGEST-LIVED FISH

A 2016 study found that one Greenland shark (*Somniosus microcephalus*) had lived for 392 years – the longest lifespan for a fish species; it is also the **longest-lived vertebrate**. This deep-dwelling creature grows roughly 1 cm (0.4 in) per year and only becomes sexually mature at 150 years old. It is found in the cold waters of the North Atlantic, an environment that is thought to contribute to its longevity.

FLUFFIEST TAIL

The tufted ground squirrel (*Rheithrosciurus macrotis*) is native to the island of Borneo. Its exceptionally bushy tail is an estimated 130% of the volume of the rest of its body, giving this species the largest tail-to-body ratio of any known mammal. The purpose of this super-fluffy appendage is not clear. However, researchers suspect that it may serve to make the squirrel appear larger, and therefore potentially more threatening to predators.

MAR 26 In 2009, the **fastest speed for a land yacht** is achieved by Richard Jenkins (UK), on board *Greenbird*, at Ivanpah Dry Lake in Nevada, USA. He pilots the carbon-composite craft to 202.9 km/h (126.1 mph).

MAR 27 The **most expensive soccer shirt sold at auction** fetches £157,750 ($225,109) in London, UK, in 2002. It is the iconic No.10 jersey worn by Pelé (BRA) in the 1970 FIFA World Cup final.

55

▶ MOST TATTOOED MAN

Chainsaw-juggling, unicycling, sword-swallowing Lucky Diamond Rich (AUS, b. NZ) has spent more than 1,000 hr having his body modified by tattoo artists. He began by having his skin covered with colourful designs from around the world, then completely overlaid this with black ink before adding white designs on top and coloured designs on top again. He now boasts more than 200% coverage, including his eyelids, the delicate skin between the toes, the upper part of the ear canals and even his gums. This reflective portrait was taken as part of an exclusive GWR photoshoot at a hotel in London, UK, in 2018.

CONTENTS

Lucky is very much his own man. "What other people think of me is none of my business," he insists. "I don't really get my self-esteem from what others think of me."

SNAPSHOT
TALLEST MAN

In Sep 2009, Sultan Kösen from Turkey arrived in London, UK, on his first-ever trip outside his homeland. He was photographed with some of the city's most iconic sights, from red telephone boxes to Routemaster buses. Here, we document that memorable day, and also see how he measures up against the **tallest man ever.**

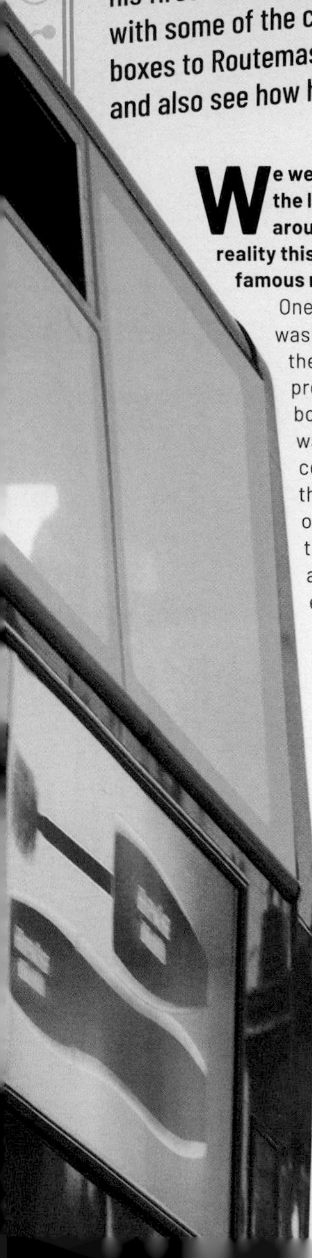

We welcomed 251-cm-tall (8-ft 2.8-in) Sultan to the UK ahead of the launch of *GWR 2010* and took the opportunity to show him around London. Pictured here waiting at a typical bus stop, in reality this mild-mannered giant would struggle to board the city's famous red buses – after all, he's more than half the height of one!

One of five children (all his siblings are average height), there was nothing extraordinary about Sultan's size until he reached the age of 10. But then a tumour on his pituitary gland – which produces a number of hormones, including those affecting body growth – caused him to shoot upwards dramatically. It wasn't until 2008 that a life-saving operation brought it under control – by which time Sultan had outgrown everyone on the planet. In fact, he's the third-tallest person on record; only John F Carroll (USA; d. 1969) at 263 cm (8 ft 7.5 in) and the remarkable Robert Wadlow (see right) were taller. He's also one of only a handful of people confirmed to have exceeded 8 ft (243.8 cm) in height.

Sultan's record-breaking stature comes with plenty of challenges, of course – he has to have his clothes and even his bed made to measure. It's not easy to buy a pair of shoes, either, when your feet are 36.5 cm (14.4 in) long! Unsurprisingly, his extraordinary height also has serious health repercussions: Sultan uses crutches to support himself when walking, as moving puts great pressure on his joints.

During his London visit, Sultan revealed to reporters that "My biggest dream is to get married... I'm looking for love." He realized that dream four years later, marrying 175.2-cm-tall (5-ft 9-in) Merve Dibo in the Turkish city of Mardin.

SULTAN VS ROBERT

Today's **tallest man** is shown above right along with two quintessential features of London: the Elizabeth Tower (aka "Big Ben", see pp.14–15) and a classic red British "K2" telephone box. Also pictured is a likeness of the **tallest man ever** – Robert Wadlow (USA, left) – whose height of 272 cm (8 ft 11.1 in) would have seen him almost level with the top of the 2.74-m-tall (9-ft) phone booth.

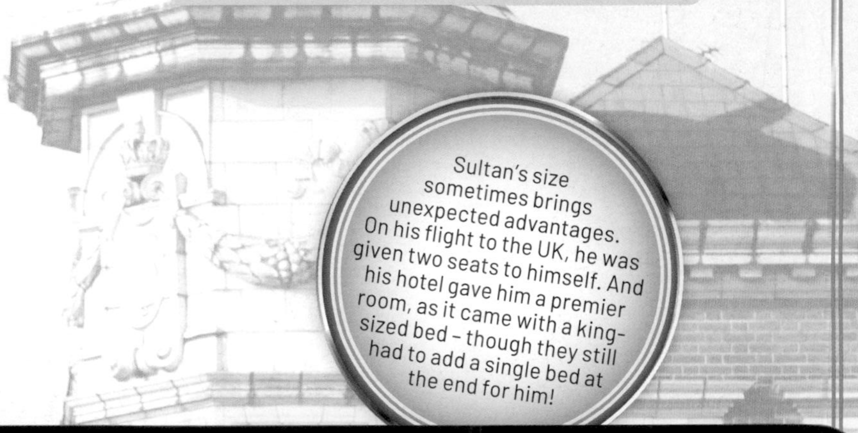

> Sultan's size sometimes brings unexpected advantages. On his flight to the UK, he was given two seats to himself. And his hotel gave him a premier room, as it came with a king-sized bed – though they still had to add a single bed at the end for him!

BUS STOP

Euston Road

towards

Oxford Circus

C2 24 hour

Buy tickets before boarding on all routes

TELEPHONE

Hea

Go big with videos of Sultan at guinnessworldrecords.com/2020

LARGEST HANDS
Sultan's hands measured 28.5 cm (11.22 in) long from the wrist to the tip of the middle finger in 2011. Currently, he also has the **widest hand span**, at 30.48 cm (12 in), as confirmed in 2010. Above, we show how the Turkish titan's right hand would measure up against the pages you're reading right now!

TALLEST MAN

59

OLDEST...

Person ever
The greatest fully authenticated age to which any human has ever lived is 122 years 164 days, by Jeanne Louise Calment (FRA). She was born on 21 Feb 1875, a year before Alexander Graham Bell patented the telephone. Jeanne took up fencing aged 85 years and cycled until she was 100. She died at a nursing home in Arles, southern France, on 4 Aug 1997.

The **oldest male ever** was Jiroemon Kimura (JPN), who was born on 19 Apr 1897 and passed away on 12 Jun 2013 aged 116 years 54 days.

Living married couple (aggregate age)
Masao Matsumoto (b. 9 Jul 1910) wedded Miyako Sonoda (both JPN, b. 24 Nov 1917) on 20 Oct 1937. As of 25 Jul 2018, the enduring couple had been married for 80 years 278 days, with Masao aged 108 years 16 days and Miyako 100 years 243 days - a combined total of 208 years 259 days.

Practising barber
As of 8 Oct 2018, Anthony Mancinelli (USA, b. ITA, 2 Mar 1911) was still cutting hair aged 107 years 220 days. He works five days a week, from noon to 8 p.m., at Fantastic Cuts in New Windsor, New York, USA.

Nobel laureate
On 3 Oct 2018, Arthur Ashkin (USA, b. 2 Sep 1922) was awarded the Nobel Prize in Physics (jointly,

HIGHEST COMBINED AGE FOR 16 LIVING SIBLINGS
The 16 children of Louis-Joseph Blais and Yvonne Brazeau of Quebec, Canada (pictured inset, seated centre), had a combined age of 1,203 years 350 days as of 11 Dec 2018. There was a 21-year age gap between the eldest sibling, 85-year-old Jean-Jacques (b. 23 Jun 1933), and the youngest, Lucie (b. 29 Mar 1954). This remarkable family (pictured above, with 15 of its members in shot) comprises six males and 10 females.

with Donna Strickland and Gérard Mourou) aged 96 years 31 days. Arthur was honoured for his work on optical tweezers.

▶ Practising pharmacist
As of 23 Nov 2018, Eiko Hiruma (JPN, b. 6 Nov 1923) was still working aged 95 years 17 days at the Hiruma Pharmacy in Itabashi, Tokyo, Japan.

Current monarch
Born on 21 Apr 1926, Her Majesty Queen Elizabeth II (UK) celebrated her 93rd birthday in 2019. She became the world's oldest monarch on 23 Jan 2015, following the death of Saudi Arabia's King Abdullah.

Heavy goods vehicle (HGV) licence holder
Great-grandfather Richard Thomas Henderson (UK, b. 13 Apr 1935) just keeps on trucking. He made a delivery

on 7 Jan 2019 aged 83 years 269 days in Selkirk, UK. He has to pass a yearly medical to stay behind the wheel.

Competitive rope skipper
On 23 Feb 2019, Annie Judis (USA, b. 23 Nov 1943) competed in the Southern California Open Jump Rope Championship aged 75 years 92 days in Coronado, California, USA.

English Premier League soccer manager
Ex-England manager Roy Hodgson (UK, b. 9 Aug 1947) took charge of Crystal Palace aged 71 years 255 days for their league match against Arsenal on 21 Apr 2019. His side won 3-2.

OLDEST ACTIVE SOCCER PLAYER
On 5 Apr 2019, goalkeeper Isaak Hayik (ISR) turned out aged 73 years 95 days for Israeli fifth-tier side Maccabi Ironi Or Yehuda against Hapoel Ramat Israel. He beat the previous record holder by almost two decades. Isaak was born in Iraq in 1945 and emigrated to Israel at the age of four. He was presented with his official GWR certificate after the match (above). "I'm ready for another game," he said.

OLDEST HEAD CHEF OF A MICHELIN THREE-STAR RESTAURANT
Aged 93 years 128 days as of 4 Mar 2019, Jiro Ono (JPN, b. 27 Oct 1925) remained head chef at Sukiyabashi Jiro, a Michelin three-star sushi restaurant in Chūō, Tokyo, Japan. Located in a subway station, Jiro's restaurant has counter space for just 10 diners and the tasting menu is determined on the morning of service. Jiro prepares all of the sushi himself.

OLDEST GAMING YOUTUBER
Aged exactly 83 years as of 2 Apr 2019, Shirley Curry (USA, b. 1936) has shot hundreds of videos for her self-titled YouTube channel, which has earned more than half a million subscribers and more than 11 million views. Shirley was introduced to gaming by her son in the 1990s, and mostly streams the action role-player game *The Elder Scrolls V: Skyrim* (Bethesda, 2011).

MAR 28 In 2016, Guy Martin (UK) attains the **highest speed on a wall of death**. He hits 125.77 km/h (78.15 mph) and completes one revolution in 3.41 sec on live TV at Manby airfield in Louth, Lincolnshire, UK.

MAR 29 Gaber Kahlwai Gaber Ali (EGY) is head over heels as he executes the **most cartwheels in one minute** - 67 - at Cairo University Stadium in Giza, Egypt, in 2015.

TOP 10 OLDEST LIVING PEOPLE

NAME	BORN	AGE
Kane Tanaka (JPN)	2 Jan 1903	116 years 73 days
Maria-Giuseppa Robucci-Nargiso (ITA)	20 Mar 1903	115 years 361 days
Lucile Randon (FRA)	11 Feb 1904	115 years 33 days
Shin Matsushita (JPN)	30 Mar 1904	114 years 351 days
Jeanne Bot (FRA)	14 Jan 1905	114 years 61 days
Shigeyo Nakachi (JPN)	1 Feb 1905	114 years 43 days
Haruno Yamashita (JPN)	19 Feb 1905	114 years 25 days
Kame Ganeko (JPN)	10 Apr 1905	113 years 340 days
Ellen "Dolly" Gibb (CAN)	26 Apr 1905	113 years 324 days
Alelia Murphy (USA)	6 Jul 1905	113 years 253 days

Source: Gerontology Research Group, as of 16 Mar 2019

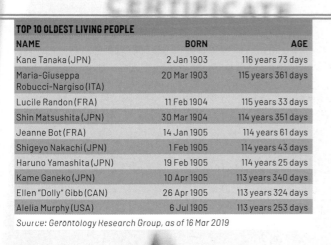

▶ OLDEST LIVING PERSON

On 16 Mar 2019, Kane Tanaka (JPN, b. 2 Jan 1903) had her age verified at 116 years 73 days in Fukuoka, Japan. She was born in the same year that the Wright brothers achieved the **first powered flight**, and grew up to run a family business selling sticky rice, sweets and noodles. Kane currently lives in a rest home, where her hobbies include mathematics and playing the board game Othello.

Kane had aspired to become the **oldest living person** since turning 100. She celebrated with chocolates.

▶ OLDEST PROFESSIONAL CLUB DJ

"DJ Sumirock", aka Sumiko Iwamuro (JPN, b. 27 Jan 1935), was still performing regularly at the age of 83 in the Shinjuku district of Tokyo, Japan, as confirmed on 25 May 2018. She took up DJing at the age of 77. Her techno sets are mixed in with jazz, anime soundtracks and classical music. Sumirock has also performed in New Zealand and France.

OLDEST PERSON TO CYCLE ACROSS CANADA (FEMALE)

Lynnea Salvo (USA, b. 21 Sep 1949) was aged 68 years 339 days when she completed her bicycle journey across the world's second-largest country on 26 Aug 2018. She rode 6,616 km (4,111 mi) in 70 days.

On 23 Oct 2016, retired teacher Lynnea became the **oldest person to cycle across the USA (female)**, aged 67 years 32 days.

OLDEST PERSON TO CYCLE FROM LAND'S END TO JOHN O' GROATS

Between 8 Sep and 25 Sep 2018, Alex Menarry (UK, b. 8 Dec 1932) rode the length of Britain, finishing at the north-eastern tip of Scotland aged 85 years 291 days. He had covered an average of 101 km (63 mi) each day. Alex, a former fell runner, said that the mental challenge of the journey was harder than the physical demands.

 MAR 30 In 2012, bass singer Tim Storms (USA) produces the **lowest vocal note** – G -7 (0.189 Hz), or eight octaves below the lowest G on a piano – at Citywalk Studios in Branson, Missouri, USA.

 MAR 31 In 1889, the Eiffel Tower is inaugurated in Paris, France. Measuring 300 m (984 ft 3 in) high, it is the loftiest structure of its time and remains the **tallest iron structure** to this day.

Beard category seven times and was crowned overall champion in 1999 and 2003. To qualify for the Imperial Partial Beard title, hair must be grown only on the cheeks and upper lip.

Kelly Hanson and Randy Carfagno Productions (both USA). It took four people to place it on the actress.

LONGEST HAIR (FEMALE)
The luxurious locks of Xie Qiuping (CHN) achieved a length of 5.62 m (18 ft 5 in), as verified on 8 May 2004. She started growing her hair in 1973, when she was just 13 years old. "It's no trouble at all, I'm used to it," she told GWR. "But you need patience and you need to hold yourself straight when you have hair like this."

At more than 5 m, Xie Qiuping's hair is almost as long as an adult male giraffe is tall.

1. Tallest Mohawk spike
Fashion designer Kazuhiro Watanabe (JPN) spent more than 15 years growing his Mohawk spike to a length of 1.23 m (4 ft), as verified at Dwango Hanzomon Studio in Tokyo, Japan, on 23 Apr 2014. Sculpting the magnificent Mohican took a team of stylists two hours and required three cans of hairspray and a jar of gel.

2. Most wins at the World Beard and Moustache Championships
Karl-Heinz Hille (DEU) won nine titles at the World Beard and Moustache Championships between 1999 and 2013. He triumphed in the Imperial Partial

3. Highest hairstyle
A tower of real and fake hair reaching 2.66 m (8 ft 8 in) was created at an event organized by KLIPP unser Frisör (AUT) in Wels, Austria, on 21 Jun 2009. Two stylists needed two days – and 22 m (72 ft 2 in) of artificial hair – to beat the record.

4. Widest wig
On 27 Jan 2017, Hollywood star Drew Barrymore (USA) appeared on the set of *The Tonight Show* in New York City, USA, wearing a humongous hairpiece measuring 2.23 m (7 ft 4 in) wide. The wig was made by

5. Youngest female with a full beard
Harnaam Kaur (UK, b. 29 Nov 1990) was 24 years 282 days old when her full beard – facial hair covering sideburns, the chin, part of the cheeks and hair above the upper lip – was confirmed on 7 Sep 2015. Her facial hair is caused by a hormonal imbalance owing to polycystic ovary syndrome. Now a freelance model and motivational speaker, Harnaam says she is driven "to show the world what true beauty is and how we can all be our own selves".

6. Longest moustache ever
A titanic 'tache belonging to Ram Singh Chauhan (IND) was measured at 4.29 m (14 ft) on the set of *Lo Show dei Record* in Rome, Italy, on 4 Mar 2010. Ram started growing his facial hair in 1970 and groomed his whiskers daily with coconut and mustard oils. His moustache even won him a cameo role in the James Bond film *Octopussy* (UK/USA, 1983).

APR 1 — A total of 114 soccer fans in scuba gear gather to watch a televised England match in a giant dive tank in 2009 at The Underwater Studio in Basildon, Essex, UK – the **most people watching TV underwater**.

APR 2 — Rémy Bricka (FRA) sets out on the **fastest "walk" across the Atlantic Ocean** in 1988, wearing buoyant 4.2-m-long (13-ft 9-in) skis. He covers 5,636 km (3,502 mi) in 59 days.

7. Largest hairy family

Jesús "Chuy" Fajardo Aceves and Luisa Lilia De Lira Aceves (both MEX) are two members of a family of 19, spanning five generations, who all have congenital generalized hypertrichosis. This rare condition is characterized by excessive facial and torso hair. The women are covered with a light-to-medium coat of hair while the men have thick hair on approximately 98% of their body, apart from their palms and soles.

8. Largest afro (female)

On 31 Mar 2012, the afro belonging to Aevin Dugas (USA) was measured at 16 cm (6.3 in) high from the crown of the head, with a total circumference of 1.39 m (4 ft 7 in). Aevin trimmed her afro two or three times a year, and used up to five conditioners at once when washing it.

The ◯ **largest afro** was 25.4 cm (10 in) high and had a circumference of 1.77 m (5 ft 10 in). Its owner, Tyler Wright (USA), was just 12 years old when his hair was measured on 19 Jun 2015.

9. Longest beard on a living male

As of 8 Sep 2011, the beard of Sarwan Singh (CAN) reached a length of 2.49 m (8 ft 2 in). Sarwan is the leader of a congregation of the Guru Nanak Sikh temple in Surrey, British Columbia, Canada.

The **longest beard ever** was 5.33 m (17 ft 6 in) and belonged to Hans N Langseth (NOR). It was measured upon his death in 1927.

LONGEST HAIR ON A TEENAGER

The tresses of 16-year-old Nilanshi Patel (IND, b. 16 Aug 2002) had achieved a length of 1.75 m (5 ft 8 in) by 21 Nov 2018. She has been growing her hair since the age of six, and calls it her "lucky charm". It is washed once a week – drying takes half an hour, combing twice that. Nilanshi usually wears her hair in a braid, but ties it in a bun to play table tennis.

APR 3 — Butcher Barry John Crowe (IRL) breaks the record for the **most sausages produced in one minute** on RTÉ's *Big Week on the Farm* in 2017. He makes 78 bangers at a rate of one every 0.76 sec.

APR 4 — In 1933, the USS *Akron* is ripped apart in a storm off the coast of New Jersey, USA, killing 73 passengers and crew – the **worst airship disaster**. There are only three survivors.

63

BODY BEAUTIFUL

Most tattoos of the same name on the body
In celebration of the birth of his daughter, Mark Evans (UK) had the name "Lucy" inked on his back 267 times, as verified on 25 Jan 2017.

▶ Most body modifications (married couple)
Victor Hugo Peralta (URY) and his wife Gabriela (ARG) have a total of 84 modifications to their bodies, as verified on 7 Jul 2014. They consist of 50 piercings, eight microdermals, 14 body implants, five dental implants, four ear expanders, two ear bolts and one forked tongue.

▶ Most flesh tunnels (face)
Joel Miggler (DEU) had modified his face with 11 flesh tunnels (hollow, tube-like pieces of jewellery), as confirmed in Küssaberg, Germany, on 27 Nov 2014. The tunnels ranged from 3 mm to 34 mm (0.1–1.3 in) in diameter.

Most people receiving henna tattoos
Henna is a natural reddish-brown dye obtained from the plant *Lawsonia inermis*. At an event organized by Shree Ahir Samaj Seva Samiti-Surat, Natubhai Ranmalbhai Bhatu and Jerambhai Vala (all IND), 1,982 people simultaneously received henna tattoos in Gujarat, India, on 3 Feb 2018.

SMALLEST WAIST EVER
In 1929, Ethel Granger (UK) began to reduce her waist of 56 cm (1 ft 10 in) by wearing ever-tighter corsets. By 1939, her waist measured just 33 cm (1 ft 1 in). A pioneer of body modification, Ethel also sported a number of facial piercings. The same waist measurement was claimed by Mlle Polaire, aka Émilie Marie Bouchaud (FRA, 1874–1939).

LONGEST NECK
Some women from the Padaung (or Kayan) tribe of Myanmar and Thailand stretch the distance between their head and shoulders using heavy brass rings. A study published in 2018 recorded Padaung women with neck lengths (taken from just above the collarbone to the lower jaw) of up to 19.7 cm (7.7 in). The neck length of a typical adult is 8–10 cm (3.1–3.9 in).

Most pierced senior citizen
"Prince Albert", aka John Lynch (UK, b. 9 Nov 1930), had 241 piercings – including 151 in his head and neck – during a single count in Hammersmith, London, UK, on 17 Oct 2008.

Most cosmetic makeovers in one hour (team of five)
On 7 Sep 2018, a five-strong team of make-up artists from Sephora Deutschland (DEU) gave 148 shoppers makeovers at the Main-Taunus-Zentrum mall in Sulzbach, Germany.

Most people applying lipstick
On 9 Sep 2018, a total of 6,900 people put on lipstick during the Ganda for All Music Festival in Quezon City, Manila, Philippines. Festival-goers had to show a Vice Cosmetics (PHL) lipstick shade to gain entry.

On 27 Jul 2018, make-up artist Melis İlkkılıç achieved the **most lipstick applications in one minute**, coating the lips of eight models with the help of Avon Türkiye (both TUR).

Most faces shaved in one hour with an electric razor (individual)
Barber Furkan Yakar (b. TUR) shaved 69 faces in Berlin, Germany, on 31 Oct 2018. The quick-fire debearding was set up by L'Oréal Men Expert and the Movember Foundation (both DEU).

Thickest make-up
Chutti is unique to the Kathakali dance-theatre tradition of India. The Redbeard characters have "masks" built up over hours using rice paste and paper. The final make-up can extend up to 15 cm (6 in) from the face.

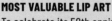

▶ MOST MARVEL COMIC CHARACTERS TATTOOED ON THE BODY
Rick Scolamiero (CAN) has 31 different characters from the Marvel Universe tattooed on his body, as verified on 3 Mar 2018. Designs include Black Widow on his torso (inset, below) and Venom on his left knee (inset, bottom). Rick also has Stan Lee's autograph inked on his wrist.

100%

MOST VALUABLE LIP ART
To celebrate its 50th anniversary, on 7 Sep 2018 Rosendorff Diamonds (AUS) decorated the lips of model Charlie Octavia with 126 diamonds worth a total of AUS$757,975 ($545,125; £421,644).

The artwork was designed and executed by make-up artist Clare Mac (pictured left, with Octavia), who initially applied a layer of matte-black lipstick before attaching each gem using false-eyelash adhesive.

OLDEST MODEL TO APPEAR IN *VOGUE* MAGAZINE
Bo Gilbert (UK, b. 1916) starred at the age of 100 in an advertising campaign for luxury department store Harvey Nichols that featured in the pages of the May 2016 edition of British *Vogue*. Bo appeared in honour of the magazine's centenary issue. "I dress to suit myself," she said. "I certainly don't dress up for boys!"

APR 5
In 1930, M K Gandhi (IND) arrives in Dandi having led 78 followers on the **longest protest march** - a 387.8-km (241-mi) journey across the Indian state of Gujarat in protest at the British levy of salt tax.

APR 6
Lucy Wardle (USA) achieves the **highest dive from a diving board (female)**, plunging 36.8 m (120 ft 9 in) into a pool at Ocean Park in Hong Kong, China, in 1985.

LONGEST NAIL EXTENSIONS

Hat-maker, Barbra Streisand superfan and self-professed *enfant terrible* Odilon Ozare (USA) created 10 colourful nail extensions, each measuring 1.21 m (4 ft), as verified on 26 Aug 2018 in Tampa, Florida, USA. They are made from 30 layers of cosmetic acrylic covered with airbrushed polyacrylic. The idea came to Odilon while he was practising "bird yoga" with his beloved cockatiels. He is currently working on the longest shoe.

Odilon is also responsible for the ● **tallest hat** (right), measuring 4.8 m (15 ft 9 in). To qualify for the record, he had to walk more than 10 m (32 ft) while wearing it.

MOST COMMON AESTHETIC NON-SURGICAL PROCEDURE

According to the International Society of Aesthetic Plastic Surgery (ISAPS), the world's most popular non-surgical cosmetic procedure performed by plastic surgeons is the injecting of botulinum toxin ("botox"). It was carried out 5,033,693 times in 2017 and accounted for 39.9% of all non-surgical procedures.

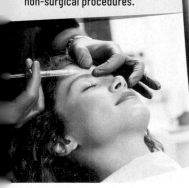

● MOST TATTOOED SENIOR CITIZEN (MALE)

Since getting his first tattoo in the 1950s, Charles "Chuck" Helmke (USA) has gone on to cover 97.5% of his body, as verified in Melbourne, Florida, USA, on 9 Dec 2016.

Chuck's partner is Charlotte Guttenberg (USA), the ● **most tattooed senior citizen (female)** and ● **most tattooed woman** overall. She had 98.75% body coverage as of 7 Nov 2017.

MOST SUBSCRIBERS FOR A YOUTUBE FASHION/BEAUTY CHANNEL

"Yuya", aka Mariand Castrejón Castañeda (MEX), boasted 23,666,883 subscribers as of 29 Apr 2019 – placing her in the top 60 most-subscribed channels on YouTube. Also known as "lady16makeup", Yuya began her vlog in 2009. She predominantly focuses on clothing and make-up, but also posts more general lifestyle videos.

APR 7 — In 2014, Jack Sexty (UK) completes the **fastest marathon on a pogo stick**, bouncing across the finish line in 16 hr 24 min at the Manchester Marathon in the UK.

APR 8 — In 2013, the **oldest pear tree** – a Manchurian variety – is given an estimated age of 458 years in the ancient orchard of Shenchuan township in Gansu Province, China.

BODY HACKING

Strongest home-made exoskeleton
"The Hacksmith" – aka James Hobson (CAN) – has designed and constructed powered exoskeletons for the upper and lower body that enable him to lift the rear wheels of a pick-up truck weighing 2,272 kg (5,009 lb) and carry a 220-kg (485-lb) barbell with ease, as demonstrated in Jan 2016. The exoskeleton is activated by Hobson's own body, but its strength comes from two powerful pneumatic cylinders.

FIRST...

Wearable computer
In 1961, mathematicians Edward O Thorp and Claude Shannon (both USA) of the Massachusetts Institute of Technology invented a computer about the size of a pack of playing cards designed to predict the outcome of roulette wheels. The device was worn strapped to the waist, with foot-switches hidden in a shoe to input the required data.

The **first wearable eyeglass camera** was created by Professor Steve Mann (CAN) in 1980. The device functioned as both a camera and an optical display, overlaying graphics in front of the wearer's eyes.

Officially recognized "cyborg"
In 2004, Neil Harbisson (see below opposite), who is totally colour blind, had an "eyeborg" antenna implanted in the back of his skull that allows him to experience colour as music. The antenna is attached to a camera in front of his eyes that converts light waves into sound waves that he can hear. He wears the eyeborg at all times, including in his passport photograph.

FIRST SELF-BUILT FUNCTIONAL LEGO® PROSTHETIC ARM
Andorra's David Aguilar, who was born without a right forearm, designed and built his own fully functioning arm using parts from a LEGO® Technic helicopter set (#9396), completing the first version in 2017. Aguilar, aka "Hand Solo", has been building LEGO prosthetics since childhood (inset) and constantly refines his designs. His most recent model (being worn above) is a motorized limb with fingers that he controls by making subtle movements of his residual arm.

Biohacker with earthquake-sensing technology
Moon Ribas (see below opposite) has implants in her feet that alert her whenever there is an earthquake anywhere on the planet. The implants, fitted in 2017, function via a smartphone app, which detects seismic activity. The intensity of the vibrations are proportional to the strength of the quake.

Sealed magnet finger implants
In 2005, body-mod pioneer Steve Haworth created the first sealed magnetic implant with Jesse Jarrell and Todd Huffman (all USA). The device was a neodymium magnet – coated in gold and silicone to seal it from the rest of the body – inserted under the skin of a fingertip.

3D-printed cornea
On 30 May 2018, scientists at Newcastle University, UK, announced that they had 3D-printed an artificial cornea. The team used a 3D bioprinter with a 200-micrometre nozzle to build up layers of "bio-ink" (made from corneal cells, collagen and alginate) into the form of a previously scanned cornea. The technique allows the reproduction of the complex internal structure of the corneal stroma.

The **first 3D-printed rib to be implanted** was announced in Jan 2019. The implant was produced by the 3D-printing service 3dbgprint (BGR) in less than 24 hr from a nylon-based material, and was implanted into patient Ivaylo Josifov at Tokuda Hospital in Sofia, Bulgaria.

FASTEST INDEPENDENT COMPLETION OF A MARATHON IN A ROBOTIC WALKING DEVICE
Simon Kindleysides (UK) completed the 2018 London Marathon in a ReWalk lower-body robotic exoskeleton. He crossed the finish line in 36 hr 46 min, after 60,373 steps and 27 hr 32 min of actual walking time. Claire Lomas (UK, bottom) – the **first person to complete a marathon in a robotic walking device** – finished the 2012 London Marathon in 16 days, also wearing a ReWalk. On 15 Apr 2018, she finished the Greater Manchester Marathon in eight days – the **fastest marathon in a robotic walking device (female)**.

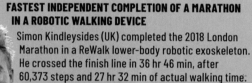

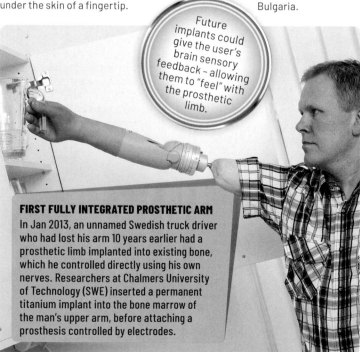

Future implants could give the user's brain sensory feedback – allowing them to "feel" with the prosthetic limb.

FIRST FULLY INTEGRATED PROSTHETIC ARM
In Jan 2013, an unnamed Swedish truck driver who had lost his arm 10 years earlier had a prosthetic limb implanted into existing bone, which he controlled directly using his own nerves. Researchers at Chalmers University of Technology (SWE) inserted a permanent titanium implant into the bone marrow of the man's upper arm, before attaching a prosthesis controlled by electrodes.

APR 9
The **first voice recording** is made in 1860 by inventor Édouard-Léon Scott de Martinville (FRA). It is a 10-sec fragment of a voice singing the folk song "Au clair de la lune".

APR 10
In 1815, a six-day eruption of the Tambora volcano on the Indonesian island of Sumbawa ends, having discharged c. 150-180 km³ (36-43 cu mi) of matter: the **largest eruption by volume**.

▶ MOST DRUMBEATS IN ONE MINUTE USING A DRUMSTICK PROSTHETIC

On 25 Jul 2018, musician Jason Barnes produced 2,400 drumbeats in 60 sec using a prosthetic arm created by Gil Weinberg (both USA) at the Georgia Institute of Technology in Atlanta, Georgia, USA. An electromyographic band picks up electrical activity within the muscle tissue of Jason's forearm, which the robotic limb then reacts to.

Jason lost his arm in an electrical accident. "I refuse to let losing an arm prevent me from fulfilling my dreams," he said. "Nothing will stop me."

FIRST BLUETOOTH-ENABLED DENTAL IMPLANTS

Cyborg artists Neil Harbisson (UK, left) and Moon Ribas (ESP, far left) each have a Bluetooth-enabled tooth implant, dubbed "WeTooth", which they can use to communicate with one another. When pressure is applied, the implants emit a signal that causes the other to vibrate via a smartphone app, allowing Harbisson and Ribas to exchange messages using Morse code.

LARGEST TETRAPOD EXOSKELETON

A 12-year labour of love for Jonathan Tippett (CAN), *Prosthesis* is a giant rideable off-road racing exoskeleton measuring 3.96 m tall, 5.1 m long and 5.51 m wide (12 ft 11 in x 16 ft 8 in x 18 ft 1 in), as verified on 26 Sep 2018. It weighs around 3,500 kg (7,716 lb). The legs and body are made from chromoly steel tubing – a high-performance material typically used in the aerospace industry.

APR 11 In 1999, the **largest koala litter** – a pair of identical twins called Euca and Lyptus – are born in Queensland, Australia. Most female koalas only have a pouch large enough to bear one offspring.

APR 12 At the 1998 World Championship Coal Skip Fill in Victoria, Australia, Christine Adams (AUS) takes 38.29 sec to move 250 kg (551 lb) with a square-mouth shovel – the **fastest coal shovelling (female)**.

SIZE MATTERS

LARGEST HANDS ON A TEENAGER
The right hand of Mathu-Andrew Budge (UK, b. 28 Dec 2001) is 22.5 cm (8.85 in) long from the wrist to the tip of the middle finger, while the left measures 22.2 cm (8.74 in), as confirmed in London, UK, on 13 Feb 2018.

Lars Motza (DEU, b. 21 Sep 2002) has the **largest feet on a teenager**. His left foot is 35.05 cm (1 ft 1.8 in) and his right foot is 34.98 cm (1 ft 1.7 in), as assessed on 19 Nov 2018 in Berlin, Germany.

TALLEST...

• **Ballet dancer**: Fabrice Calmels (FRA) stood 199.73 cm (6 ft 6.63 in) tall as of 25 Sep 2014. He is a lead dancer with Chicago's Joffrey Ballet in Illinois, USA.
• **Politician**: City councillor Robert E Cornegy Jr (USA) is 209.6 cm (6 ft 10 in) tall, as verified in Brooklyn, New York City, USA, on 14 Jan 2019.
• **Woman**: In Dec 2012, Siddiqa Parveen (IND) measured 222.25 cm (7 ft 3.5 in) when lying down. She is unable to stand upright, but the doctor who measured her estimated her standing height to be at least 233.6 cm (7 ft 8 in).
• **Woman ever**: Zeng Jinlian (CHN, 1964–82) was 246.3 cm (8 ft 1 in) tall when measured at her death.
• **Man ever**: Robert Pershing Wadlow (USA, 1918–40) is the tallest person in medical history. When last measured, on 27 Jun 1940, he had a height of 272 cm (8 ft 11.1 in).

SHORTEST...

• **Person in space**: US astronaut Nancy Currie was 152 cm (5 ft) tall when she flew on Space Shuttle mission STS-57 in Jun 1993.
• **World leader**: Benito Juárez (1806–72) served as Mexico's president from 1858 to 1872. He was 137 cm (4 ft 6 in) tall.
• **Mother**: Stacey Herald (USA, 1974–2018), who was 72.39 cm (2 ft 4.5 in) tall, delivered her first child in Dry Ridge, Kentucky, USA, on 21 Oct 2006. She went on to have two more children, one in 2008 and one in 2009.
• **Woman ever**: "Princess Pauline", aka Pauline Musters (NLD, 1876–95), measured 30 cm (1 ft) when she was born. By the time of her death, at the age of 19, she had grown to just 61 cm (2 ft) in height.

• **Spy**: As an adult, Richebourg (FRA, 1768–1858) was just 58 cm (1 ft 11 in) tall. During the French Revolution (1789–99), he carried messages into and out of Paris dressed as an infant and carried by his "nurse".
• ▶ **Man ever**: Chandra Bahadur Dangi (NPL, 1939–2015) measured 54.6 cm (1 ft 9.5 in) tall, as verified at the CIWEC Clinic in Lainchaur, Kathmandu, Nepal, on 26 Feb 2012. He is the shortest person in history whose height can be proved.

▶ LARGEST FEET
Jeison Orlando Rodríguez Hernández's (VEN) right and left feet measured 40.55 cm (1 ft 3.96 in) and 40.47 cm (1 ft 3.93 in) respectively in Parc Saint Paul, Beauvais, France, on 3 Jun 2018. His shoes are specially made for him in Germany. Jeison has held this record since 2014, when his right foot was 40.1 cm (1 ft 3.78 in) long and his left foot was 39.6 cm (1 ft 3.6 in) – so they are still growing!

The **largest feet (female)** belong to Julie Felton (UK) from Ellesmere in Shropshire, UK. As verified on 23 Mar 2019, her right foot was 32.9 cm (1 ft 0.95 in) long and her left foot measured 32.73 cm (1 ft 0.88 in).

Paulo and Katyucia married on 17 Sep 2016. Two months later, they were guests of honour at that year's GWR Day.

▶ HEAVIEST MAN
There is currently a vacancy in this category. Back in 2016, Juan Pedro Franco Salas (MEX) weighed 594.8 kg (1,311 lb 4 oz; 93 st 9 lb) when assessed by a medical team in Guadalajara, Jalisco, Mexico. After undergoing gastric-bypass surgery, however, he had reportedly dropped down to around 304 kg (670 lb; 47 st 12 lb) by Nov 2018. He's pictured here in Feb of that year, showing the benefits of his weight-loss regime. We would like to congratulate Juan Pedro on his new status as the *former* heaviest living human.

▶ THE SHORTEST MARRIED COUPLE MEET THE TALLEST MAN
Brazil's Paulo Gabriel da Silva Barros and Katyucia Lie Hoshino have a combined height of 181.41 cm (5 ft 11.4 in), as verified on 3 Nov 2016 in Itapeva, São Paulo, Brazil. They're seen here with the ▶ **tallest man**, 251-cm (8-ft 2.8-in) Sultan Kösen (TUR). The remarkable trio met up in Nov 2018 at a GWR event in Moscow, Russia. Discover more about Sultan, and see how he measures up against the **tallest man ever** (see above), on p.58.

APR 13 At the 2003 London Marathon, Paula Radcliffe (UK) runs the **fastest marathon (female)**, coming home in 2 hr 15 min 25 sec. She takes almost two minutes off her own record.

APR 14 The **heaviest hailstones** accurately recorded fall upon the Gopalganj district of Bangladesh in 1986. They weigh up to 1 kg (2 lb 3 oz) each – about the same as a pineapple – and kill 92 people.

Khagendra's father once recalled, "He was so tiny when he was born that he could fit in the palm of your hand, and it was very hard to bathe him because he was so small."

SHORTEST MOBILE MAN

Khagendra Thapa Magar (NPL, b. 14 Oct 1992) was 67.08 cm (2 ft 2.41 in) tall when measured at Fewa City Hospital in Pokhara, Nepal, on 14 Oct 2010. GWR caught up with Khagendra in Dec 2018 to document a day in his life, including time spent at his family's shop, leisure activities such as playing guitar and travelling around his home town on a motorbike with his brother (inset above).

The **shortest non-mobile man** is Junrey Balawing (PHL, b. 12 Jun 1993; right). His height was ratified at 59.93 cm (1 ft 11.5 in) – smaller than a tennis racket – on 12 Jun 2011 at Sindangan Health Centre in Zamboanga del Norte, Philippines.

Go large (and small) on GWR videos at guinnessworldrecords.com/2020

SHORTEST WOMAN

Jyoti Amge (IND) measured 62.8 cm (2 ft 0.7 in) on 16 Dec 2011 – her 18th birthday – in Nagpur, India. Up until that day, she had been the **shortest teenager (female)**. Jyoti is also the **shortest actress**, appearing as regular character Ma Petite in the FX TV series *American Horror Story*. Here, she is pictured with Erika Ervin, aka "Amazon Eve", a 201-cm (6-ft 7-in) co-star on the show and formerly the **tallest professional model**.

TALLEST MARRIED COUPLE

On 14 Nov 2013, Sun Mingming (the **tallest basketball player**) and his wife Xu Yan (both CHN) measured 236.17 cm (7 ft 8.98 in) and 187.3 cm (6 ft 1.74 in) respectively, giving them a combined height of 423.47 cm (13 ft 10.72 in). They were measured in Beijing, China – the same city in which they had married on 4 Aug that year.

APR 15 In 1934, Shankweiler's Drive-in Theater opens in Orefield, Pennsylvania, USA, with capacity for 275 cars. It is still in operation today, making it the **oldest drive-in cinema**.

APR 16 At the 2016 Baltimore Tattoo Arts Convention in Maryland, USA, Casey Severn (USA) endures the **most rat traps released on the tongue in one minute** – 13.

69

ROUND-UP

▶ LONGEST LEGS (FEMALE)

Ekaterina Lisina's (RUS) left and right legs measured 132.8 cm (4 ft 4.2 in) and 132.2 cm (4 ft 4 in) respectively when assessed on 13 Jun 2017 in Penza, Russia. The measurements were taken from the heel to the top of the hip. Ekaterina was a member of the Russian basketball team that won a bronze medal at the 2008 Olympic Games. At 205.16 cm (6 ft 8.77 in), she is also the **tallest professional model** (see the former holder on p.69).

Largest hands ever

Robert Pershing Wadlow (USA), the **tallest man ever**, had hands that measured 32.3 cm (1 ft 0.7 in) – greater than the length of an American football – from the wrist to the tip of his middle finger. He wore a size 25 ring. As you might expect, Wadlow also had the **largest feet ever**. He wore US size 37AA shoes (UK size 36 or approximately a European size 75), equivalent to 47 cm (1 ft 6.5 in) long. For more about this legendary figure, see pp.58–59.

Longest earlobes (stretched)

Monte Pierce (USA) can stretch his left earlobe a distance of 12.7 cm (5 in) and his right lobe 11.43 cm (4.5 in). In their unstretched state, his earlobes measure just under 2.54 cm (1 in).

Farthest eyeball pop

Kim Goodman (USA) can pop her eyeballs to a protrusion of 12 mm (0.47 in) beyond her eye sockets. Her eyes were measured in Istanbul, Turkey, on 2 Nov 2007.

Most body modifications

Rolf Buchholz (DEU) is adorned with 516 body mods, as verified in Dortmund, Germany, on 16 Dec 2012.

HAIRIEST TEENAGER

On 4 Mar 2010, Supatra "Nat" Sasuphan (THA) was declared the hairiest young female according to the Ferriman-Gallwey method of evaluation – which measures female hirsutism – in Rome, Italy. Nat's condition was caused by Ambras syndrome, of which there have been only 50 known cases since the Middle Ages. In early 2018, it was reported that she is now happily married (inset) and shaves regularly. GWR warmly congratulates Nat and welcomes any new applicants for this category.

His additions include 481 piercings, two subdermal "horn" implants and five magnetic implants within the fingertips of his right hand.

María José Cristerna (MEX) has the ◉ **most body modifications (female)** – 49. She has significant tattoo coverage, a range of transdermal implants on her forehead, chest and arms, and multiple piercings in her eyebrows, lips, nose, tongue, earlobes, belly button and nipples.

Most popular aesthetic plastic surgery procedure

According to the most recent annual report from the International Society of Aesthetic Plastic Surgery (ISAPS), breast augmentation is the world's most popular cosmetic operation, with 1,677,320 surgeries in 2017. In all, 10,766,848 operations were documented by ISAPS, with breast augmentation accounting for 15.6% of them.

WIDEST TONGUE

Byron Schlenker (USA) has an 8.57-cm-wide (3.37-in) tongue – broader than a baseball – as measured on 2 Nov 2014 in Syracuse, New York, USA. His daughter Emily (USA, inset) has the **widest tongue (female)**, at 7.33 cm (2.89 in), as confirmed on the same day.

The ◉ **longest tongue** measures 10.1 cm (3.97 in) from its tip to the middle of the closed top lip and belongs to Nick Stoeberl (USA), as verified in Salinas, California, USA, on 27 Nov 2012. Chanel Tapper (USA) has the ◉ **longest tongue (female)**: it measured 9.75 cm (3.8 in) on 29 Sep 2010 in California.

LONGEST MILK TOOTH

On 17 Jan 2018, a 2.4-cm-long (0.94-in) milk tooth was removed from the mouth of 10-year-old Curtis Buddie (USA). The tooth was extracted by Dr Scott Bossert (above right) at The Gentle Dentist in Columbus, Ohio, USA.

The **longest tooth removed** measured 3.67 cm (1.44 in) and belonged to Urvil Patel (IND). The extraction was carried out by Dr Jaimin Patel on 3 Feb 2017.

100%

APR 17 In 2014, Philip Joseph Santoro (USA) registers the **fastest time to eat a jam doughnut with no hands** – 11.41 sec – in San Francisco, California, USA. No lips were licked in the making of this record!

APR 18 Eagle-eyed Joe Alexander (DEU) achieves the **most arrows caught by hand in one minute** – 15 – on the set of *Lo Show dei Record* in Rome, Italy, in 2012.

▶ LONGEST FINGERNAILS ON A PAIR OF HANDS (FEMALE)

Ayanna Williams (USA) has fingernails that measure 576.4 cm (18 ft 10.9 in) overall, as confirmed in Houston, Texas, USA, on 7 Feb 2017. She's been growing them for more than 20 years now and follows a strict nail-care regime, including avoiding the washing-up and sleeping with them resting on a pillow.

The **most popular aesthetic plastic surgery for men** is blepharoplasty (eyelid adjustment), according to the same source: 292,707 surgeries took place in 2017. Globally, men opted for 1,550,263 cosmetic surgical alterations in 2017, accounting for 14.4% of all aesthetic procedures.

Most insects tattooed on the body

Joshua Thornton's (USA) skin is crawling with 281 ants, as verified on 30 Nov 2018. They were tattooed in one sitting by five artists at Skeleton Skin Tattoo in Carson City, Nevada, USA.

▶ Widest mouth

When stretched, the mouth of "Chiquinho", aka Francisco Domingo Joaquim (AGO), reaches 17 cm (6.69 in) wide – about the length of a standard pencil – as ratified in Rome, Italy, on 18 Mar 2010.

Most people painting their fingernails simultaneously

On 11 Feb 2018, a total of 1,956 people decorated their nails at an event held by Oye Foundation, Simran Jethwani and Polycab Wires (all IND) in Pune, India. The event was staged to raise awareness of breast-cancer prevention and treatment.

▶ LONGEST FINGERNAILS ON A SINGLE HAND EVER

The nails on the left hand of Shridhar Chillal (IND) had a length of 909.6 cm (29 ft 10 in) – more than twice as long as a Volkswagen Beetle – when measured in the city of Pune in Maharashtra, India, on 17 Nov 2014. Having grown them for 66 years, the octogenarian finally had them cut off with a power tool on 11 Jul 2018 in New York City, USA. They are now permanently on display at the city's Ripley's Believe It or Not! museum (inset).

100%

LONGEST FINGERNAILS ON A PAIR OF HANDS EVER

Melvin Boothe (USA, far left) had nails with a combined length of 985 cm (32 ft 3 in), as ratified in Troy, Michigan, USA, on 30 May 2009. He passed away in December of that year.

The ▶ **female** holder of this record is Lee Redmond (USA, left). In total, her nails measured 865 cm (28 ft 4.5 in) on the set of *Lo Show dei Record* in Madrid, Spain, on 23 Feb 2008. Lee lost her nails in a car accident in early 2009.

Shown here at actual size is the coiled end of Shridhar's thumbnail.

APR 19 In 1897, John J McDermott (USA) wins the first Boston Marathon – raced over 39 km (24 mi) – in 2 hr 55 min 10 sec. Today, the race remains the **oldest continuously run annual marathon**.

APR 20 In 2006, Joe Carlucci (USA) launches the **highest pizza toss** at the Mall of America in Minneapolis, Minnesota, USA. He hurls 567 g (20 oz) of dough 6.52 m (21 ft 5 in) into the air and catches it.

71

RECORDOLOGY

► LARGEST COLLECTION OF *TRANSFORMERS* MEMORABILIA

As confirmed on 11 May 2017 in Manchester, UK, Louis Georgiou (UK) has amassed 2,111 unique *Transformers*-related items, including figurines and comics. Louis started his collection in 2011 after buying Dinobot, Starscream and Grimlock toys as presents for his son. The purchases brought back memories of watching the *Transformers* TV cartoon series during his own childhood, and the resulting wave of nostalgia inspired him to start collecting.

Louis enjoys the process of tracking down new items, but also admires the creativity that went into the figurines: "the design, the illustrations, the artwork, the packaging, the clever engineering... and the clever transformations". He has always maintained that once GWR officially recognized his collection he would stop buying and perhaps even sell it. Watch this space!

Louis also has a passion for tracking down vintage 1960s vinyl records, digital watches from the 1970s and 1980s, and classic LEGO® Technic sets.

CONTENTS

LARGEST PIZZA

Take one much-loved national treasure and combine it with another... and you get St Paul's Cathedral with a delicious pizza topping! The world's **largest pizza** might not actually have been dropped on to this London landmark, but if it was, it would cover the dome and give the city's pigeons plenty to snack on!

With an overall surface area of 1,261.65 m² (13,580.28 sq ft) and an average diameter of 40.07 m (131 ft 5 in), this massive margherita could comfortably cover the famous dome of St Paul's Cathedral – although the building's lantern would make a rather big hole in the middle...

Named "Ottavia" in tribute to Rome's first emperor, Octavius Augustus, the over-the-top, gluten-free pizza was prepared by Dovilio Nardi, Andrea Mannocchi, Marco Nardi, Matteo Nardi and Matteo Giannotte (all ITA) from NIPfood at Fiera Roma in Rome, Italy, on 13 Dec 2012. Pizza may be one of the world's favourite fast foods, but the creation of this record-breaking dish was anything but speedy. The dough had to be prepared days in advance, to comply with stringent food standards. Rectangular pizza bases measuring c. 4 x 6 m (13 ft x 19 ft 8 in) were half baked and frozen, before being stuck together with edible glue to form a super-large, round pizza. In all, it took around two days to bake, in more than 5,200 individual sections. The topping – including 4,535 kg (10,000 lb) of tomato sauce and 3,990 kg (8,800 lb) of mozzarella – was then cooked under blasts of hot air at temperatures of 300–600°C (572–1,112°F).

All that remained was for GWR's adjudicators to measure up the super-sized snack and confirm that it had indeed broken the existing record, which had stood for more than 20 years! Afterwards, it was divided up and heated at a nearby pizzeria, with many of the slices then going to local food shelters.

If you *did* want to drape a gigantic margherita over a London landmark – and why wouldn't you?! – your biggest challenge would probably be getting it airborne. To save on the cost of baking such a mega-meal then hiring a transport helicopter or crane to lift it, our digital artists have simply combined photographs of a regular-sized pizza and St Paul's. If you do want to beat the record, stick to just making a really big pizza (see below).

ST PAUL'S CATHEDRAL
At least four churches dedicated to St Paul have stood on Ludgate Hill in the City district of London, the earliest dating from 604 CE. The present cathedral was built by Sir Christopher Wren between 1675 and 1710, after its predecessor burned down during the Great Fire of London in 1666. The 111.3-m-tall (365-ft) dome – one of the world's largest – weighs around 66,040 tonnes (72,790 US tons). It incorporates the famous "Whispering Gallery", so-called because a whisper directed at one wall is audible on the other side, around 34 m (112 ft) away.

RECIPE FOR SUCCESS
Have you got what it takes to recreate Ottavia? You'll need...

- 8,980 kg (19,800 lb) flour – ideally gluten-free
- 1,128 litres (298 US gal) yeast
- 675 kg (1,488 lb) margarine
- 250 kg (551 lb) rock salt
- 9,387 litres (2,480 US gal) water
- 173 litres (45 US gal) olive oil
- 4,535 kg (10,000 lb) tomato sauce
- 3,990 kg (8,800 lb) mozzarella cheese
- 125 kg (275 lb) parmesan cheese
- 100 kg (220 lb) rocket (arugula)
- 25 kg (55 lb) balsamic vinegar

1. For each pizza base section, combine the flour, yeast, margarine and salt.
2. Add the water and olive oil and turn the mixture to create a dough.
3. Knead on a lightly floured surface, then set to bake in 5,200-plus baking tins.
4. Stick these sections together with edible glue.
5. Pour on the tomato sauce, cheeses, rocket and balsamic vinegar.
6. Cook the topping with a super-powerful heater!

St Paul's was London's tallest building for more than two centuries. It was only superseded in 1939, by Battersea Power Station.

COLLECTIONS

Lip balms

As of 7 May 2017, 11-year-old Bailey Leigh Sheppard (UK) had amassed 730 lip balms over two years. They were counted in Durham, UK.

Happy Days memorabilia

Giuseppe Ganelli (ITA) had 1,439 items related to the classic US sitcom *Happy Days* in Codogno, Lodi, Italy, as of 18 Feb 2018. He has been a fan of the show since the 1970s, and his collection started with an action figure of The Fonz.

Jigsaw puzzles

For 48 years, Luiza Figueiredo (BRA) has been piecing together a collection of jigsaw puzzles. By 9 Jul 2017, she had amassed 1,047 different examples, as confirmed in São Paulo, Brazil.

Christmas tree stands

As of 10 Jul 2018, Stanley Kohl (USA) had amassed 1,197 supports for real and artificial Christmas trees. Dating from the 19th century to the present, they are displayed at Kohl's Stony Hill Tree Farm in Milton, Pennsylvania, USA.

Scooby Doo memorabilia

By 21 Mar 2018, Danielle Meger (CAN) had collected 1,806 items of Scooby Doo merchandise, as confirmed in Rocky View, Alberta, Canada.

Newspapers with different titles

There are 1,444 unique newspapers in the collection of Sergio F Bodini (ITA), as verified in Rome, Italy, on 2 Jun 2018.

LARGEST COLLECTION OF TROLLS

As of 20 Sep 2018, Sherry Groom (USA) owned 8,130 toy trolls. Sherry first broke this record in 2012 and she's added more than 5,000 trolls to her collection since then! She is the owner of The Troll Hole Museum in Alliance, Ohio, USA, where in the guise of Sigrid the Troll Queen, she hosts tours of her cache and delves into stories about these fantastical creatures of folklore.

LARGEST COLLECTION OF...

Soccer shirts

Daniel Goldfarb (USA) had 402 soccer tops as of 2 Apr 2018. They were counted in Bal Harbour, Florida, USA.

Spreadsheets

Ariel Fischman (USA) owns 506 items of physical spreadsheet software, as verified at 414 Capital in Mexico City, Mexico, on 15 May 2018.

LARGEST COLLECTION OF TEA-BAG COVERS

This record, which had remained unbroken since 2013, changed hands twice in 2018. It was set first by Márta Menta Czinkóczky (HUN), with a 743-strong cover collection (pictured), and then broken again by Louise Kristiansen (DNK), whose collection stands at 1,023 items of tea-bag packaging.

Muppets memorabilia

Rhett Safranek (USA) owns 1,841 Muppet mementoes, as counted in Merna, Nebraska, USA, on 1 Oct 2017. Rhett's favourite piece is a rare, full-sized Gonzo.

Broadcast news themes

Victor Vlam (NLD) has been curating an archive of theme music sourced from current affairs and sports news programmes since Jan 2002. As of 8 Apr 2019, his collection ran to 1,876 hr 2 min 52 sec (80 days) of music.

▶ Monopoly board games

As of 5 Sep 2018, Neil Scallan (UK) from Crawley, West Sussex, UK, owned 2,249 different Monopoly sets sourced from all over the world.

Stamps featuring birds

Jin Feibao (CHN) had collated a total of 14,558 stamps with an avian theme by 26 Oct 2018, as verified in Kunming, Yunnan Province, China.

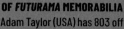

LARGEST COLLECTION OF *FUTURAMA* MEMORABILIA

Adam Taylor (USA) has 803 official items related to the cartoon *Futurama*, as confirmed in Pittsburgh, Pennsylvania, USA, on 3 Sep 2017. They include dolls, clothing and posters but also scripts, artwork and mementoes made for production staff, advertisers and convention visitors. Adam has been an avid fan of the show – created by *The Simpsons'* Matt Groening – since it first aired in 1999.

Cinderella memorabilia

As confirmed on 19 Jul 2018, there were 908 items in Masanao Kawata's (JPN) Cinderella collection when counted in Shibuya, Tokyo, Japan.

Kimono

Hironori Kajikawa (JPN) was the proud owner of 4,147 kimonos as of 22 Feb 2018, as confirmed in Kōriyama, Fukushima Prefecture, Japan.

Takako Yoshino (JPN), meanwhile, boasts the **largest collection of obi** (kimono sashes) – 4,516 – as verified in Nagoya, Aichi Prefecture, Japan, on 30 Jan 2018. It took Takako 40 years to assemble the vast array of obi.

Toy rings (jewellery)

Bruce Rosen (USA) had amassed 18,350 novelty rings in Rose Valley, Pennsylvania, USA, by 20 Oct 2018. He began his collection in 1990.

LARGEST COLLECTION OF SPATULAS

By 6 May 2017, Renee Wesberry (USA) had a total of 1,636 spatulas, as confirmed at a state cake show in Everett, Washington, USA. She began collecting them after Thanksgiving in 1998, when she realized how long it took to clean one between dishes. "I love having a crock of colourful spatulas on my counter," says Renee. "It's like having a bouquet of flowers, but they don't wilt and you can use them to make tasty treats!"

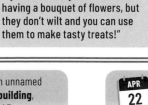

▶ LARGEST COLLECTION OF *CHARLIE'S ANGELS* MEMORABILIA

Since 1976, Jack Condon (USA) has accumulated 5,569 items of ephemera connected to the TV series *Charlie's Angels*. Jack saw the pilot for the show on 21 Mar 1976. A week after the first episode aired, on 22 Sep 1976, he bought his first piece: a copy of *TV Guide* magazine with the three original "Angels" (Kate Jackson, Farrah Fawcett and Jaclyn Smith) on the cover.

APR 21 In 2014, Fred Fugen and Vince Reffet (both FRA) – and an unnamed cameraman – perform the **highest BASE jump from a building**, leaping 828 m (2,716 ft) from the Burj Khalifa in Dubai, UAE.

APR 22 Actor Jack Nicholson (USA) is born in 1937. Between 1970 and 2003, he earns the **most Oscar nominations (actor)** – 12, eight for Best Actor and four for Best Supporting Actor. He wins three times.

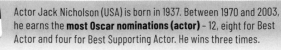

LARGEST COLLECTION OF SHEEP-RELATED ITEMS

As of 19 Feb 2017, Alessia Citti (ITA) had amassed 1,822 ovine-themed objects, as confirmed in Ciampino, Rome, Italy. Alessia was given her first toy sheep by her mother when she was just six months old. The majority of her collection is kept in her bedroom, which she has named *Il Vittoriale delle Pecore* ("The Sacred Temple for Sheep").

Alessia's prodigious cache is nearly 500 items larger than that of the previous record holder.

▶ Find GWR's collection of videos at guinnessworldrecords.com/2020

LARGEST COLLECTION OF *WIZARDING WORLD* MEMORABILIA

Victoria Maclean (UK) owns 3,686 objects relating to the *Harry Potter* and *Fantastic Beasts* franchises, as verified in Neath, West Glamorgan, UK, on 28 Feb 2019. So bewitched is Victoria by J K Rowling's creations that she has even built a replica of the Borgin and Burkes antiques shop from Knockturn Alley. Her most prized item is a 24-karat gold-plated Golden Snitch puzzle piece from Japan.

LARGEST COLLECTION OF PAPER CUPS

By 5 Sep 2017, V Sankaranarayanan (IND) had collected 736 throwaway paper cups, as confirmed in Tamil Nadu, India. The containers, which would normally hold juice, hot beverages or ice-cream, are all in mint condition.

APR 23 Kanellos Kanellopoulos (GRC) pedals his *Daedalus 88* aircraft 115.11 km (71.52 mi) from Heraklion in Crete to the Greek island of Santorini in 1988 – the **farthest human-powered flight**.

APR 24 In 2004, Chad Fell (USA) blows the **largest bubblegum bubble** – 50.8 cm (1 ft 8 in) in diameter – in Winston County, Alabama, USA. He uses three pieces of Dubble Bubble gum.

INCREDIBLE EDIBLES

100%

HEAVIEST BLUEBERRY

A "Eureka" blueberry grown by Agrícola Santa Azul S.A.C (PER) in Lima, Peru, weighed in at 15 g (0.52 oz) on a digital scale, as confirmed on 19 Jul 2018. This beat the previous holder, set earlier in 2018 in Australia, by 2.6 g (0.09 oz). Picked from a northern highbush blueberry plant, the superlative fruit had a diameter of 34.5 mm (1.35 in).

LARGEST...

Serving of noodle soup

Vietnamese instant-noodle company VIFON marked their 55th anniversary with a beef pho and rice noodle soup weighing 1,359 kg (2,996 lb) in Ho Chi Minh City, Vietnam, on 21 Jul 2018. It took a team of 31 event staff and 52 chefs to produce the soup.

▶ Portion of fish and chips

On 9 Feb 2018, Resorts World Birmingham (UK) produced a giant fillet of halibut with chips weighing a total of 54.99 kg (121 lb 3 oz). To qualify for the record, the weight of the uncooked chips could not be more than double that of the fish. The huge halibut took more than 90 min to cook.

Fishcake

On 30 Jun 2018, fish wholesalers Fonn Egersund and chef Tore Torgersen (both NOR) created a fishcake weighing 231 kg (509 lb) in the main square of Egersund, Norway. The 3.6-m-diameter (11-ft 11-in) cake, which weighed more than 50 average Atlantic salmon, required a forklift to flip it in the pan. It was served up and polished off in under 20 min by the hungry townspeople.

Menudo soup

In celebration of National Menudo Month, Juanita's Foods (USA) prepared 1,106.31 kg (2,439 lb) of the traditional Mexican favourite of cows' stomach lining (tripe) cooked in broth on 28 Jan 2018. This weighs roughly the same as 3,000 cans of soup. The dish was flavoured with 20.4 kg (45 lb) of red chilli puree, 65.3 kg (144 lb) of spices, 24.4 kg (54 lb) of chopped onion and 875 limes.

Laddu (individual)

Mallikharjuna Rao (IND) produced a spherical Indian sweet weighing 29,465 kg (64,959 lb) – equivalent to around seven Asian elephants – in Tapeswaram, Andhra Pradesh, India, on 6 Sep 2016. The laddu was made to a traditional Boondi recipe with ingredients such as cashew nuts, almonds, cardamom and ghee.

▶ LARGEST SERVING OF GUACAMOLE

On 6 Apr 2018, the town of Tancítaro in Michoacán, Mexico, celebrated its seventh Annual Avocado Festival by whipping up a huge helping of guacamole weighing 3,788 kg (8,351 lb). More than 350 people pitched in to make the avocado-based dip, which also contained tomatoes, limes and coriander (cilantro).

Baklava

On 22 Mar 2018, a filo-pastry dessert weighing 513 kg (1,130 lb) – heavier than a grand piano – was unveiled at the Ankara Gastronomy Summit 2018 in Turkey. It was prepared for the Ankara governorship by the Mado ice-cream brand and the Taşpakon Culinary Confederation (all TUR).

Cinnamon roll

Gourmet bakery Wolferman's (USA) created a cinnamon roll weighing 521.5 kg (1,149 lb 11 oz) – about the same as eight men – in Medford, Oregon, USA, on 10 Apr 2018. The mixture was heated by propane burners under a purpose-built pan.

Sweet potato pie

The Honshu-Shikoku Bridge Expressway Company (JPN) produced 319 kg (703 lb) of the traditional US dessert at the Awaji Service Area in Hyōgo Prefecture, Japan, on 7 Apr 2018. The pie measured more than 2 m (6 ft 6 in) across and was made using local Naruto Kintoki sweet potatoes.

Fruit mazamorra

On 30 Aug 2018, volunteers in Iquitos, Peru, made a 751.3-kg (1,656-lb) serving of fruit mazamorra (a soft dessert made with aguaje fruit, sugar and cornstarch). The event was organized by Universidad San Ignacio de Loyola and Gobierno Regional de Loreto (both PER).

LONGEST CAKE

Jiangxi Bakery Association (CHN) made a 3.18-km-long (1.98-mi) fruitcake on 7 May 2018 at the Zixi Bread International Tourism Festival in Jiangxi Province, China. It took 60 cake-makers and 120 assistants almost a day to assemble the cake, which is longer than the National Mall in Washington, DC, USA.

LARGEST SERVING OF SCRAMBLED EGGS

A head-scramblingly huge portion of eggs weighing 2,466 kg (5,436 lb) was made by egg production company Inicia (MUS) in Bagatelle, Mauritius, on 27 Oct 2018. The recipe also consisted of butter, milk, salt and pepper, and took more than two hours to cook. More than 250 people were involved in the preparation of 10,000-plus portions.

APR 25 — The nuclear-powered submarine USS *Triton* reaches the Saint Peter and Saint Paul Rocks in the Atlantic Ocean in 1960, having completed the **first submarine circumnavigation** in 60 days 21 hr.

APR 26 — The slave ship *Whydah* sinks in 1717, killing pirate Samuel Bellamy (UK). The **most profitable sea pirate**, "Black Sam" had built a fortune worth more than £103 m ($130 m) in today's money.

LARGEST COMMERCIALLY AVAILABLE PIZZA

Feeling peckish? Then feast your eyes on "The Bus", a rectangular pizza measuring 2.438 x 0.812 m (8 ft x 2 ft 8 in) with a total area of 1.98 m² (21.31 sq ft), as verified on 26 May 2018. Prepared by Moontower Pizza Bar (USA) in Burleson, Texas, USA, "The Bus" costs $299.95 (£224.90) plus tax and must be ordered at least two days in advance.

"The Bus" pizza only takes 30 min to bake in a rotating oven. It is delivered in a gigantic custom-made box.

Feast your eyes on foodie videos at guinnessworldrecords.com/2020

LARGEST CREAM-FILLED BISCUIT

Biscuit manufacturer Mondelēz Bahrain created an OREO cookie weighing 73.4 kg (161 lb 13 oz) in Manama, Bahrain, on 16 Apr 2018. The colossal cookie was almost three times the size of the previous record holder and 6,495 times bigger than a standard OREO.

LARGEST CUP OF HOT CHOCOLATE/COCOA

On 6 Jan 2018, the Municipio de Uruapan (MEX) filled a giant cup with 4,816.6 litres (1,272.3 US gal) of hot chocolate in Uruapan, Michoacán, Mexico. The sweet beverage was made to celebrate Three Kings' Day and contained more than 600 kg (1,322 lb) of locally grown semi-sweet chocolate.

HEAVIEST FRUIT AND VEG OF 2018

Gourd	Jeremy Terry (USA)	174.41 kg (384 lb 8 oz)
Celery	Gary Heeks (UK)	42 kg (92 lb 9 oz)
Cantaloupe melon	Danny Vester (USA)	29.89 kg (65 lb 14 oz)
Red cabbage	Tim Saint (UK)	23.7 kg (52 lb 4 oz)
Leek (right)	Paul Rochester (UK)	10.7 kg (23 lb 9 oz)
Aubergine	Ian Neale (UK)	3.06 kg (6 lb 11 oz)
Avocado	Felicidad Pasalo (USA)	2.49 kg (5 lb 8 oz)
Peach	A & L Pearson (USA)	816.46 g (1 lb 12 oz)
Bell pepper	Ian Neale (UK)	720 g (1 lb 9 oz)
Nectarine	Eleni Evagelou Ploutarchou (CYP)	500 g (1 lb 1.6 oz)
Chilli pepper	Dale Toten (UK)	420 g (14.8 oz)

APR 27 Strongman priest Kevin Fast (CAN) achieves the **most people supported on the shoulders** – 11 – in 2013 in Cobourg, Ontario, Canada. Each person weighs more than 60 kg (132 lb).

APR 28 In 2001, businessman Dennis Tito (USA) arrives at the *International Space Station* (*ISS*) on board a Russian Soyuz spacecraft. The **first space tourist**, he stays on the *ISS* until 6 May.

FUN WITH FOOD

(no hands) – 19 – and the ◉ **fastest time to drink a cup of coffee** – 4.78 sec. "He doesn't even drink coffee!" his mother marvelled.

Most chocolate spread eaten in one minute
André Ortolf (DEU) loves nothing more than polishing off a food-related record. On 30 Nov 2017, he guzzled 359 g (12.6 oz) of chocolate spread in Augsburg, Germany.

Tallest tower of cupcakes
On 19 Jan 2019, Preethi Kitchen Appliances and Food Consulate Chennai (both IND) built a 12.69-m (41-ft 8-in) cupcake stack in Chennai, Tamil Nadu, India.

Most people making kimchi
Mercedes-Benz in Korea and the Seoul Metropolitan Government invited 3,452 people to concoct the Korean dish of fermented vegetables in Seoul, South Korea, on 4 Nov 2018.

Longest cooking marathon
This record was broken twice in 2018. On 18–20 Sep, as part of National Fried Rice Day, chefs Andrey Shek (UZB) and Raymundo Mendez (MEX) of restaurant chain Benihana (USA) both separately cooked up a storm for 42 hr straight in New York City, USA.
They were out-cooked by Rickey Lumpkin II (USA), though, who

▶ LONGEST THROW AND CATCH OF A HOT DOG SAUSAGE INTO A BUN

On 24 Oct 2018, ex-Jacksonville Jaguars quarterback Mark Brunell (USA, above centre) completed a "lunchdown" pass by hurling a hot dog sausage 20.96 m (68 ft 9 in) to be caught in a bun by Ryan Moore (UK, above right) in London, UK. The hot dog was provided by event organizers Denny Fire & Smoke (IRL).

Most gummy bears eaten using a cocktail stick in one minute
Kevin "LA Beast" Strahle (USA) gobbled down 31 gummy bears in 60 sec using a cocktail stick in Ridgewood, New Jersey, USA, on 24 May 2017. It was part of his "Beast's Buffet", in which he attempted six GWR titles in one sitting. He claimed five, including the ◉ **most marshmallows eaten in one minute**

prepared his mum's secret-recipe fried chicken for 68 hr 30 min 1 sec during a fundraiser for World Vision held in Los Angeles, California, USA.

Longest habanero pepper kiss
In Puerto Vallarta, Jalisco, Mexico, on 11 Jun 2016, Carly Waddell and Evan Bass (both USA) of ABC's *Bachelor in Paradise* set temperatures soaring when they kissed for 1 min 41 sec after eating spicy habanero chillies.

Longest line of hot dogs
On 12 Aug 2018, a 1.46-km-long (0.9-mi) line of 10,000 hot dogs was laid out in Zapopan, Jalisco, Mexico. Four brands were each responsible for a different part of the jumbo treat: Embasa (ketchup), Grupo Bimbo (buns), McCormick (mustard and mayonnaise) and FUD (sausages).

The **longest line of pancakes** is 110.85 m (363 ft 7 in) and was achieved by Nutella Australia at the University of Sydney in New South Wales, Australia, on 28 Feb 2018.

Most cookies iced in one hour
On 13 Dec 2018, a team of volunteers, anchors and guests on *Good Morning America* decorated 1,696 cookies in New York City, USA. It was staged in conjunction with So Yummy (all USA).

Fastest time to find and alphabetize the letters in a can of alphabet soup
On 13 Feb 2018, Dude Perfect's Cody Jones (USA) sorted soup from A to Z in 3 min 21 sec in Frisco, Texas, USA.

MOST WINS OF THE NATHAN'S HOT DOG EATING CONTEST

The Nathan's Hot Dog Eating Contest is an annual competition held on 4 Jul in Brooklyn, New York City, USA. In 2018, Joey Chestnut (USA, above right) won his 11th men's title belt by scoffing the **most hot dogs eaten at a Nathan's Hot Dog Eating Contest** – 74 (with buns) in 10 min.
The **most wins of the Nathan's Hot Dog Eating Contest (female)** is five, by Miki Sudo (USA, above left), consecutively in 2014–18.

▶ MOST ICE-CREAM SCOOPS BALANCED ON A CONE

On 17 Nov 2018, Dimitri Panciera (ITA) balanced 125 ice-cream scoops on a cone for 10 sec on the set of *La Notte dei Record* in Rome, Italy. It was the fifth time that Dimitri had set a new benchmark for this title, having been engaged in a six-year-long struggle with Ashrita Furman (see right) to own the record outright.

MOST SKITTLES® THROWN AND CAUGHT WITH THE MOUTH IN ONE MINUTE

On 5 Feb 2018, Ashrita Furman (above right) caught in his mouth 70 fruit-flavoured sweets thrown from at least 4.5 m (14 ft 9 in) away by Bipin Larkin (above left, both USA) in 60 sec in Siem Reap, Cambodia.
Ashrita's voracious appetite for GWR titles remains undiminished. Back home in Jamaica, New York City, USA, he set the **fastest time to drink 200 ml of mustard** – 13.85 sec – on 12 May 2018.

APR 29 "Jumpin'" Jeff Clay (USA) achieves the **most cars hurdled in one hour** in 1989, completely clearing the roofs of 101 automobiles in 60 min in Fort Oglethorpe, Georgia, USA.

APR 30 In 2013, "The Midnight Swinger", aka David Scott (USA), finishes the **longest stand-up comedy show by an individual** – 40 hr 8 min – at the Diamond Jo Casino in Dubuque, Iowa, USA.

▶ FASTEST TIME TO EAT A BOWL OF PASTA

Maths teacher Michelle Lesco (USA) leads a double life as the competitive speed-eater known as the "Cardboard Shell". On 18 Sep 2017, she wolfed down a bowl of pasta in 26.69 sec at the "Carbs for a Cause" charity food drive, smashing the previous record by 14 sec. On 13 Dec 2018, in Las Vegas, Nevada, USA, Michelle gobbled up two more records: the **fastest time to eat a hot dog with no hands** (21.60 sec) and the **most mayonnaise eaten in three minutes** (2.448 kg; 5 lb 6.35 oz – or around three-and-a-half jars).

MOST GRAPES EATEN USING THE FEET IN THREE MINUTES

Arpit Lall (IND) ate 53 grapes with his feet in 180 sec at the CNI Church in Chhattisgarh, India, on 25 Feb 2018. All grapes had to be swallowed by the end of the allotted time to count towards his final total.

On 4 Sep 2018, Arpit also broke the record for the **most raw eggs cracked and eaten in 30 seconds**, slurping down nine eggs, each at least 6 cm (2.3 in) long, this time using his hands!

MOST WATERMELONS CRUSHED WITH THE HEAD IN 30 SECONDS

On 6 May 2018, Muhammad Rashid (PAK) head-butted 29 watermelons in half a minute in Karachi, Sindh, Pakistan. Each watermelon weighed at least 4 kg (8 lb 13 oz) and was ripe with firm rind, as per GWR guidelines. Muhammad, the founder and president of the Pakistan Academy of Martial Arts, beat the previous record by four.

MAY 1 In 1996, the *Ulysses* space probe passes through a stream of charged particles that forms part of the **longest measured comet tail**. The tail extends 570 million km (350 million mi) from comet Hyakutake.

MAY 2 At the Tårnby Games 2015 in Copenhagen, Denmark, Majken Sichlau (DNK) runs the **fastest 100 m wearing high heels (female)** – 13.557 sec. Her heels are 9.5 cm (3.7 in) high.

MASS PARTICIPATION

Most people showering simultaneously

Soap and body-wash brand Irish Spring (USA) rigged up a scaffold of water pipes and shower heads at the Firefly Music Festival in Dover, Delaware, USA, on 15 Jun 2018. The communal shower lured 396 dusty festival-goers.

Most people controlling soccer balls

On 14 Jun 2018, a total of 1,444 people each kept a soccer ball aloft and under control for the required 10 sec in the main square of Kraków, Poland. The record attempt was organized by media company Grupa RMF (POL). This was their second big sporting record: the previous year, on 24 Aug, they gathered 1,804 people to achieve the **most people controlling volleyballs**.

LARGEST CHARITY WALK/RUN

An impressive 283,171 people took part in a charity run organized by Filipino religious group Iglesia ni Cristo (Church of Christ) in Manila, Philippines, on 6 May 2018. The event was one of several simultaneous charity walks all over the world. Together, these events drew 773,136 participants, breaking the record for the **largest charity walk/run at multiple venues**.

Most people doing the "floss" dance

A total of 793 pupils from schools in Stockholm, Sweden, braved lows of 2°C (36°F) to perform the dance craze of the year on 4 Dec 2018. The en-masse floss was filmed by Sveriges Television (SWE) for its kids TV shows *Lilla Aktuellt* and *Lilla Sportspegeln*.

The **most people flossing on the same length of floss**, meanwhile, is 1,527, set on 12 Jul 2013. Using a 3,230-m (10,600-ft) piece of dental floss, it was achieved by the Lake Erie Crushers (USA) in Avon, Ohio, USA.

LARGEST...

Hackathon

The Hajj Hackathon 2018, organized by the Saudi Federation for Cybersecurity, Programming and Drones (SAU), drew a record-breaking 2,950 participants on 2 Aug 2018. The competition, held in Jeddah, Saudi Arabia, was won by an all-female team who built an app that would allow pilgrims to translate road signs without an internet connection.

Chess lesson

Two chess clubs and two schools from the municipality of Muttenz in Switzerland joined up to host the largest chess lesson on 20 Sep 2018. A total of 1,459 children from the area learned the rules and some basic strategies of the ancient board game.

Yoga lesson

On 21 Jun 2018, Patanjali Yogpeeth, the Government of Rajasthan and the District Administration of Kota (all IND) marked International Yoga Day by bringing together 100,984 people for a mass yoga lesson in Kota, Rajasthan, India. This almost doubled the record achieved on the previous year's International Yoga Day in Mysuru, India.

Rugby scrum

On 23 Sep 2018, a crowd of 2,586 local people locked arms to form a 200-m-long (656-ft) scrum in Toyota, Japan. The super-sized pack, which was organized by Young Entrepreneurs Group Toyota (JPN), took place at the Toyota Stadium – one of the venues for the 2019 Rugby World Cup.

Disco dance

For the DVD release of *Mamma Mia 2: Here We Go Again* (UK/USA, 2018), a "super-troupe" of 324 dancing queens (and kings) took to London, UK, on 26 Nov 2018. Led by ex-*Strictly Come Dancing* pros Ola and James Jordan, the event was staged by Universal Pictures Home Entertainment (UK).

Game of freeze tag

A total of 1,393 adults and children took part in a giant game of freeze tag organized by childcare company IBO Duffel (BEL) in Antwerp, Belgium, on 14 Sep 2018. The game was won by six-year-old Alexander Dewit.

Chocolate-tasting event

On 10 Aug 2018, Universidad San Ignacio de Loyola and Gobierno Regional de Ucayali (both PER) hosted a chocolate tasting in Pucallpa, Peru, at which 797 people tried three types of dark chocolate. The region is one of the world's top producers of cacao.

MOST PEOPLE SKINNY DIPPING

On 9 Jun 2018, Deirdre Featherstone (IRL) managed to persuade 2,505 women to bare all for a bracing swim in the Irish Sea near Wicklow, Ireland. The sun was shining on the bathers – who were taking part to raise funds for children's cancer charity Aoibheann's Pink Tie – though with temperatures of only around 20°C (68°F) it perhaps wasn't everyone's idea of beach weather!

LARGEST FOOD-TRUCK RALLY

The air was thick with the enticing smell of dishes such as *nasi dagang* (fish curry with coconut rice) and *kukus berempah* (spiced chicken and rice) in the Batu Kawan district of Penang, Malaysia, where 158 food trucks gathered to take part in the Penang International Food Festival 2018. The event was held on 28 Apr, the penultimate day of the 16-day culinary event, which celebrates street food from around the globe.

LARGEST CREAM-TEA PARTY

Fashion and homewares company Cath Kidston (UK) invited 978 guests over for tea and scones at Alexandra Palace, London, UK, on 1 Jul 2018. The quintessentially British event was held to mark the 25th anniversary of the brand and was hosted by former *Great British Bake Off* judge Mary Berry.

MAY 3 — Geelong achieve the **highest score by one team in an Australian Football League game**, racking up 239 (37-17) against Brisbane in 1992 at Carrara Stadium in Gold Coast, Australia.

The event was attended by Marvel editor C B Cebulski and actress Carolina Ravassa (who voices Sombra in Overwatch).

LARGEST GATHERING OF PEOPLE DRESSED AS SPIDER-MAN

Marvel Entertainment (USA) and Sony Interactive Entertainment Europe (UK) brought together 547 of Peter Parker's biggest fans in Stockholm, Sweden, on 16 Sep 2018. The record attempt took place at Comic Con Stockholm and was one of a series of events held to celebrate the launch of the 2018 videogame *Spider-Man*.

LARGEST HUMAN IMAGE OF A WHEELCHAIR ACCESSIBILITY SYMBOL

On 27 Feb 2018, St Britto's Institutions – an educational organization in Chennai, India – formed the largest human image of a wheelchair accessibility symbol. A total of 816 people wearing white T-shirts and caps filled out the design.

CARE FOR THE DISABLED

LARGEST EXERCISE-BALL LESSON

As part of their "sweat for good" campaign, the YMCA of Greater Toronto (CAN) held a giant exercise-ball class for 454 people on 11 Jan 2018. The event was led and hosted by celebrity fitness instructor Eva Redpath, YMCA fitness manager Sherry Perez and Canadian Olympic swimming gold medallist Mark Tewksbury.

MAY 4 — In 1536, Italian merchant Francesco Lapi uses "@" to denote *amphorae*, a unit of measurement, while recording the arrival of treasure from the Spanish conquest of Peru – the **first use of the @ (at) sign**.

MAY 5 — Prabhakar Reddy P and Sujith Kumar E (both IND) achieve the **most martial arts throws of the same person in one minute** – 42– in Andhra Pradesh, India, in 2018.

STRENGTH & STAMINA

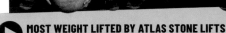

Heaviest sumo deadlift in one hour (male)

On 22 May 2018, Walter Urban (USA) lifted a total of 59,343 kg (130,830 lb) – heavier than an M1 Abrams tank – over the course of around 12,000 sumo deadlifts in 60 min. He set the record live on the set of *The Today Show* in New York City, USA. Sumo deadlifts are carried out with the feet kept wider apart than the shoulders.

Heaviest vehicle pulled over 100 ft (female)

On 31 Mar 2018, runner-turned-bodybuilder Nardia Styles (AUS) pulled a tow truck and car weighing 11,355 kg (25,033 lb) a distance of 100 ft (30.48 m) in Gold Coast, Queensland, Australia. In doing so, she raised money for the White Ribbon Campaign and Barnardo's Australia.

The **heaviest vehicle pulled over 100 ft (male)** is 99,060 kg (218,389 lb), by Kevin Fast (CAN) in Cobourg, Ontario, Canada, on 5 Jul 2017.

Heaviest ship pulled by the teeth

"Mr Tug-Tooth", aka Ukrainian paediatrician Oleg Skavysh, pulled the 614-tonne (676-US-ton) *Vereshchagino* more than 15 m (49 ft) using a cable clenched in his jaws in Chornomorsk, Ukraine, on 30 Oct 2018.

Heaviest weighted tricep dip

Trenton Williams (USA) executed a tricep dip while wearing a belt of weights totalling 106.59 kg (235 lb) in Alpharetta, Georgia, USA, on 29 Sep 2018. A retired veteran, Trenton uses physical fitness as therapy for post-traumatic stress disorder.

Fastest time to break 16 concrete blocks on the body (male)

On 18 Mar 2017 in Muğla, Turkey, Ali Bahçetepe placed 16 concrete blocks on his stomach while his assistant Nizamettin Aykemür (both TUR) smashed them with a sledgehammer in 4.75 sec. This shattered the mark of 6.33 sec, also held by Bahçetepe.

Fastest 10 km carrying a 100-lb pack (male)

Michael Summers (USA) covered 10 km (6.2 mi) with a 100-lb (45-kg) pack on his back in 1 hr 25 min 16 sec at the Milan High School athletics track in Indiana, USA, on 7 Jul 2018.

Longest chin stand

On 22 Jul 2018, Tanya Tsekova Shishova (BGR) raised her body in an elevated backbend while keeping her chin, shoulders and chest in contact with the floor for 21 min 26 sec in Sofia, Bulgaria.

Longest time to hold the scale pose (yoga)

B Prakash Kumar (IND) maintained a scale pose for 5 min 28 sec in Tamil Nadu, India, on 15 May 2018. The position is achieved by sitting with crossed legs while lifting the body up with two hands placed on the ground.

 ### Most handstand push-ups in one minute (male)

Siarhei Kudayeu (BLR) achieved 51 handstand push-ups in 60 sec in Minsk, Belarus, on 3 May 2018.

The **female** record is 12 push-ups, by Rachel Martinez (USA) representing sports brand Reebok in New York City, USA, on 1 Feb 2017.

Most chest-to-ground push-up burpees in 24 hours (female)

On 23 Feb 2018, Eva Clarke (AUS) completed 5,555 chest-to-ground push-ups in in Abu Dhabi, UAE. This figure included the **one-minute** (31) and **12-hour** (4,785) records for the same exercise.

▶ MOST WEIGHT LIFTED BY ATLAS STONE LIFTS IN ONE MINUTE (FEMALE)

On 1 Feb 2017, CrossFit athlete Michelle Kinney (USA) lifted Atlas stones weighing a total of 539.77 kg (1,189 lb 15 oz) in 60 sec in Venice, California, USA. She also set the matching **three minutes (female)** record – 1,397.06 kg (3,079 lb 15 oz) – and **most burpee pull-ups in one minute (female)** – 19.

▶ MOST ICE BLOCKS BROKEN IN ONE MINUTE

On 20 Nov 2018, J D Anderson (USA) broke 88 blocks of ice on *La Notte dei Record* in Rome, Italy. The blocks had been frozen whole in an industrial freezer to at least -2°C (28°F), and were a minimum width of 10 cm (3.9 in). Known as "Iceman", J D previously held the record for **most ice blocks broken by human battering ram** – currently 17, by Uğur Öztürk (TUR).

▶ MOST OVERHEAD PRESSES OF A PERSON IN ONE MINUTE

"Iron Biby", aka Cheick Ahmed al-Hassan Sanou of Burkino Faso, lifted GWR's 60-kg (132-lb 4-oz) Marketing Manager Emily Noakes above his head a total of 82 times in London, UK, on 23 Apr 2019. Biby – a competitive strongman – won the 2019 Log Lift World Champion by holding aloft 220 kg (483 lb).

▶ HEAVIEST AIRCRAFT PULLED OVER 100 M BY A WHEELCHAIR TEAM

On 23 Nov 2018, a team of 98 wheelchair users pulled a 127.6-tonne (281,310-lb) 787-9 Boeing Dreamliner 106 m (347 ft 9 in) at Heathrow Airport in London, UK. The "Wheels4Wings" event was a collaboration between Heathrow Airport, British Airways and Aerobility (all UK) to raise money to help people with disabilities take part in aviation.

MAY 6 In 1948, Shasta the liger is born at Hogle Zoo in Salt Lake City, Utah, USA. Sired by a lion and a tigress, she survives to the age of 24 years 74 days – making her the **longest-lived liger**.

MAY 7 Directed by Joe Castro and produced by Steven J Escobar (both USA), *The Summer of Massacre* (USA, 2011) is first screened in Hollywood. It has the **highest body count in a slasher film**: 155.

The hard-hitting couple left their mark during a visit to GWR HQ in 2017, accidentally smashing our TV during a taekwondo demonstration!

FASTEST TIME TO BREAK 1,000 ROOF TILES

In 2018, taekwondo instructors Chris and Lisa Pitman (UK) posed for a special GWR photoshoot to celebrate their love of breaking things – especially records. Lisa holds the **female** title for destroying 1,000 roof tiles (1 min 23.98 sec), while Chris has the **male** equivalent (51.08 sec). On 9 Apr 2018, they added the ◉ **most pine boards broken in one minute with one hand** – Lisa with 230 (**female**), and Chris 315 (**male**).

FASTEST TIME TO PULL A TANK OVER 10 M

On 17 Mar 2018, Eddie Williams (AUS) won the "World of Tanks PC Tank Pull" at the Arnold Strongman Australia Championships in Melbourne, Victoria, when he pulled an 8-tonne (17,630-lb) FV102 Striker 10 m (32 ft 9 in) in 36.65 sec. Arnold Schwarzenegger was in the audience to watch Eddie beat the 11-strong(man) field. A former full-time musician, Eddie now works with disabled children.

MOST CONSECUTIVE PINKY PULL-UPS

On 7 Oct 2018, Tazio Gavioli (ITA) raised himself up by his little fingers 36 times in a row in Cavezzo, Modena, Italy. He beat his own record of 23, set the previous year. A free climber and performer who calls himself the "Italian Butterfly", Tazio also lays claim to the **longest duration in the dead-hang position** (demonstrated inset) – 13 min 52 sec, set on 14 Apr 2018.

MAY 8
In 1995, a rooster named Tugaru-Ono-94 produces the **longest cock-crow** ever recorded – lasting a lung-busting 23.6 sec – in Ueda City, Nagano, Japan.

MAY 9
In 2013, Zimbabwe's Parliament approves its new Constitution. It recognizes 16 languages, including Ndau, sign language and Xhosa, making it the **country with the most official languages**.

CURIOUS ACCOMPLISHMENTS

Fastest time to put on 10 inflatable arm bands
On 25 Jul 2018, Izabelle Edge (UK) pulled on 10 pre-inflated arm bands in 7.35 sec at Blackpool Pleasure Beach in Lancashire, UK.

▶ **Most panes of tempered glass run through consecutively**
Danilo del Prete (ITA) smashed his way through 24 panes of safety glass on the set of *La Notte dei Record* in Rome, Italy, on 13 Nov 2018.

Farthest distance walking barefoot on LEGO® bricks
On 21 Apr 2018, vlogger "BrainyBricks", aka Russell Cassevah (USA), walked a distance of 834.41 m (2,737 ft 6 in) barefoot on LEGO at Brick Fest Live! in Philadelphia, Pennsylvania, USA.

Fastest time to make an origami boat with the mouth
On 2 Dec 2017, Gao Guangli (CHN) orally folded a paper boat in 3 min 34 sec in Jining, Shandong Province, China.

Farthest distance travelled on Swiss balls
Tyler Toney (USA) - one of the "dudes" from sports-trick YouTube channel Dude Perfect - covered 88.39 m (290 ft) rolling on top of Swiss balls in Frisco, Texas, USA, on 16 Oct 2018.

FARTHEST SINGLE PUSH AND RIDE OF A SHOPPING TROLLEY
On 6 Jul 2017, radio presenter Richie Firth (UK) achieved a 10.56-m (34-ft 7-in) push-and-glide in a shopping trolley in Croydon, UK. The attempt was organized after Richie stated on Absolute Radio that he is world class at travelling on these wheeled baskets.

Most push-ups while sword swallowing
Franz Huber (DEU) slid a sword down his oesophagus at the Tattoo & Piercing Expo in Eggenfelden, Germany, on 9 Sep 2017, and proceeded to complete 20 push-ups.

Most pineapples on heads cut in half in 30 seconds
On 20 Nov 2018, Reddy P Prabhakar (IND) cut through 20 pineapples with a samurai sword. His brave assistants held the fruit on their heads. The feat took place in Nellore, India.

Most motorcycles to run over a person
A total of 121 motorbikes, each weighing 257 kg (566 lb) *without* a rider, drove over Pandit Dhayagude (IND) in Mumbai, India, on 28 Aug 2016. He lay between two sections of track that broke at his stomach, leaving it exposed to the wheels of the bikes as they rode over him.

Most pencils pierced through a water-filled bag in one minute
On 21 Feb 2018, Malachi Barton (USA) popped 15 pencils through a water-filled plastic bag in 60 sec in Los Angeles, California, USA. For this record attempt, the pencils must protrude from both sides without causing any leaks.

Most skips of a rope wearing ski boots and skis in one minute
On 27 Nov 2016, Sebastian Deeg (DEU) jumped over a rope 61 times in 60 sec in ski boots and skis for *ZDF Fernsehgarten* in Garmisch-Partenkirchen, Germany.

MOST SELFIES TAKEN IN THREE MINUTES
James Smith (USA) snapped 168 self-portraits in only 180 sec on board the *Carnival Dream* cruise ship on 22 Jan 2018. James is an avid cruiser who staged this attempt on deck during one of his most recent oceanic vacations.

Fastest time to type a set sentence using one finger
On 10 Oct 2018, Kushal Dasgupta (IND) tapped out the line "Guinness World Records has challenged me to type this sentence with one finger in the fastest time" on a keyboard in 21.99 sec. The attempt took place in the city of Puttaparthi, India.

▶ **Longest time to dunk a biscuit**
A biscuit dipped into a hot drink by "Mr Cherry", aka Cherry Yoshitake (JPN), remained whole for 5 min 17.1 sec on the set of *La Notte dei Record* in Rome, Italy, on 15 Nov 2018.

Most books typed backwards
Michele Santelia typed 77 books in reverse (ATI) backwards, including the Bible (15,526 lines). His arrangements, 32,022,783, characters, 690,192 paragraphs, and 3,513,323 words, in 5,761,709, complete words, in 24 to 42 ram 2018.

MOST FOUR-LEAF CLOVERS COLLECTED IN ONE HOUR (INDIVIDUAL)
These good-luck symbols aren't quite as rare as you might think... Katie Borka (USA) picked 166 of them in 60 min in Spotsylvania, Virginia, USA, on 23 Jun 2018. Along the way, she found five- and six-leafed examples, and even one with nine leaves, although none of these counted towards her record total.

▶ **MOST STRAWS STUFFED INTO THE MOUTH**
Nataraj Karate (IND) pushed 692 drinking straws into his mouth in Salem, Tamil Nadu, India, on 25 Aug 2018. On the same day, Nataraj also broke the record for the **most straws stuffed into the mouth (no hands)** - 650.

TALLEST PAPER-CUP TOWER
Employees of the Haier Washing Machine Co. (CHN) erected a 10.08-m-tall (33-ft) sculpture made out of paper cups in Qingdao, Shandong Province, China, on 28 Jun 2017. It took 4 hr 15 min to construct the lofty tower - taller than five adult men standing on top of each other - which had four Leader cylinder washing machines as a base.

MAY 10
The Society of American Magicians, the **oldest magic society**, appears in a puff of smoke in Martinka's magic shop in New York City, USA, in 1902. Later presidents include Harry Houdini.

MAY 11
Leigh Purnell, Paul Archer and Johno Ellison (all UK) return to London, UK, in 2012 having completed the **longest journey by taxi**: 69,716 km (43,319 mi). The meter reads £79,006.80 ($127,530)!

▶ MOST TOOTHPICKS IN A BEARD

Joel Strasser (USA) stuck 3,500 toothpicks into his beard in Lacey, Washington, USA, on 7 Jul 2018. It took him 3 hr 13 min to reach this record-breaking amount. At the time of GWR's visit, Joel was training to beat the record for the **most straws in a beard**. He managed this on 18 Mar 2019, stuffing 312 straws into his whiskers (inset) to beat the record of 259 that was set by Isaac Kochman (USA) on 7 Jul 2018.

On 11 May 2017, Dean Carter (UK) achieved the **most toothpicks in a beard in one minute** – 33 – at Devon Cliffs Holiday Park in Sandy Bay, Exmouth, Devon, UK.

For a successful attempt, the participant must ensure that all the toothpicks – which he has to insert personally – remain in the beard for at least 10 seconds.

▶ Check out our top "pick" of videos at guinnessworldrecords.com/2020

MOST NECK TIES WORN AT ONCE

Jeremy Muñoz (USA) put on 287 neck ties in Lubbock, Texas, USA, on 4 Apr 2018. All the ties used in the attempt came from his personal collection. The achievement finally fulfilled Jeremy's ambition of securing a world record, which had been a dream of his ever since he began collecting *GWR* annuals aged 10 years old.

FASTEST TIME TO BURST 20 WATER BALLOONS WITH THE FEET

Farhan Ayub (PAK) burst 20 water balloons in 2.75 sec by trampling on them in Lahore, Punjab, Pakistan, on 23 Jul 2018. This beat the previous record by nearly 3 sec.

The **fastest time to burst 100 balloons with the feet** is 29.70 sec, achieved by multiple GWR title holder Ashrita Furman (USA) in New York City, USA, on 16 Dec 2015.

MOST T-SHIRTS WORN AT ONCE

Father-of-two Ted Hastings (CAN) donned 260 T-shirts in Kitchener, Ontario, Canada, on 17 Feb 2019. The tops got bigger as he progressed, starting with medium and ending with size 20X. Ted was inspired after reading *GWR 2019* with his son, William, who challenged his dad to break a GWR title. Wanting to teach his kids a lesson in hard work and commitment, Ted followed through and proved what's possible if you put your mind to it!

MAY 12 In 2002, speed cyclist Éric Barone (FRA) reaches 172 km/h (107 mph) on the steep slopes of the Cerro Negro volcano in Nicaragua. It is the **fastest speed cycling downhill on soil/gravel**.

MAY 13 Together with her owner, Samantha Valle (USA), border collie and kelpie cross Geronimo achieves the **most jump-rope skips by a dog in one minute** – 91 – in 2012.

FANTASTIC FEATS

MOST BURPEES WEARING HIGH HEELS IN ONE MINUTE (MALE)
Raneir Pollard (USA) carried out 38 burpees (squat thrusts with a vertical jump) wearing high heels in 60 sec in Los Angeles, California, USA, on 7 Dec 2017. When he's not busy training in a pair of stilettos, Raneir works as a group fitness instructor and stand-up comedian.

to another by an unseen force. On 28 Aug 2018, magician Scott Tokar (USA) instantly "transported" an assistant a distance of 285.33 m (936 ft) at the Farm Progress Show in Boone, Iowa, USA. The event was organized by Corteva Agriscience, a division of DowDuPont.

Longest duration juggling three objects on a balance board
Yutaro Nagao (JPN) juggled three balls for 41 min 19 sec while atop a balance board in Tokyo, Japan, on 8 Feb 2019.

MOST...

Waterskiers to front flip off the same ramp simultaneously
In an event organized by Chain of Records 2017 (USA), 11 waterskiers performed a simultaneous front flip from a ramp on Grassy Lake in Winter Haven, Florida, USA, on 23 Apr 2017.

Kick-scooter back-somersault twists in one minute
Dakota Schuetz (USA) flipped his kick-scooter through 21 backwards somersault twists in one minute on the set of *La Notte dei Record* in Rome, Italy, on 23 Nov 2018.

FARTHEST DISTANCE CYCLED ON A UNICYCLE USING ONE LEG
On 19 Jul 2018, unicyclist Israel Arranz Parada (ESP) covered 894.35 m (2,934 ft) – more than eight times the length of an American football field – while propelling himself only with his right leg. The unipedal ride took place in Valencia de Alcántara, Cáceres, Spain.

Farthest breakdancing head slide
In this acrobatic trick, the performer slides across the floor on the top of their head while the rest of the body is upright. The longest confirmed head slide measured 2.6 m (8 ft 6 in) and was achieved by 18-year-old breakdance champion Michele Gagno (ITA) in Rome, Italy, on 24 Nov 2018.

Farthest teleportation illusion
In terms of GWR guidelines, this magic trick is defined as an illusion in which a person or object appears to have been moved from one place

FARTHEST DISTANCE TO CATCH AN AIRBORNE ARROW WHILE TRAVELLING IN A MOVING CAR
An arrow fired by Olympic archer Laurence Baldauff (below) was caught by martial-arts pro Markus Haas, reaching out of the sun roof of a Škoda Octavia RS 245, with precision driver Guido Gluschitsch (all AUT) at the wheel. The arrow travelled 57.5 m (188 ft 7 in) before it was caught. Organized by Škoda Austria, the feat took place on 28 Jul 2018 in Zeltweg, Austria.

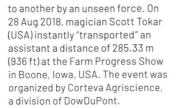

Licence plates torn in one minute
Professional strongman Bill Clark (USA) ripped 23 car number plates asunder in 60 sec in Binghamton, New York, USA, on 22 Aug 2018.

Triathlons hauling a person in one month
On 18 Nov 2018, athlete Caryn Lubetsky completed her fourth triathlon in a month towing quadriplegic journalist Kerry Gruson (both USA). The pair used an inflatable raft and a bicycle tow-hitch to adapt Gruson's racing wheelchair for each stage of the race.

Cartwheels in one minute (no hands)
On 15 Aug 2011, Zhang Ziyi (CHN) performed 45 "aerials" in 60 sec on the set of *CCTV – Guinness World Records Special* in Beijing, China.

Wine glasses balanced on the chin
Sun Chao Yang (CHN) kept 142 wine glasses balanced on his chin on the set of *La Notte dei Record* in Rome, Italy, on 11 Nov 2018. He broke his own record of 133 glasses, set in 2012.

FASTEST...

Time to lift and throw 10 people (female)
On 17 Nov 2018, Liefia Ingalls (USA) hoisted 10 people above her head and hurled them away in 39.5 sec on the set of *La Notte dei Record* in Rome, Italy.

110 m hippy jumps
In this manoeuvre, the performer jumps off a moving skateboard, clears a hurdle and lands on the board again to continue their journey. Steffen Köster (DEU) hippy-jumped a 110-m (360-ft) hurdle course in 29.98 sec

for *Wir Holen Den Rekord Nach Deutschland* at Europa-Park in Rust, Germany, on 19 Jun 2013.

100 m hurdles wearing swim fins (female)
On 8 Dec 2010, Veronica Torr (NZ) covered 100 m (328 ft) in 18.52 sec while wearing flippers on the set of *Zheng Da Zong Yi - Guinness World Records Special* in Beijing, China.

100 m on spring-loaded stilts
Ben Jacoby (USA) bounced down a 100-m course in 13.45 sec in Boulder, Colorado, USA, on 5 Oct 2018.

Time to limbo skate under 10 bars
R Naveen Kumar (IND) skated under 10 bars in 2.06 sec in Chennai, Tamil Nadu, India, on 9 Sep 2018. The bars were 24 cm (9 in) above the ground and 1 m (3 ft 3 in) apart.

FARTHEST DISTANCE COVERED JUGGLING A SOCCER BALL IN ONE HOUR (MALE)
On 12 Mar 2019, football freestyler John Farnworth (UK) juggled a ball for 5.82 km (3.61 mi) in the Sahara desert, Morocco. The previous year, John made the **greatest vertical ascent controlling a soccer ball in one hour (male)** – 197 m (646 ft) – on Kala Patthar in Nepal. In both cases, he kept the ball airborne without using his hands or arms.

MAY 14 In 2016, Gabriel Medina (BRA) lands the **first successful backflip at a Surfing World Championships event**. He is awarded a perfect score of 10 at the Oi Rio Pro in Rio de Janeiro, Brazil.

MAY 15 In 2014, Ruan Liangming (CHN) wears the **heaviest mantle of bees** – 63.7 kg (140 lb 6 oz) – in Yichun City, Jiangxi Province, China. He places 60 queen bees on his body to attract the swarm.

Brittany has been honing her acrobatic skills for years. She competed nationally and internationally as a gymnast for 12 years, retiring when she was still only 18.

▶ FARTHEST ARROW SHOT USING THE FEET

On 31 Mar 2018, using a bow that she manipulated with her feet, Brittany Walsh (USA) fired an arrow 12.31 m (40 ft 4 in) and hit a target with a radius of 30.4 cm (1 ft) almost dead centre. Her feat of inverted archery took place at Creston School in Portland, Oregon, USA. Brittany has been performing her pedestrial skills in theatre and circus shows for more than 11 years.

FARTHEST DISTANCE TO CRAWL UNDER BARBED WIRE IN 12 HOURS

On 13 Jul 2018, Eric Hutterer (CAN) covered a muddy 12.13 km (7.54 mi) on his hands and knees beneath barbed wire in 12 hr at the 2018 Spartan Death Race in Pittsfield, Vermont, USA. Eric completed more than 31 laps of the 386.79-m (1,269-ft) course, outlasting the 10 other "Death Racers" who took part.

▶ LONGEST DURATION TO PERFORM A HOLLOWBACK HANDSTAND

Jamie Stroud (USA) maintained a handstand with an arched spine for 60.03 sec in Las Vegas, Nevada, USA, on 15 Dec 2018. The attempt took place at the Rio All-Suite Hotel & Casino as part of the SkillCon 2018 event (see more on pp.98–107).

MOST CONSECUTIVE 180° SPINS ON A BALANCE BOARD

Silvio Sabba (ITA) completed 107 half-circle spins while on a balance board in Rodano, Milan, Italy, on 27 Jul 2017. Among a wealth of other GWR titles, Silvio also shares the record for the **most knee bends performed on a balance board in one minute** – 64 – with Ukraine's Dmytro Kharlov.

 MAY 16 In 1929, film stars gather at the Roosevelt Hotel in Hollywood, California, USA, for the **first Academy Awards**. The presentation ceremony lasts 15 min and isn't broadcast on TV or radio.

 MAY 17 Following the release of *Minecraft*'s public alpha version in 2009, "muku" takes just 49 min to post an image of the **first player-built structure in *Minecraft*** - a bridge formed of nine blocks.

BUBBLES!

Longest garland wand
A garland wand consists of small loops joined together, allowing the user to create lots of bubbles at once. On 23 Sep 2018, Alekos Ottaviucci, Anna Egle Sciarappa (both ITA) and Mariano Guz (ARG) created a 12.6-m (41-ft 4-in) version at Bubble Daze 5 in Caernarfon, Wales, UK (see p.91).

Longest bubble
Alan McKay (NZ) blew a 32-m (104-ft 11-in) bubble – longer than a blue whal e, the **largest animal** – in Wellington, New Zealand, on 9 Aug 1996.

Longest bubble chain (stacked)
On 13 Jan 2011, "Blub", aka Gennadij Kil (DEU), formed a free-standing tower comprising 21 stacked bubbles at the Centro de Creación y Formación Joven de Guía de Isora in Tenerife, Spain.

Longest time spent inside a bubble
"The Highland Joker", aka Eran Backler, encased his wife, Lauren (both UK), in a bubble that lasted for 1 min 2.92 sec before it burst. They achieved the feat in Peterborough, Cambridgeshire, UK, on 22 Dec 2018.

LONGEST HANGING BUBBLE CHAIN
Stefano Righi (ITA) produced a suspended string of 40 bubbles in Empoli near Florence, Italy, on 22 Feb 2017. The bubble artist had promised his son, Thomas, that he would break the previous record (35) – and delivered!

LARGEST EXPLOSIVE SOAP-BUBBLE DOME
On 20 Feb 2018, Stefano Righi (also above) created a soap-bubble dome with a diameter of 66 cm (2 ft 1 in) in Empoli, Italy. For this record, the dome must be formed on a flat surface and filled with a flammable gas (inset below). Its surface is then lit with a naked flame, with predictable results. This record is only for trained bubble-ologists!

Largest frozen soap bubble
"Samsam Bubbleman", aka Sam Heath (UK), created a frozen soap bubble with a volume of 4,315.7 cm³ (263.3 cu in) at the Absolut Vodka Bar in London, UK, on 28 Jun 2010.

"Samsam", pictured bottom right, also achieved the **most bounces of a soap bubble** at Bubble Daze 5. While wearing a glove, he bounced a bubble 215 times in his hand – surpassing the previous mark, set by Kuo-Sheng Lin (TPE) in 2012, by 20.

Largest outdoor free-floating bubble
Gary Pearlman (USA) created a 96.27-m³ (3,399.7-cu-ft) bubble – equivalent in volume to nearly 12,900 regulation NBA basketballs – in Cleveland, Ohio, USA, on 20 Jun 2015.

On 19 Jun 2017, "Marty McBubble", aka Graeme Denton (AUS), produced the **largest indoor free-floating bubble**, measuring 19.8 m³ (699.2 cu ft), at Lockleys Primary School in Adelaide, South Australia.

Most people enclosed in soap bubbles in 30 seconds
This record changed hands twice in 2018. First to achieve it was Eran Backler (UK), who created tube-shaped bubbles around nine people against the clock at Bubble Daze 5. A few weeks later, on 9 Nov 2018, Steven Langley (USA) upped the mark to 13 people in Huntersville,

North Carolina, USA. In both attempts, all of the participants were at least 150 cm (5 ft) tall.

With no time limits, artist Lyudmila Darina (RUS) enclosed 374 people in a 2.5-m-tall (8-ft 2-in) bubble in Omsk, Russia, on 2 Mar 2017 – the **most people inside a single soap bubble**.

LARGEST SOAP BUBBLE BLOWN BY HAND
Mariano Guz (ARG) dipped his hands in bubble solution then blew a 45,510-cm³ (2,777-cu-in) bubble between his index finger and thumb at Bubble Daze 5.

Most concentric soap-bubble domes
On 26 Apr 2012, Su Chung-Tai (TPE) placed 15 hemispherical bubbles inside each other in Taipei, Chinese Taipei.

Three years later, on 13 Jan 2015, he created the **most soap bubbles blown inside one large bubble** (779) in Jiangyin, Jiangsu Province, China. To do so, he first produced a large bubble, then placed his lips close to the surface and blew smaller bubbles inside.

On 28 Mar 2018, the prolific Su produced the **largest soap bubble dome** – with a diameter of 1.4 m (4 ft 7 in), a height of 0.65 m (2 ft 1 in) and a volume of 0.644 m³ (22.74 cu ft) – in the Chinese city of Tianjin.

LARGEST SOAP-BUBBLE BOTTLE AND WAND
Matěj Kodeš (CZE) presented a bottle of bubble solution and wand that stood 1.38 m (4 ft 6.3 in) tall in Lysá nad Labem, Czech Republic, on 25 Mar 2018. Five months later, on 6 Aug 2018, Kodeš generated the **most soap bubbles blown in one minute** – 1,257 – at the same location, though not with the super-sized bottle and wand.

MĚSTO

LYSÁ NAD LABEM

MAY 18 In 1968, the 200-cm-tall (6-ft 6-in) slugger Frank Howard of the Washington Senators (both USA) hits his ninth and 10th home runs in seven days – the **most baseball home runs in a week**.

MAY 19 A total of 245 climbers reach the summit of Everest in 2012 – the **most ascents of Everest in one day**. The mountain becomes congested and climbers cause a traffic jam near the summit.

BUBBLE DAZE 5

On 23 Sep 2018, GWR "popped" along to Caernarfon Castle in Wales, UK, to meet some of the world's leading bubblers (inset) at this annual celebration of bubble artistry. On the day, Dr Zigs Extraordinary Bubbles (UK) staged a number of record-breaking feats, including the **most people making bubbles with garland wands simultaneously** (317, below) and the **most people making giant bubbles with tri-string wands simultaneously** (318). You'll find a few others on these pages too...

LONGEST BUBBLE RALLY

"Ray Bubbles", aka Umar Shoaib (UK), and his son Rayhaan (FRA) passed a soap bubble between them 10 times at École la Grange in Rungis, France, on 13 Apr 2016. The "rackets" used for the record attempt featured a film of soap-bubble solution across their face, rather than strings.

MOST BOUNCES OF A BUBBLE ON A SOAP FILM

After two less successful attempts, Farhaan Shoaib (FRA) performed an impressive 113 soap-bubble bounces at Bubble Daze 5. Bubble skills are definitely a family trait – Farhaan's father and brother hold their own GWR title too (see left).

MOST BUBBLES BLOWN FROM A SINGLE WAND

From just a single wand dip, "Samsam Bubbleman", aka Sam Heath, produced 445 soap bubbles at Bubble Daze 5. Sam deliberately chose a record that didn't require specialist experience or tools, as he wanted to inspire bubble enthusiasts of all ages to try for a GWR title themselves.

Trying this at home? It's tricky! The bubble is fragile and can easily break, or merge completely with the film on the racket.

MAY 20 In 1927, Charles Lindbergh (USA) sets off on the **first solo transatlantic flight** from Roosevelt Field in New York City, USA. He lands in Paris, France, after a journey lasting 33 hr 30 min 29 sec.

MAY 21 In 1977, sharp-nosed frog (*Ptychadena oxyrhynchus*) "Santjie" makes the **farthest jump by a frog in competition** – a total of 10.3 m (33 ft 9 in) over three leaps – at a frog derby in Pietersburg, South Africa.

91

FIRE!

THE FIRE SCHOOL

GWR would like to thank The Fire School for its help in the creation of this feature. The UK's first centre for fire arts, it is located in east London and was founded in 2012 by circus performer, teacher and "fire headmistress" Sarah Harman. The school provides a safe and professional environment in which to learn a wide variety of fire skills at all levels.

Most throws and catches of a fire sword in one minute

Ashrita Furman (USA) threw and caught a burning sword 62 times in Jamaica, New York City, USA, on 20 Apr 2018. A "fire sword" is a blade coated in combustible fuel and lit.

Four months later in the same location, he achieved the **longest duration fire-torch teething** – 5 min 1.68 sec. For this record attempt, the performer tilts their head back and brings the torch down, placing it partly into the mouth and gripping it with the teeth.

▶ Most flames blown in one minute

On 9 Jan 2015, Chinese fire-breather Zhu Jiangao blew 189 flames in 60 sec on the set of *CCTV - Guinness World Records Special* in Jiangyin, Jiangsu Province, China.

On 1 Aug 2015, Tobias Buschick (DEU) blew 387 flames from his mouth one after the other – the **most consecutive flames blown without refuelling** – in Neuenbürg, Germany. Before performing, he took only a single mouthful of fire-eating fluid.

Most fire hoops spun simultaneously

Casey Martin (USA) rotated four burning hoops around herself at the same time at the Port Credit Busker Fest in Mississauga, Ontario, Canada, on 14 Aug 2014. Each hoop contained four fire wicks and Casey achieved eight revolutions during the attempt. Pippa "The Ripper" Coram (AUS)

MOST TORCHES EXTINGUISHED BY FIRE-EATING IN ONE MINUTE

"FireGuy", aka Brant Matthews (CAN), smothered 101 torches with his mouth in 60 sec in West Allis, Wisconsin, USA, on 10 Aug 2018. He performed his flame-quenching display at the State Fair.

achieved the **most fire hoops spun while in the splits position** – three – at Wonderground in London, UK, on 14 Sep 2012. As per GWR rules, she had to keep the hot hoops spinning around her arms and neck for 10 sec.

Most people spinning fire

Ameno Signum (DEU) arranged for 250 participants to spin fire pois (chain-like objects, one end of which is set alight) in Neunburg vorm Wald, Germany, on 1 Sep 2012.

Most balloons burst by a fire-breather

Colin Llewelyn Chapman (UK) popped 131 balloons by breathing fire on them – using just a single breath – in London, UK, on 22 Oct 2017.

First person to surf a wave while on fire

On 22 Jul 2015, professional surfer Jamie O'Brien (USA) was set alight then rode one of the world's largest waves – Teahupo'o, in Tahiti, French Polynesia – all in response to a suggestion on Instagram. Aside from the risk posed by the flames, the wave itself is both powerful and dangerous as it breaks on a low-lying coral reef.

Highest bungee jump into water while on fire

Yoni Roch (FRA) launched himself from a height of 65.09 m (213 ft 6 in) on a bungee rope while fully alight at the Viaduc de la Souleuvre in Normandy, France, on 14 Sep 2012. The fire was doused when he dipped into the river Souleuvre below.

▶ MOST BLINDFOLDED FIRE-EATING EXTINGUISHES WITH ONE ROD IN ONE MINUTE

On 27 Jan 2019, an unsighted Sarah Harman (UK) orally smothered the flames on a fire rod 91 times at The Fire School in London, UK, of which she is the director. In this attempt, the performer keeps one wick alight and uses it to relight the extinguished rod.

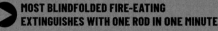

▶ LONGEST DURATION FULL-BODY BURN (WITHOUT OXYGEN)

Josef Tödtling (AUT) remained alight from his ankles to the top of his head for 5 min 41 sec without oxygen supplies in the grounds of the Salzburg Fire Department in Austria on 23 Nov 2013. He wore several layers of fire-resistant clothing and applied heat-resistant gel – particularly on his head and neck – to prevent burns.

MOST FIRE-BREATHING BACKFLIPS IN ONE MINUTE

Ryan Luney (UK) completed 14 reverse flips in 60 sec while simultaneously breathing fire at Riverside School in Antrim, UK, on 23 Jun 2017. The attempt took place as part of an event to mark the end of the academic year. He was inspired to try for this record after seeing ex-*Jackass* star Steve-O perform the stunt on the *Slow Mo Guys* YouTube channel.

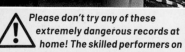

⚠ **Please don't try any of these extremely dangerous records at home! The skilled performers on these pages train for years to achieve their feats, and know exactly how to prepare and protect themselves.**

MAY 22 In 1960, the **most powerful earthquake** strikes Chile. Originating c. 160 km (100 mi) off the coast, it measures 9.5_{Mw} on the moment magnitude scale and kills more than 2,000 people.

MAY 23 In Leicester, East Midlands, UK, Rishi Thobhani (UK) displays the **largest trousers** in 2009. The pair of thermal long johns measure 12.19 m (40 ft) in length with a 7.92-m (26-ft) waist.

Laura and Noelia have performed together for years, building the mutual trust that is vital for team fire-eating feats.

▶ MOST ALTERNATE FIRE-EATING EXTINGUISHES IN ONE MINUTE (TEAM OF TWO)

In this record attempt, one performer presents a lit fire torch to the other, who douses it in the mouth and presents another flaming torch for the first performer to put out. "Isobel Midnight", aka Laura Sutton (UK, above left), and "Lady Noelia", aka Noelia Hueso Muñoz (ESP, above right), carried out 73 alternate fire-eating extinguishes in the allocated time at The Fire School on 27 Jan 2019.

During the same session, Isobel completed the **most fire-eating extinguishes in one minute (two rods)** – 78 (inset).

HIGHEST FLAME BY FIRE-BREATHER

On 11 Jan 2011, Antonio Restivo (USA) blew an 8.05-m-high (26-ft 5-in) flame in a warehouse in Las Vegas, Nevada, USA, using liquid paraffin as his fuel source. He hit the ceiling of the warehouse with the flame. The year previously, Antonio had brought his fire-handling skills to the fifth season of *America's Got Talent*, where he progressed to the semi-final stage.

▶ MOST DOUBLE JELLYFISH EXTINGUISHES IN ONE MINUTE

In a "double jellyfish", the performer raises two fire torches into the air then yanks them down sharply; the flames leave each torch, forming a jellyfish-like shape before expiring. Roman Ackley (UK) created 24 double jellyfishes in 60 sec at The Fire School on 27 Jan 2019.

He also achieved the **most single jellyfish fire extinguishes in one minute**: 34.

MAY 24 In 1991, an El Al Boeing 747 transports the **most passengers on an aircraft** – *c.* 1,088 – as part of Operation Solomon, evacuating Ethiopian Jews from Addis Ababa in Ethiopia to Israel.

MAY 25 The **oldest rat ever**, a common rat called Rodney, dies aged 7 years 4 months in 1990. He belongs to namesake Rodney Mitchell of Tulsa in Oklahoma, USA.

93

PEOPLE ARE AWESOME™

People Are Awesome is a brand dedicated to those who thrive on pushing the boundaries of human endeavour and achieving the seemingly impossible. It features videos that celebrate human physical ability, creativity and ingenuity, and shines a spotlight on the world's most talented video creators, giving them a platform to be seen. Of course, a lot of records are set along the way – the awesome people featured here are all Guinness World Records title holders featured on the channel.

FASTEST TIME TO JUMP ACROSS 10 SWISS BALLS

Neil Whyte (AUS) leaped across 10 Swiss balls – placed at least 1 m (3 ft 3 in) apart – in 7.8 sec in Beijing, China, on 12 Jan 2016. He made three attempts, but failed with his first two. On his third try, Neil successfully surpassed his previous record of 8.31 sec.

Ten years earlier, Neil had achieved the **longest jump between two Swiss balls** – 2.3 m (7 ft 6 in) – at the Zest Health Club in Perth, Western Australia, on 25 Aug 2006.

▶ **Most walnuts cracked with the head in one minute**
Muhammad Rashid (PAK) used his head – literally – to break 254 walnuts in Rome, Italy, on 11 Nov 2018.

Greatest height reached after being launched from an airbag (blobbing)
"Blobbing" is a water activity in which one participant sits on the end of a partially inflated air bag (aka a "blob") and is launched into the air when a colleague jumps on to the bag from a platform on the opposite side. On 7 Jun 2012, blobber Christian "Elvis" Guth reached a height of 22 m (72 ft 2 in), propelled there by jumpers Christian von Cranach and Patrick Baumann (all DEU). The feat was achieved in Hamburg, Germany.

Most consecutive ladder rungs climbed with one arm
Tazio Gavioli (ITA) pulled himself up 39 rungs with his left arm at Heilan International Equestrian Club in Jiangsu Province, China, on 9 Jan 2014. (For more of Tazio's records, go to p.85.)

Fastest time to climb a vertical corridor with the feet
Positioned between two walls, Fang Zhisheng (CHN) took 28.3 sec to propel himself upwards to a height of more than 18 m (59 ft) using only his feet in Beijing, China, on 21 Nov 2012.

Most Thomas flairs on a pommel horse in one minute
Well-known to breakdancers and gymnasts, a Thomas flair involves alternately supporting the torso between each arm while swinging the legs in circles. On 21 Apr 2009, Louis Smith (UK) performed 50 of these manoeuvres in London, UK. Alberto Busnari (ITA) matched the feat on 10 Jul 2014. Both men are internationally recognized gymnasts.

Fastest 10 m in the box split position (female)
In this posture, the competitor extends the legs from either side of the torso, creating an angle of about 180°. On 12 Mar 2012, Kazumi Kawahara (JPN) covered 10 m (32 ft 9 in) in this position in 16.9 sec in Rome, Italy.

▶ **HIGHEST SHALLOW DIVE**
"Professor Splash" (aka Darren Taylor, USA) dropped from a height of 11.56 m (37 ft 11 in) into just 30 cm (1 ft) of water in Xiamen, Fujian Province, China, on 9 Sep 2014.

Not scary enough? On 21 Jun that year, he made the **highest shallow dive into fire** – 8 m (26 ft 3 in). The pool's surface was set alight just before his leap.

GWR rules state that contestants must maintain a handstand position throughout the attempt.

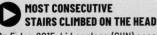

▶ **MOST CONSECUTIVE STAIRS CLIMBED ON THE HEAD**
On 5 Jan 2015, Li Longlong (CHN) ascended 36 stairs on his head in Jiangyin, Jiangsu Province, China. He surpassed his own record by two steps.

FASTEST TIME TO CRAM INTO A BOX (FEMALE)

Contortionist Skye Broberg (NZ) took 4.78 sec to squeeze into a box sized 52 x 45 x 45 cm (1 ft 8 in x 1 ft 5 in x 1 ft 5 in) in London, UK, on 15 Sep 2011.

Below, Skye is pictured passing through a tennis racket – a talent for which she once held a number of GWR titles. Today, two of her records have been surpassed by Thaneswar Guragai (NPL): **most passes through a tennis racket in three minutes** (96) and **fastest time to pass through a tennis racket three times** (4.91 sec).

MAY 26 In 1991, a team of 14 students from Stanford University in California, USA, complete the **longest distance leapfrogging**. They had travelled 1,603.2 km (996.2 mi) around a track in 244 hr 43 min.

MAY 27 The **longest daisy chain (team)** is made in 1985. A group of 16 villagers from Good Easter near Chelmsford, Essex, UK, spends seven hours forming the 2.12-km-long (1.31-mi) string of flowers.

What prompted this daring airborne record attempt? In Aaron's own words, "I want to set this record to show the world that wheelchairs can fly!"

▶ FARTHEST WHEELCHAIR RAMP JUMP

On 20 Jul 2018, Aaron Fotheringham (USA) completed a 21.35-m (70-ft) ramp jump in a wheelchair at Woodward West in Tehachapi, California, USA. This was one of three successful record attempts Aaron completed on the day, along with the **tallest quarter-pipe drop-in on a wheelchair** and the **highest wheelchair hand plant** – both 8.4 m (27 ft 6 in) – as illustrated in the inset pictures (right).

FASTEST TIME TO CLIMB A 5-M ROPE

On 30 Sep 2018, Nick "The KO Ninja" Kostreski (USA, above) scaled a 5-m-high (16-ft 4-in) rope – around the height of an adult giraffe – in only 4.11 sec in Santa Monica, California, USA.

On the same day, Natalie Duran (USA, right) achieved the **fastest 5-m rope climb (female)** in 7.67 sec.

MOST CONCRETE BLOCKS BROKEN IN ONE MINUTE

Ali Bahçetepe (TUR) split 1,175 blocks of concrete in 60 sec in Datça Cumhuriyet Meydanı, Turkey, on 17 Nov 2012. Iron-fisted Ali has also achieved the **most concrete blocks broken in 30 seconds** (683), in 2012, and the **most concrete blocks broken in one stack** (37), in 2015. (For another of his block-busting records, see p.84.)

▶ MOST ONE-FINGER PUSH-UPS IN 30 SECONDS

Xie Guizhong (CHN) performed 41 push-ups on one finger in 30 sec in Beijing, China, on 8 Dec 2011. He comfortably topped his previous record of 25.

On 11 Dec 2010, the man with the super-strong digits had achieved the **fastest time to push a car for 50 m with one finger**: 47.7 sec, in Shenzhen City, Guangdong Province, China.

MAY 28 In 2006, Xue Chen (CHN, b. 18 Feb 1989) becomes the **youngest player to win an international beach volleyball title** when she claims the China Shanghai Jinshan Open aged 17 years 99 days.

MAY 29 Rory Blackwell (UK) turns himself into the **largest one-man band** in 1989 by playing 108 different instruments (19 melody and 89 percussion) simultaneously in Dawlish, Devon, UK.

LONGEST MARATHON PLAYING ACCORDION

Between 11 and 13 Jul 2018, Anssi K Laitinen (FIN) played an accordion for 40 hr 3 min 10 sec in Kuopio, Finland. Anssi performed 610 different pieces, including Finnish as well as internationally popular music, and played entirely from memory. He is a previous record holder in the accordion-marathon category, having played for 31 hr 25 min back in 2010.

Most playing cards memorized in one hour
Mongolian teenager Munkhshur Narmandakh became the first female to win the World Memory Championships when she triumphed in Shenzhen, Guangdong Province, China, on 6–8 Dec 2017. She memorized 1,924 playing cards – 37 full decks – in 60 min and then recited them correctly in 2 hr.

At the same event, Munkhshur's identical twin Enkhshur Narmandakh (MNG) recalled 5,445 1s and 0s – the **most binary digits memorized in 30 minutes**. However, this was surpassed by Enkhtuya Lkhagvadulam (MNG) in 2018 and now stands at 5,597 digits.

Longest ice hockey pass
On 20 Nov 2018, Zach Lamppa and former National Hockey League forward Tom Chorske (both USA) joined forces to complete an ice hockey pass measuring 275.63 m (904 ft 3 in). The feat took place on the frozen Lake of the Isles in Minneapolis, Minnesota, USA.

Highest altitude soccer ball dropped and volleyed into a goal
On 24 Jul 2018, freestyle footballer John Farnworth (see p.88) and former English Premier League star Jimmy Bullard (both UK) each volleyed a ball into a goal after it had fallen 45.72 m (150 ft) from a helicopter. The extreme shooting practice took place at White Waltham airfield in Maidenhead, UK.

Fastest marathon distance in relay
A team of 59 Kansas City athletes covered a 42.1-km (26.2-mi) course in 1 hr 30 min 40.31 sec on 15 Jun 2018. The charity fundraising event, staged at Johnson County Community College in Overland Park, Kansas, USA, was organized by Joe and Phil Ratterman (all USA). High-school and collegiate sprinters joined the team, running 200-m (656-ft) legs to beat a record that had stood for 20 years.

First triple butt backflip on a slackline
Louis Boniface (FRA) landed the first ever triple backflip, starting and ending in a sitting position, on 8 Oct 2018, as verified by the International Slackline Association. The 26-m (85-ft) slackline stretched 3.10 m (10 ft) above the ground in Saint-Lambert, France.

MOST TIMES TO FOLD A PIECE OF PAPER

On 27 Jan 2002, high-school student Britney Gallivan (USA) wrote two mathematical equations that enabled her to fold a piece of paper in half 12 times. To do so, she used a section of tissue paper measuring 1,219 m (4,000 ft) long. Discussing the feat, Britney told us: "I hope that others can see this... expand on it and take on their own 'impossible' challenges!"

LARGEST GATHERING OF PEOPLE DRESSED AS DINOSAURS

On 26 Jan 2019, YouTube star Elton Castee (USA) invited 1,000 people to help him break 10 GWR titles while shooting his music video "The Fun in Life" in Los Angeles, California, USA. For one record, 252 people dressed up in dinosaur costumes; also broken were the **most nationalities kissed in one minute** and the **most nationalities in a group hug** – 50, in both cases.

Dancing dinos appear in Elton's music video performing moves like the "Carniwar" and "Tyrannosaur Twerk".

MAY 30 In 2016, Kyle Lobpries (USA) soars above Davis in California, USA, for eight-and-a-half minutes. In that time, he covers 32.094 km (19.94 mi) – the **greatest absolute distance flown in a wingsuit**.

MAY 31 In 1975, competitive-eating legend Peter Dowdeswell (UK) records the **fastest time to drink two pints of milk** – 3.2 sec – at Dudley's Top Rank Suite in West Midlands, UK.

MOST 360° DOWNWARD SPINS UNDERWATER IN ONE MINUTE

On 12 Dec 2018, mermaid performer Ariana Liuzzi (USA) achieved 32 complete downward spins underwater in 60 sec at the Silverton Casino Hotel in Las Vegas, Nevada, USA. A former synchronized swimmer, Ariana now spends her days in a 442,893-litre (117,000-US-gal) saltwater aquarium that is also home to 4,000 tropical fish, sharks and several stingrays!

Fellow mermaid Logan Halverson (USA) joined in the fun with the **most air rings blown underwater in one minute** – 48 (inset, below), also on 12 Dec 2018.

The Silverton mermaids can spend up to 15 min performing underwater, taking breaths from special "hookah ports" built into the artificial reef.

LARGEST PORCELAIN DOLL

Ten years in the making, a porcelain doll crafted by artists Wang Chu and Deng Jiaqi (both CHN) in Jiangxi Province, China, stands 172 cm (5 ft 7 in) tall. The haunting life-size creation has a chest circumference of 70 cm (2 ft 3 in), a waist width of 52 cm (1 ft 8 in) and a hip width of 74 cm (2 ft 5 in).

Heaviest vehicle pulled by hair

Mahmood Shamshun Al Arab (UAE) towed a truck weighing 10,380 kg (22,883 lb) with just his hair in Fujairah, UAE, on 2 Dec 2017.

Largest tuba ensemble

The 835-strong Kansas City Symphony (USA) performed a rendition of "Silent Night" at TUBACHRISTMAS 2018 on 7 Dec in Kansas City, Missouri, USA. The ensemble was conducted by Professor Scott Watson, with participants ranging in age from 11 to 86. For this record, lower-brass instruments including tubas, baritone horns and euphoniums are permitted.

Longest dragon boat

On 12 Nov 2018, an 87.3-m-long (286-ft 5-in) dragon boat was unveiled in Prey Veng Province, Cambodia. It had been built by the Union of Youth Federations of Cambodia in the province and financed by Prey Veng Provincial Administration (both KHM). The boat had the capacity for 179 oarsmen.

Fastest time to disassemble and assemble a *matryoshka* blindfolded

On 27 Oct 2018, Kask Georgi Togaevig (RUS) took apart and rebuilt a five-layer Russian nesting doll in 8.01 sec at a shopping mall at Kashirskaya Plaza in Moscow, Russia. The event was put on by ENKA TC (RUS).

Most people potting plants simultaneously

During a community clean-up of Portsmouth, Ohio, USA, 1,405 green-fingered volunteers from the Friends of Portsmouth (USA) potted plants on 18 Aug 2018.

Most golf holes played in 24 hours by an individual (walking)

On 23 Apr 2019, Eric Byrnes (USA) covered 169 km (105 mi) on foot at the Half Moon Bay golf course in California, USA; in that time, he played 420 holes. This bettered the mark of 401 holes, which had stood for 48 years.

FASTEST TIME TO VISIT ALL DISNEY THEME PARKS

In 2017, Lindsay Nemeth (CAN) visited all 12 Disney theme parks in 75 hr 6 min. She began in Disneyland in California, USA (pictured), before flying to Florida, USA, and then on to Paris, Shanghai and Hong Kong. Her journey ended happily ever after at Tokyo DisneySea in Urayasu, Chiba Prefecture, Japan, on 6 Dec.

JUN 1 The **longest rail tunnel** opens in 2016. The Gotthard Base Tunnel measures 57 km (35.42 mi) in length and runs beneath the Alps between Göschenen and Airolo in Switzerland.

JUN 2 In 2016, strongman Cosimo Ferrucci (ITA) completes seven squat lifts of a platform bearing 11 people – the **most people squat-lifted** – in Trani, Italy.

VIRAL SPORTS

Welcome to our chapter on fun, skills-based challenges that are video-friendly and ideal for sharing online! Our inspiration was SkillCon, an annual three-day celebration of unconventional sports (combat juggling, anyone?) staged in Las Vegas, Nevada, USA. Our adjudicators visited the event in Dec 2018 to oversee a range of record attempts, many of which you can read about over the next few pages, along with other mind-boggling demonstrations of skill and dexterity.

Check out these talented individuals, from jugglers and bottle-flippers to speed-cubers and pogo-stick jumpers. Then, go to **guinnessworldrecords.com/2020**, where some of the record holders offer performance tips and insights in videos specially made for you. Armed with your new-found knowledge, why not try out some of these challenges? Once you've got the hang of it, upload a video of yourself in action. Who knows, you may end up with a viral hit of your own – and if you're good enough, perhaps a GWR title too!

SkillCon

▶ Find more viral sports videos at
guinnessworldrecords.com/2020

LARGEST LIGHTSPEED SABER WINNER-STAYS-ON COMPETITION

On 15 Dec 2018, a group of 60 combatants battled it out at SkillCon using equipment inspired by the luminescent weapons from the *Star Wars* movies. The contest was eventually won by Cang Snow (right), founder of the Lightspeed Saber League (both USA), which organized the event.

In Feb 2019, this new form of duelling was officially recognized as a sport in France, where fencing clubs are being equipped with their very own polycarbonate lightsabers!

In a lightsaber duel, points are scored when one fighter's "blade" touches the other player. The first combatant to reach a set total wins. Bouts often take place within a demarcated area (or "light box"), the borders of which are marked out in lights.

CONTENTS

UP IN THE AIR

The ancient skill of juggling hones hand-eye coordination and much more besides – including our powers of concentration and spatial awareness. It also aids brain development and can be both relaxing and stimulating. Best of all, it's fun! If you're not yet a juggler, it's easy enough to learn the basics. And if you need encouragement, take a look at these skilled conjurors, some of whom juggle things you *definitely* shouldn't attempt. Try filming yourself – it could help you improve your technique – and putting your video online. You might get more hits than you thought – and inspire others to give it a go too!

MOST JUGGLING BACK-CROSS CATCHES IN ONE MINUTE

Back crosses are behind-the-back throws carried out continuously, alternating from left to right. On 16 Dec 2018, Matan Presberg (USA) – an International Jugglers' Association world champion – made 162 of these catches in 60 sec at SkillCon in Las Vegas, Nevada, USA.

GREATEST COMBINED WEIGHT JUGGLED

Denys Ilchenko (UKR) kept three tyres with an overall weight of 26.98 kg (59 lb 7 oz) in airborne rotation for 32.43 sec on 17 Jul 2013. His feat of pneumatic manipulation took place on the set of *Officially Amazing* in Nairn, UK.

LONGEST DURATION TO KEEP TWO BALLOONS IN THE AIR WITH THE HEAD

Juggling, but not as you know it... Abhinabha Tangerman (NLD) kept a pair of balloons aloft by heading them for 1 min 9 sec in Leiria, Portugal, on 10 Jun 2018.

> ⚠️ **Don't try these at home!** The juggling of sharp and heavy objects should be left to the professionals.

JOSH HORTON

On 6 Sep 2018, "Juggling Josh" (aka Josh Horton, above) and his wife Cassie (both USA) achieved the **most apples sliced while juggling knives in one minute (team of two)** – 36. With Jake Triplett (USA), Josh also completed the **30-second** record, cleaving 17 apples in two on 4 Sep 2017.

DAVID RUSH

A multiple GWR title holder, this US juggler tackles records to help promote STEM (Science, Technology, Engineering and Mathematics) education. On 28 Oct 2018, David achieved the **most juggling catches on a unicycle (blindfolded)** – 30 – at Centennial High School in Boise, Idaho, USA. Earlier that year, on 16 Jun, he had completed the **most consecutive axe-juggling catches** – 839 – at Rhodes Skate Park in Boise. And on 17 Aug 2018, he equalled Milan Roskopf's (SVK) 2011 record for the **most bowling balls juggled** – three.

JUN 3 In 2015, Paul Thompson (UK) sets off on the **longest journey by milk float**, travelling 1,659.29 km (1,031.03 mi) around the UK at an average speed of just 16 km/h (10 mph).

 JUN 4 In 2016, Łukasz Budner (POL) achieves the **fastest table-tennis hit** – a lightning-fast 116 km/h (72.08 mph) – during a competition in Częstochowa, Poland.

"Elbow Pop": bounce the ball off your elbow, mid-juggle. If you do it with both arms, it counts as two tricks!

"Over the Shoulder": a behind-the-back throw that can be performed on both sides of your body.

MOST JUGGLING TRICKS IN ONE MINUTE (THREE BALLS)

On 16 Dec 2018, juggler Taylor Glenn (USA) completed 39 tricks – including the three seen here (left) – with three balls in 60 sec at SkillCon in Las Vegas. She learned the basics of three-ball juggling when she was 12, moving on to four and five balls, and clubs too, in her teens.

"Under the Leg": again, you can do this with both legs – each counts as a separate trick.

DO TRY THIS AT HOME

Have you got what it takes to top Taylor's tricks total? If you think you can out-juggle her, be sure to follow the GWR guidelines...

• All the tricks that you perform should be standard juggling manoeuvres.

• We'll need you to submit a full list of all the tricks you're going to try – and the order that you'll be performing them in – ahead of your attempt.

• You can also include videos or photographs showing how the tricks are performed in your submission.

• Make sure you use three commercially available juggling balls.

• Once you start, you'll need to complete every trick before moving on to the next one. And each trick can only be performed once.

• You'll need to announce each new trick out loud as you perform it.

• Don't drop any balls! If you do, your record attempt ends.

• Two independent witnesses should be on hand to verify your attempt. They should be proficient jugglers, and proof of their expertise should be submitted with your claim.

• Your witnesses will have to review the video of your attempt, to confirm that you have completed all the tricks and in the correct order. For the full set of official GWR guidelines, go to **guinnessworldrecords.com/2020**

Catch Taylor's juggling tutorial at guinnessworldrecords.com/2020

JUN 5 Satyajit Hota (IND) achieves the **heaviest weight held with the eyelid** – 3.51 kg (7 lb 11 oz), more than an average brick – in 2013 on the set of *Rekorlar Dünyası* in Istanbul, Turkey.

JUN 6 A Colombian rainbow boa named Ben (b. 31 May 1974) passes away in 2016 aged 42 years 6 days – the **oldest snake in captivity ever**. He lived with the Hattermann family in Valdosta, Georgia, USA.

101

PLAY LIKE A PRO

Meet the record-breakers who've taken their hobbies to the extreme and turned playtime into a profession! These are the pogo-stickers, footbaggers, space-hoppers and yo-yoers who've invested thousands of hours of practice to become the best in the world at what they do. If you've got a pastime that you love, then you're already half way to joining the ranks of the record-breaking. Take inspiration from these guys and set yourself some goals – who knows, you might even get your name in next year's GWR book!

▶ MOST HULA HOOPS SPUN SIMULTANEOUSLY

Australia's Marawa Ibrahim rotated 200 hula hoops around her body at the same time in Los Angeles, California, USA, on 25 Nov 2015. Over the years, Marawa has set heaps of hoop records, including the **fastest 50 m hula hooping** – 8.76 sec – and the **fastest 100 m on roller skates while spinning three hula hoops** – 27.26 sec.

▶ PHENOMENAL FOOTBAGGERS

Controlling these mini bean bags requires stamina and fast reactions. Derrick Fogle (USA, left) needed both to record the **farthest distance covered in one hour while controlling a footbag** – 5.05 km (3.14 mi) – on 15 Dec 2018.

The **most consecutive footbag kicks with one leg using two footbags** is 71, by Mathieu Gauthier (CAN, right). The two records were set on 15 Dec 2018 during SkillCon, held in Las Vegas, Nevada, USA.

HIGHEST JUMP ON A POGO STICK

Dmitry Arsenyev (RUS) bounced 3.4 m (11 ft 1 in) into the air – around the same height as an adult African elephant – in Rome, Italy, on 20 Nov 2018.

On 5 Nov 2017, the Xpogo pro athlete also recorded the **most consecutive stick flips on a pogo stick** – 26. In this trick, Dmitry rotates his stick through 360° mid-jump before each landing!

TALLEST LEGO®-BRICK CRISS-CROSS TOWER BUILT IN 30 SECONDS WITH ONE HAND

Silvio Sabba (ITA) built a 29-block LEGO-brick tower in half a minute in Milan, Italy, on 3 Mar 2017. This super-stacker has also racked up the **most plastic bottle caps stacked into a tower in one minute** (43) and the **most CDs balanced on one finger** (247).

FASTEST 100 M ON A SPACE HOPPER (FEMALE)

Comedian and social-media superstar Ali Spagnola (USA) bounced down a 100-m (328-ft) course on a space hopper in 38.22 sec at UCLA's Drake Track & Field Stadium in Los Angeles, California, USA, on 9 Mar 2017.

Multiple record holder Ashrita Furman (USA) performed the outright **fastest 100 m on a space hopper**, covering the distance in just 30.2 sec on 16 Nov 2004.

JUN 7 In Mainz, Germany, in 2015, Christian Schäfer (DEU) achieves the **most playing cards memorized underwater**. On a single breath, he remembers 56 cards, recalling them in sequence once back on dry land.

JUN 8 In 2014, Mario Barth (DEU) finishes an epic comedy routine at the Olympiastadion in Berlin, Germany, witnessed by a total of 116,498 people – the **largest audience for a comedian in 24 hours**.

MOST SPINNING TOPS SPUN SIMULTANEOUSLY

On 17 Mar 2012, Mark kept 27 tops rotating at the same time at the Canal Park Playhouse in New York City, USA. The feat was part of a series of GWR title attempts that Mark and his stage partner, Jonathan Burns, tackled at the end of their off-Broadway comedy show *Stunt Lab*.

▶ FARTHEST DISTANCE TO "WALK THE DOG" WITH A YO-YO

Comedy entertainer Mark Hayward (USA) is also a world yo-yo and spintop champion. It's no surprise, then, that he's a record holder for "walking the dog". In this trick, the performer throws a spinning yo-yo down so that it touches the ground and rolls forward. Mark broke this record at SkillCon on 15 Dec 2018, when he made his yo-yo travel an unrivalled 8.28 m (27 ft 2 in).

▶ Mark shares his yo-yoing tips at guinnessworldrecords.com/2020

DO TRY THIS AT HOME

Can you "walk the dog" farther than Mark? If you're applying for the GWR title, be sure to follow our guidelines...

• Make sure you use a commercially available yo-yo that hasn't been modified in any way. You'll need witnesses on hand to confirm this.

• You should make your attempt on a level surface.

• Keep that yo-yo spinning throughout the trick. If it stops, so does your record attempt!

• Your witness has to measure the horizontal distance that the yo-yo travels, so they'll need to place a marker at the point where it first touches the ground.

• The measurement stops at the point where the yo-yo leaves the ground to return to your hand. Again, a witness should mark where this point is.

• As the yo-yo begins to lift off the ground, make sure that it returns to your hand in a controlled manner.

• You'll have to time your attempt and submit this reading with the rest of your evidence.

• Make sure you film your attempt from start to finish – including the measurement of the distance covered by the yo-yo. And we'll need to see slow-motion footage too. For the full set of official GWR guidelines, go to **guinnessworldrecords.com/2020**

JUN 9 At the 2018 Skowhegan Moose Festival in Maine, USA, 1,054 residents gather to break the record for the **most people moose-calling simultaneously**. All together now: "Uuuunnnnnnngggghhhhhhh!!"

JUN 10 *Sssh!* The **quietest place** is measured in 2015. Microsoft's anechoic chamber in Redmond, Washington, USA, has an ambient noise level of -20.35 dB... beyond the limits of human hearing.

103

BALANCING ACTS

If you've got a steady hand and a level head, there's a whole host of records you could try! What's more, you'll probably have many of the required objects lying around your home. Playing cards, plastic bottles and even a kitchen cutlery drawer can all provide the tools for a record attempt – check out what these inspired individuals did with them! Your balancing act might become an online hit and, who knows, your record antics could kick-start the next social-media craze...

FASTEST MILE BALANCING A MILK BOTTLE ON THE HEAD

In 2004, prolific record holder Ashrita Furman (USA) covered a mile (1.6 km) in 7 min 47 sec... with a full bottle of milk on his head! Seven years later, he took another milk bottle for a record-breaking stroll, completing a **half marathon** in 2 hr 33 min 28 sec.

TALLEST FREE-STANDING HOUSE OF CARDS

A true wizard of the decks, Bryan Berg (USA) built a 7.86-m-tall (25-ft 9-in) house of cards on 16 Oct 2007 in Dallas, Texas, USA. He also made the **tallest house of cards in one hour** – 26 levels – on *Live with Kelly and Ryan* in New York City, USA, on 12 Sep 2018.

FASTEST 100 M BALANCING A BASEBALL BAT ON THE FINGER

He's not only an adept juggler (see p.100)... On 5 Oct 2018, David Rush (USA, above and below) ran 100 m (328 ft) with a baseball bat on his finger in 14.28 sec at Boise High School in Idaho, USA. In the same year, David also broke GWR titles for the **fastest 100 m** (and **fastest mile**) **carrying an egg on a spoon in the mouth** – 18.47 sec and 8 min 2.44 sec respectively – both achieved in Boise, Idaho, USA.

MOST SPOONS BALANCED ON THE FACE

Have you got a face that keeps cutlery in place? In 2009, Aaron Caissie (CAN, above) held 17 spoons there for the full 5 sec required by GWR guidelines. Today, this record is held by Dalibor Jablanović (SRB), who raised the bar to 31 spoons in Stubica, Serbia, on 28 Sep 2013. Can you do better?

MOST TREATS BALANCED ON A DOG'S NOSE

You can even get your pet pooch in on the record-setting balancing action! How many treats can your hound keep on their snout before the stack topples (or temptation gets the better of them)? Pictured left is former record holder Monkey, who managed to balance 26 biscuits for the required minimum of 3 sec in 2013. The current top dog is husky-cross George, owned by Dima Yeremenko (UK), who between them achieved a tower of 29 treats on 9 May 2015 at the London Pet Show, UK.

 JUN 11 The **first hovercraft flight** in public is made by the 4-tonne (8,818-lb) Saunders-Roe SR.N1 at Cowes, Isle of Wight, UK, in 1959. It reaches a speed of 68 knots (126 km/h; 78 mph).

 JUN 12 The **closest approach to Earth by a comet** is made by P/1999 J6 in 1999. It passes within 0.012 astronomical units (1,795,174 km; 1,115,469 mi) – just under five times the distance to the Moon.

MOST MARSHMALLOWS CAUGHT IN THE MOUTH IN ONE MINUTE

On 17 Sep 2017, Josh (below) captured 42 marshmallows thrown by Jake Triplett (USA) in 60 sec in Dallas, Texas, USA. This record has since been broken by Ashrita Furman (see opposite) and Bipin Larkin (both USA), who exchanged 45 of the sweet treats in Ottawa, Ontario, Canada, on 30 Sep 2018.

MOST BLINDFOLDED FLIPS OF A PLASTIC BOTTLE IN ONE MINUTE

Renowned juggler and all-round entertainer Josh Horton (USA) has a number of Guinness World Records titles to his name. On 16 Dec 2018, he flipped a bottle through 360° a total of 27 times in 60 sec while wearing an eye mask. Only those turnovers in which the vessel landed on its base were counted, as per GWR rules (see below). The flipping feat took place at the Rio All-Suite Hotel & Casino in Las Vegas, Nevada, USA, during SkillCon 2018.

Josh shares his flip tips at guinnessworldrecords.com/2020

MOST TOILET ROLLS BALANCED ON THE HEAD

Josh kept a tower of 12 toilet rolls steady on his head for the required half a minute in Malibu, California, USA, on 16 May 2017. He performed the attempt during a live stream on GWR's Facebook page.

DO TRY THIS AT HOME

Are you ready to take on Josh's record for blindfolded bottle flips? Be sure to read GWR's guidelines first!

- You can use any commercially available plastic bottle for your record attempt, as long as it's 500–590 ml (16.9–20 fl oz) in size.
- Fill about one-third of the bottle with liquid. (You'll need to submit a video to confirm the measurement.)
- You'll need to wear a blindfold during the attempt. It must block your sight completely – an independent witness should confirm this.
- Start with both hands flat on a hard, level surface, and with the bottle in front of you.
- At the sound of the start signal, you must flip the bottle 360° in the air. It should land upright without toppling over. Remember: you can only use one hand and one bottle for the attempt.
- If the bottle doesn't land upright, the flip will not be counted.
- After every flip, you must locate the bottle again yourself for the next try – no peeking! Neither can you be helped by anyone else.
- Only those flips of the bottle that are completed within the 60-sec time limit will count towards the total.
- For the full set of official GWR guidelines, go to **guinnessworldrecords.com/2020**

JUN 13 In 2015, Tom Hudson (UK) and Pete Fletcher (AUS) complete the **longest distance rowed in 24 hours**, having travelled 116.76 nautical mi (216.24 km; 134.37 mi) during an Atlantic crossing.

JUN 14 *Spider-Man: Turn Off the Dark*, a musical based on the comic superhero, opens on Broadway in 2011. It is the **most expensive theatre production**, with a cost of $75 m (£46 m).

105

SPEED-CUBING

In 2020, the puzzle invented by Hungary's Ernő Rubik celebrates the 40th anniversary of its international launch. The original 3 x 3 x 3 format has now expanded to embrace the dodecahedron-shaped Megaminx, the Pyraminx, the Clock (a two-sided puzzle, each face featuring nine clocks to be aligned) and more. Grégoire Pfennig (FRA) has even made a 33 x 33 x 33 version – the **largest-order Magic Cube**, with 6,153 parts. But if you're new to Rubik's Cubes, start simple! You'll find lots of online videos on how to solve the iconic 3 x 3 x 3 puzzle. When you've mastered it, you could upload some footage of yourself in action, which might inspire others in turn. And if you'd like to try for a GWR cubing record, these are the people to beat...

FASTEST TIME TO SOLVE A RUBIK'S CUBE

Du Yusheng (CHN) took just 3.47 sec to solve a standard 3 x 3 x 3 puzzle on 24 Nov 2018 at the Wuhu Open competition in Anhui Province, China. There was no official video taken of the attempt, but CCTV footage (inset above) captured the moment the fleet-fingered Yusheng solved the cube with an official judge looking on.

TURBO-CHARGE YOUR CUBE GAME!

(All records pictured below from left to right)

Fastest time to solve...
- A Rubik's Cube on a pogo stick: 24.13 sec, by George Turner (UK)
- ▶ Three Rubik's Cubes while juggling: 5 min 2.43 sec, by Que Jianyu (CHN)
- Two Rubik's Cubes simultaneously underwater: 53.86 sec, by Krishnam Raju Gadiraju (IND)

Most Rubik's Cubes solved...
- On a caster board: 151, by Nikhil Soares (IND)
- One-handed while treading water in one hour: 137, by Shen Weifu (CHN)
- On a bicycle: 1,010, by P K Arumugam (IND)
- On a unicycle: 250, by Caleb McEvoy (USA)

FASTEST AVERAGE TIME TO SOLVE A 3 x 3 x 3 RUBIK'S CUBE IN COMPETITION

Feliks Zemdegs (AUS) achieved an average time of 5.80 sec on 15 Oct 2017 at the Malaysia Cube Open in Bangi. His feat came in the first round of the contest, with individual times of 5.99 sec, 5.28 sec, 5.25 sec, 6.13 sec and 9.19 sec. Feliks went on to win the 3 x 3 x 3 category.

He had previously recorded the overall **fastest time to solve a Rubik's Cube**, in a time of 4.22 sec, although Du Yusheng broke that record in Nov 2018 (see above left).

JUN 15
In 1982, László Kiss scores the **fastest hat-trick in a FIFA World Cup match**, finding the net three times in 7 min for Hungary while playing El Salvador in Elche, Spain.

JUN 16
In 2009, "Rutt Mysterio", aka Michele Forgione (ITA), unleashes the **longest burp** – lasting 1 min 13 sec – at the 13th annual Hard Rock Beer festival Ruttosound competition in Reggiolo, Italy.

▶ FASTEST TIME TO SOLVE A 6 x 6 x 6 RUBIK'S CUBE

It took Max (see main entry right) just 1 min 13.82 sec to complete a 6 x 6 x 6 Rubik's Cube at the WCA Asian Championship held in Taipei City, Chinese Taipei, on 17–19 Aug 2018. The prolific Max also holds titles for the quickest time to solve a host of other cube puzzles, including:

- **4 x 4 x 4:** 18.42 sec
- **5 x 5 x 5:** 37.28 sec
- **7 x 7 x 7:** 1 min 47.89 sec.

▶ FASTEST AVERAGE TIME TO SOLVE A RUBIK'S CUBE ONE-HANDED

In a mean time of just 9.42 sec, Max Park (USA) solved a 3 x 3 x 3 Rubik's Cube using only one hand at the Berkeley Summer 2018 event in California, USA, on 15–16 Sep. His individual times were 9.43 sec, 11.32 sec, 8.80 sec, 8.69 sec and 10.02 sec, with the lowest and highest times not counted towards the average, as per World Cube Association rules.

FASTEST TIME TO SOLVE A...

3 x 3 x 3	Du Yusheng (CHN, far left)	3.47 sec
2 x 2 x 2	Maciej Czapiewski (POL)	0.49 sec
3 x 3 x 3 blindfolded	Jack Cai (AUS)	16.22 sec
3 x 3 x 3 one-handed	Feliks Zemdegs (AUS, left)	6.88 sec
3 x 3 x 3 with feet	Daniel Rose-Levine (USA)	16.96 sec
Megaminx	Juan Pablo Huanqui Andia (PER)	27.81 sec
Pyraminx	Dominik Górny (POL)	0.91 sec
Clock	Suen Ming Chi (CHN)	3.29 sec
Skewb	Jonatan Kłosko (POL)	1.10 sec
Square-1	Vicenzo Guerino Cecchini (BRA)	5.00 sec

Source: World Cube Association, as of 12 Apr 2019

▶ You'll find a host of cubing videos at guinnessworldrecords.com/2020

DO TRY THIS AT HOME

The World Cube Association (WCA) has regulations for speed-solving, which GWR follows. We've provided an overview of the WCA's guidelines for attempting puzzles blindfolded here, but go to **worldcubeassociation.org** for the full details.

- You're expected to supply your own blindfold for the attempt.
- Each speed-solving record category will have a time limit, which the organizers will announce before the start of each attempt.
- If you're likely to solve the puzzle in under 10 minutes, a StackMat will be used. This is the standard timer employed at WCA events. If the solve is likely to take longer, however, the judge will use a stopwatch.

- Prior to the attempt, you'll submit your puzzle to a scrambler, who'll rearrange each face of it. The cube is then covered.
- When you're ready to start, the judge will ask "OK?" Once you respond, the puzzle will be uncovered. If you're using a StackMat, the timer is triggered when you lift your hands.
- You'll have time to memorize the appearance of the cube before you pull the blindfold over your eyes and start the solve. But you can't manipulate the puzzle until your eyes are covered.
- When you think you've finished, release your cube to stop the timer.

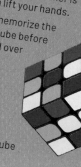

FASTEST TIME TO SOLVE A 4 x 4 x 4 RUBIK'S CUBE BLINDFOLDED

On 20 May 2018, an unsighted Stanley Chapel (USA) finished off a 4 x 4 x 4 Rubik's Cube in 1 min 29 sec in Fort Wayne, Indiana, USA. He broke the record at the World Cube Association's CubingUSA Great Lakes Championship. For the WCA's rules on solving puzzles blindfolded, see right.

▶ Stanley shares his speed-cubing tips at guinnessworldrecords.com/2020

JUN 17 Pixar's highly anticipated sequel *Finding Dory* (USA) is released in 2016. In just two days at North American cinemas, it becomes **the fastest animated movie to gross $100 m (domestic)**.

JUN 18 In 2007, Jeremy Harper (USA) starts counting for 16 hr a day, until he reaches his target of 1 million on 14 Sep, a total of 88 days later. This is the **highest number counted to out loud**.

107

SPIRIT OF ADVENTURE

FASTEST BICYCLE SPEED IN A SLIPSTREAM

On 16 Sep 2018, Denise Mueller-Korenek (USA) cycled to 296.009 km/h (183.931 mph) at the Bonneville Salt Flats in Utah, USA. A dragster towed her to a speed of around 80.5 km/h (50 mph), whereupon she was released and began pedalling, protected by the car's slipstream. (The inset shows the view from inside the dragster's fairing.) The ride not only beat her own women's record but the **male** title too – 268.831 km/h (167.043 mph), set by Fred Rompelberg (NLD) in 1995.

Denise is shown opposite just before her record-smashing ride, along with dragster driver Shea Holbrook.

Denise's carbon-frameset bike was made by KHS Bicycles. Its 43-cm (17-in) motorcycle wheels improved the stability at speed, while the suspension fork reduced surface vibrations.

CONTENTS

LARGEST CREWED BALLOON

On 14 Oct 2012, the eyes of the world turned to Felix Baumgartner. The Austrian daredevil was set to ascend to the upper reaches of the atmosphere in a capsule suspended from the largest balloon ever to carry a human passenger, then attempt a spectacular freefall back to Earth. If he succeeded, he would set multiple world records. But if he failed...

Seven years of preparation had gone into that day. It was the culmination of the Red Bull Stratos space-diving mission, a project that was to provide valuable data for NASA and the US Air Force... and shatter records that had stood for more than 50 years.

Felix took off from Roswell in New Mexico, USA, at 9:28 a.m. local time (3:28 p.m. GMT). By the time he'd reached his exit point – some two hours later – the helium balloon, constructed from 0.02-mm-thick (0.0008-in) polyethylene plastic, had expanded to almost 850,000 m³ (30 million cu ft) and reached a diameter of 129.2 m (424 ft). The **largest balloon with a human on board**, it was around 11 times the volume of the *Virgin Otsuka Pacific Flyer* flown by Richard Branson (UK) and Per Lindstrand (SWE) in 1991 during the **first Pacific hot-air balloon crossing**, and approximately 40 times more voluminous than the largest passenger hot-air balloons currently in production.

Stepping from his capsule at 38,969 m (127,851 ft), Felix began his death-defying drop, reaching Mach 1.25 (1,357.6 km/h; 843.6 mph) – the **fastest speed in freefall** (see opposite). His rapid descent also saw him become the **first human to break the sound barrier in freefall**, 65 years to the day after the **first supersonic flight** – by US Air Force officer Chuck Yeager (USA), although he was on board a Bell X-1 rocket aircraft at the time!

Here, our digital artists have brought the record balloon back down to Earth – placing it alongside another London landmark. It's hard to tell how big anything is floating nearly 39 km (24 mi) up, so to provide context, we've taken some artistic licence. In reality, the balloon could never reach its most inflated capacity hovering this close to the ground. That said, it was *taller* at take-off: 167.6 m (550 ft) versus 101.8 m (334 ft) at its apogee.

Lighter-than-air helium within the envelope could only expand to this extent on reaching the upper stratosphere, where air pressure is 2% that at sea level. By this point (aka the "float altitude"), as density inside the balloon levelled with that of the atmosphere outside, it had transformed from its elongated shape to a more egg-like form, more than twice the width of Tower Bridge's central span.

HIGH HOPES: CELEBRATING A SKYSCRAPING ACHIEVEMENT

GWR was delighted to present Felix Baumgartner with a certificate marking his extraordinary feat. "Our primary goal was always to improve aerospace safety," he explained. "But receiving the Guinness World Records certificate was a tangible reminder that my supersonic dream had finally become reality."

STANDING ON THE EDGE OF HISTORY

Felix's capsule reached such an extreme altitude that he was able to see the curvature of Earth. "I know the whole world is watching now," he said into his radio when he'd reached his take-off point. "I wish you could see what I can see. Sometimes you have to get up really high to understand how small you are... I'm going home now." Then he jumped.

Shortly after his exit, Felix began spinning and almost blacked out, but used his skydiving skills to stabilize himself. He was able to control his descent, despite his visor fogging up, deploying his parachute at an altitude of c. 1,525 m (5,000 ft) and touching down in the desert near Roswell some nine minutes after he'd exited his capsule.

Just two years later, on 24 Oct 2014, Alan Eustace (USA) broke Felix's records for the **highest freefall parachute jump** and **highest crewed balloon flight** (41,422 m; 135,898 ft).

FASTEST CYCLE JOURNEY ACROSS EURASIA

Jonas Deichmann (DEU) cycled west to east across Eurasia – from Cabo da Roca, Portugal, to Vladivostok, Russia – in 64 days 2 hr 26 min between 2 Jul and 4 Sep 2017. He faced many challenges along the way, including the sudden collapse of his bike's frame in the Czech Republic!

Most continents visited in one calendar day

On 29 Apr 2017, Thor Mikalsen and his son Sondre Moan Mikalsen (both NOR) travelled between cities on five continents: Istanbul (Turkey, Asia), Casablanca (Morocco, Africa), Lisbon (Portugal, Europe), Miami (USA, North America) and Barranquilla (Colombia, South America).

In doing so, they matched the achievement of Gunnar Garfors (NOR) and Adrian Butterworth (UK), who travelled between Istanbul and Caracas (Venezuela, South America) on 18 Jun 2012.

Longest journey by car in one country

Greg Cayea and Heather Thompson (both USA) drove 58,135.87 km (36,123.95 mi) through the USA from 11 Jul to 9 Nov 2016.

The **longest journey by motorcycle in one country** is 115,093.94 km (71,516 mi), by Gaurav Siddharth (IND) from 17 Sep 2015 to 27 Apr 2017 in India.

Most countries visited by bicycle in seven days (male)

David Haywood (UK) rode in 13 countries, from Moelingen in Belgium to Bratislava in Slovakia, between 12 and 18 Oct 2017.

Fastest time to cycle the length of Japan (north to south, male)

Hiroki Nagaseki (JPN) took just 7 days 19 hr 37 min to cross Japan by bicycle. He set out from Cape Sōya on Hokkaidō on 19 Jul 2018 and arrived a week later at Cape Sata, Kyūshū.

The **female** holder is Paola Gianotti (ITA), who crossed Japan in 8 days 16 hr 19 min on 24 May–1 Jun 2017. In 2016, she also logged the **fastest time to visit 48 contiguous US states by bicycle (female)**: 43 days.

Fastest crossing of the Simpson Desert on foot

In temperatures of up to 50°C (122°F), Pat Farmer (AUS) completed a 379-km (235.5-mi) traverse of the Simpson Desert – Australia's fourth-largest desert – in 3 days 8 hr 36 min, finishing on 26 Jan 1998. He averaged 4.75 km/h (2.95 mph) and crossed 1,162 dunes.

The **fastest crossing of the Simpson Desert by solar-powered land vehicle** took 4 days 21 hr 23 min. Husband and wife Mark and Denny French (both AUS) reached Birdsville in Queensland on 11 Sep 2017.

Longest barefoot journey

From 1 May to 12 Aug 2016, an unshod Eamonn Keaveney (IRL) covered 2,080.14 km (1,292.54 mi) in Ireland.

Youngest person to circumnavigate the globe by motorcycle (male)

Kane Avellano (UK, b. 20 Jan 1993) completed his round-the-world motorcycle ride at South Shields Town Hall, Tyne and Wear, UK, on 19 Jan 2017 – one day before his 24th birthday. Having set out on 31 May 2016, over the course of his epic journey Avellano passed through 36 countries and six continents; in all, he clocked up 45,161 km (28,062 mi).

FASTEST TIME TO CYCLE ALONG THE PAN-AMERICAN HIGHWAY

It took Michael Strasser (AUT) just 84 days 11 hr 50 min to ride from Prudhoe Bay in Alaska, USA, to Ushuaia at the southern tip of Argentina, finishing on 16 Oct 2018. He set out from Prudhoe Bay just two months after the previous record holder, Dean Stott (UK), completed his own attempt there. Stott rode the route from south to north in 99 days 12 hr 56 min between 1 Feb and 11 May.

Fastest journey from Land's End to John o' Groats on a lawnmower

On 30 Jul 2017, Andy Maxfield (UK) finished a 5-day 8-hr 36-min trip from one end of Great Britain to the other to raise funds for the Alzheimer's Society.

FASTEST CIRCUMNAVIGATION BY BICYCLE (FEMALE)

Jenny Graham (UK) cycled the globe in 124 days 11 hr from 16 Jun to 18 Oct 2018, starting and ending in Berlin, Germany. She made the journey unsupported, meaning that she carried all of her equipment with her.

Mark Beaumont (UK) achieved the **fastest circumnavigation by bicycle** overall, in 78 days 14 hr 40 min. He set off from the Arc de Triomphe in Paris, France, on 2 Jul 2017 for his "Around the World in 80 Days Challenge", returning there on 18 Sep 2017.

FASTEST CROSSING OF THE USA ON FOOT

Pete Kostelnick (USA) ran from San Francisco City Hall, California, to New York City Hall in 42 days 6 hr 30 min from 12 Sep to 24 Oct 2016.

It's a sign of how demanding this feat is that the **fastest crossing of the USA on foot (female)** has now stood for more than 40 years. Mavis Hutchinson (ZAF) set a time of 69 days 2 hr 40 min with her trans-America trip between 12 Mar and 21 May 1978.

JUN 19 — In 1963, Soviet cosmonaut Valentina Tereshkova completes a flight of 2 days 22 hr 50 min – and 48 Earth orbits – in *Vostok 6*. The **first woman in space**, she is awarded the title "Hero of the Soviet Union".

JUN 20 — The 18.04-carat Rockefeller Emerald becomes the **most expensive emerald by carat** in 2017. It sells for $5,511,500 (£4,316,250) – including buyer's premium – at Christie's in New York City, USA.

90 MILE STRAIGHT
AUSTRALIA'S LONGEST STRAIGHT ROAD
146.6 km

FASTEST CIRCUMNAVIGATION BY TANDEM BICYCLE (MEN)

British riders John Whybrow (left) and George Agate (right) cycled around the world on a tandem in 290 days 7 hr 36 min, starting and ending in Canterbury, UK, from 8 Jun 2016 to 25 Mar 2017. Travelling as the "The Tandem Men", the pair covered more than 29,946.80 km (18,608.07 mi) on their custom-made Orbit bicycle, which they nicknamed "Daisy".

The duo raised thousands of pounds for three good causes: homeless charity Porchlight, London's Great Ormond Street Hospital and Water Aid.

LONGEST JOURNEY BY SCHEDULED PUBLIC TRANSPORT IN A SINGLE COUNTRY

Durga Charan Mishra and his wife Jotshna (both IND) travelled 29,119 km (18,093 mi) across India via public transport between 18 Feb and 30 Mar 2018. They started and finished their epic trip at Puri railway station in Odisha. Impressively, the couple surpassed the previous record by more than 19,300 km (12,000 mi).

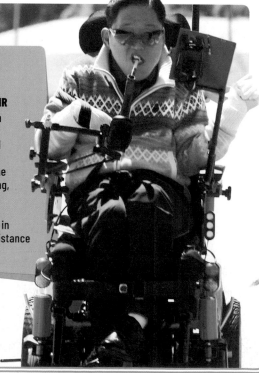

GREATEST DISTANCE IN 24 HOURS BY MOUTH-CONTROLLED MOTORIZED WHEELCHAIR

On 19–20 Apr 2017, South Korea's Choi Chang-hyun rode his motorized wheelchair along the Route 7 highway from the coastal village of Giseong, in North Gyeongsang Province, to the Goseon Unification Observatory in Gangwon Province – a distance of 280 km (173.98 mi).

JUN 21 Manikyam, the **shortest cow**, is measured at 61.1 cm (2 ft) from the hoof to the withers (i.e., the ridge between the shoulder blades) in 2014. She is owned by Akshay N V (IND) in Kerala, India.

JUN 22 In 2017, serial record-breaker Ashrita Furman (USA) sets the **farthest distance walked balancing a lawnmower on the chin (powered)** - 71.5 m (234 ft 6 in) - in New York City, USA.

BY AIR

First person to fly horizontally

On 24 Jun 2004, Swiss aviator Yves Rossy flew for 4 min at a speed of 180 km/h (111 mph) some 1,600 m (5,250 ft) above Yverdon airfield, near Lake Neuchâtel in Switzerland. His "jet-man" gear comprised two kerosene-powered jet engines fitted to 3-m (10-ft) foldable carbon wings.

Highest-altitude wingsuit jump

James Petrolia (USA) performed a jump in a wingsuit from 11,407.4 m (37,426 ft) – nearly 14 times higher than the **tallest building**, the Burj Khalifa in Dubai, UAE – above Davis in California, USA, on 11 Nov 2015.

Highest skydive without a parachute

On 30 Jul 2016, skydiver Luke Aikins (USA) leaped 7,600 m (25,000 ft) from a plane and landed safely in a 929-m² (10,000-sq-ft) net in Simi Valley, southern California, USA. He had spent a full year-and-a-half preparing for the stunt, which he named "Heaven Sent", and was filmed live for TV audiences. Using a GPS unit to guide him towards the net, Aikins reached a freefall speed of 193 km/h (120 mph) during his 2-min plunge.

▶ FARTHEST FLIGHT BY HOVERBOARD

On 30 Apr 2016, former jet-ski champion Franky Zapata (FRA) travelled 2.25 km (1.4 mi) on a hoverboard in Sausset-les-Pins, France. This was more than eight times farther than the previous record. Zapata's flying machine, the *Flyboard Air*, is propelled by a jet engine with a capacity of around 1,000 hp (745.7 kW). It is steered using a handheld controller, which regulates thrust and elevation, and by the pilot shifting their weight, as on a Segway.

FASTEST CIRCUMNAVIGATION BY SCHEDULED FLIGHTS, VISITING SIX CONTINENTS (TEAM)

Gunnar Garfors (NOR), Ronald Haanstra and Erik de Zwart (both NLD) – above, left to right - travelled to every continent except Antarctica in 56 hr 56 min between 31 Jan and 2 Feb 2018. From Sydney (Australia), they flew to Santiago de Chile (South America), Panama City (North America), Madrid (Europe), Algiers (Africa) and Dubai (Asia) before returning to Sydney.

Youngest person to circumnavigate by aircraft (solo)

On 27 Aug 2016, Lachlan Smart (AUS, b. 6 Jan 1998) ended his round-the-world flight in a Cirrus SR22 aircraft at Sunshine Coast Airport in Queensland, Australia, aged 18 years 234 days. He had stopped at 24 locations in 15 countries over the course of his epic seven-week, 45,000-km (27,961-mi) journey, which he had begun on 4 Jul 2016.

Fastest speed in speed skydiving

On 13 Sep 2016, Henrik Raimer (SWE) reached 601.26 km/h (373.6 mph) at the Fédération Aéronautique Internationale (FAI) World Championships in Chicago, Illinois, USA. By way of comparison, the peregrine falcon, the **fastest bird in a dive**, attains a terminal velocity of around 300 km/h (186 mph).

Fastest horizontal speed in a wingsuit

Fraser Corsan (UK) flew at 396.88 km/h (246.6 mph) in a wingsuit over Davis, California, USA, on 22 May 2017. He attempted the feat to raise awareness of the armed forces charity SSAFA.

Highest flight in a glider (male)

Jim Payne (USA) and co-pilot Morgan Sandercock (AUS) climbed to 15,902 m (52,172 ft) in their Airbus *Perlan 2* glider on 3 Sep 2017. They were towed to a height of 3,200 m (10,500 ft) above Argentina's mountainous Patagonian region, before air currents lifted the *Perlan 2* to its record altitude.

Longest indoor freefall

On 10 Jul 2018, Russians Viktor Kozlov and Sergey Dmitriyev carried out an 8-hr 33-min 43-sec freefall at the FreeFly Technology wind tunnel in Perm, Russia.

FASTEST TIME TO TRAVEL TO ALL SEVEN CONTINENTS

Kasey Stewart and Julie Berry (both USA) took 3 days 20 hr 4 min 19 sec to travel between seven continents, arriving on King George Island in Antarctica on 17 Dec 2017. The intrepid duo decided to break this record to push themselves outside their comfort zone and inspire others to do the same.

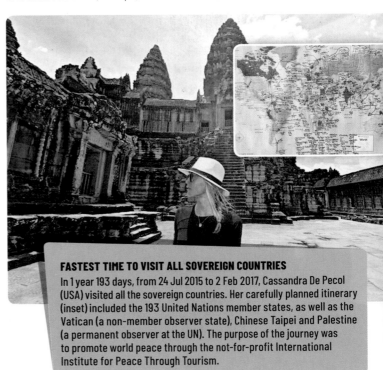

FASTEST TIME TO VISIT ALL SOVEREIGN COUNTRIES

In 1 year 193 days, from 24 Jul 2015 to 2 Feb 2017, Cassandra De Pecol (USA) visited all the sovereign countries. Her carefully planned itinerary (inset) included the 193 United Nations member states, as well as the Vatican (a non-member observer state), Chinese Taipei and Palestine (a permanent observer at the UN). The purpose of the journey was to promote world peace through the not-for-profit International Institute for Peace Through Tourism.

 JUN 23 In 2009, bride and groom Erin Finnegan and Noah Fulmor (both USA) say "I do" while weightless on board *G-Force One*, a modified Boeing 727-200 - the **first zero-gravity wedding**.

 JUN 24 Wazir Muhammand Jagirani (PAK) has the **heaviest kidney stone** removed from his right kidney in Sindh, Pakistan, in 2008. It weighs 620 g (21.87 oz) - about the same as a basketball.

GREATEST HORIZONTAL DISTANCE PARACHUTE FLIGHT

Shinichi Ito (JPN) covered a distance of 46.2 km (28.7 mi) by parachute over Davis in California, USA, on 24 Feb 2018. Having exited the plane, he opened his parachute at an altitude of around 7,600 m (25,000 ft). In flight, Ito accelerated to a maximum horizontal speed of 279 km/h (173.3 mph).

In 2011, Ito achieved the **fastest horizontal speed in a wingsuit** – but today's holder is more than 30 km/h (18.6 mph) faster (see opposite).

FASTEST CIRCUMNAVIGATION BY SCHEDULED FLIGHTS THROUGH APPROXIMATE ANTIPODAL POINTS

The speediest journey around the world exclusively via scheduled flights, through points more or less diametrically opposite to each other on Earth's surface, is 52 hr 34 min, by Andrew Fisher (NZ) from 21 to 23 Jan 2018. Fisher's route took him from Shanghai (China) to Auckland (New Zealand), Buenos Aires (Argentina) and Amsterdam (Netherlands), finishing back in Shanghai.

MOST AIRFIELDS VISITED IN 24 HOURS BY FIXED-WING AIRCRAFT

On 13 Jun 2017, Mike Roberts and Nicholas Rogers (both UK) took off from Wellesbourne, Warwickshire, UK, at 3:32 a.m. and touched down at 87 airfields before returning there at 9:38 p.m. The duo donated their landing fees to the Air Ambulance charity. Roberts had previously held this record on his own.

JUN 25 In 1977, park ranger Roy Sullivan (USA) is hit by lightning for the seventh time – the **most lightning strikes survived**. His injuries include burned eyebrows, a seared shoulder and a lost toenail.

JUN 26 Zeng Jinlian (CHN), the **tallest woman ever**, is born in 1964 in Yujiang village, Hunan Province, China. At the time of her death on 13 Feb 1982, she measures 246.3 cm (8 ft 1 in).

BY WATER

First sisters to row any ocean together

On 19 Jan 2018, Camilla and Cornelia Bull (both NOR) landed in Antigua having rowed the Atlantic in the four-woman "Rowegians" crew on board *Ellida*. They had set out from La Gomera in the Canary Islands, Spain, on 14 Dec 2017, completing their voyage in 36 days 9 hr 53 min.

Youngest person to row any ocean in a pair

Jude Massey (UK, b. 6 Mar 1999) was 18 years 318 days old at the start of his row with his half-brother Greg Bailey across the Atlantic from Gran Canaria to Barbados. They rowed from 18 Jan to 11 Mar 2018 on board *Peter*.

Youngest person to row in a team across the Atlantic (Trade Winds II route)

Duncan Roy (UK, b. 16 Aug 1990) began his row from Mindelo in Cape Verde to French Guiana on 19 Jan 2018, aged

27 years 156 days. He completed the 1,765-nautical mi (3,269-km; 2,031-mi) crossing in 27 days 16 hr 50 min, as part of a team of five on board *Rose*.

Fastest solo row west to east across the Atlantic from Canada

Between 27 Jun and 4 Aug 2018, Bryce Carlson (USA) rowed from St John's in Newfoundland, Canada, to St Mary's Harbour, Scilly Isles, UK, in 38 days 6 hr 49 min. He covered 2,302 nautical mi (4,263 km; 2,649 mi) at an average speed of 2.5 knots (4.63 km/h; 2.88 mph) on board his open-class boat *Lucille*.

First person to row an ocean sculling with a single oar moved over the stern

Hervé le Merrer (FRA) crossed the Atlantic east to west from El Hierro in the Canary Islands to Martinique in 58 days from 28 Dec 2017 to 24 Feb 2018. He propelled his purpose-built boat *Eizh an Eizh* with only a single oar.

First double-crossing swim of the English Channel by a two-person relay team (men)

On 9 Jul 2018, John Robert Myatt and Mark Leighton (both UK) swam from England to France in 10 hr 41 min and back to England in 12 hr 8 min, giving an overall time of 22 hr 49 min. The two men alternated in 1-hr swimming stints.

On 22 Jul 2018, "Sportfanatic" team members Dezider Pék, Ondrej Pék and Richard

Nyary (all SVK) achieved the **first double crossing of the English Channel by a three-person relay team**. They swam from England to France in 10 hr 14 min and back to England in 12 hr 20 min – a total time of 22 hr 34 min. Both records were set under the auspices of the Channel Swimming Association (CSA).

First person to swim the length of the English Channel

On 12 Jul 2018, Lewis Pugh (UK/ZAF) set out from Land's End, Cornwall, UK, swimming 560 km (348 mi) before reaching Admiralty Pier in Dover, Kent, UK, on 29 Aug 2018, as confirmed by the CSA. Pugh swam 10–20 km (6–12 mi) a day for 49 days.

Oldest person to complete the Triple Crown of Open Water Swimming

On 30 Jun 2018, Pat Gallant-Charette (USA, b. 2 Feb 1951) completed the 45.8-km (28.5-mi) "20 Bridges" circumnavigation swim of Manhattan aged 67 years 148 days. She had previously swum the Catalina Channel (32.5 km; 20.2 mi) between Santa

Catalina Island and the southern California mainland in the USA on 18 Oct 2011, and the English Channel (33.7 km; 20.9 mi) on 17 Jun 2017.

Largest wave kitesurfed

On 8 Nov 2017, Nuno Figueiredo (PRT) kitesurfed a wave with a height of 19 m (62 ft 4 in) in Praia do Norte, Nazaré, Portugal. This record was ratified by the International Federation of Kitesports Organisations (IFKO).

First female skipper to win a round-the-world yacht race

On 28 Jul 2018, Wendy Tuck (AUS) led her *Sanya Serenity Coast* team across the finish line to win the Clipper Round the World Yacht Race 2017–18. They had crossed six oceans and covered 40,000 nautical mi (74,080 km; 46,030 mi) in 11 months.

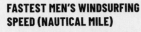

FASTEST MEN'S WINDSURFING SPEED (NAUTICAL MILE)

On 21 Jul 2018, windsurfer Vincent Valkenaers (BEL, left) hit a speed of 42.23 knots (78.21 km/h; 48.60 mph) at the Speed Sailing Event in La Palme, France. On the same day, Zara Davis (UK) achieved the **fastest women's windsurfing speed (nautical mile)**: 37.29 knots (69.06 km/h; 42.91 mph). The World Sailing Speed Record Council verified both records.

> Edgley had to endure painful wetsuit chafing, 37 jellyfish stings and a disintegrating tongue caused by seawater exposure!

FIRST STAGE SWIM AROUND GREAT BRITAIN

Between 1 Jun and 4 Nov 2018, Ross Edgley (UK) completed the first assisted stage swim around the coastlines of England, Wales, Ireland and Scotland, starting and ending in Margate, Kent, UK. He swam in multiple-hour stints through the day and night, completing up to 40,000 strokes daily. His marathon journey took a total of 209 legs over 157 days and covered 2,884 km (1,792 mi). The record was verified by the World Open Water Swimming Association.

THE OCEANS SEVEN

The Oceans Seven is a marathon swimming challenge comprising seven open-water channel swims around the world: the North Channel, the English Channel, the Catalina Channel, the Strait of Gibraltar, the Tsugaru Strait, the Molokai Channel and the Cook Strait.

On 29 Aug 2013, Darren Miller (USA, b. 13 Apr 1983, right) finished his seventh swim – the North Channel between Northern Ireland and Scotland – aged 30 years 138 days, becoming the **youngest person to swim the Oceans Seven**. He completed each swim on his first attempt – the first person to do so.

The **oldest person to swim the Oceans Seven** is Antonio Argüelles Díaz-González (MEX, b. 15 Apr 1959, below). On 3 Aug 2017, he successfully completed his final swim at the age of 58 years 110 days.

JUN 27 The 2009 World Worm Charming Championships in Willaston, Cheshire, UK, are won by 10-year-old Sophie Smith (UK). She coaxes 567 worms from the ground in 30 min – the **most worms charmed**.

JUN 28 In 2005, Smarty the cat makes her 79th airborne journey – the **most flights by a pet**. All of her trips are between Egypt and Cyprus, with owners Peter and Carole Godfrey (both UK).

FASTEST FEMALE SOLO ROW ACROSS THE ATLANTIC (TRADE WINDS I ROUTE)

Between 1 Feb and 22 Mar 2018, Kiko Matthews (UK) rowed from Gran Canaria in the Canary Islands to Port St Charles, Barbados, in 49 days 7 hr 15 min. She travelled 2,602 nautical mi (4,819 km; 2,994 mi) at an average speed of 2.2 knots (4 km/h; 2.5 mph) on board *Soma*. Her record was verified by the Ocean Rowing Society.

Matthews was diagnosed with Cushing's disease in 2009 and has battled back from two tumours. She rowed to raise money for the hospital where she was treated.

EXPLORE WHAT MATTERS

YOUNGEST BROTHERS TO ROW ANY OCEAN (AVERAGE AGE)

Between 12 Dec 2017 and 29 Jan 2018, brothers Kiran (UK, b. 11 Sep 1998, top in pic) and Jay Olenicz (UK, b. 17 Jun 1995) rowed the Atlantic east to west in tandem in 48 days 6 hr 31 min on board *White Dwarf*. At the start of their "Oarsome Odyssey", the average age of the duo was 20 years 318 days.

FASTEST TIME TO COMPLETE 10-KM MARATHON SWIMS ON SIX CONTINENTS (FEMALE)

In 2018, Jaimie Monahan (USA) completed six 10-km (6.2-mi) marathon swims on different continents in 15 days 8 hr 19 min. She began in Colombia on 13 Aug 2018 and swam in Australia, Singapore, Egypt and Switzerland/France before finishing in New York City, USA, on 28 Aug 2018.

FASTEST COMPLETION OF THE SYDNEY HOBART YACHT RACE

First held in 1945, the Sydney Hobart Yacht Race begins on Boxing Day (26 Dec) each year. Yachts sail from Sydney in New South Wales to Hobart in Tasmania, Australia. On 26–27 Dec 2017, *LDV Comanche* won in 1 day 9 hr 15 min 24 sec. It was awarded victory after the initial winner of "line honours", *Wild Oats XI*, was handed a one-hour time penalty for its role in a near-collision at the start of the race.

JUN 29 James Stephens (USA) gobbles up the **most sausages eaten in one minute** – 10 – on the set of *Guinness World Records Gone Wild!* in Los Angeles, California, USA, in 2012.

JUN 30 The personal, 173-page film script from *The Godfather* (USA, 1972) belonging to star Marlon Brando sells for $312,800 (£173,316) in 2005 – the **most expensive movie script sold at auction**.

117

BY ROCK

Most ascents of Everest in one year
The world's **highest mountain** (8,848 m; 29,029 ft) was climbed 809 times in 2018, up from 667 successful ascents in 2013.

During 2018's spring climbing season, 18 female Nepalese climbers made it to the summit – the **most ascents of Everest by women from a single nation in one year**.

Most siblings to have climbed Everest
On 23 May 2018, Dawa Diki Sherpa became the seventh child of Chhiring Nurbu Sherpa and Kimjung Sherpa (all NPL) to summit Everest. Six of her brothers had previously climbed it. This matched the record set by the offspring of Nima Tsiri Sherpa – Edmund Hillary's "mail runner" for the **first ascent of Everest** in 1953 – and Pema Futi Sherpa (both NPL), whose seventh son reached Everest's summit on 23 May 2007. Together, the latter's offspring have achieved the **most ascents of Everest by siblings (aggregate)** – an incredible total of 63.

Fastest time to climb Everest and K2
Nepalese Sherpa Mingma Gyabu climbed Everest on 21 May 2018 and K2 (8,611 m; 28,251 ft), the second-highest mountain, on 21 Jul 2018. This equalled the record of 61 days established by Robert "Rob" Hall (NZ) between 9 May (Everest) and 9 Jul 1994 (K2). Both men climbed with the use of bottled oxygen.

The **fastest female** to achieve this feat – also using supplemental oxygen – is Chinese mountaineer He Chang-Juan. She summitted Everest on 16 May 2018 and reached the summit of K2 66 days later.

Highest mountain unclimbed in winter
As of Mar 2019, K2 remains unconquered in the winter season, both calendar (20 Dec to 20 Mar) and meteorological (1 Dec to 28 Feb). So far, there have been only five attempts to climb the mountain in winter, all of them unsuccessful.

Most ascents of K2 (individual)
Fazal Ali (PAK) has climbed K2 three times: on 26 Jul 2014, 28 Jul 2017 and 22 Jul 2018. All three climbs were without supplemental oxygen.

The **most ascents of K2 in one year** was 64 in 2018, up from 51 in 2004.

Most ascents of Kangchenjunga in one year
The third-highest mountain (8,586 m; 28,169 ft) was climbed 46 times during the 2018 climbing season – six more than the previous record, set in 1989.

FIRST SKI DESCENT OF K2
On 22 Jul 2018, after summitting K2 without supplemental oxygen, Andrzej Bargiel (POL) became the first person to ski to base camp, taking around 8 hr to make the descent.

First ski descent of Lhotse
On 30 Sep 2018, Hilaree Nelson and Jim Morrison (both USA) climbed the Himalayan peak Lhotse (8,516 m; 27,940 ft) – the world's fourth-highest mountain – and skied down the couloir from summit to Camp 2 at 6,400 m (20,997 ft).

Fastest Lhotse-Everest traverse (female)
The fastest time to summit Lhotse and Everest by a woman is 21 hr 30 min by Qu Jiao-Jiao (CHN). She arrived at the summit of Lhotse at 8:20 a.m. on 20 May 2018, then reached the top of Everest at 5:50 a.m. the next day.

Most climbs over 8,000 m without supplemental oxygen
Starting with Everest on 24 May 2000, Denis Urubko (KAZ/RUS) has made 20 ascents of mountains over 8,000 m (26,246 ft) without the use of bottled oxygen. His most recent climb was Kangchenjunga on 19 May 2014.

FASTEST TIME TO CLIMB EL CAPITAN
On 6 Jun 2018, Alex Honnold and Tommy Caldwell (both USA) topped out the "Nose" of El Capitan in Yosemite National Park, California, USA, in 1 hr 58 min 7 sec. It was the third time in a week that the pair had set a new fastest climb of the 1,095-m-tall (3,593-ft) granite monolith, becoming the first to break the two-hour barrier in the process.

MOST ASCENTS OF EVEREST (INDIVIDUAL)
On 16 May 2018, Kami Rita Sherpa (aka "Thapkhe", NPL) successfully climbed Everest for the 22nd time in his career. This took the 48-year-old Sherpa one clear of the mark he had previously shared with Apa Sherpa (NPL) and Phurba Tashi Sherpa (NPL, see p.119). Kami Rita first climbed the mountain on 13 May 1994.

MOST ASCENTS OF EVEREST (INDIVIDUAL, FEMALE)
Lakpa Sherpa (NPL) reached the summit of Everest for the ninth time on 16 May 2018. She first climbed the mountain on 18 May 2000, via its south side, with her subsequent eight summits achieved via the north side. In between climbs, she lives in Connecticut, USA, where she works as a dish-washer.

FIRST DOUBLE AMPUTEE TO CLIMB EVEREST (SOUTH SIDE)
On 14 May 2018, 69-year-old Xia Boyu (CHN) summitted Everest from the south side. His feet had been amputated in 1975 on account of frostbite after an earlier attempt to scale the mountain, while in 1996 his legs were amputated below the knee owing to cancer.

The **first double amputee to climb Everest** is Mark Inglis (NZ), who summitted via the north side on 15 May 2006.

JUL 1 — "Mr Cherry", aka Cherry Yoshitake (JPN), achieves the **most baked beans eaten with chopsticks in one minute** – 71 – on the set of *Officially Amazing* at RAF Bentwaters in Suffolk, UK, in 2015.

JUL 2 — In 2011, Juicys Outlaw Grill in Corvallis, Oregon, USA, puts the **most expensive hamburger** on the menu for $5,000 (£3,115). It weighs 352.44 kg (777 lb) – about the same as five adult men.

Plain conceived of his "7 in 4" record (seven peaks in four months) in 2014 while recovering from a "hangman's fracture" – a broken neck – that he'd sustained while swimming.

▶ FASTEST TIME TO CLIMB THE SEVEN SUMMITS INCLUDING CARSTENSZ (MALE)

When Steven Plain (AUS) reached the summit of Everest on 14 May 2018, he completed his speed climb of the highest points on each of the seven continents in just 117 days 6 hr 50 min. He began on 16 Jan 2018, when he summitted Vinson in Antarctica (inset left), and went on to climb Aconcagua (South America), Kilimanjaro (Africa, inset right), Carstensz (Australasia), Elbrus (Europe), Denali (North America) and finally Everest. On 3 Mar, he also scaled the 2,228-m (7,310-ft) Kosciuszko – the highest point on mainland Australia.

FIRST WINTER ASCENT OF GORA POBEDA

At 3,003 m (9,852 ft), Gora Pobeda (aka Pik Pobeda) is not only the highest mountain in Siberia's Arctic Circle but also one of the coldest places on the planet. On 11 Feb 2018, Italians Tamara Lunger (left) and Simone Moro (right) overcame reported temperatures of -40°C (-40°F) to reach the peak's summit.

MOST CLIMBS OVER 8,000 M

On 18 Sep 2017, Phurba Tashi Sherpa (NPL) achieved his 35th successful ascent of one of Earth's 14 mountains over 8,000 m (26,247 ft) when he climbed Manaslu (8,163 m; 26,781 ft) in Nepal for the seventh time. Phurba Tashi has summitted Everest a total of 21 times - just one behind Kami Rita Sherpa (see p.118).

FASTEST TRIPLE-HEADER OF THE HIGHER 8,000ERS (FEMALE)

Nima Jangmu Sherpa (NPL) climbed three of the higher five 8,000-m mountains in 23 days 18 hr 30 min between 29 Apr and 23 May 2018. She summitted Lhotse and Everest before climbing Kangchenjunga, the world's third-highest mountain. All of the climbs were carried out with the aid of bottled oxygen.

(see p.118).

JUL 3 — In 2012, *American Ninja Warrior* competitor Brent Steffensen (USA) makes a sweet 8.8-m-high (28-ft 10-in) leap of faith on *Guinness World Records Gone Wild!* It is the **highest jump into marshmallows**.

JUL 4 — The **fastest average speed in a Tour de France stage (individual)** – 55.446 km/h (34.453 mph) – is clocked in 2015 by Rohan Dennis (AUS) in winning Stage 1.

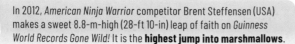

BY ICE

FIRST...

People to reach the South Pole

On 14 Dec 1911, a Norwegian party of five led by Captain Roald Amundsen reached the South Pole after a 53-day march with dog sledges from the Bay of Whales in the Ross Sea.

Crossing of Antarctica

A group of 12 headed by British explorer Dr Vivian Fuchs completed the first coast-to-coast traverse of the Antarctic continent on 2 Mar 1958. Their 3,473-km (2,158-mi) tractor-powered journey from Shackleton Base to Scott Base, via the South Pole, took 99 days.

Fuchs was preceded to the pole by a supporting party from Scott Base that laid down food and fuel supplies. It was led by Sir Edmund Hillary (NZ), who made the **first ascent of Everest** in 1953 with Tenzing Norgay (Tibet/IND).

Crossing of the Arctic Ocean

Led by Wally Herbert (UK), the British Trans-Arctic Expedition departed Point Barrow in Alaska, USA, on 21 Feb 1968 and arrived at the Seven Island archipelago, north-east of Svalbard, Norway, 463 days later on 29 May 1969. The journey, conducted on husky-drawn sleds, involved a haul of 4,699 km (2,920 mi) and a drift of 1,100 km (683 mi); the straight-line distance was 2,674 km (1,662 mi). The other expedition members were Major Ken Hedges, Allan Gill and Dr Roy "Fritz" Koerner (all UK).

Solo expedition to the North Pole

On 29 Apr 1978, Naomi Uemura (JPN) reached the North Pole, having dog-sledded c. 770 km (478 mi) across the Arctic sea-ice. He had set out from Ellesmere Island, off northern Canada, 55 days previously.

The **first solo expedition to the South Pole** was a 1,400-km (870-mi) unsupported surface trek on skis undertaken by Erling Kagge (NOR). Departing from Berkner Island, he arrived at the pole on 7 Jan 1993.

Solo circumnavigation of Antarctica in a sailboat

On board *Trading Network Alye Parusa*, Fedor Konyukhov (RUS) circled the Antarctic in 102 days 1 hr 35 min 50 sec, returning to Australia on 7 May 2008.

Lisa Blair (AUS) set the **female** record in *Climate Action Now*, reaching Albany, Western Australia, on 25 Jul 2017 after 183 days 7 hr 21 min 38 sec. The World Speed Sailing Record Council endorsed both records.

FASTEST...

1 km ice swim (female)

On 6 Jan 2019, Alisa Fatum (DEU) swam 1 km (0.6 mi) in icy water in 12 min 48.70 sec at the Ice Swimming German Open in Veitsbronn, Germany.

Sven Elfferich (NLD) claimed the **male** title on 16 Feb 2019, with a time of 11 min 55.40 sec in Freizeitverein Altenwörth, Austria. Both records were ratified by the International Ice Swimming Association.

Solo crossing of Antarctica

Also the **first solo crossing of Antarctica**, Børge Ousland (NOR) completed a 2,690-km (1,675-mi) kite-assisted ski trek on 19 Jan 1997, 65 days after setting out from Berkner Island in the Weddell Sea. He hauled a 185-kg (408-lb) supply sled all the way to Scott Base in the McMurdo Sound.

FIRST CIRCUMNAVIGATION OF ANTARCTICA IN A SAILBOAT SOUTH OF THE 60TH PARALLEL

On 23 Dec 2017, Captain Mariusz Koper and his eight-person crew (all POL) left Cape Town, South Africa, on the yacht *Katharsis II* to loop Antarctica entirely south of the 60th parallel circle of latitude (inset). On 5 Apr 2018, after a journey of 102 days 22 hr 59 min 5 sec, they reached Hobart in Tasmania, Australia. They completed the Antarctic loop south of 60° in 72 days 6 hr, between 8 a.m. UTC (Coordinated Universal Time) on 7 Jan at 2 p.m. UTC on 20 Mar 2018.

On 26 Dec 2018, US endurance athlete Colin O'Brady announced that he had completed the first unassisted solo crossing of Antarctica, skiing between the Ronne and Ross ice shelves, via the South Pole, in 54 days. The record claim has sparked a fierce debate in the polar-exploration community regarding the changing goal-posts of what constitutes a true Antarctic crossing. GWR is currently undergoing a review of its policy.

Trek to the North Pole

On 14 Apr 2010, David Pierce Jones (UK), Richard Weber (CAN), Tessum Weber and Howard Fairbank (ZAF) reached the Geographic North Pole after 41 days 18 hr 52 min. Over the 785-km (487.7-mi) trek, the team had no aids and only one resupply.

FASTEST AVERAGE SPEED FOR A ROW ON THE ARCTIC OCEAN OPEN WATERS

From 20 to 27 Jul 2017, the *Polar Row* team averaged 2.554 knots (4.73 km/h; 2.94 mph) between Tromsø, Norway, and Longyearbyen, Svalbard. The team comprised Fiann Paul (ISL), Tathagata Roy (IND), Jeff Willis (UK), Carlo Facchino (USA) and Tor Wigum (NOR).

HIGHEST ALTITUDE KAYAKING

On 7 Mar 2018, Daniel Bull (AUS) dragged a kayak up Ojos del Salado, the **highest active volcano** (summit: 6,887 m; 22,595 ft), on the border between Chile and Argentina. Upon reaching an altitude of 5,707 m (18,723 ft), he paddled 2.5 km (1.5 mi) on a semi-frozen lake.

In early 2019, Bull's record as the **youngest person to climb the Seven Summits and the Seven Volcanic Summits** fell to Satyarup Siddhanta (IND, b. 29 Apr 1983), who was 35 years 261 days old when he topped his 14th peak – Mount Sidley in Antarctica – on 15 Jan.

YOUNGEST PERSON TO TREK TO THE SOUTH POLE

Lewis Clarke (UK, b. 18 Nov 1997) was 16 years 61 days old when he reached the Geographic South Pole on 18 Jan 2014, along with his guide Carl Alvey. They had skied 1,123.61 km (698.18 mi) from Hercules Inlet, which lies some 670 km (416 mi) inland from the Antarctic coast.

The **youngest person to trek to the North Pole** is Tessum Weber (CAN, b. 9 May 1989). He was 20 years 340 days old when he completed a journey on foot to the Geographic North Pole as part of a four-person team on 14 Apr 2010.

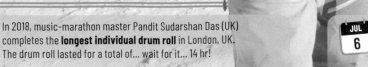

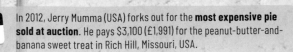

JUL 5 — In 2018, music-marathon master Pandit Sudarshan Das (UK) completes the **longest individual drum roll** in London, UK. The drum roll lasted for a total of... wait for it... 14 hr!

JUL 6 — In 2012, Jerry Mumma (USA) forks out for the **most expensive pie sold at auction**. He pays $3,100 (£1,991) for the peanut-butter-and-banana sweet treat in Rich Hill, Missouri, USA.

FIRST ICE-CLIMB OF NIAGARA FALLS

On 27 Jan 2015, veteran extreme adventurer Will Gadd (CAN) scaled the semi-frozen Horseshoe Falls – the largest of the three waterfalls that make up Niagara Falls – on the US/Canadian border, during an event sponsored by Red Bull.

Shortly afterwards on the same day, he was proceeded by Sarah Hueniken (CAN), who accomplished the **first ice-climb of Niagara Falls (female)**. Both climbers followed a 9-m-wide (30-ft) stretch of spray ice along the left-hand side of Horseshoe Falls. Below, the intrepid duo embrace after completing their successful climbs.

Recalling the sensation of ice-climbing beside one of the world's most powerful waterfalls, Gadd said: "It vibrates your intestines and makes you feel very, very small…"

MOST PISTES SKIED IN 8 HOURS

Jimmy DeMartini (USA) skied down 70 pistes in 8 hr at Beaver Creek Resort in Avon, Colorado, USA, on 17 Mar 2017. Afterwards, he stated modestly that he had accomplished the feat by "pointing downhill and letting gravity do the work".

GREATEST VERTICAL DISTANCE SNOWBOARDED IN 12 HOURS

On 12 Mar 2017, Keith Hayes (UK) descended 19,000 m (62,335 ft) on his snowboard in half a day at the Sun Peaks Resort in British Columbia, Canada. Hayes made 40 runs over a period of 9 hr 48 min, using a chairlift to return to the top each time. He spent nine months training for his attempt, which raised funds for Epilepsy Action.

GREATEST VERTICAL DISTANCE SKI-BOBBED IN 24 HOURS (TEAM OF TWO)

For this record, two riders make repeated descents of a slope and the total distance covered is calculated. Hermann Koch and Harald Brenter (both AUT) descended 63,638 m (208,786 ft) by snow bike on 11–12 Apr 2018 in Obertauern, Salzburg, Austria. That's seven times greater than Everest, the **highest mountain**. To maintain morale, they rode alongside each other for most of the runs, taking turns on a "master" ski-bob. Only the distance covered by this vehicle counted towards the total.

The pair have also achieved vertical-distance ski-bob records in **one hour** – 3,086 m (10,124 ft) – and **12 hours** – 32,736 m (107,401 ft).

JUL 7 Chad Netherland (USA) achieves the **longest time to restrain two aircraft** in 2007. He prevents the take-off of two Cessna light aircraft pulling in opposite directions for 1 min 0.6 sec.

JUL 8 In 1990, Pedro Monzón (ARG) becomes the **first player to be sent off in a FIFA World Cup final** when he sees red in the 65th minute. Argentina finish the game with nine men; Germany win 1–0.

FASTEST TIME TO RUN AN ULTRA MARATHON DISTANCE ON EACH CONTINENT (FEMALE)

As part of the World Marathon Challenge, Nahila Hernández San Juan (MEX) participated in seven 50-km (31-mi) races on different continents in 6 days 11 hr 29 min 3 sec on 23–30 Jan 2017. The epic journey took her to Antarctica (inset), Chile, the USA, Spain, Morocco, the UAE and Australia (above). Her fastest run was in Punta Arenas, Chile: 5 hr 11 min 46 sec.

GREATEST DISTANCE ON AN ELECTRIC BICYCLE IN 12 HOURS

On 26 Aug 2018, Christopher Ramsey (UK) covered 286.16 km (177.81 mi) on an electric bicycle in half a day at the Grampian Transport Museum in Alford, Aberdeenshire, UK. A self-proclaimed "sustainable adventurer", Ramsey chose to attempt this record to encourage the idea of reducing emissions in major cities.

Fastest aggregate time to complete a marathon in all 50 US states (female)

Between 3 Oct 1999 and 20 Aug 2017, Suzy Seeley (USA) ran a marathon in every state of the USA with an aggregate time of 176 hr 35 min 40 sec. She completed each race in under four hours.

Fastest cycle across Europe (Cabo da Roca to Ufa) by an individual

Leigh Timmis (UK) cycled from the westernmost point of mainland Portugal to the Russian city of Ufa in 16 days 10 hr 45 min on 10–26 Sep 2018. Charity fundraiser Timmis broke the previous record by 10 days.

The **team** record for this route is 29 days 5 hr 25 min, achieved by Helmy Elsaeed (EGY), Måns Möller, Christer Skog, Tony Duberg and Per-Anders Lissollas (all SWE) from 21 May to 19 Jun 2017.

Longest journey by bicycle in a single country (individual)

Benjamin Woods (AUS) rode 18,922.47 km (11,757.88 mi) throughout Australia from 10 Jun 2017 to 10 Feb 2018.

The **longest journey by bicycle in a single country (team)** was set two months later. From 2 Oct 2017 to 3 Apr 2018, MJ Pavan and Bhagyashree Sawant (both IND) covered 19,400.83 km (12,055.11 mi) in India. The pair passed through 21 states and five union territories, calling at some 600 schools along the way to raise awareness about polio as well as the importance of education.

Fastest crossing of the Atacama Desert by foot

Setting off from San Pedro de Atacama in Chile on 15 Sep 2018, ultramarathon athlete Michele Graglia (ITA) ran south to Copiapó in 8 days 16 hr 58 min. The journey took him across c. 1,200 km (745 mi) of the arid Atacama Desert – home to the **driest place** on Earth (see p.18). In Jul 2018, Graglia won the Badwater 135 – advertised as the "world's toughest foot race" – a testing run from Death Valley to Mount Whitney in California, USA.

Fastest time to visit all countries by public surface transport

Adventurer Graham Hughes (UK) visited 197 countries in 4 years 31 days, without once flying, between 1 Jan 2009 and 31 Jan 2013. The total included 193 UN member countries as well as Kosovo, Vatican City, Palestine and Chinese Taipei. Along the way, Hughes watched a Space Shuttle take off, dodged pirates in the Seychelles, and was arrested in Estonia and Cameroon.

Fastest time to visit all EU member states

Starting on 5 Sep 2017, Sabin Stanescu (ROM) visited all 28 countries in the European Union in 3 days 22 hr 39 min. He set off from Ireland and ended up in Bulgaria.

Fastest circumnavigation by car

The record for the **first and fastest man and woman to have circumnavigated the Earth by car** covering six continents under the rules applicable in 1989 and 1991 embracing more than an equator's length of driving (24,901 road miles; 40,075 km), is held by Saloo Choudhury and his wife Neena Choudhury (both India). The journey took 69 days 19 hours 5 minutes from 9 September to 17 November 1989. The couple drove a 1989 Hindustan "Contessa Classic" starting and finishing in Delhi, India.

▶ HIGHEST ALTITUDE ACHIEVED IN AN ELECTRIC CAR

On 24 Sep 2018, Chen Haiyi (CHN) drove a NIO ES8 electric-powered SUV to a height of 5,715 m (18,751 ft) en route to Purog Kangri Glacier in Tibet, China. The attempt was organized to demonstrate the ES8's reliability when placed under extreme conditions. On the journey to the world's third-largest glacier, the vehicle had to endure sub-zero temperatures.

▶ You'll find lots of videos to explore at guinnessworldrecords.com/2020

JUL 9
In 2011, South Sudan (capital: Juba) secedes from Sudan to become the **newest independent country**. It is the first new state since Montenegro formed in 2006.

JUL 10
In Brazil, Karoline Mariechen Meyer (BRA) achieves the **longest time breath held voluntarily (female)** – 18 min 32.59 sec – in 2009. She inhales oxygen for 24 minutes prior to the attempt.

Longest journey by solar-powered boat

MS *TÛRANOR PlanetSolar* circled the globe in a westward direction between 27 Sep 2010 and 4 May 2012, covering 32,410 nautical mi (60,023 km; 37,296 mi). It launched in Monaco and passed through the Panama Canal before returning

FASTEST COMPLETION OF 100,000 MILES BY BICYCLE (WUCA-APPROVED)

Between 15 May 2016 and 11 Jul 2017, Amanda Coker (USA) broke a 77-year-old record by riding 100,000 mi (160,934 km) in 423 days, as verified by the World UltraCycling Association (WUCA). This total included the **farthest distance cycled in one year (WUCA-approved):** 139,326.34 km (86,573.37 mi).

to the principality 1 year 220 days later – the **first circumnavigation by solar-powered boat**. The team was led by Raphaël Domjan (CHE).

On land, the **longest journey by solar electric car** is 29,753 km (18,487 mi),

by the SolarCar Project Hochschule Bochum (DEU). Having set out on 26 Oct 2011, the team spent more than a year driving around the world before coming to a stop at Mount Barker in Australia on 15 Dec 2012.

Longest journey by car using alternative fuel

Tyson Jerry and the Driven to Sustain team (both CAN) completed a 48,535.5-km (30,158.5-mi) road trip in a car powered by biodiesel and vegetable oil between 15 Nov 2009 and 4 May 2010. Jerry began in Columbia, South Carolina, USA, and collected fuel from locations such as fast-food restaurants en route to Vancouver, British Columbia, Canada.

Greatest distance by electric boat, single charge (non-solar)

Pike travelled 220.4 km (137 mi) non-stop along the River Thames in Oxfordshire, UK, on 20–21 Aug 2001. The boat was fitted with a

battery-powered electric motor from the Thames Electric Launch Company.

Fastest paddleboard across the Florida Straits (female)

On 26–27 Jun 2018, Victoria Burgess (USA) overcame high winds to paddleboard from Havana, Cuba, to Key West in Florida, USA, in 27 hr 48 min. Burgess took

on this record to raise the profile of ocean conservation and also to encourage more women into sport.

Oldest person to swim the English Channel (female)

Aged 71 years 305 days, Linda Ashmore (UK, b. 21 Oct 1946) swam from England to France on 21 Aug 2018. She first broke this record in 2007, crossing the Channel at the age of 60 years 302 days.

GREATEST DISTANCE WATERSKIED TOWED BY A BLIMP

On 13 Mar 2018, Kari McCollum (USA) waterskied around Lake Elsinore in California, USA, for 11.1 km (6.9 mi) while being towed by an airship travelling at 17 knots (31.4 km/h; 19.5 mph). The 20-year-old student triumphed over several other contenders during an aquatic contest staged by telecommunications company T-Mobile (USA).

LARGEST HUMAN WATERSKIING PYRAMID FORMATION

The Mercury Marine Pyramid (USA) built a human waterskiing formation of 80 people in Janesville, Wisconsin, USA, on 18 Aug 2018. Arranged in multiple four-tier pyramids, members of the Rock Aqua Jays Water Ski Show Team maintained an interlocked formation for more than 350 m (1,148 ft) on the Rock River, using coloured buoys to mark the distance.

FASTEST JOURNEY FROM LAND'S END TO JOHN O' GROATS BY TRIPLET BICYCLE

On 16–22 Jun 2018, the trio of Harry Fildes (middle) and brothers Alexander (right) and Fergus Gilmour (all UK) cycled the length of Great Britain on a three-seater bike in 6 days 13 hr 30 min. They embarked upon their marathon ride in order to raise money for Whizz-Kidz, a charity that helps young disabled people, as well as a local hospital.

 JUL 11 In 2014, speed-eater Takeru Kobayashi (JPN) wolfs down the **most hamburgers eaten in three minutes** – 12 – in Milan, Italy. He adds mayonnaise as his one permitted condiment.

 JUL 12 The 2014 Deja Moo Country Fair in Cowaramup, Western Australia, rustles up 1,352 participants for the **largest gathering of people dressed as cows**.

123

MOST VIEWED YOUTUBE CHANNEL FOR A "POST-POST-MILLENNIAL"

As of 1 Feb 2019, "Ryan ToysReview" had been viewed 27,143,288,795 times – and had amassed 18,052,910 subscribers – since it launched on 16 Mar 2015. It is the most watched YouTube channel hosted by someone born post-2010 (also known as a member of "Generation Alpha"). Its star is eight-year-old Ryan (USA, b. 6 Oct 2010), who uploads videos of himself (and sometimes his family) playing with toys and games, and shares his views about them. In an effort to provide their son with a little privacy, his parents have withheld Ryan's surname.

Ryan also stars in a second YouTube channel called "Ryan's Family Review". This focuses more on activities, trips and vacations undertaken by his entire family and includes his parents and his younger twin sisters, Emma and Kate.

GUS

FIRE TRUCK PLAYLAND

*INCLUDES 1 PLAYLAND + 50 SOFT

WALKS & STOMPS!

MOTORIZED!

2½ FEET TALL!

STANDS & ROARS!

CONTENTS

プラレール

●5両編成のE7系北陸新幹線かがやきと、
列車が通過するとトミカが発車する
駅前ロータリーのセットだよ！

いっぱいつなごう！

E7系 北陸新幹線かがやき
8トミカ駅前ロー

SERIES E7 HOKURIKU SHINKANS

大迫力！5両編成の
E7系北陸新幹線かがやき！

Pirate Whale

TOMICA トミカ
HYPERCITY

WINGS FLAP!

RICHEST PERSON

He's the head of all-conquering Amazon – the **largest online shop** – and owner of the *Washington Post* newspaper, so it's no surprise that Jeff Bezos (USA) is comfortably ensconced in the super-rich bracket. But just how wealthy is he? And what would his fortune look like as a mountain of cash?

With an estimated net worth of $112 bn (£81 bn) as of 6 Mar 2018, according to Forbes' Billionaires List, Jeffrey Preston Bezos is richer than anyone on the planet. Visualized as a pyramid of one-dollar bills, his fortune would rise to around 77 m (252 ft), dwarfing London's Buckingham Palace. To spend it all in a year, you'd need to pay out $3,550 (£2,570) per second!

Bezos was born on 12 Jan 1964 in Albuquerque, New Mexico, USA. His inventive genius was evident early on: he dismantled his own cot with a screwdriver while still a toddler and, as a teenager, invented an alarm to dissuade his siblings from entering his room. At high school, he devised the "Dream Institute", an inspirational summer camp for students. He eventually wound up at investment bank D E Shaw & Co. in 1990, rising to become the company's youngest-ever vice president. By now, however, Bezos was aware of the boundless potential of internet sales, and in 1994 he quit to start up an online bookshop from a garage in Seattle, Washington, USA.

FIRST CENTIBILLIONAIRE

His net worth of $112 bn puts Amazon's Jeff Bezos in a category of his own. Wealth is relative, however. Adjusted for inflation, Microsoft's Bill Gates's (USA) net worth in 1999 would have topped $136 bn (£96.8 bn) today. And oil tycoon John D Rockefeller (USA) would have been richer still (see p.132).

These are only history's *calculable* fortunes, of course. What about Genghis Khan, whose empire took in most of Asia? Or 14th-century emperor Mansa Musa I of Mali, whom *Time* magazine described as "richer than anyone could describe"? We can only guess at their immense wealth.

A dollar bill weighs around a gram, so this cash heap would weigh around 112,000 tonnes (123,500 US tons). That's more than four times heavier than the Statue of Liberty!

Bezos named his company Amazon (having considered Cadabra and the *Star Trek*-inspired MakeItSo.com) and sold his first book in Jul 1995. Business was brisk. *Time* made Bezos its "Person of the Year" in 1999 and named him as one of the world's 100 most influential people in 2018. Amazon was soon selling music, movies and more, adding a cloud-computing service in 2006. The Kindle digital reader, TV shows and films, and delivery service Amazon Prime followed.

In 2000, Bezos founded spaceflight firm Blue Origin, looking to expand into suborbital travel. In Nov 2015, the company's *New Shepard* space vehicle made the **first controlled landing by a suborbital rocket**.

Of course, Buckingham Palace's owner would no doubt have something to say about all this cash being dumped in her courtyard... You may be surprised to hear that Bezos' wealth is some 200 times greater than that of Queen Elizabeth!

BUCKINGHAM PALACE COURTYARD

First constructed as a single building in 1703, Buckingham Palace was expanded in the 1820s to include two wings and a triumphal entrance (Marble Arch), creating a "U"-shaped edifice. In 1847, the arch was moved near to Hyde Park and replaced by a fourth wing - creating the quadrangle that we've filled with Jeff Bezos's fortune above!

SKOOL DAZE

Highest enrolment rate for primary-school children
According to the UNESCO Institute for Statistics, in 2015 (the most recent year for which reasonably complete data is available) 99.94% of primary-school-age children in the UK were enrolled in primary education.

The country with the **lowest enrolment rate for primary-school children** is Liberia, where only 37.68% of eligible children were enrolled, according to the same source. Liberia also had the **lowest enrolment rate**

for secondary-school children, with just 15.48%. The **highest enrolment rate for secondary-school children** was 99.99%, in Sweden.

Highest budget for education
According to the latest available figures from *The Economist* for 2018, Denmark spends slightly more than 8% of its gross domestic product (GDP) on education. Zimbabwe and Malta follow closely behind, also devoting more than 8% to this area.

Longest career as a teacher
Medarda de Jesús Léon de Uzcátegui (VEN; b. 8 Jun 1899, d. 2002) began teaching at the age of 12 at a school she had set up with her two sisters in Caracas, Venezuela. After marrying in 1942, she ran her own school from her home in the city. She was still teaching in 1998, a total of 87 years later.

Oldest person to begin primary school
On 12 Jan 2004, great-grandfather Kimani Ng'ang'a Maruge (KEN) enrolled at the age of 84 into Standard One at Kapkenduiyo Primary School in Eldoret, Kenya. A year later, he addressed the United Nations on the importance of free primary education.

Most schools attended
Wilma Williams (USA) enrolled at 265 different schools from 1933 to 1943. Her parents were in show business.

LONGEST-RUNNING SANTA SCHOOL
We all know there's only one real Santa Claus. But for those aspiring to step into his boots one day, there's the Charles W Howard Santa Claus School. Founded in Albion, New York, USA, in Oct 1937, it still operated – now in Midland, Michigan – as of Dec 2018. Each October, the school offers a three-day intensive course exploring Santa's world, including a toy-workshop experience and sleigh-flying lessons.

Most consecutive graduation years represented at a high-school reunion
On 20 Oct 2018, the Independence High School All Class Reunion 2018 (USA) brought together former pupils from 41 consecutive graduations in San Jose, California, USA.

To celebrate this record, the alumni set another by writing the **most signatures in a yearbook in 24 hours** – 1,902. Although they were allowed the full day, they achieved the record in just three-and-a-half hours.

Longest elapsed time for a class reunion
In 1999, the 1929 class of Miss Blanche Miller's Kindergarten and Continuation School in Bluefield, West Virginia, USA, had their first reunion – after 70 years! Ten members of the class had died, but 55% of those still alive attended.

Largest school reunion
A total of 4,268 alumni attended a reunion organized by Bhashyam Rama Krishna and Bhashyam Educational Institutions (both IND) in Guntur, Andhra Pradesh, India, on 24 Dec 2017.

HIGHEST SCHOOL EVER
Between 1986 and Aug 2017, a small primary school was located at an altitude of around 5,022 m (16,476 ft) in Pumajiangtangxiang Township in Tibet, China. Its students, drawn from the local nomadic community, numbered around 100 at the time of its closing. Issues included extreme cold, lack of supplies and low oxygen levels in the air affecting pupils' concentration.

MOST TWINS IN THE SAME ACADEMIC YEAR AT ONE SCHOOL
The 2016/17 freshman year at New Trier High School in Winnetka, Illinois, USA, had 44 pairs of twins, as verified on 18 May 2017. Only three pairs (all female) were identical, while two sets were born on different days. The academic year had just over 1,000 pupils, meaning that the number of twins at New Trier High was almost triple that of the US national average for multiple births.

LONGEST CAREER AS A...
Language teacher: Middle-school Chinese teacher Ren Zuyong (b. 14 Mar 1939, above right) taught for 58 years between 1959 and 30 Aug 2017 in Xinghua, Jiangsu Province, China.
Music teacher: Charles Wright (USA, b. 24 May 1912, above left) began teaching piano privately and professionally in 1931. He continued to do so for the next 76 years until he passed away on 19 Jul 2007, aged 95 years 56 days.

JUL 13 In 2015, S K Ashraf (IND) takes just 14.88 sec to set the **fastest time to type from 1 to 50** in Hyderabad, India. To qualify for the record, he has to include a full stop between each number.

JUL 14 The **largest collection of cookbooks** is verified at 2,970 titles in 2013. It belongs to Sue Jimenez (USA/CAN), who keeps her foodie library at home in Albuquerque, New Mexico, USA.

The Institut Le Rosey has held this record since the first edition of *Guinness World Records* in 1955, when its annual fees were £1,000 ($2,800) per student.

MOST EXPENSIVE SCHOOL

The Institut Le Rosey is a co-educational boarding school located in Rolle, Switzerland, with a winter campus in the ski resort of Gstaad (inset). Annual fees for a single student are CHF115,500 ($118,299; £87,669). The school typically has no more than 400 students, overseen by around 200 staff. Notable alumni include several kings and heads of state – including Juan Carlos I of Spain, members of business dynasties such as the Rockefellers and Rothschilds, and the children of the rich and famous.

LARGEST SCHOOL (NUMBER OF PUPILS)

The City Montessori School in Lucknow, India, had an enrolment of 55,547 pupils as of 16 Jan 2019. Children are admitted from the age of three and can follow through their education all the way to senior secondary level. Founded by Dr Jagdish and Dr Bharti Gandhi, the school began in 1959 on rented premises with only five students. It continues to grow, spread across more than 1,000 classrooms on campuses across the city, and is celebrating its diamond jubilee in 2019.

LARGEST ROBOTICS LESSON

St Paul's School Pernambut, St Joseph's School Pallalakuppam and Rotary Club of Pernambut (all IND) staged a robotics engineering class featuring 1,021 students in Tamil Nadu, India, on 2 Aug 2018. During the 1-hr 4-min lesson, participants studied how to design and build robots and learned about the use of robotics in everyday life. Check out our dedicated robots chapter on pp.146–67.

JUL 15
In 2018, Muhammad Rashid (PAK) achieves the **most walnuts crushed by the hand in one minute** – 284 – in Karachi, Pakistan. He beats the previous record, set only two months earlier, by six.

JUL 16
In 2015, Burnaby Q Orbax (CAN) of the Monsters of Schlock achieves the **most nails inserted into the nose in 30 seconds** – 15 – in Saint John, New Brunswick, Canada.

BIG BUSINESS

Oldest stock exchange

The Amsterdam Stock Exchange in the Netherlands was founded in 1602. It dealt in printed shares of the United East India Company.

The **oldest active bond** was issued in 1624 by the Hoogheemraadschap Lekdijk Bovendams (NLD) to fund repairs to flood defences on the Lek river. As of 2018, the bond only pays out about €15 ($16; £13) per year, owing to inflation and currency changes.

Largest single trading floor ever

A trading floor belonging to the financial service firm UBS in Stamford, Connecticut, USA, measured 125 x 69 m (410 x 226 ft) – a total area of 8,625 m² (92,838 sq ft). This space was equivalent to 33 tennis courts. Following the banking crisis, the floor emptied as staff were moved to cheaper offices. It was finally put up for sale in 2016.

LARGEST COMPANY BY ASSETS

According to figures from Forbes in 2018, the Industrial and Commercial Bank of China (ICBC) owned $4,120.9 bn (£3,213.2 bn) in assets. This is greater than the GDP of Germany. One of China's so-called "Big Four" state-owned commercial banks, the ICBC was founded as a limited company in 1984.

Most successful chimpanzee on Wall Street

In 1999, Raven, a six-year-old chimpanzee, became the 22nd most successful money manager in the USA after choosing her stocks by throwing darts at a list of 133 internet companies. Her index – dubbed MonkeyDex – delivered a 213% gain, outperforming more than 6,000 professional brokers.

Highest share value

On 22 Feb 2000, the intraday high price of a single share in the internet service provider Yahoo! Japan (USA/JPN) hit 167,899,136 yen ($1,507,280; £942,989) on the JASDAQ stock exchange. Prices had been driven up by dot-com-era market optimism and a limited supply of shares available in the company.

Largest energy company by market capitalization

Based on the total market value of a company's shares and stocks, ExxonMobil (USA) had a value of $316 bn (£225 bn) as of 31 Mar 2018, according to the annual *Global Top 100 Companies* report by PricewaterhouseCoopers.

In the same report, the **largest bank by market capitalization** was JPMorgan Chase (USA), with a value of $375 bn (£267 bn). See left for the **largest bank by assets**.

LARGEST INITIAL PUBLIC OFFERING (IPO)

On 19 Sep 2014, American depository shares in the Alibaba Group (CHN; see p.134) were listed on the New York Stock Exchange at $68 (£41) per share. Investors rushed to buy a stake in the online marketplace, raising a record $25 bn (£15.31 bn) after additional "greenshoe" shares were released. Pictured is Alibaba Group founder, Jack Ma, raising a ceremonial mallet before striking a bell during his company's IPO.

Largest takeover

In Feb 2002, German conglomerate Mannesmann merged with Vodafone AirTouch (UK) in a deal worth £112 bn (then approximately $159 bn).

Largest trading loss sustained

In 2008, Howie Hubler, a mortgage bond trader working for US bank Morgan Stanley, lost his employer around $9 bn (then roughly £6 bn) while trading complicated credit default swaps on the subprime market. The bank's chief financial officer described it as "a very expensive and humbling lesson".

Highest closing on the Dow Jones Industrial Average (DJIA)

On 3 Oct 2018, the DJIA – a stock-market index based on the daily stock price of 30 large US companies – closed at 26,828.39. This record high was followed by a sharp fall, with the index dropping 832 points on 10 Oct.

The **largest percentage gain on the DJIA in one day** was 15.34%, on 15 Mar 1933. The **largest single-day fall** was 22.61%, on 19 Oct 1987 – better known as "Black Monday".

Easiest country in which to do business

According to the World Bank's 2018 *Doing Business* report, New Zealand has the fewest obstacles to setting up and operating a business. It scored 86.55 in the organization's "Distance-to-Frontier" rankings.

The **hardest country in which to do business** is Somalia, which scored 45.77 in the same report.

LARGEST ATTENDANCE AT AN AGM

Nicknamed the "Woodstock of Capitalism", the annual general meeting (AGM) of investment firm Berkshire Hathaway (USA) is held at the 18,975-seat CHI Health Center Omaha in Nebraska, USA. Although official attendance figures are not released, the meeting held on 6 May 2017 is estimated to have attracted around 42,000 shareholders.

JUL 17 A pot-bellied pig named Ernestine is born in Alberta, Canada, in 1991. She will live for 23 years 76 days – becoming the **oldest pig ever** – before passing away on 1 Oct 2014.

JUL 18 At the 1976 Olympics in Montreal, Canada, Nadia Comăneci (ROM) receives the **first perfect 10 awarded in Olympic gymnastics**, for her routine on the uneven bars in the team competition.

FIRST TRILLION-DOLLAR PUBLIC COMPANY

On 2 Aug 2018, tech giant Apple (USA) exceeded the $1-tr (£762.1-bn) valuation milestone when its shares hit $207.05 (£157.80) during trading. Apple's value had been boosted by strong sales of its iPhone X.

According to figures published by PricewaterhouseCoopers in their annual *Global Top 100 Companies* report, Apple had a value of $851 bn (£606 bn) as of 31 Mar 2018, making it the **largest company by market capitalization.**

Pictured are Apple customers in Australia (main) and Japan (inset) rushing to be among the first to own an iPhone XS.

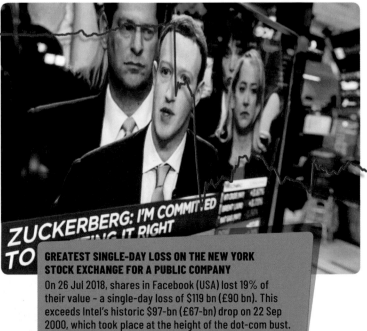

GREATEST SINGLE-DAY LOSS ON THE NEW YORK STOCK EXCHANGE FOR A PUBLIC COMPANY

On 26 Jul 2018, shares in Facebook (USA) lost 19% of their value – a single-day loss of $119 bn (£90 bn). This exceeds Intel's historic $97-bn (£67-bn) drop on 22 Sep 2000, which took place at the height of the dot-com bust. Facebook's record loss was attributed to an unexpectedly weak growth forecast in the company's earnings report.

BEST-SELLING PASSENGER CAR COMPANY (RETAIL, CURRENT)

Based on research on annual retail volume conducted on 19 Nov 2018, the best-selling passenger car company is Volkswagen (DEU), with estimated sales of 10,447,227 units in 2017. This is almost 3 million more than Toyota, at second place on the list. The Volkswagen group includes brands such as VW, Porsche and Audi.

JUL 19 In 2009, Mauricio Baldivieso (BOL, b. 22 Jul 1996) becomes the **youngest soccer player in a national top division** when he debuts for Aurora FC aged 12 years 362 days in La Paz, Bolivia.

JUL 20 At the 2014 International Quidditch Association (IQA) Global Games, the USA secure the title with a 210–0 defeat of Australia – the **highest margin of victory in an IQA World Cup final**.

THE RICH LI$T

HIGHEST CURRENT ANNUAL EARNINGS

PROFESSION	NAME	ESTIMATED EARNINGS
Soccer player	Lionel Messi (ARG)	$111 m (£84 m)
Musician	Ed Sheeran (UK)	$110 m (£83 m)
Radio host	Howard Stern (USA)	$90 m (£68 m)
Author	James Patterson (USA)	$86 m (£64 m)
Magician	David Copperfield (USA)	$62 m (£46 m)
Chef	Gordon Ramsay (UK)	$62 m (£46 m)
Comedian	Jerry Seinfeld (USA)	$57 m (£43 m)
Racing car driver	Lewis Hamilton (UK)	$51 m (£38 m)
Golfer	Tiger Woods (USA)	$43 m (£32 m)

Figures from Forbes, from 1 Jul 2017 to 1 Jul 2018

RICHEST PERSON (FEMALE)

According to Forbes' *Billionaires 2018* list, Alice Walton (USA) has an estimated net worth of $46 bn (£33.2 bn). The daughter of Sam Walton, founder of Walmart Inc., Alice is a noted patron of the arts.

Richest person ever (inflation-adjusted)

The personal fortune of oil tycoon John D Rockefeller (USA) was estimated at about $900 m (£184 m) in 1913. This is equivalent to at least $189.6 bn (£114.3 bn) in today's terms, and some estimates put its present-day value as high as $340 bn (£242.2 bn). That's around three times the net worth of Jeff Bezos (USA), the **richest person (current)** with $112 bn (£81 bn). (See pp.126–27 for more on Bezos.)

Most billionaires (city)

Of the world's 2,208 billionaires, 82 resided in New York City, USA, as of Mar 2017. Forbes estimated their combined net worth at $397.9 bn (£319.4 bn) – more than the nominal GDP of countries such as Iran ($376 bn; £301 bn) and the United Arab Emirates ($371 bn; £297 bn).

Of the 72 countries that are home to at least one billionaire, the USA has the **most billionaires**: 585.

Oldest living billionaire

Born in 1918, maritime pioneer Chang Yun Chung (CHN) appeared on Forbes' *Billionaires 2018* list aged 100 years, with a net worth of $1.9 bn (£1.4 bn). He started his shipping career in Singapore in 1949 and co-founded Pacific International Lines in 1967.

RICHEST CRYPTOBILLIONAIRE (CURRENT)

According to the first-ever cryptocurrency "rich list" by money experts Forbes, as of 19 Jan 2018 the richest cryptobillionaire was Chris Larsen (USA), whose "crypto net worth" was estimated on that day at $7.5–8 bn (£5.4–5.7 bn). Larsen is the co-founder, executive chairman and former CEO of Ripple, and owns 5.2 billion XRP – a cryptocurrency used by banks for fund transfers using the Ripple "distributed ledger" protocol.

LARGEST ACCIDENTAL BANKING CREDIT

In Jun 2013, Christopher Reynolds (USA) logged into his PayPal account and discovered he was in credit to the tune of $92,233,720,368,547,800. In theory, this $92-quadrillion (£60-quadrillion) windfall made him the richest man in the world – by around 1 million times. Sadly for Reynolds, the error was rectified moments later.

Highest current annual earnings for a male celebrity

Boxer Floyd "Money" Mayweather (USA) reportedly earned $285 m (£215.7 m) between 1 Jul 2017 and 1 Jul 2018, according to Forbes. He took $275 m (£208 m) from his headline-making fight against UFC's Conor McGregor on 26 Aug 2017, for which Mayweather also acted as a promoter. (For the **highest-earning female celebrity**, see opposite.)

LARGEST...

Loss of personal fortune

Japanese tech investor Masayoshi Son saw his net worth decline from a peak of $78 bn (£48 bn) in Feb 2000 to $19.4 bn (£12.9 bn) in July of the same year – a total loss of $58.6 bn (£38.9 bn). This was caused by the dot-com crash, which wiped out the value of his tech conglomerate SoftBank.

Charitable pledge

On 26 Jun 2006, investor and business magnate Warren Buffett (USA) made a commitment to gift 10 million shares of "Class B" stock in his investment conglomerate Berkshire Hathaway – then worth $30.7 bn (£16.7 bn) – to the Bill & Melinda Gates Foundation. As of the most recent round of payments on 16 Jul 2018, Buffett had given $24.5 bn (£18.5 bn) of the promised sum.

Severance package

In anticipation of his retirement from multinational conglomerate General Electric on 30 Sep 2001, Jack Welch (USA) negotiated a severance package valued by GMI Ratings at $417 m (£282 m). It included the lifetime use of company perks such as a private jet, a personal chauffeur and a luxurious Manhattan apartment.

Online gambling payout

On 1 Jun 2018, Lottoland Limited of Gibraltar paid out €90 m (£79 m; $105 m) to the winner of the EuroJackpot, a 36-year-old cleaner named Christina from Berlin, Germany. It was only the second time she had entered the lottery. Christina stated that she would use the money to go on her dream holiday – driving across the USA in an RV (camper van).

RICHEST LUXURY-GOODS MAKER

Described as "the ultimate tastemaker", Bernard Arnault (FRA) oversees many of the world's most prestigious brands as chairman of LVMH Moët Hennessy Louis Vuitton. His controlling stake in this luxury-goods conglomerate has made him a fortune of $72 bn (£52.1 bn), according to estimates published by Forbes on 6 Mar 2018.

YOUNGEST BILLIONAIRE (CURRENT)

As of 3 Sep 2018, the youngest billionaire was 21-year-old Alexandra Andresen (NOR, b. 23 Jul 1996). Her net worth was estimated by Forbes to be $1.4 bn (£1.08 bn), acquired when she inherited 42% of her family-owned investment company Ferd from her father Johan Henrik Andresen. Her sister Katharina – a year older – also owns 42%.

JUL 21 In 1998, Brian Milton (UK) completes the **first circumnavigation by microlight** in a Pegasus Quantum 912 flexwing, beginning and ending in Brooklands, Surrey, UK. He had set out on 22 Mar.

JUL 22 At the Delhi Monsoon Open 2018 in Ghaziabad, Uttar Pradesh, India, Shivam Bansal (IND) achieves the **most Rubik's Cubes solved while blindfolded** – 48 out of 48, in under 1 hr.

HIGHEST CURRENT ANNUAL EARNINGS FOR A FEMALE CELEBRITY

According to estimates published by Forbes on 16 Jul 2018, reality TV star and entrepreneur Kylie Jenner (USA) earned a reported $166.5 m (£126 m) between 1 Jul 2017 and 1 Jul 2018 – and all before her 21st birthday. Finding fame in the TV series *Keeping Up with the Kardashians* (on its 15th season as of 2018), Kylie built up a huge following on social media and became a major fashion and beauty influencer. Her company Kylie Cosmetics – of which she owns 100% – has been valued at almost $800 m (£600 m), only three years after it was founded in 2015.

In Nov 2018, search engine Lyst's Year in Fashion Report declared Kylie to be the most influential celebrity in fashion – just ahead of half-sister Kim.

FIRST SELF-MADE MILLIONAIRESS

The cosmetician Madam C J Walker (USA, née Sarah Breedlove) was born on a cotton plantation in Louisiana, USA, in 1867, and was orphaned at the age of seven. She built a fortune developing the "Walker System of Beauty Culture" – hair and beauty products for African-American women (see below). By 1919, she oversaw a team of 25,000 sales agents.

MADAM C.J.WALKER'S
TRADE MARK REGISTERED
WONDERFUL HAIR GROWER
NET CONTENTS 2 OZ
MADE BY
THE MADAM C.J. WALKER
MANUFACTURING CO.
INDIANAPOLIS, IND.
PRICE 50 CENTS

RICHEST FOOTBALL CLUB

As of 12 Jun 2018, Manchester United (UK) remained top of the money league with an estimated value of $4.12 bn (£3.07 bn), just ahead of Real Madrid (ESP) on $4.08 bn (£3.05 bn). United boasted an annual revenue of $737 m (£550.3 m) and a pre-tax operating income of $254 m (£189.6 m), according to Forbes' *The Business of Soccer* report.

JUL 23 In 2015, Stephen Rainey (UK) makes the **most manual wheelchair spins in one minute** (66) in Liverpool, UK, as part of an event to raise awareness of services available to local wheelchair users.

JUL 24 Under the supervision of Mike Rogiani, in 1988 Palm Dairies (both CAN) produce the **largest ice-cream sundae** in Edmonton, Alberta, Canada. It weighs 24.91 tonnes (54,917 lb).

SHOPPING

Largest shopping mall (gross leasable area)

Opened in 2005, the New South China Mall in Dongguan, Guangdong Province, China, has 600,153 m² (6.4 million sq ft) of available retail space. This is larger than the **smallest country**, the Vatican City, which has an area of 440,000 m² (4.7 million sq ft).

Longest pedestrian shopping street

A 1.21-km (0.75-mi) stretch of Zhongyang Dajie ("Central Street") in Harbin, Heilongjiang Province, China, bustles with shops. It has been pedestrianized since 1997.

Most expensive rent for shop space

According to property consultants Cushman & Wakefield's *Main Streets Across the World 2017* report, retail space on Fifth Avenue between 49th and 60th Streets in New York City, USA, costs as much as $3,000 (£2,223) per sq ft per year.

Largest fashion retail store

The Primark Stores (UK) shop in Birmingham, UK, has a retail floor space of 14,761 m² (158,892 sq ft), as ratified on 5 Apr 2019. The store is named Primark Pavilions as it has taken over the space once occupied by the city's Pavilions shopping centre.

LARGEST ONLINE RETAILER (ACTIVE BUYERS)

As of Jun 2018, Chinese e-commerce giant Alibaba Group had 552 million annual active buyers; this is almost equal to the total population of North America. (Amazon had 310 million, based on the latest available data.) The Alibaba Group owns several popular online shopping operations, including AliExpress, Alibaba.com and Tmall.

First livestream shop

Between 26 and 30 Sep 2017, cheese shoppers visiting Kaan's Stream Store could connect online with a real-time view of the shop and its staff, allowing them to start live video chats and make purchases. The livestream shop was a collaboration between Jan Kaan (NLD) and the ABN AMRO bank in Alkmaar, Netherlands.

First plastic-free supermarket aisle

On 28 Feb 2018, Ekoplaza in Amsterdam, Netherlands, opened a shopping aisle with more than 700 grocery products all wrapped in biodegradable and recyclable materials such as metal, cardboard and glass. Items included meat, rice, dairy, cereals, fruit and vegetables.

LARGEST SHOPPING MALL AQUARIUM

The Dubai Mall, in Dubai, UAE, has an unusual special feature. In addition to the 1,200 retail outlets and 548,127 m² (5.9 million sq ft) of indoor space, the mall contains a 10-million-litre (2.6-million-US-gal) aquarium. Shoppers can marvel at an impressive 140 aquatic species – including 300 sharks and rays – and can even book a shark-diving experience!

First shopping mall

Designed by Apollodorus of Damascus and built in 100–112 CE, Trajan's Forum in Rome, Italy, included a market area with 150 shops and offices on six gallery levels.

Oldest operating bookshop

The first Livraria Bertrand bookshop opened its doors in 1732 in Lisbon, Portugal. It remains part of a chain of stores in the country.

LARGEST RETAILER BY REVENUE

Retail giant Walmart Inc. (USA) had global revenues of $500.3 bn (£382.6 bn) for the 2018 fiscal year, primarily comprised of net sales of $495.8 bn (£379.2 bn). The company was founded by Samuel Moore Walton and James Lawrence Walton on 2 Jul 1962. As of Jan 2018, Walmart had 11,718 outlets in 28 countries, operating under 59 names.

HIGHEST ANNUAL REVENUE BY A SINGLE DEPARTMENT STORE

During 2016–17, Harrods department store in London, UK, had total sales of more than £2 bn ($2.7 bn), generating pre-tax profits of £233.2 m ($314.6 m). Founded by Charles Henry Harrod in 1849, Harrods now has 330 sub-departments spread over 102,000 m² (1.1 million sq ft) of floor space. It is owned by Qatar's sovereign wealth fund.

JUL 25 The **first test tube baby** is born in 1978. Louise Brown (UK) is delivered by Caesarean section in Oldham General Hospital, Lancashire, UK, and weighs 2.6 kg (5 lb 12 oz).

JUL 26 Mountaineer Karl Unterkircher (ITA) completes the **fastest ascent of Everest and K2 without supplementary oxygen**, summitting K2 in 2004 only 63 days after summitting Mount Everest.

In 2017, Amazon shipped more than 5 billion items through its Prime service alone. This is equivalent to around 158 items every second.

LARGEST ONLINE RETAILER (MARKET VALUE)

According to figures published by PricewaterhouseCoopers in their annual *Global Top 100 Companies* report, e-retailer Amazon (USA) had a value of $701 bn (£499 bn) as of 31 Mar 2018. However, its global revenue of $193.2 bn (£137.6 bn) for the 2017–18 fiscal year was less than half that of market leader Walmart (see opposite). Pictured is an Amazon distribution depot in Peterborough, Cambridgeshire, UK, preparing for "Cyber Monday" – one of the busiest online shopping days of the year – in 2013.

On 22 Jan 2018, the company opened a new flagship store in Seattle, USA, called Amazon Go (inset left). It operates without tills, cashiers or checkouts – to purchase items, customers scan in QR codes with their smartphone app and the cost is automatically charged to their Amazon account.

FIRST SHOPPING MALL FOR RECYCLED GOODS

ReTuna Återbruksgalleria in Eskilstuna, Sweden, is the world's first shopping mall dedicated to repaired, recycled and upcycled goods. Residents deposit discarded items – such as furniture, computers, audio equipment, clothes, toys, bikes, and gardening and building materials – which are then refurbished before being resold.

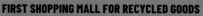

LARGEST LEGO® STORE

According to the LEGO Group, their largest store is the Leicester Square branch in central London, UK, with a total floor area of 914 m² (9,838 sq ft). The two-storey premises boasts several London-themed sculptures, including a life-size Tube carriage (above) comprising 637,902 bricks. Shown right is the shop's mascot, Lester, with a GWR certificate.

JUL 27 In 2007, Richard Rodriguez (USA) begins the **longest marathon on a roller-coaster** at Pleasure Beach in Blackpool, UK. He rides the Pepsi Max Big One and Big Dipper coasters for 405 hr 40 min.

JUL 28 Betty Lou Oliver (USA) survives a plunge of 75 storeys – more than 300 m (984 ft) – inside the Empire State Building in New York City, USA, in 1945. This is the **longest fall survived in an elevator**.

135

MOST EXPENSIVE...

1. Whisky

A bottle of "The Macallan 1926 60-year-old" single-malt whisky sold for £848,750 ($1,102,670), including buyer's premium, at Bonhams in Edinburgh, UK, on 3 Oct 2018. One of only 12 ever produced, the whisky's value was increased significantly by its label, which was designed by artist Valerio Adami and signed both by him and the then-Macallan chairman, Allan Shiach.

2. Wine

A bottle of 1945 Domaine de la Romanée-Conti red Burgundy sold for $558,000 (£422,801), including buyer's premium, at Sotheby's in New York City, USA, on 13 Oct 2018. The 73-year-old bottle sold for more than 17 times its asking price of $32,000 (£24,246).

3. Gin

In Nov 2018, the "extremely limited" Morus LXIV mulberry gin went on sale exclusively at Harvey Nichols in London, UK. For £4,000 ($5,118), buyers receive 730-ml and 30-ml porcelain jars of the spirit along with a porcelain cup housed in a leather case. The spirit is distilled from the leaves of a single mulberry tree (*Morus nigra*) that is more than a century old. It is produced by the Jam Jar Gin company, which is owned by Dan and Faye Thwaites (both UK).

▶ 4. Milkshake

As of 1 Jun 2018, the LUXE Milkshake sold for $100 (£75.15) at the restaurant Serendipity 3 in New York City, USA. The shake is the result of a partnership between the eatery, Swarovski and designer "The Crystal Ninja", aka Kellie DeFries. Its mouth-watering ingredients include three kinds of cream, *le cremose baldizzone* (a rare caramel sauce made from donkey milk) and 23-karat edible gold.

5. Handbag

A luxury matte-white "Himalaya" Hermès Birkin 30 handbag sold for 2,940,000 Hong Kong dollars ($377,238; £293,767) to an anonymous bidder on 31 May 2017. The sale took place at the Handbags & Accessories auction organized by Christie's in Hong Kong, China. Produced in 2014, the bag features 176.3 g (6.2 oz) of 18-karat white gold and 10.23 carats of diamonds.

6. Port wine

An 1863 Niepoort port in a Lalique crystal decanter sold for 992,000 Hong Kong dollars ($126,706; £97,522) at an Acker Merrall & Condit auction at the Grand Hyatt in Hong Kong, China, on 3 Nov 2018.

You'll often see the term "buyer's premium" alongside auction sales. This is a charge added to the sale price by the auction house to cover administrative costs.

7. Cheesecake

Made by chef Raffaele Ronca (ITA/USA), a white truffle cheesecake sold for $4,592.42 (£3,496.44) at Ristorante Rafele in New York City, USA, on 30 Oct 2017. The ingredients include buffalo ricotta, 200-year-old cognac, Madagascan vanilla and gold leafs.

8. Watermelon

Produced by the Inner Mongolia Green State Fertilizer Co. (CHN), an 81.75-kg (180-lb 3-oz) watermelon sold at auction for 51,000 yuan ($7,489; £5,827) in Horqin Right Front Banner, Inner Mongolia, China, on 26 Aug 2018.

9. Crab

On 7 Nov 2018, seafood retailers Kanemasa-Hamashita Shoten (JPN) purchased a snow crab, or Matsuba crab (*Chionoecetes opilio*), for 2 million yen ($17,648; £13,500). The sale took place in Tottori Prefecture, Japan. Snow crabs are a cherished treat in the country, and global shortages of the species have prompted rising prices in recent years.

JUL 29 At the 2012 Olympics, Team GB's Ryan Giggs (UK, b. 29 Nov 1973) nets against the UAE aged 38 years 243 days – the **oldest Olympic soccer goalscorer (male)**. This beats an 88-year-old record.

JUL 30 In 2017, a total of 2,325 Ivans attend a party arranged by Kupreški kosci (BIH) in Kupres, Bosnia and Herzegovina – the **largest gathering of people with the same forename**.

10. Camera
A prototype Leica 35-mm film camera sold to a private collector from Asia for €2.40 m ($2.95 m; £2.13 m) at the WestLicht Photographica auction in Vienna, Austria, on 10 Mar 2018. Known as the Leica O-series No.122, it was one of just 25 made for testing in 1923 – two years before the first Leica camera went on sale. The starting price was €400,000 ($492,000; £356,000).

11. Cognac shot
On 21 Mar 2018, a 40-ml shot of Rome de Bellegarde (UK) cognac sold for £10,014 ($14,037) to Ranjeeta Dutt McGroarty (IND) at the Hyde Kensington bar in London, UK. The brandy was decanted from a bottle that had been discovered in 2004, in the cellars of the Jean Fillioux Cognac house, and is believed to date from 1894. Proceeds from the sale went to the charity Global's Make Some Noise.

12. Box of facial tissues
Daishowa Paper Products (JPN) sold a box of facial tissues for 10,000 yen ($90.39; £68.11) as confirmed in Chūō, Tokyo, Japan, on 16 Jun 2018. "Juni-hitoe" tissues come in 12 colours; the name means "12-layer robes" and refers to an elegant type of kimono.

13. Book illustration
On 10 Jul 2018, the *Original Map of the Hundred Acre Wood*, drawn by E H Shepard (UK) for the endpapers of *Winnie-the-Pooh* (1926), sold for £430,000 ($571,369), including buyer's premium. The auction took place at Sotheby's in London, UK. The illustration is presented as the work of the character Christopher Robin, a young boy, and includes deliberate misspellings (e.g., "Big Stones and Rox" and "Nice for Piknicks").

14. Car
In May 2018, businessman and racing driver David MacNeil (USA) bought a 1963 Ferrari 250 GTO racer for $70 m (£52.7 m) in a private sale. Fewer than 40 of these cars were built. This particular model (chassis number 4153 GT) won the Tour de France Automobile in 1964, driven by Lucien Bianchi and Georges Berger.

This $70-m 250 GTO has a 3-litre "Colombo" V12 engine, enabling it to reach a top speed of 280 km/h (174 mph). Remarkably for a racing car of this vintage, it has never crashed – one reason for its record-breaking value.

NU 25

 You'll find many priceless videos at guinnessworldrecords.com/2020

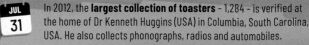

JUL 31 In 2012, the **largest collection of toasters** – 1,284 – is verified at the home of Dr Kenneth Huggins (USA) in Columbia, South Carolina, USA. He also collects phonographs, radios and automobiles.

AUG 1 During a four-day culinary event in Singapore in 2015, the Indian Chefs & Culinary Association (SGP) spice up proceedings with the **largest curry**. It weighs 15.34 tonnes (33,818 lb).

CONSUMER TECH

Fastest remote-controlled (RC) model tiltrotor aircraft

At the 75th Goodwood Festival of Speed in Chichester, West Sussex, UK, on 12 Jul 2018, Luke Bannister (UK) piloted the Wingcopter XBR at 240.06 km/h (149.16 mph). The RC tiltrotor aircraft was produced by Vodafone, XBlades Racing (both UK) and Wingcopter (DEU; see p.160).

Despite being only 17, Bannister is a veteran drone racer, having won $250,000 (then £174,695) at the World Drone Prix in Dubai, UAE, on 12 Mar 2016. With a total pot of $1 m (then £698,778), this is the **largest prize pool for a drone-racing tournament**.

Most Bluetooth speakers playing from a single source

On 25 Apr 2017, car tech and audio firm Harman International (USA) played 1,000 Bluetooth speakers from a single source at Village Underground in London, UK.

Largest touchscreen display

On 7 Apr 2017, a pair of 48.77-m² (525-sq-ft) screens – each bigger in area than 12 king-sized beds – were unveiled for the *Candy Crush* TV game show in Los Angeles, California, USA. They were used to play a supersized version of the popular mobile game by King, which – in this version – requires contestants to match up lines of colourful candies while suspended on harnesses.

Largest animated phone mosaic

Chinese electronics company Xiaomi created an image of a Christmas tree from 1,005 Xiaomi Mi Play phones in Beijing, China, on 24 Dec 2018. The animation lasted for 1 min 4 sec.

In addition to its phone business, Xiaomi is also the **best-selling wearable electronics brand**. Research conducted on 3 Dec 2018 found that Xiaomi had sold 18,643,300 pieces of wearable tech in 2018.

Highest-altitude smartphone livestream

In an event organized by Huawei Sweden on 5 Sep 2016, an Honor 8 smartphone was attached to a weather balloon and set to document its ascent. The phone streamed images of Earth live on Facebook up to an altitude of 18.42 km (11.45 mi).

Longest chain of electrical extension cables

At its annual meeting of managers in Dallas, Texas, USA, on 16 May 2018, electrical contractors IES Residential (USA) spelled out "IESR" with a 22.8-km (14.2-mi) chain of extension cables.

This monster extension might go well with another record holder: the **longest power strip**. The single unit – measuring 3 m (9 ft 10 in) long – was made by Mohammed Nawaz (IND) of the Aalim Muhammed Salegh College of Engineering and presented for measuring in Tamil Nadu, India, on 11 Oct 2018. It has 50 functioning outlets: 26 three-pin sockets and 24 two-pin.

▶ LARGEST PARADE OF AUTONOMOUS CARS

On 28 Nov 2018, the Chongqing Changan Automobile Company (CHN) arranged a 55-car parade of self-driving vehicles in Chongqing, China. The cars took 9 min 7 sec to complete the 3.2-km (1.9-mi) route, without any humans behind the wheel. This surpassed the convoy of 44 cars that the company had achieved earlier on the same day.

Most unmanned aerial vehicles (UAVs) airborne simultaneously

On 15 Jul 2018, Intel Corporation (USA) celebrated its 50th anniversary in style by flying 2,066 drones above Folsom in California, USA. The "Shooting Star" UAVs performed a five-minute choreographed routine, recreating Intel's logos from over the years as part of the story of the company's development.

On the other side of the world, in the night sky above Dubai, UAE, on 3 Jan 2019, a squadron of 30 drones formed the shape of 11 letters to spell out the words "Dubai Police". The ◗ **most consecutive formations by UAVs** was part of celebrations to commemorate 50 years of the Dubai Police Academy (UAE).

LONGEST SELFIE STICK

The Qatari Sky Climbers talent development programme celebrated its second graduation ceremony on 19 Sep 2017 with a photo taken using an 18-m (59-ft) selfie stick at the Qatar National Convention Centre in Doha. It beat the previous record, set in 2017, by 2 m (6 ft 6 in).

LONGEST-LASTING AA BATTERY CELL

In tests performed by engineering consultants Intertek Semko AB in Kista, Sweden, on 12 Oct 2018, the Energizer Ultimate Lithium battery produced by Energizer (USA) achieved the highest approved average performance score of 229.69. It underwent multiple tests against AA-size lithium-battery competitors.

▶ LONGEST DISTANCE SWUM BY A ROBOT ON A SINGLE SET OF AA BATTERIES

To mark Panasonic's 100th anniversary, the 17-cm-tall (6-in) robot "Mr EVOLTA NEO" paddled 3 km (1.8 mi) powered by two EVOLTA AA batteries. Floating on a mini-surfboard, it made the crossing from the Japanese mainland to the *torii* gate of the Itsukushima Shrine in Hiroshima Prefecture in 3 hr 22 min 34 sec.

100%

AUG 2

In 1917, E H Dunning (UK) achieves the **first landing on a moving ship** when he brings down his plane on the aircraft carrier HMS *Furious* in Orkney, UK. He dies on 7 Aug attempting the same feat.

AUG 3

In 2009, Sarah Outen (UK, b. 26 May 1985) arrives in Mauritius having rowed from Fremantle, Australia. Aged 23 years 310 days at the outset, she is the **youngest person to row the Indian Ocean solo**.

MOST PEOPLE USING VIRTUAL-REALITY DISPLAYS (MULTIPLE VENUES)

On 10 Oct 2018 – World Mental Health Day – a total of 2,340 people in five cities across China watched a virtual-reality (VR) short film entitled *The World Record of Mr.S*. The film follows a character called Mr.S and his recovery from schizophrenia. The record attempt was staged by Xian Janssen Pharmaceutical (CHN) in the hope of raising awareness about schizophrenia.

The **most people using VR displays (single venue)** is 1,867, achieved by Mobileye (ISR) on 3 Mar 2017 in Vancouver, British Columbia, Canada.

BEST-SELLING TABLET BRAND

Apple's (USA) iPad had estimated retail sales of 36,273,000 units in 2018, based on research conducted on 3 Dec. This is 12 million more than rivals Samsung (KOR), who sold approximately 24,360,900 tablets. In 2018, Apple introduced the iPad Pro, which it dubbed a "laptop killer" as it aimed to bridge the gap between tablets and laptops.

9:41
Wednesday, September 12

BEST-SELLING SMARTPHONE BRAND

Based on research conducted on 3 Dec 2018, Samsung (KOR) had estimated retail sales of 1,348,911,300 units from 2014 to 2018. It outsold iPhone – the second-highest-selling with 937,036,100 units – every year during this period, and almost tripled the total sales achieved by third-placed Huawei.

AUG 4 — Finnish heavy-metal band Agonizer play the **deepest concert underground** in 2007, performing 1,271 m (4,169 ft) below sea level in the Pyhäsalmi Mine in Pyhäjärvi, Finland.

AUG 5 — In 1971, Al Worden (USA) carries out the **first spacewalk in deep space**, retrieving film cassettes from *Apollo 15*'s scientific instrument module while 320,000 km (198,800 mi) from Earth.

URBAN LIFE

SMALLEST PARK
Mill Ends Park is set on a safety island on SW Naito Parkway in Portland, Oregon, USA. The park occupies a circle just 60.96 cm (2 ft) in diameter and has an area of 2,917.15 cm^2 (452.16 sq in). On 17 Mar 1948, at the behest of local journalist Dick Fagan, it was designated a city park for snail races and a colony for leprechauns.

Oldest continually inhabited city
Archaeologists have discovered settlements in Jericho, part of the Palestinian territories, dating back to 9000 BCE. Located near the Jordan River in the West Bank, the city is now home to around 20,000 people. The settlement that existed there in 8000 BCE is thought to have been inhabited by 2,000–3,000 people, who lived within a stone wall constructed by the community.

Smallest capital city (by population)
Melekeok, the capital of the tiny Pacific island nation of Palau, has a population of just 277 according to the country's 2015 census. This small and sparsely populated area is recognized as the capital by foreign governments, and is home to Palau's capitol building, located in an area called Ngerulmud.

Tallest residential building
Opened in 2015, the 425.5-m (1,396-ft) 432 Park Avenue in New York City, USA, is the world's tallest single-function residential building. The highest occupied storey in the 85-floor tower is at 392.1 m (1,286 ft).

Most expensive city...
To live in: The Economist Intelligence Unit's 2018 *Worldwide Cost of Living* survey ranked Singapore as the costliest city. Based on 400 prices ranging from food, drink and clothing to transport, utility bills and schools, Singapore's cost of living index is ranked at 116, compared with 100 for New York City and 26 for Damascus in Syria (the **least expensive**).
To rent in: The monthly rental cost of a two-bedroom apartment in Hong Kong is $3,737 (£2,783). This is based on Deutsche Bank's 2018 *Mapping the World's Prices* study, which lists the cost of goods and services in 50 major cities.
To dine in: A basic dinner for two at a pub or neighbourhood restaurant in Zurich, Switzerland, will cost an average of $72.30 (£53.85), according to the same 2018 report.

Most escalators in a metro system
The metro system in Washington, DC, USA, has 618 escalators. They are maintained by the costliest in-house escalator service contract in North America, with 90 technicians.

Fastest-growing city
According to *World Urbanization Prospects 2018*, the population of Rupganj in Bangladesh will be 9.35% larger in 2020 than it was in 2015. This is the result of the construction of two new planned towns – called Jolshiri Abashon and Purbachal New Town – within Rupganj's current boundaries.

The **slowest-growing** (or **fastest-shrinking**) city, by contrast, is Yichun in Heilongjiang Province, China, which is projected to have 1.35% fewer residents by 2020. This decline (which is likely greater than the statistics suggest) began following the collapse of the city's lumber industry owing to over-exploitation of the region's forests.

LARGEST CAPITAL CITY (BY POPULATION)
According to the UN's *World Urbanization Prospects 2018*, the biggest capital city is Tokyo in Japan. An estimated 37,468,302 people live within its metropolitan area.

First zebra crossing
In 1949, during a "Pedestrian Safety Week", 1,000 experimental black-and-white-striped pedestrian crossings were installed across the UK. The first permanent "zebra" crossing appeared in Slough, Berkshire, UK, in 1951.

Shortest street
On 28 Oct 2006, Ebenezer Place in Wick, Caithness, UK, was verified to be 2.05 m (6 ft 9 in) long. The UK is also home to the **shortest stretch of prohibited parking** – a 43-cm-long (1-ft 5-in) set of double-yellow lines on Stafford Street in Norwich, Norfolk.

Yonge Street, running north out of Toronto in Ontario, Canada, has been cited as the **longest street**. The oft-quoted 1,896-km (1,178-mi) length is now discounted as that incorporates Highway 11. However, the urban straight-line stretch between Toronto's harbour front and the commuter town of Newmarket is still an impressive 48 km (29.8 mi).

The **narrowest street** is Spreuerhofstrasse in Reutlingen, Germany. Measured in Feb 2006, it is 31 cm (1 ft 0.2 in) at its most slender.

CITY WITH THE WORST AIR POLLUTION
A World Health Organization (WHO) report from May 2018 revealed that Kanpur in India had an average PM$_{2.5}$ level of 173 micrograms per m^3 for 2016. That's more than 17 times higher than the WHO's advised maximum of 10 micrograms per m^3. The term PM$_{2.5}$ describes particulate matter with a diameter of less than 2.5 micrometres, such as soot, dust and ash. Prolonged exposure to these pollutants can cause lung and heart conditions.

MOST POPULAR CITY FOR TOURISM
Bangkok in Thailand is the favourite tourist destination for international travellers, according to the 2018 Mastercard Global Destination Cities Index. The influx of foreign tourists to the city grew by 3.3% to 20.05 million in 2016, helping the Thai capital surpass tourism hubs such as London, UK, with 19.83 million visitors, and Paris, France, with 17.44 million.

MOST EXPENSIVE CITY FOR A WEEKEND BREAK
A weekend visit to the Danish capital of Copenhagen will set visitors back an average of $2,503 (£1,864). The sum would cover two nights at a five-star hotel, car rental, four meals for two and some light shopping. This finding is based on Deutsche Bank's *Mapping the World's Prices* report, published on 22 May 2018. By comparison, a similar weekend in Paris, France, came in at $1,861 (£1,386).

HIGHEST PERMANENT HUMAN SETTLEMENT

La Rinconada sits on Mount Ananea in south-east Peru at an altitude of 5,100 m (16,732 ft) and is home to around 50,000 people. With temperatures usually below 0°C (32°F) and access only by means of a dangerous mountain path, it has few tourists and lacks plumbing, rubbish collection, sanitation, hospitals and hotels. The economy is mostly based on unregulated gold mines.

Miners here work unpaid for 30 days, but are then allowed a day or so when they can take away all the gold they find.

LARGEST URBAN POPULATION (AS A PROPORTION OF TOTAL)

The UN's *World Urbanization Prospects 2018* report reveals that 12 countries and/or territories have a 100% urban population. They are Singapore, the Cayman Islands, Sint Maarten, Nauru, Monaco, Gibraltar, Kuwait, Vatican City, Anguilla, Bermuda, Macau and Hong Kong (below), the most populous with 7.4 million inhabitants.

LARGEST CAR-FREE URBAN AREA

Automobiles are entirely absent from the Medina of Fez in Morocco. Also known as Fes el-Bali, it is the oldest walled section of the city of Fez, dating back to the turn of the 9th century CE. The Medina is home to more than 156,000 people, but none of them are allowed to drive cars within the city walls. It helps that the narrow ancient streets – some no more than 60 cm (2 ft) wide – make it virtually impossible for cars to get through.

AUG 8 In 2010, a total of 102 charity fundraisers bare all on the Green Scream roller-coaster at Adventure Island in Southend-on-Sea, Essex, UK – the **most naked people on a theme-park ride**.

AUG 9 Adventurer Ed Stafford (UK) becomes the **first person to walk the length of the Amazon River** in 2010. His marathon journey covers 7,226 km (4,490 mi) and lasts 2 years 129 days.

SUSTAINABILITY

Hydroelectric power: China's 332 gigawatts (GW) of installed capacity produces 1,130 TWh of electricity, or 28.4% of the world's hydroelectric energy. The term "installed capacity" refers to the maximum amount of electricity that can be generated under optimal conditions.

Wind power: the USA has 72.6 GW of installed capacity, producing some 193 TWh of electricity – or 23% of global wind energy. The wind power sector in China is rapidly expanding, however, and may soon surpass that of the USA.

The source for all of the above records is the International Energy Agency's (IEA) *Key World Energy Statistics* report from 2017. For the **largest producer of electricity from solar power**, see opposite.

LONGEST JOURNEY BY ELECTRIC VEHICLE (SINGLE CHARGE; NON-SOLAR)

On 16–17 Oct 2017, an electric car built by IT Asset Partners, Inc. (USA) travelled 1,608.54 km (999.5 mi) on one charge at Auto Club Speedway in Fontana, California, USA. Named *The Phoenix*, the vehicle was made from more than 90% recycled consumer e-waste. It was driven by its co-creator Eric Lundgren (USA, above).

Largest producer of electricity from...

Renewable sources: China generates around 25% of the world's renewable energy – some 1,398 terawatt-hours (TWh) of electricity. (A terawatt-hour represents a unit of 1 trillion watts operating for 60 min.) That would be enough energy to supply around 930 million Chinese households with electricity for a whole year.

LARGEST OFFSHORE WIND FARM

The 659-MW Walney Extension Wind Farm opened on 8 Sep 2018. Located in the Irish Sea, around 19 km (11.8 mi) off the coast of Walney Island, UK, it covers 145 km² (56 sq mi) of ocean – similar in size to 20,000 soccer pitches. The farm was developed by Danish company Ørsted at a cost of £1 bn ($1.3 bn).

Largest solar furnace

In Font-Romeu-Odeillo-Via, southern France, nearly 10,000 mirrors are arranged in an array to direct the Sun's rays on to a 2,000-m² (21,527-sq-ft) parabolic reflector. This then focuses the rays on to a small focal point where the temperature may reach 3,800°C (6,872°F). Scientists on the site, which was built in 1969, use the energy for a variety of purposes – such as creating hydrogen fuel cells and carrying out experiments in various fields, from solar engineering to testing materials for space vehicles.

FIRST HYDROGEN FUEL-CELL PASSENGER TRAIN

Developed by Alstom (FRA), the Coradia iLint is a zero-emission train powered by cells that convert hydrogen and oxygen into electricity. On 16 Sep 2018, two of these trains began commercial operation in northern Germany, running a scheduled service between Buxtehude (a suburb of Hamburg) and the nearby towns of Bremerhaven and Cuxhaven.

Most efficient solar cell (prototype)

In 2014, an experimental photovoltaic cell was produced that converts 46% of sunlight energy into electricity. It was developed jointly by the Fraunhofer Institute for Solar Energy Systems (DEU), research institute CEA-Leti and manufacturing firm Soitec (both FRA).

Most powerful tidal power station

South Korea's Sihwa Lake Tidal Power Station has an output capacity of 254 megawatts (MW), generated by 10 submerged turbines, each rated at 25.4 MW. That's enough to power around 54,000 homes.

The **most powerful wind turbine** is the V164-9.5 MW, manufactured by Danish company MHI Vestas Offshore Wind. Launched on 6 Jun 2017, it can generate 9.5 MW of energy. The turbine houses three 80-m-long (262-ft) blades, each one as long as nine double-decker London buses.

Largest solar-powered stadium

The exterior of the National Stadium in Kaohsiung, Chinese Taipei, features 8,844 solar panels spanning 14,155 m² (152,363 sq ft). It has the potential to generate 1.14 gigawatt-hours (GWh) – a gigawatt is 1 billion watts – of electricity each year. That's enough to power 80% of its operating needs. If generated by conventional power stations, this would result in some 660 tonnes (727 US tons) of CO_2 entering the atmosphere annually.

HIGHEST RATE OF WASTE RECYCLING

Germany reclaims an unrivalled 66.1% of its waste, as revealed in a 2017 report published by environmental research consultants Eunomia (UK) and the European Environmental Bureau. Shown above, workers sort plastic garbage on a conveyor belt at the ALBA Group plant in Berlin, which recycles approximately 140,000 tonnes (154,000 US tons) of material annually.

> The wind farm's 189 turbines, each 190 m (623 ft) tall, create enough renewable energy to power 590,000 homes a year.

AUG 10 — "FireGuy" Brant Matthews (CAN) lights up the 2018 Wisconsin State Fair with the **most torches extinguished by fire eating in one minute** – 101 – in West Allis, Wisconsin, USA.

AUG 11 — In 2014, illusionist and escapologist Alexis Arts (ITA, b. Danilo Audiello) achieves the **fastest time to escape from a regulated Posey straitjacket** – 2.84 sec – in Foggia, Italy.

LARGEST PRODUCER OF ELECTRICITY FROM SOLAR POWER

According to the IEA's 2017 report *Key World Energy Statistics*, China generates around 45 TWh of electricity from photovoltaic power annually, drawing on 43.2 GW of installed capacity. That represents 18.3% of all worldwide solar-energy production.

Pictured far left is a solar farm in Chunjiangyuan, Zhejiang Province, while the main photograph shows China's second panda-themed solar plant in Guigang, Guangxi Province. Seen below is a rack of solar panels in the car park at the plant of Anhui Quanchai Engine Co., in eastern China's Anhui Province.

HIGHEST ENVIRONMENTAL PERFORMANCE INDEX (COUNTRY)

The 2018 edition of the *Environmental Performance Index*, produced jointly by Yale University and Columbia University (both USA) since 2002, ranks Switzerland as the country with the best environmental record. It earned an overall score of 87.42. The index is based on an assessment of 24 indicators, including tree-cover loss, methane and CO_2 emissions, waste-water treatment and heavy-metal pollution.

MOST FLOATING DEBRIS REMOVED BY A TRASH INTERCEPTOR IN ONE MONTH

Between 1 and 30 Apr 2017, Mr. Trash Wheel, a floating trash interceptor operated by the Waterfront Partnership of Baltimore (USA), removed 57.4 tonnes (63.3 US tons) of debris from the mouth of the Jones Falls River in Baltimore, Maryland, USA. Mr. Trash Wheel is a waterwheel- and solar-powered conveyor that has prevented some 847.6 tonnes (934.3 US tons) of floating debris (including an estimated 561,180 plastic bottles) from reaching the Chesapeake Bay.

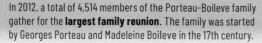

AUG 12 In 2012, a total of 4,514 members of the Porteau-Boileve family gather for the **largest family reunion**. The family was started by Georges Porteau and Madeleine Boileve in the 17th century.

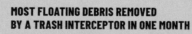

AUG 13 The **fastest speed for a car driven blindfolded** – 322.69 km/h (200.51 mph) – is set by Mike Newman (UK) in North Yorkshire, UK, in 2014. He has been blind since the age of eight.

ROUND-UP

Highest GDP

Gross domestic product (GDP) is the value of all the goods and services produced by a country in one year. World Bank ranks the USA as the country with the largest GDP – its economy was worth $19.39 tn (£14.36 tn) in 2017. If cost-of-living differences are taken into account, however, then China is the record holder, with a GDP of $23.3 tn (£17.2 tn).

Highest GDP per capita

One way of expressing a country's economic health is to divide its GDP by its population. As of 2017, the World Bank rates Luxembourg as the country with the highest GDP per capita: $104,103 (£77,148). If the cost of living is taken into account, however, then Qatar is the record holder, with a GDP per capita of $128,378 (£95,138).

The same source ranks the African country of Burundi as having the **lowest GDP per capita**, with $320 (£237). Again, allowing for cost-of-living differences, the values rise and the Central African Republic moves to last place on $725 (£537).

Largest annual trade surplus (country)

When the value of a country's exports exceeds that of its imports, it creates a trade surplus, or positive balance of trade. According to World Bank figures for 2016 (the latest year for which internationally comparable data is available), Germany has the largest trade surplus, with a balance of trade of $274.7 bn (£223.2 bn).

According to the World Bank, the USA has the **largest annual trade deficit** – $504.7 bn (£410.2 bn) – as of the same date.

Lowest rate of inflation

As noted in the Apr 2018 edition of the International Monetary Fund's (IMF) *World Economic Outlook*, Saudi Arabia and Chad both had an average rate of inflation of -0.9% during 2017.

Highest rate of VAT

Based on data collected by professional services firm KPMG, Hungary's Value Added Tax (VAT) rate was 27% in 2018.

The Caribbean nation of Aruba has the **highest top-level rate of income tax**, based on data collated by KPMG in 2018. Anyone with an annual gross income of more than 304,369 Aruban florins ($168,602; £132,708) is subject to a tax rate of 59%.

The United Arab Emirates had the **highest corporate tax rate** as of 2018, according to the same source. The emirates of Dubai, Sharjah and Abu Dhabi all levy a tax of 55% of operating profits on businesses with an income greater than 5 million dirhams ($1.3 m; £1 m).

Most journalists in jail

A total of 272 journalists were in prison in 2017 as a result of their work, according to the annual global census by the Committee to Protect Journalists (CPJ), a New York City-based non-profit organization. This makes 2017 the worst year for media imprisonment since the CPJ began documenting incarcerations in 1990.

YOUNGEST UNICEF GOODWILL AMBASSADOR

On 20 Nov 2018 – World Children's Day – Millie Bobby Brown (UK, b. 19 Feb 2004) was named as a UNICEF ambassador, aged 14 years 274 days. The actress is best known for playing Eleven on the show *Stranger Things* (inset), which has earned her an Emmy nomination (see p.205). Her new role will see Millie promote children's rights and help spotlight issues affecting young people, such as bullying.

LARGEST FLAG FLOWN

On 2 Nov 2017, Trident Support Flagpoles and Sharjah Investment and Development Authority (both UAE) flew a 2,448.56-m² (26,356-sq-ft) flag in Sharjah, UAE. At around twice the size, the **largest flag flown while skydiving (parachute jump;** inset**)** measured 4,885.65 m² (52,588.70 sq ft) and was achieved by Skydive Dubai (UAE) on 29 Nov 2018. That's around 10 times the area of a basketball court!

HIGHEST COMPARATIVE PRICE LEVELS

According to data from the Organisation for Economic Co-operation and Development (OECD) for Aug 2018, Iceland has higher prices than any other country. A standard basket of goods worth $100 (£76.81) in the USA would cost the equivalent of $149 (£114.45) in Iceland. Using the same comparison, the next priciest countries are Switzerland ($138; £106) and Denmark ($127; £97.55).

AUG 14 Maria Paraskeva (CYP) makes a childhood dream come true by walking down the aisle wearing the **longest wedding veil** in 2018 in Larnaca, Cyprus. It measures 6.96 km (4.32 mi).

AUG 15 In 2003, Ron Hunt (USA) falls face-first on to a 46-cm (1-ft 6-in) drill bit – and survives! The bit is extracted by surgeons in Nevada, USA, to become the **largest object removed from a human skull**.

HIGHEST DEFENCE BUDGET

No country spends more on defence than the USA. According to the latest figures from the Stockholm International Peace Research Institute (SIPRI), the United States Department of Defense (which coordinates budgets for the US Armed Forces) received $609.758 bn (£451.878 bn) in 2017 – up from $600 bn (£487.6 bn) in 2016.

OLDEST CURRENT PRIME MINISTER

On 10 May 2018, Mahathir bin Mohamad (MYS, b. 10 Jul 1925) was inaugurated as Malaysia's prime minister, aged 92 years 304 days, in the capital city, Kuala Lumpur. Mohamad had previously held the office from 1981 to 2003.

Most patent applications

Based on figures compiled by the World Intellectual Property Organization, 1,381,594 patents were filed in China in 2017 (the latest year for which data is available). This includes 1,245,709 patents originating from within the country and 135,885 from overseas.

Lowest urban population (as a proportion of total)

According to the United Nations' *World Urbanization Prospects 2018* report, the title of least-urbanized country is jointly held by two Pacific island nations: Tokelau and the Wallis and Futuna Islands. Neither has any settlements large enough to meet the UN's definition of an urban agglomeration. In other words, they have a 100% rural population.

Most expensive city in which to buy a car

Singapore is the priciest city in the world for purchasing new automobiles according to the *2018 Mapping the World's Prices* report by Deutsche Bank, which lists the cost of goods and services in 50 major cities. Largely as a result of taxes aimed at discouraging car ownership, an average car here will set you back $86,412 (£64,359), nearly twice that of the next most expensive city – Copenhagen in Denmark – at $44,062 (£32,817).

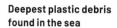

Deepest plastic debris found in the sea

A plastic bag was found at a depth of 10,898 m (35,754 ft) in the Mariana Trench in the western Pacific Ocean, as reported in Oct 2018 in the journal *Marine Policy*.

Largest recyclable material mosaic (image)

On 29 Jul 2018, Memories Events Management (UAE) and MTV SAL (LBN) presented a 971.37-m² (10,455-sq-ft) mosaic in Dbayeh, Lebanon. The artwork, which featured around 10,000 pieces of recyclable material, depicted three ships on the sea.

Most wastewater turned into potable water in 24 hours

On 16 Feb 2018, the Groundwater Replenishment System (USA) recycled 378,541,208 litres (100,000,008 US gal) of wastewater into H_2O pure enough to drink in Orange County, California, USA.

Longest career as a...

• **Hurricane hunter:** Meteorologist Dr James "Jim" McFadden (USA) has worked at the National Oceanic and Atmospheric Administration since 1962 and routinely flies into tropical cyclones to conduct storm research. The first mission he flew was to examine Hurricane Inez on 6 Oct 1966, and his most recent was on 10 Oct 2018 during reconnaissance of Hurricane Michael – giving him an active "hunting" career of 52 years 4 days.

• **Worker for the same company:** As of 2 Apr 2018, Walter Orthmann (BRA) had worked at textiles producer Industrias Renaux (now RenauxView) in Brusque, Santa Catarina, Brazil, for 80 years 75 days. His first day was on 17 Jan 1938.

HIGHEST RATE OF INFLATION

According to the Apr 2018 edition of the IMF's *World Economic Outlook*, Venezuela has the greatest rate of inflation. It averaged 1,087.5% during 2017, rising to an end-of-period rate of 2,818.4%. The IMF's projections for 2018 suggest that the rate has risen exponentially higher since then, with average annual inflation estimated at an eye-watering 13,864.6%.

MOST MONEY LOST BY A NATION TO GAMBLING

According to figures published in May 2017 by international gambling organization H2 Gambling Capital, the average adult Australian lost $1,052 (AUS$1,455; £854) on betting in 2016. Singapore came second, with an average of $674 (£547) per capita, and Ireland was third with $501 (£407). Approximately 70% of Australians are thought to participate in some form of gambling – particularly the ubiquitous electronic poker machines, or "pokies".

As of 16 Aug 2018, when this photo was taken, a chicken cost some 14.6 million bolivars ($2.20; £1.73) in Venezuela's capital, Caracas.

AUG 16 *Star of the King*, a 92-min musical tribute to Elvis Presley, debuts in Hungary in 2002. Composer Adám Lörincz (HUN, b. 1 Jun 1988) is aged 14 years 76 days – the **youngest composer of a musical**.

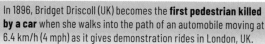

AUG 17 In 1896, Bridget Driscoll (UK) becomes the **first pedestrian killed by a car** when she walks into the path of an automobile moving at 6.4 km/h (4 mph) as it gives demonstration rides in London, UK.

145

ROBOTS

WHAT IS A ROBOT?

Over the next decade, we're going to see robots take a much more active role in our day-to-day lives. With sensors and computers that are faster and cheaper than ever before, it's becoming possible for robots to make their way out of research labs and into the real world. But depending on what you decide to call a robot, they've already been a part of our lives for years. So what is a robot, anyway?

Even among roboticists, there's no universally accepted definition of what is – and isn't – a robot. Most would probably agree, however, with this very basic definition: a robot is a device that can sense, think and act. This means that it can perceive its environment, make a decision based on what it sees, and then, as a result, do something that changes the world around it.

Beyond this, the definition starts to get tricky. The robot servants of 1950s science fiction (see Robby the Robot, pp.166–67) still haven't emerged, but many of their roles are now filled by autonomous smart devices. Even some older technologies, such as domestic thermostats, fulfil the criteria of sensing, thinking (albeit in a fairly simple way) and acting autonomously. Conversely, many things that look more like what we'd expect to see in a robot – such as most quadrotors and military robots – are actually remote-controlled by humans and don't fit with the traditional definition of a robot.

In practice, the word "robot" means different things in different contexts, covering the many ways in which humans are using automation today. A good analogy would be the word "animal", which encompasses an astonishingly broad range of things, from microscopic blobs to elephants.

AN ECOSYSTEM OF ROBOTS

The world of robots, like the natural world, is one of specialization. Roboticists can be wildly creative with their designs, shaping them to meet the needs of a particular project or to take advantage of a new technology. There are robots that look like humans, robots that look like animals and robots that look like nothing found in nature. Robots can range in size from enormous to microscopic. They can be stronger than us and faster than us and – in some ways – smarter than us.

Despite how far the technology has come (see ASIMO, below), it still has a long way to go. The robots on the following pages represent the record-breaking state of the art, but even they can't match the adaptability and intelligence of a typical toddler. Over the next few years, however, these records will be broken by even faster, stronger and smarter generations of robots.

No matter what they look like, remember that robots are designed to help us. They exist to do things that are too dull, too dirty or too dangerous for humans, and while they can't yet do everything that we might wish, there are already many amazing robots out there, hard at work making our lives better.

EVAN ACKERMAN, ROBOTICS JOURNALIST

GWR's robotics consultant, Evan Ackerman, has been writing about robots for over a decade. He started his own robotics blog in 2007, and now writes for IEEE Spectrum magazine.

What was your first experience with robots?
I didn't know much about robots when I started writing about them, but I remember going to my first robotics conference and being amazed at how many different kinds of robots there were. It's still amazing, which is why I keep writing about them.

Why are robots so bad at things people find easy?
We humans have a lifetime of experience understanding the world around us, but robots don't. They can learn to do specific things very well, but they don't have common sense like we do, which means that it's very difficult for them to adapt to new situations or understand things they haven't been specifically programmed to understand.

Should I be worried about robots taking my job or taking over the world?
Probably not! Robots are just another kind of technology. As they get to be more useful, some jobs will be changed, but they won't be replacing most humans anytime soon. And they're not likely to take over the world unless we program them to.

How can I get a robot of my own?
A robot vacuum cleaner – like a Roomba – is an easy way to add a robot to your life in a useful way. If you want to try making your own robot, a good place to start is with a simple robotics kit that also teaches you programming.

Do you have a favourite robot?
I love all robots equally, but there are some I love a little more than others… I'm especially fond of Keepon (a squishy yellow dancing robot), PR2 (a research robot with two arms) and all five of my Roombas.

BionicOpter

JAXA's Int-Ball

Boston Dynamics

ASIMO

One of the most recognizable humanoid robots is ASIMO, from Honda Research (JPN). This group began working on humanoid robots back in 1986. They started with a set of biped robots known as the "E" series, before moving on to the "P" series humanoids and then to the famous ASIMO platform in 2000. As of 2019, some 33 years after E0 took its first steps, the company was still actively involved with humanoid robot research (see p.152), making this the **longest-running humanoid robot development programme.**

These robots are shown to scale. The P2 was 182 cm (5 ft 11 in) tall.

ASIMO

2000–present

P3

P2

1993–97

P1

E5

1991–93

E1

1987–91

E0

1986

Atlas

Robocar

Kengoro

Robby the Robot

DARPA ALV

In 1985, DARPA – see far right – unveiled their ALV (Autonomous Land Vehicle): the first vehicle capable of continuous self-driving at practical speeds. ALV used a similar combination of laser scanners and cameras to navigate as the current generation of driverless cars. The hulking eight-wheeled design allowed ALV to go off-road, and it could also drive itself at night, in the rain and in snow.

STARSHIP DELIVERY ROVER

For smaller robotic vehicles, sidewalks can be a great way of getting around in cities and suburbs. Starship Technologies' robots pick up small items from local shops and deliver them to destinations within a few kilometres, using an array of sensors to navigate autonomously, avoiding pedestrians, waiting for traffic lights and using zebra crossings. The robots have been tested in 100 cities, making 20,000 deliveries and covering more than 201,000 km (125,000 mi) in the process.

WAYMO SELF-DRIVING CARS

Waymo's robot cars reached 16 million km (10 million mi) driven on public roads in Oct 2018, the **greatest aggregate distance driven by driverless cars**. Waymo, which was spun off from Google in 2016, has been testing autonomous vehicles in 25 cities across the USA, gaining experience in places with different driving conditions. Real-world testing is the best way for autonomous cars to learn how to drive safely, but Waymo is also testing in simulation — their virtual cars drive 16 million km through virtual cities every single day!

NUTONOMY SELF-DRIVING TAXI

In 2016, nuTonomy launched the **first self-driving taxi service** in Singapore. Six robotic cars could be hailed through an app and used to get around the One-North business district, reducing reliance on private vehicles. As the average car spends 95% of its time parked, nuTonomy hopes that one day autonomous taxis, which spend most of their time driving, could reduce the number of cars on Singapore's roads by more than two-thirds.

THE DRIVE TOWARDS SELF-DRIVING

ROBOTS

ROBOCAR

The robots most likely to change our lives in the near future are autonomous cars. Drivers in cities such as Los Angeles spend an average of about an hour a day commuting; if their cars were able to take care of themselves, that time might be spent working, relaxing or perhaps even sleeping.

Many important automotive technologies were first perfected for use in motor racing, and autonomous driving systems can learn a lot from the rigours of competition. Leading the pack in this field is Robocar, a futuristic self-driving vehicle from British start-up Roborace,

currently being tested at Formula E electric-car racing events.

Robocar replaces a human driver with an AI that runs on its built-in NVIDIA Drive PX2 computer. The robot's decisions are based on data from an array of sensors, including radar, LIDAR cameras and GPS. At the moment, the car is still a little slower than human drivers, but its times are improving steadily. On 21 Mar 2019, Roborace demonstrated its robot's impressive pace by taking the car to 282.42 km/h (175.49 mph) – an average confirmed by the UK Timing Association – at Elvington in Yorkshire, UK, claiming the record for ❯**fastest autonomous car**.

Lessons from the racetrack may eventually inform the design of self-driving systems on public roads. By calculating how sharp a turn can be safely taken at high speed, or identifying the point at which tyres lose traction during aggressive manoeuvres, AI-equipped vehicles will learn to drive more skilfully than most of us, especially in dangerous situations.

In the not-so-distant future, people will be able to take a ride in an autonomous taxi, comforted by the knowledge that the skills of a virtual racing driver will be on hand if anything goes wrong.

THE DARPA GRAND CHALLENGE

In 2004 and 2005, the US Government's Defense Advanced Research Projects Agency (DARPA) staged fully autonomous races across the Mojave Desert. These competitions attracted teams from all over the world (Carnegie Mellon University's *Sandstorm* pictured below) and initiated a new wave of autonomous vehicle research. Many of the self-driving car companies now active have their origins in the teams that entered these events.

FIRST AUTONOMOUS CAR TO COMPLETE THE GOODWOOD HILLCLIMB

Robocar navigated the 1.86-km (1.16-mi) Goodwood Hillclimb course in West Sussex, UK, in 1 min 15 sec on 13 Jul 2018. The driverless racing car was designed by Daniel Simon (DEU) and developed by Roborace (UK). The course – a winding, cambered (slightly convex) road running through an English country park – represents a daunting challenge for an AI-driven car. The road isn't clearly marked and a canopy of trees means that light levels vary from one part of the track to another. Trees also make GPS-based navigation patchy and unpredictable.

A top-mounted 360° camera and radio antenna are included in the car's navigation system.

Robocar uses GPS to monitor its position, checking the data against a map of the track created during practice runs.

The car's bodywork is made from carbon fibre.

The front radar is set within the nose cone. Another radar is mounted in the rear.

Each wheel has its own dedicated electric motor. Together, they generate more than 540 kW (720 hp).

Cooling outlets help maintain Robocar's 58-kWh battery at an optimum temperature.

LIDARs – light detection and ranging sensors – are fitted at the front corners, sides and rear of the vehicle.

ROBORACE

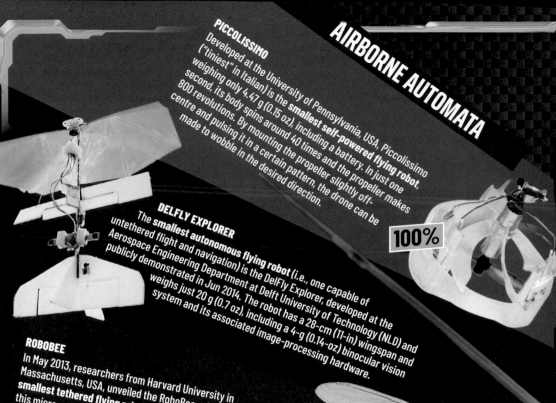

PICCOLISSIMO

Developed at the University of Pennsylvania, USA, Piccolissimo ("tiniest" in Italian) is the **smallest self-powered flying robot**, weighing only 4.47 g (0.15 oz), including a battery. In just one second, its body spins around 40 times and the propeller makes 800 revolutions. By mounting the propeller slightly off-centre and pulsing it in a certain pattern, the drone can be made to wobble in the desired direction.

100%

DELFLY EXPLORER

The **smallest autonomous flying robot** (i.e., one capable of untethered flight and navigation) is the DelFly Explorer, developed at the Aerospace Engineering Department at Delft University of Technology (NLD) and publicly demonstrated in Jun 2014. The robot has a 28-cm (11-in) wingspan and weighs just 20 g (0.7 oz), including a 4-g (0.14-oz) binocular vision system and its associated image-processing hardware.

The wings have a carbon-fibre frame and are covered with a thin foil. The wingspan is 63 cm (2 ft 0.8 in).

ROBOBEE

In May 2013, researchers from Harvard University in Massachusetts, USA, unveiled the RoboBee, which is the **smallest tethered flying robot insect**. At 80 mg (0.0028 oz), this micro aerial vehicle weighs slightly less than a real bee and it's able to do many of the same things – including taking off, flying controllably, hovering and landing again. The current version relies on its tether to supply control signals and power, but fully independent versions are in development.

100%

An electric current passes through four nitinol (nickel-titanium) shape-memory-alloy muscles, enabling the tail and head to move.

100%

IONOCRAFT

Flying robots have been able to get smaller by copying insects, but another technology might enable them to get smaller still. An ionocraft has no moving parts; instead, it generates plasma, which creates a flow of air that lifts it upwards. In a paper published on 6 Jun 2018, the University of California, Berkeley (USA) revealed the **smallest ionocraft** – a drone just 4 cm² (0.6 sq in) in size and weighing 67 mg (0.0023 oz).

ROBOTS

BIONICOPTER

Since 2006, the German automation company Festo has been experimenting with different bionic robots to explore how mechanical systems can benefit from designs inspired by animals. They've developed swarms of mechanical ants, robotic seagulls and butterflies, and even a robot kangaroo.

BionicOpter is the **largest flying robot insect**, a mechanized, 3D-printed dragonfly designed to mimic the complex movements of its real-life counterpart. Dragonflies are among the most agile and skilled aviators on the planet. They catch 95% of the prey that they hunt; by

contrast, lions are only successful about 30% of the time. Part of the insects' skill comes from the structure of their bodies and wings, enabling them to perform tricks that most birds can't, such as flying sideways or hovering. Birds tend to fly more like aeroplanes do, generating lift with wings that have an airfoil shape. Insects, however, flap their wings rapidly to push air down and themselves up.

Like a real dragonfly, BionicOpter has two sets of wings that are independently controllable. The direction and intensity of the thrust from each wing can be used to move the robot in any direction. That sounds complicated, but its on-board

systems do most of the work – you can fly BionicOpter using just a smartphone (and a little practice). BionicOpter has a 63-cm (2-ft 0.8-in) wingspan, but weighs a mere 175 g (6.1 oz). To save weight, the head and tail are controlled with shape memory alloys (SMAs) – metal wires that shrink when heated and expand when cooled.

Integrating all of these electronic and mechanical systems into a robot that flies and looks like a real dragonfly is a remarkable feat. And the insights gained from its creation could one day be used to build nimble drones capable of weaving their way through crowded spaces or cluttered environments.

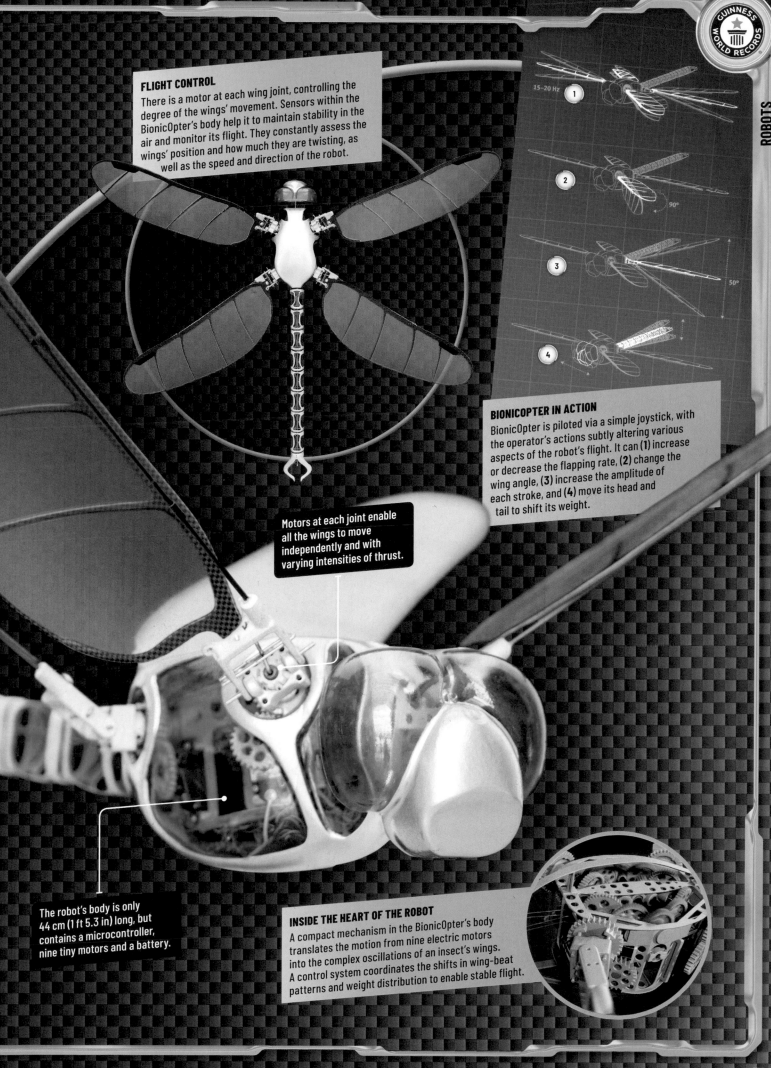

FLIGHT CONTROL

There is a motor at each wing joint, controlling the degree of the wings' movement. Sensors within the BionicOpter's body help it to maintain stability in the air and monitor its flight. They constantly assess the wings' position and how much they are twisting, as well as the speed and direction of the robot.

15–20 Hz

1

2
90°

3
50°

4

BIONICOPTER IN ACTION

BionicOpter is piloted via a simple joystick, with the operator's actions subtly altering various aspects of the robot's flight. It can (1) increase or decrease the flapping rate, (2) change the wing angle, (3) increase the amplitude of each stroke, and (4) move its head and tail to shift its weight.

Motors at each joint enable all the wings to move independently and with varying intensities of thrust.

The robot's body is only 44 cm (1 ft 5.3 in) long, but contains a microcontroller, nine tiny motors and a battery.

INSIDE THE HEART OF THE ROBOT

A compact mechanism in the BionicOpter's body translates the motion from nine electric motors into the complex oscillations of an insect's wings. A control system coordinates the shifts in wing-beat patterns and weight distribution to enable stable flight.

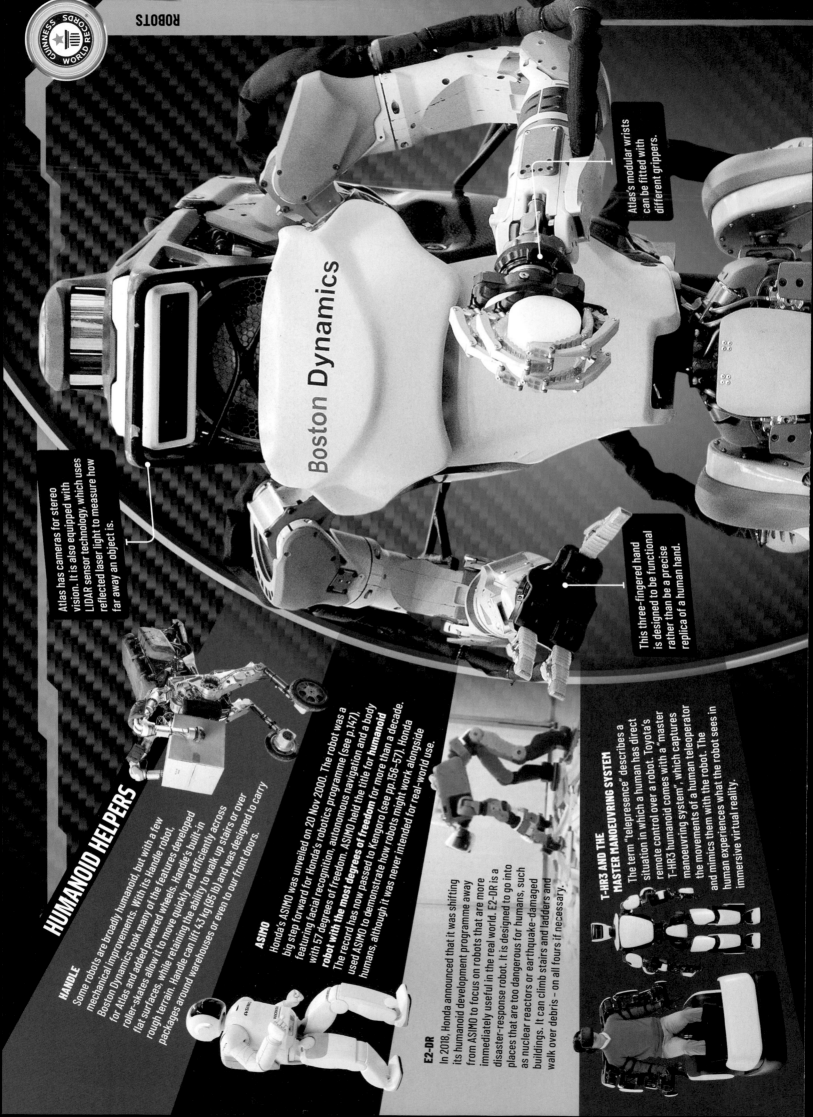

Atlas has cameras for stereo vision. It is also equipped with LIDAR sensor technology, which uses reflected laser light to measure how far away an object is.

Boston Dynamics

Atlas's modular wrists can be fitted with different grippers.

This three-fingered hand is designed to be functional rather than be a precise replica of a human hand.

HUMANOID HELPERS

HANDLE
Some robots are broadly humanoid, but with a few mechanical improvements. With its Handle robot, Boston Dynamics took many of the features developed for Atlas and added powered wheels. Handle's built-in roller-skates allow it to move quickly and efficiently across flat surfaces, while retaining the ability to walk up stairs or over rough terrain. Handle can lift 43 kg (95 lb) and was designed to carry packages around warehouses or even to our front doors.

ASIMO
Honda's ASIMO was unveiled on 20 Nov 2000. The robot was a big step forward for Honda's robotics programme (see p.147), featuring facial recognition, autonomous navigation and a body with 57 degrees of freedom. ASIMO held the title for **humanoid robot with the most degrees of freedom** for more than a decade. The record has now passed to Kengoro (see pp.156–57). Honda used ASIMO to demonstrate how robots might work alongside humans, although it was never intended for real-world use.

E2-DR
In 2018, Honda announced that it was shifting its humanoid development programme away from ASIMO to focus on robots that are more immediately useful in the real world. E2-DR is a disaster-response robot. It is designed to go into places that are too dangerous for humans, such as nuclear reactors or earthquake-damaged buildings. It can climb stairs and ladders and walk over debris - on all fours if necessary.

T-HR3 AND THE MASTER MANOEUVRING SYSTEM
The term "telepresence" describes a situation in which a human has direct control over a robot. Toyota's remote control over a robot. T-HR3 humanoid comes with a "master manoeuvring system", which captures the movements of a human teleoperator and mimics them with the robot. The and mimics them with the robot sees in human experiences what the robot sees in immersive virtual reality.

Like the hands, the flat, paddle-like feet are purely functional rather than designed to mimic human feet.

Sensors in Atlas's hydraulically powered legs help the robot to maintain its balance.

Boston Dynamics used 3D printing to integrate key systems, such as hydraulic actuators, directly into the robot's limbs. This reduces the number of individual parts required and the amount of wasted space, making Atlas lighter and more compact.

MOST EFFICIENT GAIT FOR A HUMANOID BIPEDAL ROBOT

DURUS was developed in 2016 by the AMBER Lab (USA), then located at the Georgia Institute of Technology. During treadmill tests, the robot recorded a cost-of-transport (CoT) of 1.02. A lower cost-of-transport number implies a more efficient system. The transport number implies a more efficient system. The able to move farther while using less energy. The CoT efficiency for humans is around 0.2 for walking and 0.8 for running.

ATLAS

Developing humanoid robots is a major challenge. But if we want robots to help us work, rescue us during disasters and care for us as we get older, a human-like form will make it easier for them to be useful in places designed for us.

In the short term, it's easier to make robots simpler than humans in some ways – for example, having just one or two fingers may be more than adequate for most tasks. Robots can also be designed with features that humans don't have, such as the ability to replace parts of themselves with specialized tools. This adaptability will be crucial when humanoid robots begin to be used for real-world jobs.

FIRST BIPEDAL HUMANOID ROBOT BACKFLIP

Boston Dynamics, the company that built Atlas, is famously secretive about its research projects. Most of its recent advances have been introduced to the world through short, enigmatic YouTube videos. We've seen Atlas sorting heavy boxes in a warehouse (left), jogging around the Boston Dynamics campus (below right) and, on 17 Nov 2017, performing an unprecedented backflip by a full-size humanoid robot (below left). This last feat, which took many attempts to get right, showed off Atlas's speed, strength and coordination.

In 2012, the US Defense Advanced Research Projects Agency (DARPA) announced two Robotics Challenges intended to show how robotic technology could be used to respond to catastrophic disasters. To win the challenge, robots would have to perform tasks such as clearing debris, using power tools and driving vehicles. DARPA chose Boston Dynamics to create a standard robot for the competition, and the first-generation Atlas robot was demonstrated in 2013.

Atlas uses compact hydraulic pistons to move its limbs, making it far more powerful than similar humanoid robots that use electric motors. The final DARPA Atlas was 1.9 m (6 ft 2 in) tall, weighed 156 kg (343 lb), and was strong enough to stand up by itself if it fell.

The DARPA Robotics Challenge ended in 2015, but Boston Dynamics continued upgrading Atlas's hardware while teaching it to do new things. In early 2016, they unveiled a more nimble version of Atlas that could cross rough terrain, carry heavy objects and recover from stumbles. Atlas later learned to run, jump and even perform the **first humanoid robot backflip** (see above), making it one of the most dynamic humanoid robots ever built.

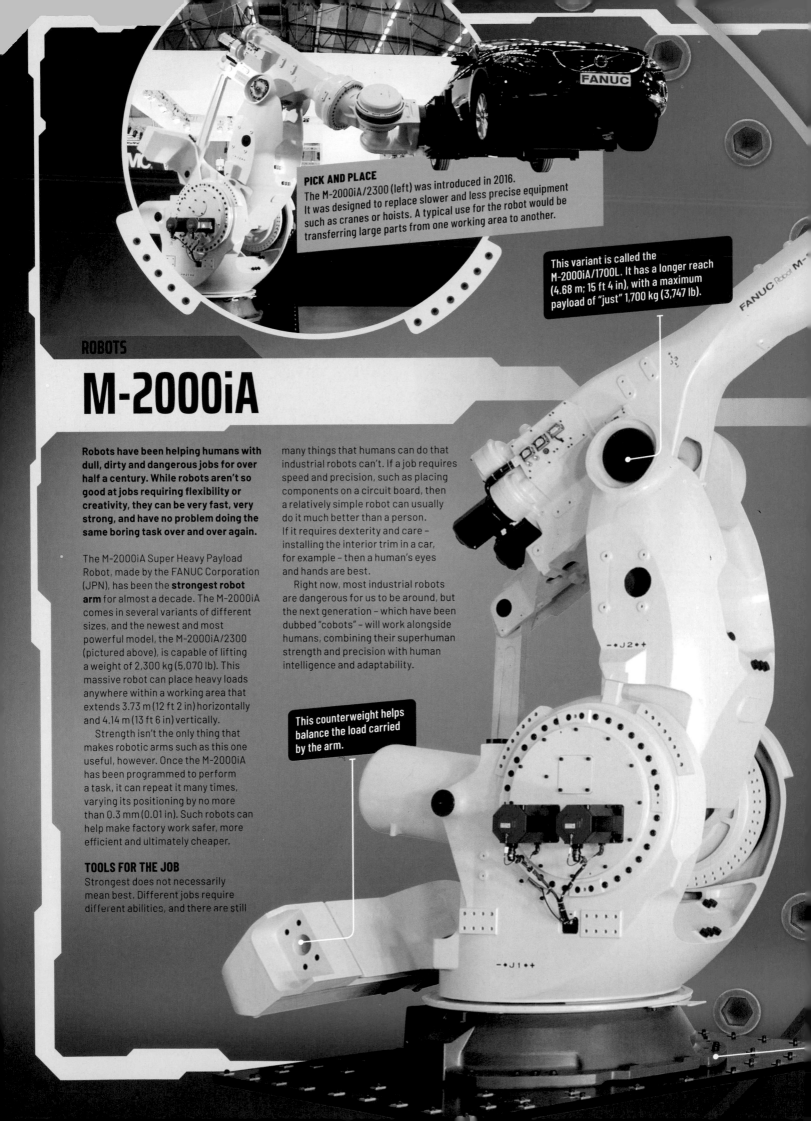

This variant is called the M-2000iA/1700L. It has a longer reach (4.68 m; 15 ft 4 in), with a maximum payload of "just" 1,700 kg (3,747 lb).

ROBOTS

M-2000iA

Robots have been helping humans with dull, dirty and dangerous jobs for over half a century. While robots aren't so good at jobs requiring flexibility or creativity, they can be very fast, very strong, and have no problem doing the same boring task over and over again.

The M-2000iA Super Heavy Payload Robot, made by the FANUC Corporation (JPN), has been the **strongest robot arm** for almost a decade. The M-2000iA comes in several variants of different sizes, and the newest and most powerful model, the M-2000iA/2300 (pictured above), is capable of lifting a weight of 2,300 kg (5,070 lb). This massive robot can place heavy loads anywhere within a working area that extends 3.73 m (12 ft 2 in) horizontally and 4.14 m (13 ft 6 in) vertically.

Strength isn't the only thing that makes robotic arms such as this one useful, however. Once the M-2000iA has been programmed to perform a task, it can repeat it many times, varying its positioning by no more than 0.3 mm (0.01 in). Such robots can help make factory work safer, more efficient and ultimately cheaper.

TOOLS FOR THE JOB
Strongest does not necessarily mean best. Different jobs require different abilities, and there are still many things that humans can do that industrial robots can't. If a job requires speed and precision, such as placing components on a circuit board, then a relatively simple robot can usually do it much better than a person. If it requires dexterity and care – installing the interior trim in a car, for example – then a human's eyes and hands are best.

Right now, most industrial robots are dangerous for us to be around, but the next generation – which have been dubbed "cobots" – will work alongside humans, combining their superhuman strength and precision with human intelligence and adaptability.

This counterweight helps balance the load carried by the arm.

The tool at the end of the arm can be custom made to suit the object it will be lifting.

HEAVY LIFTERS

MICROTUGS

MicroTugs are tiny experimental robots developed by Elliot Hawkes and David Christensen at Stanford University (all USA) in 2015. Each MicroTug weighs just 12 g (0.42 oz) but, thanks to special adhesive feet, it can drag a weight of 22.5 kg (49 lb 9 oz), making it the **strongest robot relative to size**. This is 1,875 times its own mass – equivalent to an adult human dragging a blue whale!

AUTOHAUL

Turning vehicles that have depended on humans for control into autonomous robots is an emerging trend. In Western Australia, the Rio Tinto mining company has converted a 197-tonne (217-US-ton) ore transport locomotive into the **heaviest robot**. This powerful vehicle, called AutoHaul, pulled its first 28,000-tonne (30,864-US-ton) load of iron ore on 10 Jul 2018, travelling around 280 km (174 mi) from the Mount Tom Price mine to the company's port at Cape Lambert.

UNIMATE

In 1961, the **first industrial robot** – a parts conveyor called Unimate – was installed in a General Motors assembly line at the Inland Fisher Guide Plant in Ewing Township, New Jersey, USA. The robot was used to transport die castings from a storage area to the assembly line. The first Unimate models weighed 1,814 kg (4,000 lb) and cost $25,000 (£8,900) each – that's the equivalent of around $210,000 (£160,400) in Jan 2019.

CANADARM2

Built by the Canadian Space Agency and installed on the International Space Station on 22 Apr 2001, Canadarm2 is a vital component of humanity's outpost in space. The slender 17.5-m (57-ft) arm is the **largest robotic arm in space**. It is used to ferry astronauts around during spacewalks, install parts and, because it operates in the microgravity of Earth's orbit, it can even grapple whole spacecraft to pull them up to the station's airlocks.

The massive forces exerted by the arm mean that you can't just put it anywhere. Its base has to be bolted into a reinforced concrete pad.

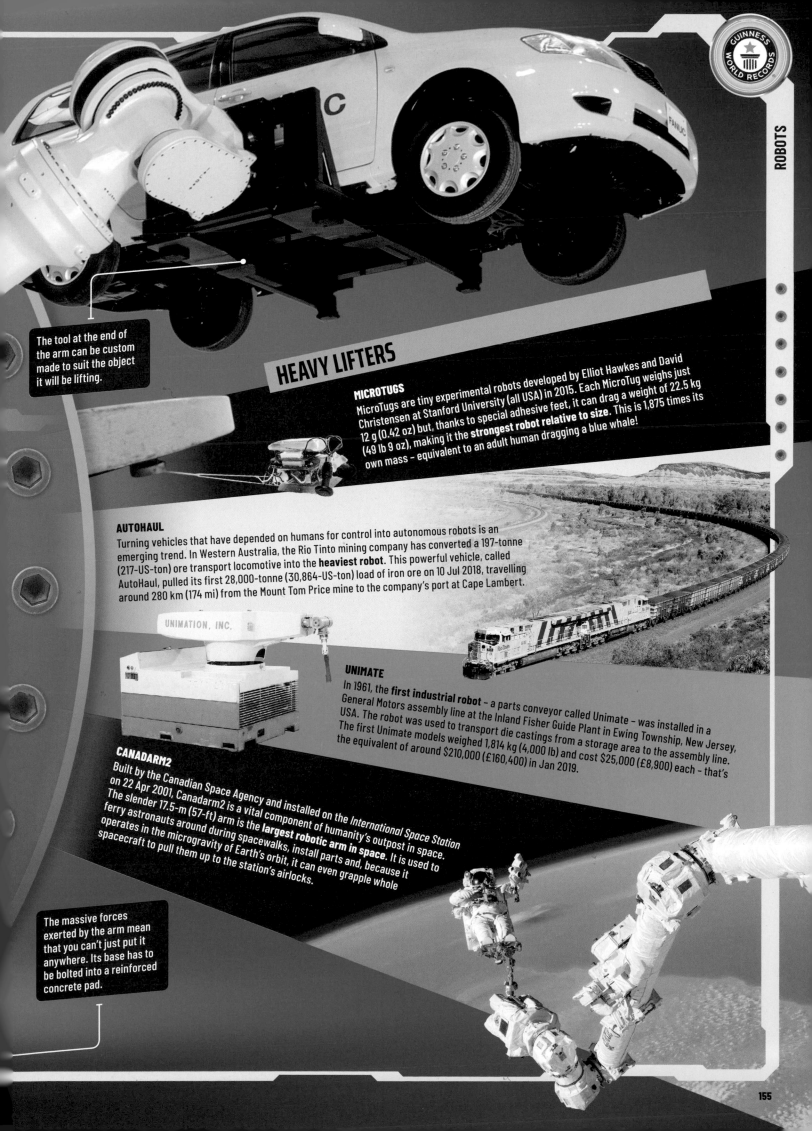

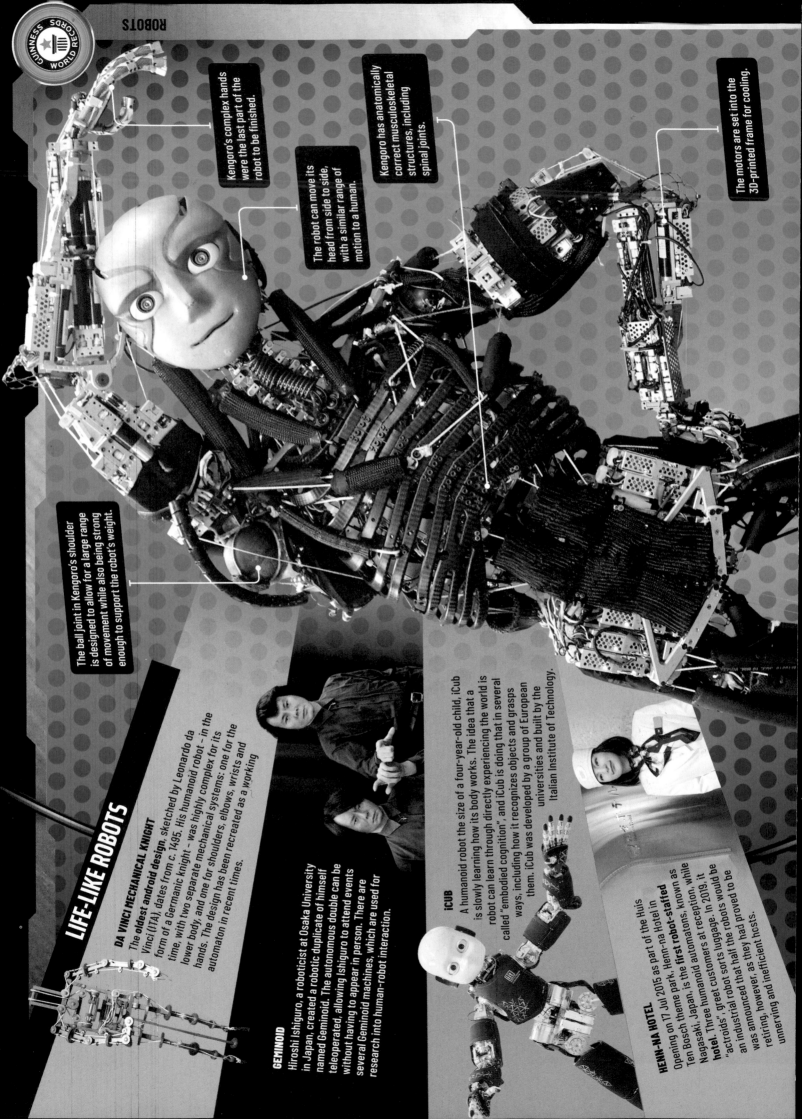

Kengoro's complex hands were the last part of the robot to be finished.

The robot can move its head from side to side, with a similar range of motion to a human.

Kengoro has anatomically correct musculoskeletal structures, including spinal joints.

The motors are set into the 3D-printed frame for cooling.

The ball joint in Kengoro's shoulder is designed to allow for a large range of movement while also being strong enough to support the robot's weight.

LIFE-LIKE ROBOTS

DA VINCI MECHANICAL KNIGHT

The **oldest android design**, sketched by Leonardo da Vinci (ITA), dates from c. 1495. His humanoid robot – in the form of a Germanic knight – was highly complex for its time, with two separate mechanical systems: one for its lower body, and one for the shoulders, elbows, wrists and hands. The design has been recreated as a working automaton in recent times.

GEMINOID

Hiroshi Ishiguro, a roboticist at Osaka University in Japan, created a robotic duplicate of himself named Geminoid. The autonomous double can be teleoperated, allowing Ishiguro to attend events without having to appear in person. There are several Geminoid machines, which are used for research into human-robot interaction.

iCUB

A humanoid robot the size of a four-year-old child, iCub is slowly learning how its body works. The idea that a robot can learn through directly experiencing the world is called "embodied cognition", and iCub is doing that in several ways, including how it recognizes objects and grasps them. iCub was developed by a group of European universities and built by the Italian Institute of Technology.

HENN-NA HOTEL

Opening on 17 Jul 2015 as part of the Huis Ten Bosch theme park, Henn-na Hotel in Nagasaki, Japan, is the **first robot-staffed hotel**. Three humanoid automatons at reception, known as "actroids", greet customers at reception, while androids greet customers and sort luggage. In 2019, it was announced, however, as they had proved to be unnerving and inefficient hosts.

Kengoro's "muscles" are actuated cables covered with protective foam to prevent them from catching on other parts.

HONDA 3E-A18

Robots don't need to look exactly like humans for us to interact with them in human-like ways. Standing about the same height as an eight-year-old, Honda's 3E-A18 is an empathic robot device with a face that can not only show emotions but also recognize and respond to people's expressions. It also has a soft exterior skin, which is designed to encourage users to touch and even hug it.

MOST CONSECUTIVE PUSH-UPS BY A HUMANOID ROBOT

In 2016, The University of Tokyo's 167-cm-tall (5-ft 5-in) robot Kengoro completed five push-ups in a row. The feat was performed as part of a test of Kengoro's evaporative cooling system, and the results were presented on 10 Oct 2016 at the International Conference on Intelligent Robots and Systems in Daejeon, South Korea.

Kengoro's knee is a hinge, just like a human knee, with added flexibility in the lower leg to allow the foot to rotate.

The replication of human body structure extends all the way to Kengoro's feet, which have fully articulated toes.

ROBOTS

KENGORO

KIROBO
On 9 Aug 2013, the **first companion robot in space** arrived at the *International Space Station* on board a supply capsule. Kirobo's purpose was to serve as a companion to astronaut Koichi Wakata, who began his mission in Nov 2013. Measuring 34 cm (1 ft 1 in), Kirobo has a wide range of physical motion and can communicate in Japanese.

Giving robots arms and legs is a good way of helping them get around environments built for humans, but most humanoid robots don't look or function exactly like we do. Human bodies are very complex and, for most tasks, it's not necessary for robots to mimic how our bodies are designed or how we look.

Robots that have certain human-like features and characteristics are called "anthropomorphic", while robots designed to replicate a human as closely as possible are called 'androids'. For example, many robots use two-fingered grippers to pick up objects, but some robots use more anthropomorphic hands, with four

fingers and a thumb. There are some things that only a human-like hand can do, but anthropomorphic hands are more expensive to build and harder to program. Androids are designed in the hope that real humans will be more comfortable interacting with robots that look like us. However, if the robot doesn't look exactly right, it runs the risk of looking creepy rather than comforting – a phenomenon known as the "uncanny valley".

Kengoro, developed at The University of Tokyo, was designed to closely mimic the humanoid body, using a similar structure of bones, joints and muscles. As a result, it has the **most degrees of freedom for a humanoid robot** – 174,

including 30 in each hand – which helps it to more accurately mirror the capabilities and range of motion of the human body.

Kengoro is strong enough to do push-ups and sit-ups, but with so many motors packed into its body, the robot can overheat if it works too hard. To mitigate this, Kengoro does what you do when you get too hot: it sweats. Its aluminium bones are constructed using a form of 3D printing called laser sintering that allows the creation of small channels to make them porous, like a sponge. The bones absorb heat from motors mounted to them, and by pumping water through its skeleton and allowing it to evaporate, Kengoro can keep cool as it works out.

Just like a human, Cassie has a hip with three degrees of freedom.

Keeping the motors close to the hips reduces the mass that has to swing during walking.

Rods transfer motion from the knee and motors that control the knee and ankle to their respective joints.

HIGH JUMPERS

SAND FLEA
The **highest-jumping robot** is Sand Flea, a shoebox-sized wheeled rover with a combustion-powered piston that can propel it to a height of 10 m (32 ft 9 in). An early version of the robot was built by Sandia National Labs in 2009 and updated by Boston Dynamics (both USA), who released a video of Sand Flea leaping on to the roof of a building in 2012.

MINITAUR
Ghost Robotics' Minitaur is the **most vertically agile quadruped robot**, with a vertical agility (a measurement of both jumping height and frequency) of 1.12 m/s (3.6 ft/s). Standing just 25 cm (9.8 in) high, it can open a full-size door by flipping itself up on to two legs, jumping upwards and punching the handle with its leading foot.

SALTO-1P
Developed at the University of California, USA, Salto-1P is almost entirely composed of a single leg, with a motor, spring, battery and controller packed in at the top. With a **vertical jumping agility** of 1.83 m/s (6 ft/s), it is the **most vertically agile robot**. Small thrusters plus a spinning "tail" keep the robot oriented in mid-air.

JUMPEN
Jumping is difficult for robots because it takes a lot of energy. Jumpen, a robot from the National Institute, Japan, has achieved – 106. Jumping is difficult for robots because it takes a lot of energy. Jumpen, a robot from the Nara College National Institute of Technology, Japan, has achieved **106. most skips by a robot in one minute** in Yamatōkoriyama.

◆ **most skips by a robot in one minute**

Cassie's actuated ankles allow it to stand in place without constantly moving its feet.

The robot's casing is made from a sturdy plastic designed to protect it during falls.

Flexible plates act as springs, cushioning the motors and allowing Cassie to cope with unpredictable terrain.

LONGEST-RUNNING ROBOT SUMO TOURNAMENT

Japanese technology firm Fujisoft has hosted the All Japan Robot-Sumo Tournament every year since 1990. The grand final of the most recent competition was held on 15–16 Dec 2018. Robot sumo is loosely based on the traditional Japanese sport. The "wrestlers" – two autonomous robots – vie to push each other out of the "ring", a 1.54-m-diameter (5-ft) circular platform. The robots' lightning-fast reactions mean that most bouts are over in seconds.

DOING THE ROBOT

Robots are known for their ability to perform precise movements over and over again. This makes them good assembly-line workers, and also surprisingly good dancers! On 1 Feb 2018, when Italian telecoms company TIM gathered 1,372 Alpha 1S robots to break the record for the ❍ most robots dancing simultaneously, there wasn't a single missed step. Other robotic dancers include SpotMini (whose dance to "Uptown Funk!" has had more than 5.5 million views on YouTube) and ANYmal (who is learning how to create its own dance moves). See p.163 for more about these quadruped robots.

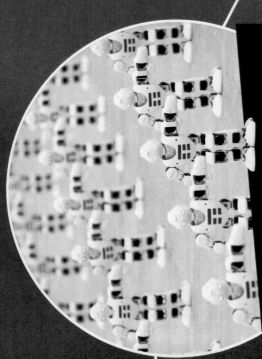

ROBOTS

CASSIE

Most robots move through the world slowly and carefully, because they tend to be both fragile and expensive. This is starting to change, however, as robots get more agile, using aggressive and dynamic movements to handle challenging terrain.

For robots, "challenging terrain" can mean anything from a steep flight of stairs to the surface of another planet. In order to navigate around different environments, robots of different shapes and sizes are learning how to do things like run and jump.

Designing robots that are agile is critical if we want them to take over the kinds of dirty and dangerous tasks that we humans would rather not do. Agility can be measured in different ways, but for robots a common agility metric is "vertical agility". This is the height a robot can reach with a single jump in Earth gravity, multiplied by the frequency with which that jump can be made.

Bipedal robot Cassie – designed by Agility Robotics (USA) and announced in 2017 – may not be able to jump, but it excels at dynamic walking. Rather than the carefully balanced and artificial-looking walk that most humanoid robots rely on, Cassie walks much more like a real human or an animal, actively maintaining its balance, even over rough terrain. It resembles an ostrich in appearance – a by-product of the roboticists developing a leg that's simultaneously lightweight, robust and very efficient.

It's hoped that the addition of sensors (to enable autonomy) and a pair of arms (to carry things) will enable Cassie to act as a robot courier, delivering packages directly to the door. During tests at the University of Michigan, USA, on 30 Jan 2019, a version of the Cassie robot (called Cassie Maize & Blue) achieved the **lowest temperature endured by a bipedal robot**, walking continuously in temperatures of -22°C (-8°F) for over an hour before collapsing.

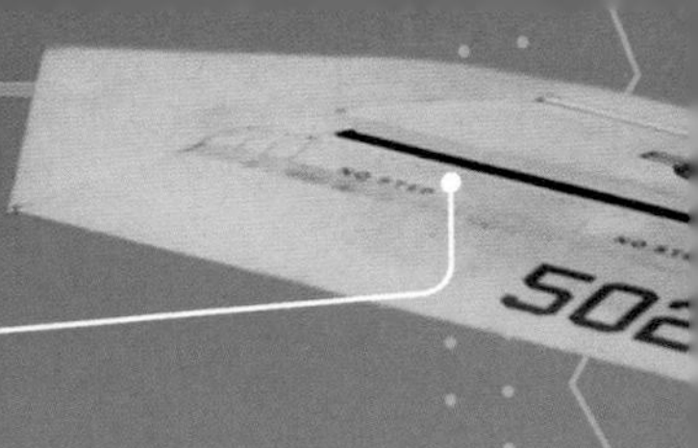

The X-47B has a high subsonic top speed and can fly at an altitude of 12,000 m (40,000 ft).

502

PILOTLESS PLANES

NASA X-43A "HYPER-X"

The X-43A was an experimental drone designed to test an engine called a scramjet. Given the risks associated with an untested engine design, a robot pilot was both safer and more efficient. The X-43A reached a top speed of Mach 9.6 (c. 10,000 km/h; 6,200 mph) during a flight test on 16 Nov 2004, making it the **fastest aircraft with an air-breathing engine**.

NASA
1
X-43A

AIRBUS ZEPHYR

A "high-altitude pseudo-satellite" (HAPS), the Airbus Zephyr is a solar-powered fixed-wing drone that can fly itself at 21,000 m (70,000 ft). Here, above other air traffic and weather, it can provide communications or surveillance services for weeks at a time. On its maiden test flight on 11 Jul–5 Aug 2018 (right), the Zephyr-S HAPS made the **longest flight by a UAV** – 25 days 23 hr 57 min – over Arizona, USA. It also achieved the **highest altitude by a fixed-wing UAV** – 22,589 m (74,113 ft) – on 13 Jul 2018.

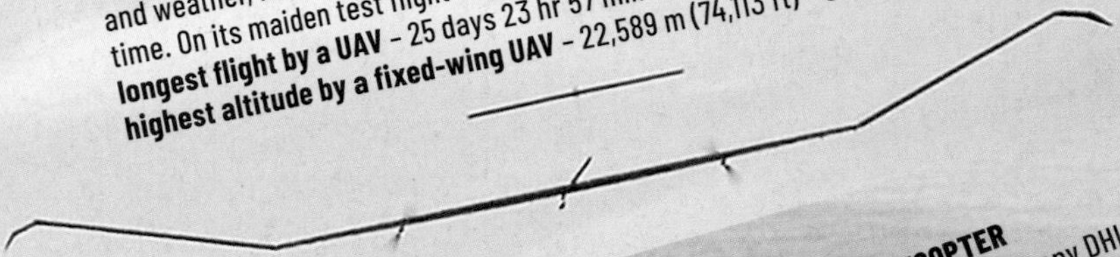

DHL PAKETCOPTER

Global shipping company DHL created its Paketcopter ("Parcelcopter") programme in late 2014, making headlines with the **first drone delivery service**, which ran between the German mainland and the island of Juist in the North Sea. The latest generation of the Paketcopter (built by Wingcopter; see p.138) made an appearance at the Oct 2018 launch of the Lake Victoria Challenge – a competition designed to test the effectiveness of drones as a way of delivering essential services to remote communities in Africa.

DHL
giz

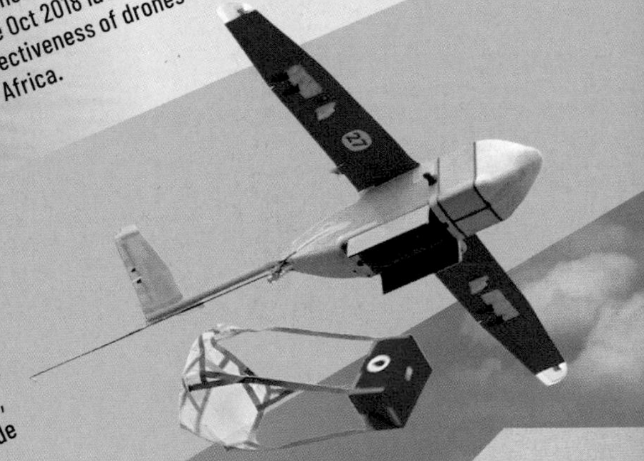

ZIPLINE DRONE DELIVERY

Many companies are trialling drone delivery technologies, but few have progressed to routine delivery operations. One company that has is the US-based Zipline, which uses relatively simple fixed-wing drones to deliver blood products and other medical supplies to remote clinics and hospitals across Rwanda and Ghana. In its first two years of operation, beginning in 2016, Zipline's drones have flown a total of 500,000 km (310,685 mi) and made nearly 10,000 deliveries, conveying more than 18,000 units of blood.

FARTHEST FLIGHT BY AN UNCREWED AIRCRAFT

On 22–23 Apr 2001, a USAF Northrop Grumman Global Hawk called *Southern Cross II* covered 13,219.86 km (8,214.44 mi) in a single flight. The High-Altitude Long-Endurance (HALE) surveillance plane took off from Edwards Air Force Base in California, USA, and landed at RAAF Base Edinburgh in Adelaide, South Australia, 23 hr 23 min later. By doing so, it became the **first unpiloted plane to cross the Pacific Ocean**.

U.S. AIR FORCE

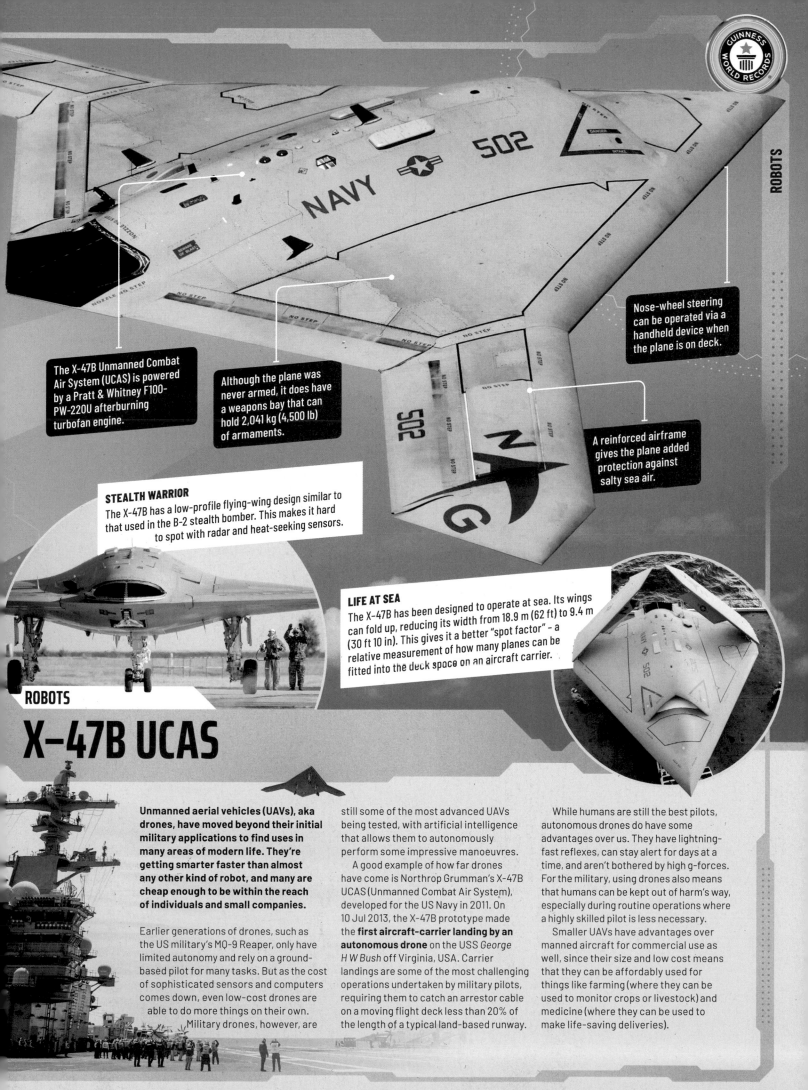

The X-47B Unmanned Combat Air System (UCAS) is powered by a Pratt & Whitney F100-PW-220U afterburning turbofan engine.

Although the plane was never armed, it does have a weapons bay that can hold 2,041 kg (4,500 lb) of armaments.

Nose-wheel steering can be operated via a handheld device when the plane is on deck.

A reinforced airframe gives the plane added protection against salty sea air.

STEALTH WARRIOR
The X-47B has a low-profile flying-wing design similar to that used in the B-2 stealth bomber. This makes it hard to spot with radar and heat-seeking sensors.

LIFE AT SEA
The X-47B has been designed to operate at sea. Its wings can fold up, reducing its width from 18.9 m (62 ft) to 9.4 m (30 ft 10 in). This gives it a better "spot factor" – a relative measurement of how many planes can be fitted into the deck space on an aircraft carrier.

ROBOTS

X-47B UCAS

Unmanned aerial vehicles (UAVs), aka drones, have moved beyond their initial military applications to find uses in many areas of modern life. They're getting smarter faster than almost any other kind of robot, and many are cheap enough to be within the reach of individuals and small companies.

Earlier generations of drones, such as the US military's MQ-9 Reaper, only have limited autonomy and rely on a ground-based pilot for many tasks. But as the cost of sophisticated sensors and computers comes down, even low-cost drones are able to do more things on their own. Military drones, however, are still some of the most advanced UAVs being tested, with artificial intelligence that allows them to autonomously perform some impressive manoeuvres.

A good example of how far drones have come is Northrop Grumman's X-47B UCAS (Unmanned Combat Air System), developed for the US Navy in 2011. On 10 Jul 2013, the X-47B prototype made the **first aircraft-carrier landing by an autonomous drone** on the USS *George H W Bush* off Virginia, USA. Carrier landings are some of the most challenging operations undertaken by military pilots, requiring them to catch an arrestor cable on a moving flight deck less than 20% of the length of a typical land-based runway.

While humans are still the best pilots, autonomous drones do have some advantages over us. They have lightning-fast reflexes, can stay alert for days at a time, and aren't bothered by high g-forces. For the military, using drones also means that humans can be kept out of harm's way, especially during routine operations where a highly skilled pilot is less necessary.

Smaller UAVs have advantages over manned aircraft for commercial use as well, since their size and low cost means that they can be affordably used for things like farming (where they can be used to monitor crops or livestock) and medicine (where they can be used to make life-saving deliveries).

The on-board computer uses information from a suite of sensors to stabilize WildCat as it runs.

Padding protects against damaging fast-paced falls.

WildCat's methanol engine makes it too loud and dangerous to use indoors.

Hydraulic actuators provide the leg strength needed to accelerate to 25 km/h (16 mph).

WildCat's 14 powered joints give it the flexibility to lean into high-speed turns.

ROBOTS

WILDCAT

As bipeds, humans have an affinity for robots with two legs, but it's hard to deny that having four legs would make a lot of things simpler. Having more legs on the ground at the same time makes it easier to lift heavy loads and much easier to stay balanced, especially over rough terrain or while moving quickly.

Quadruped robots are more versatile than robots with wheels or tracks, and more stable and reliable than human-like robots with two legs. For this reason, it's likely that quadruped robots will be among the first to make the jump from labs and carefully controlled environments to the unpredictable outside world. They'll be exploring disaster zones, inspecting equipment and even carrying packages to your front door.

CHEETAH & WILDCAT

Many of the key innovations in quadruped design were first seen in the robots produced by American firm Boston Dynamics. During the 2000s and early 2010s, the company adapted research into the gaits of quadruped animals to work with their four-legged robots. By mimicking the walk, trot, canter and gallop of quadruped animals, they hoped to achieve greater speeds and higher movement efficiency.

Boston Dynamics' first attempt at a speedy quadruped design was a tethered robot called Cheetah, which could run on a treadmill at speeds of 45.5 km/h (28.3 mph). In 2013, they took Cheetah's stabilization system and built it into a self-contained robot called WildCat, swapping out the external power supply for a methanol-fuelled motor. The 154-kg (339-lb) robot could gallop at up to 25 km/h (16 mph) over relatively flat terrain, making it the **fastest untethered quadrupedal robot**.

Four-legged robots have progressed a great deal since 2013, but no design has yet been able to match WildCat for sheer speed.

FOUR-LEGGED FRIENDS

100%

HAMR

The Harvard Ambulatory Microrobot (HAMR) was inspired by the nimble and durable cockroach. At only 4.5 cm (1.77 in) long and with a weight of just 2.8 g (0.09 oz), it is the **smallest untethered quadruped robot.** Most of HAMR's structure is made from flat sheets that are then popped up and folded together like origami. This simple construction allows for the easy assembly of large "swarms" of robots.

ANYMAL

Created at the Robotic Systems Lab at ETH Zürich in Switzerland in 2016, ANYmal is designed for harsh environments. With a modular and rugged build, ANYmal can operate in settings that are notoriously unfriendly to robots, dealing with heavy rain, dust or snow. In the future, sturdy quadrupeds may be found checking for blockages in sewers, reading gauges on offshore oil platforms or searching for people in burning buildings.

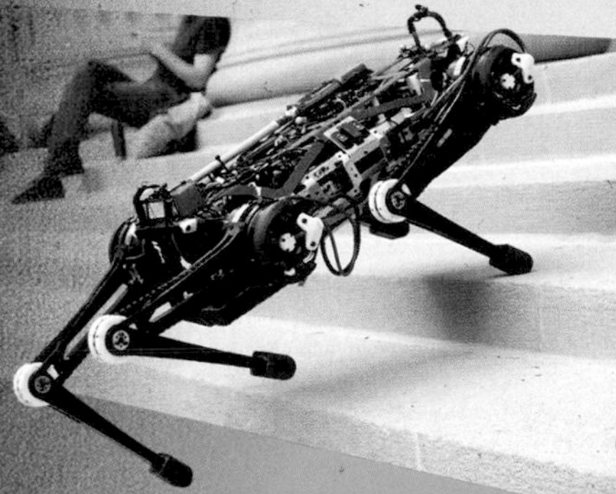

CHEETAH 3

This robot, built in 2017, is the latest in a long line of cutting-edge designs produced at the Massachusetts Institute of Technology (USA). This exceptionally agile quadruped is capable of navigating uneven and unstable terrain, and holds the record for the **highest jump by a quadruped robot** at 78.7 cm (2 ft 7 in). Cheetah 3 is currently just a research platform, but the robot's designers hope to adapt it for search-and-rescue applications. They plan to add features such as a hand for opening doors and the ability to navigate using only tactile feedback – essential for moving through spaces choked with dust or smoke that would obscure its sensors.

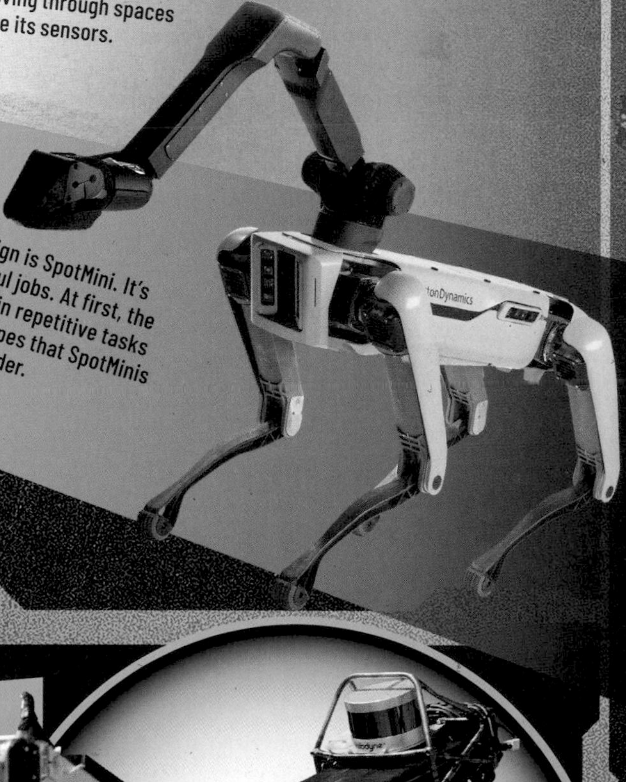

SPOTMINI

After years of research projects, Boston Dynamics' first commercialized design is SpotMini. It's expected that these quadrupeds will soon be out in the world performing useful jobs. At first, the jobs will probably be on the dull side, with the robots taking over from humans in repetitive tasks such as construction-site inspections or building security. Boston Dynamics hopes that SpotMinis will eventually be able to live with us in our homes, taking care of us as we get older.

BIGDOG & SPOT

Boston Dynamics' BigDog (left) was a donkey-sized quadruped developed for DARPA in 2005. It was designed to test the idea of a robotic "pack mule" that could carry heavy equipment for soldiers. In 2015, the lessons learned from the development of BigDog, WildCat and others were incorporated into a new design called Spot (right). Spot used batteries to power its hydraulic actuators, meaning that it could be used indoors.

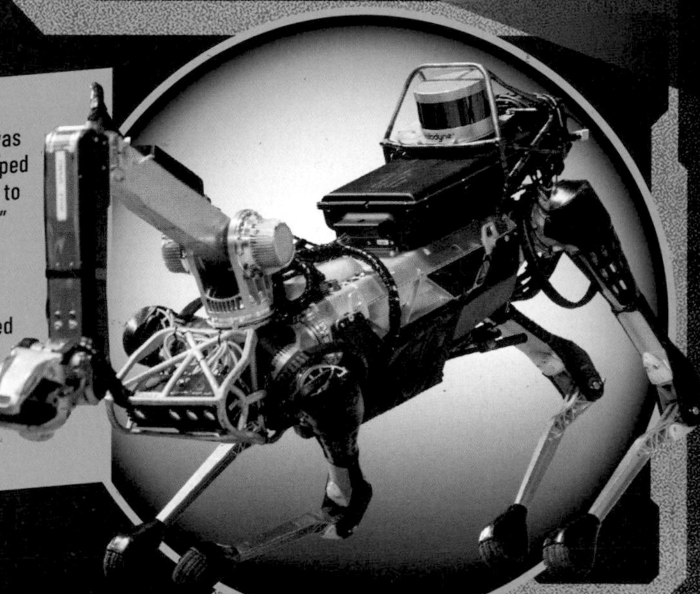

163

LUNOKHOD & YUTU-2

The **first planetary rover** was the Soviet Union's *Lunokhod 1* (right), which landed on the Moon on 17 Nov 1970. While simple by modern standards, *Lunokhod* did have a significant degree of autonomy, including systems that adapted the commands it received from Earth for the challenging terrain. The lessons learned here informed later rovers, incuding the Chinese *Yutu-2* (far right), which made the **first landing on the far side of the Moon** – carried inside the *Chang'e-4* lander – on 3 Jan 2019.

INT-BALL

Astronauts on the *International Space Station* (*ISS*) spend about 10% of each working day taking pictures and recording video of ongoing experiments. To help out, on 4 Jun 2017 the Japanese Aerospace Exploration Agency (JAXA) sent up the JEM Internal Ball Camera ("Int-Ball") – the **first autonomous camera on a space station**. Int-Ball is fitted with tiny fans that propel it around the *Kibo* module, and it can use visual markers to navigate from one experiment station to the next.

ROBONAUT 2 & VALKYRIE

The **first humanoid robot in space** was Robonaut 2 (right). Robonaut arrived at the *ISS* on board the Space Shuttle *Discovery* on 26 Feb 2011, and was first powered up on 22 Aug 2011. After spending seven years in space, Robonaut returned to Earth in May 2018 for repairs. To continue its robotics research on Earth, in 2013 NASA developed an experimental humanoid robot called Valkyrie (far right), copies of which have been distributed to research partners around the world.

SPIRIT & OPPORTUNITY

The twin rovers Opportunity (render, left) and Spirit landed on Mars in Jan 2004. They were significantly larger and more capable than the **first successful Mars rover**, *Sojourner*, which landed with the Mars Pathfinder mission in 1997. The vehicles received several software upgrades over the course of their long mission (see p.184), increasing their autonomy and testing systems that were later used in *Curiosity*.

see p.184

SOFT LANDING

Landing on Mars is hard. NASA has tried various methods over the years, including on-board rockets and airbag cocoons. The most complex, however, is the sky-crane system that lowered *Curiosity* down from a hovering rocket platform some 20 m (66 ft) above the surface.

ROBOTS

CURIOSITY

We send robots out to explore space because they're much better suited to it than humans are. We're fragile and demanding, and can't survive without things like food and water and warmth. Eventually, humans will make it back to the Moon and even to Mars, but until we have the technology to get there, robots will continue to take our place in exploring the Solar System.

On 6 Aug 2012, NASA landed the car-sized *Curiosity* rover on Mars. Weighing in at 899 kg (1,982 lb) – including 80 kg (176 lb) of scientific instruments – *Curiosity* is the **largest planetary rover**. For more than seven years, this nuclear-powered science robot has been working to answer the many questions that remain about our planetary neighbour.

GETTING AROUND

Operating a rover on Mars is not simply a matter of remote control. It can take as much as 24 min for radio signals to reach Mars from Earth, making it impractical for *Curiosity* to rely on human input for every movement. Instead, the rover is semi-autonomous for much of the time, with human operators on Earth planning routes and setting major objectives. Once these goals have been relayed to the rover, *Curiosity*'s on-board computers make decisions on the finer details of route planning, arm deployment and laser targeting.

The data gathered from the rover's cameras and instruments are transmitted back to Earth once or twice a day. These readings provide scientists with invaluable information about Mars and its history. NASA's upcoming *Mars 2020* rover – scheduled to land in Jezero Crater in Feb 2021 – is set to be even bigger than *Curiosity*, with a total mass of 1,050 kg (2,315 lb).

This part of the rover is called the "mast". It contains the primary camera system and the ChemCam laser.

The rover is powered by a radioisotope thermoelectric generator, which uses the heat from pellets of radioactive plutonium to produce electricity.

Instruments on the robotic arm include the Mars Hand Lens Imager and the Alpha Particle X-ray Spectrometer.

SNAP HAPPY
NASA's *Curiosity* rover has 17 cameras, including one on the end of its arm that it used on 31 Oct 2012 to take the **first full selfie on another planet**. The picture is actually a mosaic of 55 images digitally stitched together in a way that removes the arm from the foreground.

Curiosity's wheels have suffered on Mars's rocky surface and now sport dents, punctures and tears.

GUINNESS WORLD RECORDS

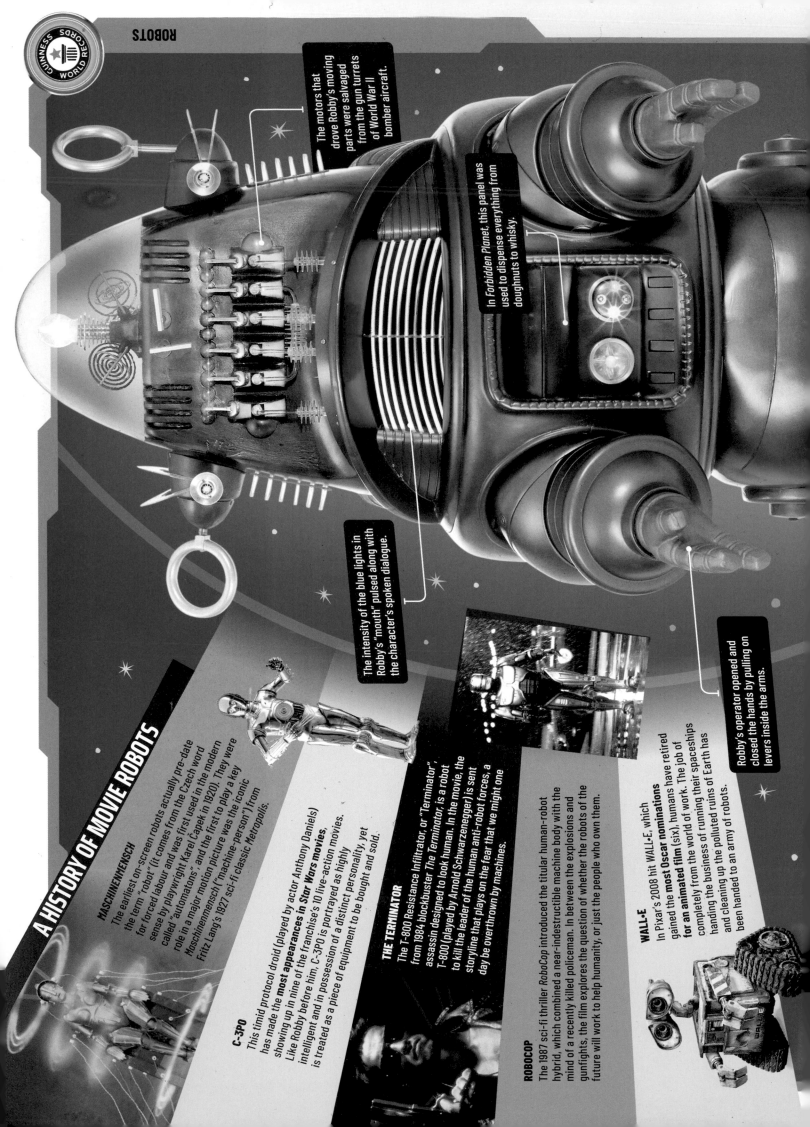

GUINNESS WORLD RECORDS

The motors that drove Robby's moving parts were salvaged from the gun turrets of World War II bomber aircraft.

In *Forbidden Planet*, this panel was used to dispense everything from doughnuts to whisky.

The intensity of the blue lights in Robby's "mouth" pulsed along with the character's spoken dialogue.

Robby's operator opened and closed the hands by pulling on levers inside the arms.

A HISTORY OF MOVIE ROBOTS

MASCHINENMENSCH
The earliest on-screen robots actually pre-date the term "robot" (it comes from the Czech word for forced labour and was first used in the modern sense by playwright Karel Čapek in 1920). They were called "automatons", and the first to play a key role in a major motion picture was the iconic Maschinenmensch ("machine-person") from Fritz Lang's 1927 sci-fi classic *Metropolis*.

C-3PO
This timid protocol droid (played by actor Anthony Daniels) has made the **most appearances in Star Wars movies,** showing up in nine of the franchise's 10 live-action movies. Like Robby before him, C-3PO is portrayed as highly intelligent and in possession of a distinct personality, yet is treated as a piece of equipment to be bought and sold.

THE TERMINATOR
The T-800 Resistance Infiltrator, or "Terminator", from 1984 blockbuster *The Terminator*, is a robot assassin designed to look human. In the movie, the T-800 (played by Arnold Schwarzenegger) is sent to kill the leader of the human anti-robot forces, a storyline that plays on the fear that we might one day be overthrown by machines.

ROBOCOP
The 1987 sci-fi thriller *RoboCop* introduced the titular human-robot hybrid, which combined a near-indestructible machine body with the mind of a recently killed policeman. In between the explosions and gunfights, the film explores the question of whether the robots of the future will work to help humanity, or just the people who own them.

WALL-E
In Pixar's 2008 hit *WALL-E*, which gained the **most Oscar nominations for an animated film** (six), humans have retired completely from the world of work. The job of handing the business of running their spaceships and cleaning up the polluted ruins of Earth has been handed to an army of robots.

The body was made from vacuum-formed ABS plastic on a metal frame.

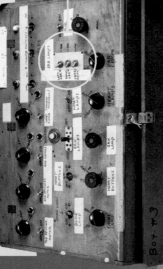

EAR LAMPS — ON ON ON — LEFT EAR RIGHT EAR EARS RELAY

Box #3

ROBOTS

ROBBY THE ROBOT

On 21 Nov 2017, an anonymous bidder at Bonhams New York paid an astonishing $5,375,000 (£4,062,120) for this iconic on-screen robot, making it the most expensive movie prop sold at auction. So what is it that's so important about this old prop?

For most people, the first robot they ever see is something in a science-fiction film, game or TV series. Robby the Robot is one of the most famous and recognizable robots in movie history. It was created for the 1956 sci-fi blockbuster *Forbidden Planet*, where it appeared as the servant and protector of the mysterious outcast Dr Edward Morbius and his daughter.

HOW IT WORKED
Unlike previous movie robots, such as Gort from *The Day the Earth Stood Still*

(1951), Robby was clearly more than simply an actor in a shiny metallic suit. With many moving parts and glowing lights, Robby was an example of how the real world's technology was gradually catching up with fiction.

The robot required at least two people to operate. The first was the actor inside the body of the robot, who shared the cramped interior of the suit with a reported 365 m (1,200 ft) of electrical wiring and looked out through the gaps between the illuminated grille that formed Robby's "mouth".

A second, off-screen operator controlled the whirring array of antennas and lights that made up Robby's head and "heart", triggering the light effects and movements needed for each scene.

Even though we're edging ever closer to a world where robots are part

of day-to-day life, it's these fictional creations that have shaped our ideas of what robots are, what they can be, and how they might change the world (for better or worse).

TOP BILLING
At the time of its construction in 1955, Robby was one of the most expensive movie props ever made. It cost a reported $125,000 – the equivalent of around $1.18 m (£898,000) today – and accounted for around 7% of *Forbidden Planet's* budget. As a result, the studio was anxious to make as much as they could of their new creation – sending it on promotional tours and putting it front and centre in the movie's poster (right).

GOOD OR EVIL?
Over the course of Robby's more-than-20-year film and TV career, it played many possible visions of what robots could be. It was a helpful servant in *Forbidden Planet* (above), and the tool of a sinister supercomputer in *The Invisible Boy* (1957). In a 1964 episode of *The Twilight Zone*, it played the robot brought in to cheaply replace the human workers in a factory.

BRINGING ROBBY TO LIFE
The operator inside Robby carried the weight of the 54-kg (120-lb) suit on a leather and metal harness (left) inside the torso. Space inside was limited, so operators needed to be 160 cm (5 ft 3 in) tall with a 76-cm (30-in) waist. The other operator stood a short distance away and ran the suit's electrical systems from the control panel pictured below.

M·G·M PRESENTS
FORBIDDEN PLANET IN CINEMASCOPE AND COLOR
STARRING WALTER PIDGEON · ANNE FRANCIS · LESLIE NIELSEN with WARREN STEVENS And Introducing ROBBY, THE ROBOT
Screen Play by CYRIL HUME · Directed by FRED McLEOD WILCOX · Produced by NICHOLAS NAYFACK AN M·G·M PICTURE

TECH & ENGINEERING

▶ TALLEST CENTRELESS OBSERVATION WHEEL

Towering 142.5 m (467 ft 6 in) over the Bailang River in Shandong Province, China, this futuristic take on the traditional ferris wheel provides panoramic views out over the Bohai Sea and inland to the city of Weifang.

The attraction, which opened to the public on 16 May 2018, uses a stationary steel lattice to form the "wheel", with the 36 gondolas travelling on rails around the rim. It was built by the China Construction Sixth Engineering Division Corp and fitted out by Zhejiang Juma Amusement Equipment for the Weifang Bailang River Scenic Spot Management Co (all CHN).

Huge though the wheel is, however, it is still smaller than the **largest observation (ferris) wheel**, which opened in Las Vegas, Nevada, USA, on 31 Mar 2014. Known as the *High Roller*, it stands 167.5 m (549 ft 6 in) tall and lifts visitors three times higher than the top of Nelson's Column in London, UK.

▶ See videos of mechanical marvels at guinnessworldrecords.com/2020

Construction of the wheel took four years. The 126.25-m-diameter (414-ft 2-in) supporting lattice alone required some 4,600 tonnes (5,070 US tons) of steel.

CONTENTS

LARGEST SPACE STATION

The *International Space Station* (*ISS*) is a state-of-the-art microgravity research laboratory that travels through low Earth orbit at a speed of 27,540 km/h (17,112 mph). It is the **largest space station**, with a mass of 419,725 kg (925,335 lb). Here, we can see how the *ISS* would look if it came to land inside one of London's most visited landmarks, Trafalgar Square.

Construction of the *ISS* in space began on 20 Nov 1998, when the *Zarya* module was launched from the Baikonur Cosmodrome in Kazakhstan. Pressurized modules were transported into low Earth orbit and connected together. The initial phase ended with the attachment of the *Leonardo Permanent Multipurpose Module* in Feb 2011. Today, the *ISS* has a total pressurized volume of 932 m³ (32,868 cu ft), similar to that of a Boeing 747, although less than half of this is accessible.

The *ISS* is a global enterprise between the space agencies of the USA, Canada, Russia, Japan and Europe. The **first *ISS* resident crew** comprised Sergei Krikalev, Yuri Pavlovich Gidzenko (both RUS) and William Shepherd (USA), who arrived to form *Expedition 1* on 2 Nov 2000 and stayed for 136 days. It has since been visited by more than 200 astronauts from at least 18 nations. Although cooperation between crew-mates is essential, not everything is shared: Russian cosmonauts on the *ISS* have access to more than 300 different food dishes on board, including mashed potatoes, broccoli with cheese, dried beef, peaches and nuts – the **largest menu in space**.

Elements continue to be added to the space station and its 16 pressurized modules. The **largest *ISS* module** is *Kibo*, developed by the Japanese space agency JAXA and launched on 31 May 2008 on board the Space Shuttle *Discovery*. It measures 11.19 m (36 ft 8 in) long with a diameter of 4.39 m (14 ft 4 in), and has a mass of 14,800 kg (32,628 lb). The *Cupola* module has a cluster of seven windows in a dome shape, made from fused silica and borosilicate glass. Its central window measures 80 cm (2 ft 7 in) across and is the **largest window in space**. *Cupola* faces towards Earth and offers the crew excellent visibility for external activities, such as the operation of the Canadarm2 robotic arm.

At the current time, the *ISS* is expected to remain in use until at least 2028. The total cost of the space station to date is estimated to be around $150 bn (£93.8 bn; €104.7 bn) – making it the **most expensive man-made object**.

As fun as it is to imagine the *ISS* landing in Trafalgar Square, the reality is that, on its retirement, it will be de-orbited in a controlled manner over 12 or so months into an open area of ocean, so tourists and pigeons can rest easy!

The *ISS* is shown here inverted, with the *Cupola* dome facing up to the skies. With an approximate width of 110 m (360 ft), Trafalgar Square would be a very snug "parking space" for the *ISS*, which has a truss length of 109 m (357 ft).

LARGEST INFLATABLE SPACE HABITAT

The *Bigelow Expandable Activity Module* (*BEAM*) is an experimental inflatable module attached to the *ISS* (not featured on the main image below) with an internal volume of 16 m³ (565 cu ft). It was inflated and fully pressurized on 28 May 2016, with plans for a two-year test period to gauge its suitability as an expandable habitat. In Oct 2017, NASA announced that the *BEAM* could remain attached to the *ISS* until the early 2020s.

Expandable modules such as the *BEAM* may be crucial in future missions to Mars, as they allow for large living spaces without needing a huge rocket to launch them.

MOST SPACEWALKS FROM A SPACE STATION

As of 11 Dec 2018, a total of 213 spacewalks – also known as extra-vehicular activities (EVAs) – had taken place outside the *ISS* in support of assembly and maintenance of the orbiting laboratory. Most of the EVAs were from the *Quest* airlock, but others include those from the *Pirs* docking compartment and the *Poisk* module. The total amount of time in space accumulated over 213 EVAs is 1,335 hr 2 min.

DRIVING YOU CRAZY

Hairiest car
Maria Lucia Mugno and Valentino Stassano (both ITA) own a Fiat 500 covered with 120 kg (264 lb 8 oz) of human hair, as verified in Padula Scalo, Salerno, Italy, on 15 Mar 2014.

Tallest rideable bicycle
Stoopidtaller is 6.15 m (20 ft 2.5 in) high. It was made by Richie Trimble (USA) and measured in Los Angeles, California, USA, on 26 Dec 2013. Why the name? One of Richie's earlier big bikes was called *Stoopidtall!*

▶ Heaviest limousine
Designed by Michael Machado and Pamela Bartholomew (both USA), *Midnight Rider* weighs 22.933 tonnes (50,558 lb) and is 21.3 m (70 ft) long and 4.16 m (13 ft 8 in) high.

Heaviest weight towed by electric car
On 15 May 2018, a Model X car supplied by Tesla Australia pulled a 130-tonne (286,600-lb) Boeing 787-9 along a 30.4-m (100-ft) course. The attempt took place at Qantas Maintenance Base in Melbourne, Victoria, Australia.

Fastest vehicle slalom
Jia Qiang (CHN) drove a Chevrolet Camaro RS between 50 markers in 48.114 sec in Shaoguan, Guangdong, China, on 16 Dec 2018. The markers were no more than 15.2 m (50 ft) apart. The event was held by Chevrolet China.

Largest parade of tow trucks
Roadside recovery firm Fier D'être Dépanneur (FRA) lined up 491 trucks in Moulins, France, on 13 Oct 2018.

Largest simultaneous car-tyre burnout
In a "burnout", a driver accelerates and brakes at the same time; the vehicle remains static and the rear tyres spin and smoke. There were 126 cars in a burnout staged by Rare Spares at Street Machine Summernats (both AUS) in Canberra, Australia, on 4 Jan 2019.

Most consecutive donuts (spins) in a car while sitting on the roof
Having set his car spinning, Naji Bou Hassan (LBN) sat on the roof as the vehicle made 52 revolutions. The head-turning feat took place in Aley, Lebanon, on 26 Aug 2018.

▶ FARTHEST DISTANCE FOR A MOTORCYCLE BURNOUT
Stuntman Maciej "DOP" Bielicki (POL, above) rode 4.47 km (2.78 mi) on a Harley-Davidson Street Rod 2017 while maintaining a burnout in Rzeszów, Poland, on 20 May 2017. It was achieved in collaboration with Game Over Cycles, the owner of the country's largest Harley-Davidson dealership, based in Rzeszów.
The **farthest distance for a car burnout**, meanwhile, is 487.07 m (1,598 ft), executed by Ron Buckholz (USA) in a 1964 Chevrolet Malibu on 13 Oct 2018. The feat was witnessed by some 600 spectators at Pacific Raceways in Kent, Washington, USA.

Most people on one motorcycle
In all, 58 members of the Indian Army's Tornadoes motorcycle team rode a 500-cc Royal Enfield in Karnataka, India, on 19 Nov 2017.

FASTEST...

Lawnmower
On 5 Nov 2015, Per-Kristian Lundefaret (NOR) clocked a speed of 214.96 km/h (133.57 mph) on his modified Viking T6 lawnmower in Vestfold, Norway.

Vehicle indoors
Mikko Hirvonen (FIN) hit 140 km/h (86.99 mph) in a Speedcar XTREM Crosskart at the Helsinki Expo Centre in Finland on 25 Feb 2013.

Mobility scooter
Sven Ohler (DEU) drove a souped-up scooter to 180.26 km/h (112 mph) during an event staged by *GRIP – Das Motormagazin* in Klettwitz, Germany, on 25 May 2017.

Motorized shopping trolley
On 18 Aug 2013, Matt McKeown (UK) rode a trolley equipped with a modified 150-hp (111-kW) Chinook helicopter starter engine to a speed of 113.298 km/h (70.4 mph) at Elvington Airfield in Yorkshire, UK.
The **largest motorized shopping trolley** is an 8.23-m-long (27-ft) and 4.57-m-tall (15-ft) cart built by Fred Reifsteck (USA) in 2012. It is displayed in South Wales, New York, USA.

LARGEST SYNCHRONIZED CAR DANCE
On 23 Oct 2018, a total of 180 vehicles performed a routine in an event staged by Nissan Middle East (UAE) in Dubai, UAE. The cars formed the shape of a falcon on the desert sands, a nod to Nissan's Patrol Safari Falcon car.

In 1960, Mickey Thompson (Danny's father) became the first American to break the 400-mph (643-km/h) barrier in *Challenger I*.

FASTEST PISTON-ENGINED CAR
Driven by Danny Thompson (USA), *Challenger 2* achieved an average speed of 722.204 km/h (448.757 mph) over two flying-mile runs at the Bonneville Salt Flats in Utah, USA, on 11–12 Aug 2018.
It's some way off the **fastest car** overall. With Andy Green (UK) at the wheel, *Thrust SSC* reached 1,227.985 km/h (763.035 mph) over a mile in the Black Rock Desert, Nevada, USA, on 15 Oct 1997.

▶ LARGEST ICE-CREAM-VAN PARADE
On 16 Oct 2018, a cavalcade of 84 ice-cream vans dubbed the "Ice Cream Van Dream Team" took to the road in Crewe, Cheshire, UK. The convoy, organized by Edward Whitby of Whitby Morrison (both UK), took 25 min to cover a 3.2-km (2-mi) route. The parade heralded a two-day showcase in the town for the ice-cream industry.

AUG 18 In 1984, Arvind Pandya (IND) embarks on his attempt to make the **fastest run backwards across the USA**. He goes on to run 2,400 km (1,500 mi) from Los Angeles, California, to New York City in 107 days.

AUG 19 French singer-songwriter Gérald Genty achieves the **most concerts performed in 12 hours** – 37 – in Brussels, Belgium, in 2015. He plays at least five songs in front of no fewer than 10 people at each venue.

Sakakibara-kikai.

MONONOFU

▶ LARGEST HUMANOID VEHICLE

Mononofu was designed by Masaaki Nagumo (JPN, inset) and developed at agricultural equipment manufacturers Sakakibara-kikai. It is 8.46 m (27 ft 9 in) tall and weighs approximately 7.3 tonnes (16,090 lb), as verified in Kitagunma, Gunma Prefecture, Japan, on 7 Dec 2018. The cockpit accommodates one driver, who can move *Mononofu*'s arms, hands and legs using levers while checking its progress on video screens.

As a child, Masaaki was a big fan of the TV anime Mobile Suit Gundam, featuring a teenage hero who pilots a giant robot. Now in his 40s, the designer has spectacularly turned fantasy into fact!

FASTEST GARDEN SHED

On 16 Sep 2017, Kevin Nicks (UK) drove a garden shed at 129.831 km/h (80.67 mph) in South Yorkshire, UK. Kevin converted his Volkswagen Passat into this fully approved, road-legal vehicle. He then drove it from Land's End to John o' Groats, accompanied by his daughter, Sophie, to raise money for a local cancer hospice that had cared for his mother.

MOST FUEL-EFFICIENT VEHICLE (PROTOTYPE)

A trial car built by Duke Electric Vehicles (USA) can travel 100 km (62 mi) on the energy equivalent of 0.01614 litres (0.0035 US gal) of petrol. That's a rate of 5,158 km/litre (14,570 mpg)! Named *Maxwell*, it's powered by hydrogen fuel cells and was tested at GALOT Motorsports Park in Benson, North Carolina, USA, on 21 Jul 2018. The team from Duke University made *Maxwell* for the Shell Eco Marathon, a contest that challenges young designers to create energy-efficient vehicles.

AUG 20 — In 2009, the **largest alphorn ensemble**, featuring 366 musicians, gathers on the Gornergrat mountain near Zermatt, Switzerland. They play six songs during a 20-min concert.

AUG 21 — The **most people riding on a regular-size skateboard** is set at 22 during filming of the music video "Troublemaker", by the band Weezer, in Los Angeles, California, USA, in 2008.

BIG SCIENCE

Most powerful laser

On 6 Aug 2015, scientists at the Institute of Laser Engineering at Osaka University in Japan fired the Laser for Fast Ignition Experiments, delivering 2,000 trillion watts (2 petawatts) of power. The duration of the beam is only 1-trillionth of a second, but it contains 1,000 times the integrated electric power consumed in the world in a typical day. The main purpose of this laser is to generate high-energy quantum beams, which have a range of possible applications including cancer treatment.

Strongest magnetic field created

In Apr 2018, Shojiro Takeyama (JPN) and his team at The University of Tokyo in Japan recorded the largest magnetic field ever generated in a laboratory test. It produced 1,200 Tesla and blew the doors off the steel containment chamber in which the experiment was housed. The field lasted for only 40 microseconds, but was about 400 times more powerful than those generated by magnets used in MRI machines, and some 50 million times stronger than Earth's magnetic field.

Such high-intensity fields may one day be required for nuclear fusion reactors (such as the Wendelstein 7-X opposite), where plasma temperatures exceed the tolerance of any known material. Magnetic fields can contain the plasma and prevent it from destroying the reactor.

Largest particle accelerator

The Large Hadron Collider (LHC) is the biggest and most complex piece of scientific equipment ever built. The collider occupies a 27-km-long (16.7-mi) circular tunnel under Geneva, Switzerland, and weighs a total of 38,000 tonnes (41,890 US tons).

Since it was activated on 10 Sep 2008, work at the LHC has led to important scientific discoveries and many more records. These include generating the **highest artificial temperature** – 5 trillion Kelvin (or 800 million times hotter than the surface of the Sun) – in 2012, and the **highest-energy ion collisions in a particle accelerator** – producing 1,045 TeV (tera electron volts) of energy – in 2015.

These experiments also require a small army of researchers. A 2015 study that provided a more accurate mass measurement for the Higgs boson elementary particle listed 5,145 authors: the **most contributors to a research paper**.

Most powerful quantum computer

At a meeting of the American Physical Society on 5 Mar 2018, researchers at Google (USA) announced an operational 72-qubit computer housing a processor called *Bristlecone*. (A "qubit" is a quantum bit.) At present, quantum computers are prone to errors, making them less useful than the cores in conventional models. Hopefully, *Bristlecone* will provide scientists with greater knowledge about how to improve them further.

Lowest artificial temperature

A team at the Massachusetts Institute of Technology in Cambridge, Massachusetts, USA, led by Aaron Leanhardt, achieved a temperature of 450 picokelvin (0.00000000045 K above absolute zero, the **lowest possible temperature**). Details of their research appeared in *Science* magazine on 12 Sep 2003.

LARGEST AIRBORNE TELESCOPE

The Stratospheric Observatory for Infrared Astronomy (SOFIA) is a Boeing 747SP fitted with a 2.5-m-aperture (8-ft 2-in) reflecting telescope. SOFIA is a joint project of NASA (USA) and DLR (DEU). It made its first airborne observations on 26 May 2010.

Largest convex mirror

In May 2017, German company Schott cast the secondary mirror (M2) for the Extremely Large Telescope (ELT), which is due to be finished by the European Southern Observatory in 2024. The mirror has a diameter of 4.2 m (13 ft 9 in) and weighs 3.5 tonnes (7,716 lb). It is made from a type of glass ceramic called Zerodur – a material that has very low thermal expansion, making it ideal for telescopes, where high image quality is vital. It took a year to cool down after manufacture, and will now be highly polished and coated in preparation for when the rest of the ELT is completed.

Largest 3D earthquake shake table

E-Defense is a table used to study the resilience of buildings and other structures against earthquakes. Located in Miki, Hyōgo Prefecture, Japan, it measures 300 m² (3,229 sq ft) and can support structures with a mass of 1,200 tonnes (1,322 US tons). The table can shake its payloads with an acceleration of 1 g horizontally in two dimensions and 1.5 g vertically.

LARGEST TILTING SHIP

The *FLoating Instrument Platform*, or *FLIP*, is a 108-m-long (355-ft) oceanic research barge capable of floating "upright" with 17 m (55 ft) of its length above the water's surface and 91 m (300 ft) below. The vessel rotates through 90° by flooding large ballast tanks. As these sink, *FLIP*'s buoyant end – containing quarters for the 16 crew and their equipment – rises. It is operated by the Scripps Institution of Oceanography at the University of California in San Diego, USA.

FLIP's design provides scientists with a stable platform to research areas such as meteorology, geophysics and underwater acoustics.

LARGEST VACUUM CHAMBER

The Space Power Facility at NASA's Glenn Research Center at Plum Brook Station in Sandusky, Ohio, USA, measures 30.4 m (100 ft) in diameter and is 37 m (122 ft) tall. The chamber is used to test spacecraft and space hardware prior to launch. It can simulate solar radiation using a 4-MW quartz heat lamp array and produce temperatures as low as -195.5°C (-320°F).

AUG 22 In 1980, Fuatai Solo (FJI) achieves the **fastest coconut tree climb**, ascending a 9-m (29-ft 6-in) tree barefoot in 4.88 sec at the annual Coconut Tree Climbing Competition in Sukuna Park, Fiji.

AUG 23 In 2007, mare JJS Summer Breeze is found to have the **longest tail on a horse**: 3.81 m (12 ft 6 in). She is owned by Crystal and Casey Socha of Augusta, Kansas, USA.

Nuclear fusion works by joining atoms' nuclei together. The name "stellarator" refers to stars, which are fuelled by the same process.

LARGEST STELLARATOR

A stellarator is a doughnut-shaped machine that confines super-hot plasma within magnetic fields to produce controlled nuclear-fusion reactions. The largest such device is the Wendelstein 7-X, which measures 15 m (49 ft 2 in) across and has an internal plasma volume of 30 m³ (1,059.4 cu ft), making it large enough to walk through (inset). It uses superconducting magnetic coils to contain plasma at temperatures of up to 130 million K (129,999,727°C; 233,999,540°F). Built in Apr 2014, the Wendelstein 7-X is located at the Max Planck Institute of Plasma Physics in Greifswald, Germany.

HIGHEST VOLTAGE FROM A FRUIT BATTERY

Professor Saiful Islam (PAK/UK) and his team generated 1,275.4 V from a battery of 2,016 lemon halves at the Royal Institution in London, UK. The attempt was filmed for the BBC Royal Institution Christmas Lectures, recorded on 13 Dec 2016 and broadcast on 29 Dec. The battery was measured using a voltmeter supplied and calibrated by the National Physical Laboratory.

FASTEST COMPUTER

On 8 Jun 2018, the US Department of Energy's Oak Ridge National Laboratory in Tennessee, USA, unveiled the *Summit* supercomputer. Constructed by IBM, it has a benchmarked performance of 143,500 trillion floating-point operations per sec (143.5 petaflops). A powerful home PC, for context, can manage around 300 gigaflops running the same benchmark tests – only 0.0002% of *Summit*'s speed.

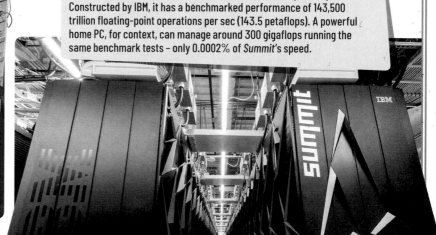

AUG 24 In 394 CE, the **last hieroglyphs** – known as the Graffito of Esmet-Akhom – are inscribed in the Temple of Isis, on the island of Philae, Egypt, in the River Nile. The date is included in the text.

AUG 25 Following a three-year journey from Uranus, *Voyager 2* completes the **first flyby of Neptune** in 1989. The probe comes within 4,800 km (2,900 mi) of the cloud tops at the planet's north pole.

Longest red carpet

On 25 Oct 2018, Bogaris Retail (ESP) rolled out a red carpet measuring 6.35 km (3.9 mi) at Centro Comercial Torrecárdenas in Almería, Spain. This is longer than the **longest runway**, at Qamdo Bamda Airport in Tibet, China, which measures 5.5 km (3.4 mi). The red carpet celebrates the history of cinematic culture in Almería, which has acted as a location for classic films such as *The Good, the Bad and the Ugly* (ITA, 1966).

Longest rug

A 10.9-km-long (6.7-mi) rug was created by The Children are Painting the World Social Fund (KAZ) and the citizens of Almaty in Kazakhstan on 16 Sep 2018.

LARGEST PARASOL

On 24 Mar 2018, Khalifa Student Empowerment Program - Aqdar (UAE) unfurled a parasol with a diameter of 24.5 m (80 ft 4 in) and a height of 15.22 m (49 ft 11 in) on the Corniche waterfront in Abu Dhabi, UAE. The canopy, in the colours of the UAE national flag, was created to celebrate the Emirates Happiness Agenda.

Most lights on an artificial Christmas tree

Universal Studios Japan were dreaming of a bright Christmas when they hung 580,806 lights on a giant artificial Christmas tree at their studios in Osaka, Japan. The record was verified on 23 Oct 2018.

LARGEST...

Dreamcatcher

On 21 Jul 2018, Vladimir Paranin (LTU) hung a dreamcatcher with a diameter of 10.14 m (33 ft 3 in) in Lithuania's Asveja Regional Park during the "Masters of Calm" festival. The dreamcatcher tipped the scales at 156 kg (343 lb) and was made from pine wood, 1,250 m (4,100 ft) of synthetic rope, 700 sticks and twigs, 319 beads and five feathers.

▶ Chess piece

The World Chess Museum (USA) unveiled a 6.09-m-tall (20-ft) king piece measuring 2.79 m (9 ft 2 in) in diameter at its base in St Louis, Missouri, USA, on 6 Apr 2018. It was 53 times the size of a standard "Champion Staunton" king piece.

Origami flower

On 1 Sep 2018, Arbnora Fejza Idrizi (KOS) made a folded floral sculpture 8.7 m (28 ft 6 in) in diameter in Skenderaj, Kosovo. She has been creating origami art for more than 10 years.

Jam jar

On 4 Jun 2018, the Instituto Tecnológico Superior de Los Reyes (MEX) presented a jam jar weighing 559.8 kg (1,234 lb) in Los Reyes, Michoacán, Mexico. It was filled with jam made using 600 kg (1,322 lb) of locally grown blackberries.

To open this jar, you might need to bulk up with the **largest container of protein powder**. Created by True Nutrition and Douglas Smith (both USA), its weight of 1,000 kg (2,204 lb 10 oz) was verified on 2 May 2018.

Steel-string acoustic guitar

Long Yunzhi (CHN) scaled up a Yamaha MG700MS acoustic guitar into an instrument measuring 4.22 m long, 1.60 m wide and 0.33 m deep (13 ft 10 in x 5 ft 2 in x 1 ft). It was verified on 8 Sep 2018. The guitar weighs 130 kg (286 lb) and requires two people to play it properly.

Functioning traditional plane

Schreinerei Fust (CHE) built a woodworking tool that was 7.13 m long, 4.37 m tall and 2.10 m wide (23 ft 4 in x 14 ft 4 in x 6 ft 10 in). It was measured on 6 May 2017.

LARGEST DIRNDL

On 4 Sep 2016, Maria Aberer (AUT) unveiled a 7.03-m-long (23-ft) traditional Alpine dress before 8,000 spectators at the harvest festival in Dorfbeuern, Austria. The dirndl had a circumference of 4.20 m (13 ft 9 in) at the waist and 5.28 m (17 ft 3 in) at the chest. Maria had been inspired by a radio report on the **largest lederhosen**, created by Gerhard Ritsch (AUT) in 2014.

Peter's other inventions include a model aeroplane with rotating fast-food buckets for wings.

▶ LARGEST OVEN LIGHTER

YouTubers Peter Sripol (above) and Samuel Foskuhl (both USA) turned up the heat with their giant oven lighter, which was verified at a length of 2.17 m (7 ft 1 in) on 26 Oct 2018, at a barbecue in Beavercreek, Ohio, USA. It was fashioned from a modified weed torch, blowtorch and an electric ignition. Now, how do you want your burgers?

 AUG 26 In 2013, trials rider Thomas Öhler (AUT) achieves the **fastest 400 m hurdles on a bicycle** – 44.62 sec – in a race against two-time Olympic gold medallist Félix Sánchez in Linz, Austria.

 AUG 27 In 1896, Britain and Zanzibar (now part of Tanzania) officially go to war at 9 a.m. The conflict ends after 45 min – the **shortest war** – with Zanzibar having suffered around 500 casualties.

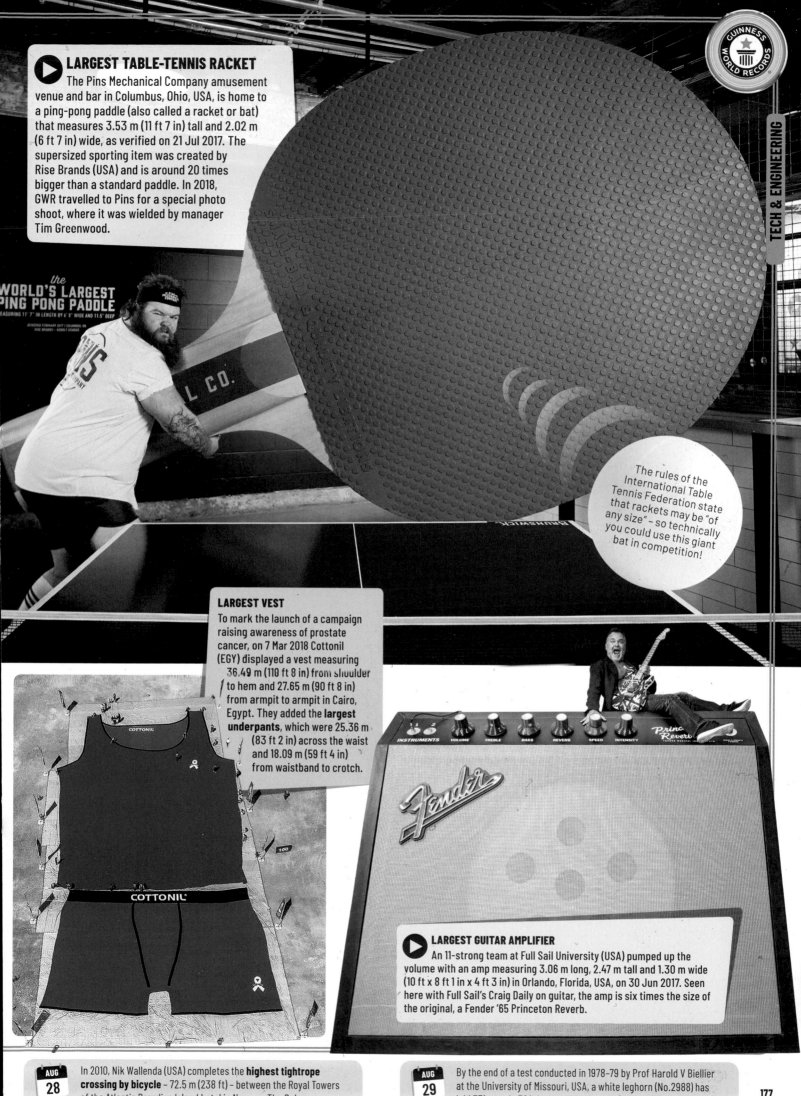

LARGEST TABLE-TENNIS RACKET

The Pins Mechanical Company amusement venue and bar in Columbus, Ohio, USA, is home to a ping-pong paddle (also called a racket or bat) that measures 3.53 m (11 ft 7 in) tall and 2.02 m (6 ft 7 in) wide, as verified on 21 Jul 2017. The supersized sporting item was created by Rise Brands (USA) and is around 20 times bigger than a standard paddle. In 2018, GWR travelled to Pins for a special photo shoot, where it was wielded by manager Tim Greenwood.

the
WORLD'S LARGEST
PING PONG PADDLE

The rules of the International Table Tennis Federation state that rackets may be "of any size" – so technically you could use this giant bat in competition!

LARGEST VEST

To mark the launch of a campaign raising awareness of prostate cancer, on 7 Mar 2018 Cottonil (EGY) displayed a vest measuring 36.49 m (110 ft 8 in) from shoulder to hem and 27.65 m (90 ft 8 in) from armpit to armpit in Cairo, Egypt. They added the **largest underpants**, which were 25.36 m (83 ft 2 in) across the waist and 18.09 m (59 ft 4 in) from waistband to crotch.

LARGEST GUITAR AMPLIFIER

An 11-strong team at Full Sail University (USA) pumped up the volume with an amp measuring 3.06 m long, 2.47 m tall and 1.30 m wide (10 ft x 8 ft 1 in x 4 ft 3 in) in Orlando, Florida, USA, on 30 Jun 2017. Seen here with Full Sail's Craig Daily on guitar, the amp is six times the size of the original, a Fender '65 Princeton Reverb.

AUG 28 In 2010, Nik Wallenda (USA) completes the **highest tightrope crossing by bicycle** – 72.5 m (238 ft) – between the Royal Towers of the Atlantis Paradise Island hotel in Nassau, The Bahamas.

AUG 29 By the end of a test conducted in 1978-79 by Prof Harold V Biellier at the University of Missouri, USA, a white leghorn (No.2988) has laid 371 eggs in 364 days, making it the **most prolific chicken**.

GIANT'S TOYBOX

▶ **Longest Hot Wheels track**
The Russian branch of Mattel laid out a 560.3-m (1,838-ft) Hot Wheels track – longer than a standard drag strip – in Moscow on 25 Aug 2018.

Largest rocking horse
Gao Ming (CHN) unveiled an 8.20-m-tall, 12.72-m-long (26-ft 10-in x 41-ft 9-in) rocking horse in Linyi, Shandong Province, China, on 7 Jul 2014. It was three times the height of a double-decker Routemaster bus.

Largest jigsaw puzzle
On 7 Jul 2018, DMCC (UAE) unveiled a 6,122-m² (65,896-sq-ft) puzzle that commemorates the late Sheikh Zayed in Dubai, UAE. That's larger than the floor space of the US White House!

Largest Monopoly board
Hasbro and the Ceres Student Association (both NLD) created a 900-m² (9,687-sq-ft) version of the property-based game in Wageningen, Netherlands. The size of three-and-a-half tennis courts, it was measured on 30 Nov 2016 at the town's university.

Fastest time to arrange a large chess set
Shurdamiev Nurzatanovich (KAZ) took 46.62 sec to align a scaled-up chess set at Kashirskaya Plaza in Moscow, Russia, on 28 Oct 2018. As per GWR guidelines, the smallest pieces (i.e., the pawns) were a minimum of 20 cm (7.8 in) tall.

LARGEST MODEL CAR POWERED BY LEGO® TECHNIC MOTORS
LEGO Technic (DNK) made a drivable plastic-brick Bugatti Chiron 1.21 m tall, 2.03 m wide and 4.54 m long (3 ft 11 in x 6 ft 7 in x 14 ft 10 in), as ratified in Aug 2018 in Kladno, Czech Republic. The model car incorporates more than a million LEGO Technic elements, took 13,438 hr to make and reaches a modest 28 km/h (17 mph).

Largest NERF gun
Engineer and inventor Mark Rober (USA) – formerly of NASA – built a 1.82-m-long (6-ft) foam-dart gun, as measured in Sunnyvale, California, USA, on 22 Jun 2016. In 2017, he also worked on the **largest water pistol**, collaborating with Ken Glazebrook, Bob Clagett and Dani Yuan (all USA). The supersized soaker was 2.22 m (7 ft 3 in) long and 1.22 m (4 ft) tall.

Largest LEGO-brick...
• **Batmobile**: On 28 Feb 2017, artist Nathan Sawaya (USA) unveiled a life-size LEGO Batmobile measuring 5.51 m (18 ft) long. Made from around 500,000 bricks, it was part of a DC Comics-inspired show in London, UK.
• ▶ **Caravan**: On 26 Sep 2018, "The Brick Builder",

aka Ben Craig (AUS), constructed a caravan from 288,630 LEGO bricks in Brisbane, Australia. Top Parks and Caravanning Queensland (both AUS) funded the attempt.
• ▶ **Cherry blossom tree (supported)**: For its first anniversary, LEGOLAND Japan built a 4.38-m-tall (14-ft 4-in) cherry tree in bloom with a total of 881,479 LEGO bricks in Nagoya, Aichi Prefecture, Japan, on 28 Mar 2018.
• ▶ **Ship (supported)**: On 17 Aug 2016, shipping firm DFDS (DNK) presented the 12-m-long (39-ft 4-in) LEGO ship *Jubilee Seaways* in Copenhagen, Denmark. The model incorporated more than 1.2 million plastic bricks. Appropriately, a LEGO champagne bottle was smashed on its hull during the naming ceremony.

▶ LARGEST LEGO®-BRICK FERRIS WHEEL
Tomáš Kašpařík (CZE) assembled a ferris wheel with a diameter of 3.38 m (11 ft 1 in) from LEGO bricks, as ratified on 22 Oct 2017 in Utrecht, Netherlands. It was 3.64 m (11 ft 11 in) tall, with 43 cars. Tomáš needed some 200 hours and 37,000 plastic bricks to design and construct it.

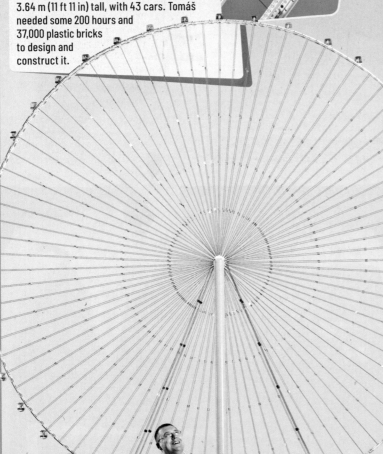

▶ LARGEST FIDGET SPINNER
Giovanni Catalano (ITA) created a 74-cm-long (2-ft 5-in) fidget spinner, as confirmed in Rozzano, Milan, Italy, on 21 Nov 2018. The toy has been around since the early 1990s, but inexplicably experienced a huge surge of popularity in 2017.

AUG 30 In 2010, professional American footballer and shampoo company spokesman Troy Polamalu (USA) has his trademark locks insured for $1 m (then £643,749) – the **highest-insured hair**.

AUG 31 The **heaviest green cabbage** tips the scales at 62.71 kg (138 lb) at the 2012 Alaska State Fair in Palmer, Alaska, USA. "Finally I reach the top of the mountain!" declares grower Scott A Robb (USA).

▶ LARGEST HULA HOOP SPUN (FEMALE)

Getti Kehayova (USA) rotated a 5.18-m-diameter (17-ft) hula hoop around herself in Las Vegas, Nevada, USA, on 2 Nov 2018. She trained every day for a full year in preparation for her attempt – and had the bruises on her body and arms to prove it! Every time the weighty hoop spun around her body, "it felt like a punch up against your ribs," Getti explained. On the day itself, her first attempt failed (and she was hit in the face by the hoop). But she persevered and her second attempt was a GWR-approved success!

The **largest hula hoop spun** overall is only fractionally larger, at 5.40 m (17 ft 8 in) in diameter. On 19 Feb 2019, Yuya Yamada (JPN) rotated it around himself in Yokohama, Kanagawa Prefecture, Japan.

A passion for hoops runs in the family. In Jul 1987, Getti's older sister, Desai, took the GWR title for **most hula hoops spun simultaneously**, with 75. Today, Marawa Ibrahim holds the record (see p.102).

▶ LARGEST WHOOPEE CUSHION

This 7.62-m-diameter (25-ft) joke cushion was created by Lee Burgess of Affordable Moonwalks for an event organized by Pastor Matt Funk of First Baptist Church Covington (all USA). Around 30 members of the church's youth group were on hand to deflate it, and so produce the characteristic flatulent sound, in Covington, Georgia, USA, on 5 Aug 2017.

▶ LARGEST RUBIK'S CUBE

TELUS Spark science museum (CAN) has produced an outsized version of the classic puzzle, each face of which spans 2.82 m² (30.35 sq ft), as confirmed in Calgary, Alberta, Canada, on 24 Sep 2018. It took staff eight weeks to create the colossal cube, which was then made available for visitors to solve.

SEP 1
In 2007, martial artist Kevin Shelley (USA) smashes the record for the **most toilet seats broken with the head in one minute** in Cologne, Germany. The 46 smashed loo lids are all made from wood.

SEP 2
In 2017, "Avery & Sylvia" – Avery Chin and Sylvia Lim (both MYS) – perform the **most costume-change illusions in one minute**, with Sylvia donning 24 different outfits in Penang, Malaysia.

ARCHITECTURE

Largest bird-shaped building
Located in Kembanglimus, Magelang, Indonesia, Gereja Ayam – or "Chicken Church" – measures approximately 56.41 m (185 ft) from beak to tail. Constructed as a dove-shaped prayer house by Daniel Alamsjah between 1988 and 2000, the building acquired its "chicken" nickname after Alamsjah placed a crown on top of the dove's head, giving it an unfortunate rooster-like appearance.

Darkest exterior for a temporary building
The Hyundai Pavilion was a 10-m-high (32-ft 10-in) pop-up structure that opened to the public on 9 Feb 2018 at the Winter Olympics in Pyeongchang, South Korea. Designed by British architect Asif Khan, the outside of the pavilion was sprayed with Vantablack Vbx2, an ultra-black coating of vertical tubes that absorbs 99% of light, creating the illusion of a void.

First building with a highway through the middle
Floors 5–7 of the 71.9-m-high (236-ft) Gate Tower in Osaka, Japan, boast an unusual design feature: the Umeda exit of the Hanshin Expressway, which passes directly through the middle of them. Completed in 1992, the building does not touch the pier-supported roadway, and has additional insulation to minimize noise and vibration.

Steepest funicular
A true funicular is a cable-operated railway where the ascending and descending cars are counterbalanced. The Schwyz–Stoos funicular railway in the Alpine resort of Stoos, Switzerland, has a gradient of 47.7° (110%) at its steepest point. Opened in Dec 2017 at a cost of 52 million Swiss francs (£39.5 m; $53 m), the four 34-person carriages are designed as rotating cylinders, which adjust to the slope and allow passengers to stay upright throughout the four-minute journey.

Largest automated parking facility
Emirates Financial Towers in Dubai, UAE, has an automated car park with 2,314 spaces, as confirmed on 21 Oct 2017. It was designed by Robotic Parking Systems (USA) and built by Mohamed Abdulmohsin Al-Kharafi & Sons (KWT). The computerized system stacks and secures cars once they have been left in the transition bays. It remembers drivers' parking history and shuffles cars towards the front before their set departure time.

LARGEST IRIS-STYLE RETRACTABLE ROOF
The Mercedes-Benz Stadium in Atlanta, Georgia, USA – home to the Atlanta Falcons NFL team – boasts a circular retractable roof. It covers an area of 5.8 ha (14.3 acres), with an oval opening measuring 104.35 m (342 ft 4 in) in diameter at its widest. The stadium roof consists of eight intersecting "petals" – each 67 m (219 ft 9 in) long, 23 m (75 ft 5 in) wide and weighing 453.5 tonnes (500 US tons) – with the whole supporting system using 19,050 tonnes (21,000 US tons) of steel and 16 electric motors.

Largest billboard
On 5 Nov 2018, Emirates Intellectual Property Association (UAE) presented an outdoor advert measuring 6,260 m² (67,382 sq ft) in Dubai, UAE. The billboard was covered in company logos to raise awareness about intellectual property rights.

Tallest building
Opened on 4 Jan 2010, the Burj Khalifa in Dubai, UAE, has 160 storeys and is 828 m (2,716 ft) tall. The building, developed by Emaar Properties (UAE), took 22 million work-hours to construct at a cost of $1.5 bn (£920 m).

The **tallest tower** is the Tokyo Skytree in Japan, which rises 634 m (2,080 ft) to the top of its mast. Completed in Feb 2012, the building functions as a broadcasting and observation tower.

FIRST HIGH-RISE MAGNETIC ELEVATOR
Installed in 2017 by ThyssenKrupp (DEU) in a 246-m-tall (807-ft) test tower in Rottweil, Germany, the prototype three-track MULTI system of elevators uses magnetized cabins moving on an electromagnetic track. This means they are not only cable-free but can also move vertically and horizontally. By switching tracks, the cabins can move upwards, downwards or sideways in order to reach their destination.

MOST SKYSCRAPERS IN A CITY
A major economic engine in East Asia located on 1,106.34 km² (427.16 sq mi) of land, Hong Kong has one of the world's highest residential densities. To house its 7 million citizens and workers, The Skyscraper Center estimated that the city was home to 2,580 buildings that were at least 100 m (328 ft) tall as of Mar 2019. Hong Kong is also the **city with the most buildings over 150 m: 385.**

LARGEST CASTLE MADE FROM PLASTIC BOTTLES
The four-storey, 14-m-high (45-ft 11-in) castle constructed in 2017 by "The Plastic King" Robert Bezeau (CAN) in Bocas Del Toro, Panama, is fabricated from 40,000 plastic bottles. Part of an ecological Plastic Bottle Village, it boasts four guest rooms, a feasting area and a viewing platform on the top.

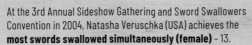

SEP 3 At the 3rd Annual Sideshow Gathering and Sword Swallowers Convention in 2004, Natasha Veruschka (USA) achieves the **most swords swallowed simultaneously (female)** – 13.

SEP 4 In 2015, Hunter Ewen (USA) achieves the **most balloons blown up in one hour by an individual** – a lung-busting 910 – at the Wild Basin Lodge Event Center in Allenspark, Colorado, USA.

Visitors to the bridge must wear special "shoe gloves" to protect the glass panels from damage.

LONGEST GLASS-BOTTOMED BRIDGE

Opened in 2017 in the Hongyagu Scenic Area, Hebei Province, China, the Red Cliff Valley Glass Suspension Bridge measures 488 m (1,601 ft) in length. Designed by Haim Dotan, it is made from 1,077 panels of 40-mm-thick (1.5-in) glass and has a deliberate swaying motion to increase the thrill of the 214-m (702-ft) drop. The bridge can bear the weight of 2,000 people, although only 600 are allowed to cross at any one time.

LARGEST SCIENCE MUSEUM

The Guangdong Science Center (CHN) in Guangzhou Province, China, has an area of 126,513 m² (1,361,780 sq ft). The centre – which is shaped to resemble a kapok flower – houses 10 permanent themed pavilions with more than 510 exhibits. It was opened in Sep 2008, and was presented with a GWR title on 7 Nov 2018 in celebration of its 10th anniversary.

HIGHEST SLIDE ON THE OUTSIDE OF A BUILDING

The Skyslide on the side of the US Bank Tower in Los Angeles, California, USA, is located at a maximum height of 280 m (918 ft) above ground. Constructed in 2016 from 32-mm-thick (1.25-in) glass, the enclosed 14-m-long (45-ft 11-in) slide curves down from the 70th to the 69th floor of the skyscraper and is designed as a tourist attraction.

SEP 5
In 2008, Herbert Weber (AUT) celebrates his 30th year at Moser Holzindustrie in Salzburg, Austria. He is responsible for the **most coffins assembled in a lifetime** – 707,335, all built by hand.

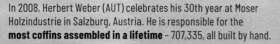

SEP 6
Coordinadora de Peñas de Valladolid assembles the **most people wearing sunglasses in the dark** – 6,774 – in Valladolid, Spain, in 2015. The attempt takes place outdoors at 10 p.m.

STICKY STUFF

First postage stamp
The Penny Black – the first postage stamp with an adhesive backing – was placed on sale in major post offices in the UK on 1 May 1840 (although not valid for use until 6 May). The stamp featured the profile of the UK's Queen Victoria, at 15 years of age, and was printed until Feb 1841.

Largest ball of stickers
As of 13 Jan 2016, John Fischer (USA) had created a 105.05-kg (231-lb 9-oz) sphere made entirely from stickers, as verified in Longmont, Colorado, USA.

Largest sticker mosaic (image)
Ahead of the 2018 FIFA World Cup final in Russia, CapitaLand Retail (CHN) presented a 385.3-m² (4,147.3-sq-ft) mosaic comprising 154,000 stickers in Shanghai, China, on 15 Jul 2018. It depicted star players from all 32 soccer teams in the tournament.

Most expensive Post-it Note
A sticky notelet featuring a pastel-and-charcoal artwork titled *After Rembrandt* sold for £640 ($939) in an online auction on 20 Dec 2000. The artist, R B Kitaj (USA), was one of a group of celebrities who created mini-masterpieces for Post-it Note's 20th anniversary. Proceeds from the auction were donated to charity.

Most sticky notes stuck on the face in one minute
At the rate of one per second, Taylor Maurer (USA) covered her face in 60 Post-it Notes in Sioux City, Iowa, USA, on 16 Nov 2014.

Largest sticky toffee pudding
A 334-kg (736-lb 5-oz) toffee sponge – weighing about the same as a horse – was baked by Farmhouse Fare Limited in Lancashire, UK, on 17 Mar 2012.

Largest tar pit
Pitch Lake at La Brea ("pitch" in Spanish) in Trinidad has an area of around 457,294.8 m² (4,922,280 sq ft), the equivalent of 85 American football fields. The lake contains more than 10 million tonnes (11 million US tons) of asphalt, and its centre is an estimated 76 m (250 ft) deep – more than enough to accommodate Nelson's Column in London, UK.

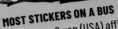

MOST STICKERS ON A BUS
STL Sticker Swap (USA) affixed 29,083 adhesive designs on a bus at LouFest in St Louis, Missouri, USA, on 10 Sep 2017. Enthusiasts from all over the world mailed in stickers for the record-breaking attempt, while the mayor of St Louis proclaimed 10 Sep 2017 as "STL Sticks Together Day" to commemorate the event.

Stickiest fish
The northern clingfish (*Gobiesox maeandricus*) is a small species native to the Pacific coast of the USA and Canada. It has an adhesive force of 80–230 times its weight, according to a 2013 study. The fish uses a modified suction cup – equipped with tiny hair-like projections called microvilli – on its belly to cling to rocks. Geckos have the same tiny structures on their feet.

Oldest spider web still containing trapped prey
The earliest known specimen of a spider's web containing entrapped insects has been dated to the Early Cretaceous period, some 110 million years ago. It was found in San Just, Spain, and reported in Jun 2006. The web takes the form of 26 strands of sticky silk preserved in a sample of ancient tree sap (amber) and contains a beetle, a mite, a fly and a now-extinct parasitic wasp.

STRONGEST NATURAL GLUE
In 2006, researchers at Indiana University, USA, found that the bacterium *Caulobacter crescentus* produces a sticky substance that enables it to attach itself to virtually any surface, even in water. This mixture of long, sugar-based molecules called polysaccharides (below) results in a stickiness about seven times stronger than that found on a gecko's sticky foot. In tests, the scientists studied 14 bacteria that had attached themselves to a glass-like base. They found that the force required to separate the microbes from the base was 7,000 Newtons per cm² (10,153 lb/f per sq in) – nearly three times greater than that needed to rip apart surfaces stuck together with commercial superglue (inset below).

OLDEST USE OF GLUE
Neanderthals made spears by bonding a flint point to a wooden shaft and joining them using tar glue made from birch bark. Scientists had presumed that the process of extracting this glue would be too advanced for Neanderthals, but evidence of the practice has been unearthed in archaeological finds from the Middle Pleistocene era (c. 200,000 years ago). In 2017, scientists at Leiden University in the Netherlands found that tar glue could be made by simply heating rolls of birch bark over an open fire.

OLDEST USE OF GLUE IN DECORATIVE WORKS
Nahal Hemar Cave, near the Dead Sea in Israel, was excavated in 1983 by a team from Harvard University (USA) and the Israel Antiquities Authority. Among the unusual discoveries were human skulls, decorated with criss-cross designs, that carbon-dated to 8,310–8,110 years ago. The patterns were made using a collagen glue produced from animal fats and tissue.

MOST PARTICIPANTS IN A DUCK TAPE FASHION SHOW
On 14 Jun 2014, at the 11th Annual Duck Tape Festival in Avon, Ohio, USA, 340 individuals took to the catwalk to model outfits made using the famous adhesive tape. GWR adjudicator Michael Empric (above right) got fully into the spirit of the event, conducting his judging duties wearing a Duck Tape jacket.

SEP 7 Ian Neale (UK) presents the **heaviest beetroot** at the 2001 National Giant Vegetables Championship in Shepton Mallet, Somerset, UK. It weighs 23.4 kg (51 lb 9 oz) – the same as an eight-year-old child.

SEP 8 In 2013, a reticulated giraffe named Jang-soon gives birth to her 18th calf at the Samsung Everland safari park in Yongin, South Korea. This is the **most giraffe offspring born in captivity**.

The special glue used for this attempt melts when heated and solidifies on cooling. The cylinders were heated to 400°C (752°F) and glue was applied to each of them. After it melted, they were joined together.

HEAVIEST WEIGHT LIFTED WITH GLUE (NON-COMMERCIALLY AVAILABLE)

On 22 Sep 2013, a super-strong glue was used to keep a 16.09-tonne (35,472-lb) truck held at around 1 m (3 ft 3 in) above the ground for more than an hour. The feat was achieved by the German Aerospace Center (DEU) at their facility in Cologne, Germany. In the test, two stainless-steel cylinders were glued together with a thermoplastic resin applied to an area of just 39.6 cm² (6.1 sq in) on each of them. A truck was connected to the cylinders, which were attached to the hook of a crane. The vehicle was then raised and suspended in the air, with only the glue on the cylinders keeping it aloft.

MOST PEOPLE MAKING SLIME SIMULTANEOUSLY

On 1 Jul 2018, a mass slime-production session involving 933 people took place at an event arranged by the City of Carson in California, USA. The attempt was held on Community Friendship Day, part of the city's Fourth of July weekend celebrations. To make the stretchy substance, participants mixed and kneaded together one-third of a cup of glue and one-quarter of a cup of liquid starch, as well as red, white and blue dye, and sometimes a touch of glitter.

FASTEST FULL-BODY CAR WRAP

Car wrapping involves covering an automobile's surface with a thin sheet of vinyl – sometimes simply to alter its colour, although the wrapping often has a design on it to advertise a brand. On 15 Jul 2018, a team from folien+zubehör (DEU) wrapped a Tesla Model X using specialist vinyl in 22 min 56.25 sec at Flugplatz Schwarze Heide in Hünxe, Germany.

LARGEST SUPERYACHT VINYL WRAP

In Feb 2015, the Rybovich boat yard, owned by the Wild Group in Miami, Florida, USA, completed a full-hull vinyl wrap of the 68-m-long (223-ft) Abeking & Rasmussen superyacht Aviva. More than 800 m (2,624 ft) of metallic vinyl wrap was used. The task took around a month, each layer being carefully overlapped by only 5 mm (0.19 in).

SEP 9 — In 1917, a letter from Admiral John "Jacky" Fisher to Minister of Munitions Winston Churchill (both UK) contains the phrase "O.M.G. (Oh! My God!)" – the **first instance of "OMG" in print**.

SEP 10 — The **last use of the guillotine** takes place in 1977 at Baumettes Prison in Marseille, France, to execute murderer Hamida Djandoubi. Capital punishment in France will be abolished in 1981.

183

Most orbital launches

The Soviet Union/Russian Federation had carried out 3,064 successful orbital launches as of 19 Mar 2019. This represents more than half of all orbital launches since the dawn of the Space Age. In 1982 alone, the Soviet Union achieved 101 – the **most orbital launches in one year**.

Of the 14,379 pieces of orbital debris logged by Space-Track.org as of 4 Jan 2019, approximately 5,075 can be traced back to Soviet or Russian activities in space, making the country the **largest contributor to space debris**. This total includes inactive satellites, used rocket stages, lost equipment and other discarded materials such as fairings.

Most satellites in orbit

As of 4 Jan 2019, the USA had 1,594 satellites in Earth orbit. This figure includes both government satellites and commercial satellites controlled by US-based organizations.

Most re-used spacecraft

NASA's Space Shuttle *Discovery* was last launched on 24 Feb 2011, its 39th space flight (STS-133) heading to the *International Space Station* (*ISS*). *Discovery* first flew on the STS-41D mission on 30 Aug 1984.

Most exoplanets discovered by a single telescope

As of 19 Mar 2019, a total of 2,697 exoplanets – i.e., planets outside our Solar System – had been identified and confirmed on the basis of observations made by the *Kepler* space telescope. This represents more than two-thirds of the 3,925 known exoplanets.

▶ Most accumulated time on spacewalks

Cosmonaut Anatoly Yakovlevich Solovyev (USSR/RUS) accrued a total of 82 hr 22 min in open space during his five space expeditions between 1988 and 1998. He made a total of 16 spacewalks, all from the space station *Mir*.

The **most accumulated time on spacewalks (female)** is 60 hr 21 min, achieved by Peggy Whitson (USA). This is the third-highest total overall. On 23 May 2017, Whitson completed her 10th spacewalk, spending 2 hr 46 min outside the *ISS* repairing a faulty relay box.

MOST CONSECUTIVE SUCCESSFUL LAUNCHES BY A ROCKET MODEL

The United Launch Alliance (USA) Delta II rocket made 100 successful orbital launches between 5 May 1997 and 15 Sep 2018. Delta II's final launch took place on 15 Sep 2018, when Delta-381 blasted *ICESat-2* from Vandenberg Air Force Base in California, USA. Delta II rockets have launched landmark missions including the *Kepler* and *Swift* space observatories.

First landing on the far side of the Moon

At 02:26 (UTC) on 3 Jan 2019, the *Chang'e* 4 lander (see also pp.164–65) – operated by the China National Space Administration – touched down in the Von Kármán Crater. While not the first man-made object to impact the far side of the Moon, it's the first to do so in a controlled way. *Chang'e* 4 contains several payloads to help us better understand this unstudied frontier, including astronomical instruments and a sealed biosphere with silkworm eggs and seeds. Also on board is a small solar-powered rover, *Yutu-2*.

Longest time survived on Mars by a rover

On 10 Jun 2018, NASA's *Opportunity* rover slipped into an emergency low-power mode as a planet-wide dust storm obscured its solar panels. This marked the first total loss of contact since its landing in 2004. *Opportunity*, along with its twin, *Spirit*, were designed to operate for 90 days, but proved to be amazingly resilient (*Spirit* shut down in 2010). On 13 Feb 2019 NASA confirmed that all attempts

MOST PROBED PLANET

A total of 25 successful or partially successful missions had been launched to the planet Mars as of 27 Nov 2018. These missions have placed 14 orbiters around the Red Planet and nine at least partially successful landers on the surface. The most recent mission to reach Mars is NASA's *InSight* lander (above), which touched down on 26 Nov 2018.

to reestablish contact had failed, and declared the rover's mission to have finally ended after 15 years 19 days.

First flyby of Pluto

Nine years after it blasted off in Jan 2006, NASA's *New Horizons* spacecraft passed Pluto at a closest approach of 12,472 km (7,749 mi) at 11:49 UTC on 14 Jul 2015. It would later arrive at the Kuiper Belt object Ultima Thule on 1 Jan 2019 (see pp.186–87).

First probe to leave the Solar System

Launched in Sep 1977, *Voyager 1* was sent to study Jupiter, Saturn, Uranus and Neptune. In Aug 2012, the probe travelled beyond the edges of our Solar System into interstellar space. Now more than 20.9 billion km (13 billion mi) from Earth, *Voyager 1* continues to transmit. It will not reach another star for some 40,000 years.

LARGEST SATELLITE DEPLOYED FROM A SPACE STATION

Built by Surrey Satellite Technology (UK), *RemoveDEBRIS* has a mass of 88.47 kg (195 lb) and measures 79 x 60 x 60 cm (31.1 x 23.6 x 23.6 in). The satellite – which aims to collect space debris – was released from the NanoRacks Kaber Microsatellite Deployer (inset) on board the *International Space Station* (*ISS*) on 20 Jun 2018.

SEP 11 In 1978, Bulgarian dissident Georgi Markov dies after a micro-engineered toxic pellet is fired into his leg by an umbrella in London, UK. It is the **first assassination by ricin poisoning**.

SEP 12 Gennady Ivanovich Padalka (RUS) returns to Earth from his fifth space mission in 2015, having spent the **longest time in space (aggregate)** – 878 days 11 hr 29 min 24 sec.

CLOSEST APPROACH TO THE SUN BY A SPACECRAFT

At 03:27:52 UTC (Coordinated Universal Time) on 6 Nov 2018, the *Parker Solar Probe* (USA) came within 24,122,872 km (14,989,257 mi) of the Sun's surface. The uncrewed spacecraft was moving at a heliocentric speed (i.e., relative to the Sun) of 95.32 km/s (343,180 km/h; 213,242 mph) – the **fastest spacecraft speed**. As its mission progresses, it should pass as close as 6.1 million km (3.8 million mi) in 2024.

On its way to the Sun, the *Parker Solar Probe* made its closest approach to Venus on 3 Oct 2018 (inset), 52 days 1 hr 13 min after its launch from Earth – the **fastest interplanetary journey**.

The probe could reach speeds of 692,000 km/h (430,000 mph) – fast enough to travel from New York City to Tokyo in under a minute!

LONGEST OPERATIONAL LIFESPAN FOR A SPACE OBSERVATORY

Launched on 24 Apr 1990, the *Hubble* space telescope (USA) was still active as of 22 Jan 2019 – an elapsed mission duration of 28 years 273 days. On 2 Apr 2018, a paper published in *Nature Astronomy* revealed that *Hubble* had located a B-type supergiant known as "Icarus" around 9 billion light years away from Earth – the **most distant star observed**.

FASTEST TRIP TO THE *ISS*

On 10 Jul 2018, the automated resupply vehicle *Progress MS-09* docked at the *ISS* after a 3-hr 40-min journey – under half the time of a flight from London to New York City. The spacecraft launched from Baikonur in Kazakhstan at 21:51 UTC on 9 Jul and docked with the *ISS*'s *Pirs* docking module at 01:31 UTC the next day.

SEP 13 In 2016, the Chicago White Sox's baseball game against the Cleveland Indians (both USA) draws 1,122 canine spectators for the "Bark at the Park" – the **most dogs attending a sports event**.

SEP 14 Acrobatic contortionist Leslie Tipton (USA) achieves the **fastest time to enter a suitcase**, zipping herself into the case in just 5.43 sec on the *LIVE! with Regis and Kelly* show in 2009.

HEAVIEST AIRCRAFT TO PERFORM AN AEROBATIC LOOP

On 18 Jul 2018, a 36,740-kg (81,000-lb) Lockheed-Martin LM-100J performed a loop as part of its demonstration flight at the Farnborough International Airshow in Hampshire, UK. The aircraft was flown by Lockheed test pilot Wayne Roberts and his co-pilot Steve Knoblock (both USA).

First self-healing glass

On 14 Dec 2017, scientists at The University of Tokyo in Japan published a paper describing their discovery of a glass-like polymer that can "heal" itself. Polyether-thiourea is hard but able to re-fuse cracks at room temperature. When broken, its pieces can be stuck back together. Just 30 sec of hand pressure at 21°C (69.8°F) is enough to rejoin the pieces, and after a few hours the material is as strong as ever.

Largest jet engine

The General Electric GE9X jet engine has a turbine blade span of 3.4 m (11 ft 1 in) – about the same as the height of an adult African elephant and 10 cm (3.9 in) larger than its predecessor, the GE90-115B (still the **most powerful jet engine**). It has been certified for use on Boeing's new 777-9 aircraft.

First simple lens to focus all colours to a single point

Conventional glass and plastic lenses have inherent problems in that they focus various colours to various points rather than all at one single point in space. On 1 Jan 2018, researchers at Harvard University, USA, published a paper in the journal *Nature* describing for the first time a "metalens" that can focus all the colours of the rainbow (our visible light spectrum) to a single point at once. In time, this will enable optical lenses to become thinner, cheaper and more effective than any other conventional lens.

First carbon-neutral gas power station

On 30 May 2018, energy company Net Power (USA) achieved a milestone in running a natural-gas-fired power station with zero carbon emissions. It did this at its prototype 25-MW electricity generating plant in La Porte, Texas, USA. The system works by driving a turbine with a loop of hot, pressurized CO_2. The CO_2 is heated by burning a mixture of natural gas and oxygen (extracted from the atmosphere in a separate facility). Additional CO_2 produced by burning the gas is siphoned off to keep the system in balance. The excess CO_2 is contained, not vented to the atmosphere, and so can be processed to avoid atmospheric pollution. The plant's running costs are as cheap as those of standard natural-gas power stations.

$$\min_G \max_D E_x\left[\log(D(x))\right] + E_z\left[\log\left(1 - D(G(z))\right)\right]$$

MOST EXPENSIVE AI-GENERATED ARTWORK SOLD AT AUCTION

On 25 Oct 2018, *Portrait of Edmond de Belamy* realized $432,000 (£334,144) at Christie's in New York City, USA. Portraying an imaginary person, it was produced by a form of artificial intelligence called Generative Adversarial Network (GAN) set up by members of the French art collective Obvious Art. This system develops new images based on existing artwork – in this case, 15,000 portraits painted from the 14th to the 20th century. The "signature" (inset) is the algorithm used to create the piece.

MOST GATES NAVIGATED BY DRONE IN ONE MINUTE

On 21 Nov 2018, Luisa Rizzo (ITA) guided a light unmanned aerial vehicle (UAV) through 57 gates in 60 sec for *La Notte dei Record* in Rome, Italy. This total represents multiple runs through a course of seven gates – at least 4 m (13 ft) apart - in a figure-eight shape. Luisa, a wheelchair user, says that drone-flying gives her a sense of freedom that transcends the limits of her condition. Her Splinter 2S UAV was built by Stefano Mirabelli of Model Drome.

Highest launch of an effervescent tablet rocket

BYU Rocketry (USA), a student team from Brigham Young University, sent a rocket powered by crushed tablets 269.13 m (883 ft) skywards at the Kennedy Space Center Visitor Complex in Florida, USA, on 12 Dec 2018. The launch took place at Bayer's second annual "Alka-Rocket Challenge", which saw five teams compete for $30,000 (£23,880).

Most active spacecraft orbiting another planet

Six operational spacecraft were in orbit around Mars as of 14 Nov 2018. The most recent is the *ExoMars Trace Gas Orbiter*, which reached the Red Planet on 19 Oct 2016.

This huge structure used 420,000 tonnes (462,970 US tons) of steel - enough for eight Sydney Harbour Bridges!

LONGEST BRIDGE-TUNNEL

The Hong Kong-Zhuhai-Macau Bridge-Tunnel is 29.6 km (18.4 mi) long. Linking Hong Kong to Macau and Zhuhai on China's Pearl River Estuary, it comprises four artificial islands, three cable-stayed bridges totalling 22.9 km (14.2 mi) and a 6.7-km (4.2-mi) undersea tunnel - located between the two illuminated islands seen above. Including approach highways, the construction measures 55 km (34.2 mi) overall.

SEP 15 At the annual Nickelodeon Slimefest in 2012, Nickelodeon arranges for 3,026 people to be gunged in Sydney, Australia - the **most people slimed simultaneously.**

SEP 16 The **highest airport** opens in 2013. Daocheng Yading Airport is situated at an elevation of 4,411 m (14,472 ft) in the Tibetan Autonomous Prefecture of Sichuan Province, China.

Most distant exploration of a Solar System object
At 05:33 UTC on 1 Jan 2019, space probe *New Horizons* passed by an asteroid in the Kuiper Belt labelled 2014 MU69 (later renamed "Ultima Thule" after a public vote). Images reveal the 31-km-long (19-mi) body to be a "contact binary" comprising two connected spheres.

Longest-running mechanical spinning top (prototype)
LIMBO is a motorized top that span for 27 hr 9 min 24 sec continuously in Tel Aviv, Israel, on 18–19 Jun 2018. It was designed by Nimrod Back of Fearless Toys (both ISR) and created in partnership with Breaking Toys (USA).

Farthest distance travelled by an electric helicopter (prototype)
On 7 Dec 2018, an experimental battery-powered electric chopper flew 56.82 km (35.3 mi) in Los Alamitos, California, USA. It was created by Martine Rothblatt, Lung Biotechnology and Tier 1 Engineering, and flown by Ric Webb (all USA).

HEAVIEST CABLE
Redaelli Tecna (ITA) produced a heavy-duty Flexpack cable weighing in at 488.366 tonnes (538.331 US tons) – heavier than the *International Space Station* – in Trieste, Italy, on 30 Oct 2017. It measured 4,050 m (13,287 ft) long overall. The total weight was extrapolated from a sample section 99.5 cm (3 ft 3 in) in length (see inset).

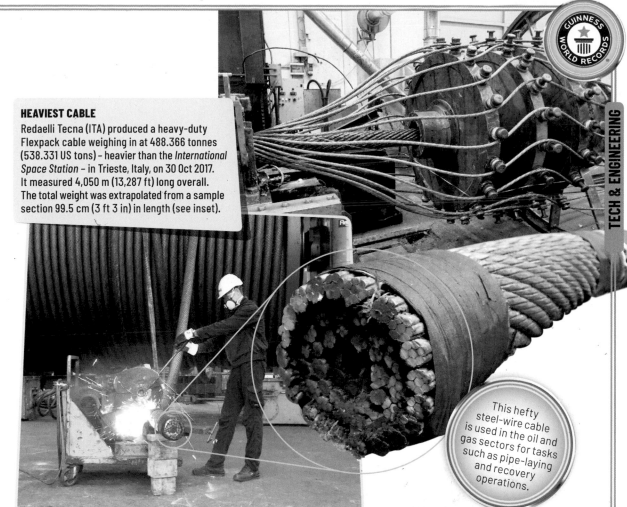

This hefty steel-wire cable is used in the oil and gas sectors for tasks such as pipe-laying and recovery operations.

CLOSEST ORBIT OF AN ASTEROID
At 19:44 UTC on 31 Dec 2018, NASA probe *OSIRIS-REx* began orbiting the small asteroid 101955 Bennu (inset). Its slightly elliptical initial orbit brought the spacecraft within 1,600 m (5,249 ft) of the asteroid's centre at its closest point.

On 3 Oct 2018, Japanese spacecraft *Hayabusa2* landed the third of four probes on the surface of asteroid 162173 Ryugu, the **most probes landed on an asteroid**.

Oldest mariner's astrolabe
Sailors once used astrolabes to calculate a ship's latitude at sea by marking the positions of certain stars. As reported in *The International Journal of Nautical Archaeology* in Mar 2019, David L Mearns (UK) found an astrolabe dated to 1498 (+/- 2 years) in a wreck off the Omani coast on 8 May 2014.

Smallest advert
On 21 Sep 2018, Dutch tech company ASML unveiled a 258.19-square-micrometre advert in Veldhoven, Netherlands. Etched and imprinted on a silicon wafer, the advert read: "To Truly Go Small You Have To Think Big #Smallest_AD ASML".

Conversely, the **largest advertising poster** measures 28,922 m² (311,314 sq ft) – big enough to cover 2,000 parking spaces. It was made by US fast-food chain Arby's to mark its partnership with Coca-Cola, and debuted in Monowi, Nebraska, USA, on 13 Jun 2018. Monowi (population: 1) was chosen because it is regarded as the smallest US town. Its sole resident is Elsie Eiler.

MOST TRAVELLED TOY SHIP
A Playmobil pirate ship named *Adventure* travelled 6,072.47 km (3,773.26 mi) between 28 May 2017 and 12 May 2018. Brothers Ollie and Harry Ferguson (both UK) launched their toy from Peterhead in Aberdeenshire, UK, and sea currents carried it to Scandinavia. The Norwegian ship *Christian Radich* picked it up, releasing it some 160 km (100 mi) off the coast of Mauritania, where it continued its journey, bobbing across the southern Atlantic to near Barbados. During its travels, a counterweight helped *Adventure* stay upright, polystyrene packing kept it buoyant and an internal tracking device reported its location.

SEP 17 In 2017, martial artist Anthony Kelly (AUS) shows off his reflexes as he achieves the **fastest tennis ball caught** – 248.09 km/h (154.15 mph) – on CBBC's *Officially Amazing* in Birchgrove, Australia.

SEP 18 In 2014, Ahmed Gabr (EGY) makes the **deepest scuba dive** – 332.35 m (1,090 ft) – in the Red Sea off Dahab, Egypt. His dive lasts for 13 hr 50 min, of which the descent itself takes just 14 min.

ARTS & MEDIA

GWR GAMER'S EDITION 2020

Can't get enough of *Fortnite*? We've devoted 14 pages to this online phenomenon in *GWR 2020*'s companion book, *Gamer's Edition*. Discover the game's biggest YouTubers and pro players, including Richard Tyler "Ninja" Blevins, and its ever-changing "Map for all Seasons". Find out about *Fortnite*'s skins and weaponry, and take on creative reader challenges. And, of course, *Gamer's Edition* is also crammed with the latest records from the rest of the videogaming world!

FIRST VIDEOGAME TO SUPPORT CROSS-PLAY ON SONY, MICROSOFT AND NINTENDO PLATFORMS

On 26 Sep 2018, after a change of policy by Sony, hugely popular third-person shooter *Fortnite Battle Royale* (Epic, 2017) became the first game to allow players on one platform to compete against those playing on others, across all the major gaming platforms. This included Sony's PS4, Microsoft's Xbox One, the Nintendo Switch and PC, as well as Android and iOS mobile devices. Sony had earlier rejected calls to enable cross-play for *Fortnite* on the PS4, but after pressure from gamers and Epic, the company finally found a solution to accommodate gamers using different hardware. It was first tested in an open beta on the above date.

CONTENTS

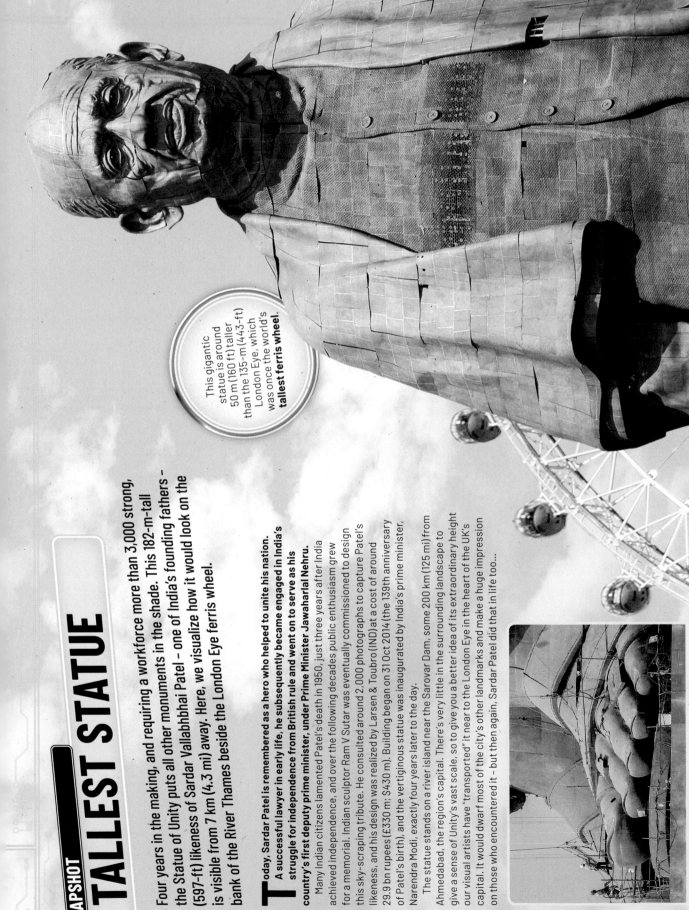

SNAPSHOT
TALLEST STATUE

Four years in the making, and requiring a workforce more than 3,000 strong, the Statue of Unity puts all other monuments in the shade. This 182-m-tall (597-ft) likeness of Sardar Vallabhbhai Patel – one of India's founding fathers – is visible from 7 km (4.3 mi) away. Here, we visualize how it would look on the bank of the River Thames beside the London Eye ferris wheel.

Today, Sardar Patel is remembered as a hero who helped to unite his nation. A successful lawyer in early life, he subsequently became engaged in India's struggle for independence from British rule and went on to serve as his country's first deputy prime minister, under Prime Minister Jawaharlal Nehru.

Many Indian citizens lamented Patel's death in 1950, just three years after India achieved independence, and over the following decades public enthusiasm grew for a memorial. Indian sculptor Ram V Sutar was eventually commissioned to design this sky-scraping tribute. He consulted around 2,000 photographs to capture Patel's likeness, and his design was realized by Larsen & Toubro (IND) at a cost of around 29.9 bn rupees (£330 m; $430 m). Building began on 31 Oct 2014 (the 139th anniversary of Patel's birth), and the vertiginous statue was inaugurated by India's prime minister, Narendra Modi, exactly four years later to the day.

The statue stands on a river island near the Sarovar Dam, some 200 km (125 mi) from Ahmedabad, the region's capital. There's very little in the surrounding landscape to give a sense of Unity's vast scale, so to give you a better idea of its extraordinary height our visual artists have "transported" it near to the London Eye in the heart of the UK's capital. It would dwarf most of the city's other landmarks and make a huge impression on those who encountered it – but then again, Sardar Patel did that in life too....

THE WEIGHT OF HISTORY

Unity required colossal quantities of building materials, including a reported 25,000 tonnes (27,557 US tons) of steel and around 135 tonnes (148 US tons) of iron crowdsourced from local farmers. It is clad in 12,000 bronze panels, weighing 1,850 tonnes (2,039 US tons) in all.

> This gigantic statue is around 50 m (160 ft) taller than the 135-m (443-ft) London Eye, which was once the world's **tallest ferris wheel.**

The Statue of Unity is built to last. It can withstand winds of 130 km/h (81 mph) and earthquakes measuring 6.5 on the Richter scale.

A TRIO OF TITANS

The Statue of Unity towers 54 m (177 ft) above the world's previous tallest sculpture – the Spring Temple Buddha in Henan Province, China. It's also nearly four times the height of New York's Statue of Liberty (minus the pedestal) – indeed, it's taller than both these famous sights stacked on top of each other.

182 m

128 m

46 m

AT THE BOX OFFICE

HIGHEST-GROSSING...

Film
Avatar (USA/UK, 2009) remains the biggest-ever box-office smash, with a lifetime gross of $2,776,345,279 (£2,109,880,000). On the weekend of 29–30 Jan 2010, director James Cameron's sci-fi blockbuster became the **first film to gross $2 billion**. Cameron was also behind the camera for the **first film to gross $1 billion**: *Titanic* (USA, 1997).

Superhero "origin" film
Ryan Coogler's *Black Panther* (USA, 2018) has earned $1,348,258,224 (£1,016,930,000), making it the ninth-highest-grossing movie ever. The storyline explains how T'Challa – aka the titular superhero, and ruler of the fictional African nation of Wakanda – must face challenges for his throne.

On 22 Jan 2019, *Black Panther* became the **first superhero movie nominated for a Best Picture Oscar**. Although it lost out to *Green Book* (USA, 2018), it won awards for Original Score, Costume Design and Production Design – the **most Oscars won by a superhero movie**.

Animated feature film
Disney's *Frozen* (USA, 2013) has taken $1,272,469,910 (£959,770,000). Its sequel, *Frozen 2*, was slated for

WIDEST FILM RELEASE (SINGLE DOMESTIC MARKET)
Family favourite *Despicable Me 3* (USA, 2017) played in 4,529 cinemas in North America during its opening weekend on Friday 30 Jun–Sunday 2 Jul. In second and third place are two movies from 2018: *Jurassic World: Fallen Kingdom* (USA), shown in 4,475 cinemas, and *Avengers: Infinity War* (USA), in 4,474 cinemas.

HIGHEST-GROSSING REMAKE
Walt Disney's 2017 live-action remake of its 1991 animated classic *Beauty and the Beast* grossed a total of $1,259,199,706 (£949,761,000). The movie, which takes its inspiration from the 1740 French fairy tale *La Belle et la Bête* – originally written by Gabrielle-Suzanne Barbot de Villeneuve – stars Emma Watson and Dan Stevens (both right).

HIGHEST-GROSSING FILM SERIES
As of 4 Apr 2019, the *Star Wars* movies had collectively grossed $9,307,186,202 (£7,072,970,000) worldwide. The seventh instalment of the blockbuster sci-fi franchise, *The Force Awakens* (USA, 2015, pictured) alone has earned $2,053,311,220 (£1,560,410,000), making it the third-highest-grossing film of all time.

The iconic score was the work of John Williams (USA, inset), the **most bankable Hollywood composer**. His value to the movie industry was rated at $10.7 m (£8 m) per film as of 28 Feb 2019.

release in Nov 2019. A teaser was unveiled on 13 Feb 2019, and received 116.4 million views in a day according to Disney – making it the **most-viewed animated film trailer in 24 hours**, overtaking *Incredibles 2* (see right).

Traditionally animated film
Disney's *The Lion King* (USA, 1994) has grossed $986,214,868 (£743,860,000). Drawn entirely by hand, it was directed by Roger Allers and Rob Minkoff, and was the top-earning film of 1994.

The **highest-grossing stop-motion animated film** is Aardman Animations' *Chicken Run* (USA/UK/FRA, 2000), with $227.8 m (£158.7 m).

Film based on a videogame
With the aid of Dwayne Johnson (see p.194), *Rampage* (USA, 2018) wreaked havoc at the global box office, earning $428,056,280 (£322,865,000). The film is based on the 1986 arcade game *Rampage* by Bally Midway.

The **highest-grossing film inspired by videogaming** is *Ready Player One* (USA, 2018), which earned $579,290,136 (£436,934,000).

Horror film
Adapted from Stephen King's 1986 novel, *It* (USA, 2017) grossed $697,457,969 (£533,182,000). Sequel *It: Chapter Two* was set to be unleashed on audiences in Sep 2019.

Opening weekend for an original film
The Secret Life of Pets (USA, 2016), a brand-new idea not based on any pre-existing storylines or characters, grossed $104,352,905 (£80,538,500) when it opened domestically in US theatres on 8–10 Jul 2016.

HIGHEST-GROSSING ANIME FILM
A romantic fantasy written and directed by Makoto Shinkai, *Your Name* (*Kimi no na wa*, JPN, 2016, above) has grossed $361,024,012 (£272,305,000) worldwide. A potential rival to its crown, *Spider-Man: Into the Spider-Verse 3D* (USA, 2018) had surpassed it with $373,735,455 (£284,019,000) as of 4 Apr 2019 – although there is debate as to whether this film could be classified as true anime.

All figures from The-Numbers.com, as of 15 Mar 2019 unless otherwise indicated

SEP 19 In 1893, New Zealand becomes the **first country to pass women's suffrage**. An electoral bill granting women the right to vote is given royal assent by Governor Lord Glasgow.

SEP 20 In 2013, *Grand Theft Auto V* (Rockstar Games) becomes the **fastest videogame to gross $1 billion** in sales. It hits the milestone after just three days of general release.

HIGHEST-GROSSING ORIGINAL ANIMATION

Incredibles 2 (USA, 2018) has grossed $1,242,532,436 (£937,227,000) at the worldwide box office, placing it sixth on the all-time list of movies with an original screenplay. The superhero sequel is the second-highest-grossing animated movie of all time, behind *Frozen* (USA, 2013, see left), which is based on the 1844 fairy tale "The Snow Queen" by Danish author Hans Christian Andersen.

LONGEST FILM TO WIN AN OSCAR

O.J.: Made in America (USA, 2016) won the Best Documentary Feature award for its creators Ezra Edelman and Caroline Waterlow (both USA) at the 89th Academy Awards on 26 Feb 2017. The feature film, which recounts the true-life rise and fall of American football star O J Simpson, has a run-time of 467 min (7 hr 47 min).

FASTEST TIME FOR A FILM TO GROSS $1 BILLION

Disney-Marvel superhero blockbuster *Avengers: Endgame* (USA, 2019) surpassed the $1-bn mark at the global box office after just five days on release on 25–29 Apr 2019. The 22nd offering from the Marvel Cinematic Universe earned $1.209 bn (£935.5 m) in that period. Could *Endgame* be the movie to finally take *Avatar*'s crown (see opposite)?

HIGHEST-GROSSING BIOGRAPHICAL FILM

Featuring Rami Malek in the central role of Freddie Mercury, the charismatic frontman of British rock band Queen, *Bohemian Rhapsody* (UK/USA, 2018) has grossed $773,633,838 (£583,519,000). The film received four Oscars at the 91st Academy Awards on 24 Feb 2019, including Best Actor for Malek.

SEP 21 Peter Pedersen (DNK) runs the **fastest marathon in armour** – 6 hr 46 min 59 sec – in 2008 at the HC Andersen Marathon in Odense, Denmark. His full battle armour includes helmet and gauntlets.

SEP 22 The University of California, Irvine (USA) stages the **largest game of capture the flag**, with 2,888 participants in 2015. UC Irvine freshmen attempt a GWR title every year.

MOVIE MAKING

Most Oscar nominations for a foreign language film

Roma (MEX/USA, 2018) received 10 nominations for the 91st Academy Awards in 2019, equalling the feat of *Wo Hu Cang Long*, aka *Crouching Tiger, Hidden Dragon* (TPE/USA, 2000). It went on to win three Oscars: Best Foreign Language Film, Best Cinematography and Best Director for Alfonso Cuarón.

First person to be nominated for Best Actress and Best New Song Oscars in one year

Singer-songwriter-actor Lady Gaga, aka Stefani Germanotta (USA), was nominated twice in 2019 by the Academy of Motion Picture Arts and Sciences: Best Actress for her role as the nightclub singer Ally Maine in the remake *A Star is Born* (USA, 2018), and Best Original Song for "Shallow", which she wrote with Mark Ronson for the same movie. Gaga went on to win the Best Original Song Oscar, following a memorable performance with co-star Bradley Cooper at the Awards.

Most Oscar nominations without winning (actress)

In 2019, Glenn Close (USA) left the Academy Awards empty-handed for the seventh time in her career. She has been nominated for Best Actress four times – for *Fatal Attraction* (USA, 1987), *Dangerous Liaisons* (USA/UK, 1988), *Albert Nobbs* (UK/IRL/FRA/USA, 2011) and *The Wife* (UK/SWE/USA, 2018) – and three times for Best Supporting Actress – for *The World According to Garp* (USA, 1982), *The Big Chill* (USA, 1983) and *The Natural* (USA, 1984).

The **most Oscar nominations without winning (actor)** is eight, by Peter O'Toole (IRL). He did receive an Honorary Academy Award in 2003.

Oldest Oscar nominee

On 4 Mar 2018, director Agnès Varda (BEL/FRA, 30 May 1928–29 Mar 2019) received a nomination for Best Documentary Feature aged 89 years 279 days. Her film *Faces Places* (FRA, 2017) follows Varda and fellow artist and "photograffeur" JR (true identity unknown) as they travel through rural France creating portraits of the characters they encounter.

Most bankable Hollywood director

Zack Snyder's (USA) value to the movie industry was rated at $15,737,661 (£11,842,900) per movie, as of 28 Feb 2019. Snyder's eight films as director – including the DC superhero movies *Justice League* (USA, 2017), *Batman v Superman: Dawn of Justice* (USA, 2016), *Man of Steel* (USA, 2013) and *Watchmen* (USA, 2009) – have grossed a total of $3,165,511,174 (£2,382,100,000).

Highest-grossing film composer

As of 23 Jan 2019, the 100 movies scored by Hans Zimmer (DEU) – including *Widows* (USA, 2018), *Interstellar* (USA/UK, 2014) and *The Dark Knight Rises* (UK/USA, 2012) – had earned $27,807,884,544 (£21,526,900,000) at the box office.

Highest-earning Bollywood actor (current)

According to Forbes, the highest-earning Bollywood star is currently Akshay Kumar, aka Rajiv Hari Om Bhatia (CAN, b. IND), who, between 1 Jun 2017 and 1 Jun 2018, earned $40.5 m (£30.4 m). Kumar is the only Bollywood star listed in Forbes' *100 Highest-Paid Celebrities* list for that year.

The **highest-earning Bollywood actress (current)** is Deepika Padukone (IND, b. DNK), who earned an estimated 112.8 crore rupees ($15.37 m; £11.79 m) between 1 Oct 2017 and 30 Sep 2018, according to data published by Forbes India.

Most deaths in a movie career

The late Christopher Lee (UK, 1922–2015) "died" in at least 61 of the 200-plus movies in which he appeared. Lee's characters have been hanged, defenestrated, struck by lightning, staked, stabbed, burned, electrocuted, dissolved, blown up, beheaded and crashed into the Moon.

LONGEST CAREER AS A LIVE-ACTION MARVEL SUPERHERO

Hugh Jackman (AUS, inset right) and Patrick Stewart (UK, inset left) have played the same Marvel superhero – the X-Men's Wolverine and Professor Charles Xavier, respectively – for a total of 16 years 232 days. They made their series debut in *X-Men* (USA, 2000) and reprised their roles most recently in 2017's *Logan* (USA, above). Both actors were presented with GWR certificates in Feb 2019 in honour of their achievement.

HIGHEST-GROSSING LEAD ACTOR

The 30 movies starring or co-starring Robert Downey Jr (USA) have accumulated $11,347,917,823 (£8,647,320,000). The actor's top-grossing movie as of Apr 2019 is *Avengers: Infinity War* (USA, 2018), which earned $2.048 bn (£1.596 bn). Co-star Scarlett Johansson (USA) is the **highest-grossing lead actress**, her 25 films grossing $10,786,897,236 (£8,409,920,000).

HIGHEST ANNUAL EARNINGS FOR A FILM ACTOR (CURRENT)

George Clooney (USA, below) earned $239 m (£180.89 m) between 1 Jul 2017 and 1 Jul 2018, according to Forbes. This was largely due to the sale of the Casamigos tequila company, which he co-founded. The next-highest-earning actor was *Jumanji: Welcome to the Jungle* (USA, 2017) star Dwayne Johnson (USA, left), who earned $124 m (£93.8 m).

HIGHEST-GROSSING LEAD ACTRESS IN MUSICAL FILMS

As of 7 Feb 2019, Meryl Streep (USA, left) had grossed $1,550,488,703 (£1,197,120,000) from four lead musical roles: *Mamma Mia!* (USA, 2008), *Mamma Mia!: Here We Go Again* (SWE/UK/USA, 2018), *Mary Poppins Returns* (USA, 2018) and *Into the Woods* (USA, 2014). Streep overtook her *Mamma Mia!* co-star Amanda Seyfried (USA, far left), who had grossed $1.4 bn (£1.08 bn).

SEP 23 At the 2016 UK National Giant Vegetables Championship in Malvern, UK, Joe Atherton (UK) presents the **longest carrot**. It measures 6.245 m (20 ft 5.86 in).

SEP 24 In 2011, students at the University of Economics Ho Chi Minh City in Vietnam complete the **jigsaw puzzle with the most pieces** – 551,232 – at the city's Phú Thọ Indoor Stadium.

Tom Cruise has been Oscar-nominated for his work in three films: *Born on the Fourth of July* (USA, 1989), *Jerry Maguire* (USA, 1996) and *Magnolia* (USA, 1999).

GUINNESS WORLD RECORDS

MOST BANKABLE HOLLYWOOD FIGURE

As of 28 Feb 2019, The Numbers' Bankability Index was topped by Tom Cruise (USA), whose value to the movie industry was rated at $20,934,185 (£15,753,300) per film. In 2018, Cruise reprised his role as special agent Ethan Hunt in *Mission: Impossible – Fallout* (USA, right). The movie grossed $787,456,552 (£592,600,000), making it the most lucrative feature film so far in his 38-year-long career.

The **most bankable Hollywood leading actress** is Sandra Bullock (USA), with an added value of $14,533,088 (£10,936,400) per film. In 2018, she led an all-female team of thieves in reboot *Ocean's 8* (USA, pictured inset, with co-star Rihanna).

MOST BANKABLE HOLLYWOOD PRODUCER

Kathleen Kennedy's (USA) value to the movie industry was rated at $15,541,558 (£11,695,300) per film as of 28 Feb 2019. Her 35 releases as a producer have earned nearly $12 bn (£9 bn), much of it grossed from *Star Wars* movies such as *The Force Awakens* (USA, 2015 – see p.192) and *Rogue One* (USA, 2016).

OLDEST OSCAR WINNER

On 4 Mar 2018, James Ivory (USA, b. 7 Jun 1928, left) won the Academy Award for Best Adapted Screenplay at the age of 89 years 271 days. His script for *Call Me by Your Name* (ITA/FRA/BRA/USA, 2017) is a retelling of the novel by André Aciman, and charts the relationship between precocious 17-year-old Elio (Timothée Chalamet, above right) and scholar Oliver (Armie Hammer, left).

FIRST PERSON TO WIN AN OLYMPIC MEDAL AND AN OSCAR

On 4 Mar 2018, two-time Olympic champion Kobe Bryant (USA) added an Oscar statuette to his trophy cabinet when *Dear Basketball* (USA, 2017) won the Best Animated Short Film category. He shared the award with the Disney animator Glen Keane. The film was based on a poem that Bryant wrote in 2015, announcing his retirement.

SEP 25 In 2016, actress and singer Selena Gomez (USA) becomes the **first person with 100 million followers on Instagram**, after the hashtag #SelenaBreakTheInternet trends worldwide.

SEP 26 A televised debate between Hillary Clinton and Donald Trump (both USA) in 2016 draws an average of 84 million viewers, making it the **most-watched TV presidential debate**.

RECORDING ARTISTS

FIRST ACT TO TOP FIVE US COUNTRY CHARTS SIMULTANEOUSLY

On 28 Oct 2017, Kane Brown (USA) crowned all five of *Billboard*'s main country charts simultaneously. The single "What Ifs", featuring Lauren Alaina, ruled Hot Country Songs, Country Airplay and Country Streaming Songs, while "Heaven" debuted at No.1 on Country Digital Song Sales. In the same week, Brown's self-titled debut album led Top Country Albums.

First rap song to win the Grammy Award for Song of the Year

At the 61st Annual Grammy Awards on 10 Feb 2019, "This Is America" by Childish Gambino (aka Donald Glover, USA) won four awards, including Song of the Year. It also became the **first rap song to win the Grammy Award for Record of the Year**.

Longest wait for a US Top 10 single

Robert "Bobby" Helms (USA, 1933–97) had his first Top 10 hit on the *Billboard* Hot 100 on 5 Jan 2019, when "Jingle Bell Rock" rose to No.8. A total of 60 years 140 days had elapsed since Helms's debut, "Borrowed Dreams", was released on 18 Aug 1958.

Most cumulative weeks at No.1 on the US Hot Country Songs chart

Nashville duo Florida Georgia Line (Tyler Hubbard and Brian Kelley, both USA) racked up their 106th non-consecutive week at No.1 on *Billboard*'s Hot Country Songs chart on 17 Nov 2018. "Meant to Be",

their collaboration with pop vocalist Bebe Rexha, extended its own record for **most consecutive weeks at No.1 on the US Hot Country Songs chart** to 50, as of the same date.

Most simultaneous entries on the US singles chart by a group

Rap trio Migos (USA) scored 14 hits on the *Billboard* Hot 100 chart dated 10 Feb 2018, matching the feat of The Beatles (UK) on 11 Apr 1964.

Most streamed track on Spotify by a lead female artist

"Havana", the 2017 chart-topper by Cuban-American singer Camila Cabello and featuring Young Thug, had accrued 1,182,041,228 streams on Spotify as of 27 Mar 2019.

The **most streamed track on Spotify** is "Shape of You" by Ed Sheeran (UK), which became the first track to pass 2 billion streams in Dec 2018.

The **most streamed track on Spotify in 24 hours** is "All I Want for Christmas Is You" by Mariah Carey (USA, see right), played 10,819,009 times on 24 Dec 2018.

The **most streamed track on Spotify in 24 hours (male)** is "SAD!" by XXXTentacion (USA, b. Jahseh Onfroy, 1998–2018), with 10,415,088 on 19 Jun 2018.

MOST US NO.1 SINGLES BY A FEMALE RAPPER

Cardi B (USA, b. Belcalis Almánzar) has scored three chart-topping tracks on the *Billboard* Hot 100: "Bodak Yellow (Money Moves)" on 7 Oct 2017; "I Like It" (feat. Bad Bunny & J Balvin) on 7 Jul 2018; and "Girls Like You" (Maroon 5 feat. Cardi B) on 29 Sep 2018. She was enlisted as guest vocalist on the remix of "Girls Like You", which originally appeared on Maroon 5's *Red Pill Blues* album in 2017.

MOST SIMULTANEOUS VIEWERS FOR A MUSIC VIDEO ON YOUTUBE PREMIERES

On 30 Nov 2018, "thank u, next" by Ariana Grande (USA) hit 829,000 simultaneous views on YouTube's Premieres scheduling feature.

Grande also achieved the **most streams on Spotify in one year for a female musician** – 3 billion in 2018 – while "7 rings" became the **most streamed track on Spotify in one week** – 71,467,874 times on 18–24 Jan 2019.

On 23 Feb 2019, she became the **first solo act to occupy the Top 3 simultaneously on the US singles chart** with "thank u, next", "break up with your girlfriend, i'm bored" and "7 rings". She is also the **first female artist to replace herself at No.1 on the UK singles chart**: "break up with your girlfriend, i'm bored" unseated "7 rings" on 21 Feb 2019.

Interest in the Florida rapper's music had spiked after he was fatally shot the previous day.

Most weeks at No.1 on *Billboard*'s Top Latin Albums chart (male)

Ozuna (PRI, b. Juan Carlos Ozuna Rosado) logged 46 non-consecutive weeks at the top with *Odisea* from 16 Sep 2017 to 1 Sep 2018.

HIGHEST-CHARTING CHRISTMAS SONG ON THE HOT 100 BY A SOLO ARTIST

First released in 1994, "All I Want for Christmas Is You" by Mariah Carey (USA) peaked at No.3 on the *Billboard* Hot 100 dated 5 Jan 2019. "The Chipmunk Song" by The Chipmunks with David Seville (below), which reached No.1 almost 60 years earlier, on 22 Dec 1958, is the only holiday song to peak higher than Carey's festive favourite.

MOST CHARTED TITLES ON ANY *BILLBOARD* LATIN AIRPLAY CHART

Salsa singer Victor Manuelle (PRI, b. USA) had achieved 72 charted titles on *Billboard*'s Tropical Songs chart, as of 12 Mar 2019. Known as El Sonero de la Juventud ("The Singer of Youths"), Manuelle is a hugely popular exponent of *salsa romántica*. He notched up his 72nd hit with "Con Mi Salsa La Mantengo" on 16 Feb 2019.

SEP 27 At the 2016 Ski Fluid International, Jacinta Carroll (AUS) completes the **longest waterski jump (female)** – 60.3 m (197 ft 10 in) – on Lake Grew in Polk City, Florida, USA.

SEP 28 In 2012, sideshow artiste "Zoe L'Amore", aka Zoe Ellis (AUS), achieves the **most mouse traps released on the tongue in one minute (female)** – 24 – in London, UK.

FIRST ALBUM TO GENERATE 1 BILLION AUDIO STREAMS IN ONE WEEK

On 29 Jun 2018, Drake (CAN, b. Aubrey Drake Graham) released the double album *Scorpion*, whose 25 tracks were streamed more than 1 billion times worldwide in the following week. Drake went on to achieve the **most simultaneous tracks on the US singles chart by a solo artist** – with 27 songs in the *Billboard* Hot 100 on 14 Jul 2018. This included the **most simultaneous Top 10 entries** – seven, all taken from *Scorpion*, including No.1 "Nice for What".

All 25 songs from Drake's *Scorpion* hit the US Hot 100. His 193 career chart entries (as of 9 Mar 2019) are the **most US Hot 100 entries by a solo artist**.

YOUNGEST FEMALE TO REACH NO.1 ON THE UK ALBUMS CHART

WHEN WE ALL FALL ASLEEP, WHERE DO WE GO?, the debut studio set by US singer-songwriter Billie Eilish (b. 18 Dec 2001), entered the UK's albums chart at No.1 on 11 Apr 2019, when she was aged 17 years 114 days.

Eilish also achieved the **most simultaneous** *Billboard* **Hot 100 entries by a female** – 14 – on the chart dated 13 Apr 2019.

BEST-SELLING SINGLE IN THE UK

"Something About the Way You Look Tonight"/"Candle in the Wind 1997" – the latter penned by Elton John and Bernie Taupin (both UK) in 1973 but reworked for Diana, Princess of Wales (1961–97) after her death – has sold 4.9 million copies in the UK. Some 50 years after his first UK Top 10 hit, "Your Song", Sir Elton has embarked on his three-year *Farewell Yellow Brick Road* world tour of more than 300 concerts. A biopic of the star entitled *Rocketman* has a May 2019 release date.

LONGEST TIME BETWEEN THE RELEASE OF AN ORIGINAL RECORDING AND A RE-RECORDING OF THE SAME SINGLE BY THE SAME ARTIST

In 1949, under the stage name Joe Bari, Tony Bennett (USA) made his recording debut with a cover of the George Gershwin-penned jazz standard "Fascinating Rhythm". On 3 Aug 2018 – a total of 68 years 342 days later – the legendary singer released a new version of the track, recorded with Diana Krall.

SEP 29 Fans of the Kansas City Chiefs (USA) unleash the **loudest crowd roar at a sports stadium**. They reach a deafening 142.2 dbA during their 41–14 defeat of the New England Patriots in 2014.

SEP 30 In 2010, the **fastest wedding chapel** hits 99 km/h (62 mph) in Shelbyville, Illinois, USA. The *Best Man* is a converted fire truck fitted out with stained-glass windows, pews and a pulpit.

197

LIVE MUSIC

First rock 'n' roll concert
The Moondog Coronation Ball at the Cleveland Arena in Ohio, USA, on 21 Mar 1952 has been described as the "Big Bang of rock 'n' roll". The concert was organized by DJ Alan Freed and music-store owner Leo Mintz, and headlined by saxophonist Paul Williams and his Hucklebuckers (all USA). The event was abandoned after approximately 30 minutes owing to overcrowding and rioting.

Largest audience for a free rock concert
On 31 Dec 1994, Rod Stewart (UK) drew *c.* 4.2 million fans for a New Year's Eve show on Copacabana beach in Rio de Janeiro, Brazil. Although some of the crowd may have come for the midnight firework display, Stewart still doubled the previous attendance record at the location.

Largest TV audience for a rock concert
The Beach Boys, David Bowie and Queen were among the acts to perform at the dual-venue Live Aid charity concerts on 13 Jul 1985, which were watched by 1.9 billion people in 150 countries. Organized by musicians Bob Geldof (IRL) and Midge Ure (UK), the event was broadcast simultaneously from Wembley Stadium in London, UK, and John F Kennedy Stadium in Philadelphia, Pennsylvania, USA.

Oldest annual pop music festival
The Reading Festival (UK) started out as the nomadic National Jazz (& Blues) Festival in 1961 before moving to its permanent home in Reading, Berkshire, in 1971. It has been staged every year bar 1984 and 1985, when the site was unavailable.

The **oldest continuous annual pop music festival** is the Pinkpop Festival, which was set to celebrate its golden anniversary in Jun 2019. It has been staged in the Dutch province of Limburg every year since 1970.

Highest-grossing music festival (current)
The Outside Lands Music and Arts Festival, staged in San Francisco, California, USA, on 10–12 Aug 2018, grossed more than $27.7 m (£21.7 m) according to Pollstar. The three-day extravaganza was headlined by The Weeknd, Florence + The Machine and Janet Jackson.

HIGHEST-GROSSING MUSIC TOUR BY A DUO (CURRENT)
Beyoncé and Jay-Z's (both USA) *On the Run II Tour* grossed $253.5 m (£195.2 m) from 48 shows in 2018, according to figures reported to Billboard Boxscore. The duo (aka The Carters) kicked off their second co-headlining stadium tour on 6 Jun and finished on 4 Oct at CenturyLink Field in Seattle, Washington, USA.

Highest-grossing music tour by a female artist (ever)
Madonna's (USA) *Sticky & Sweet Tour* grossed $407.7 m (then £250.9 m) in 2008–09. The 85-date trek, in support of the *Hard Candy* album, kicked off at Cardiff's Millennium Stadium, UK, on 23 Aug 2008 and wound up at Yarkon Park in Tel Aviv, Israel, on 2 Sep 2009. The tour drew 3.54 million fans, with each show grossing $4.79 m (£2.95 m).

Most live music performances in 24 hours (multiple cities)
As part of his *Never Give Up Tour*, Scott Helmer (USA) headlined 12 charity concerts on 28–29 Nov 2016. The singer-songwriter began his US music marathon in San Diego, California, and finished in Phoenix, Arizona, on "Giving Tuesday". Since 2012, Helmer has raised in excess of $2 m (£1.53 m) for good causes across the USA.

First musical act to perform a concert on every continent
Metallica (USA) became the first musical act to play a gig on all seven continents when they entertained 120 scientists and competition winners at Antarctica's Carlini Station on 8 Dec 2013. The hour-long show was dubbed "Freeze 'Em All".

First live music concert broadcast to space
On 12 Nov 2005, Paul McCartney (UK) serenaded astronauts on the *International Space Station* with two songs – "English Tea" and "Good Day Sunshine" – performed live from his concert in Anaheim, California, USA.

MOST LIVE ALBUMS RELEASED
Excluding bootleg recordings, rock band the Grateful Dead (USA) have released 167 full-length live albums since 1969 – of which 150 have appeared since the Californian collective disbanded in 1995. Retrospective live albums include archived concert recordings in the *Dick's Picks* (1993–2005), *Road Trips* (2007–11) and *Dave's Picks* (2012–present) series.

HIGHEST-GROSSING MUSIC TOUR
The *U2 360° Tour* (pictured left) by the Irish rock giants generated $736.4 m (then £450 m) from 110 shows staged between 30 Jun 2009 and 30 Jul 2011.
Proving their staying power, between 2 May and 28 Oct 2018, U2 earned $119.2 m (£92.8 m) from their 55-show *eXPERIENCE + iNNOCENCE Tour* – the **highest-grossing music tour by a band (current)**.

MOST PERFORMANCES BY A MUSICIAN AT MADISON SQUARE GARDEN
On 18 Jul 2018, Billy Joel (USA) played his 100th concert at Madison Square Garden in New York City, USA. He was joined on stage by Bruce Springsteen for "Tenth Avenue Freeze-Out" and "Born to Run". Joel – who had upped his total to 107 shows at the iconic venue as of 14 Feb 2019 – has been staging one show a month there since 27 Jan 2014 as part of his *Billy Joel in Concert* tour.

OCT 1 The **largest balloon village** opens in Xiamen Jimei New City, China. Made with 365,000 balloons by artist Guido Verhoef (NLD) for the 2016 International Balloon Festival, it features a palace and a panda garden.

OCT 2 In 2007, Tim Leigh (UK) has his **largest collection of salt and pepper sachets** verified at 172 matching pairs. The seasoned collector had been amassing them for nine years.

HIGHEST-GROSSING MUSIC TOUR IN A SINGLE YEAR

Ed Sheeran's (UK) ÷ [*Divide*] *Tour* of 2018 generated $429.5 m (£336.6 m) from 99 shows, with a total attendance of 4,800,441. This is the highest gross reported for a music tour in a single year since Billboard Boxscore was first published in 1990, beating the $425.1 m (then £216.9 m) made by The Rolling Stones' *A Bigger Bang* tour in 2006.

The **highest-grossing music tour by a female artist (current)** is the *Reputation Stadium Tour* by Taylor Swift (USA, right). Her fifth concert tour grossed $345.7 m (£269.4 m) in 2018.

HIGHEST ANNUAL EARNINGS FOR A MUSICIAN (FEMALE, CURRENT)

According to estimates published by Forbes, pop star Katy Perry (USA) earned $83 m (£62.37 m) from 1 Jun 2017 to 1 Jun 2018. This is thanks in large part to 80 dates of her *Witness: The Tour*, which grossed a reported $1 m (£751,515) per night.

The record for a **male musician** during the same period is held by Ed Sheeran (UK, see above), with annual earnings of $110 m (£82.66 m) according to Forbes.

BIGGEST-SELLING LIVE ALBUM

Eric Clapton's (UK) multiple-Grammy-winning 1992 album *Unplugged* has sold an estimated 26 million copies worldwide. The set was recorded live at Bray Studios near Maidenhead in Berkshire, UK, on 16 Jan 1992 and includes the single "Tears in Heaven" and an acoustic version of "Layla". As of 25 Jan 2019, *Unplugged* had been certified by the RIAA (Recording Industry Association of America) for shipments of 10 million units, making it the third-biggest-selling live album in the USA.

Left Shark, who found fame in Katy Perry's Super Bowl XLIX half-time show, joined her on stage during the tour.

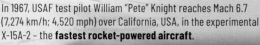

OCT 3 In 1967, USAF test pilot William "Pete" Knight reaches Mach 6.7 (7,274 km/h; 4,520 mph) over California, USA, in the experimental X-15A-2 – the **fastest rocket-powered aircraft**.

OCT 4 A *T. rex* skeleton named "Sue" fetches $8.3 m (£5.1 m) at auction in 1997. The **most expensive dinosaur bones** are acquired by The Field Museum in Chicago, Illinois, USA.

199

VIDEOGAMING

This year's *Guinness World Records Gamer's Edition* – available now – focuses on the most popular videogame characters of all time. Here, we offer a taster of the stats and facts – and design – that you'll find in the world's best-selling game-records book.

Most critically acclaimed Sonic videogame

As of 29 Mar 2019, *Sonic Mania* (Sega, 2017) had an average score of 87.02% on GameRankings. It surpassed the 86.51% rating of *Sonic Adventure* (Sega, 1999), which had long held the title. Released to mark the speedy hedgehog's 25th anniversary, retro-styled *Sonic Mania* was a return to the series' 2D roots.

Best-selling remastered videogame collection

Uncharted: The Nathan Drake Collection (Sony, 2015) is the PS4 re-release of the first three games in the series. It has proven a hit with gamers across the world: as of 21 Mar 2019, it had sold 5.7 million copies according to sales-tracking website VGChartz. The PlayStation exclusive sees Drake's PS3 adventures leap to the PS4 with improved graphics, new trophies and an added photo mode.

Most critically acclaimed action-adventure videogame

The Legend of Zelda: Ocarina of Time (Nintendo, 1998) had a rating of 97.54% on GameRankings as of 5 Feb 2019.

The **fastest completion of *The Legend of Zelda: Ocarina of Time*** is 17 min 4 sec, by Torje Amundsen (NOR) on 5 Sep 2018. The game is hotly contested at Speedrun, with more than 5,000 runs being logged by its fanbase. Although the game is more than 20 years old, skilled speed-runners are still finding ever-faster routes through it.

KNOW THE GAME? NAME THE CHARACTER!

As of 5 Feb 2019, these are the most critically acclaimed games in their respective franchises, as listed on GameRankings. Can you identify the key protagonists? Find the answers on p.249.

10. Tekken 3
A martial arts anti-hero, his Devil gene makes him as powerful as a demon.

He goes from rookie cop to a special agent tackling biothreats and zombies.
9. Resident Evil 4

8. ------ Arkham City
Childhood tragedy sees him morph into Gotham's Dark Knight.

A female bounty hunter, her arch-enemies are the Space Pirates.
7. Metroid Prime

6. Uncharted 2
This Indiana Jones-inspired figure is a rogue with endearing flaws.

Best-selling sci-fi shooter videogame series

Excluding its spin-off strategy series *Halo Wars*, Microsoft's *Halo* franchise had racked up global sales of 65.08 million as of 21 Mar 2019, according to VGChartz.

The **best-selling *Halo* videogame** is *Halo 3* (2007), which had recorded worldwide sales of 12.13 million as of the same date. The game is also the only entry in the franchise to have sold more than 10 million copies.

Most critically acclaimed videogame (current)

The critics' favourite videogame to be released in 2018 (the latest full year for which reviews are available) was Rockstar's *Red Dead Redemption 2*. According to GameRankings, this western became an instant classic, receiving an aggregate score of 96.45% across 49 reviews. Its nearest competitor was Sony's *God of War*, with a score of 94.10% across 63 reviews.

OCT 5 David Kunst (USA) completes the **first circumnavigation by walking (verified)** in 1974. He had set out more than four years earlier, covering a total of 23,250 km (14,450 mi) on foot.

OCT 6 Kurt Hess (CHE) achieves the **greatest vertical height ascended by climbing stairs in 24 hours** - 18,585 m (60,974 ft) - in 2007. He climbs and descends the Esterli Tower in Switzerland 413 times.

MOST UBIQUITOUS VIDEOGAME CHARACTER

Mario had appeared in 217 discrete videogame titles as of 5 Feb 2019, excluding remakes and re-releases. At least two more, *Dr Mario World* and *Mario Kart Tour* (both Nintendo), are set for release in 2019. The character debuted in *Donkey Kong* (1981) as a carpenter named "Jumpman".

The **best-selling Mario game** is the NES release of *Super Mario Bros.* (Nintendo, 1985), which had sold 40.24 million units as of 5 Feb 2019, according to VGChartz. It is also the **best-selling platformer**.

QUICK FACT: ○ Charles Martinet (USA) lent his voice to Mario in 100 games from 1995 to 2018 – the **most videogame voiceovers as the same character**.

He's a ruthless thug in a gang, but then develops a moral conscience.

5. Red Dead Redemption 2

4. SoulCalibur

Known as "The Dread Pirate" and "The Immortal Pirate", his real name is...?

This immigrant war veteran loses faith in the American Dream.

3. Grand Theft Auto IV

2. The Legend of Zelda: Ocarina of Time

His arch-enemy is Ganondorf and his main ally is Princess Zelda.

Mamma mia! It's the Mushroom Kingdom's favourite plumber!

1. ----- ----- Galaxy

Best-selling videogame heroine

With confirmed lifetime sales of 44.5 million as of 21 Mar 2019, Square Enix's *Tomb Raider*, starring Lara Croft, has outsold every other franchise featuring a female lead, according to VGChartz. It has inspired novels, comics and movies – including a major film reboot starring Alicia Vikander in 2018. The first game was published by Eidos Interactive on 25 Oct 1996.

Most Platinumed PlayStation videogame

A Platinum trophy is the top achievement possible in a PlayStation videogame, obtainable only by completing every other trophy challenge in the game. As of 13 Feb 2018, players of *Assassin's Creed II* (Ubisoft, 2009) on PS3 had achieved 156,569 Platinum trophies, based on the several million gamer accounts tracked by PSNProfiles.

OCT 7
In 1990, Slovenian climbers Andrej and Marija Štremfelj become the **first married couple to conquer Everest**, summitting the mountain via the South Col.

OCT 8
In 2001, David Meenan (USA) achieves the **longest distance tap-danced**, covering 51.49 km (32 mi) in 7 hr 35 min at Count Basie Track and Field in New Jersey, USA.

First battle-royale videogame with 250 million registered players

If someone talks about *Fortnite*, it's *Battle Royale* they mean. On 29 Mar 2019, Epic Games (USA) verified that the game had 250 million registered players – more than three-and-a-quarter times the population of the UK. Epic Games rarely discusses *Fortnite*'s user stats, but it was only on 27 Nov 2018 that it revealed that the game had 200 million registered players – which was itself a 60% leap from the 125 million announced in Jun 2018.

MOST DAMAGING WEAPON IN *FORTNITE* (DPS)

Looking to make a lasting impression in *Fortnite Battle Royale* (Epic, 2017)? The Legendary Double Barrel Shotgun (**1**), Legendary Minigun (**2**) and Rare Submachine Gun (**3**) all produce an unmatched 228 damage per second (DPS).

The **most damaging weapon in *Fortnite* (single shot)**, meanwhile, is the Legendary Heavy Sniper Rifle (**4**). At 157 damage per shot, this ultra-rare weapon packs the biggest punch per bullet. However with a slow reload, you'll want to make your first shot count!

First *Fortnite* player to achieve 100,000 eliminations

US gamer "HighDistortion", aka Jimmy Moreno, reached this milestone on 21 Jan 2019. He has also achieved the **most cumulative eliminations in *Fortnite*** – 101,017, as of 28 Jan 2019.

Most concurrently played videogame

In Mar 2019, *Fortnite* notched up 10.8 million concurrent players. Its success is down to a range of factors, including its availability on consoles, PC and mobile devices, and the fact that it's free to play (see p.188).

Most-watched *Fortnite*-themed video on YouTube

"The Fortnite Rap Battle | #NerdOut ft Ninja, CDNThe3rd, Dakotaz, H2O Delirious & More" by "NerdOut!" had 96,097,735 views as of 29 Apr 2019. It was first uploaded to YouTube on 10 Mar 2018 and features a comedy rap over footage from *Fortnite*.

First console-exclusive *Fortnite* skin

Owning a PlayStation 4 and being a PlayStation Plus member is the only way to acquire the Blue Team Leader skin. It was released for Sony's console on 14 Feb 2018, alongside the Blue Streak glider. Microsoft released its Eon skin for Xbox One S owners months later, and Nintendo followed with its Double Helix Outfit.

First Marvel character in *Fortnite*

On 8 May 2018, to mark the cinematic release of Marvel Studios' *Avengers: Infinity War* (USA), Thanos the mad Titan descended into *Fortnite*. The temporary crossover event was called "Infinity Gauntlet" mode. Players could transform into Thanos by finding the Infinity Gauntlet that landed at a random spot at the start of the game. If Thanos was eliminated, the gauntlet would fall to the ground, free for any other character to collect. The crossover ended on 15 May 2018.

Most Twitch channels for a videogame

By 29 Apr 2019, *Fortnite* had been streamed by 66,600 Twitch channels. Runner-up was Respawn's *Apex Legends* (2019), streamed by a peak of 18,919 channels.

Most-followed Twitch channel

Fortnite player and broadcaster "Ninja", aka Richard Tyler Blevins (USA), had accumulated 14,064,046 followers on Twitch as of 29 Apr 2018, according to Social Blade. His statistics surged by some 2 million within just a few weeks of his all-star stream on 14 Mar 2018 with American football icon "JuJu" Smith-Schuster and musicians Drake and Travis Scott, and have continued to rapidly increase since.

LARGEST LEGO®-BRICK *FORTNITE* GUN

Built by LEGO designer and YouTuber "ZaziNombies LEGO Creations", aka Kyle L Neville (CAN), this scale replica of *Fortnite*'s eviscerating Minigun was 140 cm (4 ft 7 in) long, comprised more than 5,000 LEGO bricks and topped 8 kg (17 lb 10 oz). It took some 60 hours to build over a week and was unveiled on YouTube on 22 Feb 2018.

The YouTube video in which the record-breaking Minigun was unveiled had 812,255 views as of 1 Apr 2019.

MOST PARTICIPANTS IN A VIDEOGAME EMOTE ROUTINE

"Emotes" are gestures or dances that a gamer's character can perform in play. On 28 Oct 2018, a group of 383 *Fortnite* fans donned Cuddle Team Leader hoodies for a mass emote routine during Paris Games Week in the French capital. The hooded horde emoted to "Boogie Down", "Orange Justice" and "Groove Jam" among others, in an event organized by Epic Games.

OCT 9 — Shiko Kurihara (JPN) achieves the **most kisses received in one minute** – 131 – in 2014 at the Differ Ariake sporting arena in Tokyo, Japan.

OCT 10 — A version of Ptolemy's *Cosmographia* dating from 1477 becomes the **most expensive atlas** when it sells for £2,136,000 (then $3,990,930) at Sotheby's in London, UK, in 2006.

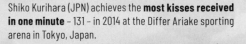

MOST WINS IN *FORTNITE*

This free, last-one-standing online game has beaten all-comers since its 26 Sep 2017 debut. The gameplay sees 100 players skydive on to an island to fight it out solo, in a duo or as a squad.

As of 30 Oct 2018, the **most wins** – playing solo or as a team – was 5,567 (in 11,746 games) by "ViniciusΔmazing ツ" (BRA). "COOLER eXzacT" (HRV) had the **longest solo winning streak** – 36 consecutive wins – while "FeroX M33P_" had notched up the **longest winning streak as part of a squad** – 66 – by the same date. The **most solo first-place finishes** was 4,351, by "SoaR PierXBL" (USA), as of 13 Dec 2018.

In late 2018, a new patch for Fortnite Season 6 saw "Cube Monsters" (zombies, effectively) enter the fray. To deal with them, players gained another weapon: the Fiend Hunter Crossbow.

▶ MOST *FORTNITE* VICTORY ROYALES USING A QUADSTICK

After a serious fall left him quadriplegic, "RockyNoHands", aka Rocky Stoutenburgh (USA), trained himself to play games using a mouth-operated joystick. As of 26 Mar 2019, he had fought his way to 509 *Fortnite* Victory Royales. He has also achieved the **most eliminations in a single *Fortnite* Battle Royale using a QuadStick**: 11, on 3 Oct 2018.

RAREST SKIN IN *FORTNITE*

If you spot a Recon Expert, make sure to take a screenshot. This Season 1 skin was only available for two weeks between 27 Oct and 12 Nov 2017, and then just to those who shelled out 1,200 V-Bucks for an otherwise bland outfit. As of 12 Nov 2018, it had spent a full year out of the *Fortnite* shop.

MOST POPULAR *FORTNITE* SKIN REQUEST

Fortnite aficionados have dreamt up hundreds of skins, but none stand (perch?) as tall as the mighty Chicken Trooper (Tender Defender). Created by Connor, the son of Reddit user "tfoust10", it wields an egg-whisk axe, wears a cracked-egg backpack and flies into battle atop a fellow chicken. The concept was posted to Reddit on 12 Sep 2018 and had earned more than 44,700 upvotes as of 31 Oct 2018.

OCT 11 The **first in-flight meal** is served up in 1919 on the Handley Page Transport (UK) service from London to Paris. It consists of a pre-packed lunch of sandwiches and fruit.

OCT 12 In 2016, the **longest radio DJ marathon** ends after 205 hr 2 min 54 sec on Radio B.B.S.I. in Alessandria, Italy. Stefano Venneri (ITA) had started his nearly nine-day broadcast on 4 Oct.

TV: MOST IN-DEMAND...

PARROT ANALYTICS

To evaluate and compare cross-platform demand for TV series, GWR has teamed up with data-analysis specialists Parrot Analytics. This company has devised a system of "television content demand measurement" that quantifies how viewers are engaging with TV shows. It does so by analysing "Demand Expressions" worldwide – everything from video consumption (streaming/downloads) to social media (hashtags, liking, sharing) and research and commentary (reading or writing about shows, etc.). The more effort – i.e., time – invested by the viewer, the greater the weighting. The interest in a programme is assessed in terms of "Demand Expressions per capita" (DEx/c) – the overall average daily global audience engagement with a show per 100 people within a set time frame. All the "in-demand" records featured here are for the 12-month period leading up to 14 Jan 2019.

MOST IN-DEMAND TV SERIES BASED ON A BOOK ADAPTATION: 6.271 DEx/c

Inspired by George R R Martin's *A Song of Ice and Fire* fantasy novels, *Game of Thrones* (HBO, USA) premiered in 2011. Over the course of eight seasons (the last of which began to air on 14 Apr 2019), the series explores the dynastic power struggles played out in the Seven Kingdoms of Westeros and on the continent of Essos. Pictured is actor Kit Harington, who plays Jon Snow, leader of the fight against the Night King and his army of undead White Walkers.

Action and adventure: 5.235 DEx/c
Medieval drama *Vikings* (History, CAN; 2013–present) follows the fortunes of Norse warriors and their oceanic raids on nearby countries.

Anime: 2.368 DEx/c
Part of a long-running Japanese franchise, *Dragon Ball Super* (Fuji TV, JPN; 2015–18) featured the adventures of the warrior Goku and his friends.

Children's show: 2.561 DEx/c
Starring the endearing eponymous yellow sponge, *SpongeBob SquarePants* (Nickelodeon, USA; 1999–present) is still soaking up fans' adulation.

Documentary: 1.246 DEx/c
Helmed by David Attenborough, the acclaimed *Planet Earth* (BBC, UK; 2006) was the BBC's most expensive nature documentary. For more about this enduring TV presenter, see p.211.

Horror: 3.016 DEx/c
Every season of *American Horror Story* (FX, USA; 2011–present) forms a discrete mini-series in itself. The fright show's stars have included supermodel Naomi Campbell, pop star Lady Gaga and Jyoti Amge, the **shortest woman** (see p.69).

MOST IN-DEMAND REALITY TV SERIES: 2.319 DEx/c
The Voice – a music talent show with "blind" judging – was first broadcast in the Netherlands in 2010 as *The Voice of Holland*. International editions swiftly followed, along with spin-off series including *The Voice Kids*, *The Voice Teens* and *The Voice Senior*. The current panel of the US show (pictured left to right) comprises Adam Levine, John Legend, Kelly Clarkson and Blake Shelton.

Medical drama: 3.850 DEx/c
In *Grey's Anatomy* (ABC, USA; 2005–present), Meredith Grey and the team face life-or-death decisions daily, while discovering that relationships are never black and white.

Remake of a previous series: 3.241 DEx/c
Shameless (Showtime, USA; 2011–present) relocates the British comedy-drama from a Manchester council estate to Chicago's South Side.

Romantic drama: 1.815 DEx/c
In *Outlander* (Starz, USA; 2014–present), nurse Claire Randall is transported from 1945 back to 1743, where she falls for a Highland warrior.

Sci-fi drama: 3.680 DEx/c
Westworld (HBO, USA; 2016–present) was inspired by the titular 1973 movie, making the futuristic Western also the **most in-demand TV series based on a film adaptation**.

Soap opera: 1.311 DEx/c
Dynasty (The CW, USA; 2017–present) reboots the classic 1980s rich-list soap for a new generation.

Superhero show: 4.605 DEx/c
A lightning bolt endows Barry Allen with superhuman speed in *The Flash* (The CW, USA; 2014–present).

TV series debut: 2.956 DEx/c
Titans (DC Universe, USA; 2018–present) sees a team of youthful superheroes unite to fight evil, led by Dick Grayson (Batman's first Robin).

Variety show: 1.640 DEx/c
The late-night *Daily Show with Trevor Noah* (Comedy Central, USA; 2015–present) offers up satire and celebrity chats.

MOST IN-DEMAND TEEN DRAMA TV SERIES: 3.817 DEx/c
Based on characters that first appeared in *Archie Comics*, Netflix's *Riverdale* (The CW, USA) stars K J Apa (centre) in the lead role of Archie Andrews. The series offers a left-field take on the comic-book original, exploring the surreal and darker side to small-town life, which has prompted comparisons to David Lynch's 1990s series *Twin Peaks*.

MOST IN-DEMAND LEGAL DRAMA TV SERIES: 2.927 DEx/c
Created by Aaron Korsh, *Suits* premiered in 2011 and is USA Network's longest-lasting show. Main character Mike Ross (Patrick J Adams, far right) is a college dropout who joins a firm of New York lawyers despite his lack of training. His girlfriend Rachel (second from right) was played by Meghan Markle until she moved to the UK in 2017 following her engagement to Prince Harry.

OCT 13
At UFC 153 in 2012, Anderson Silva (BRA) defeats Stephan Bonnar in the first round of their light-heavyweight bout. It's his 16th victory in a row – the **most consecutive UFC fight wins**.

OCT 14
In 2013, Pavel Gerasimov (RUS) has the **largest collection of squirrel-related items** counted – a total of 1,103 objects are ratified. They include a squirrel statuette made entirely of gold.

MOST IN-DEMAND TV SERIES: 6.999 DEx/c

The Walking Dead (AMC, USA) follows the adventures of deputy sheriff Rick Grimes (played by Andrew Lincoln, pictured), who wakes from a coma to find the world overwhelmed by a zombie apocalypse. Having joined up with a band of survivors, he faces danger not only from the undead (known as "walkers") but also from other groups of humans who have evolved their own moral codes. The series' 10th season is scheduled for an Oct 2019 release. It is also the **most in-demand TV series based on a comic adaptation.**

The *Walking Dead* is based on the comic-book series of the same name created by Robert Kirkman and Tony Moore. It has won two Eisner Awards since its 2003 debut.

MOST IN-DEMAND COMEDY TV SERIES: 4.793 DEx/c

The Big Bang Theory (CBS, USA) features two physicists whose brilliance is hampered by their social awkwardness. It stars Jim Parsons (USA, seated centre), whose estimated income of $26.5 m (£19.9 m) for 1 Jun 2017–1 Jun 2018 saw him named by Forbes as the **highest-earning TV actor** for the fourth year running. The show is also the **most in-demand sitcom.**

MOST IN-DEMAND DIGITAL ORIGINAL SERIES: 3.484 DEx/c

A "digital original series" is one that is produced, or was first made available, on a streaming platform. Set in the 1980s, sci-fi horror hit *Stranger Things* (Netflix, USA) debuted in 2016. Shown below, from left, are Caleb McLaughlin, Gaten Matarazzo (both USA), Finn Wolfhard (CAN) and Sadie Sink (USA).

MOST IN-DEMAND ANIMATED TV SERIES: 2.794 DEx/c

The brainchild of Justin Roiland and Dan Harmon, *Rick and Morty* (USA) premiered in Dec 2013 on Adult Swim, Cartoon Network's late-night slot. Its focus is the Smith household – Jerry and Beth and their children, Summer and Morty. Beth's father, Rick, is an eccentric scientist who lives with them and often cajoles grandson Morty into accompanying him on wild trips across the universe.

OCT 15 The British Trans-African Hovercraft Expedition sets out under David Smithers (UK) in 1969. It travels c. 8,000 km (4,970 mi) through eight West African countries – the **longest hovercraft journey**.

OCT 16 In 2013, two Italian wine merchants suspected of faking at least 400 bottles of Romanée-Conti burgundy are arrested. Estimates of the **most lucrative wine fraud** run to £1.7 m ($2.7 m).

COMICS

First comic
Most experts agree that Swiss cartoonist Rodolphe Töpffer's *Histoire de Mr. Vieux-Bois* ("The Adventures of Mr Wooden Head"), created in 1827 and first published a decade later, is the earliest comic. The story comprised around 30 pages of comic strip. Each page was cut into six panels, with a narrative caption under every drawing.

First comic with a female lead
The character Sheena, Queen of the Jungle, featured in the first issue of *Wags* published in the UK in 1937; her US debut came a year later in *Jumbo Comics* in Sep 1938. Her own comic, *Sheena, Queen of the Jungle*, in which she was the star, arrived in spring 1942. *Wonder Woman* also debuted in 1942, but not until the summer.

Best-selling edition of a single comic
X-Men #1 (Marvel Comics, 1991) enjoyed sales of 8.1 million copies. It was created by Chris Claremont (UK) and Jim Lee (USA). The latter also drew

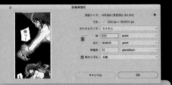

LONGEST SINGLE-PANEL GRAPHIC IMAGE IN A DIGITAL COMIC
On 19 Apr 2018, Papyless (JPN) unveiled a one-panel comic, *Hitokoma no Kuni no Alice* ("Alice's Adventures in One-derland"). It was 320 density-independent pixels (dp) wide and 163,631 dp long. "Dp" technology preserves an image's original size no matter what device it is viewed on, so to see the whole panel readers scroll down the equivalent of 25.56 m (83 ft 10 in). The panel was made to promote TateComi, a service that allows users to read digital manga seamlessly by swiping downwards.

four variant covers for this issue (1A, 1B, 1C and 1D), all with a cover date of Oct 1991. These fitted together to form a larger image, used as the gatefold cover to 1E, which appeared a month later.

Most covers for a superhero comic
Marvel's *The Amazing Spider-Man #666* – the prologue to Dan Slott's "Spider-Island" story arc – was sold with 145 variant covers. Most of them were covers dedicated to individual comic-book retailers.

Most editions of a comic
The Mexican comic *Pepin* printed its first edition on 4 Mar 1936 as a weekly anthology of comics. It eventually became a daily, running until 23 Oct 1956, with a total of 7,561 issues.

Most consecutive issues of a comic drawn and written
In all, Canada's Dave Sim created 300 editions of his indie comic *Cerebus* – describing the adventures of the eponymous aardvark – between Dec 1977 and Mar 2004.

The **most comics published by one author** is 770 titles (in 500 volumes), by Shotaro Ishinomori (JPN, 1938–98).

Largest publisher of manga
Shueisha (JPN), founded in Tokyo in 1925, is the world's biggest manga publisher, with a revenue of 123 bn yen ($1.1 bn; £887.4 m) in the 2016/17 fiscal year. Its flagship title is *Shōnen Jump*, first published in 1968.

LARGEST COMIC BOOK PUBLISHED
Turma da Mônica ("Monica's Gang"), created by Mauricio de Sousa Produções and published by Panini Brasil (both BRA), is 69.9 cm (2 ft 3.5 in) wide by 99.8 cm (3 ft 3.2 in) tall when closed, giving an area of 6,976 cm² (7.5 sq ft). It was measured in São Paulo, Brazil, on 5 Aug 2018. The 18-page edition had a print run of 120 copies.

LONGEST-RUNNING WEEKLY COMIC
British comic book *The Beano* (today simply titled *Beano*) was launched on 30 Jul 1938 (above left) by DC Thomson and has appeared every week since then, except for a period during World War II when its frequency was reduced owing to paper shortages. It is the oldest weekly comic to retain its name and numbering system. The 3,950th issue, dated 1 Sep 2018, is pictured above right.

Most valuable comic
As of 21 Jan 2019, *Action Comics #1* (Jun 1938) – produced by DC Comics (USA) – was valued at $4,620,000 (£3,585,830), according to the Nostomania comic-book price guide. It features the debut of Superman, the **first superhero with superpowers**.

Superman was also the cover star on the 1,000th issue of *Action Comics* in Apr 2018. The deluxe edition marked the 80th year of the **longest-running superhero comic-book series**.

Most strips published for the same yonkoma manga series
The term "yonkoma" describes vertical, four-panel manga cartoons. Shoji Izumi (JPN) has created 15,770 such strips for the series *Jan Ken Pon* since 30 Sep 1969, as verified on 23 Jan 2019. It appears daily in *Asahi Shogakusei Shimbun*, a newspaper for elementary-school children.

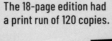

MOST EISNER AWARDS FOR...*		
Best Anthology	5	*Dark Horse Presents*, by Dark Horse Comics (USA; above left)
Best Artist/Penciller	4	P Craig Russell and Steve Rude (both USA)
Best Colourist/Colouring	9	Dave Stewart (USA)
Best Cover Artist	6	James Jean (USA)
Best New Series	4	*Saga*, by Brian K Vaughan (USA; above right)
Best Writer	9	Alan Moore (UK)
One category	17	Todd Klein (USA), for Best Letterer

*As of 8 Apr 2019

OCT 17 In 2011, a portion of an offshore gas platform weighing 23,178 tonnes (25,549 US tons) is raised 26.5 m (87 ft) at a Hyundai shipyard in Ulsan, South Korea. It is the **heaviest object lifted on land**.

OCT 18 In 1998, Ken Thompson (UK) discovers the **largest spider web (outdoors)**. Created by thousands of money spiders, it covers a 4.54-ha (11.22-acre) playing field in Kineton, West Midlands, UK.

This bespoke panel was created for GWR by Nigel Parkinson, who has drawn Beano's Dennis the Menace since 1998.

CERTIFICATE

The largest "finish the comic strip" attracted 723 entrants and was organized by V&A Dundee and Beano (both UK) at the 3D Festival in Dundee, UK, from 15 September to 7 December 2018. The winner was 9-year-old Louise Anderson from Newport on Tay, UK.

OFFICIALLY AMAZING

NIGEL PARKINSON

LARGEST "FINISH THE COMIC STRIP" CONTEST

There were 723 entrants for a competition to conclude a *Beano*-themed cartoon strip at the 3D Festival at V&A Dundee, UK, on 14–15 Sep 2018. Three months later, Louise Anderson's entry (inset) was declared the winner. The multimedia event was staged to mark the opening of the new branch of the Victoria & Albert museum, the original of which is located in London, UK. The makers of *Beano* commemorated their record-breaking achievement with this exclusive illustration.

LONGEST CARTOON STRIP BY AN INDIVIDUAL

On 1–3 Nov 2018, Claudio Sciarrone (ITA) drew a 297.5-m-long (976-ft) cartoon strip on behalf of Walt Disney Company Italia in Lucca, Italy. Claudio is a Disney artist and created the artwork (entitled *Wake-up Mickey Mouse!*) at the Lucca Comics & Games fair to mark the character's 90th anniversary.

A FOND FAREWELL TO STAN "THE MAN" LEE

The late Marvel Comics icon Stan Lee (USA, 1922–2018) held several GWR titles. As of 9 May 2019, these included the **most movies adapted from the work of a comic-book creator** (36), the **highest-grossing cameo actor in movies** ($30 bn; £23 bn) and the **highest-grossing executive producer** ($30.3 bn; £23.3 bn). The pop-up shrines at Stan's star on the Hollywood Walk of Fame attested to the fans' love for this larger-than-life character. Excelsior!

LARGEST COLLECTION OF *DRAGON BALL* MEMORABILIA

Michael Nilsen (USA) had amassed 6,148 items related to the *Dragon Ball* manga/anime series as of 1 Oct 2012, when the count was confirmed in Duluth, Minnesota, USA. The collection, which he began in 1996, includes toys, posters, DVDs, action figures, mouse pads, original animation cells and even a Master Roshi-shaped tissue dispenser.

OCT 19 The **first videogame tournament** – the Intergalactic *Spacewar* Olympics – takes place in 1972 at Stanford University's Artificial Intelligence Laboratory in California, USA.

OCT 20 Peter Wehrmann (DEU) begins the **longest human beatbox marathon** in 2012 at the Best Western Premier Hotel MOA Berlin in Germany. He finishes 25 hr 30 min later.

207

SOCIAL NETWORKS

MOST FOLLOWERS ON INSTAGRAM FOR A TV NATURALIST

Bindi Irwin (AUS; @bindisueirwin) has 2,334,912 followers. She comes from a long line of conservationists including her father, Steve Irwin (1962–2006), her mother Terri and her brother Robert, a wildlife photographer. The Irwin family own Australia Zoo in Queensland.

All records as of 29 Apr 2019, unless otherwise indicated

Largest online social network

Facebook has 2.37 billion monthly active users (defined as those who have logged in to the site within the previous 30 days). The social-media platform reached the 2-billion monthly user mark on 30 Jun 2017.

The **most-liked person on Facebook** is Juventus soccer player Cristiano Ronaldo (PRT), with 122,308,950 likes. The **most-liked female** is Colombian singer Shakira (b. Shakira Mebarak Ripoll) with 101,234,534 likes. On 18 Jul 2014, Shakira became the **first person to reach 100 million likes on Facebook**.

Largest professional online networking site

LinkedIn (USA) has attracted 303 million monthly active users.

The **most-followed LinkedIn user** is Sir Richard Branson (UK), the founder of Virgin, with 15,732,651 followers.

Most followers on Twitter

Pop singer Katy Perry (USA, b. Katheryn Hudson) currently has 107,279,315 Twitter followers. Meanwhile, former US president Barack Obama (@barackobama) has the **most followers on Twitter (male)** – 105,946,443.

Most followers on Twitter for a...

Place: The Museum of Modern Art (USA, @MuseumModernArt) in New York City, USA, has 5,404,072 followers.
Sports account: Soccer team Real Madrid (ESP, @realmadrid) has 31,892,268 Twitter fans.

Fastest time to reach 1 million followers on Twitter

It took Caitlyn Jenner (USA) just 4 hr 3 min to reach the landmark of 1 million Twitter fans on 1 Jun 2015.

Most-used hashtag on Twitter in 24 hours

On 16–17 Mar 2019, the hashtag #TwitterBestFandom achieved 60,055,339 tweets. It was employed as a tool to allow the general public to vote in the 14th Annual Soompi Awards, honouring the best in Korean television and music.

Most-downvoted comment on Reddit

An official post by videogames publisher Electronic Arts, responding to players' complaints about having to unlock characters such as Darth Vader and Luke Skywalker in *Star Wars Battlefront II* (2017) through "loot boxes", has 683,000 downvotes.

Most followers on Weibo

TV host, singer and actress Xie Na (CHN) has 123,810,773 fans on the Chinese microblogging website. On 7 Apr 2018, she became the **first person with 100 million followers on Weibo**.

Weibo's **most-followed male** is TV host and media personality He Jiong (CHN), with 111,759,484.

Most subscribers for an animal channel on YouTube

Hosted by wildlife expert Coyote Peterson (b. Nathaniel Peterson, USA), "Brave Wilderness" launched on 8 Sep 2014 and has 14,264,941 subscribers. It's also YouTube's **most-viewed animal channel**, with 2.6 billion views.

MOST-LIKED IMAGE ON INSTAGRAM

A simple picture of an egg has gained 53,427,655 likes. It was posted on 4 Jan 2019 by the Egg Gang on the account @world_record_egg. Later, it emerged that the Egg Gang are using their record-breaking Instagram image as a platform to support people who suffer from stress and anxiety brought about by the pressures of social media.

In many videos, Peterson interacts with dangerous animals and allows himself to be stung or bitten.

Most-viewed YouTube music video in 24 hours by a solo artist

On 26–27 Apr 2019, Taylor Swift (USA) had 65.2 million views of her video for "ME!", featuring Brendon Urie.

Most consecutive daily personal video blogs posted on YouTube

Charles Trippy (USA) uploaded a total of 3,653 videos from 1 May 2009 to 1 May 2019. After a decade of daily vlogging, Trippy ended his record run to spend more time with his family. Initial vlogs appeared on the channel "Internet Killed Television" (also known as "CTFxC"). He continued his video journal with "Charles and Allie".

MOST FOLLOWERS ON INSTAGRAM

Cristiano Ronaldo (@cristiano) has 163,658,939 followers on the image-sharing site. Only Instagram itself, with 296,269,356 followers, has more fans than the soccer star.

The **most followers on Instagram for a female** is 152,882,321, achieved by singer Ariana Grande (USA, @arianagrande). In second place is US singer/actor Selena Gomez, formerly the most-followed person on the site. Grande also has the **most subscribers for a female musician on YouTube** – 35,242,046.

MOST SUBSCRIBERS ON YOUTUBE

Indian music company T-Series has assembled an impressive 96,321,836 subscribers on video website YouTube. In doing so, it has edged out comedian and gamer "PewDiePie", aka Felix Arvid Ulf Kjellberg (SWE, above right), who had held this record since 2013. A heated contest has grown between the fans of each channel, with visitors going to great lengths – including hacking and issuing diss tracks – to encourage people to subscribe to their favourite.

OCT 21 In 2001, Tuomo Kostian (FIN) achieves the **fastest 5 m inverted rope climb** in 13.7 sec in Helsinki, Finland. He scrambles up feet first until his whole body clears the measured distance.

OCT 22 In 1911, during the Italo-Turkish War, Captain Carlo Piazza (ITA) flies a Blériot monoplane from Tripoli to El Azizia in Libya to reconnoitre Turkish forces – the **first use of aircraft in warfare**.

MOST-VIEWED YOUTUBE MUSIC VIDEO IN 24 HOURS

The official video for the track "Boy with Luv" by BTS (KOR) feat. Halsey (USA) had 74,600,000 views on 12–13 Apr 2019. BTS overtook fellow South Korean pop stars BLACKPINK (right), whose video for "Kill this Love" had achieved a record-breaking 56,700,000 views the week before, on 4–5 Apr.

The chart-topping BTS (@BTS_twt) have also registered the **most Twitter engagements (average retweets)** – 422,228.

MOST-VIEWED VIDEO ONLINE

The music video for "Despacito" by Luis Fonsi feat. Daddy Yankee (both PRI) has been viewed 6,159,897,341 times. Fonsi is seen below with the GWR certificates that the song and its video have been awarded, including the **first YouTube video to reach 5 billion views** (achieved on 4 Apr 2018).

MOST FOLLOWERS ON INSTAGRAM FOR A DOG

A Pomeranian pooch named Jiffpom (@jiffpom) from California, USA, has built up 9,018,251 followers on Instagram. Jiffpom's feed incorporates pictures of him in various outfits, relaxing at home, and attending movie premieres, award ceremonies, TV studios and fashion shows.

FASTEST TIME TO REACH 1 MILLION FOLLOWERS ON INSTAGRAM

It took just 5 hr 45 min for the Duke and Duchess of Sussex – aka Prince Harry (UK) and Meghan Markle (USA) – to reach 1 million followers on Instagram on 2 Apr 2019. Their joint account (@sussexroyal) more than halved South Korean singer Kang Daniel's record of 11 hr 36 min, which had been set on 2 Jan 2019.

OCT 23 Northwest Fudge Factory (CAN) produces the **largest slab of fudge** in 2010 in Levack, Ontario, Canada. The supersized treat weighs 2.61 tonnes (5,754 lb) and contains vanilla, chocolate and maple syrup.

OCT 24 The **largest collection of bagpipes** is verified at 105 playable instruments in 2013 in Cleethorpes, Lincolnshire, UK. They belong to Daniel Fleming (UK), who has been collecting since the age of 10.

ROUND-UP

£500,000

BEST-SELLING TELEVISION FORMAT

As of 2017, there had been 100 international versions of multiple-choice quiz show *Who Wants to Be a Millionaire?* (Sony Pictures Television), according to "Tracking the Giants: The Top 100 Travelling TV Formats 2017–18" by analysts K7 Media. Since first airing on the UK's ITV network on 4 Sep 1998, the show has appeared in at least 142 different variations in more than 80 languages.

HIGHEST-GROSSING SOLO SHOW ON BROADWAY

From first preview on 3 Oct 2017 to closing night on 15 Dec 2018, *Springsteen on Broadway* earned $113,058,952 (£89,771,200) in New York City, USA. The intimate show, which saw "The Boss" and E Street Band frontman reminisce about his life as a performer and sing solo at the piano or with a guitar, sold 223,585 seats in 236 performances.

Highest one-week box-office gross on Broadway

Hamilton, with music, lyrics and book by Lin-Manuel Miranda (USA), grossed $4,041,493 (£3,181,050) in the seven days ending 30 Dec 2018. A total of 10,766 people attended the show that week, shelling out an average of $375.39 (£295.46) per seat.

Hamilton's success contributed to the **highest-grossing week for Broadway theatres**: a total of $57.8 m (£45.5 m) between 24 and 30 Dec 2018.

Youngest person to write a published book (male)

Pint-sized penman Thanuwana Serasinghe (LKA) was aged just 4 years 356 days when his book *Junk Food* was published on 5 Jan 2017. His tome warns of the dangers of unhealthy eating.

Highest-earning author (female, current)

J K Rowling (UK) reportedly earned $54 m (£40.87 m) in the 12 months up to 1 Jul 2018, according to estimates by Forbes. Even without a new *Harry Potter* release, Rowling earned enough from back-catalogue sales, theatrical productions and theme parks for another substantial deposit at Gringotts.

To discover the **highest-earning author (current)** overall, turn to p.132.

Highest-paid TV host

According to estimates published by Forbes on 16 Jul 2018, talk-show host Ellen DeGeneres (USA) earned $87.5 m (£66.22 m) in the 12 months leading up to 1 Jul 2018.

The **highest-paid TV host (male)** is Dr Phil McGraw (USA), who reportedly earned $77.5 m (£58.65 m) in the same period.

Longest-running children's magazine TV programme

Blue Peter (BBC, UK) celebrated its 60th anniversary with a *Big Birthday* live special on 16 Oct 2018. The iconic children's show was first transmitted on 16 Oct 1958.

Most Primetime Emmy Awards for a TV series

NBC's *Saturday Night Live* has won 62 Primetime Emmys since it first aired in 1975. The late-night laughfest was awarded three statuettes in 2018, including Outstanding Variety Sketch Series.

Also in 2018, *The Simpsons* (Fox) received a juried prize for Outstanding Individual Achievement in Animation. That took its tally to 33 – the **most Emmy Awards for an animated TV series**.

Most Grammy nominations for a female artist

Beyoncé (USA) received 66 Grammy nominations between 2000 and 2018. She was nominated three times for the 61st Annual

Blue whales weigh around 136 tonnes (150 US tons) – the same as the amount of plastic dumped in the ocean every 9 min.

Monterey Bay Aquarium

OCT 25 In 2009, Miki Sakabe (JPN) completes the **fastest 100 m bum walk** in 11 min 59 sec. He covers the course, powered primarily by his *glutei maximi*, in Hokkaido, Japan.

OCT 26 In 2002, German dairy Edelweiss Käsewerk produces the **largest soft cheese**, weighing 180 kg (396 lb) – about the same as three adult humans – in Kempten, Germany.

MOST EXPENSIVE WORK BY A LIVING ARTIST (AUCTION)

Portrait of an Artist (Pool with Two Figures), an acrylic-on-canvas painted by David Hockney (UK) in 1972, sold for $90,312,500 (£69,547,900) – including buyer's premium – at Christie's auction house in New York City, USA, on 15 Nov 2018. Hockney completed the piece in an explosion of creative activity, working 18-hr shifts for a fortnight.

Grammy Awards – held on 10 Feb 2019 – as one half of The Carters, her husband-and-wife project with Jay-Z (see p.198 for more).

rewarded for his dedication with free tickets from the directors to the premiere of 2019's sequel *Avengers: Endgame* (USA, see p.193).

Most cinema productions attended (same film)

Anthony "Nem" Mitchell (USA) had seen *Avengers: Infinity War* (USA, 2018) a total of 103 times as of 19 Jul 2018. The superhero superfan was

Most expensive *Star Wars* figurine sold at auction

A prototype resin master of Bib Fortuna, a model used to create tie-in toys for *Return of the Jedi* (USA, 1983), sold for £36,000 ($46,540)

– including buyer's premium – on 30 Apr 2019. The rare *Star Wars* item was the top seller of three lots – the other two figurines were Ewok "Logray" and an Emperor's Royal Guard – all sold at Vectis auction house in Thornaby, North Yorkshire, UK.

LARGEST...

Anaglyph 3D mural

An anaglyph 3D artwork comprises two differently filtered coloured images

which, when viewed through special glasses, reveal a single stereoscopic image. On 14 Mar 2018, Jason Tetlak (USA) unveiled an anaglyph 3D mural of hip-hop group the Beastie Boys covering 179.36 m² (1,930 sq ft) – the equivalent area of 45 king-size beds – in Jacksonville, Florida, USA.

Tapestry

To mark the 100th year of the Peruvian town of Espinar, on 15 Nov 2018 Planta de Fibra y Lana Convenio Marco de Espinar (PER) unveiled

a 288.55-m² (3,106-sq-ft) tapestry. Twelve artisans worked for three months on the hanging, which is big enough to cover a tennis court. It depicts traditional Cuzqueño imagery and clothing associated with indigenous K'ana dancers.

▶ **Drawing by an individual** Alex Dzaghiglan (CYP) drew a 323.90-m² (3,486-sq-ft) charcoal sketch of a turtle swimming in waste plastic, as verified on 29 Dec 2018 in Nicosia, Cyprus.

LONGEST CAREER AS A TELEVISION PRESENTER

Released on Netflix on 5 Apr 2019, *Our Planet* was the latest series narrated by naturalist Sir David Attenborough (UK). His on-screen debut came on 2 Sep 1953 in BBC Children's Television's *Animal Disguises* (UK) – giving him a total career duration of 65 years 215 days to date. He is the only person to have won BAFTA awards for series in black and white, colour, HD and 3D formats. His record is set to be extended with the upcoming 2019 series *One Planet, Seven Worlds* (BBC).

Our Planet was shot over four years in 50 countries, with more than 600 members of crew involved.

LARGEST RECYCLED PLASTIC SCULPTURE (SUPPORTED)

In 2018, to bring attention to the issue of plastic pollution, the Monterey Bay Aquarium (USA) created a life-size blue whale made from plastic trash (including milk jugs, detergent bottles and toys) collected from the San Francisco Bay Area. The whale measured 25.89 m (84 ft 11 in) long, as verified on 26 Nov 2018 in San Francisco, California, USA.

The **largest sculpture made from pet tags** is *Sun Spot* (right), created from 90,000 stainless-steel dog ID tags in 2011 by artists Laura Haddad and Tom Drugan (both USA). It was commissioned for the Denver Animal Shelter in Colorado, USA.

On 22 Sep 2018, Zunyi Culture & Tourism Development Group (CHN) presented a *Triceratops* dinosaur made from 10 different kinds of vegetable (far right) in Chishui, Guizhou Province, China. The 14.31-m-long (46-ft 11-in) and 5.4-m-tall (17-ft 8-in) "veggie-saurus" is the **largest mixed-vegetable sculpture**.

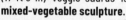

OCT 27 Steve Fossett (USA) and co-pilot Hans-Paul Ströhle (DEU) attain the **fastest speed for an airship**, reaching 115 km/h (71.46 mph) in a Zeppelin Luftschifftechnik LZ N07-100 over Germany in 2004.

OCT 28 The government of the state of Hidalgo in Mexico presents the **largest Day of the Dead altar** in Pachuca in 2017. It covers 846.48 m² (9,111.43 sq ft) and is decorated with 9,200 Mexican marigolds.

211

SPORTS

FASTEST-RUN MARATHON

On 16 Sep 2018, Eliud Kipchoge (KEN) completed the Berlin Marathon in Germany in a time of 2 hr 1 min 39 sec. He smashed the previous marathon world record – set by compatriot Dennis Kimetto in 2014, also in Berlin – by 1 min 18 sec. This represents the largest single improvement over the distance since 1967.

As athletes run faster, the prospect of a 2-hr marathon – once considered impossible – becomes increasingly likely. On 6 May 2017, Kipchoge clocked a time of 2 hr 25 sec as part of Nike's "Breaking2" marathon challenge, although this did not count as an official IAAF record owing to the use of in-out pacemakers.

CONTENTS

Kipchoge's record-breaking run was his third victory at the Berlin Marathon. In 2013, he finished second behind Wilson Kipsang, who won in a then-record 2:03:23; it remains Kipchoge's only marathon loss to date, from 12 races.

OLYMPIC PREVIEW

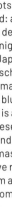

On 24 Jul 2020, a flaming torch will be carried into the New National Stadium in Tokyo, Japan, to light a cauldron that will signal the opening of the Games of the XXXII Olympiad. The world's finest athletes will compete in a variety of sports, from archery to wrestling, all hoping to return home with a gold medal. With the Paralympic Games to follow on 25 Aug–6 Sep, Japan is set for two festivals of supreme sporting excellence.

MOST OLYMPIC MEDALS

One record that won't be broken in Tokyo is that of Michael Phelps (USA), who won 28 Olympic medals between 2004 and 2016: 23 golds, three silvers and two bronze. In 2008, he won the **most Olympic golds at one Games** – eight – and set seven world records, including the **fastest men's long course 400 m individual medley**: 4 min 3.84 sec.

Tokyo will be hosting the Summer Olympics for the second time, 56 years after the Games were held there in 1964. (The city had originally been scheduled to host the 1940 Summer Olympics, but this was cancelled following the outbreak of World War II.) The 2020 Games will be staged at 42 venues dotted around Tokyo, clustered around two circular zones – "Heritage Zone" and "Tokyo Bay Zone" – with the Olympic Village sited where they border one another. Several of the venues used in 1964 will be hosting Olympic events for the second time, including the Nippon Budokan (judo) and the Yoyogi National Gymnasium (handball).

The mascots have already been unveiled: a pair of superheroes designed by artist Ryo Taniguchi and selected by Japanese elementary-school children. The Olympic mascot is Miraitowa (in blue, above left), whose name is a compound of the Japanese words for "future" and "eternity". Paralympic mascot Someity (in pink, above right) derives its name from a type of cherry blossom.

ANCIENT HISTORY
The **first Olympic Games** of which there is a certain record took place in Jul 776 BCE at a religious sanctuary in Olympia, Greece. Coroibos, a cook from the nearby city-state of Elis, won the stadion footrace. He received an olive branch for his victory. The Games went into decline during the latter days of the Roman Empire, and were officially banned, along with other "pagan festivals", by Emperor Theodosius I in 393 CE. They would not return until 1896, when the competition was resurrected by Pierre de Coubertin, founder of the International Olympic Committee. The **first modern Olympic Games** were staged in Athens, Greece, on 6 Apr 1896. It was a modest affair by today's standards, with a total of 241 participants representing 14 countries.

By contrast, the 2020 Games will feature more than 11,000 athletes, participating in 33 different sports. This total includes five events that are making their Olympic debut: karate, skateboarding, surfing, sport climbing and softball/baseball (both softball and baseball have appeared before, but not classified together). New events in established sports include 3x3 basketball, played on a half-court with a single basket, and BMX freestyle park, recognizable from the X Games. The aim is to maximize the appeal of the Olympics to younger

OLYMPIC GREATS

FIRST MODERN CHAMPION
James Connolly (USA) won the hop, skip and jump (precursor to the modern triple jump) at the 1896 Olympic Games in Athens, Greece, on 6 Apr 1896. He produced a leap of 13.71 m (44 ft 11 in) to finish ahead of the field, becoming the first recorded Olympic champion since the Armenian boxer Prince Varasdates in 369 CE, 1,527 years earlier.

OLDEST MEDALLIST
On 27 Jul 1920, Swedish marksman Oscar Swahn (b. 20 Oct 1847) won an Olympic silver medal aged 72 years 281 days in the men's 100 m running deer (double shots) shooting team event in Antwerp, Belgium. He was already the **oldest Olympic gold medallist**, having won the men's 100 m running deer (single shot) event aged 64 years 258 days in 1912.

MOST ATHLETICS GOLD MEDALS AT ONE GAMES
In 1924, Paavo Nurmi (FIN) earned five gold medals – winning the 1,500 m, 5,000 m, 3,000 m team, and individual and team cross-country in Paris, France. He claimed the 1,500 m and 5,000 m titles despite having only 42 min between finals. Nurmi might have won another, but he was not selected by Finland for the 10,000 m – much to his annoyance.

YOUNGEST GOLD MEDALLIST
Marjorie Gestring (USA, b. 18 Nov 1922) took the women's 3 m springboard title aged 13 years 268 days at the Games in Berlin, Germany, on 12 Aug 1936. Her Olympic career was interrupted by World War II, and although Gestring tried to qualify for the Games in 1948, she finished fourth in the US trials and was unable to defend her title.

MOST OLYMPIC MEDALS (FEMALE)
Soviet gymnast Larisa Latynina won 18 Olympic medals over three Games between 1956 and 1964. Latynina's nine golds is the **most Olympic gold medals (female)**. She also won five silver and four bronze. Her tally of 18 was the most by any athlete – a record that stood for 48 years, until it was broken by Michael Phelps (above) in 2012.

OCT 29 Francisco Javier Galan Màrin (ESP) lets fly with the **fastest football kick** in 2001, generating a speed of 129 km/h (80.1 mph) at the studios of *El Show de los Récords* in Madrid, Spain.

OCT 30 The **smallest cinema by seat capacity** to operate as a regular commercial venture opens in Radebeul, Germany, in 2006. The Palastkino has only nine seats and is located inside a train station.

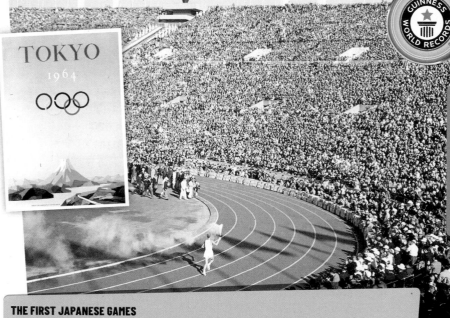

GOLDEN AMBITION

Judoka Uta Abe (b. 14 Jul 2000, in white above) promises to be one of the stars of the 2020 Olympics. She is a world champion and the **youngest winner of an IJF World Tour event**, having won the women's -52 kg category at the IJF Düsseldorf Grand Prix in Germany aged 16 years 225 days on 24 Feb 2017. Her older brother Hifumi – a two-time judo world champion at -66 kg – is also tipped to secure gold.

THE FIRST JAPANESE GAMES

The 1964 Summer Olympics in Tokyo were the first Olympics to be held in Asia. Ethiopia's Abebe Bikila set a then-world record defending his men's marathon title, while Larisa Latynina won her 18th Olympic medal (see below left). One of the most eagerly awaited victories was that of the Japanese women's volleyball team. Competing in the **first Olympic women's team sport**, they had undergone a brutal training regime that saw them practise every day after work until midnight. Led by centre Masae Kasai, the team defeated the Soviet Union 3–0 in the final, a victory that was greeted with wild acclaim in Japan.

audiences. There will also be a host of new mixed-gender events in shooting, swimming and triathlon, among others.

PRECIOUS MEDALS

Another key innovation for the upcoming Games is the Tokyo 2020 Medal Project, which aims to produce around 5,000 gold, silver and bronze medals by using recycled metal donated by Japanese citizens. In the early days of the modern Olympics, winners received a silver medal, as gold was considered too expensive.

The **first Olympic gold medals** were awarded at the 1904 Games in St Louis, Missouri, USA. The last time they were actually made from solid gold was in 1912.

In Tokyo, the USA will be looking to add to their tally of both **most Summer Olympics gold medals** – 1,022 – and **most medals**: 2,520.

Home fans will, of course, be cheering for Japanese victories. In the pool, there will be hopes for Ippei Watanabe, who recorded the **fastest long course 200 m breaststroke (male)** – 2 min 6.67 sec – in Tokyo on

29 Jan 2017. Gymnasts Kenzō Shirai (see p.231) and seven-time Olympic medallist Kōhei Uchimura will also be aiming for the podium. Meanwhile, wrestler Kaori Icho has a shot at extending her record for the **most consecutive Olympic gold medals in a women's individual event**. Icho won four golds between Athens 2004 and

Rio 2016 – three in the 63 kg freestyle and one in the 58 kg freestyle.

The Paralympics will see 4,400 athletes – potentially the **most participants at a Summer Paralympic Games**, a record currently held by Rio 2016 with 4,328 – compete over 537 medal events in 22 sports. Badminton and taekwondo make their

Paralympic debut, while returning sports include boccia, sitting volleyball and goalball, which is played by visually impaired athletes using a ball containing bells. The Paralympic flame will be extinguished on 6 Sep 2020, marking the Games' end – and the beginning of a new Olympic cycle, with eyes turning to Paris 2024.

LONGEST-STANDING OLYMPIC RECORD IN ATHLETICS

Recorded on 18 Oct 1968 in Mexico City, Mexico, Bob Beamon's (USA) long jump of 8.90 m (29 ft 2 in) has never been bettered at an Olympic Games. The 2016 men's long jump – 47 years 300 days later – was won by Jeff Henderson with a jump more than half a metre less than Beamon's extraordinary leap.

MOST SUMMER PARALYMPIC MEDALS

Swimmer Trischa Zorn (USA) won 55 medals at seven Paralympic Games between 1980 and 2004. She claimed 41 golds, nine silvers and five bronze across 13 different swimming events. At Barcelona 1992, Zorn, who was born blind, topped the individual medal table with 10 golds and two silvers.

MOST SUMMER PARALYMPIC MEDALS (MALE)

Jonas Jacobsson (SWE, above) won 30 medals in shooting events between 1980 and 2012: 17 golds, four silvers and nine bronze. Wheelchair athlete Heinz Frei (CHE) holds the overall record for the **most Paralympic medals (male)** – 34 – but he won eight of these at the Winter Paralympics.

MOST APPEARANCES BY AN ATHLETE

Equestrian Ian Millar (CAN) made his tenth appearance at an Olympics at London 2012. He made his debut in 1972 and appeared at eight consecutive Games from 1984 to 2012. Millar was also named in the Canadian team for Moscow 1980, only to miss out when Canada boycotted the Games. He won his only medal, a silver, in 2008.

MOST WINS OF THE 100 M SPRINT

Usain Bolt (JAM) won the men's 100 m Olympic title three times, in 2008-16. He also achieved the **most wins of the 200 m sprint** – also three – and two 4 x 100 m relay titles. Bolt retired in 2017, leaving behind a golden legacy and records for the **fastest 100 m** – 9.58 sec – and **fastest 200 m** – 19.19 sec – that remain unbroken.

OCT 31 In 2005, a total of 68 Jersey cows die after a lightning strike at a dairy farm near Dorrigo, NSW, Australia – the **largest recorded number of livestock killed by a single bolt of lightning**.

NOV 1 The University of Warwick Jailbreak Society (UK) squeeze the **most people in one pair of underpants** – an elastic-snapping 314 – at a 2014 charity event in Coventry, West Midlands, UK.

AMERICAN FOOTBALL

MOST WINS OF THE SUPER BOWL (TEAM)

On 3 Feb 2019, the New England Patriots triumphed 13-3 over the Los Angeles Rams in the **lowest-scoring Super Bowl**. It was their sixth victory in the annual championship game. They matched the tally of the Pittsburgh Steelers and increased their record for the **most Super Bowl appearances** to 11. Quarterback Tom Brady (jersey No.12, left) passed Charles Haley to claim the **most Super Bowl wins (individual)** with six. He also increased his tally of **most completed Super Bowl passes** – 256 – and **yards gained passing** – 2,838.

Highest average yards per carry in a game (individual)

On 7 Oct 2018, Isaiah Crowell rushed for 219 yd on 15 carries – an average of 14.6 yd per carry – while playing for the New York Jets in a 34-16 victory over the Denver Broncos.

Highest completion percentage

Los Angeles Chargers quarterback Philip Rivers finished with a 96.6% completion rate during a 45-10 win over the Arizona Cardinals on 25 Nov 2018. He surpassed the previous mark of 92.3%, set by the Cardinals' Kurt Warner vs the Jacksonville Jaguars on 20 Sep 2009.

Rivers completed 28 of 29 passes, including the **most consecutive pass completions to start a match by a quarterback** – 25. This is also the **most consecutive pass completions** outright, matched by Nick Foles for the Philadelphia Eagles on 30 Dec 2018.

Most passes thrown without an interception

From 30 Sep to 16 Dec 2018, Aaron Rodgers of the Green Bay Packers threw 402 passes in a row without once being intercepted.

Youngest Super Bowl head coach

Los Angeles Rams head coach Sean McVay (b. 24 Jan 1986) took his team all the way to Super Bowl LIII aged 33 years 10 days. It was his opposite number, the New England Patriots' Bill Belichick (b. 16 Apr 1952), who emerged triumphant, becoming the **oldest head coach to win a Super Bowl** at 66 years 293 days.

MOST CONSECUTIVE GAMES RECORDING A SACK

From 7 Oct to 23 Dec 2018, the Kansas City Chiefs' Chris Jones recorded a quarterback sack in 11 games in a row. The defensive end took the outright record when he sacked the Seattle Seahawks' Russell Wilson. The end of his streak may have come as a relief in the Kansas locker room, as Jones had been wearing the same lucky pair of (unwashed) gloves throughout!

MOST CAREER POINTS

Kicker Adam Vinatieri has scored 2,600 points playing for the New England Patriots (1996–2005) and the Indianapolis Colts (2006-18). He passed Morten Andersen's (DNK) mark of 2,544 with a 25-yd field goal against the Oakland Raiders on 28 Oct 2018. Vinatieri had also scored the **most postseason field goals** - 56 - as of the end of the 2018 season.

He tied a 35-year-old record, matching Tony Dorsett's 99-yd touchdown run for the Dallas Cowboys against the Minnesota Vikings on 3 Jan 1983.

Most consecutive 100-yard receiving games in a season (individual)

Wide receiver Adam Thielen of the Minnesota Vikings recorded 100 yd in receptions in each of the first eight games of the 2018 season from 9 Sep to 28 Oct. He equalled the mark established by Calvin Johnson of the Detroit Lions in 2012.

All teams and players National Football League (NFL) and USA, unless otherwise indicated.

Most points scored by a losing team

On 19 Nov 2018, in the highest-scoring game in the history of Monday Night Football, the Kansas City Chiefs put 51 points on the board against the Los Angeles Rams, only to lose 54-51.

The two teams may have combined for 105 points, but the **most points in a game** remains 113, set during the Washington Redskins' 72–41 victory over the New York Giants on 27 Nov 1966.

Longest run from scrimmage

Derrick Henry scored on a touchdown run of 99 yd for the Tennessee Titans against the Jacksonville Jaguars on 6 Dec 2018.

MOST CAREER PASSING YARDS

From 2001 to the end of the 2018 season, Drew Brees had thrown for 74,437 passing yards. He topped Peyton Manning's record of 71,940 during the New Orleans Saints' 43-19 victory over the Washington Redskins on 8 Oct 2018. Brees completed 364 of 489 attempts in 2018, the **highest completion percentage in a season**: 74.4%.

MOST RECEPTIONS IN A SEASON BY A ROOKIE RUNNING BACK

Saquon Barkley of the New York Giants made 91 catches in his rookie season in 2018. He surpassed Reggie Bush's mark of 88 for the New Orleans Saints in 2006.

The overall record for **most receptions in a season by a running back** also fell in 2018, to Christian McCaffrey of the Carolina Panthers with 107.

NOV 2 In 1996, the Rostrum Clubs of Tasmania begin the **longest debating marathon**, lasting until 1 Dec. They dispute the motion "Tasmania's greatest asset is its people" for 29 days 4 hr 3 min 20 sec.

NOV 3 The Harlem Globetrotters' "Thunder" Law (USA) sinks the **farthest basketball shot made backwards** - 25 m (82 ft 2 in) - in 2014 at the US Airways Center in Phoenix, Arizona, USA.

BASEBALL

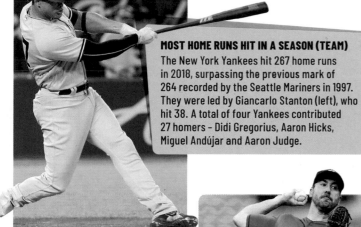

MOST HOME RUNS HIT IN A SEASON (TEAM)
The New York Yankees hit 267 home runs in 2018, surpassing the previous mark of 264 recorded by the Seattle Mariners in 1997. They were led by Giancarlo Stanton (left), who hit 38. A total of four Yankees contributed 27 homers – Didi Gregorius, Aaron Hicks, Miguel Andújar and Aaron Judge.

MOST STRIKEOUTS BY A PITCHING STAFF IN A SEASON
Houston Astros pitchers struck out 1,687 batters in 2018. They averaged 10.4 strikeouts per nine innings, the highest ever in MLB. Astros Justin Verlander (right) and Gerrit Cole threw 290 and 276 strikeouts respectively, the second- and third-highest individual totals for the season, behind Max Scherzer of the Washington Nationals (300).

All teams and players Major League Baseball (MLB) and USA, unless otherwise indicated.

Largest MLB contract
On 20 Mar 2019, the Los Angeles Angels and Mike Trout agreed on a 12-year contract worth a reported $426.5 m (£321.3 m). This exceeded the 13-year contract signed by Bryce Harper with the Philadelphia Phillies earlier that month, valued at $330 m (£249.2 m). Center fielder Trout is a seven-time MLB All-Star and six-time winner of the Silver Slugger Award.

Most career base hits
On 21 Mar 2019, Ichiro Suzuki (JPN) bid an emotional farewell to MLB in his final game, playing for the Seattle Mariners against the Oakland

FIRST INDIVIDUAL TO HIT FOR THE CYCLE (POSTSEASON)
In baseball, a cycle occurs when a batter records a single, double, triple and a home run in the same game. On 8 Oct 2018, Brock Holt achieved the feat while playing for the Boston Red Sox in Game 3 of the American League Division Series at Yankee Stadium in the Bronx, New York City, USA. He helped the Red Sox to a crushing 16-1 victory over their arch rivals, the New York Yankees.

Athletics in Tokyo, Japan. Suzuki had recorded 4,367 career base hits since 1992, playing in Japan's Nippon Professional Baseball as well as MLB.

Fewest appearances for a pitcher to reach 300 career saves
Craig Kimbrel earned his 300th career save in his 494th game, while pitching for the Boston Red Sox during a 6-5 win over the Texas Rangers on 5 May 2018. He reached the landmark from just 330 save opportunities – a save percentage of 90.9%.

Most strikeouts by a pitcher to start a game (modern era)
The Colorado Rockies' Germán Márquez (VEN) struck out his first eight batters playing against the Philadelphia Phillies on 26 Sep 2018. He equalled the feat of the Houston Astros' Jim Deshaies on 23 Sep 1986 and the New York Mets' Jacob deGrom on 15 Sep 2014.

Most strikeouts by an individual in a doubleheader
New York Yankees slugger Aaron Judge struck out eight times in two games against the Detroit Tigers on 4 Jun 2018.

The **most strikeouts in a season (team)** is 1,594, by Chicago White Sox batters during the 2018 season. They surpassed the previous mark of 1,571 by the Milwaukee Brewers in 2017.

The **most strikeouts in a season (all teams)** is 41,207, also in 2018.

Most consecutive postseason games hitting a home run (team)
The Houston Astros homered in 14 straight postseason games, from Game 6 of the 2017 American League

HIGHEST PERCENTAGE OF VOTES FOR A BASEBALL HALL OF FAME INDUCTION
Mariano Rivera (PAN) was elected to baseball's Hall of Fame in 2019 with 100% of the vote, appearing on all 425 ballots cast. The pitcher spent 19 seasons with the New York Yankees, recording the **most games pitched with one team** – 1,115 – and the **most games finished by a pitcher** – 952. He also has the **most career saves** – 652.

Championship Series (ALCS) to Game 2 of the 2018 ALCS. The Astros hit 29 homers across those 14 games.

The **most consecutive postseason games hitting a home run (individual)** is six, struck by Daniel Murphy for the New York Mets in 2015.

Most franchises played for
On 25 Jun 2018, pitcher Edwin Jackson (b. DEU) took to the mound for his 13th MLB club, the Oakland Athletics. Jackson, who made his MLB debut in 2003, matched the feat of pitcher Octavio Dotel (DOM), who between 1999 and 2013 also played for 13 teams.

LONGEST WORLD SERIES GAME
On 27 Oct 2018, the Los Angeles Dodgers defeated the Boston Red Sox 3-2 in a marathon encounter lasting 18 innings and 7 hr 20 min. The two sides called on 46 players – the **most players used in a World Series game (both teams)**. It was the Dodgers who prevailed, thanks to a walk-off home run struck by Max Muncy (pictured middle). However, it was the Red Sox who had the last laugh, winning the World Series 4-1.

NOV 4

The **fastest roller-coaster** opens in 2010 at Ferrari World in Abu Dhabi, UAE. *Formula Rossa* accelerates to 240 km/h (149.1 mph) and covers an upward distance of 52 m (170 ft) in 4.9 sec.

NOV 5

In 2013, the existence of the Hercules-Corona Borealis Great Wall galaxy superstructure is announced. Measuring c. 10 billion light years across, it is the **largest structure in the universe**.

217

BASKETBALL

All records are National Basketball Association (NBA) and all teams and players USA, unless otherwise indicated.

Most consecutive triple-doubles

Russell Westbrook recorded a triple-double in 11 games in a row for the Oklahoma City Thunder from 22 Jan to 14 Feb 2019. The previous record of nine, by Wilt Chamberlain of the Philadelphia 76ers on 8–20 Mar 1968, had stood for 51 years. Westbrook averaged 21.9 points, 13.3 rebounds and 13.5 assists over the course of his record streak.

Fastest triple-double

Nikola Jokić (SRB) recorded double figures for points, assists and rebounds in 14 min 33 sec of court time for the Denver Nuggets against the Milwaukee Bucks on 15 Feb 2018. Jokić finished the game with 30 points, 17 assists and 15 rebounds.

Most three-point field goals in a game (team)

The Houston Rockets converted 27 three-point field goals in a 149–113 win against the Phoenix Suns on 7 Apr 2019. They beat their own record of 26, set on 19 Dec 2018 during a 136–118 victory over the Washington Wizards.

During the previous season, Houston had achieved the **most three-point field goals in a season (team)** – 1,256.

MOST 30-POINT GAMES IN POSTSEASON

In Game 3 of the 2018 NBA Finals on 6 Jun, LeBron James scored 33 points for the Cleveland Cavaliers against the Golden State Warriors – the 110th postseason game in which he had passed 30, beating Michael Jordan.

Since 2006, James has racked up the **most points in playoff games** – 6,911. He leads the all-time playoff lists in **field goals made** (2,457), **free throws made** (1,627) and **steals** (419).

MOST THREE-POINT FIELD GOALS IN A GAME

Klay Thompson converted 14 three-pointers against the Chicago Bulls in Illinois, USA, on 29 Oct 2018. He surpassed his Golden State teammate Stephen Curry, who hit 13 in 2016.

In the first half against the Bulls, Thompson equalled the **most three-point field goals in a half** – 10 – set by Chandler Parsons on 24 Jan 2014.

Most three-point field goals in a Finals game

In Game 2 of the 2018 NBA Finals on 3 Jun, Stephen Curry scored nine three-pointers for the Golden State Warriors against the Cleveland Cavaliers at the Oracle Arena in Oakland, California, USA. He racked up a total of 33 points to help his team to a 122–103 victory.

In Game 1, LeBron James (see below left) scored 51 points for Cleveland, only to see his team lose 124–114 – the **most points scored in an NBA Finals game by an individual in a losing effort**. Golden State won the championship 4–0.

MOST SEASONS ON THE SAME TEAM

On 13 Dec 2018, following his recovery from ankle surgery, Dirk Nowitzki (DEU) took to the court for the Dallas Mavericks for the 21st season. He has played more than 1,400 games for the team since 1998, winning the championship in 2011. Nowitzki surpassed Kobe Bryant, who played for the LA Lakers for 20 seasons.

Most games played in a WNBA career

Sue Bird played 508 games for the Seattle Storm from 2002 to the end of the 2018 season. She surpassed DeLisha Milton-Jones's previous mark of 499 with her 500th game, against the Atlanta Dream on 22 Jul 2018.

Most field goals in a WNBA career

Nine-time WNBA All-Star Diana Taurasi has scored 2,721 field goals for the Phoenix Mercury since 2004.

MOST POINTS SCORED IN A WOMEN'S NATIONAL BASKETBALL ASSOCIATION (WNBA) MATCH

On 17 Jul 2018, Liz Cambage (AUS) scored 53 points for the Dallas Wings against the New York Liberty in Arlington, Texas, USA. The 203-cm-tall (6-ft 8-in) centre made 17 of 22 shots from the field and sank 15 of 16 free throws, sealing the record with a late three-pointer.

Most rebounds in a WNBA season

Sylvia Fowles recorded 404 rebounds while playing for the Minnesota Lynx in 2018 – one more than the single-season record previously held by Jonquel Jones. This tally included the **most defensive rebounds in a WNBA season** – 282.

The **most rebounds in a WNBA career** is 3,356, by Rebekkah Brunson for the Sacramento Monarchs and the Minnesota Lynx from 2004 to 2018.

Most assists in a WNBA season

Courtney Vandersloot recorded 258 assists while playing for the Chicago Sky in 2018. She broke Ticha Penicheiro's mark of 236, which had stood since 2000.

The **most assists in a WNBA career** is 2,831, by Sue Bird from 2002 to 2018.

HIGHEST-SCORING TRIPLE-DOUBLE

On 30 Jan 2018, James Harden of the Houston Rockets put up a 60-point triple-double – also featuring 10 rebounds and 11 assists – against the Orlando Magic.

During eight games on 13–27 Jan 2019, Harden went on a scoring spree with the **most consecutive unassisted points scored** – 304. No teammate was credited with an assist for any of Harden's points.

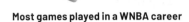

NOV 7
In 2006, the **smallest police dog** passes her Ohio Certification as a Narcotics Dog in Ohio, USA. Midge – a Chihuahua/rat terrier cross – measures 28 cm (11 in) tall and 58 cm (1 ft 10 in) long.

ICE HOCKEY

MOST SHOOTOUT WINS BY A GOALTENDER

On 30 Oct 2018, New York Rangers goaltender Henrik Lundqvist (SWE) won his 60th NHL shootout, saving two shots for a 4–3 win against the San Jose Sharks at the SAP Center in California, USA.

Earlier that year, on 16 Jan, Lundqvist had achieved the **most consecutive seasons winning 20 matches by a goaltender**: 13.

All records relate to the National Hockey League (NHL) contested in the USA and Canada. All teams and players are USA, unless otherwise indicated.

Most consecutive games with an assist to start a season

Sebastian Aho (FIN) recorded an assist in the Carolina Hurricanes' first 12 games of the 2018/19 season. When he set up Micheal Ferland's (CAN) goal against the Boston Bruins on 30 Oct 2018, Aho equalled a feat first

accomplished by Wayne Gretzky of the Edmonton Oilers (both CAN) in 1982/83 and matched by the Boston Bruins' Ken Linseman (CAN) in 1985/86.

Most career shootout goals

Frans Nielsen (DNK) scored his 49th shootout goal on 10 Nov 2018, lifting the Detroit Red Wings to a 4–3 victory over the Carolina Hurricanes. It was also his 23rd winner in a shootout – the **most career shootout-winning goals**.

Most shots on goal in a period (team)

On 21 Oct 2018, the Tampa Bay Lightning hit 33 shots on goal in the second period of their game against the Chicago Blackhawks at United Center in Chicago, Illinois, USA. This is the most since 1997/98, when "shots by period" became an official NHL statistic.

Shortest time between goals (single team)

The Montreal Canadiens (CAN) scored two goals in 2 sec against the Washington Capitals at Bell Centre in Québec, Canada, on 1 Nov 2018. Goals by Max Domi (CAN) and Joel Armia (FIN) broke the mark of 3 sec, set by the St Louis

MOST FACE OFF WINS IN A SEASON

Ryan O'Reilly (CAN) emerged victorious from the face off circle 1,274 times while playing for the Buffalo Sabres during the 2017/18 season. He surpassed the previous mark of 1,268 by the Carolina Hurricanes' Rod Brind'Amour (CAN) in 2005/06. The NHL began tracking face off statistics in 1997.

Eagles on 12 Mar 1935 and matched by the Minnesota Wild in 2004 and the New York Islanders in 2016.

Most consecutive games played

On 13 Jan 2018, Andrew Cogliano's (CAN) streak of 830 consecutive NHL games – fourth on the all-time list – ended when he was hit with a two-game suspension. The

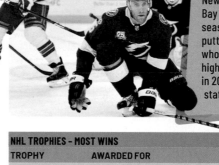

all-time leader remains Doug Jarvis (CAN), who played 964 games in a row for the Montreal Canadiens (CAN), the Washington Capitals and the Hartford Whalers from 8 Oct 1975 to 10 Oct 1987.

Most overtime (OT) goals in a regular-season career

Alex Ovechkin (RUS, see below) scored his 22nd OT winner during the Washington Capitals' 5–4 win over the Carolina Hurricanes on 2 Jan 2018.

MOST BLOCKED SHOTS IN A CAREER

As of 8 Jan 2019, Dan Girardi (CAN) had blocked or deflected wide 1,873 shots while playing for the New York Rangers and the Tampa Bay Lightning since the 2006/07 season. The defenceman has been putting his body on the line his whole career, recording a season-high figure of 236 blocked shots in 2010/11. The NHL began tracking statistics for this category in 1998.

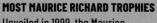

MOST WINS IN A SEASON BY AN EXPANSION TEAM

The Vegas Golden Knights won 51 games during the 2017/18 season, their first in the NHL. Vegas beat the previous record of 33 wins, achieved by the Anaheim Ducks and the Florida Panthers in 1993/94. They went on to become only the third expansion team to reach the Stanley Cup Finals in their first season, losing 4–1 to the Washington Capitals.

NHL TROPHIES – MOST WINS

TROPHY	AWARDED FOR	PLAYER*	WINS
Art Ross	Most regular-season points	Wayne Gretzky	10
Hart Memorial	Most valuable player	Wayne Gretzky	9
Lady Byng	Most sportsman-like behaviour/ highest standards of play	Frank Boucher	7
Vezina	Best goaltender	Jacques Plante	7
Jack Adams	Biggest contribution by a coach	Pat Burns	3
Conn Smythe	Most valuable player in Stanley Cup playoffs	Patrick Roy	3

All players Canadian

MOST MAURICE RICHARD TROPHIES

Unveiled in 1999, the Maurice Richard Trophy is awarded each year to the NHL's leading goal-scorer. In 2018, the Washington Capitals' Alex Ovechkin (RUS, far right) secured his seventh trophy after a 49-goal season. His fifth win in six seasons, it meant he tied Bobby Hull's record for **most seasons to finish as NHL top goal-scorer**.

NOV 8 The **tallest rose bush** – grown, appropriately, by Christopher Rose (USA) – is verified at a height of 5.68 m (18 ft 8 in) in La Puente, California, USA, in 2017.

NOV 9 In 2007, Trever McGhee (CAN) achieves the **farthest distance firewalking** – 181.9 m (597 ft) over embers reaching a temperature of up to 853.3°C (1,568°F) in Calgary, Alberta, Canada.

SOCCER

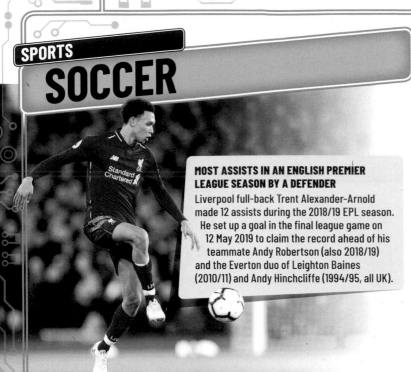

MOST ASSISTS IN AN ENGLISH PREMIER LEAGUE SEASON BY A DEFENDER

Liverpool full-back Trent Alexander-Arnold made 12 assists during the 2018/19 EPL season. He set up a goal in the final league game on 12 May 2019 to claim the record ahead of his teammate Andy Robertson (also 2018/19) and the Everton duo of Leighton Baines (2010/11) and Andy Hinchcliffe (1994/95, all UK).

Most regular-season goals in the National Women's Soccer League

Samantha Kerr (AUS) scored 63 goals in the US domestic women's soccer league from 20 Apr 2013 to 12 May 2019, playing for three clubs.

In Australia, Kerr has recorded the **most W-League goals** – 70, for Perth Glory and Sydney FC between 7 Dec 2008 and 16 Feb 2019.

Most goals scored during a Major League Soccer (MLS) season

Atlanta United's Josef Martínez (VEN) hit 28 goals during the 2018 MLS season. Between 30 Jun and 24 Aug, he also achieved the **most consecutive MLS games scored in** – nine, equalling Diego Valeri (ARG) from 29 Jul to 24 Sep 2017.

YOUNGEST PLAYER NOMINATED FOR THE BALLON D'OR

Kylian Mbappé (FRA, b. 20 Dec 1998) was nominated for *France Football*'s Ballon d'Or award aged 18 years 293 days on 9 Oct 2017. Mbappé starred in France's 2018 World Cup-winning team, becoming only the second teenager to score in the final after Pelé (BRA), the **youngest goal scorer in a FIFA World Cup**: 17 years 249 days, on 19 Jun 1958.

Youngest player to win the English Premier League (EPL)

Manchester City's Phil Foden (UK, b. 28 May 2000) received an EPL winner's medal aged 17 years 350 days at the end of the 2017/18 season. He made his fifth appearance of the season against Southampton on 13 May to qualify for the award.

On 4 May 2019, Harvey Elliott (UK, b. 4 Apr 2003) became the **youngest EPL player** when he appeared aged 16 years 30 days for Fulham against Wolverhampton Wanderers.

Fastest goal scored in the EPL

On 23 Apr 2019, Southampton's Irish striker Shane Long hit the back of the net after just 7.69 sec against Watford at Vicarage Road in Watford, UK. This was the fastest strike of the Premier League era, pipping Ledley King's 9.82-sec goal for Tottenham against Bradford on 9 Dec 2000.

Most consecutive Serie A games scored in (single season)

On 26 Jan 2019, Sampdoria's Fabio Quagliarella (ITA) scored twice against Udinese to record his 11th Serie A game in a row with a goal. He equalled the single-season feat of Fiorentina's Gabriel Batistuta (ARG) between 4 Sep and 27 Nov 1994.

Youngest player to score a hat-trick in the UEFA Europa League

On 11 Apr 2019, João Félix (PRT, b. 10 Nov 1999) scored three times for Benfica against Eintracht Frankfurt aged 19 years 152 days at the Estádio da Luz in Lisbon, Portugal.

The **youngest UEFA Europa League goalscorer (excluding qualifiers)** is Romelu Lukaku (BEL, b. 13 May 1993), aged 16 years 218 days on 17 Dec 2009 for Anderlecht.

MOST WINS OF THE EUROPEAN CUP/UEFA CHAMPIONS LEAGUE

On 26 May 2018, Real Madrid (ESP) won their 13th top-echelon European title – and their third in succession – when they defeated Liverpool 3–1 at the Olimpiyskiy Stadium in Kiev, Ukraine. The Spanish giants claimed six European Cups between 1956 and 1966, including five consecutive titles, and have won the Champions League seven times since 1998.

MOST EPL HAT-TRICKS

Sergio Agüero (ARG) recorded his 11th EPL hat-trick for Manchester City during a 6–0 defeat of Chelsea on 10 Feb 2019. The Argentine hitman equalled the record of Alan Shearer (UK), who bagged 11 three-goal hauls for Blackburn Rovers and Newcastle United from 23 Nov 1993 to 19 Sep 1999. Agüero alone holds the **most EPL hat-tricks for one club**.

MOST GOALS SCORED IN AN ASIAN CUP TOURNAMENT

Almoez Ali scored nine goals for surprise package Qatar at the 2019 Asian Cup. The Sudan-born striker surpassed Ali Daei's record of eight from 1996 with a spectacular overhead kick (pictured) in the final against Japan, which Qatar won 3–1. Ali scored four times against North Korea on 13 Jan, matching four players for **most goals in an Asian Cup match (individual)**.

 NOV 10 In 2000, Rob Williams (USA) rustles up the **fastest sandwich made using feet**. He makes a bologna, cheese and lettuce sandwich, complete with olives on cocktail sticks, in 1 min 57 sec.

 NOV 11 To celebrate GWR Day 2009, Toufic Daher (LBN) builds the **tallest matchstick model** – a scale replica of the Eiffel Tower standing 6.53 m (21 ft 5 in) tall. It is unveiled at City Mall in Beirut, Lebanon.

MOST GOALS SCORED IN LA LIGA

FC Barcelona striker Lionel Messi (ARG) had scored 417 goals in 451 matches in the Spanish top flight as of 12 May 2019. This gave him a strike rate of 0.92 goals per La Liga match.

On 18 Sep 2018, Messi increased his tally of **most UEFA Champions League hat-tricks** to eight. This was equalled on 12 Mar 2019 by Cristiano Ronaldo.

Most Bundesliga goals by a foreign player

The most goals scored in the Bundesliga by a non-German player is 202, by Robert Lewandowski (POL), playing for Borussia Dortmund and Bayern Munich from 19 Sep 2010 to 4 May 2019. Lewandowski overtook his former teammate, Claudio Pizarro (PER), with a brace on 9 Mar 2019. On 4 May 2019, Pizarro (b. 3 Oct 1978) scored his 196th league goal aged 40 years 213 days to become the **oldest goalscorer in the Bundesliga**.

Youngest UEFA Champions League manager

Julian Nagelsmann (DEU, b. 23 Jul 1987) was in the dugout for TSG 1899 Hoffenheim aged 31 years 58 days during their Champions League tie with Shakhtar Donetsk on 19 Sep 2018.

Most UEFA Women's Champions League wins

Olympique Lyonnais Féminin (FRA) have won the UEFA Women's Champions League five times: in 2011, 2012 and 2016–2018. They claimed their fifth trophy on 24 May 2018, beating VfL Wolfsburg 4–1 after extra time in Kiev, Ukraine.

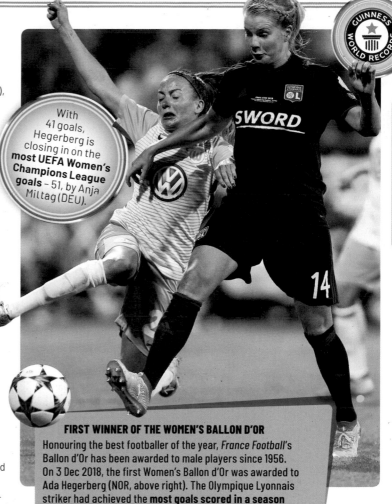

With 41 goals, Hegerberg is closing in on the **most UEFA Women's Champions League goals** – 51, by Anja Mittag (DEU).

FIRST WINNER OF THE WOMEN'S BALLON D'OR

Honouring the best footballer of the year, *France Football*'s Ballon d'Or has been awarded to male players since 1956. On 3 Dec 2018, the first Women's Ballon d'Or was awarded to Ada Hegerberg (NOR, above right). The Olympique Lyonnais striker had achieved the **most goals scored in a season of the UEFA Women's Champions League** – 15, in 2017/18.

FIFA WORLD CUP 2018

The 2018 FIFA World Cup, held in Russia from **14 Jun to 15 Jul**, saw France emerge victorious for the second time in their history, defeating Croatia 4–2 in the final. But they weren't the only players who had cause to remember the tournament with pride.

Before a ball had been kicked, Iceland had created history by becoming the **smallest country (by population) to play at the World Cup**. The Icelandic population of 337,669 was almost 1 million fewer than the previous record holder, Trinidad & Tobago, in 2006.

On the touchline, Uruguay's Óscar Tabárez equalled the **most World Cup appearances as a coach with the same national team** – four. He matched the feat of England coach Walter Winterbottom (UK) in 1950–62 and Helmut Schön (DEU) with West Germany in 1966–78. Man in the middle Ravshan Irmatov (UZB) achieved the **most World Cup matches refereed** when he oversaw his 10th fixture, Croatia's 3–0 defeat of Argentina on 21 Jun.

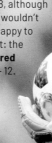

The players were also keen to put their names in the record books. On 17 Jun, Rafael Márquez achieved the **most World Cup finals as captain**, donning the armband for Mexico at his fifth tournament since 2002. On 24 Jun, Panama's Felipe Baloy became the **oldest player to score on World Cup debut** when he struck aged 37 years 120 days during a 6–1 defeat to England. (The **oldest player to score at a World Cup** remains Cameroon's Roger Milla, aged 42 years 39 days against Russia on 28 Jun 1994.)

By their own high standards, Brazil were disappointing in Russia, knocked out in the quarter-finals 2–1 by Belgium. But at least they were able to increase their total of **most World Cup matches won by a team** to 73 since 1930. Nor is their record for **most wins of the World Cup** – five – under threat yet.

One final notable record was also achieved in 2018, although the players involved wouldn't have been quite so happy to have helped create it: the **most own goals scored during a World Cup** – 12.

OLDEST PLAYER AT A FIFA WORLD CUP

Goalkeeper Essam El-Hadary (EGY, b. 15 Jan 1973) took to the field against Saudi Arabia aged 45 years 161 days on 25 Jun 2018. Although Egypt had already failed to qualify for the next round, El-Hadary celebrated his record-breaking appearance in style by saving a first-half penalty.

MOST FIFA WORLD CUP TOURNAMENTS SCORED IN

Cristiano Ronaldo (PRT) joined an elite club when he found the net in his fourth World Cup tournament in 2018, equalling Miroslav Klose (DEU), West Germany's Uwe Seeler and Pelé (BRA).

On 15 Jun, Ronaldo (b. 5 Feb 1985) became the **oldest player to score a World Cup hat-trick**. He struck three times during Portugal's 3–3 draw against Spain, aged 33 years 130 days.

 NOV 12 Lars Clausen (USA) completes the **longest unicycle journey** in 2002 in Los Angeles, California, USA. He had covered 14,686.82 km (9,125.97 mi) while crossing the USA twice.

 NOV 13 In 2010, Dominic Cuzzacrea (USA) achieves the **highest pancake toss**, catching a 9.47-m (31-ft 1-in) flip at the Walden Galleria mall in Cheektowaga, New York, USA.

221

RUGBY

80–0 demolition of Scotland at Twickenham, UK, on 16 Mar 2019. They scored a total of 45 tries and 278 points on their way to the title.

Most career tries scored in the Top 14 (individual)

Vincent Clerc (FRA) signed off his final season in professional rugby in style, overhauling Laurent Arbo's long-standing record of 100 tries in the top flight of French domestic rugby. Clerc scored his 101st Top 14 try in his final match, during RC Toulon's 38–26 defeat to Pau on 5 May 2018.

The **most tries scored in a Top 14 season** is 24, by Chris Ashton (UK) for RC Toulon during the 2017/18 season.

Most tries scored in a Super Rugby season (individual)

Ben Lam (NZ) scored 16 tries for the Hurricanes during the 2018 Super Rugby season. He claimed the outright record at the last second, touching down in the 80th minute during the Hurricanes' semi-final defeat to Crusaders on 28 Jul.

Most Super Rugby appearances

Prop Wyatt Crockett (NZ) played 202 Super Rugby matches for the Crusaders from 2006 to 2018. He made his final bow against the Sharks on 21 Jul 2018.

MOST APPEARANCES IN THE FIVE/SIX NATIONS CHAMPIONSHIP

Sergio Parisse made 69 appearances for Italy in the Five/Six Nations between 15 Feb 2004 and 16 Mar 2019. He broke the tournament record of Ireland's Brian O'Driscoll with his 66th tournament appearance, against Scotland on 2 Feb 2019. Parisse has finished on the winning side in just nine matches, compared with O'Driscoll's 45 victories.

Most Six Nations Championship Grand Slams

The first Six Nations tournament took place in 2000, when Italy were added to the Five Nations of England, Ireland, Scotland, Wales and France. On 16 Mar 2019, Wales sealed their fourth clean sweep with a 25–7 defeat of Ireland at the Principality Stadium in Cardiff, UK.

Most Women's Six Nations titles

England secured their 10th Women's Six Nations title – and their ninth Grand Slam – with an

MOST WINS OF THE HEINEKEN CUP/EUROPEAN RUGBY CHAMPIONS CUP (TEAM)

Irish side Leinster secured their fourth top-tier European title with a hard-fought 15–12 victory over Racing 92 on 12 May 2018, having previously won in 2009, 2011 and 2012. They equalled the record of Toulouse (or Stade Toulousain, FRA), winners in 1996, 2003, 2005 and 2010. The French side also finished as runners-up in 2004 and 2008.

Two weeks later, the Crusaders secured their ninth championship – the **most Super Rugby titles won**. The Christchurch-based side defeated the Lions 37–18 on 4 Aug 2018.

Most Rugby Championship matches won

New Zealand won 35 of their 39 matches at the international southern-hemisphere tournament between 18 Aug 2012 and 6 Oct 2018.

Most National Rugby League (NRL) career points (individual)

During the Melbourne Storm's 18–12 win over the North Queensland Cowboys on 12 Apr 2019, Cameron Smith (AUS) overtook Hazem El Masri (LBN) to become the NRL's all-time highest point scorer, with 2,422. Smith also extended his record for **most NRL appearances** to 389.

MOST WORLD CLUB CHALLENGE TITLES

On 17 Feb 2019, Sydney Roosters (AUS) beat Wigan Warriors (UK) 20–8 to equal Wigan's four rugby league World Club Challenge titles. On his debut for Sydney, Brett Morris (AUS, pictured) scored the **most tries in a World Club Challenge match**, three, matching the Roosters' Michael Jennings (AUS) in 2014 and Wigan's Joe Burgess (UK) in 2017.

MOST CLEAN BREAKS MADE IN WORLD RUGBY SEVENS SERIES TOURNAMENTS

As of 16 Apr 2019, Perry Baker (USA) had made 235 clean breaks through the opposition's defensive line in the World Rugby Sevens Series. The jet-heeled winger has become one of the most dangerous strikemen in rugby, scoring 179 (often spectacular) tries in 202 matches. In 2018, Baker became the first player to win the World Rugby Sevens Player of the Year award twice.

MOST ENGLISH PREMIERSHIP FINAL WINS BY AN INDIVIDUAL

Scrum-half Richard Wigglesworth (UK) secured his fifth Premiership Final victory on 26 May 2018, when Saracens defeated the Exeter Chiefs 27–10. He had previously triumphed in 2011, 2015, 2016 and – with Sale Sharks – in 2006.

On 23 Sep 2018, Wigglesworth also claimed the record for the **most appearances in the English Premiership**. He had played 273 matches as of 16 Apr 2019.

WORLD SEVENS SERIES			
MOST...	PLAYER	COUNTRY	TOTAL
Matches (male)	D J Forbes	New Zealand	512
Tries (male)	Dan Norton	England	332
Points (male)	Ben Gollings	England	2,652
Matches (female)	Sarah Hirini	New Zealand	183
Tries (female)	Portia Woodman	New Zealand	195
Points (female)	Ghislaine Landry	Canada	1,090

All figures correct as of 16 Apr 2019

NOV 14 Crooner Al Martino (b. Jasper Cini, USA) has the **first UK No.1 single** with "Here in My Heart" in 1952. The song stays at the top of the chart for nine consecutive weeks, until 9 Jan 1953.

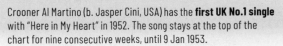

NOV 15 In 2012, TV weatherman Steve Jacobs (AUS) prepares for a cold snap by reclaiming his record for the **most pairs of underpants worn** – 266 – in Sydney, New South Wales, Australia.

TENNIS

FIRST POST-MILLENNIAL TO WIN A WTA TITLE

On 29 Jul 2018, Olga Danilović (SRB, b. 23 Jan 2001) won the Moscow River Cup in Russia, defeating Anastasia Potapova aged 17 years 187 days. She became the first player born in the 21st century to win a WTA tournament, and also the first "lucky loser" to win a WTA singles title – entering the main draw despite suffering a loss in the final round of qualifying.

Slam main draw. Players faced the potential docking of points for repeated failure to complete their service motion before the clock counted down to zero.

Longest Grand Slam semi-final match

Kevin Anderson (ZAF) and John Isner (USA) served up a strength-sapping Centre Court epic lasting 6 hr 36 min in the semi-finals of the Wimbledon Championships in London, UK, on 13 Jul 2018. Anderson eventually prevailed 7-6, 6-7, 6-7, 6-4, 26-24, with the last set alone clocking in at 2 hr 54 min.

Most Grand Slam singles matches won

As of 18 Jan 2019, Roger Federer (CHE) had won 342 singles matches at Wimbledon and the Australian, French and US Opens. Serena Williams (USA) held the **female** record with 335 victories at the four Grand Slams, as of 21 Jan 2019.

MOST WINS OF A GRAND SLAM SINGLES TOURNAMENT (OPEN ERA)

Clay-court maestro Rafael Nadal (ESP) won the French Open for an 11th time on 10 Jun 2018 when he defeated Dominic Thiem (AUT) 6-4, 6-3, 6-2 at Stade Roland Garros in Paris, France. Nadal had previously triumphed in 2005-08, 2010-14 and 2017.

Between 29 May 2017 and 10 May 2018, Nadal completed the **most consecutive sets won on a single surface** – 50 on clay.

Most Grand Slam singles tournaments played consecutively

As of the 2019 Australian Open, Feliciano López (ESP) had taken part in 68 consecutive Grand Slam tournaments since 2002. He has reached four Grand Slam quarter-finals – at Wimbledon in 2005, 2008 and 2011, and at the US Open in 2015.

First Grand Slam to adopt a shot clock for the main draws

At the 2018 US Open in New York City (27 Aug–9 Sep), a 25-sec shot clock was used for the first time in a Grand

MOST GRAND SLAM WHEELCHAIR SINGLES TITLES WON (MALE)

Shingo Kunieda (JPN) has won 22 wheelchair singles titles: nine Australian Opens (2007-11, 2013-15, 2018), seven French Opens (2007-10, 2014-15, 2018) and six US Opens (2007, 2009-11, 2014-15). Kunieda has also won 20 doubles titles, including eight at the Australian Open (2007-11, 2013-15).

First singles player to achieve a "Career Golden Masters"

On 19 Aug 2018, Novak Djokovic (SRB, see below) completed a career slam of all nine ATP (Association of Tennis Professionals) Masters 1000 events at the Cincinnati Masters. The others were Indian Wells, Miami, Monte Carlo, Madrid, Rome, Montreal/Toronto, Shanghai and Paris.

Djokovic has amassed the **highest earnings in a tennis career (male)**, with $129,000,709 (£98,920,200) in career prize money since 2003.

The **most ATP Masters 1000 singles titles won in a career** is 33, by Djokovic's great rival Rafael Nadal (see above left).

MOST AUSTRALIAN OPEN SINGLES TITLES WON (MALE)

On 27 Jan 2019, Serbia's Novak Djokovic secured his seventh title on the hard courts of Melbourne – more wins than any other man in the event's 114-year history – with a 6-3, 6-2, 6-3 victory over Rafael Nadal. Djokovic had previously won the Australian Open in 2008, 2011-13 and 2015-16.

FASTEST ASCENT TO WTA NO.1 RANKING FOLLOWING TOP 10 DEBUT

It took Naomi Osaka (JPN) just 138 days to climb to the top of the WTA (Women's Tennis Association) world rankings after making her debut as a Top 10 player on 10 Sep 2018. Back-to-back Grand Slam titles at the US Open on 8 Sep 2018 and the 2019 Australian Open took her to No.1 on 26 Jan 2019.

Djokovic won the 2012 Australian Open after the **longest Grand Slam final** – 5 hr 53 min, also against Nadal.

In 2010, Sweden's Magnus Andersson has his **largest collection of stamps featuring popes** verified at 1,580 individual items at the public library in Falun, Sweden.

Art Arfons (USA) walks away from the **fastest car crash survived** in 1966, after a wheel on his jet-powered car fails at c. 981 km/h (610 mph) on the Bonneville Salt Flats in Utah, USA.

BALL SPORTS

Highest-scoring Women's Softball World Championship final

On 12 Aug 2018, the USA defeated Japan 7–6 in the final of the Women's Softball World Championship at ZOZO Marine Stadium in Chiba Prefecture, Japan. They came back from 6–4 down in the 10th innings to snatch victory with a walk-off single. It was the seventh time in a row that the USA and Japan had contested the final.

The USA have now lifted the trophy 11 times – the **most wins of the Women's Softball World Championship**.

Most wins of the Federation of International Lacrosse (FIL) World Lacrosse Championship

The USA's lacrosse team have been crowned world champions 10 times: in 1967, 1974, 1982, 1986, 1990, 1994, 1998, 2002, 2010 and 2018. They took their latest title with a last-gasp winner in a 9–8 victory over Canada in Netanya, Israel, on 21 Jul 2018.

The **most wins of the FIL World Indoor Lacrosse Championship** is four, by Canada in 2003, 2007, 2011 and 2015. They have won every tournament staged to date, and are yet to lose a single match.

Most deflections in a Super Netball regular season (individual)

Goalkeeper Geva Mentor (UK) finished the 2018 Super Netball season with 102 deflections playing for Sunshine Coast Lightning (AUS). She beat her own record of 90 from 2017. Mentor captained the Lightning to back-to-back Super Netball titles, before signing for the Collingwood Magpies in Sep 2018.

Most wins of the men's team title at the World Table Tennis Championships

On 6 May 2018, China claimed their 21st Swaythling Cup, the trophy awarded to the winning men's team at the World Table Tennis Championships. China beat Germany 3–0 in the final, staged in Halmstad, Sweden.

A day earlier, China had won the **women's team title** for a record 21st time. They claimed the Corbillon Cup with a 3–1 victory over Japan.

MOST GOALS SCORED IN A SUPER NETBALL SEASON

Jhaniele Fowler (JAM) marked her debut Super Netball season with 783 goals for West Coast Fever (AUS) in 2018. She also led the league in goal attempts – 846 – giving her a success rate of 92%.

In Rounds 1 and 8 of the season, Fowler scored the **most goals in a Super Netball game**, 66, both times against the Adelaide Thunderbirds.

FIRST TRIPLE CHAMPION AT AN ITTF WORLD TOUR EVENT

Jang Woo-jin (KOR) won the men's singles, men's doubles and mixed doubles titles at the International Table Tennis Federation (ITTF) World Tour Platinum Korea Open in Daejeon, South Korea, on 19–22 Jul 2018. His gold medal in the mixed doubles alongside North Korea's Cha Hyo-sim was the first ITTF World Tour title for a unified Korean team.

YOUNGEST GOLD MEDALLIST AT THE FIVB BEACH VOLLEYBALL WORLD TOUR FINALS

On 19 Aug 2018, Eduarda "Duda" Santos Lisboa (BRA, b. 1 Aug 1998, above right) won the women's gold medal match aged 20 years 18 days at the Fédération Internationale de Volleyball (FIVB) Beach Volleyball World Tour Finals. Alongside Ágatha Bednarczuk (above left), she defeated a Czech team 21–15, 21–19 in Hamburg, Germany.

MOST WINS OF THE FIH WOMEN'S HOCKEY WORLD CUP

On 5 Aug 2018, the Netherlands secured their eighth Fédération Internationale de Hockey (FIH) world title since 1974 with a 6–0 win over Ireland in London, UK. The Dutch scored four goals in seven minutes on their way to recording the **highest margin of victory in a Women's Hockey World Cup final**.

On 29 Jul 2018, the Dutch beat Italy 12–1 – the **highest margin of victory at the FIH Women's Hockey World Cup**.

Most goals scored in the EHF Champions League FINAL4

Held in the Lanxess Arena in Cologne, Germany, the FINAL4 stage of the European Handball Federation (EHF) Champions League comprises the semi-finals and final of the competition. Kiril Lazarov (MKD) scored 14 times in two games for HBC Nantes (FRA) in the 2017/18 season to take his tally to 65 since 2011.

The free-scoring right back had also scored the **most EHF Champions League goals** – 1,299, as of 26 Mar 2019. He made his competition debut in 1998 and has featured for seven different sides.

Most Women's EHF Handball Champions League goals

As of 26 Mar 2019, Anita Görbicz (HUN) had scored 939 goals in the Women's EHF Champions League. She found the back of the net 70 times in the 2017/18 season, on her way to her fourth league title with Hungarian side Győri Audi ETO KC.

NOV 18 — In 2010, Christian Schäfer (DEU) gives a whole new meaning to the term "airmail" when he sets the **fastest time to blow a stamp one mile** – 1 hr 57 min 38 sec – in Netphen, Germany.

NOV 19 — Professional unicycle rider Satomi Sakaino (JPN) achieves the **most spins on a unicycle in one minute** – 131, more than two every second – on the set of *Kinsma* in Tokyo, Japan, in 2011.

CRICKET

MOST INDIAN PREMIER LEAGUE (IPL) TITLES WON

The Chennai Super Kings sealed their third IPL title with an eight-wicket win against Sunrisers Hyderabad at Mumbai's Wankhede Stadium on 27 May 2018. They matched the feat of the Mumbai Indians, winners in 2013, 2015 and 2017. Chennai previously lifted the IPL trophy in 2010 and 2011, and have been runners-up on four occasions (2008, 2012-13, 2015).

MOST TEST WICKETS TAKEN BY A FAST BOWLER

On 11 Sep 2018, England's James Anderson surpassed Australian paceman Glenn McGrath when he claimed the 564th wicket of his Test career with the final ball of the match against India at The Oval in London, UK. Anderson is now the fourth-highest wicket-taker in Test history, behind three spinners. He had amassed 575 as of 26 Feb 2019.

Most consecutive Test matches played

England's Alastair Cook played 159 consecutive Tests between 11 May 2006 and 7 Sep 2018. In an international career spanning 161 games, he missed only one match – against India in Mar 2006, owing to an upset stomach. Cook announced his retirement in 2018 having scored 12,472 runs – the **most Test runs scored by a left-handed batsman**. He hit 11,845 runs batting at either No.1 or No.2 – the **most Test runs scored by an opening batsman**.

Most balls bowled in Test matches without bowling a no-ball

As of 15 Feb 2019, Ravichandran Ashwin (IND) had sent down an incredible 18,372 balls (3,062 overs) in Test cricket without bowling a no-ball. The all-rounder has taken 342 wickets in 65 matches, at an average of 25.43 runs per wicket.

Highest team score in a One Day International (ODI)

New Zealand's women hit 491 for 4 against Ireland at the YMCA Cricket Club in Dublin, Ireland, on 8 Jun 2018.

The White Ferns' total is 10 runs more than the **highest team score in an ODI (male)** – 481 for 6, set by England against Australia on 19 Jun 2018.

Fastest time to reach 10,000 ODI runs

It took India's Virat Kohli 205 innings to make 10,000 runs in the ODI format. He reached the milestone with his 37th hundred, against the West Indies on 24 Oct 2018. Kohli capped a remarkable year by winning the International Cricket Council's (ICC) Test and ODI Player of the Year awards, along with the Sir Garfield Sobers Trophy for Cricketer of the Year – an unprecedented treble.

Youngest player to take five wickets in an ODI

Mujeeb Ur Rahman (AFG, b. 28 Mar 2001) took an ODI five-for aged 16 years 325 days against Zimbabwe in Sharjah, UAE, on 16 Feb 2018.

Most hundreds scored in an ODI career (female)

Meg Lanning scored 12 ODI centuries for Australia in 69 matches between 5 Jan 2011 and 22 Oct 2018. Her top ODI score is 152 not out.

Most wins of the ICC Women's World Twenty20 (T20) tournament

Australia have won the ICC Women's World Twenty20 four times, in 2010, 2012, 2014 and 2018. They defeated England in the final of the most recent competition in Antigua on 24 Nov 2018.

Most runs scored by a player in a T20 International career (male)

On 8 Feb 2019, Rohit Sharma (IND) became the all-time leading scorer in men's T20 internationals when he scored 50 against New Zealand at Eden Park in Auckland, New Zealand. As of 26 Feb 2019, Sharma had moved on to 2,331 career runs in the format.

The **most runs scored by a player in a T20 International (male)** is 172, by Aaron Finch (AUS) against Zimbabwe at Harare Sports Club in Zimbabwe on 3 Jul 2018. He hit 16 fours and 10 sixes.

Highest team score in a T20 International (female)

England Women amassed 250 for 3 against South Africa Women in a Tri-Nations Series match in Taunton, Somerset, UK, on 20 Jun 2018. They beat New Zealand's previous record score of 216 for 1, set earlier the same day – also against South Africa.

The **highest team score in a T20 International** is 278 for 3, achieved by Afghanistan's men against Ireland on 23 Feb 2019.

Lowest team score in a T20 International

Mexico Women were dismissed for just 18 runs against Brazil Women at Los Pinos Polo Club 2 in Bogotá, Colombia, on 24 Aug 2018. Only two Mexico players avoided making a duck in the South American Women's Championships match.

MOST INTERNATIONAL WICKETS TAKEN BY A TEENAGER

Afghanistan's Rashid Khan (b. 20 Sep 1998) took 176 international wickets before his 20th birthday. The spinner claimed 110 ODI victims, 64 in T20 Internationals and two in his sole Test match. Pakistan's Waqar Younis is the only other player to have taken more than 100 international wickets as a teenager (125).

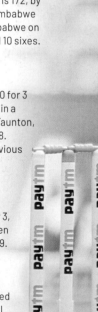

YOUNGEST CRICKETER TO SCORE AN INTERNATIONAL DOUBLE CENTURY

On 13 Jun 2018, Amelia Kerr (NZ, b. 13 Oct 2000) hit 232 not out aged 17 years 243 days old for New Zealand against Ireland at the YMCA Cricket Club in Dublin, Ireland. This is the **most runs scored by a female cricketer in a One Day International (ODI)**. Kerr's innings included two sixes and 31 fours.

NOV 20 In 2011, the **largest collection of grey alien memorabilia** – 547 – is ratified in Florida, USA. Belonging to Lisa Vanderperre-Hirsch (USA), it includes figurines, masks and alien-themed toilet paper.

NOV 21 In 1783, François Pilâtre de Rozier and the Marquis d'Arlandes (both FRA) make the **first free crewed balloon flight**, staying airborne for 25 min above Paris, France.

COMBAT SPORTS

WBO, WBC, WBA and IBF women's welterweight titles for 4 years 201 days – the **longest reign as a four-belt undisputed world boxing champion**.

Most individual gold medals won at the IBJJF World Championships

Marcus Almeida (BRA) has won 11 gold medals at the International Brazilian Jiu-Jitsu Federation World Championships – commonly known as the Mundials. He secured medal No.11 – in the +100 kg ultra heavyweight category – at the 2018 Mundials, which were held in Long Beach, California, USA, on 31 May–3 Jun 2018. Almeida had the opportunity to win a 12th gold but stood aside for his friend Leandro Lo, who had suffered a dislocated shoulder and was unable to compete in the absolute final.

Oldest winner of an IJF World Tour event

On 11 Aug 2018, Miklós Ungvári (HUN, b. 15 Oct 1980) won the men's –73 kg category aged 37 years 300 days at the International Judo Federation (IJF) Budapest Grand Prix in Hungary. Ungvári defeated three-time world champion Masashi Ebinuma in the final.

FEWEST FIGHTS TO BECOME A FOUR-BELT WORLD BOXING CHAMPION

On 21 Jul 2018, Oleksandr Usyk (UKR) became the first-ever cruiserweight undisputed world champion in only his 15th professional fight since 9 Nov 2013. Already the WBO and WBC title holder, Usyk won the IBF and WBA belts with victory over Murat Gassiev in the final of the World Boxing Super Series at Olimpiysky Sports Complex in Moscow, Russia.

Most bouts undefeated by a world champion boxer in a career (female)

Cecilia Brækhus (NOR) completed her 35th consecutive victory with a unanimous decision over Aleksandra Magdziak Lopes at StubHub Center in Carson, California, USA, on 8 Dec 2018. As of 2 Apr 2019, the "First Lady" of boxing had held the

Most medals won on the IJF World Tour

As of 2 Apr 2019, Urantsetseg Munkhbat (MNG) had claimed 34 medals on the IJF World Tour since 17 Dec 2010. She had won 11 golds, 10 silvers and 13 bronze in the women's –48 kg and –52 kg categories.

Most UFC fights

On 15 Dec 2018, Jim Miller (USA) fought his 31st bout in the Ultimate Fighting Championship (UFC). He was defeated in the first round by Charles Oliveira

YOUNGEST JUDO WORLD CHAMPION

At the 2018 World Judo Championships in Baku, Azerbaijan, Daria Bilodid (UKR, b. 10 Oct 2000, in blue above) became a judo world champion aged 17 years 345 days. In the final of the women's –48 kg on 20 Sep, Bilodid defeated Funa Tonaki by scoring *ippon* with her trademark *ōuchi-gari* throw.

MOST GOLD MEDALS AT THE AIBA WORLD BOXING CHAMPIONSHIPS

Mary Kom (IND) has won six golds at the International Boxing Association (AIBA) Women's World Boxing Championships since 2002, matching the feat of Félix Savón (CUB) in 1986–97. On 24 Nov 2018, Kom beat Hanna Okhota in the final of the light flyweight category (above) to claim her sixth title before a home crowd in New Delhi, India.

(see opposite), taking his record to 18 wins, 12 losses and one no contest. Miller claimed 17 of his victories at lightweight, the most ever in that division.

The **most UFC wins** is 22, achieved by Donald "Cowboy" Cerrone (USA) between 5 Feb 2011 and 19 Jan 2019.

First female UFC fighter to hold two titles simultaneously

At UFC 232 on 29 Dec 2018, reigning women's bantamweight champion Amanda Nunes (BRA) defeated Cris Cyborg in a devastating 51-sec knockout to claim the

LARGEST UFC TELEVISION AUDIENCE

There were an estimated 2.4 million pay-per-view buys for *UFC 229: Khabib vs McGregor*, staged at T-Mobile Arena in Las Vegas, Nevada, USA, on 6 Oct 2018. The fiercely anticipated match between Conor McGregor (IRL, left) and Khabib Nurmagomedov (RUS, right) for the UFC Lightweight Championship saw Nurmagomedov win via a fourth-round submission. However, the event would descend into chaos and controversy following widespread brawls after the end of the bout.

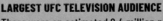

NOV 22 At the 2015 Philadelphia Marathon in Pennsylvania, USA, Christmas comes early for Brian Lang (USA) as he runs the **fastest marathon dressed as Santa Claus**: 2 hr 54 min 2 sec.

NOV 23 In 2007, in Cologne, Germany, Thomas Blackthorne (UK) achieves the **heaviest object sword-swallowed** – a DeWALT D25980 demolition hammer weighing 38 kg (83 lb 12 oz).

Most UFC fights won by submission

Charles Oliveira (BRA) won 13 UFC fights via submission between 1 Aug 2010 and 2 Feb 2019. He moved past Royce Gracie's record of 10 when he forced Christos Giagos to tap out with a rear-naked choke at UFC Fight Night 137.

Most ONE Championship title defences (female)

On 18 May 2018, Angela Lee (SGP, b. CAN) made her third successful defence of her women's atomweight title. She defeated her rival Mei Yamaguchi by unanimous decision.

Most gold medals won at the World Fencing Championships by a country

Italy has won 116 gold medals at the FEI World Fencing Championships – 54 in individual events and 62 in team events. At the 2018 World Championships in Wuxi, Jiangsu Province, China, Italy added four golds: in men's and women's individual foil, women's individual épée and men's team foil.

MOST MEN'S WORLD TAEKWONDO TEAM CHAMPIONSHIPS WINS

On 25 Sep 2018, Iran secured their third World Taekwondo Team Championships title with a one-point victory over Russia in Fujairah, UAE. Instituted in 2006, the competition was previously known as the World Cup Taekwondo Team Championships.

The **most women's titles won** is five, a record shared by South Korea and 2018 champions, China.

Women's Featherweight Championship. She became only the third fighter to hold two UFC titles at the same time, after Conor McGregor (featherweight and lightweight) and Daniel Cormier (USA; light heavyweight and heavyweight). This is the **most UFC world titles held in different weight divisions simultaneously**.

Nunes's victory over Cyborg was her 10th in UFC – the **most UFC wins by a female fighter**.

MOST SUMO TOP-DIVISION WINS

As of 25 Mar 2019, Hakuhō Shō (MNG, b. Munkhbat Davaajargal) had won 1,026 bouts in the *makuuchi*, sumo's top division. He claimed his 1,000th victory at the 2018 Autumn Grand Sumo Tournament, defeating Gōeidō on 22 Sep (pictured). Hakuhō won the 2019 Spring tournament with a perfect record of 15 wins from 15 bouts, increasing his tallies for **most top-division sumo championships** – 42 – and **most undefeated top-division sumo championships** – 15.

FEWEST FIGHTS TO BECOME A THREE-WEIGHT BOXING WORLD CHAMPION

In only his 12th pro fight, staged on 12 May 2018, Vasyl Lomachenko (UKR) became WBA lightweight world champion having previously won titles at featherweight and junior lightweight. He claimed the latter on 11 Jun 2016, in just his seventh fight – the **fewest fights to become a two-weight boxing world champion**.

Henry Cejudo was the third Olympic gold medallist to join UFC, after Mark Schultz and Kevin Jackson.

FIRST ATHLETE TO WIN OLYMPIC AND UFC WORLD TITLES

On 4 Aug 2018, Olympic gold medallist Henry Cejudo (USA) defeated Demetrious Johnson for the UFC Flyweight Championship at UFC 227. Cejudo beat Johnson – who had previously recorded the **most consecutive UFC title defences** (11) between 26 Jan 2013 and 7 Oct 2017 – by split decision at the Staples Center in Los Angeles, California, USA. Cejudo won gold at the 2008 Beijing Olympics in the men's freestyle wrestling 55 kg category (inset).

 NOV 24 In 1963, TV audiences watch as Lee Harvey Oswald, the accused assassin of US President John F Kennedy, is shot by nightclub owner Jack Ruby (all USA) – the **first murder on live television**.

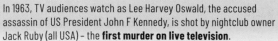 **NOV 25** Scouts Australia organize the **largest piggyback race** in Pascoe Vale South, Victoria, Australia, in 2012. A total of 1,274 participants join in the fun.

227

CYCLING

Most gold medals won at the UCI Track Cycling World Championships (female)

Kristina Vogel (DEU) tied Anna Meares's (AUS) tally of 11 golds with her victory in the women's team and individual sprints at the 2018 UCI World Championships in Apeldoorn, Netherlands. On 26 Jun 2018, Vogel saw her track-cycling career cut tragically short when she was left paralysed by a collision with another rider in training.

Farthest distance in one hour – unpaced standing start (female)

On 13 Sep 2018, Vittoria Bussi (ITA) rode 48.007 km (29.83 mi) in 60 min in Aguascalientes, Mexico. She set a new women's hour record only a day after an unsuccessful attempt that had seen her withdraw after 44 min.

Fastest 3 km individual pursuit (C4, female)*

Para-cyclists who are able to use a standard bicycle compete in classes C1–5. C1 athletes have the most severe activity limitation, while C5 athletes meet the minimum impairment criteria. At the 2019 Para-Cycling Track World Championships on 16 Mar, Emily Petricola (AUS) won the C4 individual pursuit final in 3 min 43.620 sec, smashing her previous

*pending ratification by the UCI

FASTEST 3 KM INDIVIDUAL PURSUIT (FEMALE)

On 3 Mar 2018, Chloé Dygert (USA) won the women's individual pursuit in 3 min 20.060 sec at the Union Cycliste Internationale (UCI) Track Cycling World Championships in Apeldoorn, Netherlands. She broke Sarah Hammer's record twice in one day, achieving a qualifying time of 3:20.072 before going even faster in the final. Dygert has now won five World Championships gold medals.

FASTEST WOMEN'S FLYING 200 M TIME TRIAL (B)

Visually impaired para-cyclist Sophie Thornhill and pilot Helen Scott (both UK) won gold in 10.891 sec at the 2018 Para-Cycling Track World Championships on 25 Mar. The duo followed up with an as-yet unratified 10.609 sec at the Commonwealth Games on 5 Apr 2018 (above).

world record by 10 sec. Petricola, a teacher, was diagnosed with multiple sclerosis in 2007.

Fastest 4 km individual pursuit (male)

On 31 Aug 2018, gravel-rider-turned-track-cyclist Ashton Lambie (USA) recorded a time of 4 min 7.251 sec in the men's individual pursuit at the Pan-American Championships in Aguascalientes, Mexico.

Fastest men's 4 km team pursuit

Sam Welsford, Kelland O'Brien, Leigh Howard and Alex Porter (all AUS) triumphed at the UCI Track Cycling World Championships in 3 min 48.012 sec on 28 Feb 2019.

Most appearances in the Tour de France

In 2018, Sylvain Chavanel (FRA) rode his 18th Tour de France at the age of 39, finishing 39th in the general classification. Chavanel, who made his Tour debut in 2001, finished every race bar 2007 and 2012, tying Dutch rider Hendrik "Joop" Zoetemelk's tally of 16 in 1970–73 and 1975–86: the **most Tour de France races completed**.

Most downhill titles at the UCI Mountain Bike World Cup (female)

Downhill racer Rachel Atherton (UK) has won the UCI Mountain Bike World Cup six times: in 2008, 2012–13, 2015–16 and 2018.

Most wins of the UCI Cyclo-cross World Cup (female)

On 28 Jan 2018, Belgian rider Sanne Cant secured her third cyclo-cross title with victory at Hoogerheide, Netherlands. She matched the feat of Daphny van den Brand (NLD) in 2005/06, 2009/10 and 2011/12.

Peter Sagan has also claimed the **most stage wins of the Tour de Suisse** – 16, from 2011 to 2018.

MOST WINS OF THE TOUR DE FRANCE'S POINTS CLASSIFICATION

Peter Sagan (SVK) won his sixth Tour de France points classification in 2018, matching the feat of Erik Zabel (DEU) in 1996–2001. Established in 1953, points are awarded to riders according to the position in which they finish each stage of the Tour, with additional points for intermediate sprints. The rider heading the classification traditionally wears the *maillot vert* (green jersey).

MOST CONSECUTIVE GRAND TOUR FINISHES

Adam Hansen (AUS, above centre, pictured with fellow rider Alberto Contador, right, and Giro d'Italia race director Mauro Vegni) completed 20 consecutive Grand Tour races – i.e., the Tour de France, the Giro d'Italia and the Vuelta a España – between 11 Sep 2011 and 27 May 2018. His incredible streak of sporting endurance ended at the 2018 Giro, with his announcement that he would not be entering that year's Tour de France.

 NOV 26 Dr Vijaypat Singhania (IND) pilots the **highest hot-air balloon flight**, reaching 21,027 m (68,986 ft) in a Cameron Z-1600 hot-air balloon over Mumbai, India, in 2005.

 NOV 27 In 2014, Norbert Selmaj, aka Norberto Loco (POL), completes the **longest marathon club DJ-ing**, having spun the decks for 200 hr at The Underground Temple Bar in Dublin, Ireland.

AUTO SPORTS

FIRST FEMALE MOTORCYCLE WORLD CHAMPION

Ana Carrasco (ESP) won the 2018 Fédération Internationale de Motocyclisme (FIM) World Supersport 300 Championship, finishing 13th in the final race of the season on 30 Sep to clinch the title by a single point. She won races at Imola, Italy, and Donington Park in Leicestershire, UK, finishing on 93 points.

Most Superbike World Championship race wins

Jonathan Rea (UK) capped another record-breaking Superbike season with his 71st race victory in Qatar on 26 Oct 2018. At the Automotodrom Brno in the Czech Republic on 9 Jun 2018, he overtook Carl Fogarty's mark of 59, which had stood since 1999.

Rea sealed the 2018 championship with an unprecedented run of 11 consecutive victories. In the process, he matched Fogarty's record of **most Superbike World Championship titles** – four, although only Rea has managed to win them consecutively (2015–18).

Youngest rider to win a motorcycling Grand Prix

On 18 Nov 2018, Moto3 rider Can Öncü (TUR, b. 26 Jul 2003) took the chequered flag aged 15 years 115 days at the Valencian Community Grand Prix in Spain. On his Grand Prix debut, Öncü qualified fourth and won a dramatic race that saw several riders crash out in wet conditions at the Circuit Ricardo Tormo.

Fastest speed in a National Hot Rod Association (NHRA) Drag Racing Pro Stock Motorcycle race

On 11 Nov 2018, Matt Smith (USA) recorded a speed of 323.83 km/h (201.22 mph) at the Auto Club NHRA Finals at Auto Club Raceway in Pomona, California, USA. Smith sealed his third Pro Stock Motorcycle world championship with his victory over Eddie Krawiec in the final elimination round.

Fastest speed in an NHRA Drag Racing Top Fuel race (1,000 ft)

Tony Schumacher (USA) achieved a speed of 541.65 km/h (336.57 mph) at the NHRA Arizona Nationals on 23 Feb 2018 in Chandler, Arizona, USA.

Most race wins in the NASCAR Truck Series

Kyle Busch (USA) had won a total of 54 NASCAR Truck Series races as of 26 Mar 2019. He surpassed Ron Hornaday Jr's record of 51 with victory at the Ultimate Tailgating 200 on 23 Feb 2019 in Atlanta, Georgia, USA.

Highest average lap speed at an F1 Grand Prix

Ferrari's Kimi Räikkönen (FIN) recorded a single-lap average speed of 263.587 km/h (163.785 mph) during qualification for the Italian Grand Prix on 1 Sep 2018 at the Autodromo Nazionale Monza. He lapped the iconic 5.7-km (3.5-mi) course in a time of 1 min 19.119 sec to take pole.

Most World Rally Championship (WRC) race wins

Nine-time world champion Sébastien Loeb (FRA) won his 79th WRC race at the Rally de Catalunya on 25–28 Oct 2018. Loeb retired from full-time rallying in 2012, and won his first race in more than five years during a guest appearance for Citroën Racing.

MOST CONSECUTIVE FORMULA 1 (F1) POINTS FINISHES

Lewis Hamilton (UK) scored points in 33 consecutive races for Mercedes from 9 Oct 2016 to 24 Jun 2018. His run ended at the Austrian Grand Prix on 1 Jul 2018, when a loss of fuel pressure forced him to retire. In 2018, Hamilton secured his fifth world title and increased his tally of **most F1 pole positions** to 83.

On 27 Jan 2019, Citroën celebrated its 100th WRC victory at the Monte Carlo Rally – the **most WRC race wins by a manufacturer**.

Most wins of the FIA World Rallycross Championship

PSRX Volkswagen's Johan Kristoffersson (SWE) won 11 of 12 events in 2018 to secure his second rallycross world title in succession. He matched the feat of Petter Solberg (NOR), who was champion in 2014–15.

FASTEST OUTRIGHT SPEED AT THE ISLE OF MAN TT RACES

Peter Hickman (UK) recorded an average lap speed of 217.989 km/h (135.452 mph) at the Senior TT race on 8 Jun 2018. It capped a scorchingly fast year at the TT, where ideal racing conditions led to fastest-ever lap times in many classes (see table).

FASTEST-EVER LAPS AT THE ISLE OF MAN TT

CLASS	DATE	RIDER(S)*	TIME
Superbike TT	2 Jun 2018	Dean Harrison	16:50.384
Superstock TT	4 Jun 2018	Peter Hickman	16:50.501
Supersport TT	4 Jun 2018	Michael Dunlop	17:31.328
Lightweight TT	6 Jun 2018	Michael Dunlop	18:26.543
TT Zero	6 Jun 2018	Michael Rutter	18:34.956
Sidecar TT	8 Jun 2018	Ben and Tom Birchall	18:59.018

*All riders UK

FASTEST COMPLETION OF THE BROADMOOR PIKES PEAK INTERNATIONAL HILL CLIMB

On 27 Jun 2018, Romain Dumas (FRA) won the "Race to the Clouds" in 7 min 57.148 sec. Behind the wheel of the Volkswagen electric race car *I.D. R Pikes Peak*, Dumas drove at an average speed of more than 144 km/h (90 mph) along the 19.98-km (12.42-mi) mountain course, climbing 4,302 m (14,115 ft) and navigating 156 turns.

NOV 28 Blue Water Recoveries (UK) locates the **deepest shipwreck** in 1996. The SS *Rio Grande*, a World War II German blockade runner, lies 5,762 m (18,904 ft) at the bottom of the South Atlantic Ocean.

NOV 29 In 1976, the **first plane crash caused by a dog** occurs when an unrestrained German shepherd interferes with the controls of a Grand Canyon Air Piper 32-300 in Arizona, USA.

WEIGHTLIFTING

Para powerlift –55 kg (female)
On 9 Feb 2019, Ukraine's Mariana Shevchuk lifted 131 kg (288 lb 12 oz) at the 10th Fazza World Para Powerlifting World Cup in Dubai, UAE.

Weightlifting 55 kg clean & jerk (male)
Om Yun-chol (PRK) clean & jerked 162 kg (357 lb 2 oz) at the IWF World Championships in Ashgabat on 2 Nov 2018. He went on to take the title with a total of 282 kg (621 lb 11 oz).

Weightlifting 59 kg clean & jerk (female)
On 24 Feb 2019, Chen Guiming (CHN) clean & jerked 136 kg (299 lb 13 oz) at the IWF World Cup competition held in Fuzhou, Fujian Province, China.

HEAVIEST WEIGHTLIFTING 59 KG TOTAL (FEMALE)
At the 2018 International Weightlifting Federation (IWF) World Championships in Ashgabat, Turkmenistan, Hsing-chun Kuo (TPE) took gold with 237 kg (522 lb 7 oz) on 4 Nov. She followed up the **heaviest 59 kg snatch (female)** – 105 kg (231 lb 7 oz) – with a 132-kg (291-lb) clean & jerk. The IWF had created all-new weight categories in 2018, resetting world records from 1 Nov.

HEAVIEST...

Para powerlift –107 kg (male)
Sodnompiljee Enkhbayar (MNG) bench-pressed 244 kg (537 lb 14 oz) on 12 Oct 2018 at the Asian Para Games in Jakarta, Indonesia. It was the last of five world records set during the competition.

Yujiao Tan (CHN) achieved the **heaviest para powerlift –67 kg (female)** – 140.5 kg (309 lb 11 oz) – on 9 Oct 2018. She set the record with her fourth bonus lift of the competition. On the same day, Roohallah Rostami (IRN) took gold with 229 kg (504 lb 13 oz) – the **heaviest para powerlift –72 kg (male)**.

On 10 Oct 2018, Lili Xu (CHN) achieved the **heaviest para powerlift –79 kg (female)** – 141 kg (310 lb 13 oz).

On 11 Oct 2018, Jixiong Ye (CHN) won gold with a lift of 234 kg (515 lb 14 oz) – the **heaviest para powerlift –88 kg (male)**. He broke his own record of 233.5 kg, which he had set in Japan the previous month.

HEAVIEST PARA POWERLIFT –50 KG (FEMALE)
On 10 Apr 2018, Esther Oyema (NGA) lifted 131 kg (288 lb 12 oz) to win a Commonwealth Games women's lightweight gold medal – part of a Nigerian clean sweep of all four para powerlifting titles in Gold Coast, Queensland, Australia. Para powerlifters compete in just one discipline, the bench press.

HEAVIEST WEIGHTLIFTING 96 KG TOTAL (MALE)
Sohrab Moradi (IRN) set three records in Ashgabat on 7 Nov 2018, with a final total of 416 kg (917 lb 1 oz). He lifted the **heaviest 96 kg snatch (male)** – 186 kg (410 lb) – and the **heaviest 96 kg clean & jerk (male)** – 230 kg (507 lb 1 oz). Three months earlier, Moradi had set the final IWF record before reclassification in the 94 kg snatch.

Weightlifting 64 kg total (female)
Deng Wei (CHN) lifted a total of 254 kg (559 lb 15 oz) in Fuzhou on 25 Feb 2019: the **heaviest 64 kg snatch (female)** – 113 kg (249 lb 1 oz) and the **heaviest 64 kg clean & jerk (female)** – 141 kg (310 lb 13 oz).

Weightlifting 71 kg total (female)
On 6 Nov 2018, Wangli Zhang (CHN) secured a World Championship title in Ashgabat with a total lift of 267 kg (588 lb 10 oz). This included the **heaviest 71 kg clean & jerk (female)** – 152 kg (335 lb 1 oz).

Weightlifting +109 kg total (male)
On 10 Nov 2018, Lasha Talakhadze (GEO) won gold in the super heavyweight category with a total of 474 kg (1,044 lb 15 oz) at the IWF World Championships in Ashgabat. He set seven world records in one day, including the **heaviest +109 kg snatch (male)** – 217 kg (478 lb 6 oz) – and the **heaviest +109 kg clean & jerk (male)** – 257 kg (566 lb 9 oz). Talakhadze had held all three records at +105 kg before the IWF's weight-division reclassification.

Olympic weightlifters compete in two disciplines: the snatch and clean & jerk. Powerlifters have the bench press, snatch and deadlift.

HEAVIEST ELEPHANT BAR DEADLIFT
Hafþór Björnsson (ISL) deadlifted an elephant bar weighing 472.1 kg (1,041 lb) at the 2018 Arnold Strongman Classic in Columbus, Ohio, USA, on 3 Mar 2018. He beat Jerry Pritchett's previous record of 467.65 kg (1,031 lb). Björnsson, familiar to many as Gregor Clegane in HBO's *Game of Thrones* TV series, capped an incredible year by winning the Arnold Strongman Classic, Europe's Strongest Man and World's Strongest Man.

* All records organized by the weight class of the athlete, as per the relevant federation

NOV 30 In 1954, Ann Hodges of Sylacauga, Alabama, USA, becomes the **first person injured by a meteorite**, when a 5.5-kg (12-lb) piece of chondrite crashes through the roof of her home.

DEC 1 Jonas Livet (FRA) has his record for the **most zoos visited by an individual** verified at 1,068 in 2017. He has travelled to wildlife parks and sanctuaries in 50 countries since 1987.

ARTISTIC SPORTS

The **female** record is seven, achieved by the former Soviet gymnast Nellie Kim. She has three original skills on vault, two on balance beam and two on the floor.

Most medals won on a single apparatus at the World Artistic Gymnastics Championships

Oksana Chusovitina (UZB) won nine medals on the vault at the World Artistic Gymnastics Championships between 1991 and 2011: one gold, four silvers and four bronze. At the age of 43, she finished fourth in the vault at the 2018 World Championships.

Chusovitina plans to compete at the 2020 Olympics in Tokyo. She is already the **oldest Olympic gymnast (female)**, having competed at the 2016 Olympic Games in Rio de Janeiro, Brazil, aged 41 years 56 days.

Most Senior Men Inline titles at the Artistic Skating World Championships

On 4 Oct 2018, Yi-fan Chen (TPE) claimed his fourth consecutive Inline title at the Artistic Skating World Championships, staged at the Vendéspace arena in Mouilleron-le-Captif, France.

The **most Senior Women Inline titles** is 11, achieved by Silvia Marangoni (ITA) in 2002, 2004, 2006–13 and 2015. She also took silver in 2003, 2005 and 2014.

HIGHEST SCORE AT THE FINA ARTISTIC SWIMMING WORLD SERIES (WOMEN, SOLO FREE)

On 11 Mar 2018, Svetlana Kolesnichenko (RUS) scored 95.500 at a FINA Artistic Swimming World Series event in Paris, France. Kolesnichenko has won 13 World Championship gold medals – six behind Natalia Ishchenko (RUS), whose 19 is the **most synchronized swimming FINA World Aquatics Championships gold medals**.

Most consecutive men's individual titles at the Trampoline Gymnastics World Championships

On 10 Nov 2018, Gao Lei (CHN) secured his third consecutive world title in St Petersburg, Russia. He matched the feat of Alexander Moskalenko (RUS) in 1990, 1992 and 1994.

The **most consecutive women's individual titles** is five, by Judy Wills Cline (USA) in 1964–68.

MOST MEDALS WON AT THE INTERNATIONAL SKATING UNION (ISU) WORLD SYNCHRONIZED SKATING CHAMPIONSHIPS (TEAM)

On 7 Apr 2018, Team Surprise (SWE) secured their 12th medal, a silver, at the World Synchronized Skating Championships. Finnish team Marigold IceUnity have also won 12 medals, but Team Surprise's tally includes the **most gold medals**: six. Originally called precision skating, synchronized skating was introduced in the 1950s, and the first World Championships were held in 2000.

Highest score in figure skating – short programme (female)

Rika Kihira (JPN) scored 83.97 points for her short programme on 11 Apr 2019 at the ISU World Team Trophy event in Fukuoka, Japan. For more ice skating, see pp.240–41.

Highest score for an individual clubs routine in rhythmic gymnastics

On 18 Aug 2018, Linoy Ashram (ISR) scored 20.65 for her clubs routine at the Fédération Internationale Gymnastique (FIG) World Challenge Cup in Minsk, Belarus. Rhythmic gymnastics traditionally has five different pieces of apparatus: ribbon, hoop, ball, rope and clubs.

Most elements named after a gymnast in the FIG Code of Points (male)

Kenzō Shirai (JPN) has six elements (original skills) named after him in the FIG's 2017–20 Code of Points: three for the floor exercise and three on vault. His sixth element to be accepted was the "Shirai 3" vault, first performed in competition by Shirai on 25 Feb 2017.

HIGHEST SCORE IN UCI ARTISTIC CYCLING (WOMEN, SINGLE)

Compared by the UCI (Union Cycliste Internationale) to ice skaters and gymnasts, artistic cyclists present a 5-min programme set to music on fixed-gear bicycles. The highest score by a solo female is 191.86, by Iris Schwarzhaupt (DEU) at the German Masters #1 in Wendlingen, Germany, on 8 Sep 2018.

MOST GOLD MEDALS WON AT THE WORLD ARTISTIC GYMNASTICS CHAMPIONSHIPS

At the 2018 World Artistic Gymnastics Championships in Doha, Qatar, Simone Biles (USA) won four golds to take her career tally to 14, overtaking Vitaly Scherbo's record of 12. Her haul includes the **most individual all-around World Championship titles** – four, achieved in 2013–15 and 2018.

Biles has now also won the **most medals at the World Artistic Gymnastics Championships (female)** – 20 – matching Svetlana Khorkina (RUS, from 1994 to 2003).

HIGHEST SCORES IN UCI ARTISTIC CYCLING

CATEGORY	COMPETITOR(S)	POINTS	DATE
Men, Single	David Schnabel (DEU)	208.91	6 Nov 2011
Women, Pair	Katrin Schultheis and Sandra Sprinkmeier (both DEU)	165.12	21 Sep 2013
Open, Pair	André Bugner and Benedikt Bugner (both DEU)	168.68	28 Aug 2015
Women, ACT-4	Céline Burlet, Jennifer Schmid, Melanie Schmid and Flavia Zuber (all CHE)	234.44	30 Sep 2017

All information correct as of 1 Feb 2019

DEC 2 The **tallest Buddha** is measured in 2009. The Zhongyuan Buddha in Lushan County, Henan Province, China, rises 127.64 m (418 ft 9 in) – nearly three times the height of the Statue of Liberty.

DEC 3 NASA spacecraft *Pioneer 10* completes the **first Jupiter flyby** in 1973. It passes the gas giant planet at a distance of 130,000 km (80,778 mi) above the cloud tops.

231

TARGET SPORTS

Most points scored in 30 m 36-arrow outdoor recurve archery (male)

On 15 Jun 2018, Kim Hyun-jong (KOR) scored 360/27x at the 36th National Tournament for President Challenge Flag in Gwangju, South Korea. He hit the 10-point gold target with all 36 arrows, with 27 landing in the inner X-ring. At the age of just 18, Hyun-jong surpassed his compatriot Kim Woo-jin's record of 360/26x.

Most points scored in 70 m 72-arrow outdoor recurve archery (female)

Kang Chae-young (KOR) scored 691 with 72 arrows during the ranking round at the World Cup event in Antalya, Turkey, on 21 May 2018.

Most points scored in 60 m 36-arrow outdoor compound archery (female)

On 31 Mar 2018, Danelle Wentzel (ZAF) shot 357 with 36 arrows at a distance of 60 m (196 ft) during the South African National Archery Championships at the Marks Park Archery Club in Johannesburg. Wentzel beat Gladys Willems's record of 356, which had stood for more than a decade, by a single point.

Most points scored in a 15-arrow outdoor compound archery match (female)

Linda Ochoa-Anderson (MEX) shot 150/11x with 15 arrows during a match round at the Easton Foundations Gator Cup in Newberry, Florida, USA, on 12 May 2018. She landed all of her arrows in the 10-point gold target, with 11 in the inner X-ring.

HIGHEST SCORE IN PARA SHOOTING MIXED 50 M RIFLE PRONE SH2

At the 2018 World Shooting Para Sport Championships in Cheongju, South Korea, 16-year-old Kristina Funkova (SVK) shot 250.7 in the mixed 50 m rifle prone SH2 on 11 May. The event will make its Paralympic debut in Tokyo in 2020. Competitors require a firearm support to shoot.

The **male** record for the event is 150/12x, shot by six-time world championship gold medallist Reo Wilde (USA) on 7 May 2015 at the Archery World Cup stage in Shanghai, China.

Highest score in ISSF 10 m air pistol (male)

Chaudhary Saurabh (IND) scored 245 points at an International Shooting Sport Federation (ISSF) World Cup competition in New Delhi, India, on 24 Feb 2019. It was the 16-year-old's first-ever senior event.

The next day, Commonwealth Games gold medallist Apurvi Chandela (IND) achieved the **highest score in ISSF 10 m air rifle (female)** – 252.9 points – also in New Delhi. Hungary's Veronika Major followed up with the **highest score in ISSF 25 m pistol (female)**, hitting 40 out of a maximum 50 targets in the final on 24 Feb 2019.

Highest score in ISSF Trap (female)

On 5 Mar 2018, Ashley Carroll (USA) hit 48 of 50 targets at an ISSF World Cup event in Guadalajara, Mexico. Trap is one of the major disciplines of clay pigeon shooting, in which targets are launched from a single machine.

Most wins of the Horseshoe Pitching World Championships (male)

Alan Francis (USA) won his 23rd men's title at the NHPA World Horseshoe Tournament in 2018. He emerged victorious from 14 of his 15 matches.

Most World Croquet Championship appearances by an individual

Stephen Mulliner (UK) has competed at the World Croquet Championship 15 times since 1989. He surpassed David Openshaw and Robert Fulford with his appearance at the 2018 World Championship in Wellington, New Zealand, on 3–11 Feb. Mulliner has won the title once, in 2016.

MOST PROFESSIONAL BOWLERS ASSOCIATION (PBA) MAJOR CHAMPIONSHIPS

On 21 Mar 2019, Jason Belmonte (AUS) defeated Jakob Butturff 236-227 at Thunderbowl Lanes in Allen Park, Michigan, USA, to secure his second PBA World Championship and his 11th major title overall. Belmonte – famous for his two-handed "shovel" technique – has also won two Players Championships, four USBC Masters and three Tournament of Champions. Of the five PBA majors, only the US Open eluded him as of Apr 2019.

Highest match average in a Premier League Darts final

On 17 May 2018, Michael van Gerwen (NLD) defeated Michael Smith 11–4 in the final of the Premier League Darts tournament with a three-dart average of 112.37. He fell just short of his own record for the **highest match average in a televised darts final** – 112.49, recorded at The Masters on 1 Feb 2015.

FIRST SNOOKER PLAYER TO MAKE 1,000 COMPETITIVE CENTURIES

On 10 Mar 2019, Ronnie O'Sullivan (UK) compiled his 1,000th century in professional snooker. He reached the milestone with a 134 break in the final frame of his 10-4 victory over Neil Robertson at the Coral Players Championship in Lancashire, UK. O'Sullivan's century tally includes the **most competitive 147 breaks** - 15 - and the **fastest 147 break** - 5 min 8 sec, set at the 1997 World Snooker Championship. This maximum has been officially recognized as even faster than previously thought, following analysis of video footage.

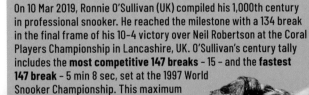

MOST WORLD WOMEN'S CURLING CHAMPIONSHIP TITLES

Canada has won the World Women's Curling Championship 17 times since 1980. They collected their most recent title on home ice under skip Jennifer Jones, beating Sweden 7-6 in the final on 25 Mar 2018 in North Bay, Ontario, Canada. The **most World Men's Curling Championship titles** is 36, also by Canada between 1959 and 2017.

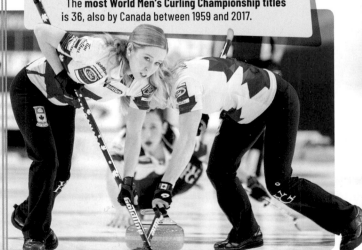

A stellar 2018/19 season saw O'Sullivan equal Stephen Hendry's (UK) tally of **most career ranking snooker titles** - 36, as of 28 Mar 2019.

DEC 4

Charlie Bigham's "Swish Pie" is launched in the UK in 2013 - at £314.16 ($514.73), it is the **most expensive ready meal**. It contains lobster, turbot and oysters, all poached in Dom Pérignon sauce.

DEC 5

In 2015, Ratnesh Pandey (IND) achieves the **longest continuous ride standing on the seat of a motorcycle**, covering 32.3 km (20 mi) on a Honda Unicorn in Indore, Madhya Pradesh, India.

GOLF

HIGHEST CAREER EARNINGS ON THE PGA TOUR

Tiger Woods (USA) had earned $118,309,570 (£90,473,700) on the Professional Golfers' Association (PGA) Tour as of 15 Apr 2019. He won his first event in five years on 23 Sep 2018, and secured his 15th career major title at The Masters on 14 Apr 2019 (above). It capped a remarkable comeback from a career-threatening back injury that saw him drop out of the Official World Golf Ranking's top 1,000 in 2017. Woods now stands one away from equalling the **most PGA Tour wins** – 82, by Sam Snead (USA).

Most PGA Tour tournament victories by a left-hander

On 11 Feb 2019, Phil "Lefty" Mickelson (USA) won his 44th PGA Tour title at the AT&T Pebble Beach Pro-Am in California, USA. It was his second win on the tour in a year. Mickelson, who learned his golf swing by mirroring his father's, is right-handed at everything except golf.

Mickelson ended 2018 by achieving the **most Ryder Cup tournament appearances** – 12 consecutively since 1995. A captain's pick for the 2018 event at Le Golf National in Guyancourt, France, he played two matches, losing both times.

Most consecutive birdies in a professional golf tournament

On 7 Feb 2019, James Nitties (AUS) sank nine birdie putts in a row at the ISPS Handa Vic Open in Geelong, Victoria, Australia. He equalled the mark set by Mark Calcavecchia (USA) at the Canadian Open on 25 Jul 2009, and matched by Amy Yang (KOR), Beth Daniel, Omar Uresti (both USA), Rayhan Thomas (IND) and Bronte Law (UK).

Highest career earnings on the PGA European Tour

Lee Westwood (UK) had won €36,499,627 (£31,520,800; $41,236,600) on the European Tour as of 15 Apr 2019. On 11 Nov 2018, he won his first European Tour title in four years, claiming the Nedbank Golf Challenge in Sun City, South Africa, with his girlfriend Helen Storey caddying for him. Westwood, who first played on the Tour in 1994, has won 24 tournaments and finished in the money 451 times.

LOWEST TOTAL SCORE AT AN LPGA TOUR EVENT

On 5-8 Jul 2018, Kim Sei-young (KOR) tore up the record books at the Thornberry Creek Ladies Professional Golf Association (LPGA) Classic in Oneida, Wisconsin, USA. She carded rounds of 63, 65, 64 and 65 for a lowest-ever total of 257. This equated to -31, the **lowest LPGA 72-hole score to par**. Kim also shot the **most birdies in an LPGA 72-hole event**: 31.

Longest drive on the PGA Tour

Officially, the PGA's longest drive in the era of ShotLink is 476 yd, struck by Davis Love III (USA) at the Mercedes Championships in Kapalua, Hawaii, USA, on 11 Jan 2004. ShotLink is the laser-based system that the PGA have used to measure the length of golf shots since 2003.

On 23 Mar 2018, Dustin Johnson hit a 489-yd drive at the WGC-Dell Technologies Match Play at Austin Country Club in Texas, USA. However, it doesn't count as an official record owing to the differences between match play and regular stroke-playing events.

Lowest score in a US Open round

On 17 Jun 2018, Tommy Fleetwood (UK) shot a final-round 63 at the US Open at Shinnecock Hills in New York, USA. He equalled the feat of Johnny Miller in 1973, Jack Nicklaus and Tom Weiskopf (all USA) in 1980, Vijay Singh (FJI) in 2003 and Justin Thomas (USA) in 2017. Fleetwood missed a 9-ft putt on the final green that would have secured the outright record.

Most major tournaments played before winning

Angela Stanford (USA) recorded her maiden major victory in her 76th tournament at the 2018 Evian Championship on 13-16 Sep. Her previous highest finish was tied-second at the 2003 US Women's Open. This eclipsed the feat of Sergio García, who won his first major at the 74th attempt in 2017.

LOWEST SCORE IN A ROUND ON THE PGA EUROPEAN TOUR

On 21 Sep 2018, Oliver Fisher (UK) became the first player to record a sub-60 round on the European Tour when he shot 59 at the Portugal Masters in Vilamoura. Fisher sunk 10 birdies and an eagle during his second round. This is the lowest score in almost 700,000 rounds of the European Tour's history.

LOWEST TOTAL SCORE AT THE US PGA CHAMPIONSHIP

Brooks Koepka (USA) claimed the 2018 US PGA Championship at Bellerive Country Club in Missouri, USA, with a four-round total score of 264 (69, 63, 66, 66; 16 under par). His round of 63 equalled the **lowest score in a round at the PGA Championship**, a record he currently shares with 15 other golfers.

MOST RYDER CUP POINTS WON BY AN INDIVIDUAL

Europe's Sergio García (ESP) won 25.5 points at the Ryder Cup in nine appearances from 1999 to 2018. His match record stands at 22 wins, 12 defeats and 7 halves. Selected as a wildcard for the 2018 event, García won three matches, overtaking Nick Faldo's previous record of 25 points in the process.

DEC 6 In 2002, the **shortest baby** is discharged from hospital in Minneapolis, Minnesota, USA. When born 108 days premature on 20 Jul, Nisa Juarez (USA) measured just 24 cm (9.44 in) long.

DEC 7 In 1995, a probe released by the *Galileo* spacecraft begins a fiery descent into Jupiter's atmosphere, reaching a speed of 170,000 km/h (105,600 mph) – the **fastest atmospheric entry**.

TRACK & FIELD

MOST POINTS IN A DECATHLON

On 15–16 Sep 2018, Kevin Mayer (FRA) scored a total of 9,126 points at the Décastar IAAF Combined Events Challenge in Talence, France. Mayer, who only entered the event after fouling out of the decathlon at the European Athletics Championships the previous month, became the first decathlete to surpass 9,100 points.

FASTEST…

Indoor one mile (male)*

On 3 Mar 2019, Yomif Kejelcha (ETH) broke a 22-year-old record when he clocked 3 min 47.01 sec for the Bruce Lehane Invitational Mile in Boston, Massachusetts, USA. He took 1.44 sec off the previous best, by Hicham El Guerrouj (MAR) on 12 Feb 1997.

El Guerrouj also saw his record for the **fastest indoor 1,500 m (male)*** fall in 2019,

*pending ratification by the IAAF

when Samuel Tefera (ETH) ran 3 min 31.04 sec on 16 Feb at the IAAF World Indoor Tour meeting in Birmingham, UK.

Indoor 400 m (male)*

Michael Norman (USA) won the men's 400 m in 44.52 sec on 10 Mar 2018 at the NCAA Men's Division I Indoor Track and Field Championships in College Station, Texas, USA. The 20-year-old, competing for the University of Southern California (USC), beat the

record of 44.57 sec by Kerron Clement (USA), which had stood for almost 13 years.

Later that day, Norman ran the anchor leg for the USC 4 x 400 m team, which won in a world-best time of 3 min 0.77 sec. However, this could not qualify as a world record under IAAF regulations, as relay teams must be the same nationality and USC team member Rai Benjamin was not eligible to run as a US athlete until 3 Oct 2018, having represented Antigua at youth level. Instead, it was second-place Texas A & M – Ilolo Izu, Robert Grant, Devin Dixon and Mylik Kerley (all USA) – who set the **fastest indoor 4 x 400 m (men)***, coming home in 3 min 1.39 sec.

Indoor 4 x 800 m (men)

On 25 Feb 2018, the Hoka NJ/NY Track Club team – represented by Joe McAsey, Kyle Merber, Chris Giesting and Jesse Garn (all USA) – won the men's 4 x 800 m relay in 7 min 11.30 sec at the 2018 Boston University Last Chance Meet in Massachusetts, USA.

Wheelchair 100 m (T34, female)

On 22 Jul 2018, Kare Adenegan (UK) won the women's T34 100 m in 16.80 sec at the Anniversary

FASTEST 3,000 M STEEPLECHASE (FEMALE)

Beatrice Chepkoech (KEN) won the women's 3,000 m steeplechase at the IAAF Diamond League meeting in Monaco in 8 min 44.32 sec on 20 Jul 2018. She beat the previous fastest time by more than eight seconds, becoming the first Kenyan woman to hold the world record in the event.

MOST DIAMOND RACE ATHLETICS TITLES WON (FEMALE)

On 30–31 Aug 2018, Caterine Ibargüen (COL) won Diamond League titles in both the triple jump and the long jump to take her overall tally to six. In doing so, she matched the feat of Sandra Perković (HRV), who triumphed in the discus in 2012–17 (see right). Ibargüen was named IAAF Female Athlete of the Year on 4 Dec 2018, capping a remarkable year.

Games in London, UK. Aged just 17, she became the first female T34 athlete to go under the 17-sec mark over the distance.

The **fastest wheelchair 100 m (T34, male)** is 14.80 sec, by Rheed McCracken (AUS) at the World Para Athletics Grand Prix in Nottwil, Switzerland, on 26 May 2018. He broke his own record of 14.92 sec, set at the same event the previous year.

400 m (T11, female)

Cuiqing Liu (CHN) ran the 400 m in exactly 56 sec at the World Para Athletics Grand Prix in Beijing, China, on 13 May 2018. She broke Terezinha Guilhermina's 2007 record of 56.14 sec. The T11 classification is for athletes with a visual impairment.

FARTHEST…

Long jump (T64, female)

Marie-Amélie Le Fur (FRA) took gold in the long jump with a leap of 6.01 m (19 ft 8 in) on 26 Aug 2018 at the World Para Athletics European Championships, held in Berlin, Germany.

Le Fur, whose left leg was amputated below the knee following a motorcycle accident in 2004, also holds the record for the **fastest 400 m (T64, female)** – 59.27 sec, recorded at the 2016 Paralympic Games.

YOUNGEST ATHLETE TO RUN A FOUR-MINUTE MILE

On 27 May 2017, Norwegian middle-distance runner Jakob Ingebrigtsen (b. 19 Sep 2000) ran a mile in 3 min 58.07 sec, aged 16 years 250 days, in Eugene, Oregon, USA. In 2018, Ingebrigtsen won gold in both the 1,500 m and 5,000 m (pictured above) at the European Athletics Championships at the age of just 17.

DEC 8 Procter & Gamble (BRA) airs the **longest TV commercial** in 2018. It lasts for 14 hr and promotes Old Spice deodorant on TV channel Woohoo in São Paulo between 6 a.m. and 8 p.m.

DEC 9 *Departure of the Argonauts*, by "a Master of 1487" (thought to be Pietro del Donzello of Italy), sells at Sotheby's in London, UK, in 1989 for £4.2 m ($6.6 m) – the **most expensive anonymous painting**.

FASTEST INDOOR 4 x 800 M (WOMEN)

On 3 Feb 2018, a United States team comprising Chrishuna Williams, Raevyn Rogers, Charlene Lipsey and Ajeé Wilson won the women's 4 x 800 m relay in 8 min 5.89 sec at the New York Road Runners Millrose Games in New York City, USA. They beat a record that had stood since 2011. Wilson (second from right) brought the team home with a fastest leg of 1 min 58.37 sec.

MOST...

Medals won at the IAAF World Indoor Championships (country)

Since 1985, the USA has won 257 world indoor medals – 114 golds, 77 silvers and 66 bronze. They earned 18 of those medals at the 2018 IAAF World Indoor Championships on 1–4 Mar, setting four championship records into the bargain.

The **most medals won at the IAAF World Indoor Championships (individual)** is nine, achieved by Maria Mutola (MOZ) in the 800 m from 1993 to 2008, and Natalya Nazarova (RUS) in the 400 m and 4 x 400 m relay between 1999 and 2010.

Diamond League victories

Croatian discus thrower Sandra Perković triumphed in 42 Diamond League competitions from 12 Jun 2010 to 22 Jul 2018 – more than any other athlete, male or female. She won four out of four events in 2018 before suffering a surprise defeat in the series final.

YOUNGEST WINNER AT A DIAMOND LEAGUE MEETING (FEMALE)

On 3 May 2019, at an IAAF Diamond League event in Doha, Qatar, Yaroslava Mahuchikh (UKR, b. 19 Sep 2001) won the women's high jump aged 17 years 226 days. Mahuchikh, a gold medallist at the 2018 Summer Youth Olympics, recorded a lifetime-best outdoor jump of 1.96 m (6 ft 5 in) to take the honours.

Discus throw (F53, female)

On 20 Aug 2018, Iana Lebiedieva (UKR) won gold at the World Para Athletics European Championships with a throw of 14.93 m (48 ft 11 in). She broke Cristeen Smith's 23-year-old record of 14.46 m (47 ft 5 in) twice at the same competition, achieving world-record throws in the fifth and sixth rounds.

Discus throw (F11, male)

Oney Tapia (ITA, b. CUB) threw 46.07 m (151 ft 1 in) at the World Para Athletics European Championships on 22 Aug 2018. He broke his own record of 45.65 m (149 ft 9 in), set in Chiuro, Italy, on 28 Apr 2018. Tapia lost his sight in 2011 when he was hit by a falling branch while working as an arborist. In 2017, he became a household name in Italy when he won its *Dancing with the Stars* TV programme.

Club throw (F51, male)

On 13 May 2018, two-time Paralympic gold medallist Željko Dimitrijević (SRB) threw a club 32.90 m (107 ft 11 in) in Split, Croatia. The F51-57 classifications are for seated throwers.

Diamond League appearances

As of 31 Aug 2018, Blessing Okagbare-Ighoteguonor (NGA) had participated in 67 Diamond League meetings since 3 Jul 2010. She competed in the 100 m, 200 m and long jump, emerging victorious on 10 occasions.

Wins of the IAAF Hammer Throw Challenge

Anita Włodarczyk (POL) has won the IAAF Hammer Throw Challenge six consecutive times, in 2013-18. She claimed her sixth title with a score of 228.12 points.

The **most wins of the IAAF Hammer Throw Challenge (male)** is four, by Paweł Fajdek (POL) in 2013, 2015, 2016 and 2017.

FARTHEST LONG JUMP (T64, MALE)

On 25 Aug 2018, "Blade Jumper" Markus Rehm (DEU) won gold at the World Para Athletics European Championships in Berlin, Germany, with a leap of 8.48 m (27 ft 9 in). He broke his own world record by 1 cm (0.3 in). Rehm's record leap equalled the distance of non-Paralympian Luvo Manyonga's winning jump at the IAAF World Championships the previous year.

DEC 10 Dzmitry Dudarau (BLR) achieves the **longest duration to hang suspended by the teeth** in 2017, supporting his body weight for 7 min 15 sec in Jimo, Shandong Province, China.

DEC 11 In 2004, more than 5 million people join hands to form the **longest human chain**. It stretches 1,050 km (652.4 mi) from Teknaf to Tentulia in north-west Bangladesh.

235

MARATHONS

Most wins of the World Marathon Majors series (male)

Inaugurated in 2006, the World Marathon Majors is a points-based competition that encompasses the annual marathon races in Boston, Tokyo (added in 2013), Berlin, Chicago, London and New York City, and also the IAAF World Championship and Olympic marathons. Competing athletes score points for top-five finishes. In 2018, Eliud Kipchoge (KEN) underlined his dominance over the distance by claiming his third consecutive men's series title.

The **most wins (female)** is also three, by Irina Mikitenko (DEU, b. KAZ) in 2007/08–2009/10, and Mary Keitany (KEN) in 2011/12, 2015/16 and 2017/18.

Most wins of the London Marathon (male)

On 28 Apr 2019, Eliud Kipchoge claimed his fourth London Marathon title, following victories in 2015–16 and 2018. His winning time of 2 hr 2 min 37 sec was the **fastest-run London Marathon (male)** and the second-fastest marathon in history, just 58 sec behind his own world record (see p.213 for more).

The **most wins of the London Marathon (female)** is four, by Norway's Ingrid Kristiansen in 1984–85 and 1987–88.

MOST WINS OF THE GREAT NORTH RUN

On 9 Sep 2018, Mo Farah (UK, b. SOM) claimed his fifth consecutive title at the Great North Run half-marathon in Newcastle upon Tyne, UK. He had previously shared the record with four-time winner Benson Masya (KEN). A month later, former track star Farah won the Chicago Marathon in 2 hr 5 min 11 sec – his first victory over the distance.

FASTEST TIME TO COMPLETE THE IRONMAN® WORLD CHAMPIONSHIP (FEMALE)

Daniela Ryf (CHE) won the women's IRONMAN® World Championship in 8 hr 26 min 18 sec on 13 Oct 2018 in Hawaii, USA. She recovered from a painful jellyfish sting just before the start of the race to beat her own record, set in 2016, by 20 min 28 sec. Ryf completed the 3.8-km (2.4-mi) swim in 57 min 27 sec, the 180-km (112-mi) bike ride in a record 4 hr 26 min 7 sec (inset), and the 42.1-km (26.2-mi) marathon in 2 hr 57 min 5 sec. It was her fourth consecutive IRONMAN® World Championship victory.

Most wins of the Ultra-Trail du Mont-Blanc (male)

First staged in 2003, the Ultra-Trail du Mont-Blanc is a c. 167-km (103-mi) race held annually in the Alps across France, Switzerland and Italy. Three male athletes have triumphed three times: Kilian Jornet (ESP) in 2008–09 and 2011; François D'Haene (FRA) in 2012, 2014 and 2017; and Xavier Thévenard (FRA) in 2013, 2015 and 2018.

FASTEST-RUN...

IRONMAN® World Championship (male)

On 13 Oct 2018, Patrick Lange (DEU) became the first athlete to break the eight-hour barrier at the IRONMAN® World Championship, coming home in 7 hr 52 min 39 sec. It was Lange's second win in a row in Hawaii, USA.

Marathon on debut

On 25 Jan 2019, Getaneh Molla (ETH) won the Dubai Marathon in his first competitive race over the distance, crossing the finish line in 2 hr 3 min 34 sec in the UAE. This was not only the **fastest Dubai Marathon (male)** – by 26 sec – but also the ninth-fastest marathon time ever run on a record-eligible course.

In the women's race, Ruth Chepngetich (KEN) recorded the **fastest Dubai Marathon (female)** – 2 hr 17 min 8 sec. She moved to third

On 28 Apr 2019, around 43,000 runners lined up for the 39th annual London Marathon in the UK. GWR partnered with the event for the 12th year, and saw a host of records fall to fleet-footed fancy-dress runners (all UK, unless stated):

Awareness ribbon (male) Oliver Williams – 2:36:52

Scout (male) Oliver Jones – 2:41:45

Zombie (male) Matthew Berry – 2:43:54

Bride (male) Lee Goodwin – 2:49:17

Doctor (male) Greg Kelly – 2:50:17

Golfer (male) Jonni Suckling – 2:59:35

Love heart (male) Thomas Brockwell – 3:05:32

Nurse (female) Jessica Anderson – 3:08:22

Skeleton (male) David Course – 3:08:59

Nun (male) Paul Nelis – 3:12:19

Postbox (male) Matthew Collins – 3:14:32

In a non-racing wheelchair (male) Joshua Landmann – 3:18:59

Scientist (male) Angelos Michaelides – 3:22:51

Brownie (female) Elise Rendall – 3:26:51

Fairy-tale character (female) Alison Stewart, as Snow White – 3:29:58

Shoe (male) Charlie Field – 3:35:19

Cavewoman (female) Nicky McKenzie – 3:35:20

Hospital patient (female) Eileen Naughton – 3:40:16

In a sleeping bag (male) Ben Burfoot – 3:41:59

Soccer player (male) Daniel Newman – 3:42:32

Two runners handcuffed (mixed pair) Rebecca (UK) and Nuno César de Sá (PRT) – 3:43:17

DEC 12 After exactly 24 hr, Richard Glover wraps up the **longest radio interview** with writer Peter FitzSimons (both AUS) in 2011. The pair chat in a pop-up studio in a shop window in Sydney, Australia.

DEC 13 In 1972, Eugene Cernan and Harrison Schmitt (both USA) set the **lunar speed record** while driving the Apollo 17 Lunar Rover at 18 km/h (11.18 mph) east of their landing site on the Moon.

of 1 hr 6 min 11 sec. Gudeta surpassed Lornah Kiplagat's mark of 1 hr 6 min 25 sec, set at the World Road Running Championships in 2007 – the first women-only record ratified by the IAAF over this distance.

The **fastest half marathon (female)** is 1 hr 4 min 51 sec, by Joyciline Jepkosgei (KEN) on 22 Oct 2017 in a mixed-gender race in Valencia, Spain.

Berlin Marathon (female)
Kenya's Gladys Cherono took the 2018 Berlin Marathon women's title in 2 hr 18 min 11 sec on 16 Sep. It was Cherono's third victory in Berlin and the eighth-fastest women's marathon at that time.

Rotterdam Marathon (male)
Marius Kipserem (KEN) crossed the finish line in Rotterdam, Netherlands, in 2 hr 4 min 11 sec on 7 Apr 2019.

He beat compatriot Duncan Kibet's course record of 2 hr 4 min 27 sec, which had stood for a decade.

100 miles (female)
Camille Herron (USA) continues to rewrite the ultra-distance record books. In Nov 2018, her time of 12 hr 42 min 40 sec – which she clocked on 11 Nov 2017 at the Tunnel Hill 100 in Vienna, Illinois, USA – was ratified by the IAU. She added the **farthest run in 24 hours (female)** – 262.193 km (162.919 mi) – at the Desert Solstice Track Invitational on 8–9 Dec 2018 in Phoenix, Arizona, USA.

Herron also holds the GWR title for the **fastest marathon dressed as a superhero (female)**. On 18 Nov 2012, she completed the Route 66 Marathon wearing a bright pink Spider-Man costume in 2 hr 48 min 51 sec in Tulsa, Oklahoma, USA. She won the women's category of the race.

FASTEST ROAD RUN 100 KM
On 24 Jun 2018, Nao Kazami (JPN) won the Lake Saroma 100 km Ultramarathon in 6 hr 9 min 14 sec in Kitami City, Hokkaido Prefecture, Japan. He took four minutes off the record set by his compatriot Takahiro Sunada, which had stood for 20 years.

This time also constitutes the **fastest ultra-distance 100 km** – as sanctioned by the International Association of Ultrarunners (IAU). Kazami bettered the mark of 6 hr 10 min 20 sec, set by British athlete Don Ritchie (1944–2018) in London, UK, on 28 Oct 1978.

on the all-time women's marathon list, behind Mary Keitany (2 hr 17 min 1 sec, at the 2017 London Marathon) and Paula Radcliffe (UK), whose **fastest marathon (female)** – 2 hr 15 min 25 sec, also at London on 13 Apr 2003 – remains as yet unchallenged.

Half marathon (female, women-only race)
At the IAAF World Half Marathon Championships in Valencia, Spain, on 24 Mar 2018, Netsanet Gudeta (ETH) took the women's honours in a time

FASTEST WHEELCHAIR MARATHON T54 (FEMALE)
On 16 Sep 2018, Manuela Schär (CHE) completed the fastest female wheelchair marathon on a world-record-eligible course in 1 hr 36 min 53 sec at the Berlin Marathon in Germany. Schär beat the previous record by more than one minute.

The **male** record is 1 hr 20 min 14 sec, set by Schär's compatriot Heinz Frei on 31 Oct 1999 in Ōita, Japan.

YOUNGEST WINNER OF THE WOMEN'S LONDON MARATHON
Brigid Kosgei (KEN, b. 20 Feb 1994) won the women's London Marathon aged 25 years 67 days on 28 Apr 2019. She crossed the finish line in 2 hr 18 min 20 sec – the ninth-fastest women's time over the distance – having run the fastest-ever second half of a marathon by a female athlete: 1 hr 6 min 42 sec.

Christmas tree (male) Laurence Mumford – 3:43:41

Tree (male) Alan Dean – 3:48:17

Full-body animal costume (female) Kate Carter, as a panda – 3:48:32

Elvis (female) Elizabeth Sampson – 3:49:53

Toiletry item (female) Katie Simpson, as toothpaste – 3:51:17

Tooth (female) Fiona Henderson – 3:51:17

Astronomical body (male) Philip Rose, as the Sun – 3:52:40

Stationery item (female) Belinda Neild, as a crayon – 3:54:25

Videogame character (female) Shaolin Loke, as Chun-Li – 3:56:18

In a tent (male) Oscar White – 3:57:05

Mythical creature (male) Andy Taylor, as a unicorn – 3:58:05

Egg (female) Katy Garnham-Lee – 3:58:43

Mummy (male) Pardip Singh Minhas – 3:59:04

Nut (female) Sally Orange – 4:09:51

DNA double helix (female) Marie Evans – 4:20:07

Dragon (male) James Cook – 4:46:50

Snowboarder (male) James Williams – 5:21:50

In ski boots (male) Paul Harnett – 5:30:27

In a six-person costume Charlotte Farge, Cey Uzun, Rob Jones, Helen Smith, Andy Moulden and David Brennan, as the Thunderbirds – 5:55:33

DEC 14 In 1952, Dr Jac Geller completes the **first successful separation of conjoined twins**, on xiphopagus (joined at the sternum) girls at Mount Sinai Hospital in Cleveland, Ohio, USA.

DEC 15 The seven-masted schooner *Thomas W Lawson* is wrecked off the Isles of Scilly, UK, in 1907. Built in 1902 at Quincy, Massachusetts, USA, the *Lawson* had the **most masts on a sailing ship**.

MOST FINA MARATHON SWIM WORLD SERIES TITLES (FEMALE)

Ana Marcela Cunha (BRA) has won the FINA Marathon Swim World Series four times: in 2010, 2012, 2014 and 2018. She won two of eight races during the 2018 Series – at Balatonfüred in Hungary and Lac Saint-Jean in Quebec, Canada – to seal the title and increase her tally of **most World Series race wins (female)** to 20.

FASTEST...

Long course 1,500 m freestyle (female)

Katie Ledecky (USA) destroyed her own 1,500 m freestyle record by 5 sec when she touched home in 15 min 20.48 sec in Indianapolis, Indiana, USA, on 16 May 2018.

Long course 50 m butterfly (male)

Andriy Govorov (UKR) beat a "supersuit" record from 2009 (see above right) when he swam the 50 m fly in 22.27 sec at the Sette Colli Trophy in Rome, Italy, on 1 Jul 2018.

Long course 50 m backstroke (female)

Liu Xiang (CHN) won the women's 50 m backstroke in 26.98 sec at the 18th Asian Games in Jakarta, Indonesia, on 21 Aug 2018.

Long course 100 m breaststroke (male)

On 4 Aug 2018, Adam Peaty (UK) won the men's 100 m breaststroke in 57.10 sec at the European Aquatics Championships in Glasgow, UK. He currently owns the 14 fastest-ever times for the event.

Long course relay 4 x 100 m freestyle (female)

The Australian team of Cate Campbell, Emma McKeon, Bronte Campbell and Shayna Jack delighted the home crowd at the 2018 Commonwealth Games by winning the 4 x 100 m relay in 3 min 30.05 sec on 5 Apr.

Short course 50 m breaststroke (female)

At the 2018 FINA Swimming World Cup meet on 6 Oct in Budapest, Hungary, Alia Atkinson (JAM) won the women's 50 m breaststroke in 28.56 sec. She beat her own record by 0.08 sec.

On the same night, Nicholas Santos (BRA) broke another "supersuit" record with the **fastest short course 50 m butterfly (male)** – 21.75 sec.

At the World Cup meet on 11 Nov 2018 in Tokyo, Japan, Xu Jiayu (CHN) swam the **fastest short course 100 m backstroke (male)** – 48.88 sec.

FASTEST SHORT COURSE 100 M INDIVIDUAL MEDLEY (MALE)

During the 2018 FINA Swimming World Cup, Vladimir Morozov (RUS) won the 100 m individual medley in 50.26 sec - twice: on 28 Sep in Eindhoven, Netherlands, and on 9 Nov in Tokyo, Japan. Morozov has won 88 World Cup races, behind only Chad le Clos (ZAF; 143 wins) for the **most FINA Swimming World Cup gold medals (male)**.

FASTEST LONG COURSE 50 M BACKSTROKE (MALE)

Kliment Kolesnikov (RUS) took gold in 24.00 sec at the European Aquatics Championships in Glasgow, UK, on 4 Aug 2018. The 18-year-old beat Liam Tancock's mark of 24.04 sec, achieved in 2009 during the "supersuit era", when swimmers wearing (now banned) hi-tech, non-textile swimsuits set a host of long-standing records.

MOST GOLD MEDALS WON AT A FINA WORLD CHAMPIONSHIPS (INDIVIDUAL)

Olivia Smoliga (USA) won eight gold medals at the 14th FINA World Swimming Championships (25 m) on 11-16 Dec 2018 in Hangzhou, China. She triumphed in the women's 50 m and 100 m backstroke, and six relays (four women's and two mixed). The previous best from a single FINA championships had been seven, achieved by Caeleb Dressel in 2017 and Michael Phelps in 2007.

S11 400 m freestyle (female)

Liesette Bruinsma (NLD) beat an eight-year-old record by almost 6 sec when she won the 400 m freestyle in 5 min 4.74 sec at the World Para Swimming European Championships in Dublin, Ireland, on 15 Aug 2018. The S11 category is for swimmers with visual impairments.

Also in Dublin, Bruinsma achieved the **fastest S11 100 m freestyle (female)** – 1 min 5.14 sec – and the **fastest SM11 200 m individual medley (female)** – 2 min 46.58 sec.

SB14 100 m breaststroke (male)

Scott Quin (UK) swam the 100 m breaststroke in 1 min 5.28 sec at the British Para-Swimming International Meet in Glasgow, UK, on 27 Apr 2019. The SB14 category is reserved for swimmers with an intellectual impairment.

FASTEST SM6 200 M INDIVIDUAL MEDLEY (FEMALE)

On 25 Apr 2019, Maisie Summers-Newton (UK) swam the 200 m individual medley in 2 min 57.99 sec at the British Para-Swimming International Meet in Glasgow, UK. The 16-year-old improved on her own record of 2 min 59.60 sec, set on 14 Aug 2018 (above).

Summers-Newton, who is short-statured, has also swum the **fastest SB6 100 m breaststroke (female)** – 1 min 33.63 sec, set on 15 Aug 2018.

DEC 16

In 2016, Todd Simpson (CAN) builds the **smallest snowman** – measuring 3 micrometres in height – at Western University Nanofabrication Facility in Ontario, Canada.

DEC 17

A J Hackett (NZ) makes the **highest bungee jump from a building**, plunging 199 m (652 ft 10 in) from a platform on the Macau Tower in Macau, China, in 2006.

WATER SPORTS

HIGHEST SCORE SLALOM WATERSKIING (FEMALE)

On 16 Jul 2018, Regina Jaquess (USA) passed four buoys on a 10.25-m (33-ft 7-in) line at 55 km/h (34 mph) at the July Heat tournament in Florida, USA. It was her eighth slalom record, as ratified by the International Waterski & Wakeboard Federation. Slalom waterskiers negotiate a zigzag course around six buoys: with each successful pass, the boat speed increases to a maximum rate and then the rope line is gradually shortened.

Most points waterskiing (men)

On 16 Jul 2018, Adam Sedlmajer (CZE) scored 2,819.76 points at the July Heat event. He slalomed three buoys on a 10.25-m line at 58 km/h (36 mph), scored 10,750 points in tricks, and jumped 66.3 m (217 ft 6 in). This record was approved by the International Waterski & Wakeboard Federation.

On 6 Oct 2018, Erika Lang (USA) scored the **most points from waterskiing tricks (female)** – 10,850 – at the Sunset Fall Classic in Groveland, Florida, USA.

Youngest surfer to qualify for the World Surf League Championship Tour

Caroline Marks (USA, b. 14 Feb 2002) took her place on the 2018 World Surf League Championship Tour, having qualified aged 15 years 264 days at the conclusion of the Women's Qualifying Series on 5 Nov 2017. She finished her debut season in seventh place, earning herself the Rookie of the Year award.

Largest wave surfed (female)

Maya Gabeira (BRA) surfed a 20.72-m-tall (68-ft) wave at Praia do Norte in Nazaré, Portugal, on 18 Jan 2018. The seven-storey-sized wave was verified by the World Surf League's Big Wave Awards panel.

Gilmore won events in Australia, Brazil and South Africa en route to the 2018 World Surf League title.

Fastest men's kite-surfing speed (nautical mile)

Christophe Ballois (FRA) reached 35.78 knots (66.26 km/h; 41.17 mph) over 1 nautical mi (1.8 km; 1.1 mi) at the Speed Sailing Event at La Palme, France, on 21 Jul 2018. The record was ratified by the World Sailing Speed Record Council (WSSRC). Born without a left forearm, Ballois learned to sail one-handed, but used a prosthetic arm for this attempt.

Fastest women's sailing speed (nautical mile)

Also at the Speed Sailing Event at La Palme on 21 Jul 2018, windsurfer Zara Davis (UK) achieved a speed of 37.29 knots (69.06 km/h; 42.91 mph), as verified by the WSSRC.

FASTEST 2,000 M SINGLE SCULLS PARA-ROW (FEMALE)

Birgit Skarstein (NOR) won the PR1 women's single sculls in 10 min 13.630 sec at the World Rowing Championships in Plovdiv, Bulgaria, on 16 Sep 2018. She broke her own world-best time by more than 10 sec. Skarstein also represented Norway in cross-country skiing at the 2014 and 2018 Winter Paralympic Games.

Fastest 2,000 m lightweight single sculls row (male)

On 9 Sep 2018, Jason Osborne (DEU) won his heat of the men's lightweight single sculls in 6 min 41.030 sec at the World Rowing Championships in Plovdiv, Bulgaria.

Farthest freediving dynamic apnea with fins (female)

Magdalena Solich-Talanda (POL) swam 243 m (797 ft) underwater with fins on a single breath in Belgrade, Serbia, on 29 Jun 2018. She smashed the record of 237 m (777 ft) by Natalia Molchanova, which had stood for four years.

FASTEST INTERNATIONAL CANOE FEDERATION (ICF) C1 1,000 M (MALE)

On 26 May 2018, Martin Fuksa (CZE) won the C1 (solo canoe) 1,000 m event in 3 min 42.385 sec at the ICF Canoe Sprint World Cup in Duisburg, Germany.

Six days earlier, Fuksa had achieved the **fastest ICF C1 500 m (male)** – 1 min 43.669 sec – at the Canoe Sprint World Cup event in Szeged, Hungary.

DEEPEST CONSTANT-WEIGHT FREEDIVE (MALE)

On 18 Jul 2018, Alexey Molchanov (RUS) dived to 130 m (426 ft 6 in) at the Vertical Blue freediving competition at Dean's Blue Hole on Long Island in The Bahamas. This is the deepest self-propelled dive in history. During a record-packed Vertical Blue, Molchanov also achieved the **deepest free-immersion freedive (male)** – 125 m (410 ft 1 in) – on 24 Jul 2018.

MOST ASP/WORLD SURF LEAGUE WORLD CHAMPIONSHIPS (FEMALE)

Stephanie Gilmore (AUS) won the World Surf League in 2018 to seal her seventh world championship. She matched Layne Beachley (AUS), winner in 1998–2003 and 2006. Gilmore first qualified for the Association of Surfing Professionals (ASP) World Tour in 2007, winning in her rookie season and adding titles in 2008–10, 2012 and 2014. The World Surf League replaced the ASP World Tour in 2015.

DEC 18 In 1898, Gaston de Chasseloup-Laubat (FRA) sets the **first recognized land-speed record** in Achères, Yvelines, France. He reaches 63.15 km/h (39.24 mph) in the electric *Jeantaud Duc*.

DEC 19 In 2014, Puskar Nepal (NPL) achieves the **most kicks to the head in one minute (self)** – 134 – in Kathmandu, Nepal. He sets the record in front of an audience of invited guests.

WINTER SPORTS

FASTEST SPEED SKATING 3,000 M (FEMALE)

Martina Sáblíková (CZE) triumphed at the ISU World Cup Speed Skating Final in 3 min 52.02 sec on 9 Mar 2019 in Salt Lake City, Utah, USA. She beat her own record of 3 min 53.31 sec, set just a week earlier at the World Allround Speed Skating Championships, where she also set the **fastest 5,000 m (female)** – 6 min 42.01 sec.

FASTEST SHORT TRACK SPEED SKATING 500 M (MALE)

On 11 Nov 2018, Wu Dajing (CHN) won the men's 500 m in 39.505 sec at the ISU Short Track Speed Skating World Cup in Salt Lake City, Utah, USA. He took full advantage of the conditions at the high-altitude Utah Olympic Oval, where skaters face less air resistance and there is less oxygen frozen into the ice, making the track harder and faster.

Fastest speed skating 500 m (male)

Held on 9–10 Mar 2019 in Salt Lake City, Utah, USA, the ISU World Cup Speed Skating Final witnessed a slew of super-fast times. Pavel Kulizhnikov (RUS) skated his first race in the men's 500 m in a record 33.61 sec on 9 Mar, the same day that Brittany Bowe (USA) achieved the **fastest 1,000 m (female)** – 1 min 11.61 sec.

On 10 Mar, Japan's Miho Takagi completed the **fastest 1,500 m (female)** – 1 min 49.83 sec – while Kjeld Nuis (NLD) set the **fastest 1,500 m (male)** – 1 min 40.17 sec.

Fewest points for speed skating long track mini combination (female)

The mini combination comprises four separate races held over 500 m, 1,000 m, 1,500 m and 3,000 m.

Using the *samalog* system, times over each distance are converted into points, with the lowest overall score winning the event. On 9–10 Mar 2018, at the World Junior Speed Skating Championships in Salt Lake City, Utah, USA, Joy Beune (NLD) recorded a total score of 153.776 points. She also set world junior records over three of the four distances.

Fastest short track speed skating 5,000 m relay (men)

The Hungarian team of Csaba Burján, former US speed skater Cole Krueger and brothers Shaoang Liu and Shaolin Sándor Liu skated the 45 laps of the men's 5,000 m relay in 6 min 28.625 sec on 4 Nov 2018. They were competing at the ISU Short Track World Cup in Calgary, Alberta, Canada.

MOST WORLD LUGE CHAMPIONSHIPS TITLES (FEMALE)

At the 2019 World Luge Championships in Winterberg, Germany, Natalie Geisenberger (DEU) collected her eighth and ninth career world titles. She won the women's singles and women's sprint to add to her four relay and three singles titles. Geisenberger also has the **most Women's Luge World Cup titles** – seven, won consecutively from 2012/13 to 2018/19.

Chen's quadruple Lutz at the World Championships earned the highest-ever Grade of Execution for a jump: 4.76.

FIGURE SKATING: A NEW ERA

At the beginning of the 2018/19 season, the International Skating Union (ISU) increased the range of its Grade of Execution scoring system from –3/+3 to –5/+5 and reset all of its figure skating highest scores. World records were set throughout the season in each of the four disciplines, with the 2019 World Championships in Saitama, Japan, seeing a host of superlative performances.

HIGHEST SCORES IN FIGURE SKATING

MEN	SKATER	POINTS	LOCATION	DATE
Short programme	Yuzuru Hanyu (JPN)	110.53	Moscow, Russia	16 Nov 2018
Free skating	Nathan Chen (USA, right)	216.02	Saitama, Japan	23 Mar 2019
Combined total	Nathan Chen	323.42	Saitama, Japan	23 Mar 2019
WOMEN				
Short programme	Rika Kihira (JPN)	83.97	Fukuoka, Japan	11 Apr 2019
Free skating	Alina Zagitova (RUS)	158.50	Oberstdorf, Germany	28 Sep 2018
Combined total	Alina Zagitova	238.43	Oberstdorf, Germany	28 Sep 2018
PAIRS				
Short programme	Evgenia Tarasova & Vladimir Morozov (RUS)	81.21	Saitama, Japan	20 Mar 2019
Free skating	Sui Wenjing & Han Cong (CHN, left)	155.60	Saitama, Japan	21 Mar 2019
Combined total	Sui Wenjing & Han Cong	234.84	Saitama, Japan	21 Mar 2019
ICE DANCE				
Rhythm dance	Gabriella Papadakis & Guillaume Cizeron (FRA)	88.42	Saitama, Japan	22 Mar 2019
Free dance	Gabriella Papadakis & Guillaume Cizeron	135.82	Fukuoka, Japan	12 Apr 2019
Combined total	Gabriella Papadakis & Guillaume Cizeron	223.13	Fukuoka, Japan	12 Apr 2019

All figures correct as of 12 Apr 2019

DEC 20 The **longest Christmas cracker** – 63.1 m (207 ft) – is made by the parents of children at Ley Hill School and Pre-School in Chesham, Buckinghamshire, UK, in 2001. It contains balloons, toys and a joke.

DEC 21 In 2012, "Gangnam Style" by South Korean pop/rap superstar PSY becomes the **first video to receive 1 billion views**. It had been uploaded to YouTube in July, just 159 days earlier.

MOST INDIVIDUAL RACE WINS AT THE FIS WORLD CUP

No skier has won more races at the Fédération Internationale de Ski (FIS) World Cup than Amélie Wenger-Reymond (CHE). She claimed her 141st in the Telemark discipline on 17 Feb 2019. Only two other skiers have recorded more than 100 World Cup victories: Marit Bjørgen (114, cross-country) and Conny Kissling (106, freestyle).

most downhill race wins (female) – 43 – and **most Super-G race wins (female)** – 28. Injuries forced Vonn into retirement during the 2018/19 season, leaving her just four victories shy of the overall record for **most World Cup victories** – 86, by Sweden's legendary Ingemar Stenmark in 1974-89.

Oldest medallist at the FIS Alpine Ski World Championships

On 6 Feb 2019, Johan Clarey (FRA, b. 8 Jan 1981) won a World Championships silver medal aged 38 years 29 days in the men's Super-G race in Åre, Sweden. Clarey had spent much of his career focusing on the downhill discipline: on 19 Jan 2013, he achieved the **fastest World Cup downhill skiing speed** – 161.9 km/h (100.6 mph) – at Wengen in Switzerland. He was the first skier to break the 100-mph barrier in competition.

MOST RACE WINS IN AN FIS ALPINE SKI WORLD CUP SEASON

Mikaela Shiffrin (USA) enjoyed a dazzling 2018/19 season, winning 17 races on the Alpine Ski World Cup calendar. This is three more than the previous best, set by Vreni Schneider in 1988/89. Shiffrin became the first skier to win overall, slalom, giant slalom and Super-G titles in the same season. Her career total of 60 World Cup victories includes the **most slalom race wins (female)** – 40.

Most ISU World Single Distances Speed Skating Championships (male)

Sven Kramer (NLD) picked up his 20th career title at the 2019 World Single Distances Speed Skating Championships. His total comprises eight 5,000 m, five 10,000 m and seven team pursuit titles.

The most **female titles** is 15, by Martina Sáblíková (see above left) between 2007 and 2019. She has won five golds at 3,000 m and 10 at 5,000 m.

Most FIS Alpine Ski World Cup victories (female)

Lindsey Vonn (USA) won 82 races at the FIS Alpine Ski World Cup between 3 Dec 2004 and 14 Mar 2018. Her tally includes the

MOST WINS OF THE FIS FREESTYLE SKI WORLD CUP (MALE)

Mikaël Kingsbury (CAN) has won eight consecutive freestyle World Cup titles since 2011/12. In 2018/19, he won seven out of nine World Cup events to dominate the moguls discipline and claim the overall freestyle crystal globe for the eighth year in a row. Kingsbury's tally of 56 victories is the **most Freestyle Ski World Cup race wins.**

Most Ski Jumping World Cup individual victories (female)

Sara Takanashi (JPN) won 56 events at the Ski Jumping World Cup between 3 Mar 2012 and 10 Feb 2019.

Most skeleton race wins at the IBSF World Cup (male)

On 18 Jan 2019, Latvia's Martins Dukurs claimed his 51st career race victory in the skeleton at the International Bobsleigh & Skeleton Federation (IBSF) World Cup in Innsbruck, Austria.

Most countries at a Bandy World Championships

Similar to ice hockey, bandy is contested by teams of 11 players on a soccer-pitch-sized rink, using a ball instead of a puck. A total of 20 nations, including China, Great Britain and Somalia, took part in the Federation of International Bandy World Championships from 21 Jan to 2 Feb 2019 in Vänersborg, Sweden.

The **most Bandy World Championships wins (men)** is 14, by the Soviet Union from 1957 to 1991. Sweden and Russia have both won 12. The **women**'s record is eight, by Sweden from 2004 to 2018. They have won every edition bar one, in 2014.

Most wins of the Canadian Curling Championships

The provincial curling competition known as the Brier was first held in 1927. On 10 Mar 2019, Alberta won their 28th title when they beat Team Wild Card in Brandon, Manitoba, Canada.

MOST FIS ALPINE SKI WORLD CUP OVERALL TITLES (MALE)

Marcel Hirscher (AUT) won eight consecutive overall titles at the FIS Alpine Ski World Cup from 2011/12 to 2018/19. He has won 67 races: 32 slalom, 31 giant slalom, three parallel and one Super-G. In 2017/18, Hirscher won 13 races, tying Ingemar Stenmark (SWE; 1978/79) and Hermann Maier (AUT; 2000/01) for **most race wins in an Alpine Ski World Cup season (male).**

DEC 22 Wilhelm Röntgen (DEU) unveils the **first published x-ray**, of his wife Anna's hand, at the University of Würzburg, Germany, in 1895. Upon seeing the image of her bones, she exclaims: "I have seen my death!"

DEC 23 In 2013, Pabba Soujanya (IND) achieves the **most consecutive one-handed claps by an individual** – 1,233 – in Andhra Pradesh, India. It takes her just 3 min 59 sec to break the record.

241

EXTREME SPORTS

On 25 Jan 2019, Kelly Sildaru won ski Slopestyle gold with the **highest Winter X Games Slopestyle score** – 99.00.

Longest indoor formation four-way skydive sequence (women)

The Aerodyne Weembi Girls – Clémentine Le Bohec, Paméla Lissajoux, Christine Malnis and Sophia Pécout (all FRA) – completed 45 consecutive formations at the FAI European Indoor Skydiving Championships in Voss, Norway, on 13 Apr 2018.

Lowest Para-Ski combined score

Para-Ski combines two sports: giant slalom skiing and parachute accuracy landings. The lowest combined score after two ski runs and six jumps by a **male** is 7, by Sebastian Graser (AUT) in Bad Leonfelden, Austria, on 16 Feb 2019.

The **female** record is 10, set by Magdalena Schwertl (AUT) at the same event.

Longest downhill bicycle stair race

Beginning at the summit of a hill overlooking Bogotá in Colombia, the Devotos de Monserrate follows a 2.40-km (1.49-mi) downhill course along tight paths featuring 1,060 steps. The latest edition of the race – organized by Red Bull Colombia – was won by Marcelo Gutiérrez in 4 min 42.48 sec on 16 Feb 2019.

FASTEST SPEED PARACHUTING CANOPY PILOTING (FEMALE)

On 4 Jul 2018, Cornelia Mihai (UAE, b. ROM) cleared a 70-m (229-ft) canopy piloting course in 2.273 sec at the World Canopy Piloting Championships in Wrocław, Poland. This equates to an average speed of 110.86 km/h (68.88 mph).

The **male** record is 2.019 sec, by Mohammed Baker (UAE) in Dubai, UAE, on 24 Apr 2015. This equates to an average speed of 124.81 km/h (77.55 mph). Both records have been ratified by the Fédération Aéronautique Internationale (FAI).

Highest unicycle platform high jump (male)

Unicyclist and three-time world champion Mike Taylor (UK) leapt on to a platform at a height of 148.5 cm (4 ft 10 in) at Unicon XIX in Ansan, South Korea, on 3 Aug 2018.

Also in 2018, Lisa-Maria Hanny (DEU) completed the **farthest unicycle long jump (female)** – 3.35 m (10 ft 11 in) – on 16 Jun in Warendorf, Germany. Both records were approved by the International Unicycling Federation.

MOST MEDALS WON AT A SINGLE WINTER X GAMES (FEMALE)

At the 2019 Winter X Games on Buttermilk Mountain in Aspen, Colorado, USA, freestyle skier Kelly Sildaru (EST) won three medals in 25 hr: a gold medal in Slopestyle, a silver in Superpipe and a bronze in Big Air. She equalled the tally of snowboarder Jennie Waara (SWE) in 1997, who took gold in Boardercross, silver in Halfpipe and bronze in Slopestyle at Big Bear Lake in California, USA.

Youngest Winter X Games gold medallist (female)

On 19 May 2018, Kokomo Murase (JPN, b. 7 Nov 2004) won the women's Snowboard Big Air at X Games Norway aged 13 years 193 days. She became the first female to land a backside double-cork 1260 in competition, earning a score of 49.66 out of 50.

Most medals won at the X Games (female)

Snowboarder Jamie Anderson (USA) won 16 Winter X Games medals from 2006 to 2019: 14 in the women's Slopestyle (five golds, seven silvers and two bronze) and two in Big Air (both bronze).

Most appearances at the Winter X Games

On 26 Jan 2019, seven-time gold medallist Kelly Clark (USA) made her 22nd and final Winter X Games appearance.

MOST WINS OF MOTO X BEST TRICK AT THE SUMMER X GAMES

Australia's Jackson Strong has ridden off with the X Games Moto X Best Trick title four times: in 2011–12, 2016 and 2018. He earned his fourth gold on 21 Jul 2018 with a no-handed front flip on his first run that earned him a score of 93.00. Strong also won a silver medal in the Snow Bike Best Trick event at the Winter X Games in 2018.

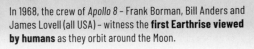

YOUNGEST X GAMES DOUBLE GOLD MEDALLIST

At the 2018 X Games in Minneapolis, Minnesota, USA, Brighton Zeuner (USA, b. 14 Jul 2004) defended her Skateboard Park title aged 14 years 8 days. A score of 90.33 was enough to secure Zeuner her second gold medal. She won her first on 15 Jul 2017, aged 13 years 1 day, making her the **youngest X Games gold medallist (female)**.

MOST WINS OF THE RED BULL CLIFF DIVING WORLD SERIES (MALE)

Gary Hunt (UK) has triumphed in the Red Bull Cliff Diving World Series seven times: in 2010–12, 2014–16 and 2018. He wrapped up his latest title at Polignano a Mare in Italy on 23 Sep (right), recording his 34th victory in 72 individual competitions.

The **most wins (female)** is three, achieved by Rhiannan Iffland (AUS) in 2016–18.

DEC 24 In 1968, the crew of *Apollo 8* – Frank Borman, Bill Anders and James Lovell (all USA) – witness the **first Earthrise viewed by humans** as they orbit around the Moon.

DEC 25 In 2017, Beijing Hyundai and Mohe Tourism Bureau (both CHN) put the finishing touches to the **longest wish list to Santa** in Mohe, Heilongjiang Province, China. It consists of 124,969 wishes.

WORLD OF SPORT

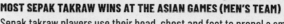

MOST WINS OF THE WORLD GRAVY WRESTLING CHAMPIONSHIPS

The world's gravy-est grappling event has been held annually since 2007 outside the Rose 'n' Bowl pub in Stacksteads, Lancashire, UK. The two-minute bouts are judged on fancy dress, entertainment and wrestling ability. Joel Hicks (above) holds the **male** record, having triumphed five times. The **female** record is two, shared by Roxy Afzal, aka "The Oxo Fox" or "Foxy Roxy" (inset), and Emma Slater (all UK).

Longest-running finger wrestling contest

Finger wrestling contests known as Fingerhakeln have been staged in Bavaria, Germany, since the 14th century. Competitors select a finger (usually the middle) to be interlocked with their opponent's by a leather strap, and then vie to pull each other across the table between them.

Most wins of the Toe Wrestling World Championships

Alan "Nasty" Nash (UK) secured his 15th men's toe wrestling title – and his seventh in a row – by defeating Ben Woodroffe in the final of the 2018 tournament on 22 Jun in Fenny Bentley, Derbyshire, UK.

Fastest time to complete the World Bog Snorkelling Championships

On 26 Aug 2018, Neil Rutter (UK) snorkelled his way to victory in 1 min 18.81 sec at Llanwrtyd Wells in Powys, UK. Entrants have to complete two lengths of a murky 55-m (180-ft) trench.

MOST SEPAK TAKRAW WINS AT THE ASIAN GAMES (MEN'S TEAM)

Sepak takraw players use their head, chest and feet to propel a small rattan ball over a volleyball net. Thailand have won the men's team *regu* (i.e., three-person) event at the Asian Games six times: in 1998, 2002, 2006, 2010, 2014 and 2018. They secured their most recent title with a two-set victory over Malaysia on 22 Aug 2018 at Ranau Hall in Palembang, Indonesia.

MOST TEAMS AT A QUIDDITCH WORLD CUP

A total of 29 teams, including Vietnam, Slovenia and Catalonia, took part in the 2018 International Quidditch Association World Cup, held on 27 Jun–2 Jul in Florence, Italy. The USA secured their third title – the **most wins of the Quidditch World Cup** – by defeating Belgium 120-70 in the final, with seeker Harry Greenhouse grabbing their opponents' snitch to end the game. The only other country to win the cup is Australia, in 2016.

The fastest time by a **female** is 1 min 22.56 sec, by Kirsty Johnson (UK) on 24 Aug 2014.

Farthest canal jump (male)

The farthest distance jumped across a canal with an aluminium pole in the West Frisian sport known as fierljeppen ("far leaping") is 22.21 m (72 ft 10 in), by Jaco de Groot (NLD) on 12 Aug 2017 in Zegveld, Netherlands.

The **female** record is 17.58 m (57 ft 8 in), by Marrit van der Wal (NLD) on 16 Jul 2016 in Burgum, Netherlands.

Longest successful 360° kiiking swing (male)

Competitors in the Estonian sport of kiiking try to complete full rotations on giant swings. On 25 Aug 2018, Sven Saarpere (EST) went head over heels on a swing with a 7.38-m-long (24-ft 2-in) shaft in Tallinn, Estonia.

First FootGolf World Cup winner (female)

Sophie Brown (UK) took the inaugural women's title at the 2018 Federation for International FootGolf (FIFG) FootGolf World Cup, staged on 9–16 Dec in Marrakesh, Morocco. Brown finished on 280 after her four rounds, six shots clear of the field. FootGolfers complete a round of golf by kicking a soccer ball towards a 53-cm (1-ft 9-in) cup.

Most All-Ireland Senior Camogie Championships

Camogie is a stick-and-ball women's team sport, similar to hurling. The "Rebelettes" of Cork claimed their 28th title since 1934 on 9 Sep 2018, defeating Kilkenny 0-14 to 0-13 with an injury-time free at Croke Park in Dublin, Ireland.

Most Rodeo World Championships

On 15 Dec 2018, Trevor Brazile (USA) won his 24th golden buckle at the Professional Rodeo Cowboys Association Rodeo World Championship. His tally includes the **most all-around world titles** – 14. These are awarded each season to the leading money winner in two or more events.

Most NATwA National Championships titles

Legendary winker Larry Kahn (USA) squidged his way to 30 singles and 25 pairs titles at the North American Tiddlywinks Association (NATwA) National Championships between 1976 and 2018.

MOST WINS OF THE WOMEN'S FISTBALL WORLD CHAMPIONSHIPS

On 28 Jul 2018, Germany secured their third consecutive and sixth overall Women's Fistball World Championships title with a 4-1 defeat of Switzerland at the ÖBV Arena in Linz, Austria. They had previously triumphed in 1994, 1998, 2006, 2014 and 2016.

MOST CABER TOSSES IN THREE MINUTES

On 20 Jul 2018, Daniel Frame (CAN) tossed the caber 16 times in 180 sec at the Middleton Heart of the Valley Festival in Nova Scotia, Canada. He claimed the record on his second attempt, after a caber had broken in two during his first.

The **female** record is 15, by Heather Boundy (CAN) on 10 Sep 2016 in Trenton, Ontario, Canada.

DEC 26 Three-year-old Cranston Chipperfield (UK) becomes the **youngest ringmaster** in 2005 at the Circus Royale in Strathclyde Country Park, Lanarkshire, UK.

DEC 27 Maria Leijerstam (UK) arrives at the South Pole in 2013 having travelled from the edge of the Ross Ice Shelf in Antarctica on a recumbent tricycle – the **first person to cycle to the South Pole**.

243

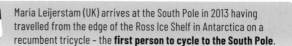

The first World Orienteering Championships were held in 1966. The event is now staged annually.

MOST WINS OF THE WOMEN'S BASEBALL WORLD CUP

Japan won the Women's Baseball World Cup for a sixth consecutive time in 2018, securing the trophy with a 6–0 shutout of Chinese Taipei on 31 Aug in Viera, Florida, USA. They won all nine matches at the tournament, allowing just four runs and scoring 63. Japan hasn't lost a game at the biennial World Cup since 2012, winning 30 in a row.

FASTEST...

15 m speed climb (female)

On 26 Apr 2019, Song Yi Ling (CHN) won her speed climb quarter-final in 7.101 sec at the International Federation of Sport Climbing World Cup in Chongqing, China. She beat the previous women's world record, held jointly by two climbers, by 0.219 sec.

The **fastest 15 m speed climb (male)** is 5.48 sec, by Reza Alipour (IRN) on 30 Apr 2017.

2,000 m row on a Concept2 Indoor Rower (male)

On 10 Mar 2018, Josh Dunkley-Smith (AUS) rowed 2 km (1.24 mi) on a Concept2 indoor rowing machine in 5 min 35.8 sec at the Senior Australian Rowing Team Trials. He beat the time of 5 min 36.6 sec by Rob Waddell (NZ), which had stood for a decade.

Also in 2018, on 10 Jul Jennifer Casson (CAN) set the **fastest Concept2 2,000 m (female, lightweight)**: 6 min 53.8 sec, at the Rowing Canada Aviron National Training Centre in Victoria, British Columbia, Canada.

Finswimming 400 m bi fins (female)

On 18 Jul 2018, Maria Patlasova (RUS) won gold in 3 min 44.92 sec at the Finswimming World Championships in Belgrade, Serbia. It was her second world record in three days, having been a part of the victorious Russian team that set the **fastest finswimming 4 x 100 m bi fins relay (mixed)** – 2 min 58.04 sec – on 16 Jul. Patlasova's teammates were Lev Shtraikh, Aleksey Fedkin and Vitalina Simonova.

Also on 16 Jul, Sun Yi Ting (CHN) swam the **fastest finswimming surface 400 m (female)** – 3 min 12.10 sec.

ILSF 100 m manikin carry with fins (male)

In this International Life Saving Federation (ILSF) event, competitors swim 50 m before retrieving a submerged manikin, which is then carried across the surface back to the finish. Jan Malkowski (DEU) came home in 44.21 sec at the DLRG Cup Pool 2018 event in Warendorf, Germany, on 23 Sep 2018.

The **female** record is 50.43 sec, by Lucrezia Fabretti (ITA) at the Italian Open Championships in Milan, Italy, on 16 Dec 2018. She broke her own record of 50.78 sec, set on 12 Sep 2018 at the European Youth Championships.

MOST...

Water Polo World League wins (women)

The USA have won the FINA Women's Water Polo World League 12 times: in 2004, 2006–07, 2009–12 and 2014–18. The competition has been contested every year since 2004 and features the world's best national teams competing in a league format.

The **men's** record is 11, by Serbia in 2005–08, 2010–11 and 2013–17.

MOST WORLD ORIENTEERING CHAMPIONSHIPS LONG DISTANCE TITLES (MALE)

Norwegian Olav Lundanes won his fifth long distance title at the World Orienteering Championships in 2018. He came home in first place on 11 Aug with a time of 1 hr 37 min 43 sec in Riga, Latvia. It was Lundanes's third consecutive victory in the event, with two earlier titles in 2010 and 2012.

MOST INDOOR AND OUTDOOR MOTORCYCLE TRIALS WORLD CHAMPIONSHIPS

In a remarkable display of sporting dominance, Antoni Bou (ESP) won the FIM Trial World Championship (main picture) and FIM X-Trial (inset) every year between 2007 and 9 Mar 2019, a combined tally of 25 titles. Bou rode to victory in 104 outdoor and 61 indoor trials. Motorcycle trials are non-speed events in which riders navigate a series of obstacles and hazards without touching the ground with their feet.

DEC 28 In 2010, Thomas Müller and Heiko Becher (both DEU) achieve the **greatest distance walked using snowshoes in 24 hours** – 94.41 km (58.66 mi) – between Gräfenwarth and Saalburg, Germany.

DEC 29 The **highest bridge** opens in 2016 in Dugexiang, Guizhou Province, China. The Beipanjiang Bridge Duge has a clearance at mean high water of 565 m (1,854 ft) above the Beipan River.

MOST GROUP 1 HORSE RACING VICTORIES BY A HORSE

On 13 Apr 2019, racehorse Winx crowned a glorious career with her 25th Group 1 race win, achieved at the Queen Elizabeth Stakes in Sydney, NSW, Australia. She had surpassed Hurricane Fly's tally of 22 with victory at the 2019 Chipping Norton Stakes on 2 Mar. Winx was retired to stud following her win in the Queen Elizabeth Stakes – her 33rd consecutive victory in all races.

Mile-High NHRA Nationals, staged at Bandimere Speedway in Colorado, USA. The 69-year-old Force also increased his record for the **most NHRA finals** to 251.

Hockey Champions Trophy wins (men)

Australia secured their 15th Champions Trophy in the final edition of the competition on 1 Jul 2018. They beat India 3–1 in a penalty shoot-out.

The **most Champions Trophy wins (women)** is seven, achieved by Argentina and 2018 champions the Netherlands. For more hockey, see p.224.

Prix de l'Arc de Triomphe wins by a jockey

Frankie Dettori (ITA) claimed Europe's richest horse race for a sixth time in 2018, riding Enable to victory for the second successive year. Dettori also won on board Lammtarra (1995), Sakhee (2001), Marienbard (2002) and Golden Horn (2015).

World Sailing World Cup gold medals (men)

As of 1 Mar 2019, Australia had accumulated 53 gold medals at the World Sailing World Cup in men's events since 2008.

The **most gold medals won (women)** is 26, achieved by Great Britain. This is one more than China and two ahead of the Netherlands.

Dakar Rally races (consecutive)

Yoshimasa Sugawara (JPN) competed in his 36th straight Dakar Rally in 2019. This streak does not include the 2008 race, which was cancelled but for which he had also registered.

National Hot Rod Association (NHRA) career wins

On 22 Jul 2018, John Force (USA) claimed his 149th victory in the Funny Car class since 1979, at the Dodge

FASTEST TIME TO WIN THE MONTANE SPINE RACE

On 16 Jan 2019, Jasmin Paris (UK) became the first woman to win the Montane Spine Race, crossing the finish line in a course record of 83 hr 12 min 23 sec. The race is a 431-km (268-mi) non-stop winter ultra-marathon that runs from Derbyshire to the Scottish Borders in the UK. It involves a total climb of 13,106 m (43,000 ft).

MOST WINS OF THE BADMINTON WORLD CHAMPIONSHIPS SINGLES (FEMALE)

On 5 Aug 2018, Carolina Marín (ESP) secured her third women's singles title at the Badminton World Federation World Championships in Nanjing, China. In a repeat of the 2016 Olympic final, Marín defeated India's P V Sindhu to claim the title, winning 21–19, 21–10. Her previous wins came in 2014 and 2015.

Squash World Championship titles (female)

Malaysia's Nicol David announced her retirement from squash in 2019 after a glittering career. She had spent an unprecedented nine years as world no.1 (2006–15), amassing 81 tour titles and eight women's individual World Championships (in 2005–06, 2008–12 and 2014).

HIGHEST...

Score for barefoot waterskiing tricks (male)

On 14 Aug 2018, David Small (UK) "tricked" his way to a score of 13,350 points at the 2018 World Barefoot Championships, staged at Dream Lake in Napanee, Ontario, Canada.

Small also holds the record for the **longest barefoot waterskiing jump (male)** – 29.9 m (98 ft 1 in) – set in Brandenburg, Germany, on 11 Aug 2010.

Ioseba Fernández also holds the record for **fastest inline speed skating road 200 m (male)** – 15.879 sec – which he recorded on 9 Dec 2012.

FASTEST INLINE SPEED SKATING ROAD 100 M (MALE)

At the 2018 Inline Speed Skating World Championships in Arnhem, Netherlands, Ioseba Fernández (ESP, right) won his semi-final of the men's road 100 m in 9.684 sec on 7 Jul. As well as a new world record, he also sped away with a gold medal, going on to pip Colombia's Edwin Estrada (left) in the final.

DEC 30 The **largest piano** is played at a concert in Poland in 2010. Built by Daniel Czapiewski (POL), it has 156 keys and is 2.49 m wide, 6.07 m long and 1.9 m high (8 ft 2 in x 19 ft 10 in x 6 ft 3 in).

DEC 31 In 2008, the Sun Bowl Association celebrates the New Year by organizing the **largest "YMCA" dance** in Texas, USA. A total of 40,148 participants join in with the Village People classic.

245

INDEX

QUIZ ANSWERS (pp.200–01)

1. Super Mario
2. Link
3. Niko Bellic
4. Cervantes
5. Arthur Morgan
6. Nathan Drake
7. Samus Aran
8. Batman
9. Leon S Kennedy
10. Jin Kazama

CONSULTANTS

Guinness World Records 2020 has been compiled from applications made by the general public and also submissions from a global network of consultants and contributors, whom we'd like to thank:

School of Ants: Dr Kirsti Abbott is an ant ecologist and science communicator who runs School of Ants in Australia, a citizen-science project that aims to document and understand the diversity and distribution of ants in urban landscapes. She has a passion for inspiring younger generations to connect with their inner ant lover. *www.schoolofants.net.au*

Centre for Mountain Studies: Professor Martin Price is the Director of the Centre for Mountain Studies, which is based at Perth College, University of the Highlands and Islands, UK. Its staff undertake research and consultancy at all levels from Scotland to the world, and have organized major mountain-science conferences. Professor Price is currently the holder of the UNESCO Chair in Sustainable Mountain Development. *www.perth.uhi.ac.uk/mountainstudies*

University of Liverpool: Dr João Pedro de Magalhães leads the Integrative Genomics of Ageing Group at the UK's University of Liverpool. The team's research focuses on understanding the genetic, cellular and molecular mechanisms of ageing. He also created AnAge, a curated database of ageing and life history in animals, including extensive longevity records. *pcwww.liv.ac.uk/~aging/*

Berkeley Seismology Lab: Professor Michael Manga is chair of Earth and Planetary Science at UC Berkeley in California, USA, specializing in volcanic eruptions and geysers on Earth and other planets. His research has been recognized by a MacArthur Fellowship and election to the National Academy of Sciences. *seismo.berkeley.edu/~manga*

American Society for Ichthyologists and Herpetologists: The ASIH was founded in 1913 and is dedicated to the scientific study of fishes, amphibians and reptiles. The primary emphases of the Society are to increase knowledge about these organisms, to disseminate that knowledge, and to encourage and support young scientists who will make future advances in these fields. *www.asih.org*

National Speleological Society: Scott Engel is the Executive Vice President of the National Speleological Society (NSS), a non-profit membership organization dedicated to the scientific study, exploration, protection and conservation of caves and karst, and to the promotion of responsible cave exploration and management. Founded in 1941 in the USA, the NSS is the largest organization of its kind in the world. *caves.org*

Jane Goodall Research Center, USC: Primatologist Dr Craig Stanford is the Professor of Anthropology and Biological Sciences at the University of Southern California, where he is also the co-director of the Jane Goodall Research Center. He has conducted extensive field research on wild great apes, monkeys and other animals in East Africa, Asia, and Central and South America. Dr Stanford has authored more than a dozen books and 100 scholarly articles. *dornsife.usc.edu/labs/janegoodall*

International Society of Limnology: Dr Tamar Zohary is a senior research scientist at the Kinneret Limnological Laboratory at Israel Oceanographic & Limnological Research. Her research focuses on phytoplankton ecology and the impact of water-level fluctuations on lake ecology. Since 2013, she has also been the General Secretary-Treasurer of the International Society of Limnology (SIL), an international society devoted to the study of inland waters. *limnology.org*

Desert Research Institute: Dr Nick Lancaster is Research Professor Emeritus of the Desert Research Institute (DRI) in Nevada, USA, where his specialisms are desert geomorphology and the impacts of climate change on desert regions. He is a fellow of the Royal Geographical Society and the Geological Society of America. The DRI is a world leader in basic and applied interdisciplinary research. *www.dri.edu*

MonumentalTrees.com: Tim Bekaert is the administrator of MonumentalTrees.com, a community website listing tens of thousands of photos, girth and height measurements, as well as location details of often otherwise undocumented remarkable tree specimens around the world. *www.monumentaltrees.com*

UltimateUngulate.com: Brent Huffman is a zoo professional from Toronto, Ontario, Canada, who specializes in ungulate (hoofed-mammal) biology. Brent has contributed to a diverse range of scholarly and popular publications, but is best known for founding UltimateUngulate.com in 1996, the first online resource dedicated to this diverse group of animals. *ultimateungulate.com*

International Ornithologists' Union: Dr Dominique Homberger is an alumni professor at the University of Louisiana, USA, and President of the International Ornithologists' Union (IOU). Her research has centred on comparative anatomy as a means to answer functional and evolutionary questions, and she has a particular interest in the order Psittaciformes (i.e., parrots and cockatoos). The IOU is a body of around 200 bird experts that puts on the International Ornithological Congress every four years; the first congress was conducted in 1884. *www.internationalornithology.org*

Royal Entomological Society: Dr Luke Tilley is the Director of Outreach & Development at the RES, which was founded in 1833 for the promotion and development of insect science. The Society supports international collaboration, research and publication. It aims to promote excellence in entomology and demonstrate the importance of studying insects. *www.royensoc.co.uk*

World Meteorological Organization: Dr Randall Cerveny is a President's Professor in Geographical Sciences who specializes in weather and climate in the School of Geographical Sciences and Urban Planning at Arizona State University, USA. He has also been the Rapporteur of Weather and Climate Extremes for the WMO since 2007. *wmo.asu.edu*

Natural History Museum Vienna: Dr Ludovic Ferrière is a geologist and expert on meteorites and impact craters. He is chief curator of the prestigious meteorite and rock collections at the Natural History Museum Vienna in Austria. Together with colleagues, he has confirmed four impact craters to date: Keurusselkä in Finland, Luizi in the Democratic Republic of the Congo, Hummeln in Sweden and Yallalie in Australia. *www.nhm-wien.ac.at*

British Ecological Society: Professor Richard Bardgett is the President of the British Ecological Society and also Professor of Ecology at the University of Manchester, UK. Areas of expertise include plant-soil interaction and grassland ecosystems. A Senior Editor for the *Journal of Ecology*, he has published more than 260 scientific papers as well as several books, including *Earth Matters: How Soil Underpins Civilization* (2016). *www.britishecologicalsociety.org*

Royal Botanic Gardens, Kew: The Royal Botanic Gardens, Kew is a world-famous scientific organization, globally respected for its outstanding collections as well as its scientific expertise in plant diversity, conservation and sustainable development in the UK and around the world. Its remit includes all aspects of botany and fungal research, with dedicated departments for species identification, biodiversity informatics, and comparative plant and fungal biology, among others. Kew Gardens in London, UK, is a major international visitor attraction, which was accredited as a UNESCO World Heritage Site in 2003. *www.kew.org*

The Cornell Lab: Directed by Dr Holger Klinck, the Bioacoustics Research Program (BRP) at The Cornell Lab of Ornithology in New York, USA, is an interdisciplinary team of scientists, engineers, students and research support staff working on a wide variety of terrestrial, aquatic and marine bioacoustic research projects. BRP's mission is to collect and interpret sounds in nature by developing and applying innovative conservation technologies across multiple ecological scales to inspire and inform conservation of wildlife and habitats. *brp.cornell.edu*

University of Maryland: Dr Andrew Baldwin is Professor in the Department of Environmental Science & Technology at University of Maryland, USA. In addition to teaching courses on wetland ecology and restoration, he conducts research on global change ecology and restoration of wetlands. He is Fellow and Past President of the Society of Wetland Scientists. *www.enst.umd.edu*

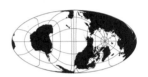

International Association for Bear Research and Management: The International Association for Bear Research and Management (IBA) is a non-profit tax-exempt organization open to professional biologists, wildlife managers and others dedicated to the conservation of all bear species. The organization has 550-plus members from more than 60 countries. It supports the scientific management of bears through research and the distribution of information. *www.bearbiology.org*

Scott Polar Research Institute: The SPRI, of Cambridge University, UK, was founded in 1920 as a memorial to the men who died during Captain Scott's 1910-13 South Pole expedition. Its resources cover the entire Arctic and Antarctic with an extensive library and archives, research departments in several polar specialities, and a small public museum. It has become a global centre for history, geography and research, both in the field and laboratory, for these two regions. *www.spri.cam.ac.uk*

Royal Veterinary College: Alan Wilson is Professor of Locomotor Biomechanics and head of the Structure and Motion Laboratory at the RVC, University of London. He qualified as a veterinary surgeon and physiologist at Glasgow University and obtained his PhD on the mechanics of tendon injury at Bristol University. His research focuses on mechanical and physiological limits to locomotor performance in species ranging from racing pigeons to cheetahs. Currently he is studying iconic African mammals such as lion and wildebeest in Botswana using novel GPS and motion-tracking equipment.*www.rvc.ac.uk*

International Gem Society: Donald Clark, CSM founded the International Gem Society (IGS) in 1998. IGS's mission is to make gemology information accessible and affordable to everyone. IGS has members on every continent (except Antarctica), who range from seasoned professionals to hobbyists. IGS offers members multiple resources, including a reference library that is updated weekly and gemology certification courses. *www.gemsociety.org*

National Oceanic and Atmospheric Administration: NOAA's reach extends from the surface of the Sun to the depths of the ocean floor as it works to keep the public informed of the changing environment around them. Its scope ranges from daily weather forecasts, severe storm warnings and climate monitoring to fisheries management, coastal restoration and supporting marine commerce. *www.noaa.gov*

University of Essex

Coral Reef Research Unit, UoE: Professor of Marine Biology at the University of Essex, UK, and Director of the Coral Reef Research Unit, David Smith has focused on coral-reef ecology and conservation for 20 years. He is Associate Editor for the journal *Global Change Biology* and advises governments and organizations on research strategies and conservation solutions. *www.essex.ac.uk/departments/biological-sciences/research/coral-reef-research-unit*

International Mineralogical Association: The IMA held its first meeting in Apr 1958. Today, the IMA consists of 39 member societies representing all six populated continents. In addition to sponsoring and organizing conferences, the IMA facilitates interactions within the global mineralogical community through the activities of its commissions, committees and working groups. Its mandate ranges from streamlining the nomenclature and classification of minerals to the preservation of mineralogical heritage to outreach. *www.ima-mineralogy.org*

Whale and Dolphin Conservation: WDC is the leading global charity dedicated to the conservation and protection of whales and dolphins. It defends cetaceans against the many threats they face through campaigns, lobbying, advising governments, conservation projects, field research and rescue. WDC believes that whales and dolphins have the right not to be hunted or kept in captivity for human entertainment and encourages all those that agree to join them. *whales.org*

World Open Water Swimming Association: WOWSA is the international governing body for the sport of open-water swimming. WOWSA provides membership and certification programmes as well as publications and online resources that foster community, celebrate achievements and codify the rules, records and vernacular to help the sport grow. *www.worldopenwaterswimmingassociation.com*

Channel Swimming Association: The CSA has been the governing body of Channel swimming and helping swimmers since its formation in 1927. The organization only recognizes swims that are conducted under its rules and that are accompanied by its appointed observers. *www.channelswimmingassociation.com*

World Sailing Speed Record Council: The WSSRC was recognized by the International Yacht Racing Union (now renamed World Sailing) in 1972. Early on, the decision was taken to base such outright speed ratifications on a one-way leg of exactly 500 m (a sub-section for speeds over one nautical mile was subsequently introduced). The expert council draws members from Australia, France, Great Britain and the USA. *www.sailspeedrecords.com*

World Surf League: The WSL is dedicated to celebrating the world's best surfing on the world's best waves through a variety of best-in-class audience platforms. The WSL has been championing competitive surfing since 1976, annually running more than 180 global events across the Women's and Men's Championship Tours, the Big Wave Tour, Longboard Tour, Qualifying Series and Junior Championships, as well as the WSL Big Wave Awards. The League possesses a deep appreciation for the sport's rich heritage while promoting progression, innovation and performance at the highest levels, and in doing so crowns the undisputed Women's and Men's World Champions across all tours. *www.worldsurfleague.com*

The Numbers: The-Numbers.com is the web's biggest database of movie financial information, with figures on more than 38,000 movies and 160,000 people in the film industry. It was founded in 1997 by Bruce Nash and is visited by more than 8 million people every year. As well as movie fans, the major studios, independent production companies and investors use the site and its services to decide which movies to make and when to release them. The site gathers data from the movie studios, retailers, news reports and other sources to compile its comprehensive database, known as OpusData. The database contains in excess of 14 million facts about the movie business. *www.the-numbers.com*

Council on Tall Buildings and Urban Habitat: The CTBUH – based in Chicago, Illinois, USA – is the world's leading resource for professionals focused on the inception, design, construction and operation of tall buildings and future cities. It facilitates the exchange of the latest knowledge available on tall buildings through publications, research, events, web resources and international representation. *www.ctbuh.org*

8000ers.com: Eberhard Jurgalski has been fascinated by mountains since early childhood, and in 1981 he began formally chronicling the high mountains of Asia. He has developed the system of "Elevation Equality", a universal method of classifying mountain ranges and peaks, and his website, 8000ers.com, has become the main source of statistics for altitude in the Himalayas and Karakorum ranges. He is also co-author of *Herausforderung 8000er*, the definitive guide to the world's 14 mountains that stand over 8,000 m (26,246 ft). *www.8000ers.com*

Ocean Rowing Society: The ORS was established in 1983 by Kenneth F Crutchlow and Peter Bird, later joined by Tom Lynch and Tatiana Rezvaya-Crutchlow. It keeps a record of all attempts to row the oceans and major bodies of water such as the Tasman Sea and Caribbean Sea, as well as rowing expeditions around Great Britain. The Society also classifies, verifies and adjudicates ocean-rowing achievements. *www.oceanrowing.com*

Great Pumpkin Commonwealth: The GPC's mission cultivates the hobby of growing giant pumpkins, as well as other super-sized vegetables, by establishing standards and regulations that ensure quality of fruit, fairness of competition, recognition of achievement, fellowship and education for all participating growers and weigh-off sites. *gpc1.org*

CANNA UK National Giant Vegetables Championship: Every September at the Three Counties Showground in Malvern, Worcestershire, UK, Martyn Davis – a National Vegetable Society Judge – welcomes expert growers to the CANNA UK National Giant Vegetables Championship, held in association with Westons Cider Mill. Martyn checks that the vegetables comply to the strict competition criteria, and that they are weighed and documented appropriately. *www.malvernautumn.co.uk*

World UltraCycling Association: WUCA (formerly the UltraMarathon Cycling Association, or UMCA) is a non-profit organization dedicated to supporting ultra-cycling throughout the world. It holds the largest repository of cycling records for any type of bike, and continues to certify records for its members. WUCA members also participate in yearly challenges and support each other at events. *worldultracycling.com*

The Bartlett School of Architecture: Iain Borden is Professor of Architecture & Urban Culture, and Vice-Dean Education, at The Bartlett, University College London, UK. An active skateboarder, photographer, film watcher and urban wanderer, he has written more than 100 books and articles on these subjects, as well as several titles on architects, buildings and cities. *www.ucl.ac.uk/bartlett/architecture*

The Penguin Lady: Dyan deNapoli is a penguin expert, TED Speaker and award-winning author of *The Great Penguin Rescue* (2011), which chronicles the dramatic rescue of 40,000 penguins from the *Treasure* oil spill that took place off South Africa in 2000. She lectures for National Geographic in Antarctica, and can be found on social media as "The Penguin Lady". *thepenguinlady.com*

Mark O'Shea: Mark is Professor of Herpetology at the University of Wolverhampton and Consultant Curator of Reptiles at West Midland Safari Park – both in the UK. With over five decades' experience working with reptiles, both in the wild and in captivity, his career has taken him to 40 different countries across six continents. To date, Mark has authored six books, including *The Book of Snakes* (2018), which discusses 600 of the 3,700-plus species of snake. Mark is also a wildlife TV presenter, with 40 documentaries, including four seasons of *O'Shea's Big Adventure* for Animal Planet and Channel 4 (UK). *www.markoshea.info*

CONTRIBUTORS

Mark Aston has served as a Science & Technology consultant for GWR since 2010. He brings nearly 30 years of experience of high-technology science and engineering to ensure GWR's sci-tech records are accurate and informative. Mark's involvement in both academia and commercial companies has led to a lively career in optics development.

Tom Beckerlegge is an award-winning writer whose books have been translated around the world. A sports consultant for GWR, Tom has worked on five compendia of record-breaking, and researched hundreds of records across athletic disciplines as diverse as artistic cycling, canopy piloting and beach taekwondo.

David Fischer has acted as the senior US sports consultant for GWR since 2006. He has written for *The New York Times* and *Sports Illustrated for Kids*, and has worked at *Sports Illustrated*, *The National Sports Daily* and NBC Sports. David is the author of *The Super Bowl: The First Fifty Years of America's Greatest Game* (2015) and *Derek Jeter #2: Thanks for the Memories* (2014). He also edited *Facing Mariano Rivera* (2014).

Rory Flood has a BA in Geography, MSc in Environmental Sciences and PhD in Physical Geography, and is a Lecturer in Physical Geography at Queen's University Belfast in Northern Ireland, UK. He has authored articles on geomorphology, sedimentology and geochemistry, with a focus on marine and terrestrial environments. Rory is particularly interested in how coastal landscapes and landforms are shaped and change under the influences of marine, climate and human processes.

Jonathan McDowell is an astrophysicist at the Harvard-Smithsonian Center for Astrophysics, where he is part of the team that operates the Chandra X-ray Observatory. He maintains a website documenting the history of space exploration (*planet4589.org*) and has published a monthly newsletter – *Jonathan's Space Report* – since 1998.

James Proud is a writer and researcher specializing in unusual facts and stories from around the world, with a particular focus on technology and extreme feats. He is the author of several books on a wide variety of subjects, including historical oddities, urban legends and pop culture.

Karl P N Shuker has a PhD in Zoology and Comparative Physiology from the University of Birmingham, and is a Scientific Fellow of the Zoological Society of London, a Fellow of the Royal Entomological Society and a Member of the Society of Authors. He has penned 25 books and hundreds of articles covering all aspects of natural history. Karl's work has an emphasis on anomalous animals, including new, rediscovered and unrecognized species.

Matthew White is GWR's music, cricket and tennis consultant. Between 2009 and 2019, he has pored over an estimated 40,000 published records as proofreader during the course of 12 editions of the world's **best-selling annual**.

Robert D Young is GWR's lead consultant for gerontology – the study of various aspects of ageing. He has maintained lists of the world's oldest people for the Gerontology Research Group (GRG; *grg.org*) since 1999, and has worked with the Max Planck Institute for Demographic Research and the International Database on Longevity. Robert became Director of the Supercentenarian Research Database Division for the GRG in 2015. He is also the author of *African-American Longevity Advantage: Myth or Reality?* (2009).

ACKNOWLEDGEMENTS

Editor-in-Chief
Craig Glenday

Layout Editors
Tom Beckerlegge,
Rob Dimery

Senior Editor
Adam Millward

Editor
Ben Hollingum

Gaming Editor
Mike Plant

**Proofreading
& fact-checking**
Matthew White

**Head of Publishing
& Book Production**
Jane Boatfield

**Head of Pictures
& Design**
Fran Morales

Picture Researcher
Alice Jessop

Artworker
Billy Waqar

Design
Paul Wylie-Deacon
and Rob Wilson
at 55design.co.uk

Cover Design
Paul Wylie-Deacon,
Edward Dillon

3D Design
Joseph O'Neil

Product Manager
Lucy Acfield

**Head of Visual
Content**
Michael Whitty

Content Producer
Jenny Langridge

Production Director
Patricia Magill

Production Coordinator
Thomas McCurdy

Production Consultants
Roger Hawkins, Florian
Seyfert, Tobias Wrona

Reprographics
Res Kahraman and Honor
Flowerday at Born Group

Original Photography
James Ellerker,
Jon Enoch, Paul
Michael Hughes,

Prakash Mathema,
Kevin Scott Ramos,
Alex Rumford, Ryan
Schude, Trevor Traynor

Indexer
Marie Lorimer

Researcher
Ben Way

Printing & Binding
MOHN Media Mohndruck
GmbH, Gütersloh,
Germany

British Library Cataloguing-in-publication data:
a catalogue record for this book is available from
the British Library
UK: 978-1-912286-81-2
US/Canada: 978-1-912286-83-6
US: 978-1-912286-87-4
US PB: 978-1-912286-93-5
Middle East: 978-1-912286-86-7

Records are made to be broken – indeed, it is one
of the key criteria for a record category – so if you
find a record that you think you can beat, tell us
about it by making a record claim. Always contact
us before making a record attempt.

Check www.guinnessworldrecords.com
regularly for record-breaking news, plus video
footage of record attempts. You can also join and
interact with the Guinness World Records online
community.

Sustainability
The trees that are harvested to print *Guinness
World Records 2020* are carefully selected from
managed forests to avoid the devastation of
the landscape.

The paper contained within this edition is
manufactured by Stora Enso Veitsiluoto, Finland.
The production site is Chain-of-Custody certified
and operates within environmental systems
certificated to ISO 14001 to ensure sustainable
production.

Guinness World Records Limited has a very
thorough accreditation system for records
verification. However, while every effort is made
to ensure accuracy, Guinness World Records
Limited cannot be held responsible for any
errors contained in this work. Feedback from
our readers on any point of accuracy is always
welcomed.

Guinness World Records Limited uses both
metric and imperial measurements. The sole
exceptions are for some scientific data where
metric measurements only are universally
accepted, and for some sports data. Where
a specific date is given, the exchange rate is
calculated according to the currency values that
were in operation at the time. Where only a year
date is given, the exchange rate is calculated
from 31 Dec of that year. "One billion" is taken to
mean one thousand million.

Appropriate advice should always be taken when
attempting to break or set records. Participants
undertake records entirely at their own risk.
Guinness World Records Limited has complete
discretion over whether or not to include
any particular record attempts in any of its
publications. Being a Guinness World Records
record holder does not guarantee you a place in
any *Guinness World Records* publication.

GLOBAL HEADQUARTERS
Global President: Alistair Richards
Professional Services
Alison Ozanne
Category Management: Benjamin
Backhouse, Jason Fernandes,
Sheila Mella Suárez, Will Munford,
Shane Murphy, Luke Wakeham
Finance: Tobi Amusan,
Jusna Begum, Elizabeth Bishop,
Jess Blake, Yusuf Gafar, Lisa Gibbs,
Kimberley Jones, Nhan Nguyen,
Sutharsan Ramachandran, Jamie
Sheppard, Scott Shore, Andrew Wood
HR & Office Management: Jackie
Angus, Alexandra Ledin, Farrella Ryan-
Coker, Monika Tilani
IT: Céline Bacon, Ashleigh Bair,
John Cvitanovic, Diogo Gomes,
Rob Howe, Benjamin Mclean, Cenk
Selim, Alpha Serrant-Defoe
Legal: Catherine Loughran,
Raymond Marshall, Kaori Minami,
Mehreen Moghul
**Brand Strategy,
Content & Product, Creative**
Sam Fay, Katie Forde, Paul O'Neill
Brand Partnerships: Juliet Dawson
Design: Edward Dillon, Alisa Zaytseva
Digital: Veronica Irons, Alex Waldu
Product Marketing: Lucy Acfield,
Rebecca Lam, Emily Osborn,
Mawa Rodriguez, Louise Toms
Visual Content: Sam Birch-Machin,
Karen Gilchrist, Jenny Langridge,
Matthew Musson, Joseph O'Neil,
Catherine Pearce, Alan Pixsley,
Jonathan Whitton, Michael Whitty
Website & Social Content: David
Stubbings, Dan Thorne

EMEA & APAC
Nadine Causey
Brand & Content
Marketing & PR: Nicholas Brookes,
Lauren Cochrane, Jessica Dawes,
Imelda Ekpo, Amber-Georgina
Gill, Lauren Johns, Doug Male,
Connie Suggitt
Publishing Sales: Caroline Lake,
Helene Navarre, Joel Smith
Records Management: Lewis
Blakeman, Adam Brown,
Tara El Kashef, Daniel Kidane,
Mark McKinley

Consultancy - UKROW
Neil Foster
Client Account Services: Sonia
Chadha-Nihal, Fay Edwards,
Samuel Evanson, Andrew Fanning,
William Hume-Humphreys, Soma Huy,
Irina Nohailic, Sam Prosser, Nikhil
Shukla, Sadie Smith
Event Production: Fiona
Gruchy-Craven, Danny Hickson
Marketing & PR: Lisa Lambert, Iliyan
Stoychev, Amanda Tang
Records Management: Matilda Hagne,
Paul Hillman, Christopher Lynch,
Maria Raggi
Consultancy – MENA
Talal Omar
Client Account Services: Naser
Batat, Mohammad Kiswani,
Kamel Yassin
HR & Office Management: Monisha
Bimal
Marketing & PR: Aya Ali, Leila Issa
Records Management: Hoda Khachab,
Samer Khallouf

EAST ASIA
Marco Frigatti
China
Client Account Services: Blythe
Fitzwilliam, Catherine Gao, Chloe Liu,
Tina Ran, Amelia Wang, Elaine Wang,
Ivy Wang, Jin Yu, Jacky Yuan
HR & Office Management: Tina Shi,
Crystal Xu
Legal: Paul Nightingale, Jiayi Teng
Marketing & PR: Tracy Cui, Karen Pan,
Vanessa Tao, Angela Wu, Echo Zhan,
Naomi Zhang, Yvonne Zhang, Delling
Zhao, Emily Zeng
Records Management: Fay Jiang,
Ted Li, Reggy Lu, Charles Wharton,
Winnie Zhang, Alicia Zhao
Japan
Erika Ogawa
Client Account Services: Blythe
Fitzwilliam, Wei Liang, Takuro
Maruyama, Yuki Morishita, Yumiko
Nakagawa, Masamichi Yazaki
HR & Office Management: Emiko
Yamamoto
Marketing & PR: Kazami Kamioka,
Vihag Kulshrestha, Aya McMillan,
Momoko Satou, Masakazu Senda,
Yumi Uota, Eri Yuhira

Records Management: Aki Ichikawa,
Kaoru Ishikawa, Momoko Omori, Koma
Satoh, Lala Teranishi, Yuki Uebo

AMERICAS
Alistair Richards
North America
Client Account Services: Alex Angert,
Mackenzie Berry, David Canela,
Danielle Levy, Nicole Pando, Kimberly
Partrick, Michelle Santucci
HR & Office Management: Vincent
Acevedo, Jennifer Olson
Marketing, PR & Publishing Sales:
Valerie Esposito, Lauren Festa,
Michael Furnari, Rachel Gluck,
Elizabeth Montoya, Morganna Nickoff,
Rachel Silver, Kristen Stephenson,
Sonja Valenta
Records Management: Spencer
Cammarano, Christine Fernandez,
Hannah Ortman, Callie Smith, Claire
Stephens, Kaitlin Vesper
Latin America
Carlos Martinez
Client Account Services: Carolina
Guanabara-Hall, Ralph Hannah,
Jaime Rodriguez
Marketing & PR: Laura Angel, Alice
Marie Pagán-Sánchez
Records Management: Raquel Assis,
Jaime Oquendo

OFFICIAL ADJUDICATORS
Camila Borenstain, Joanne Brent,
Jack Brockbank, Sarah Casson, Dong
Cheng, Christina Conlon, Swapnil
Dangarikar, Casey DeSantis, Brittany
Dunn, Michael Empric, Pete Fairbairn,
Victor Fenes, Fumika Fujibuchi, Ahmed
Gabr, John Garland, Şeyda Subaşı
Gemici, Andy Glass, Sofia Greenacre,
Iris Hou, Rei Iwashita, Louis Jelinek,
Kazuyoshi Kirimura, Mariko Koike, Lena
Kuhlmann, Maggie Luo, Solvej Malouf,
Mike Marcotte, Mai McMillan, Rishi
Nath, Chika Onaka, Anna Orford, Douglas
Palau, Kellie Parise, Pravin Patel, Justin
Patterson, Glenn Pollard, Natalia
Ramirez, Stephanie Randall, Cassie Ren,
Philip Robertson, Paulina Sapinska,
Tomomi Sekioka, Hiroaki Shino, Lucia
Sinigagliesi, Brian Sobel, Kevin Southam,
Richard Stenning, Carlos Tapia,
Lorenzo Veltri, Xiong Wen, Peter Yang

Picture credits

1 Shinsuke Kamioka/GWR, Shutterstock; **2** Alamy, Jon Enoch/GWR, Paul Michael Hughes/GWR, Shutterstock; **3** Boston Dynamics, NASA, Shutterstock; **4 (UK)** Getty, CPL Productions; **5 (UK)** Alex Rumford/GWR; **6 (UK)** GWR; **7 (UK)** Matt Alexander, Shutterstock; **4 (US)** Michael Simon, Philip Robertson; **5 (US)** Geoff Heith, Christine Cater, Carol Kaelson; **6 (US)** Shutterstock, Disney ABC Home Entertainment and TV Distribution; **7 (US)** Ben Gibbs; **4 (AUS)** Qantas Airways Limited, Shutterstock; **5 (AUS)** Shutterstock, Kate Roberge; **6 (AUS)** Jane Howie, Tanya McCulloch; **7 (AUS)** Dean Treml/Red Bull Content Pool, Jeremy Guzman; **5 (ARAB)** Musthafa Photography ; **6 (ARAB)** Shubayqa Project, Zia Creative Network; **14** Roger Culos; **15** Alamy, Shutterstock; **16** Shutterstock, Alamy; **17** Shutterstock, Alamy, SPL; **18** Shutterstock, Alamy; **19** Shutterstock; **20** Shutterstock, Alamy; **21** Alamy, Shutterstock; **22** Shutterstock, Karl Brodowsky, M. San Félix; **23** Shutterstock, Alamy; **24** Alamy, Shutterstock; **25** Shutterstock, Getty, Alamy, Robin Brooks; **26** Shutterstock, Mick Petroff/NASA, Alamy; **27** Shutterstock, Alamy, **28** Shutterstock, Alamy, SPL, Jason Edwards/National Geographic; **29** Shutterstock, Alamy; **30** Shutterstock, Alamy; **31** Alamy, Robbie Shone, Neckton; **32** Jon Enoch/GWR; **34** Shutterstock, Science Source/ARDEA, Nobu Tamura, Alamy; **35** Shutterstock, Alamy; **36** Alamy; **37** Alamy, Shutterstock; **38** Alamy, Shutterstock; **39** Alamy, Shutterstock; **40** Nature PL, Shutterstock; **41** Shutterstock, Nature PL, Ardea, Alamy; **42** Alamy, Shutterstock; **43** Alamy, Shutterstock; **44** Shutterstock, Alamy; **45** Alamy, Shutterstock; **46** Shutterstock, Ardea, Alamy, Getty; **47** Shutterstock; **48** Shutterstock, Alamy; **49** Alamy, Shutterstock; **50** Shutterstock, Alamy; **51** Shutterstock, Alamy; **52** Jon Enoch/GWR, Kevin Scott Ramos/GWR; **53** Shutterstock, Paul Michael Hughes/GWR; **54** Alamy, Shutterstock, Clay Bolt: claybolt.com; **55** Ardea, Alamy; **56** Jon Enoch/GWR; **58** Paul Michael Hughes/GWR; **59** Tim Anderson/GWR; **60** Reuters, Alamy, Kevin Scott Ramos/GWR; **61** Getty, Shinsuke Kamioka/GWR; **62** John Wright/GWR, Paul Michael Hughes/GWR, Richard Bradbury/GWR, NBC/NBCU Photo Bank; **63** Chris Granger/GWR, John Wright/GWR, Paul Michael Hughes/GWR; **64** Alamy, Aleksandar Terzic, Harvey Nichols; **65** Kevin Scott Ramos/GWR, Shutterstock, Al Diaz/GWR; **66** Reuters, Shutterstock, Ortiz-Catalan et al; **67** Paul Michael Hughes/GWR, Fernanda Figueiredo; **68** UGLY Enterprises LTD, Paul Michael Hughes/GWR, Getty, Evgeny Nikolaev; **69** Paul Michael Hughes/GWR, Shutterstock; **70** Paul Michael Hughes/GWR, John Wright/GWR, Kimberly Cook/GWR; **71** Kevin Scott Ramos/GWR, Reuters, Ranald Mackechnie/GWR; **72** Paul Michael Hughes/GWR; **74** Shutterstock; **75** Shutterstock, Craig Glenday; **77** Jon Enoch/GWR; **79** Brian Braun/GWR; **80** Alamy, Richard Bradbury, Sam Christmas/GWR, Shutterstock; **81** Ryan Schude/GWR; **82** Getty, GWR, Karen Wade/GWR; **83** Marvel/Sony/GWR; **84** Kevin Scott Ramos/GWR, Paul Michael Hughes/GWR, GWR; **85** Alex Rumford/GWR, Jon Enoch/GWR; **87** James Ellerker/GWR, Alex Rumford/GWR; **88** Christian Houdek/GWR; **89** James Ellerker/GWR, Ryan Schude/GWR; **90** Paul Michael Hughes/GWR, Jon Enoch/GWR; **91** Paul Michael Hughes/GWR; **92** Richard Bradbury/GWR, Paul Michael Hughes/GWR; **93** Ryan Schude/GWR, Paul Michael Hughes/GWR; **94** Richard Bradbury/GWR, Paul Michael Hughes/GWR, John Wright/GWR; **95** Trevor Traynor/GWR, Paul Michael Hughes/GWR, John Wright/GWR; **97** Ryan Schude/GWR, Jenna Henderson; **98** Ryan Schude/GWR; **100** Ryan Schude/GWR, Ranald Mackechnie/GWR, Kevin Scott Ramos/GWR, James Ellerker/GWR; **101** Ryan Schude/GWR, Shutterstock; **102** Ryan Schude/GWR, Paul Michael Hughes/GWR, James Ellerker/GWR; **103** Ryan Schude/GWR, Shutterstock; **104** James Ellerker/GWR, Drew Gardner/GWR, John Wright/GWR; **105** Ryan Schude/GWR, Kevin Scott Ramos/GWR; **106** Shutterstock, Mark Dadswell/GWR, Maria Marin; **107** Ryan Schude/GWR, Shutterstock; **108** Matt Ben Stone; **109** Alamy; **110** Red Bull/GWR, Jörg Mitter/Red Bull Content Pool; **111** Shutterstock, Jay Nemeth/Red Bull Content Pool; **112** Samuel Renner; **116** Raphael Thomas/Prince of Speed, Alex Broadway/Red Bull Content Pool, Dan Speicher; **117** Anthony Ball, Reuters, Shutterstock; **118** Samuel Crossley, Shutterstock, Marek Ogień/Red Bull Content Pool, Getty; **119** Matteo Zanga; **120** Christian Pondella/Red Bull Content Pool, Keith Ladzinski/Red Bull Content Pool; **123** AP Images for T-Mobile US, Jenna Henderson; **124** Kevin Scott Ramos/GWR; **126** Shutterstock; **127** Shutterstock, Alamy; **128** Alamy, Getty; **129** Iwan Baan, Getty; **130** Shutterstock, Getty; **131** Shutterstock, Alamy; **132** Alamy, Courtesy Chris Reynolds, Frédéric Boudin/Ferd, Shutterstock; **133** Alamy, Shutterstock; **134** Alamy, Shutterstock; **135** Shutterstock; **136** Courtesy Bonhams, Alamy, Shutterstock; **137** Alamy, Raphaël Dauvergne, Shutterstock; **139** Shutterstock; **140** Getty, Shutterstock; **141** Alamy, Shutterstock; **142** Shutterstock, Alamy; **143** Shutterstock; **144** Shutterstock, Alamy; **145** Lt.Chad Dulac, Shutterstock, Getty, Reuters; **146** JAXA, Boston Dynamics, Roborace; **147** Festo AG & Co.KG, JSK Lab/University of Tokyo, Bonhams, Honda; **148** DARPA, Roborace; **149** Roborace, DARPA, Shutterstock; **150** University of Pennsylvania, TU Delft, Kevin Ma and Pakpong Chirarattananon/Harvard University, Adam Lau/Berkeley Engineering; **151** Adam Lau/Berkeley Engineering, Festo AG & Co.KG, Shutterstock; **152** Boston Dynamics, Honda, Toyota; **153** Shutterstock; **154** FANUC, Karen Ladenheim; **155** Christian Sprogoe, The Henry Ford, NASA, Shutterstock; **156** Hiroshi Ishiguro Laboratory, IIT-Istituto Italiano di Tecnologia, Shutterstock, Kibo Robot Project; **157** Honda Motor Co, JSK Lab/University of Tokyo; **158** Shutterstock, Boston Dynamics, Ethan Schaler; **159** Shutterstock, Joseph Xu/Michigan University College of Engineering; **160** NASA, Airbus, DHL, Getty, Northrop Grumman Corporation; **161** Northrop Grumman Corporation, U.S. Navy; **162** Boston Dynamics; **163** Wyss Institute/Harvard University, ANYbotics, MIT, Boston Dynamics, Alamy; **164** Alamy, CNSA, JAXA, NASA; **165** NASA; **166** Shutterstock, Alamy, Bonhams; **167** Bonhams, Shutterstock; **168** VCG/Getty; **169** Alamy; **170** Alamy; **171** NASA/BEAM, NASA; **172** Jon Enoch/GWR, Holly Martin/MetalAndSpeed, Paul Michael Hughes/GWR; **173** Shinsuke Kamioka/GWR, Shutterstock; **174** NASA, U.S. Navy; **175** Alamy, ORNL & Carlos Jones; **176** Kevin Scott Ramos/GWR; **177** Kevin Scott Ramos/GWR, Shutterstock; **178** Paul Michael Hughes/GWR; **179** Ryan Schude/GWR, Kevin Scott Ramos/GWR; **180** Getty, Thyssenkrupp, Marcus Ingram/dreamstime, Plastic Bottle Village, Shutterstock; **181** Shutterstock; **182** Alamy, Shutterstock, Diederik Pomstra/Leiden University; **184** Lockheed Martin Corporation, NASA, NanoRacks; **185** NASA; **186** Alamy, Christies, Getty, Paul Michael Hughes/GWR, Shutterstock; **187** NASA; **190** Shutterstock; **191** Shutterstock; **192** David James/Lucasfilm Ltd, Shutterstock; **193** Walt Disney Pictures, Marvel Studios, ESPN Films, 20th Century Fox; **194** Ken McKay/ITV/Rex Features/Shutterstock; **195** Alamy, Shutterstock, Believe Entertainment Group; **196** Shutterstock; **197** Universal Music Group, Shutterstock; **198** Alamy, Shutterstock; **199** Alamy, Shutterstock; **204** NBCUniversal Media, Alamy, Ian Watson/USA Network, Warner Bros; **205** AMC, Warner Bros, Shutterstock, Alamy; **206** Beano, Todd Klein, Image Comics; **207** Nigel Parkinson/Beano, Shutterstock, Alamy; **208** Getty; **209** Kevin Scott Ramos/GWR, Shutterstock; **210** Getty, Sony Pictures Television; **211** Shutterstock, AMC/BBC; **212** Shutterstock; **213** Shutterstock; **214** Alamy, Shutterstock, Getty; **215** Alamy, Getty, Shutterstock; **216** Getty, Alamy; **217** Getty, Shutterstock; **218** Getty; **219** Getty, Shutterstock; **220** Shutterstock, Getty; **221** Alamy, Shutterstock; **222** Shutterstock, Mike Lee/KLC Fotos, Getty; **223** Shutterstock, Alamy, Getty; **224** Getty, Shutterstock, PA; **225** Shutterstock; **226** Alamy, Shutterstock; **227** World Taekwondo, Getty, Shutterstock; **228** Shutterstock, Getty; **229** Alamy, Shutterstock, Volkswagen AG, **230** International Weightlifting Federation, Shutterstock, Arnold Sports Festival; **231** Getty, Leo Zhukov, Alamy; **232** PBA LLC, Jeffrey Au/WCF, Getty; **233** Getty, Shutterstock; **234** Getty, Alamy, Shutterstock; **235** Shutterstock, Alamy; **236** Getty, Shutterstock; **237** Saroma 100km Ultra Marathon Organising Committee, Shutterstock; **238** FINA, Alamy, Shutterstock, Seb Daly/Sportsfile; **239** USA Water Ski & Wake Sport, Balint Vekassy, Shutterstock, World Surf League/Sloane, Alex St. Jean; **240** Shutterstock, Alamy, Getty; **241** Shutterstock; **242** Christian Pondella/Red Bull Content Pool, Peter Morning/Red Bull Content Pool, Michal Rotko, Getty, Ricardo Nascimento/Red Bull Content Pool; **243** Alamy, Getty, Reuters, Wolfgang Benedik; **244** Torben Utzon, Alamy, Getty; **245** Getty, Shutterstock, Eline Hooghiemstra; **254** Shutterstock, EHT Collaboration, Anthony Upton

GWR would like to thank: Stuart Ackland (Bodleian Library), David C Agle (NASA JPL), American Society of Ichthyologists and Herpetologists (Bruce Collette, JP Fontenelle, Kirsten Hechtbender, David Smith, Leo Smith, Milton Tan, Tierney Thys, Luke Tornabene, Peter Wainwright), ATN Event Staffing, Baltimore City Department of Public Works (Jeffrey Raymond, Muriel Rich), British Aerobatic Association (Alan Cassidy, Steve Todd, Graeme Fudge), Jochen Brocks (Australian National University), Peter Brown (Rocky Mountain Tree-Ring Research), Benson Brownies, Buena Vista Television, Michael Caldwell (University of Alberta), Steve Campbell, Canada Running Series, CBS Interactive, Che John Connon (Newcastle University), John Corcoran, Jon Custer (International Energy Agency), Adriene Davis Kalugyer (Lilly Family School of Philanthropy), Ryan DeSear, Suzanne DeSear, Disney ABC Home Entertainment and TV Distribution, Dude Perfect, Christopher Duggan, Péter Fankhauser (ANYBotics), Matias Faral, Corrine Finch (King's School Canterbury), FJT Logistics Ltd (Ray Harper, Gavin Hennessy), Marshall Gerometta (Council on Tall Buildings and Urban Habitat), Emily D Gilman, Megan Goldrick, Jessy Grizzle (University of Michigan), Götz Haferburg (Freiburg University of Mining and Technology), Nora Hartel (Foundation for Environmental Education), Timothy Hoellein (Loyola University Chicago), Joe Hollins, Paul Holmes, Kelly Holmes, Marsha K Hoover, Chuanmin Hu (University of South Florida), Integrated Colour Editions Europe (Roger Hawkins, Susie Hawkins), International Association for Bear Research and Management (Djuro Huber, Svitlana Kudrenko, Martyn Obbard, Bernie Peyton, Ioan-Mihai Pop, Hasan Rahman, Agnieszka Sergiel, Siew Te Wong, Jennapher Teunissen van Manen, Renee Ward), IUCN (Craig Hilton-Taylor, Dan Laffoley), Johns Hopkins University Applied Physics Laboratory (Geoffrey F Brown, Justyna Surowiec), Carol Kaelson, Almut Kelber (Lund University), Priya Kissoon (University of the West Indies), KWP Studios Inc., Robert D Leighton, Brian Levy (Metropolitan Water Reclamation District of Greater Chicago), Roy Longbottom, Stefano Mammola (University of Turin), Mastercard, Amanda McCabe (Port Lympne Hotel & Reserve), Gary McCracken (University of Tennessee), Lisa McGrath, Giorgio Metta (Istituto Italiano di Tecnologia), William C Meyers, Mohn Media (Anke Frosch, Theo Loechter, Marina Rempe, Reinhild Regragui, Jeanette Sio, Dennis Thon, Christin Moeck, Jens Pähler), Michael Moreau (NASA Goddard Space Flight Center), Shon Mosier (Elastec), Carolina Muñoz-Saez (University of Chile), Adriaan Olivier (Klein Karoo International), William Pérez (Universidad de la República), Simon Pierce (Marine Megafauna Foundation), Print Force, Xinpei Qitong, Rachael Ray, Rick Richmond, Ripley Entertainment, Kieran Robson, Royal Botanic Gardens, Kew (Martin Cheek, Elizabeth Dauncey, Aljos Farjon, Michael Fay, Peter Gasson, Christina Harrison, Heather McCleod, William Milliken, Paul Rees, Chelsea Snell), Kate Sanders (The University of Adelaide), Etsuro Sawai (Ocean Sunfishes Information Storage Museum / Hiroshima University), Scott Polar Research Institute (Peter Clarkson, Robert Headland), Robert Sieland (Wismut GmbH), John Sinton (University of Hawai'i at Mānoa), Southern California Timing Association (Dan Warner, JoAnn Carlson), StackOverflow (Sarah Caputo, Khalid El Khatib), Stephanie Stinn (Lockheed Martin), Stora Enso Veitsiluoto, Mike Szczys (Hackaday), Andy Taylor, Ginnie Titterton (Chronicle of Philanthropy), University of Arizona LPL (Erin Morton, Dante Lauretta), University of Birmingham (Rebecca Lockwood, Stuart Hillmansen), University of Tokyo (Yuki Asano, Rohan Mehra), Beverley Wiley, Beverley Williams, Eddie Wilson, Alexandra Wilson (Foreign and Commonwealth Office), WTA Networks Inc., XG Group, Liam Yon (St Helena Government), Xuexia Zhang (Southwest Jiaotang University), Paul Zimnisky Diamond Analytics (paulzimnisky.com), ZSL (James Hansford, Samuel Turvey), 55 Design (Hugh Doug Wylie, Linda Wylie, Hayley Wylie-Deacon, Tobias Wylie-Deacon, Rueben Wylie-Deacon, Anthony "Dad" Deacon, Vidette Burniston, Lewis Burniston)

Endpapers

Front/row 1: Largest human image of a pencil, most licence plates torn in one minute, fastest remote-controlled model tiltrotor aircraft, largest papier-mâché sculpture, highest launch of an effervescent tablet rocket, largest cheerleading cheer.

Front/row 2: Longest journey by elliptical cycle in a single country, longest duration chair balancing on a tightrope, largest inflatable (bouncy) castle, fastest solo row across Atlantic from Canada, largest collection of *Happy Days* memorabilia, most active spacecraft orbiting another planet.

Front/row 3: First barometric weather implant, farthest flight by an electric helicopter (prototype), fastest time to limbo skate under 10 bars, longest duration balancing a basketball on a toothbrush, fastest half marathon dressed in a baseball uniform (male), greatest vertical height stair climbing in one hour (male).

Front/row 4: First ski descent of Lhotse, largest animated mobile-phone mosaic, largest pair of jeans, largest dreamcatcher, largest gathering of people dressed as rabbits, largest automated parking facility, largest collection of *The Muppets* memorabilia.

Back/row 1: Most people blowing train whistles simultaneously, longest duration to spin a fidget spinner on one toe, largest scone, fastest journey from Land's End to John o' Groats on a lawnmower, most cosmetic makeovers in one hour (team of five), most combine harvesters working simultaneously.

Back/row 2: Longest time balancing a football on the knee, largest pillow fight, longest charcuterie board, largest steel-string acoustic guitar, largest chess piece, largest serving of beshbarmak, most guide dogs trained by an organization.

Back/row 3: Longest Hot Wheels track, most sticky notes stuck on the face in 30 seconds, longest chain of electrical extension cables, largest T-shirt, most escape rooms attended in one day, youngest person to row the Atlantic in a team (Trade Winds II).

Back/row 4: Largest parade of tow trucks, largest rugby scrum, most ping-pong balls bounced against a wall with the mouth in 30 seconds, longest time spent inside a bubble, largest collection of ties, largest sticker mosaic (image).

Country codes

Code	Country
ABW	Aruba
AFG	Afghanistan
AGO	Angola
AIA	Anguilla
ALB	Albania
AND	Andorra
ANT	Netherlands Antilles
ARG	Argentina
ARM	Armenia
ASM	American Samoa
ATA	Antarctica
ATF	French Southern Territories
ATG	Antigua and Barbuda
AUS	Australia
AUT	Austria
AZE	Azerbaijan
BDI	Burundi
BEL	Belgium
BEN	Benin
BFA	Burkina Faso
BGD	Bangladesh
BGR	Bulgaria
BHR	Bahrain
BHS	The Bahamas
BIH	Bosnia and Herzegovina
BLR	Belarus
BLZ	Belize
BMU	Bermuda
BOL	Bolivia
BRA	Brazil
BRB	Barbados
BRN	Brunei Darussalam
BTN	Bhutan
BVT	Bouvet Island
BWA	Botswana
CAF	Central African Republic
CAN	Canada
CCK	Cocos (Keeling) Islands
CHE	Switzerland
CHL	Chile
CHN	China
CIV	Côte d'Ivoire
CMR	Cameroon
COD	Congo, DR of the
COG	Congo
COK	Cook Islands
COL	Colombia
COM	Comoros
CPV	Cape Verde
CRI	Costa Rica
CUB	Cuba
CXR	Christmas Island
CYM	Cayman Islands
CYP	Cyprus
CZE	Czech Republic
DEU	Germany
DJI	Djibouti
DMA	Dominica
DNK	Denmark
DOM	Dominican Republic
DZA	Algeria
ECU	Ecuador
EGY	Egypt
ERI	Eritrea
ESH	Western Sahara
ESP	Spain
EST	Estonia
ETH	Ethiopia
FIN	Finland
FJI	Fiji
FLK	Falkland Islands (Malvinas)
FRA	France
FRG	West Germany
FRO	Faroe Islands
FSM	Micronesia, Federated States of
GAB	Gabon
GEO	Georgia
GHA	Ghana
GIB	Gibraltar
GIN	Guinea
GLP	Guadeloupe
GMB	Gambia
GNB	Guinea-Bissau
GNQ	Equatorial Guinea
GRC	Greece
GRD	Grenada
GRL	Greenland
GTM	Guatemala
GUF	French Guiana
GUM	Guam
GUY	Guyana
HKG	Hong Kong
HMD	Heard and McDonald Islands
HND	Honduras
HRV	Croatia (Hrvatska)
HTI	Haiti
HUN	Hungary
IDN	Indonesia
IND	India
IOT	British Indian Ocean Territory
IRL	Ireland
IRN	Iran
IRQ	Iraq
ISL	Iceland
ISR	Israel
ITA	Italy
JAM	Jamaica
JOR	Jordan
JPN	Japan
KAZ	Kazakhstan
KEN	Kenya
KGZ	Kyrgyzstan
KHM	Cambodia
KIR	Kiribati
KNA	Saint Kitts and Nevis
KOR	Korea, Republic of
KWT	Kuwait
LAO	Laos
LBN	Lebanon
LBR	Liberia
LBY	Libya
LCA	Saint Lucia
LIE	Liechtenstein
LKA	Sri Lanka
LSO	Lesotho
LTU	Lithuania
LUX	Luxembourg
LVA	Latvia
MAC	Macau
MAR	Morocco
MCO	Monaco
MDA	Moldova
MDG	Madagascar
MDV	Maldives
MEX	Mexico
MHL	Marshall Islands
MKD	Macedonia
MLI	Mali
MLT	Malta
MMR	Myanmar (Burma)
MNE	Montenegro
MNG	Mongolia
MNP	Northern Mariana Islands
MOZ	Mozambique
MRT	Mauritania
MSR	Montserrat
MTQ	Martinique
MUS	Mauritius
MWI	Malawi
MYS	Malaysia
MYT	Mayotte
NAM	Namibia
NCL	New Caledonia
NER	Niger
NFK	Norfolk Island
NGA	Nigeria
NIC	Nicaragua
NIU	Niue
NLD	Netherlands
NOR	Norway
NPL	Nepal
NRU	Nauru
NZ	New Zealand
OMN	Oman
PAK	Pakistan
PAN	Panama
PCN	Pitcairn Islands
PER	Peru
PHL	Philippines
PLW	Palau
PNG	Papua New Guinea
POL	Poland
PRI	Puerto Rico
PRK	Korea, DPRO
PRT	Portugal
PRY	Paraguay
PYF	French Polynesia
QAT	Qatar
REU	Réunion
ROM	Romania
RUS	Russian Federation
RWA	Rwanda
SAU	Saudi Arabia
SDN	Sudan
SEN	Senegal
SGP	Singapore
SGS	South Georgia and South SS
SHN	Saint Helena
SJM	Svalbard and Jan Mayen Islands
SLB	Solomon Islands
SLE	Sierra Leone
SLV	El Salvador
SMR	San Marino
SOM	Somalia
SPM	Saint Pierre and Miquelon
SRB	Serbia
SSD	South Sudan
STP	São Tomé and Principe
SUR	Suriname
SVK	Slovakia
SVN	Slovenia
SWE	Sweden
SWZ	Swaziland
SYC	Seychelles
SYR	Syrian Arab Republic
TCA	Turks and Caicos Islands
TCD	Chad
TGO	Togo
THA	Thailand
TJK	Tajikistan
TKL	Tokelau
TKM	Turkmenistan
TMP	East Timor
TON	Tonga
TPE	Chinese Taipei
TTO	Trinidad and Tobago
TUN	Tunisia
TUR	Turkey
TUV	Tuvalu
TZA	Tanzania
UAE	United Arab Emirates
UGA	Uganda
UK	United Kingdom
UKR	Ukraine
UMI	US Minor Islands
URY	Uruguay
USA	United States of America
UZB	Uzbekistan
VAT	Vatican City
VCT	Saint Vincent and the Grenadines
VEN	Venezuela
VGB	Virgin Islands (British)
VIR	Virgin Islands (US)
VNM	Vietnam
VUT	Vanuatu
WLF	Wallis and Futuna Islands
WSM	Samoa
YEM	Yemen
ZAF	South Africa
ZMB	Zambia
ZWE	Zimbabwe

STOP PRESS

The following entries were approved and added to our database after the official closing date for this year's submissions.

Most tornadoes sighted by one person
Professional storm chaser Roger Hill (USA) witnessed 676 twisters between 7 Jul 1987 and 13 Jul 2017, as verified on 15 Feb 2018.

Longest chain of pipe cleaners
On 9 Mar 2018, students at Brookman Elementary School in Las Vegas, Nevada, USA – together with teacher Alana London and her husband, comedy magician Adam (all USA) – laid out an 18.09-km-long (11.2-mi) chain of pipe cleaners. The record attempt was part of a literacy programme in which students earned pipe cleaners by reading books.

Tallest toilet-roll pyramid
To celebrate the opening of a new superstore in Appleton, Wisconsin, USA, on 24 May 2018, Kimberly-Clark Corporation and Meijer (both USA) constructed a 4.36-m-tall (14-ft 3-in) pyramid out of toilet rolls. It took 14 people 10 hr to build the tissue-paper ziggurat, which comprised 25,585 individual rolls.

First baby snake preserved in amber
The remains of an embryonic snake encased in amber, dated to around 99 million years ago, have been unearthed in Kachin State in Myanmar. The specimen – a new species since named *Xiaophis myanmarensis* – was 4.75 cm (1.8 in) long and missing its skull; it's estimated that the creature's full length would have been nearer to 8 cm (3.1 in). The discovery was reported in *Science Advances* on 18 Jul 2018.

▶ Largest hand-knitted blanket (non crochet)
Valery Larkin (IRL) and Knitters of the World hand-knitted a blanket measuring 1,994.81 m² (21,471.95 sq ft) – about the size of four basketball courts – as verified on 26 Aug 2018 in Ennis, Ireland. More than 1,000 people worked on the blanket, which was subsequently divided up and donated to the Red Cross.

Fastest sport stacking individual 3-3-3 stack
Hyeon Jong-choi (KOR) completed a 3-3-3 stack in 1.322 sec at the SPEED STACKS World Championship Challenge 1st in Seoul, South Korea, on 4 Nov 2018. He shaved 0.005 sec off his previous record, set on 16 Sep 2018.

Largest water-screen projection
On 20 Sep 2018, the Moscow International Festival "Circle of Light" in Russia presented a light display across a curtain of water measuring 3,099.24 m² (33,359 sq ft).

The festival, coordinated by LBL Communication Group (RUS), also achieved the **most flame projections launched simultaneously** – 162.

Largest human image of a country
On 29 Sep 2018, a total of 4,807 people celebrated Romania's 100th Great Union Day by forming an image of their country at a renovated 17th-century citadel in Alba Iulia, Romania. The event was organized by Asociația 11even, Primăria Alba Iulia and Kaufland (all ROM).

Largest hurling lesson
To mark its 20th birthday, on 30 Sep 2018 The Gaelic Athletic Association Museum (IRL) taught hurling to 1,772 people at Croke Park in Dublin, Ireland. Hurling Development Officer Martin Fogarty led the lesson.

Most escape rooms attended in one day
On 3 Oct 2018, Richard Bragg, Daniel Egnor, Amanda Harris (all USA) and Ana Ulin (ESP) – aka "Bloody Boris's Burning Bluelight Brigade" – visited 22 escape rooms in 24 hr in Moscow, Russia. The team were able to extricate themselves from all but one of the rooms in the allotted time.

Youngest person to circumnavigate by aircraft (solo)
Mason Andrews (USA, b. 26 Apr 2000) flew around the world in a single-engine Piper PA-32 in 76 days, completing his journey on 6 Oct 2018 in Monroe, Louisiana, USA, aged 18 years 163 days.

Most people assembling hunger-relief packages (multiple venues)
Rise Against Hunger (USA) organized a hunger-relief package assemblage with 832 participants on 16 Oct 2018. More than 4,500 meal packages were completed in locations across the USA, India, Italy, the Philippines and South Africa.

Fastest time to complete 10 m on hind legs by a dog
On 11 Nov 2018, a three-year-old cavapoo named Oliver covered 10 m (32 ft 10 in) on his hind legs in 3.21 sec in Nashville, Tennessee, USA. Oliver was accompanied by his owner and trainer Rayner Fredrick (USA).

Most empanadas served in 8 hours
On 11 Nov 2018, the Asociación de Propietarios de Pizzerías y Casas de Empanadas (ARG) broke two records in Buenos Aires, Argentina. They served 11,472 Latin-American pastries in 8 hr and then successfully attempted the **most pizzas made in 12 hours (team)**, baking 11,089 12-in (30.5-cm) pizzas.

Most people blowing out candles simultaneously
To celebrate the 90th birthday of Mickey Mouse, Disney partner King Power International (THA) had 1,765 people blow out candles at the same time on 18 Nov 2018 in Bangkok, Thailand.

Smallest vacuum cleaner
Talabathula Sai (IND) created a mini vacuum cleaner with a length of 5.4 cm (2.1 in) in Peddapuram, India, as verified on 10 Dec 2018. The body of the vacuum was made using a pen cap, 12-v battery, DC motor and a small copper sheet.

Most people crushing cans simultaneously
A total of 463 people crushed cans at the same time at an event organized by Coca-Cola HBC Ireland & Northern Ireland Ltd in Belfast, UK, on 17 Jan 2019.

▶ Highest catch of a cricket ball
On 31 Jan 2019, Australian women's wicket-keeper Alyssa Healy (AUS) securely gathered a cricket ball dropped from a drone at a height of 82.5 m (270 ft 8 in) in Melbourne, Victoria, Australia. The record attempt was staged to publicize the 2020 ICC Men's and Women's T20 World Cups.
Also part of the promotional drive was the **most signatures on a piece of sports memorabilia** – 1,033, on a supersized cricket shirt – as verified in Melbourne on 8 Mar 2019.

Largest pair of jeans
Paris Perú (PER) exhibited a pair of jeans measuring 65.5 m (214 ft 10 in) long and 42.7 m (140 ft 1 in) wide at the Mall del Sur in Lima, Peru,

LARGEST AIRCRAFT BY WINGSPAN
The brainchild of Microsoft co-founder Paul Allen (1953–2018) and aerospace engineer Burt Rutan (both USA), *Stratolaunch* has a 117.35-m (385-ft) wingspan. On 13 Apr 2019, it made its maiden test flight from the Mojave Air & Space Port in California, USA. The plane is designed to carry space rockets to launch at the edge of Earth's atmosphere.

FIRST DIRECT IMAGE OF A BLACK HOLE
On 10 Apr 2019, the Event Horizon Telescope Collaboration unveiled this image of the black hole at the heart of a galaxy known as M87. The picture shows a disk of superheated matter spiralling towards the dark "event horizon" – where the black hole's gravitational pull is strong enough to prevent any light escaping.

OCEAN ROWING ACHIEVEMENTS (2018–19)
Source: Ocean Rowing Society

Achievement	Details	Date
Fastest solo row from Europe to South America	60 days 16 hr 6 min by Lee "Frank" Spencer (UK) in *Rowing Marine* (pictured right)	26 Jan–11 Mar 2019
First amputee to row an ocean solo	Lee "Frank" Spencer, as above	As above
Youngest all-male team of four to row an ocean	22 years 246 days (average) for Lee Gordon, Cole Barnard, Matthew Boynton & Grant Soll (aka "Mad4Waves", all ZAF) in *Jasmine 2*	12 Dec 2018–20 Jan 2019
First related team of four to row the Atlantic east to west	Caspar Thorp, Toby Thorp, George Blandford & Justin Evelegh (aka "Oar Inspiring", all UK) in *Lionheart*	12 Dec 2018–16 Jan 2019
First male pair to row the Atlantic from continental Europe	John Wilson & Ricky Reina (aka "Atlantic Avengers", both UK) in *Sic Parvis Magna*	27 Nov 2018–23 Feb 2019
Fastest average speed to row the Atlantic east to west on the Trade Winds I route by a pair (open class)	2.875 knots (5.32 km/h; 3.30 mph) by Alex Simpson & Jamie Gordon (both UK) in *Hyperion Atlantic Challenge*	29 Jan–8 Mar 2019
Youngest person to complete three ocean rows	27 years 4 days old for Alex Simpson (b. 25 Jan 1992)	As above
Oldest person to complete three ocean rows	66 years 359 days for Fedor Konyukhov (RUS, b. 12 Dec 1951), New Zealand to South America in *Akros*	6 Dec 2018–9 May 2019
First multi-crewed team to row across the Atlantic and the Caribbean Sea	Isaac Giesen (NZ), Jógvan Clementsen, Niclas Olsen & Jákup Jacobsen (all FRO) in *SAGA*	12 Mar–13 May 2018

on 19 Feb 2019. The jeans weighed 4.8 tonnes (10,582 lb) and took a team of 50 people six months to create.

Fastest time to arrange the periodic table
On 25 Feb 2019, student Ali Ghaddar (LBN) took a series of jumbled-up images of elements and placed them in the correct order of the periodic table in 6 min 44 sec at Safir High School in Saida, Lebanon. The record attempt took place during the international celebrations for the 150th anniversary of the first organization of the periodic table, by Dmitri Mendeleev in 1869.

Highest score in UCI artistic cycling (women's single)
Milena Slupina (DEU) scored 194.31 at the UCI Artistic Cycling World Cup in Prague, Czech Republic, on 9 Mar 2019. She surpassed the record score of compatriot Iris Schwarzhaupt (see p.231).

Fastest road walk 50 km (female)
On 9 Mar 2019, Hong Liu (CHN) became the first woman to break the 4-hr barrier for the 50 km race walk when she completed the Chinese Race Walk Grand Prix in 3 hr 59 min 15 sec in Huangshan, China. She beat the record of compatriot Rui Liang (4 hr 4 min 36 sec), although Liu's time is yet to be ratified by the IAAF.

Most people to pass an egg
A total of 353 residents of Misaki Town in Kume, Okayama Prefecture, Japan, used dessertspoons to pass a fresh, unbroken and uncooked hen's egg between them on 10 Mar 2019.

Lowest elapsed time in an NHRA Drag Racing Pro Stock motorcycle race
Andrew Hines (USA) won a 440-yd (402-m) NHRA Pro Stock motorcycle race with an elapsed time of 6.720 sec on 17 Mar 2019 at the 50th Amalie Motor Oil NHRA Gatornationals at Gainesville Raceway in Florida, USA.

Most expensive pigeon
Racing pigeon Armando sold for €1,252,000 ($1,417,650; £1,065,870) through the PIPA online auction house on 17 Mar 2019. He was part of a collection of birds put up for sale by pigeon breeder and retired abattoir manager Joël Verschoot (BEL). Although recently retired, five-year-old racing pigeon Armando came with an impeccable competitive pedigree, having won his last three events: the 2018 Ace Pigeon championship, the 2019 Pigeon Olympiad and the Angoulême. His value

skyrocketed when two Chinese fanciers became involved in a last-minute bidding war.

Deepest dive by a sea snake
As described in *Austral Ecology* on 18 Mar 2019, a *Hydrophis* sea snake (species undetermined) was captured on video on 16 Nov 2014 swimming at a depth of 245 m (803 ft 9 in) by a remotely operated vehicle (ROV) in the Browse Basin, which lies off north-west Australia. A subsequent ROV recorded another *Hydrophis* sea snake in the same location on 18 Jul 2017 at a depth of 239 m (784 ft 1 in), appearing to forage on the seabed.

Highest note whistled
On 20 Mar 2019, Andrew Stanford (USA) whistled a note measured at 8,372.019 Hz (C9 standard notation) in Hanover, New Hampshire, USA. He was recorded in a sound booth at Dartmouth College.

Highest combined age for two living siblings
Portuguese brothers Albano (b. 14 Dec 1909) and Alberto (b. 2 Dec 1911) Andrade had a combined age of 216 years 284 days, as verified in Santa Maria da Feira in Aveiro, Portugal, on 2 Apr 2019.

Oldest participant in the University Boat Race
James Cracknell (UK, b. 5 May 1972) rowed for Cambridge in the 165th University Boat Race on 7 Apr 2019 aged 46 years 337 days. He finished in the winning boat, as Cambridge beat Oxford in a time of 16 min 57 sec. Cracknell was eight years older than the previous oldest participant (Cambridge cox Andrew Probert, in 1992) and 10 years older than the next-oldest rower (Oxford's Mike Wherley, in 2008).

Largest display of LEGO® *Star Wars* Minifigures
At the 2019 *Star Wars* Celebration on 11 Apr,

LEGO Group (USA) displayed 36,440 *Star Wars* Minifigures – arranged in the shape of a Stormtrooper helmet – in Chicago, Illinois, USA. The image measured 6.93 m wide by 6.88 m tall (22 ft 9 in x 22 ft 7 in) and took a team of 12 people 38 hr to build; 16 hr were spent simply assembling the Minifigures.

Largest whisky tasting
On 13 Apr 2019, Nigab (SWE) and Bruichladdich (UK) organized a whisky-tasting event for 2,283 people in Gothenburg, Sweden.

Farthest distance cycled in one hour (unpaced, standing start)
On 16 Apr 2019, Victor Campenaerts (BEL) rode 55.089 km (34.230 mi) in 60 min in Aguascalientes, Mexico. Situated at an altitude of 1,800 m (5,905 ft), Aguascalientes was also the setting for Vittoria Bussi's women's one-hour record (see p.228).

Widest tongue (male)
Verified on 16 Apr 2019, the tongue of Brian Thompson (USA) is 8.88 cm (3.49 in) at its widest point, as measured in La Cañada Flintgrade, California, USA, on 30 Jul 2018. He claimed the record from previous holder Byron Schlenker (see p.70).

Largest gold bathtub
On 22 Apr 2019, Huis Ten Bosch theme park (JPN) unveiled an 18-karat bath weighing 154.2 kg (339 lb 15 oz) in Sasebo, Nagasaki, Japan. The golden tub has a diameter of 1.3 m and a depth of 55 cm (4 ft 3 in x 1 ft 9 in) – making it large enough to accommodate two adults.

▶ **OLDEST TAPIR IN CAPTIVITY**
On 13 Mar 2019, a Malayan tapir (*Tapirus indicus*) called Kingut (b. 27 Jan 1978) was verified to be 41 years 45 days old at Port Lympne Hotel & Reserve in Kent, UK. Kingut was born in Jakarta, Indonesia, where he was originally called Huta, before relocating to the UK in 1992. He loves to be brushed by his keeper, Alice Elliot (left), and his favourite snacks are sweet treats such as bananas.